Willie Nelson
Sings America!

". . . the life I love is makin' music with my friends . . ."

Steven Opdyke

EAKIN PRESS ★ Austin, Texas

FIRST EDITION

Contents

The Introduction

Section I. The Early Recordings

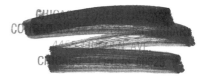

Section II. The RCA Albums and Compilations

Section III. The Atlantic and Columbia Years

Section IV. The Non-Columbia and Post-Columbia Recordings and Film Career

Section V. The "Guest" Projects and Tributes

The Appendices (With a Special Bonus Section: The Complete Willie Nelson RCA Sessionography)

Acknowledgements and Appreciations

The front cover of the book came from an exclusive photo "shoot" of Willie Nelson taken by Will van Overbeek of Austin, Texas. The computer composition of the cover was done by Steve Bourdon of Gainesville, Florida. Steve also did the computer design and layout for all the photos. Six other van Overbeek originals were featured in the book, as well, the Kinky Friedman (with cigar) and Willie shot, the shot of the golf cart, the portrait of a "swinging" Willie, the "face" of Willie, and the two "IRS" photographs. Will holds the copyrights and all were used by permission. Thank you Shelley and Phil Bentley for all your help and enthusiasm.

The back cover shot of Willie with the author and the book's editor came from the author's private collection, as did the picture of the Country Music Hall of Fame poster and the Willie Nelson "coin" shot. The still of Kris and Willie from *Songwriter* and the picture of Willie playing the guitar came courtesy of Evelyn Shriver Public Relations and the author's private collection. The two publicity pictures from *Red Headed Stranger* came courtesy of Alive Films, Evelyn Shriver Public Relations, and the author's private collection.

The picture of Willie and Willie Nelson, Jr. came courtesy of Promised Land Music and Evelyn Shriver Public Relations. The four recent publicity photos of Willie (taken from slides) came courtesy of Evelyn Shriver Public Relations. The publicity photo of Willie in the cowboy hat came courtesy of Evelyn Shriver Public Relations and Columbia Records. The Lone Star logo came courtesy of Willie Nelson and the author's private collection. The picture of the young Willie Nelson came from the Lana Nelson collection. The picture of Willie as a young "live" performer, of him singing into a studio microphone, the two RCA publicity photos, the Hal Smith publicity shot, and the

Atlantic Records promotional photo all came courtesy (and with permission) of the Michael Ochs Archives.

I have worked as diligently and carefully as possible to track all the copyrights or permission requirements of all photographs, to accurately credit them, and gain permissions where appropriate. On some I could find no information. If I have omitted credit where due or have been incorrect, please notify and all changes where required will be made for subsequent printings and editions. I would be indebted to anyone who calls with pertinent information to ensure that all copyrights are protected.

I have worked just as painstakingly to ensure complete accuracy in the text and appendices of the manuscript. I have put the book through the most stringent process of checking and editing as possible, by my chief editor, Pamela Meister, and by the editors at Eakin Press. I directly contacted personal and private sources where information appeared to be in doubt, contradictory, or even just unsubstantiated. The printed and computerized sources I cited have all been compiled into the "Source Listing and Bibliography" section. The lyrics to the song, 'Country Music Crazy', a loving remembrance of country music icons past and present, have a 1998 copyright and were used by permission, courtesy of Co-op Music.

I have had the pleasure of many hours of Mr. Nelson's time to probe his memory of events and recordings to ensure the maximum possible correctness. He carefully and in detail answered every question I posed on his recording career, even though he more than once said, "I don't want to spend too much time on me." Mr. Nelson's friend and associate, Mark Rothbaum, also graciously spent hours on numerous occasions by phone answering lists of questions, especially about Willie's split from Columbia in 1993. I am grateful that he reviewed much of what I wrote and told me that not only was the writing "excellent," his only concern was that I might have made him appear to be a "guru." I also very much appreciated Lana Nelson looking over the information in the appendices and making available her personal photograph collection. David Anderson, Willie's road and business manager, made possible all the backstage visits and the various interviews. He even stopped the buses as they were leaving one concert site so I could review, with Willie, some of the finished parts of the book. Thank you very much , David.

Bill DeYoung, editor of *Scene* (the *Gainesville Sun*) made many pictures available, passed on a great deal of information about Willie, and graciously read and critiqued much of the manuscript as it evolved. His assistance and time were greatly appreciated. Thanks Bill! If it wasn't for you putting me in touch with Willie, Evelyn Shriver, and Promised Land, this book might never have been written. An especially heart-felt thanks goes to Amy at Evelyn Shriver Public Relations. She got me in to see Willie in concert and set up interviews on several occasions. She reviewed the manuscript and made a great deal of publicity information (slides, pictures, press releases) available. Thank you, Amy!

All of the people at RCA Nashville (especially Katherine Woods, Vice President, Legal and Business Affairs, who got everything rolling there and Steve Lindsey, the person to whom she referred me), BMG Entertainment (in New York), Sony Music (Nashville - where Vicki Rowland was a huge help), Promised Land Music, Sony ATV Tree Music (especially Todd Ellis and Judy Roberts who were extremely helpful), Sony Music (New York, thanks Scott Pascucci of the Business Office) and Justice Records (who opened their publicity files for me), were wonderful, informative, and eager to help me track down permissions, session information, and anything else pertinent to Mr. Nelson's career. Everyone I contacted at the Country Music Hall of Fame was extremely helpful and patient and took as much time as I needed to answer my questions. I am very grateful with a special thanks to Kent Henderson and Ronnie Pugh.

The Michael Ochs Archive in Venice, California, made their stock of Willie photos available to me and granted me permission to use some of them. Thank you Helen and Jonathan for all the work you did in research and copying. The Willie Nelson Museum in Nashville has always been a fun-filled place to visit. Jeannie and the others who work there opened the doors to me and I was able to see many pictures of Willie and his fans, the very personable side of Willie that is not made visible often enough in the media. From them I learned Willie's rules of golf and discovered the specifics of various awards I had not heard of before.

Willie once told me that even he did not have all the various albums he recorded or were attributed to him. He even asked to borrow several RCA albums so he could listen to some of his songs to perhaps rerecord them. Thanks to the Great Escape store in Nashville, Bill Perry of Hyde and Zeke Records (Gainesville) and Ted Sharpe, I have obtained just about every Willie Nelson album.

DEDICATION

To Pamela, my editor, best friend, wife, partner, and soulmate.

To Trevor, Jason, and Sara, family, friends, and my hopes for the future.

To the writer who got me started on this book, Bill DeYoung.

To Jack and Theresa, the best parents/in-laws anyone could have.

Thanks all of you for all the hard work, support, review, and recommendations.

To Willie, Mark, Steve, Will, Ed, and so many others, you kept the dream going.

The Introduction

. . . I'M CRAZY, COUNTRY MUSIC CRAZY . . .

He began writing songs at a very young age.
(Photo from the Lana Nelson collection)

Willie designed the "Lone Star" logo.

"One Step Beyond":

Willie Nelson's Place in Country Music

American popular (pop) music in the twentieth century has been based on several very broad categories, jazz, rhythm and blues (R & B), gospel, and country. Rock music (or Rock and Roll) was the outgrowth of a fusion of country and R & B, with a great deal of gospel influence thrown in. It has been a dominant force in popular tastes for the past several decades.

Pop singers, those performers who have been typecast as "middle of the road," have drawn from all formats, including rock music, to come up with "national" hits. Tony Bennett took Hank Williams' country hit, 'Cold Cold Heart', to the top of the national pop charts in the early fifties. Later that decade, Pat Boone had a big hit with Little Richard's 'Tutti Frutti', which became both an R & B and Rock and Roll hit.

Two of the categories, jazz and R & B, were mainly created by Black Americans. Country music, was derived from the folk and ballad traditions of the early European and British settlers. It has remained largely a creation and cultural attribute of white America. One of the strengths of most of the major country artists from Jimmie Rodgers to Merle Haggard has been to bring black music into their art.

Tompall Glaser, who had a top forty country hit (number thirty-six) with Rodgers' 1927 song, 'T for Texas (Blue Yodel No. 1)', told *American Songwriter* that Jimmie "tackled my kind of music, Hawaiian and blues." Texas performer, Don Walser, observed that the language used by African Americans "is the same used in most of Rodgers' lyrics." Bob Dylan, who compiled (in 1997) a Jimmie Rodgers tribute album, understood that Rodgers was "combining elements of blues and hillbilly sounds before anyone else had thought of it."

When Jimmie recorded with jazz greats Louis Armstrong and Lillian Hardin Armstrong on July 12, 1930, he showed just how far beyond the normal range of country music he could go. He even included the St. Louis blues guitarist Clifford Gibson in a 1931 session, but the results were never issued and presumed lost. Posthumously, Jimmie was awarded the W. C. Handy Blues Award "for his contributions to blues music."

A recent *New York Times* column (by Ben Ratliff writing in the March 13, 1998 issue) pointed out some very striking parallels between Willie and Louis Armstrong. The strongest similarity came in phrasing, especially when Willie, like Armstrong, suddenly accelerates his. Another obvious comparison lay in the "clipped rhythms and earned vibratos" distinctive to both artists. Beyond that, Willie and Louis both toured endlessly, uniquely interpreted pop standards, played themselves in countless movie roles, and embodied a specific style of music.

Another country pioneer, Hank Williams, learned (early in his career) the blues-based forms of a traveling black performer, Rufus Payne. Ernest Tubb grew up working side by side with the black workers on his father's tenant farms and from a young age, listened to and particularly liked Ethel Waters and Bessie Smith. Tex Ritter said he learned one of his most famous songs, 'The Boll Weevil', from a black musician, Robert Williams.

The Carter Family collaborated with a fellow native of the Eastern mountain country, a black musician by the name of Leslie Riddles. For Bill Monroe, Bluegrass legend, there were two men, as he was growing up, whose music "found an important place in his music as it developed." He told interviewer James Rooney that "one was a black blues player who used to live near Rosine called Arnold Schultz." The blues were what he heard and as he remembered, "you would gradually touch the blues someplace."

Willie Nelson learned and listened to the music of the black cotton pickers in his rural Texas. At the same time, a black artist like DeFord Bailey ended up playing country music because he grew up within "a rich tradition of string band music that was shared by both blacks and whites." DeFord liked to call it "black hillbilly music."

Because of that interchange of black and white musical influences, black artists like Charlie Pride have, in the past, found success in the predominantly white province of country music. It was also the basis for Conway Twitty knowing he could turn the Pointer Sisters' classic, 'Slow Hand', into a number one country hit, which he did. Correspondingly, R & B musicians have brought many country classics, from 'Little Green Apples' to 'Release Me', into their repertoire and made them "soul" classics.

Jerry Wexler, formerly head of Atlantic Records, for whom Willie recorded in the early seventies, first met Willie in 1973, "when Willie was looked down on by Nashville's assembly-line producers." The Atlantic recordings Willie made were the catalyst for the excellent Columbia ones that put him on top of modern country. Wexler knew Willie would be outstanding because "I heard the blues in him." He further said that Willie:

> shares with Sinatra a gift for incredible vocal rubato - prolonging one note, cutting short another, swinging with an elastic sense of time that only the finest jazz singers understand.

Country Music historian and scholar, Bill Malone, made a case that, by the late seventies into the early eighties, country music had "indeed" become American music. One of the artists he cited for making the music so culturally diverse and rich was Willie Nelson, "whose blues-tinged voice was one of the most distinctive since Jimmie Rodgers." Malone wrote that Willie:

> absorbed a heavy diet of gospel, honky-tonk, pop, and western swing music, all of which would later show up in his own highly individualistic style.

What Willie succeeded in doing, "in a way that has been unequaled before or since by any other country singer," concluded Malone, was to "build an audience among the rock oriented youth" and to attract listeners "to gospel and earlier varieties of country music, including honky-tonk." The audience Willie built "would not have listened to such music without Willie's sanction."

From 'Without a Song' to 'Stardust' and 'Red Headed Stranger', Willie refocused the nation back to its rich musical heritage like never before. He also added his own standards, from 'Crazy' and 'Night Life' to 'On the Road Again'. Indeed, Willie's recording choices have encompassed the best of American popular song interspersed with unique original and personal perspectives. All the songs were delivered in a singing style that Malone described as "consistently excellent."

Country music historians Douglas B. Green and Bob Pinson placed Willie, "the de facto leader of the outlaw movement," in some very exclusive company when they discussed his place in the annals of country music. Writing in the 1979 book, *The Illustrated History of Country Music*, they postulated that:

> whenever the music gets too complicated, too sophisticated, too formulaic, somebody - be it Jimmie Rodgers or Hank Williams or Elvis or Willie Nelson - comes up with music of urgency, of intensity, and most of all, of simplicity.

Critic Fred Dellar took a mid-nineties view of influential country artists and concluded, for the British music magazine, *Mojo*, that there was a "fast" line from Jimmie Rodgers and Hank Williams to Willie. Texas compatriot, Waylon Jennings, also put Willie's country music stature in perspective, saying,

> I think he will go down as one of the greatest, if not the greatest songwriter ever in country music ... even greater than Hank Williams. He can write the most complex song, like 'And So Will You My Love', that will shoot over most people's heads, and then he will turn around and write a little song like 'On the Road Again' that everyone can appreciate.

Willie not only brought to country music some of the greatest and longest lasting original material, he infused it with music from all areas of American and world culture, jazz, classic pop, blues, and even Jamaican reggae. He became the last great artist to command and successfully put across such a repertoire because, as he explained, he was among the last to work in a country music industry that "was more run by musicians than by lawyers." As author Rob Patterson observed, Willie's unique greatness lay not only in his restless creativity, but in his ability to "bridge genres" and "break down walls."

RCA put Willie in the studio and said, "Sing, shorty!"
(Photo from the Michael Ochs Archives)

SECTION I
The Early Recordings

I CAN'T STOP THIS JUKE BOX IN MY HEAD . . .

Willie started his own label!
(Photo from Willie Nelson and the author's private collection)

An album full of "demo" recordings.

(Photo from Willie Nelson and the author's private collection)

"No Place for Me":

The First Recordings

Willie Nelson's first "officially released" commercial recording was a single that paired his own composition, 'No Place for Me', with 'Lumberjack', written by Leon Payne, writer of such classics as 'Lost Highway' and 'I Love You Because'. The single was "marketed" (on the "Willie Nelson Records" label) in 1957, when Willie was twenty-four. A first pressing of five hundred copies, available exclusively through Willie's KVAN (Vancouver, Washington) radio show (where he was often billed as "Wee Willie"), completely and quickly sold out.

Because of his show's popularity, the sell-out was not surprising. In the 10 AM to 2 PM time slot, Willie's broadcast moved into the second spot in the Vancouver market behind the Arthur Godfrey CBS network program. Overall, he was able to sell three thousand copies of the single through mail order, with the only promotion being Willie, himself, during the show. Each single was priced at one dollar and came complete with an autographed picture of the artist. Original copies have become very hard to find.

In making the recording, which consisted of him singing and playing guitar through a small amp, he used both the KVAN facility in Vancouver and a converted garage in Portland, Oregon (across the bridge from Vancouver). Willie's recalled the year as being 1957 and added that he "was working as a deejay over in Vancouver, but I cut the record in a basement in Portland." After recording the songs, he said,

> I had five hundred copies pressed by Pappy Daily's D Records down in Houston. I sold the five hundred over the air with an eight by ten glossy included with each one.

1

He said he had run into Daily (or Dailey, as Willie wrote it) before, "when I was working in the Houston area." Willie said he also knew Gabe Tucker through Daily. Tucker was a publicist who at one time worked with Colonel Tom Parker (who managed Elvis).

Other sources have stated that Starday Records (of Nashville) manufactured the single. The distribution was done solely by Willie on the Willie Nelson Records label. Starday supposedly had the option to release the record on their own label if they so chose, but they did not exercise that option.

Prior to his move to Vancouver, Willie and his family had lived in San Diego. That was his first major time out of Texas, except for a short-lived army hitch (which ended in a medical discharge - for a back disorder). Willie relocated to Vancouver at the behest of his mother, Myrle. She had left her two children (Willie and sister Bobbie) and divorced their father soon after Willie was born, leaving them to be raised by grandparents in the tiny hamlet of Abbott, Texas.

It was Mae Boren Axton (writer of the 1956 Elvis Presley hit, 'Heartbreak Hotel' and mother of Hoyt Axton) who gave Willie his first encouragement, his first assurance that he indeed had talent, especially as a writer. Writing in 1973, Ms. Axton recalled that she was in a Tacoma, Washington, (later she wrote she was actually in Vancouver) radio station visiting a friend. At the time she was working for Colonel Tom Parker to promote the early Elvis recordings (and push Hank Snow, as well). When leaving the station, she remembered that:

> a very thin, extremely shy, dee jay, with a tape recorder in his hand, hesitatingly stopped me, introduced himself, said he loved the songs I wrote, and asked if I had time to listen to just one song of several he had on tape, that he had written, and see if I thought he had any talent.

The "dee jay" was, of course, a twenty-four year old Willie Nelson. Ms. Axton later disclosed that the first song she listened to was none other than 'Family Bible' and that it took only four bars for "her chin to hit the proverbial floor." Mae recalled that she listened to four or five songs and they figuratively knocked her out "with their beauty and power," or as she elaborated, a "beauty that caressed my ears." When she told him how beautiful his songs were, she recollected that "his eyes lighted up, and he asked me what he should do." She advised him to go to Nashville and "write, write, write."

Willie and Mae discussed jobs Willie could get in Texas while working on getting to Nashville. She gave him her address and unlisted phone number and offered help to get him established, if he needed it. She remembered urging him to "get on with it" and told him it "wasn't fair to the world not to get to hear his beautiful songs."

The songs on the tape Mae Axton heard and the single marketed to Vancouver radio listeners were not actually Willie's first recorded attempts to get his songs across. The "A" side song was not even his first published song. One of Willie's biographer's, Lola Scobey, wrote that the honor belonged to a song entitled 'Pullamo', co-written with a "friend" named Steve Pulliam and published in 1949 by Sophisticate Music (when Willie was a high school sophomore).

She wrote that his next writing venture came in 1956, when he co-authored 'Too Young to Settle Down' with Jack Rhodes (composer of songs cut by Sonny James and Hank Snow). It was published by a California-based publisher, Central Songs. In a recent interview with Willie, he said he never wrote a song with Pulliam. He said, "I never knew him. I wasn't part of writing that song." He did say he wrote "that one song" ('Too Young to Settle Down') with Jack Rhodes, who "was a deejay in Ft. Worth, who had his own publishing company."

His first recording occurred prior to 1957, in 1955, when he made an audition tape and sent it to the Sarg label in Luling, Texas, fifty miles Southeast of Austin. At the time, Willie was disc jockey for KBOP in Pleasanton, Texas (later that year, 1955, he would work for KCNC in Houston and meet his long-time drummer, Paul English). Willie sent the tape to Charlie Fitch, who founded the label in April, 1954, naming the company after his service rank (sergeant). The two songs sent were 'When I Sang My Last Hillbillie Song' and 'A Storm Is (Has) Just Begun'. The 'Storm' song was one that Willie cut again in 1959 for "D" Records of Houston. Interestingly, Fitch's recollection was that Willie's tape showed up sometime in 1954.

The tape Willie sent to Fitch was a reel-to-reel on which he first introduced himself, saying hello to Sarg Records and that he had already worked for them on a Dave Isbell session "down at ACA in Houston." What Willie did was record his introduction and two songs over some previously-aired farm reports. The first song on the tape was the 'Hillbillie' song, which Willie said he wrote back when he was about five or six years old.

The release of those songs, together as a single, came about at an unknown later date. The single carried a Sarg 260-45 catalog label and number. Interestingly, some were pressed as 78's and those today are valued at more than a hundred dollars by the serious collector (according to Jerry Osborne's *Official Price Guide to Country Music Records*). Fitch remembered receiving the tape and his reaction to it, telling Richard Zelade (as captured in his book, *Hill Country*) that:

> Nobody - but nobody - would have recorded it, so I just threw the tape in the corner, where it stayed for years. It wasn't recordable, just two times two stuff, you know. Willie was a deejay back then, and the tape he sent me had been recorded over that day's stock market report, so the last song trailed

> off into the last of that day's stock market quotations. He sent it to me and said, 'If you like it, tell me. If you don't like it, tell me. It won't hurt my feelings'.

The two songs did not impress Fitch, so he did nothing with them. He did hold on to them and was later able to tell *Goldmine* the story that:

> the tape he sent me sat there on the shelf for 25 years. Then when he got real popular I thought I'd make something that would make a nice collector's item. You know, you're not gonna make a million bucks off something like that, but I thought it would be good for people who collected his records, and I put the story there with it on the jacket.

When I asked Willie about the belated release of the two songs, he smiled and said, "he [Fitch] was smart to make money on it."

The session Willie referred to on his audition tape, the Dave Isbell one, did result in two 1955 single releases on which Willie was featured playing guitar. He worked the Isbell sessions because he had been playing in Dave's band in the San Antonio area in 1954. As Willie described it, the band was "Dave, his brother, and a left-handed steel player named Carl." During 1954, Willie also played in Johnny Bush's first band when it gigged in San Antonio. That band "included Billy Deaton, who went on to become Faron Young's manager," as well as a powerful friend for Willie when Willie finally moved to Nashville.

The first of the two Isbell singles (they came out on Sarg), carried the catalog number 108-45. The second was numbered 109-45. The "108" single featured Isbell doing 'No Longer Afraid' and 'Satisfied or Sorry'. Number "109" featured 'Let's Do It Up Brown' and 'A Make Believe Christmas'.

Neither of the Isbell 1955 recordings has been made available as part of any Willie Nelson album collections. The audition tape, containing the songs, 'Hillbillie' and 'The Storm', was finally released, not on a conventional music collection, but on a CD-ROM entitled, *Willie: The Life and Music of Willie Nelson*, Graphix Zone GZ10760. The voice, even then, was unmistakably Willie.

Included on the CD-ROM was a version of 'What a Way to Live' (the "A" side of the second "D" label single) done by Willie with his old band, the Repeat Offenders. The "A" side of Willie's first commercial single, 'No Place for Me' also appeared. A live version of 'We Don't Run', a song on the *Spirit* album, was an unexpected treat.

The CD-Rom, itself, showed another of the inventive, "ahead-of-his-time" sides of Willie. As *ICE: The CD News Authority* noted, "not many country artists have jumped on the multimedia bandwagon yet." What a multimedia event it was, from extensive pictures to numerous sound-bites from friends, family members, musical associates, and others who have surrounded Willie for up to five decades. There was an extensive study of the the songs with lyrics to more than thirty. The detailed information imparted throughout the CD ranged from the story behind Patsy Cline's first attempt to record 'Crazy' to Willie's "discovery" of Julio Iglesias.

Following the 1957 self-released single that Willie sold from his Vancouver radio show, it would not be until 1959 that he would again record his own singles. That occurred after a move back to Texas, to the Houston area specifically. Once again he went to work at a radio station, KCRT, and once again played the local music scene.

The first single he recorded in 1959 was for Harold "Pappy" Daily's "D" Records. It paired 'Man with the Blues' with 'The Storm Has Just Begun' (the song which in 1955 he had sent to Sarg Records). It has also been titled 'The Storm Within My Heart'. The "Storm" song was one of the two or three earliest songs Willie ever wrote. He recalled writing it at the age of twelve, about "the same clouds" taking away the sun. Looking back on the song, he said, "that's kind of looking on the dark side for a twelve-year-old kid." Appraising his very first attempts at songwriting, Willie mused that "I always seemed to be able to write the sad side of everything."

Recorded at the Gold Star Studios in Houston, the "D" label single (D-1084) was released in August, 1959. Paul Buskirk, who purchased some of Willie's songs and who hired him as a guitar teacher, played guitar on the session. The resulting single did not become a big hit but a version, by fellow-Texan and country superstar Billy Walker, of that same song, also released in 1959 (the session was done in April) should have become a big seller. At least that's what Walker remembered.

He said that disc jockey Tommy Edwards of WERE in Cleveland, Ohio, "picked it up and so did Edwards' pop counterpart on the station, Bill Randle." Walker even supported the record by doing a number of shows in the area. Unfortunately, though the song caught on in that part of the Midwest, it "didn't catch fire nationally." Nonetheless, the "significant" airplay did show how good the song was.

The next song Willie tried to record in 1959 was 'Night Life', a song he had written going to and from a gig. Unexpectedly, Daily did not want Willie to record it for "D" Records, supposedly because it was too "bluesy" or not "country" enough. Willie's determination to record the song transcended a threatened Daily lawsuit and behind Pappy's back and in violation of his contract with Daily, Willie recorded the song for another small independent Houston label, "RX" (originally Rx as in the sign for drugstore prescriptions, with the slogan, "prescriptions for happy tunes").

The single, 'Night Life' and 'Rainy Day Blues', was cut at a session financed by Willie from proceeds he amassed (all of $150) from the sale of 'Night Life' to Buskirk and a Houston businessman, Walter Breeland (which is why for so long the credits on Willie's song read

"Buskirk/Breeland"). In a hastily conceived attempt to fool Daily, the recording credits for the single (RX 502) listed "Paul Buskirk and His Little Men, featuring Hugh Nelson."

A version of the "RX" single (with the song listed as 'Nite Life') went out as a "promotional" recording with a note that supposedly read, "congratulations and many thanks. Your purchase of this record benefits a non-profit organization for cardiac research." The signature read, "Mary Hill, Ladies Guild." Nowhere was the affiliation or the origination of either the signer or the guild ever revealed. This version was likely the one featured on the Rhino Records collection, *Nite Life: Greatest Hits and Rare Tracks (1959-1971)*, which accounts for the spelling of the word "nite." I was able to ask Willie if he knew anything about the "charity" version, and he replied, "no, I was never aware of it."

Though 'Night Life', as a recorded song, did eventually sell millions of copies for numerous artists, it did not sell this time for Willie. So, Willie tried one more single, in 1960, for "Pappy" Daily and D Records, 'What a Way to Live' and 'Misery Mansion'. It, too, failed to sell. From 1959 and 1960, there were six cuts that comprised three singles for "RX" and "D" Records, 'Night Life', 'Rainy Day Blues', 'Man With the Blues', The Storm Within My Heart' (aka 'The Storm Was in My Heart' and 'The Storm Has Just Begun'), 'Misery Mansion', and 'What a Way to Live'.

The songs have appeared in various formats, from rereleased singles to selections on many of the compilations that focused primarily on the Pamper Music "demos." 'Man with the Blues' and 'The Storm Has Just Begun' went out again as a single in 1961 under the catalog number D-1179. In 1964, it was rereleased by Betty Records as Betty 5703. As a single, 'Night Life' and Rainy Day Blues also appeared in 1959 as Bellaire 107, again in 1963 as Bellaire B-45-107 and once again in 1964 as Oldies 64-6756.

Two more appearances of the single occurred in 1976 as American Gold 7601 and Bellaire B-5000. In 1964, 'What a Way to Live' and 'Misery Mansion' was released by Betty Records as Betty 5702. On the Bellaire b-45-107 single, writer credits for 'Night Life' actually went to "Buskirk-Breeland-Matthews." Even then it would appear that Willie held on to a one-third interest in the song in his wife's name (or at least used her last name to retain his partial credit).

'Night Life' was one of several songs that Willie "sold" early in his career, when he needed the money. The money supposedly went to pay for recording the song, though Willie has also said that some of the proceeds went "to buy an old car that took me to Nashville." The song has since become one of the most recorded songs in history, thanks initially to Ray Price's great version released in 1963 as the "B" or flip side of a single. Even as the flip side, the song was so good that it reached number twenty-eight, giving Price a rare "two-sided" hit. The

"A" side was 'Make the World Go Away', written by none other than Hank Cochran, Willie's mentor and friend.

Rusty Draper also had a 1963 hit with 'Night Life', this time taking it to number fifty-seven on the *Billboard* pop singles chart. It was, after a long and successful career of selling records, Draper's last charting single (and his only one on Monument Records, the company for whom Willie recorded in 1964). Later, Draper and Nelson would co-own a night club in Jackson, Wyoming, according to Mae Axton. Fortunately, Draper's excellent rendition was not forgotten. In 1993, it reappeared as part of the soundtrack for the film, *A Perfect World*. The soundtrack album came out on Reprise Records.

In spite of the money the song made, Willie initially only realized a one hundred and fifty dollar payback, the amount he got for selling the rights to Paul Buskirk, who was then employing Willie at the Buskirk School of Guitar. Later Willie told *Billboard* magazine that "I eventually got the rights to that one back." He did get his name back on the copyright as one of three co-writers. He recently told me that "I did get back one-third of 'Night Life'." So, Willie has had no regrets, later telling a group of writers that "I needed the hundred and fifty dollars a lot worse then than I do the millions now."

In addition, the fact that someone would buy the song at the time told him that he could become a successful writer. He later observed, without regret, that even though 'Night Life' has "sold more than thirty million records," and further had been performed by artists in all musical categories, "all I got out of it was $150. But so what? At the time I needed the money. The fact that both songs (Willie also sold 'Family Bible' to Buskirk) became hits encouraged me to think I could write a lot more songs that were just as good."

In reality, the fifty dollars he got for 'Family Bible' was a lot of money in those days to the men involved. Willie said he was only able to get that much for the song and "it took all three of them (Buskirk, Breeland, and Claude Gray) to get together $50." He recently said he did not know "if I ever got back any part of 'Family Bible'."

'Night Life' was as great a first commercial effort as a songwriter could hope to make. His daughter, Susie, wrote about "the feeling" Willie had "that made 'Night Life' a classic." She said he told her that:

I first heard the blues picking cotton in a field full of black people. One would sing a line at this end of the field, another at that end. I realized they knew more about music, sound, feeling than I did.

Willie said he wrote the song while working days in Houston, "driving back and forth to Pasadena, over to a place across town called The Esquire Club. It was about a thirty-mile drive over there and I had plenty of time to think, so I wrote it on the way over there." At the club, he worked with Larry Butler's band. During the evening's work, he tried to remember the song. On the way home, he said he "remembered it again, and went over it some more. When I got home, I finally got around to working it out and writing it down."

That wouldn't be the only time he wrote a great song while driving. 'Funny How Time Slips Away' also came to him while driving to work in Nashville, "right after I'd gotten to town." In fact, he observed that "most of the songs I write come to me when I'm drivin'." To him, back then, the night life was not a good life from two points of view. First, from the "religious standpoint," Willie recounted,

> the night life is beer joints and the women of the evening and the honest man blowing his hard-earned money in some beer joint on some dance-hall floozy.

"Plus the fact that it is a hard life," Willie continued, "for a musician who works six nights a week, four hours a night, for just a little money." Once Willie's career took off the night life became a "great life," but back then he was getting "ten dollars a night, six nights a week."

Did Willie make the "right" choice in selling his songs? One of the songs he sold to Buskirk, 'Family Bible', did become a top ten country hit in March 1960 (for Claude Gray on D Records, of all places). It was probably one of the key factors that convinced Willie he could go to Nashville and be a hit songwriter. So, who could possibly answer the question? In reality, who could do more than speculate or look at other situations?

When Willie's old buddy Kris Kristofferson won the first Roger Miller Songwriter award at the Music City News Country Songwriters Awards show in 1995, it was yet another major honor in more than twenty years of recognitions for the man who wrote such classics as 'For the Good Times', 'Help Me Make It Through the Night', and 'Me and Bobby McGee'. Nonetheless, it took him years of writing, starving, living broke, and plugging his songs to finally make it. Actually, Kris told interviewer Bill Flanagan that "it took me five years to make any money at anything but a daytime job." He added that he:

> lived in a slum tenement, condemned, fifty dollars a month. It was the pits, but at the same time I always thought I was making it, you know?

He worked as a janitor for CBS and tried to pitch his songs to anyone he could. The artist he targeted most often was Johnny Cash, so much so that Kris was prohibited from soliciting Johnny while on the job. Legend had it that Kris hired a helicopter to land him on Johnny's lawn so he could, beer in hand, present him with a tape of his compositions. John recalled the contact a little differently (according to author Frye Gaillard), saying that Kris slipped his tapes to June (Johnny's then soon-to-be wife) Carter who passed them on to Cash who would "sit up all night long listening."

Even with that inside track, Kris' writing efforts didn't take off. Why not? Johnny explained:

> 'Sunday Morning Coming Down' was the story of my life at that time. He had another one called 'The Best of All Possible Worlds', which is about getting thrown into jail, and I heard it right after I got out. I held on to his songs for three or four years before I ever recorded any of them. That didn't do him any good, but they were just too personal for me at the time.

Finally Cash did record Kris' songs after getting his own network TV show (on ABC). By then, he "was no longer in and out of jails" and "could look at Kristofferson songs with the mind of a performer or an artist." They finally became something Cash "could sing without it hurtin' so bad."

Frances Preston, former president of BMI, wrote that because Kris' songs were so different, "they weren't accepted at first." Only when an artist of the stature of Johnny Cash took a chance on recording those songs, did Kris make it big. Similarly, the chain of events unleashed after Willie sold a song to Paul Buskirk, who turned around and got it to Claude Gray whose recorded version went top ten country, put Willie on the road to songwriting acclaim and recognition.

The success of 'Family Bible' in Houston in 1960 took Willie to the next point in his journey, where according to Ms. Preston (in her introduction to the Dorothy Horstman book, *Sing Your Heart Out, Country Boy*) , he and two other similarly "special" songwriters, Roger Miller and Mel Tillis, worked:

> behind the scenes in the bands of big stars, quietly perfecting their crafts. Then seemingly out of nowhere, they emerged from their apprenticeship as full-blown stars themselves.

Another great writer, Kostas, appeared to have become, almost overnight, one of Nashville's hottest songwriters, penning the 1989 number one hit, 'Timber I'm Falling in Love', for Patty Loveless. Prior to that, however, he had spent years in Montana, destined for the oblivion of singing his material in small clubs while making an occasional tape of his songs, hoping to get them cut by other unknown artists. One unknown group did record a bunch of his songs and then moved on to sell the tape at concerts in other parts of the country.

Quite a while later, MCA producer, Tony Brown, heard a song from that tape while visiting in the Baltimore/Washington area. He immediately liked the song and eventually tracked down the writer and the rest, as the cliche always goes, was history. The point was that except for one chance listen to a great but unknown song, Kostas would probably still be in Montana.

Willie might never have made a cent on any of his songs and he might never have discovered he was a "commercial" writer. He could still be poor (and older) somewhere in Texas had he not sold his songs to Buskirk and gotten that intricate slow-moving song-selling machinery going (with the Claude Gray "top-tenner" on 'Family Bible' for D Records). No, Willie sold the songs and went on to write many more over many more years. He also never worried about the money saying once he hoped he owed a million dollars when he died.

Writer Don Cusic summarized Willie's situation only too well, that he was unique among aspiring country music songwriters because even before moving to Nashville, he had, "in his Texas days," crafted "a batch of first class songs." The problem was, "he had no immediate way of knowing whether they'd work in Nashville." More to the point, as Cusic understood, Willie didn't know how good his songs were "until he began offering to sell them outright." So intent was he on making it big as a songwriter that in 1960 in Nashville when Hank Cochran told him he had been given a staff writing job at Pamper Music, Willie said he "broke down and cried."

Should this man be kept off the radio?
(Photo from Evelyn Shriver Public Relations)

The First Recordings - Album Listings

The Classic, Unreleased Collection. Rhino Records (and QVC Marketing) R2 71462. (1993).

CD 1 Track Listing: Introduction by Willie, *The First Recordings:* No Place for Me, Lumberjack, *The Pamper Music Recordings:* Why Are You Picking on Me, The Shelter of Your Arms, (A) Moment Is Not Very Long (Isn't), Any Old Arms Won't Do, December Day (s), Healing Hands of Time, Things to Remember, (The) Face of a Fighter, Suffering in Silence, Who Do I Know in Dallas, Slow Down Old World, I Hope So, *The Atlantic Recordings:* I Gotta Have Something I Ain't Got, I'm So Ashamed, My Cricket and Me, Both Ends of the Candle, Slow Down Old World, Under the Double Eagle.

CD 2 Track Listing: So Much to Do, (How Will I Know) I'm Falling in Love Again, Bloody Mary Morning, No Love Around, After the Fire Is Gone (w. Tracy Nelson), *Live at the Texas Opry House:* Whiskey River, Me and Paul, Medley: Funny How Time Slips Away/Crazy/Night Life, Stay All Night (Stay a Little Longer), Walkin', Bloody Mary Morning/Take Me Back to Tulsa, The Party's Over, Truck Drivin' Man, She Thinks I Still Care, Good Hearted Woman, Sister's Coming Home, *Sugar Moon:* Sugar Moon, I'm a Fool to Care, Rosetta, I'll Sail My Ship Alone.

CD 3 Track Listing: I'll Take What I Can Get, If It's Wrong to Love You, Struttin' with Some Barbeque, I'm Gonna Sit Right Down and Write Myself a Letter, Till the End of the World, I'll Keep on Lovin' You, *Willie Alone:* It Should Be Easier Now, Will You Remember Mine, Who'll Buy My Memories, Jimmy's Road, *Willie Sings Hank Williams:* I'm So Lonesome I Could Cry, A House Is Not a Home, My

Bucket's Got a Hole in It, Why Don't You Love Me, Mind Your Own Business, They'll Never Take Her Love From Me, Move It On Over, Why Should We Try Anymore, My Son Calls Another Man Daddy, I Saw the Light.

Recording Notes: The 1957 self-recorded single was made available on this initially mail-order only 1993 package, marketed by Rhino Records, through QVC Marketing, a joint venture production between the W.N. Collection and Rhino. James Austin, senior director of A & R/Special Projects, said that finding Willie's first single was one of the most difficult undertakings he had ever been through (even Willie did not have a copy). Austin was quoted as saying,

> I spent weeks calling every collector, and nobody had it. Then we found a D.J. in Portland, Ore., who had a near-mint copy.

The two sides of that first single were but one of many delights and surprises presented within this set.

The three disc release also contained some of the "least-issued" 1961 Pamper Music demos (*The First Recordings*). A live recording originally done for but not released by Atlantic Records along with outtakes and unreleased material from the Atlantic sessions dominated most of the rest of the first and almost all of the second disc. The remainder of the second disc and all of the third disc consisted of an unreleased set of standards, *Sugar Moon*, from the mid-eighties, four songs done by Willie with just the accompaniment of his guitar, and a tribute album to Hank Williams.

One of the unreleased Atlantic cuts (from the *Shotgun Willie* sessions), 'I Gotta Have Something I Ain't Got', was written by one of Willie's musical heroes, Floyd Tillman. Another, 'Me and My Cricket', was written by Leon Russell. The *Sugar Moon* material drew from jazz and pop standards and featured Freddie Powers, who had done considerable work previously with Merle Haggard. That set of recordings was not planned. In fact, the whole thing came about by accident. Willie recalled that:

> Freddie had a guy he wanted to record, so he brought Merle's band down to my studio in Austin and recorded the guy, and Merle was gonna come down and do some tracks while the band was there. And Merle didn't show up after they got through. I was there, so I said, 'Why don't we pick some together?' We went in and in one day, we did that whole album. Most of them were old standards that most of those pickers had played all their lives, anyway.

The eclectic group of standards ranged from Louis Armstrong's 'Struttin' with Some Barbeque', a song whose melody line was written around a major seventh chord, to Earl "Fatha" Hines' 'Rosetta'. The Hines song was written, according to Hines, himself,

> as a ballad, but later it was played in all kinds of ways, as a waltz, as a Latin number, as a brass section number, and so on.

The Hank Williams tribute album was done with Jimmy Day, who once played steel guitar with Hank. Day also backed Ray Price when Willie became Ray's bass player. In 1962, when Willie left the Price band, he took Day with him. Jimmy stayed with Willie for about six months, leaving to join George Jones' band. In 1966, he rejoined Willie's band, then called "The Record Men." He stayed seven years full-time and after that he played every so often behind Willie. Willie also explained how the "Hank" set came about. According to him,

> I just had the songs there, the studio was there and I had Jimmy Day there and a good band that was just hangin' out around the studio. And Jimmy used to play steel guitar with Hank Williams years ago on the Louisiana Hayride. Jimmy also learned from Sammy Pruett who played guitar with Hank in The Drifting Cowboys to play that 'snap' rhythm. Hank didn't use a drum, but he had that real 'snap' rhythm. Jimmy Day knew how to do that. So I got out my Hank Williams collection and did the Hank album with Jimmy playin' steel, then I had him go in and overdub 'snap' rhythm on electric guitar.

As Willie remembered, they did the songs:

> one after the other, really, most of them in one take. We'd all lived with that material for years.

He sang them "in the same key Hank did 'em in and did 'em in exactly the same tempo." He also followed "Hank's phrasing as much as I could do it." This was an unusual approach for Willie, because as he observed, Hank, unlike himself, "did most everything right on the beat." In the end it was a fitting tribute that merged the Willie Nelson interpretive method with songs from the most universally accepted country singer/songwriter, who loved good covers of his songs. Hank's second wife, Billie Jean, remembered:

> when Tommy Edwards came out with 'You Win Again' and they sent Hank a copy. We sat on the floor and listened to it

and tears was running out of his eyes. He said, 'Just think, a pop artist cuttin' ol' Hank's songs.'

The Longhorn Jamboree Presents Willie Nelson & His Friends. (Willie Nelson & Friends). Plantation Records PLP-24. (1976).

Track Listing: What a Way to Live, Misery Mansion, Rainy Day Blues (*), Night Life (*), Man With the Blues (*), The Storm Within (Was in) My Heart (Has Just Begun) (*).

Recording Notes: This 1976 release from the Shelby Singleton label featured all the sides (six cuts in all) of Willie's 1959 and 1960 singles for the Houston-based Rx and D labels. Pappy Daily, early producer for George Jones, founded and owned D Records. His refusal to record 'Night Life' (also written as 'Nite Life') caused Willie to record it for the Rx label under the name Hugh Nelson.

The cover picture showed a bearded Willie as he appeared in the seventies. The back photo came from a seventies live performance (though there were no live recordings on this album). Also included on this collection, along with the Willie selections, were two cuts each by Jerry Lee Lewis (original Sun recordings), Carl Perkins (also Sun recordings), and David Allan Coe. Coe was an artist with whom Willie would later record a duet. That occurred after David signed with Columbia Records.

Other Releases: In England this album was released (in 1977) on the Charly label as CR 30120. In 1980, four of the cuts (*) were marketed along with four David Allan Coe sides as *Willie and David,* (credited to Willie and David Allan Coe) Plantation Records PLP-41. That particular compilation was also released in England as *Outlaws,* Topline TOP-133 and in Portugal as *Willie and David,* Pronit PLP-0062. Several of the cuts were also released on a Plantation album credited to Willie, Johnny Lee, and Mickey Gilley.

* = the four cuts included on the album, *Willie and David,* Plantation Records PLP-41.

Early Tracks. Sun R4 70345. (1990).

Track Listing: I Can't Find the Time, (The) End of Understanding, A Moment Is Not Very Long, Blame It on the Times, What a Way to Live, Misery Mansion, Rainy Day Blues, Night Life, Man With the Blues, Everything But You.

Recording Notes: This 1990 ten cut compilation was released through Such a Deal Records, a division of Rhino Records. The tracks were licensed from Sun Entertainment Corp. and the actual release came out under the Sun logo. Of the ten selections, five were the original songs released as singles on the RX and D labels. Only 'The Storm Within My Heart' was not included.

The remainder of the tracks were Pamper Music "demos." All of the Pamper "demo" tracks originated from Willie. Four came from the tapes retrieved and saved by his dad (from Willie's burned out house in Nashville) and one came via a group called Tax Planners that administered many of those recordings. The front cover depicted Willie in an early "promo" shot with turtleneck and short hair.

Nite Life: Greatest Hits & Rare Tracks: (1959-1971). Rhino Records R2 70987. (1990).

Track Listing: Man With the Blues, What a Way to Live, Nite Life, Rainy Day Blues, You'll Always Have Someone, Everything But You, Mr. Record Man, Hello Walls, Crazy, Touch Me, Funny How Time Slips Away, Am I Blue, Half a Man, Opportunity to Cry, San Antonio Rose, One in a Row, Bring Me Sunshine, Me and Paul.

Recording Notes: The first four tracks on this 1990 compilation came from the 1959 and 1960 singles Willie did for D and Rx Records in Houston. The next two tracks, 'You'll Always Have Someone' and 'Everything But You', were Pamper Music "demos," both co-written with Hank Cochran. They were both "previously unissued" (according to Rhino Records).

After that came eight Liberty recordings, including the first song, 'Touch Me', Willie cut for the label, though it was not part of the first single. Instead, it became the "A" side of his second solo single for the label and peaked at number seven on the country singles charts. Among the other Liberty cuts were three Willie standards and four surprising choices, especially the song, 'Am I Blue', which had failed to chart as the "A" side of Willie's next-to-last Liberty single (while under contract to the company).

The final four cuts came from Nelson's RCA catalog, including his most successful single for the company, 'Bring Me Sunshine'. Also featured was his first top twenty RCA single, 'One in a Row', along with its "B" side, 'San Antonio Rose'. The final and fourth RCA cut, 'Me and Paul', came from the *Yesterday's Wine* album.

King of the Outlaws. Charly Records CDCD 1088. (1993).

Track Listing: What a Way to Live, Misery Mansion, Rainy Day Blues, Night Life (RX Records single), Man With the Blues (D Records single), The Storm Within My Heart (Was in), A Moment Is Not Very Long (Isn't), Some Other Time, Blame It on the Times, The Shelter of

Your (My) Arms, Touch Me, Half a Man, Will You Remember Mine, Everything But You, I Hope So, Is There Something on Your Mind.

   Recording Notes: This 1993 English compilation consisted of six cuts obtained from Shelby Singleton's holdings, Sun Entertainment Corp. They comprised the singles released on RX and D Records in 1959 and 1960. The remainder of the set consisted of Pamper Music demos along with two songs only known to have been released on Liberty, 'Touch Me' and 'Half a Man'.

Willie was ahead of his time at RCA.
(Photo from the Michael Ochs Archives)

"Face of a Fighter":

The Pamper Music "Demos"

None of the three singles Willie made in Houston on the "RX" and "D" labels sold enough to make any charts. So, by 1960, he became even more determined to try to make it as a songwriter in Nashville. He traversed that legendary trek in an ancient (1946, or 1941 or 1951, depending on the source or the story) "gun-grey" Buick that "died" in downtown Nashville. Through one of his first Nashville friends, Hank Cochran, he signed with Pamper Music (later sold to Tree Music) for a fifty dollar per week draw, or advance on future royalties.

Hank recalled first meeting Willie at Tootsie's Lounge. "This new guy was there and he had some of the best songs I had ever heard," was the way Cochran remembered the event. Willie told Hank, "I don't write for nobody. Nobody wants me." In fact, Willie had gotten the message that "my songs weren't what they considered commercial - some had more than three chords in them."

Nonetheless, Hank got Willie signed to Pamper after Willie impressed the "talent guy, Hal Smith." Actually, Hal was co-owner of Pamper along with singer, Ray Price, and at the same time he was Ernest Tubb's booking agent (Curtis Artists Productions). Hank turned down an impending fifty dollar a week raise so Pamper could pay Willie that same fifty dollars to be a staff writer. Willie remembered the Pamper years and how they began for him, saying that:

> when I was a songwriter at Pamper Music, Ray Price was an owner. I had a few songs that had gotten recorded. In the meantime, Ray was touring and Johnny Paycheck was playin' bass for Ray. And Ray called me from on the road and wanted to know if I knew a bass player, that Johnny was leaving. I

said, 'Sure.' He said, 'Who?' I said, 'Me.' I'd never played bass in my life, but I didn't figure Ray would notice for a while.

It was fellow musician, Jimmy Day, who quickly taught Willie the rudimentary aspects of playing bass. Day would later often play with Willie, most noticeably on Willie's tribute to Hank Williams. At the time, Price was very impressed with Willie, recalling that "when I first heard 'Night Life', Willie was in my band at the time. Willie sang it for me, and I thought it was a great blues song."

A fellow songwriter at Pamper, Harlan Howard remembered (for *American Songwriter*) his "first impressions" of Willie, saying that:

Willie Nelson was a great writer. He didn't write a lot, but everything he touched turned to gold. I'd write a dozen songs to his one, but I'd have a bunch of mediocre songs that didn't get recorded.

Willie eventually recorded 'Yours Love', one of Harlan's better copyrights, a song that also became a classic duet in the hands of Dolly Parton and Porter Wagoner.

One of the major accomplishments Willie had while with Pamper was the recording of forty-six high quality "demo" selections, beginning in 1961. These "demos," or to be more specific, demonstration recordings, were intended to showcase Nelson's compositions to other artists to hopefully interest them in using one or more of the songs on a forthcoming album or as a single release. The recordings were effective, getting Johnny Bush, for example, to record 'Undo the Right' (he took it country top ten as a single) and Ray Price to cut 'I Let My Mind Wander' (it did not chart).

All of the "demos" Willie recorded were a cut above most demos of the time (by other writers) in that Willie, himself, did the singing and playing, often with some of Nashville's top session players. Pianist Hargus 'Pig' Robbins, guitarist Pete Wade, bass-player Bob Moore, and veteran steel guitarist, Jimmy Day (once with Hank Williams), played on many of the sessions. The songs, themselves, were substantially superior to the average country composition of the time, although many in the business unhesitatingly told Willie he was not "commercial."

He was always commercial, but back in the early 1960's he was not following the accepted country formula. In many ways, he was more than country. Though one of Willie's producers at Liberty Records, Joe Allison, "didn't think he was a pop star back in those days," others came to that conclusion, such as the critic who wrote that "Nelson is the Sinatra of this generation." Frank Sinatra also saw the pop possibilities in Willie songs, going as far as working on recording a full album of Willie's material.

The only difficulty was, Frank couldn't release the album because of problems encountered in gaining permission to use the copyrighted music. To solve those problems, Willie and Hank Cochran got the money together (mostly Willie's to the tune of about fifty thousand dollars) to buy control of Pamper Music (from none other than Ray Price). That still didn't result in a full resolution of the problems. Meanwhile, Willie very quickly began to find the ownership of Pamper financially draining with a continuing barrage of bills for all sorts of things.

He sold his interest and Pamper eventually was sold to Tree Music, which has since become part of the Sony Entertainment empire. Tree actually bought Pamper in 1969 from majority owner, Hal Smith. Hal and Ray Price had initially been the principal founders of the company. Though Sinatra never did release (or even complete) his intended Willie album, the fact that it was conceptualized stood as testimony to the greatness of Willie's early works.

In Willie's case, instead of his "demo" recordings remaining with other artists or with his publishing company, they eventually made their way into the commercial world. The question of how they came into the commercial realm has always been an intriguing one. The first major source was a set of tapes found in the effects of Willie's father, Ira Nelson, when Ira died. Twenty-one songs were saved from those tapes (out of about thirty). The twenty-one songs were as follows:

Blame It on the Times, Both Ends of the Candle, Broken Promises, Country Willie, The End of Understanding, Everything But You, Face of a Fighter, The Ghost, Happiness Lives Next Door, I Hope So, I'll Stay Around, I'm Going to Lose a Lot of Teardrops, Is There Something on Your Mind, Let's Pretend, A Moment Isn't Very Long, A New Way to Cry, No Tomorrow in Sight, Pride Wins Again, Shelter of Your Arms, Some Other Time, Will You Remember Mine (Me)?

Of the twenty-one tracks, twenty were initially released in 1977 on the 1961 album (on the Double Barrel label), making it the first commercial collection of Pamper "demos."

So, how did Ira Nelson come to have, in his effects, tapes of Willie's songs? The tapes were actually ones the elder Nelson recovered from the ruins of Willie's burned down Ridgetop house outside of Nashville. That fire supposedly occurred the Christmas of 1969 (there have been some discrepancies in the reporting of the date). The aftermath of the fire precipitated Willie's first move out of Nashville, since arriving in 1960, back to Texas to foreshadow his eventual move to Austin and the firming up of that city's "sound."

After the fire was extinguished, Willie's father, Ira, went poking in the ruins and found charred boxes of tapes. The boxes were later rediscovered in his effects after he died. Next, as Willie's buddy, Larry Trader, related, Trader took the most salvageable boxes (four in all) to a studio in Dallas and began to listen. He said that the tapes had been made in a "little studio" Willie had built "in the storm cellar" of his Ridgetop home. The recording machine was nothing more than "a little two-track tape machine."

Larry played the tapes and what he heard was a lot of original music "made when guys would be sitting in the cellar rehearsing or passing time if somebody didn't show up for a session." He said he ended up with enough great material to do at least three full albums. Armed with twenty-two of the best cuts, he played them for Willie, who when he heard the quality, "thought he'd just finished cutting them." According to Trader, Willie was so impressed he said, "why don't we go into the record business? You're the president."

That was Trader's recollection of how he "became president of Willie's Lone Star Records label" and how Lone Star Records became, in 1978, a separate company not affiliated with Columbia Records. This time it was headquartered at the Austin Opera House and had a worldwide distribution deal with Phonogram Inc. (parent company of PolyGram and Mercury Records). In 1975, Lone Star had served initially as a logo under which two Willie albums were released, the first two following his signing of his new Columbia contract.

The 1978 opening (or re-opening) of Lone Star was accompanied by a good deal of fanfare. According to *Billboard*, there was "a Texas-size grand opening celebration and showcase" at the Austin Opry House (on Monday June 19). The party was "climaxed with a performance by the label's founder and chairman of the board, Willie Nelson." Other performers (on the Lone Star roster) who appeared at the opening day gala included Larry G. Hudson (with whom Willie would later record a single), Don Bowman, Cooder Browne, the Geezinslaw Brothers, Steve Fromholz, and Ray Wylie Hubbard.

Guerry Massey was introduced as president of the label. Larry Trader was listed as vice-president while Willie's attorney, Joel Katz, was listed as the company's attorney. Massey spoke of wanting to "present a variety of talented artists," while Willie said he planned "for the label to deal with artists the way I like to be dealt with." When he was asked if he would ever record exclusively for Lone Star, Willie replied that:

> it's hard to say what will happen in three years when my contract is up with CBS, but it only seems natural that if everything works like we plan that I would eventually be on my own label.

As a company, Lone Star eventually put out (starting in 1978) several albums by other artists, most of which Willie was involved in as guest star. A collection of ten of Willie's Pamper "demos" from the tapes found at Ridgetop went out as a single album on Lone Star in 1978, entitled *Face of a Fighter*, distributed by Mercury (PolyGram). Unfortunately, in 1979, due to marketing (and financing) problems, Willie decided to "shut the company down for awhile."

The *Face of a Fighter* album became the initial major nation-wide release of ten of the Pamper "demos." Previously, there had been a localized release of a double album of "demos" Larry did not discuss, yet it was one in which he was involved. That collection, entitled *1961*, consisted of twenty of the twenty two songs he first played for Willie. It came out on the Double Barrel label in 1977, one year earlier than *Face of a Fighter*, making it the first commercial (though geographically limited) release of some of the Pamper "demos."

Larry was listed as producer and according to his own hand-written liner notes, this was a "double album that was recorded in 1961. These were Willie's first songs to ever be recorded." The label, Double Barrel Records, was described as "a laidback Division of Shotgun Productions." Trader further wrote that the tapes:

> have been through fire, that destroyed Willie's home, in and
> out of suit cases, pick up trucks, farms and apartments.

Willie recently told me that, "yes, the Double Barrel label was done through me."

Nine of the songs on the *1961* album were included on the *Face of a Fighter* album, along with one more cut, 'Will You Remember Mine'. Together the two albums comprised twenty-one of the twenty-two songs that Trader first played for Willie after salvaging the four reels of tape. 'Will You Remember Mine' demonstrated the commerciality of the Pamper "demo" songs when it was released as a single in 1978 (on the Lone Star label, catalog number 703), getting to the bottom reaches of the national country singles charts, in spite of the company's marketing difficulties. Some of the other "demo" songs on these two albums eventually wound up rerecorded by Willie on his Liberty and RCA albums.

Of the remaining twenty-five Pamper "demos," twenty-one (that did not come from Ira Nelson's tapes), came from Willie, through an organization known as Tax Planners & Associates (also referred to as Tax Planners Associates). The demos originating from this group came "courtesy of Just Willie Ltd., Lone Star Ltd., and West Star Ltd." That meant that Willie, himself, released the recordings, as a result of another past income tax problem (circa 1983, well before the 1990's tax bill of more than seventeen million dollars which took several years to settle). The twenty-one songs, recorded between 1961 and 1963, that came from the Tax Planners were, as follows:

And So Will You My Love, Any Old Arms Won't Do, Building Heartaches, Go Away, The Healing Hands of Time, Home Is Where You're Happy, I Can't Find the Time, I Didn't Sleep a Wink, I Feel Sorry for Him, I Just Don't Understand, I Let My Mind Wander, One Step Beyond, Right from Wrong, Slow Down Old World, Suffering in Silence, Things to Remember, Undo the Right (Wrong), Waiting (Wastin') Time, Why Are You Picking on Me, You Wouldn't Cross the Street to Say Goodbye, You'll Always Have Someone.

Beyond the two major sources (Ira Nelson and the Tax Planners), there were two other sources that covered the remaining four "demos." The first was Shelby Singleton (or "Sun Classics"), purchaser of Sun Records and founder of Plantation Records. He eventually released (on Plantation Records) two "demos" that had not been released before, along with seventeen others that came from the Tax Planners. Shelby also rereleased Willie's 1959 and 1969 singles. How Shelby came into possession of the two "demos" has never been revealed. The two demos for which he was the source were, as follows:

Follow(ing) Me Around, So Much to Do

The final source was Rhino Records, which released twelve of the "demos" (they came to the label courtesy of Willie) as part of the box set they marketed on Willie (through QVC, the telemarketers), and listed them as being "previously unissued." In the enclosed booklet, they conceded the cuts were really "less issued" ones. In fact, ten had previously been issued by "Tax Planners." That left only two for this category, as follows:

December Day, Who Do I Know in Dallas

Ever since Willie's sales success with Columbia, all forty-six tracks have been commercially marketed by more than a hundred different record companies. They have been released and rereleased over a twenty year span (1977 to 1997) on more than a hundred different album collections (over fifty in the United States alone). How has Willie felt about the plethora of albums containing his Pamper "demo" recordings? "They've been coming out of the cracks," was the answer he gave. When asked if he was getting paid for all the albums, he replied, "Yeah, as far as I know. I love it. I wish they'd come out with some more."

The Pamper Music "Demos" - Album Listings

1961. Double Barrel Records LT-1961. (1977).

Track Listing: Blame It on the Times, A Moment Is Not (Isn't) Very Long (*), I'm Going to Lose a Lot of Teardrops, No Tomorrow in Sight, A New Way to Cry, Both Ends of the Candle, The End of Understanding, The Shelter of (My) Your Arms (*), I Hope So, Everything But You (*), Pride Wins Again, I'll Stay Around, Face of a (the) Fighter, A Broken Promise, Is There Something on Your Mind, Country Willie, Happiness Lives Next Door, Let's Pretend, The Ghost, Some Other Time.

Recording Notes: In 1977, Willie and friend, Larry Trader (listed as "producer"), marketed this first commercial release of the early sixties Pamper "demos." It consisted of twenty of the twenty-two songs on the tape found in Willie's father's effects. As a double album, it wound up on both the Double Barrel and Shotgun logos with the same catalogue number.

Some of the songs were later rerecorded and released on other labels in newer (usually more ornate) arrangements. 'Country Willie', for example, sounded much more lively when released as it was redone for Liberty. When rerecorded for RCA, the song featured a more sedate, string-backed arrangement. When 'I Hope So' was rerecorded for Liberty, it was given a much smoother backdrop.

Of all the songs in this collection, 'I Hope So' became the only one to experience chart success after being rerecorded, going to number thirty-six on the country singles chart in 1970. Liberty released it that year even though Willie had left the label and had been signed to RCA (since 1964), where he was having some chart success. Though the song possessed a definite Willie "sound," sole writing credit went to Shirley (Collie) Nelson.

Despite the fact that all the cuts were intended to serve specifically as demonstrations of individual songs, the sound was close to commercial quality. The album credits noted that the original recordings were done "somewhere in Nashville." In reality, there were only two likely places for them to have taken place, either at the spur of the moment in Pamper Music's converted garage/studio or in the basement of Willie's house.

The string players behind Willie were often found on studio recordings coming out of Nashville at the time, Pete Wade on guitar, Jimmy Day on pedal steel, and Ray Edenton on guitar. In 1966, Jimmy joined Willie's band, The Record Men, and has often toured, since then, as part of Willie's bands. Willie has also worked on Jimmy's projects.

The piano player, Hargus 'Pig' Robbins was about the best around (right up there with Floyd Cramer). He was good enough to be named, in 1976, the Academy of Country Music's "Keyboardist of the Year." That same year he was chosen "Musician of the Year." Bob Moore on bass and Willie Ackerman on drums rounded out a talented cast of supporting musicians.

Other Releases: Three tracks (*) appeared on an undated Quicksilver collection entitled *Alabama, Willie Nelson, Jerry Lee Lewis*, catalog number 1013. Quicksilver also distributed a 1982 Intermedia Records collection (QS-5005), *Willie Nelson and Johnny Lee*. Half of the cuts were Willie's "demos" while the other half consisted of older Johnny Lee tracks. A year later (1983) Quicksilver distributed another Intermedia collection, *Broken Promises*, QS-5048, consisting entirely of Willie's "demos." The Lee/Nelson material was distributed overseas (Germany) as Astan ASTAN-20022 (same title).

* = the three cuts included on the Quicksilver collection entitled *Alabama, Willie Nelson, Jerry Lee Lewis*, catalog number 1013.

Face of a Fighter. Lone Star Records/Mercury Records L-4602. (1978).

Track Listing: Face of a (the) Fighter, The Shelter of (My) Your Arms (*), The End of Understanding, Is There Something on Your Mind, Some Other Time, Will You Remember Mine, Everything But You, I Hope So, A Moment Is Not (Isn't) Very Long, Blame It on the Times.

Recording Notes: Nine of the ten tracks that made up this collection came from the 1977 Double Barrel album, *1961*. The tenth track was, 'Will You Remember Mine', which, when released as a single, made the country charts in October 1978, rising to number sixty-seven. On the back cover of the album, it was noted that all the songs were recorded in Nashville, Tennessee in 1961.

The Lone Star label was founded by Willie along with several other financiers. Two of the others, the president and the secretary-treasurer, were largely blamed for the label's eventual demise in 1979. Bud Doss, then Willie's publicist, revealed in a 1979 (datelined June 12) statement carried by *Variety* that "the blame may be laid upon the shoulders of former Lone Star Records prez Guerry Massey and former secretary-treasurer Wes Day." Doss elaborated that "the duo went through the capitalization in just 10 months."

For its first official album release early in 1978, Lone Star combined two Willie tracks ('Face of a Fighter' and 'Some Other Time' - both from this album) with additional cuts by Steve Fromholz, Don Bowman, the Geezinslaw Brothers, Cooder Browne, and Ray Wylie Hubbard. One of the Bowman cuts was 'Willon and Waylee' which featured the collective talents of Willie and Waylon. The collection was marketed as *Six Pak Vol. I* (there was never a Volume 2), under the catalogue number, L-4600. Willie told me he was the one who "designed the logo" for the label.

The album cover consisted of pictures of six beer cans, each featuring the likeness of one of the artists or groups. The legend on each can read "brewed with pure country music" and "certified country quality." Willie was listed as the album's producer. His two cuts were "recorded in 1961." Special thanks were given to Larry Trader.

Other Releases: The *Face of a Fighter* album also appeared as a picture disc. Two undated reissues were marketed, one on Audio Fidelity as L-4602/PD-213 and the other in England on Hallmark (catalog number 300042). The cuts on the collection have since appeared on other similar collections. *The Poet (Early Recordings)*, Accord 4N-7236, from 1982, was an abridged rerelease of the *Face of a Fighter* album with one cut (*) deleted. In England, the Accord set was released on the Breakaway label (same title) as BWY-62.

The Legend Begins, Takoma Records DCA-1151 (marketed by Allegiance Records), was a 1983 complete rerelease of the *Face of a Fighter* album with a reordering of cuts. It was interesting to see a set of Willie's "demos" on Takoma because the original intention behind the founding of the label was to release new recordings by guitarist John Fahey. In 1994, the ten "Lone Star" tracks were put out (with a resequencing of cuts) as *Remember Me*, Chicago Music CMR-94-106. Production credits, on both the Takoma and Chicago Music sets, went to Willie, for Abbott Ltd. The Chicago Music label has marketed sets of early cuts from other country artists, such as Johnny Cash.

* = the cut deleted from the *Face of a Fighter* album to make up the abridged set, *The Poet (Early Recordings)*, Accord 4N-7236, from 1982.

Just Plain Willie (The Unreleased Tapes - Vol. 1, Vol. 2, Vol. 3). Back-Trac Records (CBS Records) BT-17726, 7, 8. (1983).

Vol. 1 Track Listing: Is There Something on Your Mind (+), A Moment Is Not (Isn't) Very Long (+), Some Other Time (+), Blame It on the Times (%) (+), The Shelter of Your (My) Arms (*) (@), The End of Understanding (+), Will You Remember Mine? (+), Everything But You (+), I Hope So (+), Face of a Fighter.
Vol. 2 Track Listing: I Feel Sorry for Him (*) ($) (%) (@) (&), Suffering in Silence (*) ($) (%), You Wouldn't Cross the Street to Say Goodbye (*) ($) (%) (&), I Didn't Sleep a Wink (*) (@) (&), I Can't Find the Time (*) ($) (@) (&), (If You Can't Undo the Wrong,) Undo the Right (%) (@), I Let My Mind (Wander) Wonder (*) ($) (@) (&), Why Are You Picking on Me (@) (+), Home Is Where You're Happy ($) (%) (@) (#).
Vol. 3 Track Listing: One Step Beyond ($) (%) (@), Any Old Arms Won't Do (*) (%) (@) (#), I Just Don't Understand (*) ($) (%) (@) (&) (#), You'll Always Have Someone (*) (%) (@) (#), Things to Remember (@) (#), And So Will You My Love ($) (@) (#), Healing Hands of Time, Slow Down Old World (@) (#), Building Heartaches (+).
Recording Notes: This 1983 three volume set (twenty-eight tracks) featured ten of the twenty "demo" cuts found on the 1961 album. In addition, the selection that appeared on both the Lone Star album and as a Lone Star single, 'Will You Remember Mine?', was included. For the seventeen other tracks, this collection marked their first commercial release.

One cut, 'Building Heartaches', found on Volume Three, only appeared again on two other (and later) compilations. One was a set from the English label, Premier (which itself was made up of a subset of cuts from these three volumes)and the other came from Success Records. 'Suffering in Silence', from the second volume, was one of those listed on the Rhino boxed collection as being "previously unreleased." Every cut was credited as being "from Tax Planners & Associates courtesy of Just Willie Ltd., Lone Star Ltd., and West Star Ltd."

The first volume of this three volume compilation contained the same cuts that were on the Lone Star Records (Mercury) release, *Face of a Fighter*, but in a different order. All three volumes, though released on the Back-Trac label, were distributed by CBS, the parent company for Columbia Records, the label to which Willie was then currently signed. In 1983, the three Back-Trac volumes appeared as one on the Orbit label (a subsidiary of CBS) with a catalog number of P3-17131. That combined collection was likewise entitled *Just Plain Willie.*

Other Releases: Since the initial 1983 release of the three individual sets, the twenty-eight cuts have been resequenced into numerous other, usually smaller collections. A 1984 budget compilation from Premier (also released on Evergreen), *A Portrait in Music,* catalog number KCBR 1016, combined eighteen of the cuts (in a different sequence, of course), omitting ten (*) selections. Almost all of the first volume was included, with the exception of 'The Shelter of Your Arms'. Most of the second volume was omitted, except for three cuts. Only three cuts of the third volume were not included. Most of the cuts on the Premier set were listed as being from Tree Music, owners of Nelson's Pamper catalog.

The 1983 Allegiance Records collection, *Willie or Won't He*, AV 5005, consisted of ten tracks ($) from the last two volumes (with some reordering of selections). Its cover illustration showed a caricature of a smiling Willie holding two dice that totalled up to seven. The same ten cuts were released (same title) in Australia on the Axis label as AX.260312.

The undated budget set, *Super Hits*, Evergreen 2690252, consisted of ten cuts (%), all (except for 'Blame It on the Times') from volumes two and three. It was printed in West Germany and "made" in Korea. Evergreen has specialized in marketing sets of obscure cuts on artists ranging from Little Richard to Fats Domino, calling them some variation on "greatest hits"). This collection was also released in 1990 as *Super Hits,* on both Point 2661114 and Black Tulip 2690254, out of Holland. The source for the Point set was listed as Creative Sounds of New Mexico.

Creative Sounds was originally based in Pennsylvania, then moved to New Mexico. It has specialized in rereleasing catalogs of hundreds of older artists, from Hank Williams to James Brown. The sources for and royalty payments on the recordings they have marketed have been questioned in past court cases. In the early 1990's, the company did market its own collection of Pamper "demos" (SSI 3548), entitled *Things to Remember,* Fifteen (@) of the cuts came from this three volume set while one other cut, 'A Broken Promise' (which led off the set), came from the Ira Nelson tapes. In 1984, Media Music had released the Creative Sounds collection (same title) as MM-37184.

At about the same time, Classic Sound, Inc. of Norcross, Georgia, released the same set of cuts (resequenced slightly) that appeared on the Creative Sounds compilation. The Classic Sound collection was entitled *I Just Don't Understand* and given a catalog number of CLASSIC 7560. Licensing came from Peachtree Music, Inc., while the cover photo came from the Michael Ochs archive. Additionally, the company marketed their Willie "demos" as *Super Hits*, CLASSIC 40022.

In 1994, a two compact disc twenty track compilation entitled, *Willie Nelson-Volume 1* and *Willie Nelson-Volume 2*, Eclipse Music Group 64705-2/64708-2, was released without a given country of origin. The cover jackets were printed in Canada, while the discs were made in the United States. The company responsible for the release, Eclipse Music, had no address. The San Juan Music Group, often cited as the origin for foreign compilations by companies like England's Charly

Records, licensed the tracks. Eighteen of the twenty tracks came from the Back-Trac volumes, meaning ten tracks (+) were not utilized. The two additional tracks on the Eclipse collection were the RX single "A" side, 'Night Life' and 'December Days'.

In 1997, Promo Sound, under the series name, "The Entertainers," released a twenty-eight cut collection, catalogue number CD 257. It was credited to Willie and entitled, *His 28 Greatest Hits*. The country of origin was not specified. With the exception of six cuts, the collection was identical to this Back-Trac set. The first exception was 'Dream Baby', and although credited to Willie as writer, it was the well-known Roy Orbison song as sung by Waylon Jennings.

'Dream Baby' and five other tracks, 'Night Life', 'Both Ends of the Candle', 'No Tomorrow in Sight', 'I'll Stay Around', and 'Waiting Time' took the place of six cuts (&) that had been on the Back-Trac volumes. Otherwise, the remaining twenty-two cuts came from the Back-Trac volumes. All writing credit went to Willie, except for three songs, two of which were correctly given to Willie and Hank Cochran. On the third, 'Night Life', the writer credits were also correct.

In 1997, Boomerang Records, marketed and distributed by BRL (USA), released seven cuts (#) from the last two volumes. They were packaged with five old Waylon cuts under the title, *Burning Memories*, catalog number BEA-51582. One track, 'And So Will You My Love', was mistitled as 'And So Will You Love Me'.

* = the ten cuts omitted from the Premier collection, *A Portrait in Music*, KCBR 1016.

$ = the ten cuts used on the 1983 Allegiance Records collection, *Willie or Won't He*, AV 5005.

% = the ten cuts used on the undated budget set, *Super Hits*, Evergreen 2690252.

@ = the fifteen cuts used on the 1990 Creative Sounds compilation, *Things to Remember*, SSI 3548.

& = the six cuts replaced by six other tracks on the twenty-eight cut Promo Sound collection, *His 28 Greatest Hits*, CD 257.

+ = the ten cuts not utilized by the Eclipse Music Group sets, *Willie Nelson-Volume 1* and *Willie Nelson-Volume 2*, 64705-2/64708-2.

= the seven cuts on the Boomerang Records release, *Burning Memories*, BEA-51582.

"20 Early Memories". Plantation Records PLC-2000. (1983).

Track Listing: I Can't Find the Time, The End of Understanding (*), Rainy Day Blues, Follow Me Around, Any Old Arms Won't Do, I Just Don't Understand, Suffering in Silence, I Didn't Sleep a Wink, So Much to Do, A Moment Is Not (Isn't) Very Long (*), Some Other Time (*),

Blame It on the Times (*), The Shelter of Your Arms (*), You Wouldn't Cross the Street to Say Goodbye, You'll Always Have Someone, Will You Remember Mine? (*), Everything But You (*), I Hope So (*), Is There Something on Your Mind.

Recording Notes: In the late 1960's, Shelby Singleton, who had previously interned in the record business as head of Smash Records, managed to establish Plantation Records and acquire all of the assets of Sun Records from its original founder, Sam Phillips. He quickly had a huge hit with Jeannie C. Riley's rendition of Tom T. Hall's 'Harper Valley PTA'. At the same time, he obtained at least nineteen (and possibly more) of the Willie Nelson Pamper Music "demo" recordings.

This twenty selection 1983 compilation from Shelby featured eight songs from the tape found in Ira Nelson's effects. Added to those eight songs were eight other Pamper "demos" that had already come out (in 1983) on the Back-Trac (CBS) label via the Tax Planners & Associates. 'Rainy Day Blues' had been previously released as part of a 1959 "D" label single, while 'Will You Remember Mine' previously appeared as a single on Willie's Lone Star label,

Rounding out the collection were two more "demo" cuts, 'Follow Me Around' and 'So Much to Do', both of which came out for the first time on this collection. Singleton's source for the two cuts has never been disclosed. Willie would later rerecord both songs for RCA in the sixties. Interestingly, both songs appeared on a 1983 Intermedia Records collection (distributed by Quicksilver), *Past Times Behind Rock and Roll*, QS-5055. Added to the two Willie tracks were eight more selections by the Beach Boys, Hall and Oates, among others.

Other Releases: Singleton went on to release his acquired Nelson cuts on numerous albums featuring Willie's name, with one exception. In 1983, the cuts came out under a "various artists" credit (Willie, Johnny Lee, and Mickey Gilley) on the album, *Texas Tornadoes*, Plantation PLP-54. Otherwise, over an approximate fourteen year period, Singleton has both released and licensed other companies to release numerous Pamper "demo" tracks under the Willie Nelson name.

Specifically, cuts from the *20 Early Memories* collection (along with the tracks that made up the RX and D label singles) did reappear on two other (undated) Plantation "budget" collections, *Night Life*, PLC-207, and *Rainy Day Blues*, PLC-224. Eight of the cuts (*) were previously marketed together in 1982 as *The Hungry Years*, Plantation Records PLC-53. The original cover of *The Hungry Years* showed Willie with a local Western swing band, The Frontiersmen. Later covers showed only the flag of the state of Texas.

* = the eight cuts on the 1982 collection, *The Hungry Years*, Plantation Records PLC-53.

Vintage Willie Nelson. Delta Records CTA 7104. (1984).

Track Listing: Night Life (#) (+) (@), A New Way to Cry, Both Ends of the Candle (*) (@), I'll Stay Around (@), A Broken Promise (Broken Promises), Happiness Lives Next Door, Let's Pretend (*) (#), I'm Going to Lose a Lot of Teardrops, Country Willie (*) (#) (+) (@), Rainy Day Blues (*) (#) (+) (@), The Ghost (#), Waiting (Wasting) Time, Go Away, Right from Wrong, Pride Wins Again (#) (@), No Tomorrow in Sight.

Recording Notes: This 1984 release from Delta Records, based in Nacogdoches, Texas, contained the original versions of 'Night Life' and 'Rainy Day Blues' as released on a single for RX Records. Eleven of the remaining cuts came from the *1961* album. Three other "demos" (from the Tax Planners), 'Waiting Time', 'Go Away', and 'Right from Wrong', rounded out the set. All three appeared for the first time.

Other Releases: Delta originally released their "demo" compilations under two titles, *Vintage Willie Nelson*, DLP-1151, in 1982, and *Diamonds in the Rough*, DLP-1157, in 1984, which itself was a reissue of the Lone Star album, *Face of a Fighter*. In the same year, 1984, that Delta released this set, Allegiance Records came out with a subset of the collection, entitled *Wild & Willie*, AV 5010. Six (#) cuts were omitted. The Allegiance compilation was subsequently paired with one from Takoma, *The Legend Begins* (itself a reissue of *Face of a Fighter*), and the two were released together on compact disc as *'Allegiance Extra'*, CDP 72922.

Again in the same year, 1984, Tudor Records of Merrick, New York, utilized ten of the Delta tracks to create a two volume set. The first volume, Tudor Records TR 1144-04, was entitled *Tudor Records Vintage Series: Volume I* and it featured five cuts by Willie and five by David Houston. The second volume, TR 1143-04, was similarly titled *Tudor Records Vintage Series: Volume II* and it contained five Nelson cuts along with five by Mickey Gilley.

The cuts on Tudor's volume one were 'Go Away', 'Right from Wrong', 'Waiting Time', 'No Tomorrow in Sight', and 'A New Way to Cry'. The cuts on the second volume were, in order, 'Both Ends of the Candle', 'I'll Stay Around', 'A Broken Promise (Broken Promises)', 'Happiness Lives Next Door', and 'Let's Pretend'. The stated source for these cuts was the Tax Planners Associates, the same source for the three volume set from Back-Trac Records (CBS Records), which was released in 1983.

In 1986, Bridge, a label out of Switzerland, released another subset (with a resequencing of cuts) of this collection as *Historic Reissue*, Bridge 100.027-2, this time omitting only three (+) cuts. The label gave credit to these selections as being from 1961 and Tree Music. In the liner notes, it was stated that "this album was previously released as *1961* on the 'Double Barrel' record label." That was not quite true since some of the titles on the *1961* album weren't included, replaced, on the Bridge collection, by other "demo" cuts.   The Bridge collection actually derived from this Delta set.

In 1988 (though the recording, itself, was not dated), Premore, Inc. of Urbana, Illinois, issued ten of the Delta tracks as *Willie Nelson: Collector's Edition Promo*, PL66, choosing not to use six (@) tracks. The Premore collection was used as a promotional item for Solo cups (for TV marketing).   One further collection, *Night Life*, Laserlight (part of Delta Music Inc. of Los Angeles) 15 485, was a 1992 abridged version (twelve cuts) of the original sixteen song release with a resequencing of cuts and four (*) cuts deleted.

= the six cuts on this collection omitted from *Wild & Willie*, Allegiance Records AV 5010.

+ = the three cuts omitted from the Swiss collection, *Historic Reissue*, Bridge 100.027-2.

* = the four cuts omitted from the collection entitled, *Night Life*, Laserlight 15 485.

@ = the six cuts omitted from the Premore collection, *Willie Nelson: Collector's Edition Promo*, PL66.

Early Willie: Collector's Edition. Potomac Records P7-1000. (1984).

Track Listing: (The) End of Understanding, (The) Shelter of Your Arms (*), Undo the Right (Wrong), One Step Beyond, A Moment Is Not (Isn't) Very Long (*), You Wouldn't Cross the Street to Say Goodbye, So Much to Do, I Let My Mind Wonder (Wander), I Can't Find the Time, Some Other Time, Will You Remember Mine, Everything But You (*), I Hope So, Blame It on the Time(s), And So Will You My Love, Healing Hand(s) of Time, You'll Always Have Someone, I Just Don't Understand, Follow Me Around, Any Old Arms Won't Do.

Recording Notes: This 1984 compilation featured seven "demos" from the Ira Nelson tapes along with ten from the Tax Planners & Associates.   Additionally, the Lone Star single, 'Will You Remember Mine?' was included. The other two tracks, 'So Much to Do' and 'Follow Me Around' were released a year earlier on the Plantation Records compilation, *20 Early Memories*.

Interestingly, two songs, 'Healing Hands of Time' and 'Any Old Arms Won't Do', even though they had been on the Tax Planners set, were later listed on the Rhino collection as being "previously unissued." Potomac Records was distributed by Music Factory Outlet, located in Hendersonville, just outside Nashville. Other than this collection, the label did not have many releases.

Willie Nelson Sings 28 Great Songs. Highland Music HT/HCD-405. (1989).

Track Listing: Any Old Arms Won't Do, Slow Down Old World (%), Healing Hands of Time (*) (%), And So Will You My Love, Things to Remember (%) (&), One Step Beyond (+), Undo the Right (Wrong), Home Is Where You're Happy (+) (%) (&), Why Are You Picking on Me (%) (&), No Tomorrow in Sight (@) ($) (&), A New Way to Cry (*) (#) (@) ($) (&), A Broken Promise (Broken Promises) (#) (@) ($) (&), Happiness Lives Next Door (*) (@) (&), Let's Pretend (@) ($) (&), I Let My Mind Wonder (Wander) ($), December Days (%), I Can't Find the Time (%) ($) (&), I Didn't Sleep a Wink (&), You Wouldn't Cross the Street to Say Goodbye (*) (+), Suffer(ing) in Silence (*) (+) (%), I Feel Sorry for Him (+) ($), You'll Always Have Someone (+) (%), I Just Don't Understand (+) (%), I'm Going to (Gonna) Lose a Lot of Teardrops (#) (+) (@) ($) (&), The Ghost (@) ($) (&), Waiting (Wastin') Time (#) (+) (@) ($) (&), Go Away (@) ($) (&), Right from Wrong (@) (&).

Recording Notes: This 1989 compilation from Highland Music (on the Hollywood label) has stood as the most inclusive of the "demo" collections. However, it featured only one track, 'December Days', that had not been released before. Seven of the cuts on this set were from Ira Nelson's tapes. Twenty came from the Tax Planners. Seven cuts, though released here and in an earlier collection, were among twelve tracks that Rhino Records had billed as being "previously unissued."

Other Releases: Over the years, Highland Music has become known for releasing material from such early independent ("indie") label powerhouses as King and Chess Records. In 1993, the company rereleased five (*) of Willie's cuts along from this compilation along with five old Conway Twitty tracks as a compilation on their King label, entitled *Willie & Conway*, King Special KSCD-473. Yes, that's the old King label once owned by Sidney Nathan and former home to James Brown and Hank Ballard, as well as old-time country stars like Grandpa Jones and T. Texas Tyler.

Two Andover (Aura) sets from 1982 (ten cuts each) were exactly incorporated - same order of cuts - into this collection, along with nine other titles. The first ten cuts of this collection were the ones on the first Andover set, *Slow Down Old World*, catalog number A 1002. The next nine cuts beginning with 'I Let My Mind Wonder' and ending with 'I Just Don't Understand' comprised the second Andover set, *Love and Pain*, A 1003. The source for the cuts on both albums was Soundwave, Inc. of Los Angeles.

On the jacket of the *Love and Pain* set, a tenth cut was listed, entitled 'I Write You Letters'. The writing credit was given solely to Willie, though in actuality the song was co-written by Willie and Harlan Howard. It was listed on the collection between 'December Days' and 'I Can't Find the Time'. Inside on the record label, however, the song did not appear. There were only nine selections on the recording. The track, itself, has remained a mystery. Was there a Pamper "demo" track by that title? Did Willie ever record the song? It has never shown up anywhere on any Willie Nelson album.

Andover's *Slow Down Old World* set came out in England (same title) in 1984 on Sundown Records (Magnum Music Group) as SDLP-1006. In the U. S., it came out, in 1984, through a company called Out of Town Distributors (OTD). The same title was used with a catalog number OTD-8642. In 1996 (same title again), the collection was released (catalog number 0411) by the Forever Music Group Inc. of Edison, New Jersey. Only the first nine cuts were included, with 'No Tomorrow in Sight' deleted. The *Love and Pain* album also came out in the U.S. on the Out of Town label as OTD-8641. Forever Music rereleased the *Love and Pain* set (using the same title) in 1996, giving it a catalog number of 0403. The phantom track, 'I Write You Letters' was, of course, not included.

The Magnum Music Group released in England, in 1987, a subset of the Highland collection on the Starburst label entitled *One Step Beyond*. In 1995, Retro Music of Canada (Excelsior) released a deceptively titled compilation, *Greatest Hits*, 1332/EXL 10732, consisting of nine cuts (+) from this collection along with 'Blame It on the Times'. The same company put four (#) of the Willie cuts (along with 'A Moment Isn't Very Long') together with five from Waylon to make a 1996 collection credited to Willie & Waylon, entitled, *Crying*, EXL20072.

An undated compilation out of Italy, *20 Golden Hits*, Masters MA MC 911121183, contained eighteen of the tracks on this Highland collection. Ten cuts (@) were deleted while two were added, 'I Hope So' and 'Pages'. The 'Pages' track was not an original Pamper "demo," but a cut from Willie's RCA album, *Good Times*.

Another undated collection, from Tring International, combined eleven cuts ($) from this collection (plus 'A Moment Isn't Very Long') with twelve older selections by Waylon Jennings and called it *Outlaw Reunion* (catalog number GRF058) in an obvious attempt to garner sales off the successes the two had based on their reputations together as "outlaws." The Tring collection was manufactured in the EEC (the European community). According to the notes on the back of the disc, the tracks were licensed from Long Island Music Co. Ltd.

In 1983, Masters released a set of the "demos," originating from Germany, called *18 Golden Hits*, MA-11141183. The label has been responsible for similar sets on artists such as Bob Marley, James Brown and others. A recent, though not specifically dated, budget subset (also from West Germany) of ten (%) cuts from the Highland set, entitled *Golden Hits*, was released as Masters MACD 61020.

In 1997, Kingfisher Records, distributed by Ichiban Records of Atlanta, released a thirteen track subset of the Highland collection. It was entitled *I Let My Mind Wander*, with the catalog number, KF6 0019-2. Fifteen cuts (&) were not used. Ichiban has been, in the past, best known for its issuance of Curtis Mayfield albums. Curtis was one of the founders of the modern Chicago Soul sound, writing such great hits as 'People Get Ready', 'Monkey Time', and 'Freddie's Dead'.

* = the five cuts released as part of the collection, *Willie & Conway*, King Special KSCD-473.

+ = the nine cuts released on *Greatest Hits*, Retro/ Excelsior EXL 10732.

= the four cuts included on the Waylon and Willie collection, *Crying*, Retro Music/Excelsior EXL20072.

@ = the ten cuts not included on the Masters collection, *20 Golden Hits*, MA MC 911121183.

$ = the eleven cuts, along with 'A Moment Isn't Very Long', that made up the undated Tring International collection, *Outlaw Reunion*, GRF058, along with twelve tracks by Waylon Jennings.

% = the ten cuts on the collection, *Golden Hits*, Masters MACD 61020.

& = the fifteen cuts not used on the Kingfisher Records collection, *I Let My Mind Wander*, KF6 0019-2.

Willie Nelson: Original Artist. Fat Boy Records FAT CD 125. (1993).

Track Listing: A Moment Is Not (Isn't) Very Long, Some Other Time, Blame It on the Time(s) (*), (The) Shelter of Your Arms (*), (The) End of Understanding, Will You Remember Mine(?), Everything But You, I Hope So, Face of a Fighter (*), Is There Something on Your Mind (*), Follow Me Around (*), Any Old Arms Won't Do (*), You'll Always Have Someone (*), I Just Don't Understand (*), I Feel Sorry for Him, Suffer(ing) in Silence (*), You Wouldn't Cross the Street to Say Goodbye (*), Ashamed (*), I Can't Find the Time, So Much to Do, I Let My Mind Wonder (Wander) (*), Why Are You Picking on Me, Home Is Where You're Happy (*), Undo the Wrong (Right), December Day(s), Things to Remember (*), And So Will You My Love (*), Healing Hands of Time.

Recording Notes: In 1993, this twenty-eight cut collection was released in the EEC (also known as the European Union). It became the definitive foreign collection. All but one of the tracks, 'Ashamed' (though it was published by Tree Music), were Pamper "demos." According to notes included with the collection, the tracks were obtained from Shelby Singleton and licensed from Sun Classic Communications Group. Other than on this set, 'Ashamed' has only appeared as an Atlantic outtake ('I'm So Ashamed' on the Rhino box set) and on a 1968 RCA album.

Interestingly, the publishing credit for 'You Wouldn't Cross the Street to Say Goodbye' was not given to either Willie, Pamper,

Copyright Control, or Tree Music. It was credited to Acuff-Rose Opryland Music, which held the foreign rights. Another title, 'So Much to Do', also appeared on the Rhino box as an Atlantic outtake.

In 1994, a Scotti Bros. Records set (released in the U. S.), *The Early Years*, 72392 75437-2, incorporated thirteen (including two CD "bonus tracks") of these tracks and added one, 'One Step Beyond'. Fifteen cuts (*) were not used. 'One Step Beyond' and one of the "bonus tracks," 'Some Other Time', were listed as being "previously unreleased." Inside the CD cover were some excellent liner notes by Barry McCloud, author of *Definitive Country: The Ultimate Encyclopedia of Country Music and Its Performers*. The Scotti Bros. label, a BMG subsidiary, was the same label that recorded James Brown through the early nineties.

* = the fifteen cuts from this collection not used on the Scotti Bros. set, *The Early Years*, 72392 75437-2.

Home Is Where You're Happy. Success 16182CD. (Undated).

Track Listing: Home Is Where You're Happy, Ashamed, Blame It on the Times, A Moment Is Not (Isn't) Very Long, (The) Shelter of Your (My) Arms (*), December Day, Things to Remember, Any Old Arms Won't Do, I Just Don't Understand, Why Are You Picking on Me, Will You Remember Mine, Slow Down Old World (*), Building Heartaches (*), Who Do I Know in Dallas, I Don't Feel Anything.

Recording Notes: At an undated time, an American label, Blossum Gap, released a three LP collection of "demos," entitled, *Willie Treasures* BGR-WN, that did not stay in print very long, mainly because of the limited marketing and distribution resources the label possessed. In 1993, Success Records (a division of Pickwick in England) marketed a newer version of that small label LP, under license from that company. The collection was most notable for the inclusion of the rarely featured 'Who Do I Know in Dallas'. The cut, 'I Don't Feel Anything', actually came from one of Willie's later RCA albums.

Broken Promises. Century Records/PNEC Records PLCD 1010. (1997).

Track Listing: Night Life, Why Are You Picking on Me, (The) Shelter of Your (My) Arms, You Wouldn't (Even) Cross the Street to Say Goodbye, Blame It on the Times, I Just Don't Understand, You'll Always Have Someone, Any Old Arms Won't Do, Right from Wrong, Suffering in Silence, One Step Beyond, (A Broken Promise) Broken Promises, No Tomorrow in Sight, I Didn't Sleep a Wink, I Can't Find the Time, I Let My Mind Wonder (Wander), Waiting Time, A New Way to Cry, Home Is Where You're Happy, I Feel Sorry for Him.

Recording Notes: In late 1997, Century Records (a division of Planet Entertainment) put out this twenty selection set (or fifty minutes of music) with a bonus "multimedia" track that would play on a personal computer's CD ROM. The tracks were all ones that had been readily available. They either came from the Ira Nelson tapes or from Tax Planners, so actually, every one came out via Willie, himself.

The Minor Collections of Pamper Music Demos.

The compilations listed above were major collections of Pamper "demos," each presenting a set of the tracks in some unique way. There were also numerous domestic and foreign compilations that did not qualify as sets of major importance. They were little more than rehashes of minimal value. As long as Willie's name was on a collection, consumers didn't seem to notice its origins. In all, the forty-six (Pamper Music) "demo" titles have appeared on more than a hundred foreign and American compilations. The American collections, by themselves, have totalled in excess of fifty. All of the minor compilations have been listed below (without any listing of contents).

The Undocumented Collections of Pamper Music "Demos" - The United States and English-speaking Countries (E = England, C = Canada)

Label & Number	Title	Date
Aura A-1010	**Outlaw Reunion Vol. 1** (w. Waylon) (also Out of Town Distributors OTD-8647- same title, 1984, Sundown SDLP 1005 - England, same title, 1983, and South Africa - same title, 1985, MNC 1106)	1982
Aura A-1011	**Outlaw Reunion Vol. 2** (w. Waylon) (also Out of Town Distributors OTD-8648 -same title, 1984 and Sundown SDLP 1007- England, same title, 1984)	1982
Heritage HSRD 181920WN	**Bandanna Land** (also on Aura)	1983
82 Records 122982 (TV only)	**Willie Nelson: Nashville** (2 record set)	1983
Country Fidelity CFX-213	**Even Then**	1983
Exact EX-249	**Original Artists Collector Series**	1983
Design DELP-308 (E)	**18 Great Songs** (w. Waylon) (also South Africa undated)	1984

Audio Fidelity		
ZCGAS 757 (E)	**Willie Nelson**	1984
Classic Collection		
KC-10101	**The Original Willie Nelson**	1984
Casino CASINO-151	**Just Willie**	1984
Romulus A-6056	**Willie Nelson and Faron Young**	1984
	(also Mid South T-6056 - undated)	
Hot Schaltz		
HS-0052-1	**The Ghost of the Ghost**	1984
Golden Circle		
GC-47503	**Willie Nelson Vol. I**	1984
Merit MC-101	**Willie Nelson and His Texas Friends**	1984
Merit MC-105	**Willie Nelson and Bob Wills**	1984
Blue Ribbon BR-47541	**Let's Pretend**	1985
82 Music Co. LSM 906	**Home Is Where You're Happy**	
(TV only)	(2 record set)	1985
82 Music Co. LSM-609	**Mellow Moods of the Vintage Years:**	
(TV only)	**Written and Sung by Willie Nelson**	1985
Topline TOP-133 (E)	**"Outlaws"** (w. David Allan Coe)	1985
Showcase SHLP-111	**Home Is Where You're Happy**	1985
(E)	(also ONN ONN-39 (Switzerland -	
	same title) - undated)	
Warwick WW 2004	**The World of Willie Nelson**	1985
(E)		
Sierra FEDB 5007 (E)	**Replay**	1985
Object OR-0028 (E)	**The Best of Willie Nelson**	1987
Castle Communica-		
tions CCSLP-178	**Willie Nelson: The Collection**	1988
(E)	(2 record set)	
Object FPF05A (E)	**Country Legends**	1989
16 Tons CD-11006 (E)	**16 Great Songs**	1990
16 Tons CD-11009 (E)	**16 Great Songs** (w. Waylon Jennings)	1990
That's Country TC-006	**Things to Remember**	1990
(E)		
That's Country TC-007	**Suffering In Silence**	1990
(E)		
Jerden 7010	**Pure Willie**	1992
Legacy Entertainment	**Country Legends Reunion**	
ATP 034	(Waylon and Willie)	1996
Prestige CDSGP-096	**One Step Beyond** (also Starburst SM	
(E)	11, undated England, and Magnum	
	Music, same title, England, 1987)	n/d
The Classic Series	**Willie Nelson - Lone Star**	n/d
JEM PB-55007	(Deluxe)	
Ditto DTO-10087 (E)	**Willie Nelson's World of Country**	
	(2 records)	n/d

CD Sounds CDFX-6741		
(C)	**Willie Nelson**	n/d
Soundsational		
CDMA-4011 (C)	**Country Outlaw**	n/d
AIM AIM-3003CD (E)	**Classic Collection: 23 of His Best**	n/d
Taylors COL-026 (E)	**Collection**	n/d
AR-Express 295047 (E)	**Country Heroes**	n/d
Prestige CDSGP-052	**Heartaches**	n/d
(E)		
Ronco CDSR-016 (E)	**Great Willie Nelson**	n/d
Javelin' HADCD-132	**Spotlight on Willie Nelson**	n/d
(E)		
Pickwick PWKS-4041	**Old Friends** (Waylon and Willie)	n/d
(E)		

The Undocumented Collections of Pamper Music "Demos" - Europe and Pacific Rim Countries (G = Germany, P = Portugal, F = France, EE = EEC, I = Italy, H = Holland, A = Australia, K = Korea)

Astra ASTRA-102 (I)	**Country Classics**	1984
Astan ASTAN-20020		
(G)	**20 Outlaw Reunion Hits** (w. Waylon)	1984
Astan ASTAN-20021	**20 Golden Classics**	
(G)		1984
Axis AX.701238 (A)	**Willie Nelson Second Fiddle**	1986
Amiga 8-56-363 (G)	**20 of the Best Willie Nelson**	1988
Starlight CDS-51023		
(EE)	**The Best of Willie Nelson**	1988
Masterpiece CD-	**The Country Store Collection**	
CST-42 (F)	(w. Waylon)	1988
Point 2661114 (H)	**Super Hits**	1990
	(also Black Tulip 2690254 - 1990)	
Goldies GLD 63125 (P)	**Willie Nelson & Waylon Jennings**	n/d
Success 204310 (H)	**Willie Nelson and Don Williams**	n/d
Galaxy 1-3884122 (G)	**Golden Hits**	n/d
Galaxy 1-3884132 (G)	**Twenty Golden Hits** (w. Waylon)	n/d
Eagle Rock 0000016-		
EAB (G)	**Masters**	n/d
Big Country 2430513	**20 Golden Classics**	u/d
(K)	(printed in W. Germany)	
Tring GRF032	**Is There Something on Your Mind**	u/d

"Mr. Record Man":

The Liberty Recordings

The Pamper "demos" and the acclaim for Willie's songs when done by other artists led quickly to his first commercial recording contract, with Liberty Records. He began his Liberty recording stint in 1961 after one of his first Nashville friends, Hank Cochran, got a tape of his songs to Joe Allison, who was, at the time, head of Liberty's country music division. It was a venture Allison started in 1959 at the request of label president, Al Bennett. Allison proceeded to work with session player and leader, Harold Bradley, to get the best recordings of Willie they could. Allison felt that Willie had not been recorded because people thought he "sung funny."

Bradley explained it further by saying that Willie sang both in front of and behind the beat making it very difficult for the players to keep time. Nelson's recordings turned out well enough for the first album to yield one top ten single, unusual for a debut record. Liberty and Willie remained together for three years, until 1964, when he moved over to Monument Records (for a very brief stay). During Willie's tenure at Liberty, only two albums worth of material were issued along with numerous singles.

Only three of his single releases charted country while two of those three hit the "bubbling under" part of the national sales chart (according to *Billboard* magazine). His first single was 'The Part Where I Cry'/'Mr. Record Man'. Neither side of that first single sold well enough to reach the country charts.

It should be noted here that Tim Neely, in his *Goldmine Price Guide to 45 RPM Records*, did credit Willie with a 1958 Liberty single, 'Susie'/'No Dough', catalog number 55155, which would fit in with that year's set of Liberty singles. Unfortunately for Tim (and other collectors who have been charging upwards of twenty-five dollars for a mint to near mint copy at "oldies" conventions), the "Willy" Nelson on that single was not the one known and loved by country fans everywhere. He was the cousin of teen idol, Ricky Nelson, and, in fact, went on to manage Rick for a while. In 1958, Ricky's cousin (Willy) was a fourteen year old would-be recording star.

It was in March of 1962 that Willie first charted a country single as part of a duet with label-mate Shirley Collie. The song was 'Willingly', written by none other than Hank Cochran. According to Bif Collie, then Shirley's husband as well as a disc jockey, the duet came about at the request of Joe Allison. "Joe Allison phoned and asked if Shirley would like to do a duet with Willie Nelson," was what Bif recalled in a segment included in Willie's autobiography. He elaborated that:

> the story I got was Willie offered Joe a piece of one of his songs if Joe could put him and Shirley in the studio together.

Soon after the record was made, Shirley "ran away from Bif." She said she "flew to Seattle to meet Willie" in order to "prove to Willie that I was serious about being with him." Their relationship flourished in 1962 (all the way to marriage) but fell apart by 1965, ending for good in 1969. In all, four duets pairing Willie and Shirley were cut.

A second duet single, with 'You Dream About Me' as the "A" side (and a Helen Carter song, 'Is This My Destiny', as the "B" side), was released but failed to chart. Just as the follow-up duet single failed to click, so did their marriage. Willie moved on (he's now in his fourth marriage) but, as author Janet Byron noted, Shirley did not. Writing in 1988, Shirley said:

> I have never come close to remarrying. I can't make a commitment to anyone, because I love Willie. I'm happy with that. At last, I can handle knowing there's nobody else for me.

After the Willie/Shirley 'Willingly' duet charted (with a Willie composition, 'Our Chain of Love', as the "B" side), Willie's 'Touch Me' single reached the seventh spot on the country charts (in May of 1962). Two follow-on releases, 'Half a Man' (also released on the second Liberty album) and 'You Took My Happy Away' charted in the twenty-fifth and thirty-third positions respectively. 'You Took My Happy Away' was not released on an album until 1994 as part of the two CD set of Willie's Liberty material.

In 1969, long after Nelson left Liberty, the single 'I Hope So' reached the thirty-sixth spot. Following that, two United Artists singles (inheritors of the Liberty material), 'The Last Letter' and 'There'll Be No Teardrops Tonight' reached the forty-sixth spot in 1976 and number eighty-six in 1978, respectively. The Liberty material has remained fresh, even today, thanks not only to Willie's great and timeless songs, but to the outstanding session players, specifically Leon Russell, known for his hit, 'Delta Lady', and his Hank Wilson persona or alter ego.

There were only two officially released Willie Nelson Liberty albums, but they contained quite a few of what became his standards, from 'Funny How Time Slips Away' to 'Crazy'. Most of the great songs were hits for others and, to their credit, Liberty did not later release any of the "standards" as singles to capitalize on Willie's name. 'Funny' was at one point, according to Willie,

> my most successful song financially to date. It has been recorded maybe 80 or 90 times so far - on the average, someone records it once a month.

It was recorded by artists beyond the country vein, including a 1972 Junior Parker rendition. Understatedly, Willie recounted that:

> I wrote this song one afternoon while driving to the office. Somewhere during the trip the line that I had heard someone say probably a thousand times in my life, 'It's funny how time slips away,' came to me. I thought, 'It's funny there's never been a song by that title,' and it started coming to me.

Willie also admitted one more insight about 'Funny', saying, "that's the only time I've written a song consciously for somebody else to sing." He wrote it for Billy Walker, at whose house he stayed when he first came to Nashville. The first place he and the family lived was, of course, the trailer court where Roger Miller once resided, the one which inspired Roger to write 'King of the Road'. Billy had previously covered 'Mr. Record Man' and Willie wanted to write something else especially for him.

In an interview for *Country Weekly* (the April 21, 1998 issue), Willie offered a little different perspective on 'Funny How Time Slips Away'. He told interviewer Larry Holden that while still in Houston,

> I wrote three songs - 'Crazy', 'Funny How Time Slips Away' and 'Night Life' - the same week. After that, I felt like I could make it in Nashville.

Since he had already met Walker in Texas, he still could have had Billy in mind when he wrote the song. However, did Willie really write the song in Texas, or, as he has previously stated, while "driving to work" in Nashville soon after he arrived in town? In yet another interview, this one with Dave Hoekstra (published by *Country Song Roundup*), Willie said he wrote 'Funny How Time Slips Away':

> for Faron to follow up 'Hello Walls' with. But he thought it was too much like 'Hello Walls', so Billy Walker recorded it.

Walker did recall that Willie offered to sell him four songs for five hundred dollars. That did occur soon after Willie came to Nashville and was living at Billy's house. Billy said he told Willie, "I can't let you do that." He told Willie how he had done that once and the song had gone to number three nationally. Faron Young said he turned down the chance to record 'Funny' because its opening line starting with "hello there" sounded too much like his previous hit, 'Hello Walls'.

'Hello Walls' was another "standard" that Willie wrote (and which he recorded on the first Liberty album) soon after he came to Nashville (in 1961). He later recalled, "I just looked up and said, 'Hello, walls'." Actually, Willie was writing in an old garage remodeled into a studio. As he put it,

> there was a door, and a window, and a guitar, and that was about it. I started writing this song - I started talking to the walls.

Hank Cochran said he was there in the studio when Willie came up with the idea. They started to write the song. Then Hank got called away. When he came back "just ten minutes later," Willie had "written the whole damn thing." Between Hank and Willie, the song was pitched to almost everyone and everyone turned it down, deeming it quirky and too comical.

The definitive version belonged to Faron Young because it was his phrasing style that made the song a hit with the public. Remaining at number one on the country charts for nine weeks, Faron's version crossed over to the pop singles chart, where it peaked in the twelfth spot, the highest one of his singles ever reached. It's a version that has never completely gone away. Recently, it surfaced as part of the soundtrack for the movie, *The People vs. Larry Flynt*.

It wasn't just Faron's version of 'Hello Walls' that has proven to be so timeless. The song, itself, has stood the test of time. In 1998, thirty-seven years after Willie composed it, it made the news (in *Billboard*) again via young country singer David Kersh's "very uptempo" version. Kersh said there was initially some negative criticism of his treatment, though "overall it's been positive," in spite of one "classic country guy," who said Kersh "had mutilated Willie's song."

Reflecting on the greatness of the song, Kersh mused that he didn't have to "change the words, just the feel."

Except for Faron's sense of fair play, the song might not have remained Willie's. When he decided to record the song, early in 1961, Willie offered to sell Faron the rights. Faron explained to Willie the many thousands of dollars of potential royalties inherent in a hit song. Instead, he offered to lend Willie four hundred dollars (Faron recently said it was fifteen hundred dollars) until those royalties began to roll in. And roll in they did!

When Nelson got his first big check from the Young recording, he went up to Faron at Tootsie's and supposedly laid a great big appreciative "kiss" on him and repaid the loan. Faron recalled that he told Willie, "you don't owe me a thing. If anybody owes anybody here, it's me that owes you." Talent agent, Billy Deaton, who worked closely with Faron over many years, clearly recalled Willie trying to sell Faron the rights to 'Hello Walls'. Deaton explained that:

> Willie Nelson was living here and was real broke and ran into Faron down at Tootsie's Orchid Lounge. He said, 'Faron I want to sell you the rights.' Faron said, 'Son, I don't want to buy that song from you. You're about to get a big check on it. How much money do you need, Willie?' He said, 'About $500.' Faron handed him the money and told him to hang on to the song.

A close friend of Faron's, Billy Galvin, said that Faron "would complain that Willie never paid him back the $500." On the other hand, Galvin heard from Willie that Faron "refused the money" whenever Willie offered it to him. Galvin closed the story by saying that Willie finally paid Faron back by:

> having a $50,000 bull delivered to Young's house with a sign on it that read 'Paid in Full'.

The Liberty relationship with Willie fell apart for a number of reasons. First of all, between the first and second albums, Joe Allison left the label. The recordings turned from Allison's basic productions to Tommy Allsup's over-done tracks. Secondly, Willie had his success early on with the label and the later recordings went nowhere.

Third, Liberty was based in Los Angeles and even though Pamper Music was willing to set Willie up as their office manager there, he (and second wife Shirley) wanted to be back in Nashville. In the fourth place, Liberty was not, at that time, a strong country label. Finally, as Willie told daughter Susie, the Liberty offer to renew his contract was not good enough. So, Willie left the label, appearing for all intents and purposes like he was going to sign with RCA Victor. Instead, he signed with Monument Records and Fred Foster.

A third and final album for Liberty was planned, recorded, but the release never materialized. It was never even titled, though its release date was set to be November 1963. Some of the tracks were first released on two albums compiled after Willie left Liberty and found some success on RCA and finally Columbia.

Only three of the third album cuts did not see release at that time, 'I Hope So' 'Cold War With You', and 'At the Bottom'. They had to wait until the complete contents were finally released together on Liberty's 1994 Willie Nelson box set, *The Early Years: The Complete Liberty Recordings Plus More*, C2 7243-8 28077-2-8. Tracks seventeen through twenty-seven (of disc two) were the cuts intended for that ill-fated third album.

The project, though completed at the time, died when Willie decided not to re-sign with Liberty. It would have featured 'River Boy', the Floyd Tillman standard, 'Cold War With You' (which Willie has since done in even better versions), and George Jones' 'Seasons of My Heart'. Two pop standards, 'Am I Blue' and 'I'll Walk Alone', were also intended to be part of the lineup. No Willie originals were planned.

In addition to three major collections of Liberty material, there have been other compilations, the majority being budget sets. United Artists also marketed a "various artists" compilation in 1976, *Texas Country*, UA-LA574 (released in England as USD 309/310). It featured six Willie tracks on side one of the two LP release. The six tracks were 'Second Fiddle', 'Night Life', 'Funny How Time Slips Away', 'Take Me As I Am (or Let Me Go)', 'Hello Walls', and 'Crazy'.

The Sunset budget label had one collection containing Nelson material, *Country Get Together*, SUS 5283. In 1994, Liberty issued a "various artists" compilation, *Classic Duets*, CDP-7243-8-30851-2-5. It featured Willie's 1962 duet with Shirley, 'Willingly', and the 1978 duet by Hank Cochran and Willie, 'Ain't Life Hell'.

The Liberty Recordings - Album Listings

... and Then I Wrote. Liberty LSP/LRP-7239. (1962).

Track Listing: Touch Me, Wake Me When It's Over, Hello Walls, Funny How Time Slips Away, Crazy, The Part Where I Cry, Mr. Record Man, Three Days (*) (#), One Step Beyond (#), Undo the Right (*) (#), Darkness on the Face of the Earth (*) (#), Where My House Lives (#).

Recording Notes: Willie's first Liberty album release came together in 1962 with Joe Allison producing. Half of it was recorded in Nashville and the remainder in Los Angeles. One of the L. A. session players was Leon Russell, who would later make a critically acclaimed album with Willie. All the songs were written by Willie, except one, 'Undo the Right', which was co-written with Hank Cochran. Two of the songs were originally Pamper Music "demos" and at least three others have since become country standards.

One, 'Crazy', became a Patsy Cline standard. Willie recalled that he had "problems immediately with my song 'Crazy' because it had four or five chords in it." He elaborated that "it just wasn't your basic three-chord country hillbilly song." When fellow Texan, Billy Walker, presented 'Crazy' to the president of Starday Records (in the hope of getting Willie a writer's contract), the reaction was, "that song sounds like a piece of shit."

It took Hank Cochran to personally get the song to Cline's producer, Owen Bradley, who took it to Patsy (he was convinced it was perfect for Patsy). Willie always knew the song was great, once musing, "I figure that if any of the songs are around for any length of time, that one will be." When he heard Cline's version (on Decca), he was incredulous, saying, "it was magic." Willie further stated that

Patsy's recording was his "favorite of anything I ever wrote." Bradley appraised 'Crazy' as:

> probably the finest [record] I've ever been involved with. It's country and a little bit pop, though it's not supposed to be either. The steel guitar sounded more like a vibraphone or something.

Strings were also used, which sent considerable criticism Bradley's way, causing him to reflect that "you can't please everybody." Actually the sound Bradley achieved came after criticism from the label's New York office. They wanted a record that leaned away from traditional country music, or as Owen remembered, "they didn't say 'pop,' but that's what they meant." So, according to country music author Dan Daley, in his 1998 book, *Nashville's Unwritten Rules: Inside the Business of Country Music,* that thoroughly explored the business of country music, Bradley:

> toned down the distinctively country elements like the steel guitar, leaving them present, but only subliminally, and letting the shimmering strings dominate the sound.

Once 'Crazy' hit for Patsy, it became a concert favorite for her, proving that country audiences could connect with a complex song. Barbara Mandrell recalled that Patsy:

> had a great way of introducing her newest hit. She would tell the audience, 'I recorded a song called 'I Fall to Pieces', and I was in a car wreck. Now I'm really worried, because I have a brand new record, and it's called 'Crazy'.

Patsy's interpretation was magical, so much so that the combination of her voice and Willie's song sent the record high up both the pop and country charts. Willie remembered that:

> when Hank took 'Crazy', my demo of it, and played it for Patsy Cline. She liked it and recorded it. It's funny, I'd always heard my voice on it, and hearing her sing it was a brand-new thing. A lot of times when your songs are recorded, they come off a little below what you hoped for. But this was so far above what I had expected. So far above.

That "far above" version brought Cline her one and only top ten pop single (and has since been named the number one juke box song of all times). It made Willie lots of money, which might not have happened had Willie accepted an earlier, tempting Paul Buskirk offer. Paul

recalled that Willie wrote 'Crazy' while he was working at the Esquire Ballroom, back in Texas.

He said Willie brought in the song, calling it a "Floyd Tillman special." Once Buskirk heard it he tried to buy it, offering Willie first fifty dollars, then one hundred and fifty. Willie didn't sell it to "Brother Paul," saying if it was that good, he would keep it for himself.

Willie's own first top ten country single, 'Touch Me', was a featured track. According to Allison, 'Touch Me', as a recording, was:

> the epitome of ... how we tried to record Willie Nelson. There were no funny frills, nothing fancy in the background. We were just playing rhythm and sticking his voice out in front.

The song, 'Willingly', a duet with Shirley Collie (soon-to-be the second Mrs. Nelson), had been Willie's first taste of chart success, while it was Shirley's first and only top ten hit and the last of only three singles she was able to chart. Strangely, it was not featured on this album. Neither were Willie's other two charting singles for Liberty, 'Half a Man' and 'You Took My Happy Away', though 'Half a Man' was included on the second album.

That was more than made up for by the inclusion of 'Three Days', a song which didn't catch the kind of attention it should have, a similar fate for many Willie originals. Faron Young did take the song to number seven on the *Billboard* country singles chart in early 1962 (approximately a year after he took Willie's 'Hello Walls' to number one) and even received co-writing credit on it for a while. Dwight Yoakam summarized why such a song didn't catch on, saying,

> when I go back and listen to what you were doing in 1962, 'Three Days' or any of them - I mean, you had to be from Mars to them.

According to Willie, 'Three Days' came from a joke, in which the person telling it said he hadn't eaten in three days, yesterday, today and tomorrow. Willie turned the joke into a timeless song about three days when he couldn't forget his true love, "yesterday, today, and tomorrow."

In 1989, k. d. lang recorded a "campy" version of the song that brought out a whole new unanticipated meaning, especially for women. According to critic Martha Mockus, "the frequency and exaggeration" of lang's "vocal cries, glides, whimpers, and hiccups" effectively reinterpreted "the three days much more physically." They now "suggest menstruation." More specifically,

lang's campy vocal maneuvers represent the 'dread,' the 'tears and sorrow,' and the knowledge that it will 'start over again' to form a menstrual narrative.

Her entire performance "pokes fun at the cultural taboos surrounding menstruation."

Other Releases: The album, itself, was rereleased in May 1973 as *The Best of Willie Nelson*, United Artists UA-LA086-F. An abridged version, minus three cuts (*), appeared as Liberty LN-10118, in February 1981. A Liberty Special Products version (also abridged) appeared in 1982 with a catalogue number SLL-8296. Five (#) cuts were missing with one added, 'Country Willie'. EMI had a European release in 1983 entitled, *The Best of Willie Nelson*, EMI 1C 064 82878.

Another abridged Special Products (from Capitol and later CEMA) release appeared in 1986, catalogue number 4XLL-9391. It had the same lineup as the Liberty Special Products edition of 1982 (SSL-8296), with the same five cuts deleted and 'Country Willie' added. In September 1987 (with the same "Best of" title) the album went out as EMI Manhattan Records CDP 7 48398 2, with a reordering of the original cuts. One cut, 'Half a Man', originally on the second Liberty album, was added to the set. Finally, in 1995, the entire album (under the original title, *...and Then I Wrote)* was released on compact disc as Liberty CDP-7243-8-32464-2 (minus the 'Half a Man' cut).

* = the three cuts omitted when this album was rereleased in abridged form as a 1981 budget set, *The Best of Willie Nelson*, Liberty LN-10118.

= the five cuts deleted when Liberty Special Products rereleased this album again as a 1982 budget set, *The Best of Willie Nelson*, SLL-8296 (and added the 'Country Willie' cut).

Here's Willie Nelson. Liberty LRP/LSP-3308/7308. (1963).

Track Listing: Roly Poly, Half a Man, Lonely Little Mansion, The Last Letter, Second Fiddle, Take My Word, Right or Wrong, Feed It a Memory, Let Me Talk to You, The Way You See Me, The Things I Might Have Been, Home Motel.

Recording Notes: Willie's second and final Liberty album came out the following year, in June of 1963. Unlike its predecessor, it has yet to be rereleased in the compact disc age. Tommy Allsup produced this one, after Joe Allison had left the label. Where the production on the first album had been on the sparse side, this went to the other extreme, with overdubbed strings and voices.

Bob Wills wrote the liner notes, saying that in his "nearly 35 years" as an entertainer, he has hardly ever "seen the likes of Willie Nelson." He concluded that "Willie's style is just right for his

material." Fittingly, 'Roly Poly, a Fred Rose song associated with Wills, was the opening cut.

Of the twelve selections, only four were written by Willie, 'Half a Man', 'Lonely Little Mansion', 'Take My Word', and 'Home Motel'. Single-wise, 'Half a Man' reached the twenty-fifth spot on the country singles chart. One of the other cuts, 'The Last Letter', became a single release in 1976, topping out at the forty-sixth spot and lasting for seven weeks.

Of the remaining cuts, 'Second Fiddle' was Willie's buddy Roger Miller's composition, while former Hank Williams band member, Jimmy Day, wrote 'The Way You See Me'. One of the premier Nashville song-writing teams, Danny Dill and Don Davis, wrote 'Let Me Talk to You', which was also recorded (without chart success) by Ray Price. Willie's Nashville mentor Hank Cochran co-wrote (with the late Justin Tubb) 'Feed It a Memory'.

Haven Gillespie, lyricist for the standard, 'That Lucky Old Sun', was one of three writers who co-authored 'Right or Wrong'. The writers of 'The Things I Might Have Been', Richard M. and Robert B. Sherman, were much more well known for other compositions, including 'You're Sixteen' (a top ten pop hit for Johnny Burnette), 'Chim Chim Cher-ee' (from *Mary Poppins*) and 'Chitty Chitty Bang Bang'. Yes, they also wrote 'Supercalifragilisticexpialidocious'.

Willie turned 'Right or Wrong' into one of his first recordings of a song not specifically written as a country song. To most Texans, however, it was already quite familiar via the version Bob Wills did years prior (back in 1936). In 1984, George Strait would make it even more familiar to both Texans and country fans with his hit single, which reached the number one slot in April of that year.

Country Willie. Liberty Records LN-10013. (1975).

Track Listing: Country Willie, There'll Be No Teardrops Tonight, Right or Wrong, I'll Walk Alone, Take Me As I Am (or Let Me Go), Night Life, Seasons of My Heart, Columbus Stockade Blues, There Goes a Man, The Last Letter.

Recording Notes/Other Releases: Four cuts from Willie's never-released third Liberty album wound up on this 1975 collection. One of them, 'There'll Be No Teardrops Tonight' (written by Hank Williams), went out as a single in 1978 (peaking at number eighty-six), well after Willie had gone to Columbia. It also became the title cut for the second (next) compilation of Willie's Liberty material. Ironically, the song had not charted on the post-War country singles charts prior to Willie's single release.

Of the other three cuts, two were straight country songs, 'Seasons of My Heart' and 'Take Me As I Am'. George Jones was the co-writer of

'Seasons of My Heart', although he did not have the hit version. Cajun country singer Jimmy Newman did, in 1956. Four years later, in 1960, Johnny Cash took the song back into the country top ten.

In November 1963, Willie became one of the first artists to record Boudleaux Bryant's classic country composition, 'Take Me As I Am'. George Jones made the song an album cut in 1965. It did not become a hit single, however, until Ray Price cut it in 1968 and succeeded in taking it all the way to number eight.

The non-country song was 'I'll Walk Alone', composed by Sammy Cahn and Jule Styne. It was originally written as a World War II song. Later it became a part of the Ethel and Jule Styne divorce skirmish, when she told the judge she had "become a living example of Jule's song, 'I'll Walk Alone'."

Another non-country song on this album, 'Right or Wrong', was not intended for the cancelled third album. It was released earlier, in 1963, on the second of Willie's two original Liberty albums. Six years later, in 1969, it was marketed by Liberty as a single, though it failed to chart.

The song, itself, was one of Tin Pan Alley lyricist Haven Gillespie's lesser known songs. Some of his better known creations were 'That Lucky Old Sun' and 'Santa Claus Is Coming to Town'. Both of those songs were later recorded by Willie on Columbia.

Rex Griffin's country classic, 'The Last Letter' also previously appeared (in 1963) on Willie's second Liberty album. Thirteen years later, in 1976, United Artists (the company that purchased Liberty Records) released it as a single and it climbed to number forty-six on the country singles charts for Willie, even though he was then signed to Columbia. According to one of Griffin's wives, Dorothy, the song was not about Rex "or his life in general." It was "just a song."

Rex had told her he wrote it when "he lived in New Orleans at the Tutweiler Hotel," early in his career. He was married to a young girl, Margaret, with whom he did not "get along too well." One of the few times they got along was when he was able to sit down by himself at the piano and write this song, which presumably had nothing to do with their lives.

Nelson's own compositions, 'Country Willie', 'Night Life', and 'There Goes a Man' appeared on an album for the first time. For a final bonus, there was Willie's rendition of the Jimmie Davis country classic, 'Columbus Stockade Blues'. Though Davis claimed the copyright on the song, as he did with his classic, 'You Are My Sunshine', the real authorship has been questioned because Davis had been known for purchasing other writers' songs.

The first "hit" version of 'Columbus Stockade Blues' was by Tom Darby and Jimmie Tarlton back in the late twenties. It was their first hit and as it turned out, their biggest. Tarlton was one of the best of the early country steel guitar players, while Darby was both an excellent singer and blues-influenced guitarist. Though it has become a country standard, it did not hit the modern country charts until a 1970 version by Danny Davis and the Nashville Brass peaked at number seventy.

The album, itself, was first released in March 1975, on Liberty. After United Artists acquired the Liberty masters, it was reissued in October 1980, as United Artists LA410-G. It finally made its compact disc debut in September 1987 as CDP 7 48399 2, on EMI-Manhattan Records, a subsidiary of Capitol Records, which had purchased the United Artists catalog.

There'll Be No Teardrops Tonight. United Artists LA930-H. (1978).

Track Listing: River Boy, I'll Walk Alone, Take Me As I Am (or Let Me Go), Tomorrow Night, Am I Blue, Take My Word, Home Motel, Blue Must Be the Color of the Blues, There'll Be No Teardrops Tonight, Feed It a Memory.

Recording Notes: Released in November 1978, this collection contained seven of the cuts intended for the cancelled third album. One of them, 'There'll Be No Teardrops Tonight' (the well-known Hank Williams song), had been on the previous Liberty compilation, *Country Willie.* It became the title cut of this collection after United Artists experienced some chart action with it when they released it as a single earlier in the year. It wound up peaking at number eighty-six on the country singles chart.

The song was also included on the 1993 Hank Williams tribute collection, compiled by EMI Records (of England), entitled *A Tribute to Hank Williams,* 0777 7 81301. Two other cuts from the *Country Willie* compilation, 'I'll Walk Alone' and 'Take Me As I Am', were likewise added to this set. 'River Boy', written by Fred Carter, Jr. (guitarist and father of country songstress Deanna Carter), was intended for the ill-fated third album. It was also the "A" side of Willie's final Liberty single, released when he was about to leave the label.

In addition to 'River Boy', other cuts on this set originally intended for the (never-released) third album were 'Tomorrow Night', 'Am I Blue', and 'Blue Must Be the Color of the Blues'. 'Blue Must Be the Color of the Blues' was a George Jones top-ten hit from 1958. 'Tomorrow Night', written by Hank Thompson, had been the "A" side of singles by both Carl Smith and Charlie Rich, though neither version went top twenty.

Harry Akst and Grant Clarke wrote 'Am I Blue' in 1929. There were five hit versions of the song that same year from artists as diverse as Libby Holman and Ben Selvin. Beginning with 1929's *On With the Show,* starring Ethel Waters and Joe E. Brown, it has been included in a number of musical films. Rounding out the song selection was Willie's own composition, 'Home Motel', and the Justin Tubb/Hank Cochran piece, 'Feed It a Memory', both from Willie's second original album.

The Early Years: The Complete Liberty Recordings Plus More. Liberty Records 7243-8 28077-2. (1994).

Disc One Track Listing: Night Life, Rainy Day Blues, Touch Me, Wake Me When It's Over, Hello Walls, Funny How Time Slips Away, Crazy, The Part Where I Cry, Mr. Record Man, Three Days, One Step Beyond, Undo the Right, Darkness on the Face of the Earth, Where My House Lives, How Long Is Forever (Version # 1), Country Willie, Go Away, The Waiting Time, You Wouldn't Even Cross the Street (Original Version), There's Gonna Be Love in My House, Take My Word (Version # 1), There Goes a Man, Columbus Stockade Blues (Version # 1), Chain of Love, Willingly, Columbus Stockade Blues (Version # 2), You Dream About Me, Is This My Destiny, Together, Columbus Stockade Blues (Version # 3).

Disc Two Track Listing: How Long Is Forever (Version # 2), You Took My Happy Away (Version # 1), Roly Poly, Half a Man, Lonely Little Mansion, The Last Letter, Second Fiddle, Take My Word (Version # 2), Right or Wrong, Feed It a Memory, Let Me Talk to You, The Way You See Me, The Things I Might Have Been, Home Motel, Opportunity to Cry, You Took My Happy Away (Version # 2), I Hope So (Original Version), River Boy (Original Version), At the Bottom (Original Version), Cold War With You, Seasons of My Heart, Blue Must Be the Color of the Blues, Am I Blue, There'll Be No Teardrops Tonight, Take Me As I Am (or Let Me Go), Tomorrow Night, I'll Walk Alone, You Wouldn't Even Cross the Street (Overdubbed Version), I Hope So (Overdubbed Version), River Boy (Overdubbed Version), At the Bottom (Overdubbed Version).

Recording Notes: This was the giant of the Willie Nelson Liberty rereleases. A 1994 release, it contained sixty-one selections on two compact discs, all of his recordings for the company, overdubbed and undubbed versions alike. Of all the Liberty reissues, this one has become the most crucial for his fans because it was chronologically compiled (from early singles to his first recordings for the label, culminating with his final ones) and contained some material available on album for the first time. In England, a subset of this collection went out as *Forty-Five Original Tracks* while the entire set went out (undated) as *EMI Country Masters*, EMI CDEMC-1505.

One of those tracks was Willie's third charting Liberty single (presented on this collection in two versions), 'You Took My Happy Away', which reached number 33 in early 1964. Both sides of the RX single, 'Night Life' and 'Rainy Day Blues' led off the first disc of the compilation. Also featured (again for the first time on an album) were two versions of a Willie track, 'I Hope So' (credited to Shirley Nelson as writer), one as originally cut and one with considerable overdubbing.

The overdubbed version, released in 1969 - after Willie had some chart success on RCA, reached number 36 and stayed on the chart for nine weeks. On this compilation, the original version was track number seventeen on compact disc two. It was intended to be the first cut of Willie's cancelled third Liberty album.

This collection contained other gems, such as 'You Dream About Me', a beautiful, wistful love song. Susie Nelson said that once when her dad was leaving for a long trip, she "hollered" at him, "you dream about me, Daddy, and I'll dream about you." When Willie returned from that trip, he "looked like hell." He explained it was because he "had to finish a song." The song was 'You Dream About Me'.

It was released as the "A" side of a Willie-Shirley duet single, which unfortunately never charted. Like so many of Willie's originals that were recorded early in his career, it never received the recognition and appreciation it deserved. Maybe Willie could redo it someday as he has done with so many of his beautiful songs that were not noticed, for one reason or another, the first time around.

Six additional Nelson originals appeared on this compilation (for the first time on any collection), beginning with the song, 'Go Away'. Additionally, there were 'Chain of Love', done as a duet by Willie and Shirley, 'Opportunity to Cry', a song Willie would recut several times, 'There's Gonna Be Love in My House', 'The Waiting Time', and You Wouldn't Even Cross the Street'. The latter song was presented as originally recorded and in an overdubbed form (other instrumentation added after the session was completed).

The Willie/Shirley duet on the song, 'Is This My Destiny', became available for the first time on an album. Two other songs, both by unknown authors, according to the liner notes, also saw release for the first time. The songs were 'Together' and 'At the Bottom'.

Classic Willie Nelson. Liberty Records (Music for Pleasure) MFP 5602. (1975).

Track Listing: Funny How Time Slips Away, Hello Walls, Wake Me When It's Over, Crazy, Touch Me, Half a Man, Darkness on the Face of the Earth, Mr. Record Man, Country Willie, There'll Be No Teardrops Tonight, Right or Wrong, Night Life, Seasons of My Heart, Columbus Stockade Blues.

Recording Notes: Issued in England in 1975 and again in 1983, this collection was part of a popular English low budget "Music for Pleasure" series. Six cuts were taken from the *Country Willie* album. The remaining eight came from *The Best of Willie Nelson.* Two of his three early sixties singles were included ('You Took My Happy Away' was the missing one). The "MFP" series had another Willie release, this one entitled *The Very Best of Willie Nelson*, CDMFP-6110.

Other Releases: This set was also issued (using the same title) in 1975 (and again in 1979) as Sunset SLS-50430. Sunset was the budget label arm of Liberty Records. In 1976, United Artists released the set as UAS 29945 (still the same title). In Australia, it was released (no given date) on the Axis label as AX.1177.

"Hello Walls". Sunset Records SUM-1138/SUS-5138. (1978).

Track Listing: Hello Walls, Funny How Time Slips Away (*), Home Motel, Half a Man, Touch Me, Three Days, One Step Beyond, Take My Word, Lonely Little Mansion.

Recording Notes: This collection was originally released in 1978 on the United Artists' budget label, Sunset Records. All nine tracks were songs written by Willie alone. Later in 1978, when Pickwick rereleased the set as SPC-3584 (same title), one cut (*) was deleted.

'Take My Word', a Willie original, previously appeared as a track on his second Liberty album and as a 1963 Liberty single that failed to chart. 'Touch Me' was the first single Willie charted for Liberty. Peaking at number seven, it became his only top ten hit for the label. 'Half a Man' was the second of only three singles he took to the charts during the time he actively recorded under contract for the company (1961 through 1963). In 1969, 1976, and 1978, both Liberty and United Artists (which purchased Liberty) were able to sell enough copies of older material to return Willie to the country singles charts even though he had recorded with, by then, several other labels.

* = the one cut deleted when Pickwick rereleased this set as SPC-3584 under the same title.

Take Me As I Am. Capitol Records (Special Projects) 4XLL-8312. (1982).

Track Listing: Funny How Time Slips Away, There'll Be No Teardrops Tonight, Hello Walls, Take Me As I Am (or Let Me Go), Am I Blue?, Wake Me When It's Over, Right or Wrong, Half a Man.

Recording Notes: This collection was a 1982 Capitol Records Special Projects release of Liberty material. It later became a Cema budget release, catalog number 8312, under the title, *Funny How Time Slips Away*. Capitol acquired the cuts for this set and the CEMA compilation by gaining control of the Liberty catalog through its buyout of United Artists, which had earlier purchased Liberty.

As was the norm for most budget compilations, this one featured only eight cuts, less than the previous given number of ten or twelve cuts for most full-priced albums of the time. Among the eight cuts were two Willie standards, 'Hello Walls' and 'Funny How Time Slips Away', a Hank Williams song, 'There'll Be No Teardrops Tonight', a pop standard, 'Am I Blue?', and a classic country song, 'Take Me As I Am (or Let Me Go)'. The final three cuts were written by Willie.

Country Willie. Liberty Records TC-EMS 1252. (1987).

Track Listing: Country Willie, River Boy, Darkness on the Face of the Earth, Mr. Record Man, Night Life, I'll Walk Alone, Take Me As I Am (or Let Me Go), Tomorrow Night, Take My Word, Home Motel, Blue Must Be the Color of the Blues, Feed It a Memory, Three Days, One Step Beyond, Undo the Right, Right or Wrong, Columbus Stockade Blues, The Part Where I Cry, Where My House Lives, There Goes a Man.

Recording Notes: Twenty Liberty recordings made up this definitive 1987 anthology on the English EMI label. It featured twelve Nelson compositions and eight interpretations including the Tin Pan Alley standard, 'I'll Walk Alone'. It followed a not quite-so-satisfying twenty track 1985 EMI collection (on the Liberty label), *Touch Me*, ED-2606831, which featured ten originals, among them, 'Funny How Time Slips Away' and 'Half a Man', along with all four Willie/ Shirley duets, even their hit, 'Willingly'.

Greatest Songs. CURB Records D4-77366. (1990).

Track Listing: Good Hearted Woman, Night Life, One Day at a Time, Hello Walls, Crazy, Funny How Time Slips Away, Touch Me, Three Days, Undo the Right, Half a Man, Darkness on the Face of the Earth.

Recording Notes: Eight of the eleven cuts on this 1990 compilation were Liberty recordings. The other three (the first three) were from RCA. The Liberty tracks were all Willie originals. The three RCA tracks, 'Night Life', 'One Day at a Time', and 'Good Hearted Woman', were either written or co-written by Willie.

The version of 'Good Hearted Woman' was the one Willie did by himself. According to the liner notes, 'Crazy' was written for Patsy Cline, 'Night Life' for Ray Price, 'Hello Walls' specifically for Faron Young, and 'Funny How Time Slips Away' for Billy Walker. That's how "tall tales" get started.

The Legend Begins. Capitol Records (Pair Records) PCD-2-1333. (1994).

Track Listing: Hello Walls, Mr. Record Man, Funny How Time Slips Away, Touch Me (*), Country Willie (*), Take Me As I Am (or Let Me Go), Right or Wrong (*), I'll Walk Alone (*), Where My House Lives (*), Seasons of My Heart (*), Crazy (*), Night Life (*), The Part Where I Cry, Three Days (*), Am I Blue?, Willingly (with Shirley Collie) (*), There'll Be No Teardrops Tonight, Half a Man, Home Motel, One Step Beyond (*).

Recording Notes: Pair Records released this compilation in 1994, the same year Willie's complete box set of Liberty recordings came out. It contained twenty selections highlighting the best of Willie's Liberty recordings. The top ten duet with Shirley Collie on 'Willingly' was featured.

Cema, using the catalog number 8349, released an abridged budget nine song version of this set, entitled, *Country Legend*. The Cema set was the same as one first released in 1983 by Capitol Records (same title) as 4XLL-8349. Eleven cuts (*) on this collection were not utilized on the nine track Capitol and CEMA budget collections.

* = the eleven tracks excluded from the 1983 Capitol set, *Country Legend*, 4XLL-8349 and the later CEMA set of the same name, catalog number 8349.

A contemplative Willie!
(Photo from Will van Overbeek)

"I Never Cared For You":

The Monument Project

Monument Records was founded in 1958 in Baltimore, Maryland, by Fred Foster, an erstwhile songwriter, producer, and sometime singer. Foster was born and raised on an Appalachian foothills farm until he moved to Washington D. C. There he met Billy Strickland, who liked to write songs in addition to owning a nightclub. Somehow Strickland came to trust Foster with writing words to his melodies and the result was 'Picking Sweethearts', recorded in 1953 by the McGuire Sisters (best known for their 1957 number one smash, 'Sugartime').

From there, Foster did his first record production work, for a session by a then-unknown group called Jimmy Dean and the Texas Wildcats. That led him to a record promotion position with Mercury Records, followed by a series of spots with other labels, through 1958, when he opened Monument, using his life savings to start the company. The former guitarist for Dean's Texas Wildcats, Billy Grammer, became the label's first hit artist that year with the song, 'Gotta Travel On'.

The company really took off in 1959, when it signed Roy Orbison and began a string of hit singles that culminated in 1964 with 'Oh, Pretty Woman'. 1964 was the same year Foster signed Willie to a Monument contract (after his contract with Liberty expired). It was also the year (November 24, 1964, to be exact) Willie became a cast member of the Grand Ole Opry. Haze Jones and Ott Devine signed him for an initial first Opry appearance payment of thirty-five dollars.

Willie had a chance then to sign with RCA, a major player in the Nashville country music business. Why did he choose a small independent label like Monument over one of the majors, especially when it appeared that he was on the verge of joining RCA? Daughter

Susie felt that "what influenced Dad" to sign with Monument was the fact that it "was not a typical, formula Nashville label."

Fred had also wanted Willie on his label ever since he first heard him singing one of his Pamper "demos." In fact he said, according to Susie Nelson, that:

> I heard that phrasing and said to myself, 'This is going to be a gigantic star.' Then I heard he was on Liberty and it depressed me to no end. I probably went out and had a drink.

After that first listen, Foster did get to know Willie and invited him to call if he ever left Liberty. In 1964, Willie did call, much to the surprise of both RCA and Chet Atkins. One reason he finally chose Monument (over RCA) was because Foster wanted to record him "with just a small group, and even let him play guitar." Fred recalled that one of Willie's two Monument sessions produced the song, 'I Never Cared for You'. He remembered cutting "five songs" at that session and having the bass player tell him:

> You just can't do this. Willie is all over the place. Things are out of meter. He's hard to follow.

Fred's reply to the bassist was, "you got to follow." After those sessions were completed in July 1964, the song written by Willie, 'I Never Cared for You', was quickly released as the "A" side of his "kickoff" single for the label. The "flip" side, 'You Left Me a Long, Long Time Ago', was also written by Willie. Chet Atkins' opinion of the "A" side was that it was a "kind of weird record that wasn't a hit." He was right; it never charted.

Though more songs were recorded with the intent of putting out an album, Willie abruptly exited Monument without ever completing enough single tracks to fill an album. He signed with RCA after his short and unproductive tenure with Monument ended. He joined RCA just as suddenly in 1965 as he had previously gone with Monument in 1964. Daughter Susie, in her biography of her famous father, concluded that it was an incident over an unplaced but promised *Billboard* magazine full page ad that ultimately caused the severing of relations between dad Willie and Monument Records.

Lloyd Price had signed with Monument just about the same time as Willie, within a week or two of each other. As part of kicking off their new recordings, Monument planned to do full page ads on both artists in *Billboard* magazine, a major promo shot coveted by any popular performer. Price's ad came out as scheduled but Willie's did not, through no fault of the record company or the magazine (so they claimed).

The producer of the ad simply needed more time because the inks in the full-color ad did not come out right. Unfortunately, label president, Foster, was not able to inform Willie personally. Willie learned of the missing ad only when he tried to find it in that week's issue. Susie felt that soured Willie on the label. That may well have been the big factor, but the fact remained that Monument had no success with Willie, from the first single on, not that RCA would do better.

For Monument, Willie cut seven tracks consisting of six songs (recording 'King of a Lonely Castle' at the only two sessions he did for the company). His first session was held July 6, 1964, with a wide array of session players, Harold Bradley, Wayne Moss, and Ray Edenton, guitars, Bob Moore, bass, Murrey Harman, Jr., drums, Charlie McCoy, harmonica, and Bill Pursell, piano. In addition, there was the unusual addition of Douglas Williams playing xylophone and vibes, as well as Dan King on French horn and Glenn Baxter and George Tidwell on trumpets. Renowned instrumentalist Bill Justis (a number two hit from 1957, 'Raunchy') was listed as "contractor."

The other songs cut at the first session were (in addition to 'King of a Lonely Castle') 'Someone Waiting for You' and 'To Make a Long Story Short' (the first two songs were Willie originals and the third was co-written with Foster). At the second session (July 28, 1964), there were far fewer musicians; this time only Boots Randolph, sax, David Parker, guitar, Bob Moore, bass, and John Greubel, drums were listed. The songs cut at the second session (in addition to 'King of a Lonely Castle' again) were 'I Never Cared for You', 'You Left Me a long, Long Time Ago' and I Feel That Old Feeling' (all three written by Willie). On August 7 (1964), Foster brought guitarist Parker back in to the studio to overdub guitar on the four tracks done July 28. Then all too soon, Willie was gone from Monument.

With his abrupt departure in the latter part of 1964, the other recordings Willie completed, in addition to that first single, sat unreleased in the company's vaults until 1982. That was the year the two record album, ... *The Winning Hand*, was put together. It was credited to Brenda Lee, Dolly Parton, Kris Kristofferson, and Willie. They were listed on the cover as Brenda, Dolly, Kris & Willie.

The entire collection of tracks was actually a soundtrack to an accompanying TV show, released into syndication. Together, both the show and the soundtrack were intended to spark a successful reactivation of the Monument label, dormant since 1981, following a bankruptcy filing. Willie's material, the songs recorded in 1964, was included though he was no longer signed to the label. Neither were the others (remember the label had been out of business).

For the album and TV show, duets were overdubbed on some of Willie's songs by either Brenda, Dolly, or Kris. Mark Rothbaum, Willie's manager/advisor, said that since Foster was a friend of

Willie's, Willie did go back into the studio in 1983 to overdub on Dolly's song. He also did that for the songs with Lee and Kristofferson.

For the actual TV show, performances were either specifically filmed or compiled from existing footage. As a distributed videotape, it received a limited short-lived circulation. When the soundtrack was first released in 1982, according to *Billboard*, it was the subject of a major ($100,000) radio, retail, and advertising campaign designed to sell it in Pop, Country, and AC (Adult Contemporary) markets.

The *Billboard* article, in the November 20, 1982, issue, disclosed that the cuts were primarily "material from the label's vaults." Monument had some extensive vault material, having been the label that first signed a very young Parton soon after she arrived in Nashville from her mountain home in Eastern Tennessee. The company also was home to Kristofferson from 1971 through 1978.

Several tracks had either new or rerecorded parts added specifically for this release. As a result, it finally became possible to hear most of Willie's original 1964 Monument recordings. As far as new material went, in early 1983, Brenda recorded 'You're Gonna Love Yourself in the Morning' with Willie specifically for this project. Sometime after 1983, since CBS really owned Monument and all its product, *The Winning Hand* album was rereleased as a CBS Special Product album/cassette/compact disc (though it was still dated 1982).

In 1993, a full decade after *The Winning Hand* project (show and soundtrack) had been marketed, the Special Products division of Sony Music (parent company of CBS and Columbia Records) released six songs from Willie's 1964 Monument recordings. This time the tracks were unadorned, meaning that no extra overdubbing had been done. It was all Willie singing alone with only the originally recorded backing instrumentation.

Several songs on the soundtrack album (notably 'You'll Always Have Someone') were not included on this compilation while one previously unreleased song, 'I Feel That Old Feeling' was added to what became a Willie Nelson/Eddie Rabbitt album entitled *Singer Songwriters*, BT 21130. Willie's one official Monument release, the unadorned original version of his only single for the label, 'I Never Cared for You', appeared on both *The Winning Hand* soundtrack and the 1993 *Singer Songwriters* compilation. In 1994, it was also included on the Sony Music collection, *The Monument Story*.

During the late eighties and into the nineties, Foster remained relatively inactive in the music business. The pair did work together again after Willie signed with Columbia, as the producer of Willie's 1989 album project, *A Horse Called Music*. So even though Willie left the label hurriedly in 1964, seemingly no hard feelings remained.

The Monument Project - Album Listings

... *The Winning Hand*. (Brenda, Dolly, Kris & Willie). CBS Records PT 38389/JWG-2784. (1982)

Track Listing: You're Gonna Love Yourself (in the Morning) (Brenda Lee & Willie), You'll Always Have Someone (Willie), Happy, Happy Birthday Baby (Dolly Parton & Willie), You Left Me a Long, Long Time Ago (Willie & Brenda), To Make a Long Story Short, She's Gone (Willie & Kris Kristofferson), Everything's Beautiful (in It's Own Way) (Dolly & Willie), I Never Cared for You (Willie), Casey's Last Ride (Kris & Willie), King of a Lonely Castle (Willie).

Recording Notes: This was the soundtrack as originally released (and also released as JWG-2784) in 1982 on Monument Records. Two singles featuring Willie were pulled from the album. Up first was the duet with Dolly Parton, 'Everything's Beautiful (in Its Own Way)', which hit number seven (and remaining twenty weeks) on the country singles charts in early 1983. The main parts of the version on this album were done in October 1981 at Nashville's Sound Emporium. The song was one Dolly said she:

> brought with me when I moved to Nashville in 1964 and it helped me get my first recording contract.

In 1983, Dolly included the Willie duet version on her RCA album, *Burlap & Satin* (AHL1-4691). Late in her tenure with RCA, Dolly cut one other duet with Willie, 'I Really Don't Want to Know' (released only on a 1985 German RCA anthology, *The Love Album 2*, RCA ND-90455). The next Willie single from the album turned out to be 'You're

Gonna Love Yourself (in the Morning)', a duet with Brenda Lee. That collaboration peaked at number forty-three in the Spring of 1983. The album itself peaked at number one hundred and nine on the national album sales charts in early 1983.

Singer Songwriters. (Willie Nelson/Eddie Rabbitt). Columbia Records (Sony Music Special Products) BT/A 21130. (1993).

Track Listing: Someone Waiting for You, To Make a Long Story Short, She's Gone, I Never Cared for You, You Left Me a Long, Long Time Ago, King of a Lonely Castle, I Feel That Old Feeling.

Recording Notes: This 1993 compilation featured (unadorned) most of what Willie cut for Monument back in 1964, including that first and only single, 'I Never Cared for You', as well as 'To Make a Long Story Short, She's Gone', co-written with label head, Fred Foster. Actually, all of the songs (six) that Willie recorded for Monument were included on this collection. He did cut seven tracks but one song, 'King of a Lonely Castle' was cut twice, first at the recording session of July 6, 1964 and again July 28 of the same year.

'I Never Cared for You', also appeared on the 1994 Sony Music Special Products "various artists" album, *The Monument Story,* A2K 66106. That collection featured the highlights from Monument Records' greatest recording achievements, from Grammer's 'Gotta Travel on' to Billy Swan's Pop smash, 'I Can Help'. Liner notes were by label president Foster. They gave a detailed overview of how he saw the beginnings and growth of the company, up to the demise of the company as an independent label, which, unfortunately, was never discussed.

Willie's on the course again.
(Photo from Will van Overbeek)

SECTION II

The RCA Albums
and Compilations

BECAUSE I'M CRAZY . . .

Live in Fort Worth!
(Photo from RCA Records and Willie Nelson)

RCA never really promoted Willie.
(Photo from the Michael Ochs Archives)

"My Own Peculiar Way":

The Original RCA Albums

After stints with Liberty and Monument, Chet Atkins signed Willie to RCA Victor in late 1964. He then proceeded to record two Christmas songs with Nelson on November 12th (of 1964), 'Pretty Paper' (a Willie original) and 'What a Merry Christmas This Could Be' (written by Harlan Howard and Hank Cochran). With a major recording contract in hand, Willie not only went to work cutting his first album, he put a band together and went back on the road regularly. He also began appearing regularly on the Ernest Tubb show.

The company, RCA, and the artist, Willie, embarked on a multi-year relationship that did not result in major sales success (although Willie did chart twenty-four singles, the last in 1981, nine years after he left the label), but which did significantly expose Nelson's songwriting abilities to other artists. Most of the recordings (singles and albums) were not produced to put Nelson's voice and singing style on display, instead he was mixed as if he couldn't sing (or play) very well. His voice was buried under strings and other instrumentation.

As a producer, Chet Atkins used what he liked best, smooth studio pickers, strings, and vocal choruses (i.e. "the Nashville Sound"). Back then, Chet was quoted as saying that Willie "doesn't play good enough to accompany himself." From a mid-1990's perspective, Chet recently observed about Willie that, "he's pretty good. He plays a helluva lot better than when I used to record him." He added that, "I think he should change strings and tune up his guitar a little more often."

Chet acknowledged that he held the production reigns pretty tightly back then. He told Rick Clark of *Mix Magazine* that:

at one time, I fought a little bit against Waylon and Willie and all of those guys who wanted to produce their own records. It was because I had a whole bunch of producers, and I knew that they would lose their jobs. I was thinking of them. But Waylon and Willie, of course, are some of my dearest friends, and they don't hold any of that against me, I'm sure.

Overall, Willie's records were not enthusiastically marketed. RCA marketing experts could not figure out how to sell his records so the one (and only) place where he remained hot was Texas, the "only place we could sell him," according to Atkins. The records were also not enthusiastically received because, as drummer Paul English related, people would tell him, "we like to hear you (Willie and his band - formed around 1966), but we don't like your records."

Chet, himself, admitted that "I just didn't have the time - or take the time - to promote and sell records, mine or anybody else's." He finally resigned from RCA in 1981 because he found himself overwhelmed by budgets, paperwork, and just too much in the way of corporate demands. At least it wasn't true that Chet didn't believe in Willie. In fact, Chet once said, in effect, that it would be unbelievable "if Willie Nelson don't make it."

Chet philosophized further about why Willie and RCA did not click together. He mused that Willie was "probably too different for the average country public." He further recalled that he "used to have meetings with Willie and Lucky Moeller all the time, trying to decide how we could spread his sales out of Texas where he always sold records and did well in personal appearances. But we couldn't seem to spread them anywhere else."

Willie had his own view on why his singing/recording career did not take off at RCA. His insight was that:

there was no money being spent production-wise on Willie Nelson, and it seemed like I was only cutting my albums there like dub sessions. They would release them and see if anybody wanted to record them, I just didn't feel like the promotional department of RCA was behind me. In fact I knew they weren't, and they admit they weren't.

To put it bluntly, he said, "I didn't have any promotion." But why?

In his autobiography, Willie was even more insightful. He wrote that "it's always been fashionable for the record companies to find a good songwriter and sign him to a contract for his songs." He was obviously referring to RCA when he further explained that:

they grudgingly allowed me to sing as long as they could cover up my voice with horns and strings and hope the songs were strong enough to carry the album. They didn't bother to promote me. They figured, hey, when we need a good song for one of our twenty other singers we'll just go pick one off of Willie's latest album and people will think it is new work.

Danny Davis, who fronted the group Danny Davis and the Nashville Brass and who also did production work for RCA, including some with Willie's material, confirmed that "Chet and the Nashville office always believed he was a giant." Unfortunately, Davis added, "we never could convince the top brass at RCA about Willie..." Thus, no matter what Willie recorded and no matter how hard the people in Nashville, like Chet Atkins, worked, as even Willie himself observed, "everything had to be cleared through New York, and once the computer got it, it was going to say, 'Willie Who?'."

How did Willie feel about the way he was recorded? "I just didn't feel comfortable in that kinda situation," he admitted. He said:

you'd walk into the studio and they'd put six guys behind you who'd never seen your music before, and it's impossible to get the feel of it in a three hour session. That was true for me, at least.

He further elaborated that "the music I played on a bandstand was better than the music I played in the studio."

He was hardly at his best when he went into a studio and "they pointed a finger at me and said, 'Sing, Shorty'." Yet, Willie went "along with what I was told, even though I didn't agree with it particularly." That's likely why, in his autobiography, Willie barely mentioned his years at RCA. What little he discussed centered around his *Yesterday's Wine* album which he still considered one of his best.

Colin Escott, in his liner notes to RCA's summation compilation of Willie's RCA recordings, *The Essential Willie Nelson*, speculated that the lack of mention by Willie probably "says something about his disappointment." Willie remarked on numerous occasions that Ernest Tubb's label, for example, would not have stripped him of his backing band. Most of the time, the music played at Willie's sessions did not sound like the music his band was making or would have made had they been allowed to back Willie in the studio.

It also was not that Willie failed to receive a good amount of "other" exposure. In late 1964, as he was leaving Monument, he signed with the Grand Ole Opry. Author Ronnie Pugh explained that in 1965, when Hal Smith put together a syndicated TV show for Ernest Tubb, "The Ernest Tubb Show," Smith "billed Willie as Ernest's co-star." According to Smith, "that's the way Ernest wanted it, to help Willie."

Yet, it didn't help, as Smith recalled, "nothing we ever did for Willie seemed to help him! His records then weren't going anywhere."

Being a co-star on someone else's show didn't suit Willie and it didn't take long for him to realize that. He went to Smith and "asked to leave the show." Tubb clearly saw the problem, recounting that the show's "producer kept after me to get Willie to say something." Ernest said that he told the producer, "you get him to say something, I can't." Tubb's observation was that "Willie's a great singer, but he didn't have just a whole lot of exuberance on TV." Willie had learned from Bob Wills not to talk but to continually play the music.

Still other people have speculated that back when Willie began his Nashville career, he was ahead of his time. Even Chet Atkins concluded that, "nobody admired him more than people in the business, but Willie was kind of ahead of his time." There will always be some merit to that kind of conclusion because, as even Willie himself observed, he was writing songs with five or more chords back when three chord songs were the "norm" for country music.

A friend of Willie's, Crash Stewart, offered that view once to Willie. Willie replied that he wished the world would hurry up and catch up because he needed the money. The world did eventually catch up and follow. For each new turn that Willie made, he found the audience with him. Most often it was the record executive that dragged behind. Willie quickly concluded that:

> the executive producers and the record company producers had a very small opinion of the intelligence of people who listened to country music. They felt the public was not capable of hearing words that had more than three syllables, of songs that had more than three chords.

Willie just as immediately decided that "as soon as I hit town I realized I was in the wrong place."

He had a fundamentally different way of looking at his chosen profession, making music. Referring to the executives who ran the country music business in Nashville, Willie noted that:

> they'd stay in their offices all day expecting people to call 'em up and tell 'em what was going on in the music world. You can't do that, you gotta get out on the streets and find out what people are into. But, you know, they were in charge.

Meanwhile he was "out on the streets trying to make it against these people who were all in offices."

When he chose to do a sparse concept album like *Red Headed Stranger*, it was the heads of the label who didn't think it would sell. His audience bought the album en masse. The same proved true when

Willie did his first complete album of standards. He knew the audience that loved Bob Wills also loved 'Stardust'. When Willie did what he knew was right, he became the all-time best seller of country music albums. Unfortunately, he wasn't able to do things his way at RCA, nor did RCA try to fit his musical style into his recordings.

After Willie left the label in 1972, RCA did meet with much more success when it remarketed his material, mostly because he had become such a huge star on Columbia Records and demand for his product, any of it, was high. Though the company never did fully realize just how commercial the material was, others did.

In 1982, Merle Haggard and George Jones not only "proved" the greatness of the song, 'Yesterday's Wine', they definitively demonstrated its commerciality, taking their version to number one on the *Billboard* country singles chart. Merle had just finished recording the *Pancho and Lefty* album with Willie. After that he went to work on a duet album with Jones that would wind up being called *Yesterday's Wine*. Producer Billy Sherrill recalled that Merle brought 'Yesterday's Wine':

> to the session, and Jones didn't care what he sang. Whoever or whatever comes up, is fine with him. Merle brought most of the stuff in there, and we just did it.

Even though Chet Atkins signed Waylon Jennings to the label in 1965, RCA also didn't know what they had in Waylon and Willie together. Strangely, the two artists didn't record together until after Willie had left the company. However, during their tenures with RCA, they did write one extremely famous country classic, 'Good Hearted Woman'. Willie's recollection of the creation of that song went like this,

> I was at the Fort Worther Motel in Ft. Worth, Texas, playing poker with a man named Billy Gray. My wife, Connie, was there, and Waylon came in. He had the idea for the song and the first line. Waylon joined the poker game and told me about it. Connie took the words down as we played.

Supposedly, Willie only contributed two lines, though he did begin picking out the beginnings of the tune. Waylon added more detail about the song's origins, saying,

> I'd been reading an ad for Ike and Tina Turner, and it said, 'Tina Turner singing songs about good-hearted women loving good-timing men.' I thought, 'What a great country song title that is!'

Willie's daughter, Susie, told a more detailed version of the songwriting effort, relating that Waylon mentioned to Willie "he was stalled on a song he wanted to record." The recording session, according to Susie, was scheduled for the next day. Waylon had completed the first verse and chorus. He read the beginnings of the song to Willie and told him "if he could finish it, he could have half the song." Susie wrote that Willie "stayed the night" and finished the song "right after breakfast." Willie specifically remembered that "I woke up the next morning writing that song." He said he:

> told Waylon about it at the breakfast table, so we finished it after breakfast. We weren't scheduled to record, but Waylon called the studio and set up some time for that day.

Waylon did give Willie half the writer's royalties, so who knows who did exactly what and how much. Willie later remarked that:

> I think Connie and Jessi (Colter - Waylon's wife) both were the object of that song. Naturally, we started thinking about the ones who were having to put up with us at that particular time.

The song, as recorded by Willie and Waylon in 1985, made it to the number one spot (staying there for three weeks), unusual for the country charts at the time. In 1972, Waylon had taken his solo version (recorded for RCA) to number three on the same charts. Tina Turner was but one of several artists who eventually cut a version of the song.

Over the years, much of Willie's RCA material has become unavailable, in spite of several comprehensive compilations. In 1998, Willie's fans were finally able to take heart with the announcement that Bear Family Records of Germany was rereleasing all the original RCA material (along with all the Monument tracks). The eight disc boxed set was advertised as being "very complete." It turned out to be, containing all seven Monument tracks and everything he did with RCA (even 'Chet's Tune') except for his 1964 version of Cole Porter's 'Don't Fence Me in', which was listed as "lost." At one hundred and fifty plus dollars, the collection had to have been "complete."

Sue Thrasher wrote, in *Southern Exposure*, a very succinct synopsis of Willie's tenure on RCA. She stated that he "was under contract to RCA Victor for years, produced a number of albums for them, and wrote a good many of Nashville's hit songs." Billy Joe Shaver was considerably more pointed in his comments about Willie and RCA when he observed that "I don't think they knew what they had a hold of."

The Original RCA Albums - Album Listings

Country Willie: His Own Songs. RCA LSP-3418. (1965).

Track Listing: Mr. Record Man, Healing Hands of Time, Funny How Time Slips Away, It Should Be Easier Now, Are You Sure, One Day at a Time, Hello Walls, So Much to Do, Within Your Crowd, Night Life, Darkness on the Face of the Earth, My Own Peculiar Way.

Recording Notes: Nelson's first album for RCA was produced by Mr. "Nashville Sound," Chet Atkins, and released in 1965. According to session notes, Willie was both the leader and guitar player for all the tracks, which were completed over a three day period (April 7, 8, and 9, 1965), each night from six to nine PM at RCA's Studio A. The song, 'Buddy' was done at the April 9th session but not released until it became a cut on the 1968 album, *Good Times.*

Players at the April 7th session included Henry Strzelecki, bass, Murrey Harman, Jr., drums, Pete Drake, steel guitar, Jerry R. Hubbard, electric guitar, and Ray Edenton, guitar. On April 8th, there were three lineup changes, Jerry Carrigan, drums, Jerry G. Kennedy, electric guitar, and Velma Smith, guitar, while the April 9th session substituted Bob Moore on bass, had Harman coming back on drums, and added Hubbard as a second electric guitarist to complement Kennedy. The Jerry R. Hubbard, who played April 7 and 9, later became known as Jerry Reed. Velma Smith was married to promoter Hal Smith.

Interestingly, Willie rerecorded some of his Liberty material (both written by him and others) for this and the next album. The Liberty songs re-done for this album were some of his best known originals, 'Mr. Record Man', 'Funny How Time Slips Away', 'Hello

Walls', 'Night Life', and 'Darkness on the Face of the Earth'. Not one of Willie's first RCA singles was included, unfortunately.

The final selection on the album, 'My Own Peculiar Way' (a Willie original) would become the title track for one of his later RCA albums, released in 1969. Another original, 'So Much to Do', had previously been recorded as a Pamper Music "demo." Two more Pamper "demo" recordings, 'Healing Hands of Time', and 'It Should Be Easier Now' were released commercially for the first time on this album.

The 'Healing Hands of Time' track came from the April 7th session, though Willie had previously recorded it for RCA on January 12, 1965, with the backing of six session players, four violins, and one viola. Willie would rerecord it and 'It Should Be Easier Now' for Columbia Records, in 1976 and 1977, respectively. 'Healing Hands of Time' also became the title cut for his 1994 Liberty Records album.

'Within Your Crowd' was a beautiful Nelson original that has remained obscure, appearing only on this first RCA set. Two songs, 'One Day at a Time' and 'It Should Be Easier Now' were both classified by Willie (in his autobiography) as "philosophical" songs. The album's fifth selection, 'Are You Sure', was co-written with steel guitar player, Buddy Emmons. Willie would later rerecord the song, for Step One Records on a 1994 album he did with Curtis Potter, *Six Hours at Pedernales*. That same Step One album contained a rerecorded version of 'It Should Be Easier Now'.

Country Favorites: Willie Nelson Style. RCA LFT/LSP-3528. (1966).

Track Listing: Columbus Stockade Blues, Seasons of My Heart, I'd Trade All of My Tomorrows (for Just One Yesterday), My Window Faces the South (*), Go on Home, Fraulein, San Antonio Rose, I Love You Because, Don't You Ever Get Tired (of Hurting Me), Home in San Antone (*), Heartaches by the Number, Making Believe (*).

Recording Notes: Chet Atkins also produced this 1966 release, which featured Willie mixing country standards with the only two Hank Cochran songs he recorded for RCA, 'Go on Home' (not to be confused with Willie's song, 'Goin' Home') and 'Don't You Ever Get Tired (of Hurting Me)'. Once again, unfortunately, none of his first RCA singles were included on the album. No original Willie compositions made the album either.

The musical emphasis was on Western Swing with backing by fiddler Wade Ray and others who had played with Ernest Tubb's Texas Troubadours (Grant Shofner, rhythm guitar, Elmer "Buddy" Charleton, steel guitar, Jack Greene, drums, Jack Drake, bass, and Leon Rhodes, lead guitar). Willie was listed only as leader (though he later said the album was "my idea"). Hargus Robbins on piano and

James Wilkerson on bass were the other session players for the two days of recording, December 15 and 16, 1965 (six to nine PM at Studio A).

Two songs Willie had recorded for Liberty, 'Columbus Stockade Blues' and the George Jones oldie 'Seasons of My Heart', appeared here as re-recordings. The selection emphasis was on songs made popular by other artists. Bobby Helms' 1957 pop hit, 'Fraulein' was featured, as was Guy Mitchell's 1959 number one pop song, 'Heartaches by the Number', which was written by Harlan Howard, based on his time in the Army where "everything was done by the numbers."

Kinky Friedman once said that 'Fraulein' was the first song both he and Townes Van Zandt ever learned. Fitting in with those two songs was Willie's version of the Leon Payne composition, 'I Love You Because', which Mrs. Payne said was written "for me." In 1963, the song had gone to number three on the pop singles charts for Capitol Records artist Al Martino. The original hit versions of the song came from Payne in 1949 and Ernest Tubb in 1950. Jim Reeves recorded the song in 1964 and hit the charts with it posthumously in 1976 for RCA.

Willie's rendition of 'San Antonio Rose' was his first cover of a Bob Wills song, a man whose music Willie greatly admired, once writing that "it was just a good sound. I'm sure I have taken a lot of influence from Bob Wills." Wills wrote the song as an instrumental in 1938 and "it sold very well" for him.

According to his biographer, Charles Townsend, "the original melody came out of an old fiddle tradition." Once the song was successful as a music-only piece, Wills found his record company requesting him "to record it again with lyrics." That took him two years before he "finally finished the words and recorded 'New San Antonio Rose' in April 1940."

Another "San Antonio" song, 'Home in San Antone', was written by Floyd Jenkins. Roy Acuff has since divulged that Fred Rose wrote "under the name Floyd Jenkins." Country music historian and author, Dan Daley, discussed Rose's writing credits in more depth, saying,

> he wrote under several pen names, including Bart Dawson and Floyd Jenkins, with the idea that country-sounding names would more quickly get songs placed in that genre.

Other Releases: When released in Germany, the catalog number became NK 90006. In 1970, RCA rereleased most of it as a Camden budget product, *Columbus Stockade Blues and Other Country Favorites*, RCA Records (Camden) CAF-2440. Unfortunately, they shortened it to nine cuts and resequenced the tracks.

The three cuts (*) that were eliminated were three of the better songs on the album, especially 'My Window Faces the South'. That song, written by Abner Silver and Mitchell Parish (lyricist for 'Stardust'), was one of Willie's earliest and best attempts at cutting Tin

Pan Alley pop. The other eliminated cuts were Rose's 'Home in San Antone' and 'Making Believe', a song written by former automobile assembly-line worker, Jimmy Work.

In 1976, the shorter resequenced Camden set came out again on Camden but with a 7018 catalog number. Pickwick also released the set in 1976 as ACL-7018. Using a similar catalog number, CK-7018, Pickwick rereleased the collection as *Seasons of My Heart*. Finally, in 1985, Camden released it again as CAK-2444, through the Special Music Company, Hackensack, New Jersey.

* = the three cuts deleted from this album to make up the 1970 budget set, *Columbus Stockade Blues and Other Country Favorites*, RCA Records (Camden) CAF-2440 and the 1976 Camden set, 7018, as well as the 1976 Pickwick set, ACL/CK-7018, which was entitled, for the CK-7018 release, *Seasons of My Heart*.

Live Country Music Concert. RCA LSP-3659. (1966).

Track Listing: Introduction: Bo Powell, Willie Introduces Band, Medley: Mr. Record Man/Hello Walls/One Day at a Time, Medley: The Last Letter/Half a Man, I Never Cared for You, Yesterday, Touch Me, Something to Think About, I Just Can't Let You Say Goodbye, How Long Is Forever, Night Life, Medley: Opportunity to Cry/Permanently Lonely, My Own Peculiar Way.

Recording Notes: Felton Jarvis, at the time an assistant to Chet Atkins, took over production on this live 1966 release, which was recorded at Panther Hall in Fort Worth. Jarvis became better known through his attachment to Elvis Presley as producer and friend. Supposedly when Jarvis needed a kidney transplant, Elvis helped arrange a speedy proceeding.

This was one of Willie's best RCA releases because the live sound as well as his singing was not lost in the mixing. That should not have been unexpected. Willie often stated he made better music live than he did in the studio at RCA because,

> for one thing. I'd be using my own band, and we'd have a better feel for it - be more relaxed. We'd have an audience to play for, and it was just a whole lot more fun.

Not only did Willie present some of his best-known songs, he used this concert to introduce some unfamiliar gems, such as his own very different 'I Just Can't Let You Say Goodbye', a song about strangling one's object of affection. Willie explained (and made it sound merely routine) that he had read in the paper:

> where some guy killed his old lady and I thought, well, that would be a far-out thing to do, to write this song where you're

killin' this chick, so I started there. ...I brought it up to where she was really pissin' him off, she was sayin' bad things to him and so he was tryin' to shut her up and started chokin' her.

The song, strange as it was in subject matter, became Willie's second RCA single, going only as far as number forty-eight and exiting after only two weeks. Two other Nelson originals, ones that have remained relatively unknown, 'Something to Think About' and 'How Long Is Forever', were presented here for the first time. The performance of 'My Own Peculiar Way', a Nelson original from his first RCA album, closed the show.

Other Releases: In 1975, this album was recataloged (same title and artwork) as ANL1/ANS1-1354. A year later, in 1976, RCA rereleased it as *Willie Nelson Live*, (RCA APL1-1487 and AYL1-4165), with one track deleted, 'Night Life', and one added, 'I Gotta Get Drunk', which had been earlier released on the *What Can You Do to Me Now* album (RCA APL1-1234). The added track was grafted in right after the Bo Powell introduction, creating an album that contained material from two different sources.

Obviously, live effects had to be added. New artwork was also added. The updated picture of Willie as he looked in 1976 (he was by this time being hailed as a "bearded" outlaw) gave the appearance that the album was a "new" live set. New liner notes by Don Cusic of Record World appeared on the back.

RCA felt it necessary to get 'I Gotta Get Drunk' on an album because it had reached number fifty-five on the country singles chart in April of 1976. This "live" album charted for seven weeks (the original album failed to chart), reaching number one-hundred forty-nine on the national album sales chart as tracked by *Billboard*. About the same time, Willie's Columbia album, *The Sound in Your Mind*, was charting nationally at a much higher ranking. His Atlantic album, *Phases and Stages*, was also charting, two years after its initial release.

Make Way for Willie Nelson. RCA LSP-3748. (1967).

Track Listing: Make Way for a Better Man, Some Other World, Have I Stayed Away Too Long, Born to Lose, Lovin' Lies, You Made Me Live, Love and Die, What Now My Love, Teach Me to Forget, A Mansion on the Hill, If It's Wrong to Love You, Have I Told You Lately That I Love You, One in a Row.

Recording Notes: This was a joint production effort by Atkins and Jarvis, issued in 1967. The title was from the first track, 'Make Way for a Better Man', written by Cy Coben, one of Nashville's oldest and most varied writers. After studying musical theory and composition in the thirties, Coben began as a pop writer in New York but liked country music so well he wrote it on the side.

Then he moved to Nashville where he has written more than six hundred songs. He "genuinely loved" country music and was convinced he succeeded at it "because I stuck by two rules: don't write about something you don't know about, and don't look down on Country music." In addition to having written 'The Name of the Game Was Love', Hank Snow's next-to-last top twenty hit, he composed 'Piano Roll Blues' and several selections for Walt Disney's "Alice in Wonderland."

On this album, Willie introduced his ability to interpret standards such as Ted Daffan's 'Born to Lose' and Scotty Wiseman's 'Have I Told You Lately That I Love You'. This was where he first sang Frank Loesser's 'Have I Stayed Away Too Long'. It was a song he would do again in 1994 for his *Moonlight Becomes You* album.

Scotty Wiseman and his wife Lulu Belle were a hot country comedy act when Scotty wrote the classic love song, 'Have I Told You Lately That I Love You'. Scotty was in the hospital and at the end of his wife's visit, she leaned over and told him, "have I told you lately that I love you?" Scotty recalled that after she left, he "lay there thinking tender thoughts about her."

It occurred to him that her words would make a good song title. By her next visit he was singing part of the new song to her. When he finished, a friend of his "took a copy to Gene Autry in Hollywood," who "made the first recording." According to Scotty's figures, the song has sold "approximately 10 million records here and abroad."

'Born to Lose' was credited to Frankie Brown (F. Brown), though it was written by the great Ted Daffan. That seeming contradiction had an interesting history. In 1942, following some very strong regional success, Ted Daffan and His Texans were brought by Columbia Records to California to cut twenty four sides, most of them written by Ted.

As Daffan and his band were in the midst of recording, the A & R man (the legendary Art Satherley) for the session took Ted aside and told him the label for whom he was recording, Columbia (specifically Okeh, a Columbia subsidiary), would not publish more than a few songs by any one writer. In a highly unusually move, Daffan published his songs through the recording company "rather than go through a publisher." Satherley told Daffan he had too many originals, that the label wouldn't even "take twenty-four songs from Irving Berlin." So, Ted put his own name on half of his songs and the pseudonym, Frankie Brown, on the other half. Columbia then published everything.

Of the songs done at that session, 'Born to Lose' (with vocals by Leon Seago) became the second single issued by Okeh. It was first a pop smash, peaking at number nineteen in August 1943. Then it went on to dominate the newly documented "hillbilly" charts throughout the Summer of 1944.

The phrase, "born to lose," had such an obvious reference to losing at cards, it was long speculated that card playing was the origin of the song idea. At first Daffan would say "the source of inspiration for 'Born to Lose' will have to remain my secret." He also hinted at the card-playing possibility, adding, "it is true that I sometimes played penny ante poker, but I almost always won."

Then Ted got very specific in an interview, revealing that the station wagon he and his band traveled in throughout Texas had its seats placed so that several of the band members could play cards. One of the players thought he had an amazing hand but it turned out that another player's four three's had him beaten yet again. Ted recalled saying, "you were just born to lose." He said he immediately realized, "now that is a hell of a song title."

One of Willie's originals, 'One in a Row', was written, according to Crash Stewart, a promoter and friend of Willie's, after he taught Willie to rope calves. He told Willie, after his first successful roping, that was "one in a row." Stewart claimed Willie sat down and immediately wrote, 'One in a Row'.

The song was also his third single for RCA and finally, his first top twenty entry (debuting in October 1966), peaking at number nineteen and lasting for thirteen weeks. The song, 'A Mansion on the Hill', that Hank Williams wrote with his mentor, Fred Rose, became one of only two Hank songs that Willie recorded for RCA. Willie also covered two Floyd Tillman songs, 'You Made Me Live, Love and Die' and 'Some Other World', and a Leon Payne number, 'Teach Me to Forget'.

From such great country material, Willie did an about face to record the 1966 torch song, 'What Now My Love' co-written by a French composer, Gilbert Becaud. Both Sonny and Cher and Herb Alpert and the Tijuana Brass had hit versions of the song that year. Alpert's instrumental rendition won him a couple of Grammy's. For Columbia, Willie would record another Becaud song, the perennial 'Let It Be Me'.

Sessions for ten of the twelve cuts on this album were done over a two day period, November 28 and 29, 1966 (both days went from ten AM to one PM). The ten cuts featured six backing players, ranging from James Day on steel to Johnny (Bush) Shinn on drums. The two cuts not done in November, 'One Day at a Time' and 'Make Way for a Better Man', were recorded June 8, 1966 (with Atkins producing). Buddy Emmons replaced Day on steel and four violins were added. The mix on both tracks submerged Willie's vocals under the layer of strings.

Two tracks, 'Something to Think About' and 'Tender Years', were recorded at the November 29th session but not used on this album. They would be held until they were included on the 1968 RCA Camden budget set, *Good Ol' Country Singin'*. The June 8th session also produced 'The Party's Over', which would become the title track for Willie's next album, and 'A Wonderful Yesterday', which would appear on the *Good Times* album.

Liner notes were by Joe Allison, the man who oversaw Willie back on Liberty Records. He attempted to answer the question, "what is a Willie Nelson...?" Allison imparted some very insightful evaluations, from noting Willie's 'jazz-country' execution to the observation that he "is so relaxed that he makes Chet Atkins look like a nervous wreck." Chet was so relaxed that he was supposedly replaced by Felton Jarvis as Elvis' producer at RCA when it appeared he had fallen asleep at the console during one of Presley's sessions.

The Party's Over. RCA LSP-3858. (1967).

Track Listing: Suffer in Silence, Hold Me Tighter, Go Away, The Ghost, To Make a Long Story Short (She's Gone), A Moment Isn't Very Long, The Party's Over, There Goes a Man, Once Alone, No Tomorrow in Sight, I'll Stay Around, The End of Understanding.

Recording Notes: This 1967 release, with production by Chet Atkins, consisted of all Nelson originals (though 'I'll Stay Around' was co-written with Hank Cochran). The majority of the tracks were songs Willie had already recorded as "demos" for Pamper Music. 'Hold Me Tighter' and 'Once Alone' made their first appearances on this set. 'There Goes a Man' had been previously recorded for Liberty.

Though the title song (a Willie original) has since become very familiar, it was only a top ten hit in England, for Lonnie Donegan. Donegan was known for recording novelty songs, his biggest being 'Does Your Chewing Gum Lose Its Flavor (on the Bedpost Overnight?). The stateside familiarity for 'The Party's Over' came about when it was used (by Don Meredith) on ABC's Monday Night Football to note that one team was being defeated so badly that the game was really over before it was officially over.

Willie actually recorded the title cut June 8, 1966 with backing by seven session players and four violins. When RCA released it as his fourth single, it did go to number twenty-four. It also stayed on the charts for sixteen weeks, the longest a Willie single would chart until Columbia's 'Blue Eyes Crying in the Rain'. Another of the cuts, 'To Make a Long Story Short (She's Gone)', was co-written with Fred Foster and had been previously recorded by Willie (but not released right away) for Monument Records.

The sessions for the other eleven cuts on the album were held over a two day period (June 13 and 14, 1967 - ten AM to one PM both days). Those tracks featured three violins, a viola, and a cello. Six regular session players were also used. Johnny Bush and James Day played drums and steel, respectively. Both times, Jerry Hubbard (soon to become Jerry Reed) played electric guitar.

Texas in My Soul. RCA LSP-3937. (1968).

Track Listing: Dallas, San Antonio, Streets of Laredo, Who Put All My Ex's in Texas, The Hill Country Theme (From Lyndon Johnson's Texas), Waltz Across Texas, Travis Letter, Remember the Alamo, Texas in My Soul, There's a Little Bit of Everything in Texas, Beautiful Texas.

Recording Notes: This was a 1968 release and a Chet Atkins production. In a way it was a "concept" album in that it brought together some of the best songs about Nelson's home state of Texas. 'San Antonio' became Willie's sixth RCA single, peaking at fifty but lingering on the charts for nine weeks. Several classics, 'Waltz Across Texas' (written by Ernest Tubb's nephew, Talmadge Tubb), 'There's a Little Bit of Everything in Texas', and 'Texas in My Soul', associated with Texas favorite son, Ernest Tubb, were naturally included.

'Waltz Across Texas' was not a big seller for Ernest when he first released it in 1965, but through the following years it became one of his most requested songs. This was the first but not the only time Willie would record the song. In 1978, when Tubb rerecorded most of his major songs for Pete Drake, Willie came in and recorded an electronic duet with Ernest on 'Waltz Across Texas'. Though Tubb also wrote 'Texas in My Soul' (with help from then eleven year old son Justin), he did not record it. Both Tex Williams and Hank Penny recorded it, though it was not a big hit for either.

The 'Travis Letter' was actually written by the legendary Colonel Travis, who died at the Alamo. The song, 'Who Put All My Ex's in Texas', was a co-composition from Eddie Rabbitt, the great country singer/songwriter by way of New Jersey. It was not to be confused with the 1987 George Strait hit, 'All My Ex's Live in Texas', written by Whitey and Lyndia Shafer.

The sessions for this album were done over a two day period, August 10 and 11, 1967, the first day extending from ten AM to 1PM and the second from nine-thirty AM to twelve-thirty PM. In addition to Grady Martin, guitar, James Day, steel, and four other Nashville session regulars, country funnyman Ray Stevens (real name: Harold Ray Ragsdale) contributed vibes and organ backing. Chet Atkins added his guitar sound to the six cuts recorded on the first day of sessions.

Other Releases: The album was rereleased in its entirety 1986 on the German Bear Family Records (LP only) as *Beautiful Texas, 1836-1986*, BFX 15256. Additional cuts on the Bear Family release were 'San Antonio Rose' (from Nelson's second RCA album), the 1966 single release of 'San Antonio Rose', and 'Home in San Antone', also from Nelson's second RCA album. Richard Weize, the head of Bear Family, was listed as "the producer of the re-issue."

Good Times. RCA LSP-4057. (1968).

Track Listing: Good Times, December Day, Sweet Memories, Little Things, Pages, She's Still Gone, Ashamed, A Wonderful Yesterday, Permanently Lonely, Down to Our Last Goodbye, Buddy, Did I Ever Love You.

Recording Notes: Another joint Jarvis and Atkins work, this album was also issued in 1968. Included were more rerecordings of Willie's legendary Pamper demos. Finally, RCA began featuring Willie's singles with a corresponding album. This time his seventh RCA single, 'Little Things' was included.

It was co-written by Willie and his former duet partner, then wife, Shirley (Collie) Nelson. As a single, it peaked at number twenty-two and remained chart-bound for eleven weeks. In fact, ten of the twelve songs were either written or co-written by Nelson. Three of those co-written songs were done with second wife, Shirley. They were 'Pages', 'Little Things', and 'She's Still Gone'.

'December Day' (as recorded December 12, 1967) was introduced on this album. It would be rerecorded in 1971 for Willie's concept album, *Yesterday's Wine*. Only 'Sweet Memories', by Mickey Newbury (the same gentleman who tried to marry Willie's daughter, Lana, when she was only fourteen), and 'Down to Our Last Goodbye' (by Wayne Moss and Jan Crutchfield) were not composed by Willie. His eighth single, 'Good Times', led off the album.

It did not fare as well on the singles chart (as often happens to an album cut that later becomes a single), stopping at the number forty-four position and fading away after only eight weeks. Nonetheless, in 1981, RCA was able to push the same song, as a rereleased single, all the way to number twenty-five. Of course, by 1981, Willie was a big star for Columbia Records.

As a song, 'Good Times' was great, being recorded by none other than pop star Jack Jones. 'Sweet Memories' was not initially pulled from the album as a single. However, in 1979, it became the sixth post-contract Willie single that RCA was able to chart. It peaked at number four, making it Willie's highest charting RCA single ever.

The original album cover art consisted of a relaxed Willie closely showing a young woman how to putt on some golf course. Willie and golf have always been close, so much so that his recording studio in Texas had a golf course around it so Willie could golf in the afternoon and record at night or "half-past dark." The whole setup was called "Cut and Putt."

The selections on the album came from three different recording sessions and one "remake" session. 'Ashamed' (co-produced by Jarvis) and 'Permanently Lonely' came from a January 12, 1965 Atkins-produced session, while 'December Day', 'Pages', and 'Little Things' were recorded by Jarvis December 12, 1967, and 'Good Times', 'She's Still

Gone', and 'Sweet Memories' were cut by Atkins and Jarvis March 27, 1968. Four violins and one viola were featured on the January 12 recordings (arrangements by Anita Kerr) along with six session players (drummer included).

Atkins played guitar on both of the other sessions along with another picker and a bass player. No drums were used at either session. The December 12 date had James Day on guitar while the other guitarist, Thomas G. Martin, was listed as "leader." Willie was not involved in the "remake" session, held August 17, 1965. Atkins was listed as leader and guitarist.

What he did was add his guitar, six violins, and the piano playing of Harold R. Ragsdale (who arranged the "remakes"), to four tracks, 'Did I Ever Love You', 'Down to Our Last Goodbye', 'I Just Can't Let You Say Goodbye', and 'And So Will You My Love', that Willie had previously recorded. The latter two tracks were excluded from this album. 'And So Will You My Love' never did appear on any Willie Nelson album or compilation. 'Buddy' came from one of the sessions (held April 9, 1965) done for Willie's first album.

My Own Peculiar Way. RCA LSP-4111. (1969).

Track Listing: My Own Peculiar Way, I Walk Alone, Any Old Arms Won't Do, I Just Don't Understand, I Just Dropped By, The Local Memory, That's All, I Let My Mind Wander, Natural to Be Gone, Love Has a Mind of Its Own, The Message, It Will Come to Pass.

Recording Notes: This was a 1969 release produced by Atkins with help on four of the cuts from Danny Davis. The title song, a Willie original, 'My Own Peculiar Way', also appeared on his first album and on his "live" set from Panther Hall. The song actually appeared eleven times on Willie's various RCA albums and compilations.

Texas songwriter, Arleigh Duff (author of the song, 'Ya'll Come'), was impressed by the title song. He wrote, in his autobiography, that:

> Willie's weepers were so beautiful, one of them 'My Own Peculiar Way', influenced me to write one similar. Mine was called 'It's the Little Things', recorded by Sonny James and a BMI award winner in 1968. Thanks Willie, I needed that.

Of the twelve songs on the album, six were by Willie alone. A seventh tune had Willie as a co-writer (with Hank Cochran on 'Any Old Arms Won't Do'). The five remaining cuts were by a wide assortment of writers from John Hartford ('Natural to Be Gone') to Merle Travis ('That's All'). Each cover brought out Willie's eclectic interpretive abilities. Hartford, one of Nashville's finest banjo pickers, has become most well known as the writer of the classic,

'Gentle on My Mind', first recognized and published by Tompall and the Glaser Brothers. Travis, the legendary guitarist from Muhlenberg County, gained his greatest fame as composer of 'Sixteen Tons'.

The 1968 Marty Robbins number one hit, 'I Walk Alone', written by Herbert Wilson, received a very different Willie interpretation. Two more covers of other writers' songs came toward the end of the album. One was a Dallas Frazier song, 'Love Has a Mind of Its Own', and the other, 'It Will Come to Pass', was penned by Don Baird.

Of the Willie originals, there were more rerecordings of the Pamper Music "demos," specifically 'I Just Don't Understand', 'I Let My Mind Wander', and 'Any Old Arms Won't Do' (co-written with Cochran). 'The Local Memory', 'I Just Dropped By', and 'The Message' were three more recently written Nelson originals (they had not been done initially as Pamper Music "demos"). Though they were all beautiful songs, they joined the dozens of incredible Willie originals that have remained forgotten on his RCA albums.

Arrangements (and conducting) for the album came from Bergen White. Bob Baker, program director for radio station WHOO, wrote the liner notes, in which he recognized that "when Willie sings a song, it suddenly becomes a 'Willie Nelson song,' regardless of who wrote it." He also noted what has become accepted dogma, that Willie was both "the standard of excellence in the field of songwriting" as well as "twenty years ahead of his time."

The sessions were held November 5, 6, and 7, 1968, from ten AM to one PM each day. For every track on the album, producer Atkins really went all out towards achieving his version of the "Nashville Sound," then in vogue, with an overload of stringed and orchestral-type sounds. Arranger White played vibes and celeste on four cuts, the title track, two other of Willie's compositions, 'The Message' and 'Any Old Arms Won't Do', as well as Travis' song, 'That's All'. For those same four tracks, six violins, two trumpets, a baritone and a tenor sax, and a trombone were added along with the usual drums, two electric guitars, piano, and bass.

On the other eight cuts, the six violins remained, joined by two violas, and a cello. Four tracks, 'Natural to Be Gone' (when released as a single, it failed to chart), 'Love Has a Mind of Its Own', 'I Walk Alone', and 'It Will Come to Pass', featured bass, piano, drums, two electric guitars along with Nashville veteran Charlie McCoy on piano and vibes. On the remaining four ('I Let My Mind Wander', 'I Just Dropped By', 'I Just Don't Understand', and 'The Local Memory'), the same stringed instruments were used along with the bass, piano, drums, and two electric guitars. McCoy played guitar as well as the vibes and piano. Willie's voice was very much buried in the mix and preponderance of instruments.

Both Sides Now. RCA LSP-4294. (1970).

Track Listing: Crazy Arms, Wabash Cannon Ball, Pins and Needles (In My Heart), Who Do I Know in Dallas, I Gotta Get Drunk, Once More With Feeling, Both Sides Now, Bloody Merry Morning, Everybody's Talkin', One Has My Name (The Other Has My Heart), It Could Be Said That Way.

Recording Notes: The Joni Mitchell title track, 'Both Sides Now', headed this Jarvis-produced 1970 album. Mitchell once said of her composition that it "is like an old person reflecting back on their life." Along with 'Both Sides Now, there was another pop standard, Fred Neil's 'Everybody's Talkin' (from the film *Midnight Cowboy*). A few country classics, such as 'One Has My Name', were also featured.

A further album highlight was the first recorded appearance of 'I Gotta Get Drunk', a Willie original. About that song, Willie once told George Jones, "I wrote that song for you back in the fifties but I didn't have the nerve to pitch it to you." It appeared on a 1991 Jones CBS compilation album as a duet between Willie and George. When it was released by RCA as a single by Willie (in 1976 - almost a year after he joined Columbia and 'Blue Eyes Crying in the Rain' had hit), it reached the number fifty-five slot.

'Who Do I Know in Dallas' (written by Willie and Hank Cochran) was a rerecording of one of the rarer Pamper demos, while, 'Bloody Mary Morning' (an original Willie classic) was introduced in its original incarnation as 'Bloody Merry Morning'. The final album track, 'It Could Be Said That Way', was yet another of many beautiful but neglected Willie originals.

'Once More with Feeling' was written by the former Mrs. Nelson, then billed as Shirley Nelson. It became the lead single off the album, reaching number forty-two and staying only nine weeks. In time, it wound up serving as the title for two of RCA's budget Willie albums.

The cut, 'Crazy Arms', a hit for Ray Price, was later culled from this collection and released as a single in 1979 at which time it rose to number eighteen on the charts. Willie's corresponding hits for Columbia Records in 1979 were 'Help Me Make It Through the Night (reaching number four) and 'My Heroes Have Always Been Cowboys' (reaching number one). The song was written by Ralph Mooney, whose wife had left him because of his drinking.

Ralph, who had a productive tenure as Waylon Jennings' steel guitarist, said he "wrote the whole song in a few minutes." After he finished the song, he went "to get my wife back a few days later." The track was included, along with two others, 'I Gotta Get Drunk' and 'Bloody Merry Morning', on RCA's 1979 "various artists" compilation, *Honky Tonkin'*.

'Pins and Needles' was written by "Floyd Jenkins," a pseudonym for Fred Rose, according to Roy Acuff. It was originally recorded and turned into a pop hit on Okeh Records by the country duo Bob Atcher and Bonnie Blue Eyes. As a pioneer artist in country music, Acuff was irrevocably tied to the song, 'Wabash Cannon Ball', though it was first formally published in 1905 as a composition credited to William Kindt. His version was based on an older song, 'The Great Rock Island Route'. That song was traced to 1882 with authorship (words and music) credited to J. A. Roff.

Hugh Cross first recorded 'Wabash Cannon Ball' in 1929 but Roy's vocal interpretation, finally recorded in 1947, quickly became the definitive version. Roy said he first learned the song when he was a youngster working as a callboy for the L & N Railroad in Eastern Tennessee, over by Knoxville. When he made his recording, credit for the song (at least the arrangement) had been given to A. P. Carter, one of the three relatives who made up (along with is then-wife Sara and his sister-in-law, "Mother" Maybelle) the legendary Carter Family.

According to Roy, he once performed the song as a train passed, whistle blowing and all, near where he was performing, giving him the idea to always include a whistle sound during every rendition (live and studio) of the song. He also paced the song to emulate a fast moving train. Willie's version was "laidback," with a trademark Willie guitar solo in the middle, resulting in the feel of a train rolling across the plains rather than speeding down some mountain.

In a surprising about face, the instrumental excesses of the previous album, *My Own Peculiar Way*, were eliminated. The sound on this album foreshadowed the work Willie would eventually turn out for Atlantic and Columbia. His voice was in peak form, he accompanied himself in the studio for the first time in awhile, and was allowed to use spare arrangements with a familiar set of backing musicians (from his own band), Billy English, drums, David Zettner, bass and guitar, and Jimmy Day, bass.

Sessions for the tracks took place over three days, November 12, 13, and 18, 1969 (ten AM to one PM each day). On January 15, 1970, Jarvis brought in bass player Norbert "Curly" Putnam and bongo player James Isbell to overdub on three tracks, 'Pins and Needles', 'Everybody's Talkin'', and 'Both Sides Now'. James was the brother of Dave Isbell, who had a local Texas band in which Willie played (off and on) during the early fifties. When Dave recorded for Sarg Records in 1954, Willie backed him for at least two sessions.

Laying My Burdens Down. RCA LSP-4404. (1970).

Track Listing: Laying My Burdens Down, How Long Have You Been There, Senses, I Don't Feel Anything, I've Seen That Look on Me (A Thousand Times), Where Do You (We) Stand?, Minstrel Man,

Happiness Lives Next Door, When We Live Again, Following Me Around.

Recording Notes: Willie's second 1970 album release featured production by Jarvis and six Nelson originals. A seventh original, 'If You Could See What's Going Through My Mind', was also recorded at the album sessions, but never released. Once again, there were three days of recording, June 1, 2, and 3, 1970 (the first two days went from ten AM to one PM while the last went from two to five PM).

Jerry Carrigan, drums, David Briggs, piano, Jerry Stembridge, rhythm guitar, and Norbert Putnam, bass worked all three sessions. Herman Wade added electric guitar June 1, at which time 'Following Me Around', 'Minstrel Man', 'Where Do You Stand?', and 'When We Live Again' were recorded. On June 2, one of Willie's friends, Grady Martin, played electric guitar and served as leader for the session that produced 'If You Could See What's Going Through My Mind', 'I've Seen That Look on Me', 'Happiness Lives Next Door', and 'I Don't Feel Anything'. Thomas G. Martin served as session leader and electric guitarist June 3, during which 'Laying My Burdens Down', 'How Long Have You Been There', and 'Senses' were cut.

The title track, 'Laying My Burdens Down' (a Willie original), was also a 1970 single though not a strong seller, peaking at sixty-eight and falling off the charts after only two weeks. A song originally done as a Pamper "demo," 'Happiness Lives Next Door' was featured on side two with three other originals, 'Where Do You Stand?', 'When We Live Again', and 'Following Me Around. The remaining Nelson original, 'I Don't Feel Anything' (side one, track four), was one of his most unique conversational type of song.

'Minstrel Man', by Eddie Rager and Stan Haas, completed side two. That song would become the title track for one of RCA's "new" Willie Nelson releases (compiled after Willie had left the label) comprised entirely of previously released tracks. Liner notes were by songwriter, Dee Moeller, who contributed the song, 'How Long Have You Been There'.

Two of the non-Nelson original tracks were 'I've Seen That Look on Me', by Harlan Howard and Shirl Milete, and the beautiful and touching, 'Senses', co-written by two diverse country stars, Glen Campbell and Jeannie Seely. Seely was, for a time, the wife of Willie's writing mentor, Hank Cochran. On a another creative note, the album cover art was a full shot of an ancient rusting automobile.

Willie Nelson & Family. RCA LSP-4489. (1971).

Track Listing: What Can You Do to Me Now?, Sunday Morning Coming Down, I'm So Lonesome I Could Cry, Fire and Rain, Yours Love,

I'm a Memory, Kneel at the Feet of Jesus, I Can Cry Again, That's Why I Love Her So, Today I Started Loving You Again.

Recording Notes: Jarvis produced this 1971 album featuring some of Willie's most mournful performances, most notably his rendition of the Hank Williams classic, 'I'm So Lonesome I Could Cry'. Organist Glen Spreen, arranged all but two tracks on the album ('Fire and Rain' and 'Kneel at the Feet of Jesus') while playing the organ on all of them. In a stroke of diversity, Willie recorded a Kristofferson song for the first time, 'Sunday Mornin' Comin' Down'. As with the rest of the album, this version was too "busy" to be as appreciated as the interpretation he later recorded for his Columbia album devoted to Kris' songs.

Three days of sessions (November 19, 20, 24, 1970) produced eleven cuts, including the poignant Cindy Walker piece, 'The Loser's Song', which went unreleased. The first day of recording, which resulted in not only the Walker tune, but Kristofferson's 'Sunday Mornin' Comin' Down' and 'What Can You Do to Me Now?', was filled with an overabundance of instrumental backing. In addition to three guitars, drums, piano, bass, and Spreen's organ, there were four violins, two each of violas, cellos, trumpets, trombones, french horns, and flutes, along with percussion.

The four tracks recorded the next day ('Fire and Rain', along with three Willie originals, 'I'm a Memory', 'I Can Cry Again', and 'That's Why I Love Her So') had only drums, bass, two guitars, piano, and organ. However, the final session saw the same huge set of instruments as the first day (no extra percussion, though). Weldon Myrick on electric guitar was added while David Zettner, who had played guitar on the 19th, wasn't included. 'I'm So Lonesome I Could Cry', 'Yours Love', 'Kneel at the Feet of Jesus' and 'Today I Started Loving You Again' were all recorded at the final session.

In Willie's words, the album came out and "went into the dumper, commercially." The single from the album (a Willie original), 'I'm a Memory' did not exactly bomb, however. It pulled Willie back to number twenty-eight (and stayed on the charts eleven weeks), the highest one of his singles had reached in a while. RCA had such success with the 'I'm a Memory' track that it rereleased it as a single in 1977 and pushed it all the way to number twenty-two. Each time it resided on the charts for eleven weeks.

Two country classics, Merle Haggard's 'Today I Started Loving You Again' and Harlan Howard's 'Yours Love', were featured along with the contemporary pop hit, James Taylor's 'Fire and Rain'. The Taylor song later became, in 1975, the first RCA single by Willie to chart after he had left the label. It went to number twenty-nine, about four months after 'Blue Eyes Crying in the Rain' reached number one for Columbia Records. It stayed chart-resident for eleven weeks.

'Yours Love' was one of the most beautiful and different songs Harlan ever wrote. It started out as a poem to his wife, to be read to her on their wedding day. The poem, 'My Wedding Prayer', contained "all the things I really felt, hoped and wished for her." When he saw that almost every line ended with "yours love," he said his songwriter's mind took over. He changed the title, put the words to music, and sang it to her at the ceremony. In 1969, Waylon Jennings took the song to number five while the duo of Dolly Parton and Porter Wagoner saw their version peak at number nine.

The legendary story, according to Susie Nelson, concerning 'What Can You Do to Me Now?', was that Willie and Hank Cochran composed it "not long before Christmas of 1969." She said it "kind of summed up the last year or so. Four or five wrecked cars. Shirley gone. The whole thing." She added that "a few days later, the farmhouse at Ridgetop [Willie's home outside Nashville] burned down." On the upbeat side, one of Willie's greatest original gospel songs, 'Kneel at the Feet of Jesus', made its first album appearance.

Yesterday's Wine. RCA LSP-4568. (1971).

Track Listing: Intro - Willie Nelson and Band, Medley: Where's the Show/Let Me Be a Man, In God's Eyes, Family Bible, It's Not for Me to Understand, Medley: These Are Difficult Times/Remember the Good Times, Summer of Roses, December Day, Yesterday's Wine, Me and Paul, Goin' Home.

Recording Notes: Willie described the songs on this 1971 Jarvis-produced release as being about "before life and after life." He reminisced about the album, saying "that's still my favorite album of all, and even it didn't sell." Under "Album Idea" in the session notes, was the inscription, "story of a man from birth to death - each song giving a phase of his life."

Yesterday's Wine was one of the few albums Willie ever analyzed, disclosing that "in *Yesterday's Wine*, I wrote that some people were put here to show how perfect a guy can be." He also said the album was "about a guy - an imperfect man, watching his own funeral and reviewing his life." With such an underlying though weighty idea, it became country music's first concept album, or as Willie wrote, "an album that tells a story." The "editor's note" on the back cover (of the original LP), stated that:

this album is the story of a man from birth to death. Each song recalls different incidents of his life - gathering around the Family Bible as a child... a Summer of Roses, of love, followed by a December Day... the bitterness of reflecting, Yesterday's Wine... and finally, full cycle - back to God - a time for Goin' Home.

This coincides with what some critics have said, that *Yesterday's Wine* was a life-cycle album. Actually, one analyst saw the artist or writer as an "imperfect man" who stood in contrast to the "perfect man," who has already been and gone. One critic noted that the album started with the singer talking to God while another saw the final song, 'Goin' Home' as a "funeral song."

Another song, 'In God's Eyes', was seen by a theologian as being about the doctrine of revelation, or how God sees our lives and human situations. The same theologian saw 'December Day' being about "each ending in life," while 'A Summer of Roses' dealt with the "meaning of gifts for relationships."

That old Willie chestnut, 'Family Bible', found its way on to the album and, interestingly, its inclusion caused the statement on the back cover that "with the exception of 'Family Bible', all songs were written by the artist, Willie Nelson." According to Willie, "seven of those songs" were written "the night before the session." Producer Jarvis told him on a Saturday morning that sessions were scheduled for Monday and Willie "had better get busy." Willie said that he:

> stayed up all night and wrote several songs, then I went back over some of my old scribblings I had stored in a closet and came up with the rest of the songs.

One of the results (direct or indirect) of the forced schedule was that some members, such as David Zettner, of Willie's road band were allowed to play on the album with hired Nashville session guys.

The sessions were held over only two days, May 3 and 4, 1971 (from two to five PM the first day and ten AM to one PM the second). In all, fifteen tracks were recorded, though only ten were used in the the final album configuration. Of the ten tracks, two were medleys, both consisting of songs written by Willie. One was made up of two songs recorded separately but spliced together to make one cut because of RCA's insistence that only ten album tracks would be allowed.

A memo from Felton Jarvis confirmed this development. It read,

> 'Where's the Show' originally carried master no AWA4-1444 ... but because only ten sides could be included in album this song was made part of medley with master no AWA4-1445 and medley given this master no in order that numbers run consecutively ... no other song could be eliminated and carried complete theme of album idea.

As it was, five tracks were not used, four recorded on May 4th, Kristofferson's 'Help Me Make It Through the Night', and three by Willie, 'Rainy Day Blues', 'Will You Remember?', and 'Wake Me

When It's Over', along with one done May 3rd, 'Will You Remember?'. The five cuts all appeared on Willie's last two RCA albums.

Willie seemed to agree with the theological nature of the critiques, saying, "It's pretty much a gospel album, a spiritual album in a sense." It was the last album Willie would record in Nashville for some time, according to biographer, Bob Allen. 1971 was also the year Willie married his third wife, Connie (Koepke) and moved his family to Bandera, Texas.

Saleswise, 'Yesterday's Wine' was released as the "A" side of a single released in the Fall of 1971. The "B" side, the autobiographical (and later title cut for a Columbia album) 'Me and Paul' also charted, making this Willie's first two-sided single. Unfortunately neither side sold enough to move the single past the number sixty-two spot.

Other Releases: In 1972, the album was released in a second pressing as ANL1-1102 (excellent liner notes omitted) and again in a third pressing (same year) under the number AYK1/AYL1-3800. In 1997, Willie obtained the rights to rerelease the album in its entirety on the Texas-based Justice label as JR 1603-2. The forward to the insert was a brief excerpt from Willie's autobiography, part of which told about the whitewashed wall in South America where the face of Jesus was thought to have miraculously appeared. Instead, as further rains revealed, it turned out to be an old Willie poster.

The Words Don't Fit the Picture. RCA LSP-4653. (1972).

Track Listing: The Words Don't Fit the Picture, Good Hearted Woman, Stay Away from Lonely Places, Country Willie, One Step Beyond, My Kind of Girl, Will You Remember?, Rainy Day Blues, If You Really Loved Me, London.

Recording Notes: Willie did have another Nashville-recorded album in him. Over four days of sessions (October 19, 21, 26, and 28, 1971), he recorded fifteen tracks, using eight of them, along with two left over from the *Yesterday's Wine* sessions, 'Will You Remember?' and 'Rainy Day Blues'. The standout track recorded at the October sessions was Willie's solo version of 'Good Hearted Woman'.

Of the tracks recorded but not used, only one, 'I Want a Girl', was never released (on any RCA or affiliate album or compilation). It was written by Willie with Paul Buskirk's name also on it. Otherwise, the remaining six unused tracks wound up on the next album, the final one created with Willie still technically under contract.

Some of the cuts, 'Country Willie', 'One Step Beyond', 'Will You Remember?', and 'Rainy Day Blues' were reprised from his Liberty years or before. 'Stay Away From Lonely Places' was a joint writing effort by Willie and country comedian, Don Bowman. Strangely, on the session notes for the album, Bowman's name was crossed off as co-writer.

The rest of the songs on the album, 'London', 'If You Really Loved Me', 'My Kind of Girl' and the title cut, 'The Words Don't Fit the Picture' were all written by Willie. The title cut was also Willie's final charting single for RCA while still under contract. After debuting on the *Billboard* country singles chart in February 1972, it reached number seventy-three but died after only two weeks. It would be almost a year and a half (July 1973) before another Willie single, 'Shotgun Willie' (on Atlantic Records), would hit the charts again.

The Willie Way. RCA LSP-4760. (1972).

Track Listing: You Left a Long, Long Time Ago, Wonderful Future, Mountain Dew, Help Me Make It Through the Night, Wake Me When It's Over, Undo the Right, Home Is Where You're Happy, A Moment Isn't Very Long, What Do You Want Me to Do?, I'd Rather You Didn't Love Me.

Recording Notes: This 1972 Jarvis-produced album became the final Nelson (album) product released (or at least conceived of) by RCA with Nelson still under contract. 'A Moment Isn't Very Long' appeared again, though this particular cut was recorded, along with five others, during the sessions for the previous album, *The Words Don't Fit the Picture.* In an earlier recorded version, the song had been part of the album, *The Party's Over.*

'I'd Rather You Didn't Love Me' was written by Willie before he left Texas to come to Nashville for the first time. According to credits in Lana Nelson's book, *Willie Nelson Family Album,* it was another composition to which he sold some of the rights, the buyers being, not surprisingly, Walter Breeland (one-quarter share) and Claude Gray (one-quarter share). Buskirk did not participate this time. In the RCA session notes, however, Willie was listed as sole author (and the publisher as Willie Nelson Music).

Willie's second cover of a Kristofferson song, 'Help Me Make It Through the Night', and two of his own songs, 'Wonderful Future' and 'Wake Me When It's Over', were recorded during the *Yesterday's Wine* sessions.   The classic, 'Mountain Dew', was recorded at his last documented recording session for RCA, April 27, 1972. It became the final single of Willie's that RCA was able to chart years after he and the company parted ways (in 1981, nine years after Willie left).

At the April 27th session and one two days prior, Willie, with only Paul English and Dan Spears, recorded most of the songs that would later become the major components of his second Atlantic album, *Phases and Stages.* On the 25th, he cut what became his final RCA single (while still under contract), 'Phases, Stages, Circles, Cycles and Scenes'. The two days of sessions were intended for a "pop" album.

"The Party's Over":

The "New" Albums of "Old" Material

By 1972, Willie and RCA had parted company. The last Nelson RCA single to chart, 'The Words Don't Fit the Picture', (the title song to Willie's next to last album under RCA's contract with him) peaked at seventy-three in February of 1972 and lasted there for only two weeks. RCA did try one more single, 'Phases, Stages, Circles, Cycles and Scenes', (later recut for Atlantic Records) but it failed to chart. Willie then signed with Atlantic.

When Willie moved to Columbia in 1975 (two years after his first Atlantic album) and immediately "boomed" onto the charts, both pop and country, RCA began a program of marketing "new" albums consisting of old, or more precisely, "previously released" material. They also released "new" singles consisting of old album cuts. The first of these was released four months after Willie hit it big with his first Columbia single. It was the old James Taylor song, 'Fire and Rain'.

The strength of his Columbia success helped to carry the RCA single to the number twenty-nine slot on the country singles chart. That was higher than eleven of his charting singles released by RCA when Willie was actually under contract to the company. In 1978, RCA moved a Willie single up to the number five slot, higher than any of his previous singles. The marketing was obviously better. Then too, Willie's sound on Columbia had become hot!

Willie briefly "returned" to RCA in both 1976 and 1978 thanks primarily to Waylon Jennings. The 1976 "return" was not really a return in the physical sense, but in the sense that his material was resurrected for use in the *Outlaws* project, which was principally spearheaded by Waylon. Willie's voice did return in that Waylon overdubbed it on one of his own live tracks to create the classic duet, 'Good Hearted Woman'.

The *Outlaws* album was essentially a compilation, a "primer" for the burgeoning outlaw movement in country music. It was also the first platinum-selling country album. Because of its success, Willie did "return" in 1978 for the *Waylon and Willie* album RCA asked Waylon to do as a successor to the *Outlaws* set.

Colin Escott wrote that "if there was ever a period of Willie Nelson's career in need of some serious re-evaluation, it was the RCA years." He felt that "the genesis of so much that Willie did in the years ahead is here." How would such an evaluation go? The singing was not emphasized like Willie wanted it. He felt that the way he was being recorded reflected the prevailing opinion at RCA, that he was a great songwriter but could not sing.

Willie was told what to do and he went along with it. Later, he would do what he knew was best. On RCA, he didn't push back. Looking back on one time when he was in the studio with Chet and Grady Martin (who would later become part of his traveling band), he admitted he was "so intimidated being in the studio with those two guys that I couldn't find my ass with a search warrant." He told one interviewer, "I didn't have the authority to say, 'Hey, wait a minute, I don't want to do it this way'."

In putting together this review of Willie's RCA period, I was referred, by Katherine Woods, Vice President for RCA Nashville of Legal and Business Affairs, to the person who has taken over producing the RCA "Essential" series, Steve Lindsey. Steve used to work for RCA but has been on his own as a music industry consultant. He has become so good at what he does that RCA has given him the only authorized access to their archives.

I had a chance to talk with him in mid-April of 1998 about what RCA has in their files on Willie. He was the one who made available all the information I needed to compile a complete Willie sessionography. That sessionography unearthed enough unreleased tracks to make possible a very interesting compilation of Willie originals, perhaps as a follow-up to the 1995 compilation, *The Essential Willie Nelson*.

If any successor compilation ever became possible, most of the Willie fans with whom I have spoken would especially love to see 'Pins and Needles', 'Truth No. 1', and 'Jimmy's Road' on an RCA compact disc collection (along with any unreleased originals). Sorting through the RCA archives for whatever could be utilized might be quite a job. Justice Records claimed that when they rereleased the *Yesterday's Wine* album, the only session notes they could find were "not complete."

The "New" Albums - Album Listings

What Can You Do to Me Now. RCA APL/AFL1-1234. (1975).

Track Listing: I'm a Memory, What Can You Do to Me Now?, Fire and Rain, Once More With Feeling, I've Seen That Look on Me (a Thousand Times), Wake Me When It's Over, My Own Peculiar Way, Permanently Lonely, I Gotta Get Drunk, You Left a Long, Long Time Ago.

Recording Notes: The "new" RCA albums consisting of previously released material began with this 1975 release, two years after Willie left RCA and the same year he signed with Columbia. The title cut had particular meaning to Willie, who once told Ralph Emery, a Nashville TV and Radio host,

> I wrote that the year I had gotten a divorce and wrecked four cars and a pickup, I wrote the tune and the next day my house burned down.

The album was also released as AYK1/AYL1-3958.

Building off the strength of his new-found popularity on Columbia, the album charted for three weeks on the *Billboard* pop album charts. It peaked at number one hundred ninety-six. Though he was no longer with the label, it became his first RCA album to chart nationally. RCA's repackaging of collections of old material as new albums appeared to pay off.

Their rereleasing of old cuts as "new" singles also bore fruit as the first selection on this album, 'I'm a Memory' (as a 1971 single it had peaked at number twenty-eight) reached number twenty-two on the *Billboard* country singles chart in early 1977. Previously, in late 1975 and early 1976, two other cuts, 'Fire and Rain' and 'I Gotta Get Drunk', had been released as singles and went to number twenty-nine and number fifty-five respectively. The following year, 'I Gotta Get Drunk' wound up being crafted on to *Willie Nelson Live*, itself a modified rerelease of Willie's classic 1966 set, *Live Country Music Concert*. The fourth cut on the album, 'Once More With Feeling', had been a 1970 RCA single that peaked at number forty-two.

Before His Time. RCA AFL1-2210. (1977).

Track Listing: One in a Row, I'd Trade All of My Tomorrows (for Just One Yesterday), She's Not for You, You Ought to Hear Me Cry, To Make a Long Story Short (She's Gone), I'm a Memory, Stay Away from Lonely Places, It Should Be Easier Now, Little Things, How Long Have You Been There.

Recording Notes: Waylon Jennings gathered ten previously released cuts and, in 1977, with the help of his drummer, Richie Albright, remixed them to produce a clean uncluttered collection featuring Willie without the RCA "overproduction." It became quite popular, charting for fifteen weeks and reaching number seventy-eight on the national album charts. It was the highest that any RCA album attributed to Willie was able to chart.

Of the chosen cuts, the premier standout was the original Willie song, 'She's Not for You'. It was recorded at a January 12, 1965, session, and though it had been his first charting single for the label, this marked the first time it was included on an album. When initially released back in 1965, it reached number forty-three, though it only charted five weeks.

Another original Willie song from this compilation, 'You Ought to Hear Me Cry', was released as a single in September 1977. It broke the top twenty barrier by reaching number sixteen and staying chart-bound for thirteen weeks. It, too, had not been previously included on an album. Since then, this album has been reissued under a new catalogue number, AYL1-3671.

Sweet Memories. RCA AHL1-3243. (1979).

Track Listing: Sweet Memories, Everybody's Talkin' (*), Wonderful Future (*), December Day, Help Me Make It Through the Night, Both Sides Now (*), Wake Me When It's Over, Little Things, Buddy, Will You Remember?.

Recording Notes: This 1979 compilation featured Willie's voice overdubbed by five violins, one cello, one viola, and even one harmonica, putting it square in the middle of the Nashville sound (as characterized by an overload of strings). Pat Carter served as overdub producer with string arrangements by Mike Leech. The set, itself, charted for five weeks on the national pop album charts, reaching number one hundred fifty-four. The event that prompted its release was having the title cut go top five in 1979 on the country singles chart.

In 1969, ten years before Willie's hit single version, the team of Dottie West and Don Gibson could only take the song to number thirty-two for RCA. It was a poignant tune, written, according to its composer Mickey Newbury, "after a broken engagement with a girl from Westphalia, Texas." Willie's RCA material once again proved quite commercial when marketed aggressively, something RCA couldn't seem to do the first time around. The song, 'Will You Remember?' was not only included on this collection, but on the next set from RCA, as well.

Other Releases: Because of its popularity, the collection was also released as AYL1-4300. In 1987, it was rereleased in abridged form on compact disc and cassette with the catalogue numbers 5975-4-R and 55975-2. Though the album title stayed the same, three of the best cuts (*) were deleted.

* = the three cuts that were deleted when this album was released in abridged form.

The Minstrel Man. RCA AFLI-4045. (1981).

Track Listing: Good Times, Will You Remember?, Laying My Burdens Down, Mountain Dew, Blackjack County Chain, Minstrel Man, Senses, You Left a Long, Long Time Ago, Where Do You Stand?, It Should Be Easier Now.

Recording Notes: This 1981 "new" release contained all previously released material (with lots of "new" overdubs). RCA must have been pleased that it charted nationally for seven weeks, hitting number one hundred forty-eight. The featured single, 'Good Times' went to number twenty-five in mid-1981 on the *Billboard* country singles chart.

During its first time out as a single, in 1968, the song only placed at number forty-four. In 1968, it lasted eight weeks, while in 1981, it stayed on for twelve. A second single, 'Mountain Dew', also came out in 1981 and peaked at number twenty-three, making it the last rereleased Willie Nelson RCA single to chart. To continue marketing the album, RCA also released it using another catalog number, AYL1-4655.

'Mountain Dew' peaked at the number twenty-three position. That was three places better than his previous Columbia single, 'I'm Gonna Sit Right Down and Write Myself a Letter' and sixteen slots better than his next Columbia charter, 'Heartaches of a Fool'. As a song, Willie's version dated back to Scotty Wiseman's 1939 rewrite of an earlier set of words and music by Bascom Lamar Lunsford.

The best account of Lunsford's life and career was captured by Bill Finger in an issue of *Southern Exposure*. Finger wrote that Bascom:

> gained world-wide acclaim as a collector and preserver of pure mountain music, serving as U. S. representative to the first International Folk Festival in Venice (Italy).

His most famous work turned out to be, 'Mountain Dew'. It was written during the nineteen-twenties as a description of:

> the moonshine business of those Madison County folk [the North Carolina county in which Lunsford was born] untouched by the labors of the Baptist preachers, Christian mission schools and the Methodist Circuit Riders.

Bascom recorded his version of the song for the Library of Congress in 1949 along with a treasure trove of traditional mountain tunes.

After Wiseman and his wife Lulu Belle had a good deal of success with Scotty's rewrite of the Bascom tune, he and Lunsford met in Chicago. Scotty remembered that Bascom "was elated with what we had done" to his song. As a result of the meeting, Lunsford sold Wiseman his interest in the song for twenty-five dollars (to raise enough money for his bus fare back to Asheville, North Carolina). Unbeknownst to Lunsford, at the time, Scotty instructed his publishing company to go ahead and pay Lunsford "50 per cent of all royalties on the song during his lifetime." As one who had to sell his songs in times of financial need, Willie, as much as anyone, could appreciate the magnanimous gesture Scotty made to Lunsford.

One cut, 'Blackjack County Chain', was a Red Lane song about a black chain gang prisoner who killed a sheriff in Georgia. It had not previously been on a Willie Nelson album. Though Willie was the first to record it, the song had initially been offered to Charley Pride, one of the few black country singers.

When asked to record the song, Pride, then on RCA, recalled that he replied, "Red, you're out of your mind. Somebody else will have to do that one." Not long after, Willie recorded the song for RCA. When released as a single in 1967 (Willie's fifth for the label), the song went to number twenty-one on the *Billboard* country singles chart.

My Own Way. RCA AHL1-4819. (1983).

Track Listing: I'm a Memory, My Own Peculiar Way, Both Sides Now, Funny How Time Slips Away, Hello Walls, One in a Row, Stay Away from Lonely Places, Pins and Needles (in My Heart), Rainy Day Blues.

Recording Notes: This was a 1983 collection from RCA, released more than ten years after Willie had left RCA. It became the final album of his "previously released" material to chart nationally, peaking at the number one hundred eighty-two spot. In keeping with RCA's then current policies, the total number of cuts on the album was limited to nine. RCA also rereleased the set as AYL1-5438.

The album title was derived from the cut, 'My Own Peculiar Way'. That same cut had served as the full title track of one of Willie's original RCA albums. His original composition, 'One in a Row', had been his third RCA single. The version of 'Rainy Day Blues' came from the May 4, 1971 sessions for the *Yesterday's Wine* album.

In 1980, Danny Davis and the Nashville Brass had overdubbed their unique sound on top of Willie's rendition of 'Funny How Time Slips Away' and wound up with a charting single, which peaked at number forty-one on the country singles charts. On this album, the listener could once again hear Willie's solo version. The lead-off cut, 'I'm a Memory', had also been the lead cut on the 1975 album, *What Can You Do to Me Now*. As a 1977 single, it had peaked on the charts at number twenty-two.

Don't You Ever Get Tired of Hurting Me. RCA CPL1-5174. (1984).

Track Listing: Don't You Ever Get Tired of Hurting Me, One Has My Name (The Other Has My Heart), The Party's Over, Mr. Record Man, Johnny One Time, I've Seen That Look on Me (a Thousand Times), Heartaches by the Number, Crazy Arms.

Recording Notes: This 1984 compilation was comprised of material all previously released on album, except for the cut, 'Johnny One Time', written by A. L. "Doodles" Owens and Dallas Frazier. It had been released as a Willie Nelson single in 1968, but did not sell very well, going only to number thirty-six in the fall of 1968. Brenda Lee had a medium sized pop hit with the song in early 1969.

This set and the following one were the final "new" Willie Nelson albums consisting of rereleased material. Neither one made the album sales charts. Though RCA limited the number of selections on the album to eight, the company did include several of Willie's more popular tracks, namely 'Crazy Arms', which, when released as a single in 1979, peaked at the sixteenth spot on the country singles chart, three months before he took one of his Columbia singles, 'Help Me Make It Through the Night', to number four. Another cut, 'The Party's Over', had gone to number twenty-four when released as a single in early 1967. In 1966, the title song, 'Don't You Ever Get Tired of Hurting Me' had been a number eleven hit for Ray Price.

Willie. RCA CPL1-7158. (1985).

Track Listing: Me and Paul, Hello Walls, Making Believe, I've Seen That Look on Me (a Thousand Times), Sunday Morning Coming Down, Good Hearted Woman, Night Life (*), One Day at a Time.

Recording Notes: This 1985 compilation consisted entirely of previously released material. It was the last of the pseudo "new" albums. By this time RCA was no longer putting ten selections on an album, but eight. In 1987, this set was rereleased in abridged form as 5988-4-R, minus one (*) cut.

To RCA's credit, all of the selections were strong songs. Five of them were either written or co-written by Willie. The remaining three came from three premier writers, Kris Kristofferson, Harlan Howard, and Jimmie Work. Nonetheless, there was just no excuse for limiting this or any album to only eight (then seven) tracks.

In this limited setting all the tracks stood out to prove once again that Willie did record some excellent songs and performances for RCA. For example, the cut, 'Making Believe', got lost among all the other classics Willie recorded for his second album, *Country Favorites: Willie Nelson Style.* It had previously been a standout hit for other people. Back in 1954, it went top ten for both its author, Jimmy Work, and Kitty Wells. Emmylou Harris took it top ten again in 1977.

For Work, his 1954 triumph subsequently led to disappointment. While working on an automotive assembly line in Detroit in 1953, he began writing the song, first coming up with the title that he had "running through my mind for some time." Then one day he began really working on it, "fooling with some words," and in no time "I had all the lyrics and the music to a song that I believed could be a hit."

After finishing the song he got it to publisher Fred Rose (of Acuff-Rose). Rose liked it so well he took it to Dot Records and not only sold President Randy Wood on it but got Work a recording contract with the label. Jimmy's recording of the song shipped in January 1954 and went country top five. Wells covered it and took it to number two.

Work was on his way or so he thought. He had a hit with a great original song. The reigning queen of country music, Kitty Wells, thought so much of it she recorded it. Work's next single went to number six. Then it was all over. Unable to come up with any more hit material, Work faded from the limelight. Fortunately, he left one great song behind, 'Making Believe'.

* = the one cut that was deleted from this album when it was released in abridged form as 5988-4-R.

"Heaven or Hell":

The Album Projects with Others

For seven of the years that Willie was with RCA, from 1965 to 1972, Waylon Jennings was also signed to RCA. Yet during that time, they did not record together. It wasn't until 1973 (October) that the pair sang together for the first time in the studio on Willie's song, 'Heaven or Hell' (for Waylon's *This Time* album).

Their next venture, Willie's overdubbed vocals on the Jennings live cut, 'Good Hearted Woman' brought them unbelievable results. It was not only a hit single but the featured cut on the outlaw music primer, *Wanted! The Outlaws*, which became the first platinum-selling country album. That album was the most unexpected best-selling country music album ever.

Never intended as anything more than a "sampler," *Wanted! The Outlaws* came about because RCA producer Jerry Bradley decided to capitalize on the "outlaw" trend by rereleasing old Waylon, Willie, and Jessi Colter (who became Waylon's wife) tracks. Initially, Waylon did not want the compilation put together, but Bradley pushed for it. He told *New York Times* writer Bruce Feiler that:

> we had a meeting and I said, 'Here's how it is. What did you make last year? Three, four, five million dollars? I have a job that pays me fifty grand. I enjoy my job. If I put this album out, I might get to keep it another year.'

That convinced Waylon to do the album and use the name, "outlaws."

The album went beyond mere sales success to become the Country Music Association's 1976 album of the year. Two of the other albums Jennings and Nelson did together on RCA, *Waylon & Willie* and

WWII, also grew out of the close musical kinship and overall friendship of the pair. So close did they become in the public eye that the top man at RCA, according to Waylon, "some South American guy, I think he was," believed them to be one person.

RCA forced another "collaboration" on Willie when it dubbed in the sound of Danny Davis and the Nashville Brass over a set of Willie's "previously released" recordings. Such overdubbing was not an unheard of practice. MGM Records layered strings on top of old minimally recorded Hank Williams songs and called the resulting album *The Legend Lives Anew*. They also added Hank, Jr.'s voice on top of dad's for a time-warped duet effect.

RCA was the first company to consistently release full-price albums with less than ten average length cuts. The company claimed it was necessary because list prices of albums had been kept artificially low and did not adequately cover sharply rising production and manufacturing costs. Therefore, the number of songs per album and subsequently the amount of royalties paid had to be cut.

Following their initial releases, *The Outlaws* album, as well as the *Waylon & Willie* and *WWII* sets, fell victim to RCA's practice and reappeared in abridged form only (less than the original number of tracks). *WWII* did come out initially on compact disc with its full contingent of eleven tracks. Some of Willie's other albums reflected this policy, an abridged rerelease of a full-length original album.

Then, surprisingly, in 1996, RCA did a turnabout and rereleased the *Outlaws* compilation album as a twenty-one track compilation, produced by Steve Lindsey for MaxAmor Productions. It was billed as the twentieth anniversary edition. The original had eleven cuts while the first rerelease was reduced to eight. Each one of the ten "new" cuts had been considered for inclusion on the original compilation.

It must have become increasingly difficult for a company like RCA (now BMG) to sell albums with only seven or eight tracks, even budget ones, in an age where compact discs can and do contain more than seventy minutes of music. Unfortunately, the *Waylon & Willie* album has not reappeared on compact disc in its original form. Most of the Willie Nelson RCA albums, both the original ones and those consisting of "previously released" material, have remained out of print because they were too short, time-wise, to be turned into compact discs.

The Danny Davis overdubbed album has also remained out of print. That's probably a form of justice for Willie, given that Davis, when he was just a producer for RCA, favored the "sweetened" overdubbed (with layers of strings) sound as opposed to the sparse cleaner sound Willie wanted. Even though the overdubbed version of 'Night Life' went out and sold well as a single, there was really nothing to recommend the collection.

The Albums with Others - Album Listings

Wanted! The Outlaws: Waylon Jennings, Willie Nelson, Jessi Colter, Tompall Glaser. RCA AP/AA/AFL1-1321. (1976).

Track Listing: Good Hearted Woman (w. Waylon Jennings), Heaven or Hell (w. Waylon Jennings), Me and Paul, Yesterday's Wine, You Left a Long, Long Time Ago, Healing Hands of Time, Nowhere Road (w. Waylon Jennings) (last three cuts only on 1996 version).

Recording Notes: For the original 1976 release of this trend-setting collection, RCA compiled eleven different cuts. Waylon constructed a duet version of 'Good Hearted Woman' based on his own previously recorded live rendition (at the Texas Opry House). That original Jennings live cut was previously released on the *Waylon Live* album. It had also been a hit 1972 single for Waylon (as a studio recording, not a live one). To make the duet version, Waylon brought Willie back to cut new vocals long after Willie had left RCA. Waylon explained,

> I just took my voice off and put Willie's on in different places. Willie wasn't within 10,000 miles when I recorded it.

Later, Waylon recalled that Willie "was so high when he was doing his part he was dancing a jig out in the studio." Waylon also said he added some canned audience in several places, including where he called out "Willie!" (which was also added in the studio). It was this version that became a classic, and, in 1976, the Country Music Association's Single of the Year.

The two Willie (solo) songs, 'Me and Paul' and 'Yesterday's Wine', on this compilation came from the *Yesterday's Wine* album. The first

RCA album appearance of the Waylon and Willie duet, 'Heaven or Hell', was on Waylon's album, *This Time*. Willie also did a solo version of that song for his final Atlantic set (with an "and" in place of the "or"). During his tenure with Columbia, Willie would again rerecord the song for his *Honeysuckle Rose* soundtrack.

With 'Good Hearted Woman' leading the way (along with Waylon's solo version of 'My Heroes Have Always Been Cowboys'), this set, in spite of containing previously released material and being a compilation ("a sampler"), became one of the all-time best selling country albums, reaching number ten and spending almost a year on the *Billboard* national album charts. As Waylon once said, "to understand what all the fuss was about, it was a perfect introduction." In trying to comprehend why the album was so successful, Robert Hilburn of the *Los Angeles Times* quoted an RCA official as saying that:

> there were a lot of people curious about all they had read or heard about the so-called 'outlaws' of country music - particularly Waylon and Willie - and they decided to take a chance on the package rather than buy a whole album by one of the artists.

"Outlaw" was simply a term that had buzzed around Nashville, most likely originating with Waylon's cut of the Billy Joe Shaver song, 'Ladies Love Outlaws'. Producer Jerry Bradley said:

> there wasn't no outlaw movement. It was a damn album cover called *The Outlaws*, but folklore made it into this great story.

Nonetheless, the outlaw "movement" became one of the most popular phenomenons ever in country music, even larger than the early 1980's sharply-dressed "urban cowboy" country boom.

Jennings remembered the project, itself, as something "dear to my heart." He told Deborah Evans Price in a 1996 interview (for *Billboard* magazine), that:

> I didn't know how it was going to come out, because most of the songs were ten years old. I went in there and doctored them up and sweetened them up. Jessi came in and worked on hers and I went back and got a couple more of Willie's songs from the vault.

His appraisal to her was that "the music is forever." Jessi Colter (Waylon's wife) remembered that it "was a surprise to all of us" when the album sold more than a million copies. It was also funny to her, because Waylon just does things and doesn't have any big goal in mind. It was exciting and a surprise. I was really proud to be a part of it. And I was very proud for him.

The album was basically Waylon's idea, or as Jessi emphatically said,

Waylon masterminded the whole thing. He put it together for practically nothing and they packaged it. He didn't like the name - 'Outlaws' - it never appealed to him, for a number of reasons. But it was a good packaging idea.

Chet Atkins observed that the "outlaw" concept sure gave the press "something to write about." One of the other names on the album belonged to Tompall Glaser, of Tompall and the Glaser Brothers, an erstwhile songwriter, lead singer, and publishing company and studio owner. The album had a very special significance to Tompall. He told an interviewer that:

Waylon and I were disgusted with the way radio was handling country music. There was logjam like it gets every once in a while where everything gets repetitious and labels are too much in charge. We were just trying anything that might break it.

Most of the work in compiling the album was done by Waylon, as Jessi again (her comments were all made to *Country Weekly*) recalled:

when we were in the studio and Waylon was putting all those old songs together, it was almost an undercover thing, because nobody else was involved. He'd call Willie and say, 'Hey, Willie, does this song sound good?'

In addition to the Willie solo and the Waylon and Willie duet cuts, there were previously released solo tracks by Waylon, Jessi, and then-close friend, Tompall, as well as a Waylon and Jessi duet. Because of their inclusion on this album, the four became the leading "outlaws" of country music. Yet that was not even the intended line-up.

Billie Joe Shaver, who wrote one of the Waylon cuts on this collection, disclosed in a *Goldmine* interview, that "Waylon asked me to be on the *Outlaws* album with Willie and Jessi." Why would Shaver, a songwriter trying hard to become a major recording artist, decline the chance to be part of this history-making set? He elaborated that:

my wife - we were fussin' and fightin' - she said, 'Hell, you ain't no damn outlaw. What's your mama gonna think of you?' So I passed that up and Tompall Glaser wound up on *Outlaws.*

The "outlaw" movement in country music that effectively coalesced around this album had specific meanings to different people. According to sociology professor, George H. Lewis, the record buying public saw the outlaw movement as a "romantic vision of the lonely, suffering, outsider as creator." The outlaw was a rebel living the kind of carefree life every country music fan dreamed of being able to live. According to that same critic, the songs were an "invitation to the listeners to share" in an "outcast" kind of "community."

Obviously, the country music industry knew that the concept of "outlaw music" was a profitable promotion as well as a "battle against the Nashville establishment" that had become controlled by "the Nashville producer" in which the creation of music had "become highly routinized" and turned into productions that were "predictable and sounded so much the same." When the "battle" was won, what resulted, for the industry, was a commercial success "on a scale undreamed of by the Music City moguls." The outlaws were great business and although they disrupted business as usual, they generated much profitable new business.

To Hazel Smith, currently columnist for *Country Music* magazine and Tompall's former publicist, "outlaw music" was a suggested concept for a North Carolina radio show. For Neil Reshen, manager of both Willie and Waylon at the time, outlaw was an image that began when Willie "grew his beard" following which "we've been very successful with the image." Jerry Bradley, producer of *The Outlaws*, said he put:

> Willie and Waylon and Tompall together as the Outlaws, because that's the way they are regarded here in town.

Chet Atkins found it funny to have Willie, especially, cast as an outlaw. He told a story about how Waylon:

> once said that, 'Willie thinks that fighting the establishment in Nashville is double parking on Music Row'.

Willie, of course, saw his greatest commercial success result from people perceiving him as an outlaw. According to one musical analyst, it took the notoriety and resulting fame of the "outlaw" movement to get Willie's music to a massive audience. Even though he had written huge commercial hits like 'Crazy', this analyst concluded that many of Willie's songs (especially his newer ones) would not have been appealing to record company executives because of their "unusual metric patterns." The analyst, Charles T. Brown, stated that:

no record company really wanted to do his tunes with him performing because they thought his voice was wrong for a country star.

The problem wasn't really "the voice" but Willie's "irregular" phrasing and the fact that his songs were "word-oriented." In Willie's songs, according to Brown, "the melodic structure is second in importance to the words" while the traditional country music approach had always maintained "a careful relationship between melody and word phrasing." Willie was, in essence, "a narrator in the way he communicates to an audience." It took "a move to a different audience" (the audience Willie found in Austin as opposed to the traditional audience for Nashville-based country music) "to provide the necessary catalyst" for Willie's becoming a superstar.

The "outlaw" movement opened the doors for Willie to do just about anything he wanted, musically. He embarked on cutting pop standards, making movies, and writing more great songs. To Waylon, the whole outlaw bit "done got out of hand." To many critics, "outlaw music" had a creative integrity that all too soon became co-opted by the overly commercialized "urban cowboy" craze.

Other Releases: In the end, the concept lived on, haltingly at first but still successful today. The first compact disc release of the album, 5976-2-RRE, was reduced to only eight cuts. In 1996, for the compilation's twentieth anniversary, a special edition (same title) was issued, BMG Entertainment (RCA) 66841-2. It consisted of twenty-one cuts, the original eleven with nine "lost" tracks (that meant these "previously released" tracks were intended to be included on the original "LP") and one "new" previously unreleased track, a duet by Willie and Waylon on Steve Earle's 'Nowhere Road', cut in 1996. Not only was it used in this updated *Outlaws* package, it became featured on the soundtrack of the movie, *Switchback* (RCA 66993-2).

The "lost" tracks that featured Willie were 'You Left a Long, Long Time Ago' and 'Healing Hands of Time' (both were solo Willie). The 'Healing' cut came from Willie's first RCA album, *Country Willie: His Own Songs*, while the 'You Left a Long, Long Time Ago' track came from his final original RCA album, *The Willie Way*. What these two specific songs had in common with "outlaws" was anyone's guess.

Earle produced the "new" cut, which got Willie and Waylon working together directly in the studio for the first time in a long time. One of the youngest of the seventies' "outlaws," Earle, for whom the song had previously been one of several signature tunes, experienced quite a few drug-induced hard years prior to a 1996 "comeback" of his own. Waylon said that "Steve brings three dogs with him to the sessions. One bites. You don't know which one it is."

According to Bruce Feiler, author of *Dreaming Out Loud*, when Waylon and Willie came to the Nashville studio to cut Earle's track for the updated "anniversary" edition of the album, the first question Waylon had was, 'you got any idea how to split this up?" Willie told him, "you sing one verse, I'll sing the other. Then we'll split the chorus." Earle added that "it's probably best to split the last verse."

At the end of take one, as Feiler told the story, Waylon wanted to do another, saying to Willie, "I think you and me got one better in us." Willie warned him that "my phrasing won't be the same twice." When Waylon wasn't pleased with the second take, Earle suggested the two singers could "practice." Waylon set him straight, telling him that "we don't know how to practice."

After the third take. Waylon was happy that Willie had really stretched his part out. "You Willied it," he complimented his partner. Soon after, Willie left, but Waylon had ideas on parts he wanted to improve and harmonies he wanted to add or change. After numerous retakes, Earle finally said, "that was a really good take." Waylon still wanted "to do it one more time."

Earle was done and told Waylon not to worry, that any remaining minor changes could be "comped," a process by which, as Feiler explained, the best sounding word was taken from one of a number of takes and digitally pieced together. That did it for Waylon. He told Earle, "I don't like that comping shit. One word here, one word there. Where's the feeling in that?" In today's country music, as Earle pointed out, "everyone does it." That really got Waylon "steaming," so much so that he told Steve, "I think you'll regret this. You just don't do shit like that! I've made a lot of those myself, you know."

In reality, the 1996 remake of *The Outlaws* reflected a "new" country music. Waylon, the "outlaw" who put together the original album, was no longer either tinkering on his own or in charge. Steve Earle was the man who completed the new track, not Waylon, who finally "stormed" out of the studio. Waylon couldn't redo the album the way he wanted. As Earle concluded, Waylon "hates this modern stuff. He likes doing things the old-fashioned way."

Looking back on the "storm" between him and Steve Earle, Waylon admitted that he "had ideas he wanted to try that night. I had a guitar part I wanted to do. I never got it out of the case." The problem, as he and Willie talked about it, was that neither one wanted "to do a Steve Earle record. We wanted to do our own version." Steve felt bad about the "storm," saying that Waylon was gone "before I really realized he was uncomfortable."

From a twenty years after perspective, Travis Tritt explained the importance of the Outlaws album. In the September 1997 issue of *New Country*, he wrote that:

> I think the Outlaw movement was one of the most significant times in country music history. Pointing to that is the fact that the *Outlaws* album with Willie, Waylon, Jessi Colter

and Tompall Glaser was the first platinum album we had in country music.

The album also had a significant impact on the business of country music. Tritt explained that:

> the mindset of people like Willie and Waylon opened doors for people like myself who wanted to do things a little differently and have more control over their music. Being able to be involved in writing, production, choosing singles and marketing the album, that was made possible by Willie and Waylon, who broke up the good ol' boy network Nashville had been running on. For artists who want control over their projects, and I'm one of those people, without the outlaw movement, that couldn't have happened.

Chet Flippo understood that the success of *The Outlaws* meant that the "feudal notion" of producer as king was over. He wrote that:

> country artists gained control over their own record sessions, their record production, everything else related to their careers, including the right to make their own mistakes.

Waylon & Willie. (Waylon Jennings & Willie Nelson).   RCA AA/AP/AFL1-2686. (1978).

Track Listing: Mammas Don't Let Your Babies Grow Up to Be Cowboys (Waylon & Willie), The Year 2003 Minus 25 (Waylon & Willie) (*), Pick Up the Tempo (Waylon & Willie), If You Can Touch Her at All (Willie), Lookin' for a Feeling (Waylon), It's Not Supposed to Be That Way (Willie), I Can Get Off on You (Waylon & Willie), Don't Cuss the Fiddle (Waylon & Willie) (*), Gold Dust Woman (Waylon) (*), A Couple More Years (Willie), The Wurlitzer Prize (I Don't Want to Get Over You) (Waylon).

Recording Notes: Willie "returned" to RCA in this 1978 collaboration with Jennings (ostensibly the successor to the "compilation" album, *The Outlaws*). Willie told the press that "Waylon picked most of the songs, there wasn't a lot of research in this album." Nationally the album sold very well, reaching the twelfth spot on the charts.

It was Jerry Bradley who first began to envision this project as an *Outlaws* successor. "After the *Outlaws* album," Bradley said he told Waylon, look, we are going to put out a Waylon and Willie album. It can be five old songs of you and five old songs of Willie. We can do that. We don't have to talk to anybody.

Then Jerry proposed some additional work, asking Waylon,

but what do you think about going in and recording on Willie's tracks and putting your voice on it and let's make some duets?

Waylon told Bradley he would pursue the idea. According to Bradley, Waylon:

talked to Willie and we decided we would try because that would make a better album than five old tracks of Waylon and five old tracks of Willie.

Bradley worked out the permission problem with Rick Blackburn at CBS and the result came close to the original idea, five duets, three Willie solos, and three Waylon solos.

The key single, 'Mammas Don't Let Your Babies Grow Up to Be Cowboys', went to number one on the country charts almost immediately and to number forty-two on the pop charts. It also won a Grammy. Waylon initially recorded the song as a solo performance and the recording was complete, but he wasn't happy with it. Later he said he told Willie,

I said, 'Willie, I cut this thing, but I ain't sure about it.' I said, 'It don't sound right, but it might be a great duet.' The whole record was finished, and I just took part of my voice off and put his on.

To Waylon, when the song was completed, it became "mine and Willie's tip of the cowboy hat to our mustang values."

Another single, Willie's 'If You Can Touch Her at All', went top ten (peaking at number five) on the country singles chart, making it his first RCA single to go that far, ironically nearly six full years after he left the label. It entered the charts in March 1978, the same month that his Columbia single, 'Georgia on My Mind' debuted and began its climb to the number one chart spot. Liner notes were very interestingly written by Chet Flippo, then Associate Editor of *Rolling Stone Magazine*. To him, "Willie and Waylon invoke the sheer beauty and power of real, honest country music."

Other Releases: The album, itself, had a limited pressing as gold vinyl release. Later it was rereleased as both AYK1-5134 , and in 1995, in an abridged form as 8401-4-R (cassette) and 58401-2 (compact disc)

with three cuts (*) eliminated. On the 1995 abridged version, the cut 'If You Can Touch Her at All' was credited to Waylon and Willie. It had been previously credited to Willie alone.

* = the three cuts that were eliminated in the 1995 abridged rerelease of this set as 8401-4-R (cassette) and 58401-2 (compact disc).

Danny Davis & Willie Nelson with the Nashville Brass. (Danny Davis & Willie Nelson). RCA AFLI-3549. (1980).

Track Listing: Night Life, December Day, Rainy Day Blues, Hello Walls, The Local Memory, Funny How Time Slips Away, Bloody Mary (Merry) Morning, My Own Peculiar Way, Good Hearted Woman, Yesterday's Wine.

Recording Notes: 1980 saw the release of these previously released Nelson vocal tracks with the Danny Davis and the Nashville brass sound electronically added to them through "modern recording techniques". A terse set of liner notes that had Willie thanking Danny were included over Willie's reproduced signature. With Davis' sound selling well and Willie off the label, Davis got top billing, though Nelson's Columbia album sales still made his name hot property. The album got another catalog number of AYL1-4301.

Surprisingly, for previously available material, this album reached number one-hundred fifty on the *Billboard* national album sales chart (and stayed on that chart for five weeks). Making an album chart run at the same time was Willie's Columbia duet project with Ray Price, *San Antonio Rose.* As a single, 'Night Life' went top twenty (number twenty) on the country singles chart. It was followed, in May, by 'Funny How Time Slips Away', which stopped at number forty-one, making it the third time the song hit the country charts. The 'Night Life' cut from this album appeared on compact disc in 1996 as part of the Willie Nelson & Friends collection entitled, *Pure Country,* PCD-4601, marketed by Coyote Sound Cuisine and Sony Music Special Products.

WWII. (Waylon and Willie). RCA PCD1-4455. (1982).

Track Listing: Mr. Shuck and Jive (*), Roman Candles (#), (Sittin' on) the Dock of the Bay, The Year That Clayton Delaney Died (*), Lady in the Harbor (#), May I Borrow Some Sugar from You (#), Last Cowboy Song (#), Heroes, The Teddy Bear Song (#), Write Your Own Songs, The Old Mother's Locket Trick (*) (#).

Recording Notes: Willie again returned to RCA to work with Waylon on this 1982 release. The two performers were so well known by this time that only their first names were featured, putting them right up there with Elvis, Fabian, Dolly, and Prince. The album, which charted as high as number fifty-seven, was later rereleased in abridged form as 6329-4-R/56329-2 with three cuts (*) deleted.

Six solo Waylon tracks (#) dominated the track lineup. The five remaining cuts were Waylon and Willie duets. Together, the tracks formed an eclectic bond, from Jimmy Webb's 'Mr. Shuck and Jive' to the Tom T. Hall classic, 'The Year That Clayton Delaney Died'.

According to Tom T., Clayton was a real person, though renamed for the sake of the song. The real "Clayton" was an original style country picker and singer, who inspired Hall to do original work, not copy someone else's. The song was Tom T.'s way of remembering his teacher who died fairly young from either TB or cancer.

Of the other songs the two did together, one, a Willie original, 'Write Your Own Songs', later showed up on an Asleep At the Wheel album as a duet between Willie and Ray Benson. The Otis Redding soul and pop hit, '(Sittin' on) The Dock of the Bay' became a country hit via this Waylon and Willie version. It went to number thirteen in late 1982. 'Heroes' came from one of Willie's favored writing teams, Bobby Emmons and producer Chips Moman (they also wrote 'May I Borrow Some Sugar from You' for this album, which Waylon recorded alone).

Another of the songs Waylon did by himself, '(The) Last Cowboy Song', previously appeared in 1980 on an album by the man who wrote it (along with his wife), Ed Bruce. Surprisingly enough, Ed recorded it as a duet between himself and none other than, Willie Nelson. Waylon also did the Barbara Fairchild number one country hit, 'The Teddy Bear Song' by himself. The authors were old friend of Fairchild's. One was a former homicide detective while the other was a would-be performer (both came from St. Louis).

One last Waylon-by-himself cut, 'The Old Mother's Locket Trick', was written by Guy Clark, legendary Texas songwriter (of songs like 'Desperados Waitin' for a Train'). Guy once told an interviewer that 'The Old Mother's Locket Trick' song was the first of his compositions to be recorded. It was done by someone named Harold Lee on Cartwheel Records. Waylon's version had to be the definitive one.

Waylon and Willie continued working together through the Epic album, *Clean Shirt* (in 1991) and on the Highwaymen projects. With all the ways RCA tried to record Willie, it was interesting in hindsight to note that they never envisioned the two Texans together on record. Then again, RCA seemed to mainly want Willie's songs on record, not necessarily Willie, and definitely with nothing else but studio musicians.

* = the three cuts that were deleted when this album was rereleased in abridged form.

= the six cuts that Waylon recorded by himself.

"Once More With Feeling":

The Greatest Hits Collections

Even though Willie did not generate many hit singles for RCA, the company has continually exploited his back catalog. One avenue of exploitation has been the "greatest hits" packages. There were six major "hits" packages, beginning in 1982 and continuing through 1995, with an "essential" set. Two of the collections, *Help Me Make It Through the Night* and *20 of the Best* were foreign releases only.

The two foreign releases accounted for the only RCA (or affiliate) appearances of Willie's seasonal favorite (as it was cut for RCA), 'Pretty Paper'. Because his final single for RCA (while under contract), 'Phases, Stages, Circles, Cycles and Scenes', didn't chart, it was not included on a Willie compilation or album until the foreign collection, *20 of the Best*, featured it. In 1995, it appeared on *The Essential Willie Nelson*.

The "hits" compilations actually began in 1976 with *The Best of Willie Nelson*, a set that initially included ten tracks, but has since been rereleased with as few as eight cuts. *The Essential Willie Nelson* was the most valuable collection because it included four cuts, 'Waltz Across Texas', 'Some Other World', Goin' Home', and 'Darkness on the Face of the Earth', that appeared nowhere else but on one of Willie's original RCA albums (all of which have, of course, gone out of print - except for the Justice Records rerelease of *Yesterday's Wine*). It was also the final RCA compilation, to date, and, along with *20 of the Best*, the most inclusive, boasting twenty selections.

There were fourteen albums credited to Nelson while he was under contract to the label. After he left the label, twelve more albums, with his name associated, were released through 1985. The twelve included the "various artists" album, *The Outlaws*, and two Waylon and Willie sets. In addition to the six sets of "greatest hits," there have been many more budget "hit" compilations marketed as recently as 1997.

In 1979, RCA released a "various artists" (Willie, Gary Stewart, Bobby Bare, Guy Clark, and Waylon Jennings) collection entitled, *Honky-Tonkin'* (RCA AHL1-3422). Perhaps the label was trying to make another successful "concept" compilation similar to its 1976 platinum-selling *The Outlaws*. Three sides from Willie's *Both Sides Now* album were included. Subsequently, those sides were rereleased on newer "greatest hits" collections, making that compilation expendable and unnecessary, which led to its going out of print.

As far as album releases and catalogue numbers, RCA used AA, AF, AH, AP, AY followed by either K1 or L1 to prefix most albums released from 1971 through 1982. Most of the prefix codes reflected either price or price change information. During the latter part of the 1960's RCA used LPM, LFT, and LSP to prefix release numbers. Many albums, after initial issue, were rereleased under different catalogue numbers. The budget Camden releases were prefixed by either CAS or ACL1.

One hundred seventy-five cuts by Willie (solo and with others) were presented on all of the various RCA albums and compilations credited to him. Five of the tracks were "live" medleys. Of the remaining one hundred and seventy (that were not medleys), ninety-one were rereleased (some - several times) on the many packages and compilations RCA put together after Willie had left the company, either as "greatest hits" collections, subsidiary (Camden) budget sets, foreign releases, or as compilations of previously released material dressed up to appear as "new" albums (despite the fact he was no longer with the label).

Seven cuts appeared only on the albums or compilations put together after 1972 (when Willie left RCA), of which two appeared first on a foreign release. In addition, Willie cut twenty-two songs (according to RCA session logs) that neither the company nor any affiliate included on a Willie album or compilation. Six of those twenty-two did go out as singles.

'Truth # 1' was the "B" side of the 1970 single featuring 'Laying My Burdens Down'. One of his Pamper "demos," 'And So Will You My Love' only went out commercially as the "B" side of the 1965 single that had 'I Just Can't Let You Say Goodbye' as the "A" side. One more "B" side was 'Don't Say Love or Nothing', a Willie original. It was paired with 1968's 'Bring Me Sunshine', his best-selling RCA single. Another Willie-written song, 'Jimmy's Road', was the "flip" side of a 1971 single headed up by John Hartford's 'Natural to Be Gone', which did not chart. 'Whiskey Walzer' and 'Little Darling (co-written by Willie), were marketed in 1964 only as a German single.

The Greatest Hits Collections - Album Listings

The Best of Willie. RCA Records AHK/AHL1-4420. (1982).

Track Listing: Everybody's Talkin' (*), Mountain Dew, Sweet Memories, Minstrel Man (*), Good Times, Little Things, Bloody Mary Morning, Night Life, Me and Paul, Yesterday's Wine.

Recording Notes: Originally released in 1982, this compilation featured six well-known Willie compositions, 'Me and Paul', 'Yesterday's Wine', 'Good Times', 'Bloody Mary Morning', 'Night Life', and 'Little Things', which was co-written with his second wife, Shirley Collie. That same year, 1982, the combined interpretive talents of Merle Haggard and George Jones reworked 'Yesterday's Wine' and watched their version zoom to the top of the country singles charts. That was reason enough to recycle Willie's original version.

The first four album tracks were songs by other writers. Of those four, one, 'Everybody's Talkin'', had been a Nilsson pop hit (and the featured song in the movie, *Midnight Cowboy*) though it was written by Fred Neil. Two of the remaining three selections, 'Mountain Dew' (by Scott Wiseman and Bascom Lamar Lunsford) and 'Sweet Memories' (by Mickey Newbury), were country standards.

In the previous year, 1981, 'Mountain Dew' had peaked, for Willie, at number twenty-three, after RCA released it as a single. In that same year (1981), 'Minstrel Man', written by Eddie Rager and Stan Haas, had been the title track of a "new" album RCA put together of previously released Willie tracks. Earlier, in 1979, 'Sweet Memories' had peaked at number four for Willie, even though he had been gone from RCA, by then, for nearly seven years.

Other Releases: This set was released again in 1985 on RCA Camden, CL85143, with the title *Greatest Hits*. On the RCA parent label, it received a new catalog number of AYK1-5143. In 1992, it was rereleased in abridged form on compact disc with the catalog number 56335-2, minus two (*) cuts.

* = the two cuts deleted when this set was released in abridged form as 56335-2.

20 of the Best. RCA NK 89137/ITNS 5208. (1982).

Track Listing: Funny How Time Slips Away, Night Life, My Own Peculiar Way, Hello Walls, Mr. Record Man, Family Bible, Me and Paul, Good Times, She's Still Gone, Little Things, Pretty Paper, Bloody Merry Morning, What Can You Do to Me Now, December Day, Yesterday's Wine, To Make a Long Story Short (She's Gone), Good Hearted Woman, She's Not for You, It Should Be Easier Now, Phases & Stages (Circles, Cycles & Scenes).

Recording Notes: This was a much better "hits" package which unfortunately was limited to a foreign distribution, West Germany and England, to be exact. As a 1982 English RCA release, the catalog number was INTS-5208. It contained the first and, until 1995, only album appearance of the "A" side of Willie's final single released on RCA (while he was still under contract), 'Phases & Stages (Circles, Cycles & Scenes)'. Willie wrote or co-wrote all twenty selections on this package, which ranged from some of his most well known such as 'Night Life' to his more obscure like 'She's Not for You'.

This collection also featured the first RCA album appearance of Willie's original composition, 'Pretty Paper', as it was cut for the label at Willie's first (RCA) recording session, produced by Chet Atkins, which took place November 12, 1964. Otherwise, the track could only be found on several "various artists" compilations, 1982's *A Country Christmas*, AYL1-4812/4812-2-R (sometimes listed as Vol. 1)/CPK1-4396, *Wishing You a Merry Christmas*, LSP-4973/ANK1-1952, 1985's *The Best of Christmas*, CPL1-7013/7013-2-R, and 1972's *Nipper's Greatest Christmas Hits*, 9859-2-R. The classic version of 'Pretty Paper', for Willie, was the one he cut for Columbia Records in 1978. Since then, he has rerecorded it several more times, for two Christmas albums he released in the nineties and as a guest cut on a 1997 Asleep at the Wheel Christmas collection.

Though 'Pretty Paper' was marketed as the "A" side of Willie's first single, it failed to chart. The flip side, 'What a Merry Christmas This Could Be' (not included on this compilation), was recorded during the same session. Although written by Harlan Howard and Hank Cochran, the song went unnoticed and was not included on an RCA album or compilation attributed to Willie. It could only be found on the 1990

RCA "various artists" compilation, *We Wish You a Merry Christmas*, 2294-2-R. 'Pretty Paper' had its greatest success as a Roy Orbison single. Roy recorded the song in 1963 when he and Willie were both with Monument Records.

Help Me Make It Through the Night. RCA NL 89475. (1984).

Track Listing: Help Me Make It Through the Night, I Love You Because, Heartaches by the Number, Both Sides Now, Have I Told You Lately That I Love You, I'm So Lonesome I Could Cry, Bring Me Sunshine, What Now My Love, Born to Lose, Everybody's Talkin', Fire and Rain, Funny How Time Slips Away, Yesterday, Pretty Paper.

Recording Notes: This 1984 set, released in England and Germany, featured the only other album release of 'Pretty Paper'. The rest of the cuts were among the finest tracks Willie recorded, while at RCA, of other people's songs, especially the pop songs, from the Beatles' 'Yesterday' to the Gilbert Becaud classic, 'What Now My Love'. With the inclusion of 'Bring Me Sunshine', this became one of the best foreign RCA compilations of Willie material. The only other foreign RCA compilations that came close to being satisfactory were 1975's twenty-eight cut *Famous Country Musicmakers* (from England), DPS-2062, and 1989's *Country Heroes*, BMG/RCA 56335-2 (from Germany).

Collector's Series. RCA AHLI-5470. (1985).

Track Listing: Night Life, Funny How Time Slips Away, Crazy Arms, Healing Hands of Time, Yesterday's Wine, Today I Started Loving You Again, Rainy Day Blues, San Antonio Rose, Heartaches by the Number, Born to Lose, Have I Told You Lately That I Love You, One in a Row, Good Hearted Woman, Help Me Make It Through the Night.

Recording Notes: This fourteen cut compilation from 1985 was part of a series that RCA marketed utilizing many of its most popular artists (from Waylon Jennings to Dolly Parton). Half of the cuts, ranging from 'Night Life' to 'Yesterday's Wine', were written or co-written by Willie. Three years prior, 1982, an inspired duet by George Jones and Merle Haggard had turned 'Yesterday's Wine' into a number one country smash.

The other seven tracks, including 'Crazy Arms' and 'Born to Lose', were all oft-recorded country (and pop) standards. It too quickly became another of many RCA releases reissued in abridged form. Six cuts were eliminated for the later abridged version. On the positive side, this set was one of only three Willie Nelson RCA albums that featured 'Have I Told You Lately That I Love You'. The other two were

Sixteen Top Tracks, RCA 90116 (a short-lived English release) and the album on which it was first released, *Make Way for Willie Nelson.*

All Time Greatest Hits Vol. 1. RCA 8556-2-R. (1988).

Track Listing: One Day at a Time, Night Life, The Party's Over, My Own Peculiar Way, Hello Walls, Sunday Morning Coming Down, Fire and Rain, San Antonio, The Words Don't Fit the Picture, Good Hearted Woman, Blackjack County Chains, You Ought to Hear Me Cry, Bring Me Sunshine, Funny How Time Slips Away, She's Not for You, Mr. Record Man, Healing Hands of Time, I Just Can't Let You Say Goodbye, I'm a Memory, Yours Love.

Recording Notes: Until the 1995 release of *The Essential Willie Nelson,* this 1988 set stood as the most comprehensive compilation of RCA material. Volume 2 had previously been cataloged (as RCA 2695-2) but never released. The selections were not surprising as all had some impact during Willie's RCA tenure. The digital remastering, done at RCA's New York City studios, was excellent.

The Essential Willie Nelson. RCA Records (BMG) RCA07863-66590-2. (1995).

Track Listing: Me and Paul, Yesterday's Wine, December Day, Bloody Mary Morning, Healing Hands of Time, Darkness on the Face of the Earth, Funny How Time Slips Away, Family Bible, My Own Peculiar Way, Mr. Record Man, I Gotta Get Drunk, Hello Walls, Sweet Memories, Night Life, Waltz Across Texas, The Party's Over, Some Other World, Goin' Home, Once More With Feeling, Phases, Stages, Circles, Cycles and Scenes.

Recording Notes: In 1995, RCA finally put together a definitive collection of sides Willie recorded during his nine year tenure. Many of the songs were ones he subsequently made famous at other labels, 'Me and Paul' (album title cut for Columbia), 'Healing Hands of Time' (recently done again for Liberty), and 'Phases, Stages, Circles, Cycles and Scenes' (key part of his song cycle recorded for Atlantic).

This was only the second time that 'Phases, Stages, Circles, Cycles and Scenes' appeared on an album. The first time was for a 1982 foreign RCA collection. Featured were five cuts from the concept album, *Yesterday's Wine.* Seven tracks came from Willie's first RCA album. Paul Williams produced the set while Colin Escott wrote the excellent liner notes and selected the repertoire. Will there be a "Volume 2" sequel? RCA does own quite a bit of unreleased material but if such a collection ever happens it will not likely be within calendar 1998.

"Both Sides Now":

The Camden and Budget Compilations

Beyond the original RCA album releases (even those with previously released material or greatest hits packages), there were numerous compilations of Willie's material made available at lower retail prices. These sets either came out on the RCA (domestic or foreign) or Camden labels. Some of the budget sets, particularly the first one, contained cuts that had not been previously released on any of Willie's regularly priced sets for the label.

The first budget release was marketed in 1968. That was only three years after Willie's first full-priced album came out in 1965. The fact that his first set of albums did not sell well prompted RCA to market the first budget collection. The company hoped that a lower price might attract customers who hadn't wanted to take a chance on Willie Nelson at the regular retail price. They also included several cuts that had not been on an album before.

The budget collections continued long after Willie and RCA parted company, thus far as late as 1997. They were especially prevalent during the time Willie was experiencing his greatest sales on Columbia Records. By then, they were being released solely in an attempt to cash in on that surge of popularity and marketability.

Pair Records of New Jersey was responsible for the best budget releases, packaging sixteen tracks on each of three collections. Candlelite Music released an excellent cross-section, which was, for a time, sponsored by a Tequila company. It not only had some great RCA cuts, there were several Atlantic Records tracks, as well. An English company, Everest, marketed a comprehensive compilation, courtesy of the English RCA affiliate. The English Camden subsidiary put out its own undated budget set, *The Best of Willie Nelson*, 74321-37840-2.

It took until 1997, however, for the definitive budget RCA collection to come out in the form of a three CD package originating from BMG Direct Marketing. Entitled *Sweet Memories: 36 All-Time Favorites*, it featured, for the first time on CD, the old Hank Williams classic, 'A Mansion on the Hill'. One cut was a Waylon/Willie pairing from a Waylon Jennings album and two came from a Waylon/Willie album, WWII. Two of Willie's best selling singles, 'Johnny One Time' and 'Bring Me Sunshine' were also included. Closing out the set was the Willie Monday Night football favorite, 'The Party's Over'.

Overall, the thirty-six cuts ranged from such pop classics as 'What Now My Love' and 'Fire and Rain' to several of the many country standards Willie recorded for RCA. One of them, 'One Has My Name', stood out, according to its lyricist, Hal Blair, as:

> the first of the cheating songs and daring enough at the time to be banned by certain church leagues and others.

The other two co-writers on that song were the old-time Western actor, Eddie Dean and his wife, Dearest. Eddie recalled that:

> my wife Dearest and I had been discussing the idea for a song for about six years but couldn't come up with the right title. One day Hal Blair and I were out writing a song - actually a rewrite - entitled 'Wake Me in the Morning by the Swanee River'. I was going to record it. Dearest came out to our little studio and said, 'I have the title for the song we've been trying to write.' I said, 'Honey, we're busy; wait just a minute. We're finishing this song.' She said, 'But I have the title; forget everything else. I've got the title.' I said, 'What title?' She said, 'One Has My Name, The Other Has My Heart.' Well, we put 'Swanee River' aside. Each one of us wrote lyrics and I started singing it. I did the music and within fifteen minutes I had it on the tape. That's the way that song came about.

Another "singing cowboy" star of Hollywood Westerns, Jimmy Wakely, got his version of the song out on Capitol Records in 1948, three weeks before Dean marketed his rendition on a smaller label. Needless to say, the larger label, Capitol, was able to push Wakely's version to the top of the charts, while Dean, the co-writer, came close (his single peaked at number eleven). In May 1969, Jerry Lee Lewis, by then a country artist, released a version of the song that went to number three on the *Billboard* country singles chart. With material like that, most of Willie's budget RCA collections were excellent buys.

The Camden and Budget Sets - Album Listings

Good Ol' Country Singin'. RCA Records (Camden) CAL-2203. (1968).

Track Listing: I'm Still Not Over You, I Don't Feel Anything, You Ought to Hear Me Cry, Ashamed, Tender Years, He Sits at My Table, Did I Ever Love You, Blackjack County Chain, Something to Think About, Down to Our Last Goodbye.

Recording Notes: The first budget compilation of Nelson's recordings released by RCA went out on their Camden label in May of 1968. Most of the cuts included had not been previously released on an album. One example was Willie's original song (from 1966) 'I'm Still Not Over You', the "A" side of his seventh single for the label, which, by the way, did not chart, although when Ray Price recorded it for Columbia in 1967, it went top ten (peaking at the number six spot). Willie's version would only appear on this album.

The "A" side of Willie's thirteenth single, 'Blackjack County Chain', was also accorded its first album appearance, though it would reappear on later album compilations. As a single, it did make the charts, going all the way to number twenty-one. Three of the tracks, 'Ashamed', 'Did I Ever Love You', and 'Down to Our Last Goodbye' had previously appeared on the 1968 release, *Good Times*.

The Willie original, 'Something to Think About', was recorded November 29, 1966, and had been slated to be part of the album, *Make Way for Willie Nelson*, while the Willie-written 'I Don't Feel Anything' previously appeared on *Laying My Burdens Down*. This compilation also served as the only album release of Willie's cover of George Jones' 'Tender Years' (also recorded in November 1966) and 'He Sits at My Table', written by Chip Taylor (it had been the "B" side of

Willie's sixth single). Willie's composition, 'You Ought to Hear Me Cry', was a 1977 single and part of the 1977 RCA album, *Before His Time,* the one constructed by Waylon and Richie Albright by remixing previously released tracks.

Country Winners by Willie Nelson. RCA Records (Camden) ACL1-0326. (1973).

Track Listing: The Party's Over, One Day at a Time, Night Life, Hello Walls, Mr. Record Man, My Own Peculiar Way, Funny How Time Slips Away, I Walk Alone, Streets of Laredo.

Recording Notes: This 1973 release contained nine selections, seven of which were written by Willie. Of the two covers, 'I Walk Alone', was by Herbert Wilson while 'Streets of Laredo' belonged to the "public domain." This collection, with uncredited liner notes, bore little similarity to the later *Country Winners* compilation marketed through Pair Records.

The hand-drawn bucking bronco part of the cover art was remarkably similar to the one done for the Liberty album, *Country Willie.* All selections had been previously released on at least one of Willie's earlier RCA albums. Pickwick also released the set (same title) as ACL-0326.

Spotlight on Willie Nelson. RCA Records (Camden) ACL1-0705. (1974).

Track Listing: Bloody Merry (Mary) Morning, One Has My Name (The Other Has My Heart), Yours Love, Everybody's Talkin', Today I Started Loving You Again, Bring Me Sunshine, San Antonio, I'm So Lonesome I Could Cry, Wabash Cannon Ball.

Recording Notes: This 1974 release also contained nine selections, eight of which were previously released. One, 'Bring Me Sunshine', was released for the first time on an album. Actually, the song was a strange choice for Willie to record at the time, since it was not even remotely a country song, but the theme song for the British comedy duo, Morecambe and Wise (as written by Sylvia Dee and Arthur Kent).

Strange as it may seem, it was Willie's most successful RCA single. It reached number thirteen on the country singles chart in early 1969. That success proved what Willie had always claimed, a great song was a great song without categorical differentiation. He more than once pointed out that a G chord is a G chord no matter who played it. Then again, Willie has been called one of the greatest song interpreters in pop music, not just country music.

He proved his assertion for Columbia Records when he took pop standards like 'Blue Skies' to the top of the country charts. Why RCA waited until 1974 to include Willie's most successful single (from 1968) on an album (and a budget album besides) probably best underscored the inconsistent and underemphasized marketing approach RCA used on his product. Pickwick rereleased this set as ACL-0705.

Country Club: The Hits of Willie Nelson. RCA KEL1-8015. (1979).

Track Listing: I Love You Because, I Never Cared for You, I'd Trade All of My Tomorrows (for Just One Yesterday), You Left a Long, Long Time Ago, One Has My Name (The Other Has My Heart), Crazy Arms, Heartaches by the Number, Yesterday, Fraulein, Everybody's Talkin', One in a Row, Help Me Make It Through the Night, Me and Paul.

Recording Notes: This 1979 Canadian budget release featured thirteen Nelson cuts produced by either Atkins or Jarvis with one cut produced jointly. Four original Nelson compositions were featured, as well as some country and pop standards. Nothing about this collection made it stand out from the other budget releases RCA seemed to have been haphazardly creating.

Country Winners. RCA (Pair) PDK2-1007. (1987).

Track Listing: The Party's Over, Born to Lose, San Antonio, Mr. Record Man, Texas in My Soul, I Just Can't Let You Say Goodbye, I Walk Alone, Streets of Laredo, Columbus Stockade Blues, Heartaches by the Number, Seasons of My Heart, San Antonio Rose, What Now My Love, Fraulein, Go on Home, I'd Trade All of My Tomorrows (for Just One Yesterday).

Recording Notes: With much of the original RCA catalog no longer available, this 1987 album became one of the best available sources for RCA material. That remained true until the 1995 release of the collection, *The Essential Willie Nelson.* The formula for this album was the combination of a few strong Willie originals with great country standards. Several of the cuts came from Willie's *Texas in My Soul* album. 'Go on Home' was the one by Hank Cochran.

Once More With Feeling. RCA (Pair) PDK2-1032. (1983).

Track Listing: What Can You Do to Me Now?, Sunday Morning Coming Down, I'm So Lonesome I Could Cry, Fire and Rain, I'm a Memory, Yours Love, That's Why I Love Her So, Today I Started Loving You Again, Crazy Arms, Pins and Needles (in My Heart), Who

Do I Know in Dallas, Once More With Feeling, Both Sides Now, Everybody's Talkin', One Has My Name (The Other Has My Heart), It Could Be Said That Way.

Recording Notes: This album was a 1983 compilation available through RCA Special Products and Pair Records. Much of the album's emphasis, with songs like 'Fire and Rain', 'Both Sides Now', and 'Everybody's Talkin'', was on Willie's interpretations of modern pop songs. Interspersed were two great Hank Cochran and Willie originals, 'Who Do I Know in Dallas' and 'What Can You Do to Me Now', Willie's own 'I'm a Memory', along with old and new country classics, from Kristofferson's 'Sunday Morning Coming Down' to Merle Haggard and Bonnie Owens' 'Today I Started Loving You Again' (which Willie would later rerecord and place on a 1994 Merle Haggard tribute).

Good Hearted Woman. RCA (Pair) PDK2-1114. (1985).

Track Listing: Country Willie, You Left a Long, Long Time Ago, Mountain Dew, One Step Beyond, Good Hearted Woman, Home Is Where You're Happy, If You Really Loved Me, My Kind of Girl, Rainy Day Blues, What Do You Want Me to Do?, The Words Don't Fit the Picture, Undo the Right, Stay Away from Lonely Places, I'd Rather You Didn't Love Me, A Moment Isn't Very Long, London.

Recording Notes: This 1985 collection complemented the other Pair albums available through RCA Special Products. Featured were many of Willie's early songs (also recorded as Pamper "demos," pre-Nashville singles, or Liberty recordings) such as 'Country Willie' and 'Rainy Day Blues'. The track, 'London', appeared for only the second time on one of Willie's RCA albums.

Monte Alban Mezcal Proudly Presents Willie Nelson, Country Superstar. Candlelite Music (RCA Special Products) DVL-1-0446A. (1980).

Track Listing: Funny How Time Slips Away, Whiskey River, I'm So Lonesome I Could Cry, Bring Me Sunshine, I Love You Because, After the Fire Is Gone (Willie Nelson & Tracy Nelson), Touch Me, Both Sides Now, Night Life, Born to Lose, Help Me Make It Through the Night (vocal accomp. by Suzee Waters), Stay All Night, One in a Row, Yesterday, San Antonio Rose, Once More With Feeling, Crazy Arms, Fire and Rain, Bloody Mary Morning, Sweet Memories (vocal accomp. by Suzee Waters).

Recording Notes: The cover of this 1980 special collection stated that Mezcal was presenting Nelson, while the inside record label said Candlelite Music was presenting him. Candlelite did release the set separately under two catalog numbers, G-101 and DVL-1-0446. Through Candlelite, the album was available mail-order only.

'Stay All Night', 'Bloody Mary Morning', 'Whiskey River', and the Tracy Nelson duet, 'After the Fire Is Gone', were 1973 and 1974 Atlantic recordings. Tracy Nelson's identity was well-known, but who was Suzee Waters? She was a singer whose voice was overdubbed on to the two cuts in 1978, six years after Willie stopped recording for RCA.

Once More With Feeling. RCA (Realistic) DPK1/DPL1-0496. (1981).

Track Listing: Once More With Feeling, Yesterday's Wine, Help Me Make It Through the Night, How Long Have You Been There, My Own Peculiar Way, Bloody Merry Morning, You Left a Long, Long Time Ago, Hello Walls, I'd Trade All of My Tomorrows (for Just One Yesterday), Will You Remember?.

Recording Notes: This compilation from 1981 was sold through Radio Shack (Realistic brand) with the word "Realistic" prominently featured on the front. It was not even barely similar to the Pair Records compilation having the same title. For a time, the collection had a Realistic catalog number of 51-7008.

There were some pleasant surprises among the selections, such as Dee Moeller's 'How Long Have You Been There' and two Willie originals, 'You Left a Long, Long Time Ago' and 'Will You Remember?'. The title track, 'Once More With Feeling' was written by Willie's former wife, Shirley Collie. It was a good time for rereleasing 'Yesterday's Wine' since Merle Haggard and George Jones were about to turn it into one of the biggest hits of 1982.

The Magic of Willie Nelson. Banner Records BTR 2452. (1981).

Track Listing: I Gotta Get Drunk, Once More With Feeling, Johnny One Time, The Party's Over, I'm a Memory, Little Things, Good Times, Fire and Rain, Bring Me Sunshine, San Antonio, If You Can Touch Her at All, You Ought to Hear Me Cry, One in a Row, Blackjack County Chain.

Recording Notes: This 1981 compilation of RCA tracks released by a Canadian label was notable for featuring Willie's single, 'Johnny One Time', for only the second time on an album collection. 'Johnny One Time' was the A. L. Owens/Dallas Frazier tune popularized by Brenda Lee. Willie's top twenty single, 'Bring Me Sunshine', was included, as was the song he once wanted to pitch to George Jones, 'I Gotta Get Drunk'. It became a hit for Willie when released by RCA as a single in 1976, four years after he left the label.

As a single, Lee Clayton's song 'If You Can Touch Her at All' had gone top five for Willie and RCA in 1978, three years after he left the label. Otherwise, there was a mixture of familiar Nelson compositions, such as 'The Party's Over', 'I'm a Memory', and 'One in a Row', and the less familiar, namely, 'You Ought to Hear Me Cry'. The authorship of the fourteen songs was evenly split between seven Willie wrote or co-wrote and seven that other writers composed. On only one song was Willie the co-writer. That was with second wife, Shirley, on 'Little Things'. Shirley was also the writer (by herself) of 'Once More With Feeling'. The songs written by others included James Taylor's 'Fire and Rain' and Red Lane's 'Blackjack County Chain'.

Greatest Hits. (Willie Nelson/Waylon Jennings). Era Records/RCA Special Products DPK1-0675. (1984).

Track Listing: Heartaches by the Number, Sweet Memories, San Antonio Rose, I'd Trade All of My Tomorrows (for Just One Yesterday), Night Life.

Recording Notes: This 1984 Waylon/Willie budget set featured Waylon's solo version of 'Good Hearted Woman', as well as five Willie tracks. 'Night Life' appeared for what seemed like the "umpteenth" time on an RCA album or compilation. Except for 'Night Life' the five Willie tracks were all his versions of someone else's songs.

One was the classic Jenny Lou Carson song, 'I'd Trade All of My Tomorrows (for Just One Yesterday)', which had first been a hit in 1952 for the RCA Records superstar, Eddy Arnold. Carson, a struggling recording artist through the 1940's, became a songwriter after meeting the legendary songwriter and publisher Fred Rose and having an affair with him. She not only wrote several other hits for Arnold (and Red Foley and Tex Ritter as well), she had a top pop success with 'Let Me Go, Lover', recorded by Joan Weber in 1955.

RCA Special Products seemed to like featuring old cuts from two artists together so they did one with Willie and Ronnie Milsap (also in 1984) entitled *Ballads: Willie and Ronnie,* DPL-1-0700. It was later recataloged as JCI-4103. RCA/ERA released another budget Waylon/Willie set entitled *Two Greatest Hits Collections,* BU-3830, as well as a Willie compilation, *Songs from My Heart,* NU-5540 (recataloged as DPL1-0686).

Country Showdown: Waylon & Willie. RCA Special Products DPK1-0783. (1987).

Track Listing: Bring Me Sunshine, Night Life, Good Times, Sweet Memories.

Recording Notes: With the success RCA had on its Waylon and Willie collaborations, it was only natural that the company would compile more than one budget set featuring the two superstar names. In 1987, RCA of Canada did just that, including only individual cuts from the catalogs of the two artists and none of their duets. Three of the four Willie cuts had all been RCA single hits at one time or another. 'Night Life' was, of course, one of Willie's most famous compositions.

Waylon's solo version of 'Good Hearted Woman' was again featured on his side of the collection, as was his rendition of Kris Kristofferson's 'The Taker'. The other two Waylon cuts were hit singles of his from 1969 and 1970.

Night Life. Everest Records KCBR 1039. (Undated).

Track Listing: Today I Started Loving You Again, Everybody's Talkin', I'm So Lonesome I Could Cry, One Day at a Time, Sunday Morning Coming Down, The Party's Over, Night Life, A Couple More Years, Fire and Rain, If You Can Touch Her at All, It's Not Supposed to Be That Way, Funny How Time Slips Away.

Recording Notes: This collection was released at an unknown date in England. It was compiled by Ron Winter, courtesy of RCA Ltd, Record Division. The set was also released (same title) in England and Germany (at an unknown date) as Premier CBR 1039. All in all, it was a balanced mix of Willie originals and satisfactory cover versions. Willie's solo cut, 'A Couple More Years', was one he did for the *Waylon & Willie* album.

Classic Willie. BMG Special Products 44525-2. (1997).

Track Listing: Night Life, Once More With Feeling, I'm So Lonesome I Could Cry, Streets of Laredo, Everybody's Talkin', Crazy Arms, Funny How Time Slips Away, Help Me Make It Through the Night, Born to Lose, I'd Trade All of My Tomorrows (for Just One Yesterday).

Recording Notes: In 1997, twenty-five years after Willie and RCA had parted contractual company, RCA (the direct marketing arm of RCA's German-based parent company, BMG Entertainment) was still rereleasing Willie cuts to the record consumer. This time the company called their product *Classic Willie* and noted that it was "the encore collection." The ten cut compilation drew from many of the various albums Willie recorded for RCA. The same cuts (and quite a few more) appeared on the 1997 thirty-six selection GSC/BMG Special Products collection, *Sweet Memories.*

To begin with, there were two of his best-known originals, 'Night Life' and 'Funny How Time Slips Away'. Then there was the cut, 'Streets of Laredo', from his all-Texas album, *Texas in My Soul,* as well as a Hank Williams cover, 'I'm So Lonesome I Could Cry', a Kristofferson cover, 'Help Me Make It Through the Night', and a few country standards along with a pop classic. For good measure, RCA threw in 'Once More with Feeling', a song written by then-wife Shirley Collie Nelson.

Sweet Memories. GSC Music/BMG Special Products 15331. (1997).

Volume One Track Listing: Funny How Time Slips Away (*), Night Life (*), Once More with Feeling (*), One Day at a Time, Good Hearted Woman, She's Not for You, If You Can Touch Her at All, How Long Have You Been There, Don't You Ever Get Tired of Hurting Me, Heroes, A Mansion on the Hill, Just to Satisfy You.

Volume Two Track Listing: What Now My Love, Sweet Memories, Good Times, Bring Me Sunshine, Little Things, One in a Row, Streets of Laredo, Born to Lose, Minstrel Man, Mountain Dew, Crazy Arms (*), Johnny One Time.

Volume Three Track Listing: Wabash Cannon Ball, Help Me Make It Through the Night, The Year That Clayton Delaney Died, I'm So Lonesome I Could Cry (*), One Has My Name (The Other Has My Heart), I Gotta Get Drunk, Blackjack County Chain, I'd Trade All of My Tomorrows (for Just One Yesterday), Fire and Rain, Everybody's Talkin' (*), I'm a Memory, The Party's Over.

Recording Notes: This 1997 compilation (all three discs worth) encompassed all of the previously listed 1997 budget release, *Classic Willie,* and a lot more. 'Johnny One Time' and 'Bring Me Sunshine', two of Willie's more successful RCA singles also appeared. One cut, 'Just to Satisfy You', featured Willie's singing, but came off the Waylon Jennings album, *Black on Black.*

Two of the selections, 'Heroes' and 'The Year That Clayton Delaney Died', came from the Willie/Waylon album, *WWII.* For the first time, Willie's version of the Hank Williams classic, 'A Mansion on the Hill' was released as part of an RCA Willie collection. Other cuts, like 'She's Not for You', had been included on previous compilations, but not that often, nowhere near the number of times 'Night Life' and 'Funny How Time Slips Away' had been. Six of the cuts (*) appeared on another budget compilation, *Nightlife,* a joint release by BMG Special Products and KRB Music Companies. It was part of a cassette tape series called "Six Pack Hits."

* = the six cuts from this set that comprised the 1997 budget collection, *Nightlife,* BMG Special Products/KRB Music DRK 11770.

"Who'll Buy My Memories":

The Conclusion to the RCA Years

Because the initial sales of Willie Nelson albums never reached satisfactory levels for RCA, the company became less than enthusiastic about marketing his recordings (singles and albums). When his contract was up, many of the songs he had recorded had yet to appear on an album. After 1975, when Willie became successful with Columbia, RCA packaged and remarketed selected groups of songs as albums that either appeared to be new releases or were, in fact, collections of "hits."

Due to this remarketing effort, the recorded track, 'Night Life', appeared on a total of thirteen albums and compilations. Similarly, many other cuts placed on later albums or collections had previously been released in album format. Surprisingly, quite a few had not, including his best selling single from 1968, 'Bring Me Sunshine'.

One hundred and ninety-seven tracks (five of which consisted of medleys of two or more songs) were known to have been recorded by Willie (alone or with others) for RCA (when he was under contract and when he came back to record with Waylon Jennings, including the new track, 'Nowhere Road', for the anniversary edition of *The Outlaws* album). Not counted was the duet he was credited with doing with Dolly Parton (only released on an German RCA anthology).

Twenty-two of the tracks were never placed on even one Willie album or compilation, although the Christmas song, 'What a Merry Christmas This Could Be', did appear on the "various artists" collection, *We Wish You a Merry Christmas,* and did go out as the "B" side of a seasonal single ('Pretty Paper' was the "A" side). Three other tracks, 'Truth Number One' (by Aaron Allen), 'Jimmy's Road', and 'And So Will You My Love' (both by Willie), were also released as singles but never included on an RCA (or subsidiary) album. 'Whiskey Walzer' and 'Little Darling' (co-written by Willie) only went out as a German single (in 1964)

That meant that sixteen (of the twenty-two tracks) were never commercially released in any form by either RCA (or an affiliate). Three were by others, 'Don't Fence Me in' (Cole Porter), 'Someday You'll Call My Name' (Jean Branch and Eddie Hill), and 'The Loser's Song' (Cindy Walker). Thirteen were Willie originals, as follows, 'If You Could See What's Going Through My Mind', 'I Want a Girl', 'Talk to Me', 'When I Don't Have You', 'Wild Memories', 'Pretend I Never Happened', 'Sister's Coming Home', 'Down at the Corner Beer Joint', 'I'm Falling in Love Again', 'Who'll Buy My Memories', 'No Love Around', and 'Come on Home'.

Of those thirteen, Willie has never rerecorded six ('If You Could See What's Going Through My Mind', 'I Want a Girl', 'Talk to Me', 'When I Don't Have You', 'Wild Memories', and 'Come on Home'), meaning they have remained unheard for up to a quarter of a century. The best service RCA could provide would be to create an anthology comprised completely of the twenty-two tracks. The alternative would be for Willie to make it a priority to recut the six original songs RCA has kept isolated in their vaults. Fortunately, the 1998 eight CD Bear Family Records collection (from Germany) *Nashville Was the Roughest...*, BCD 15831 HK, contained all the unreleased material (except for the Cole Porter song which has been noted as "lost").

Eight years of Willie's life went into his attempts to become a country star via his RCA recordings. Was there any kind of satisfactory or productive end result? To Willie, the company "just didn't think my records were worth a damn." He has seemingly closed off any revisiting of that period of his career. Yet no less stellar a critic than Chet Flippo (writing for *Rolling Stone*) concluded that Willie "recorded a string of brilliant LPs" for the label. How about Chet Atkins, the man who signed him to RCA and produced his early work back when, in Chet's words, Willie "looked like a banker?" In 1998, with a more than twenty-five year distance (or perhaps perspective) he was finally able to humorously relate to Jane Sanderson of *People* magazine that:

> I tell him when I see him, 'You never did start selling until you started getting ugly and funky.' It's true. He went out to Texas and kind of uglified himself up and got smoking dope, and people started writing about him.

The Atlantic and Columbia Years

WILLIE TOLD US THAT . . .

Shotgun Willie in his underwear!
(Photo from Willie Nelson and Atlantic Records)

Willie's picnics became the place to appear in Texas.
(Photo from the Lana Nelson collection)

"Phases and Stages":

The Atlantic Albums

Following Willie's stint with RCA from 1964 to 1972, he signed with Atlantic Records at the urging of new manager, Neil Reshen. Willie released his first album for Atlantic in 1973. He was a hot commodity in spite of RCA's failure to successfully market him. That year he was honored by being inducted into the Nashville Songwriter's Association Hall of Fame.

Leon Russell wanted to sign him to his own label, Shelter Records. Instead, it was Jerry Wexler who signed Willie to Atlantic after hearing him perform at Harlan Howard's house during a 1972 Christmas party. Accompanied only by his own guitar, Willie sang the songs built around the concept inspired by his final (under contract) RCA single, 'Phases, Stages, Circles, Cycles and Scenes'.

Atlantic Records of New York had always been primarily a rhythm and blues and rock and roll label. Some of its most famous artists at one time included Ray Charles, Bobby Darin, and the Drifters. In 1972, the company decided to start a country division. Wexler explained his signing of Nelson, saying,

> I've always loved good country music. Good, genuine country music is the blues, and I think the blues is the best music there is. There isn't a note Willie plays, not a note he sings, that isn't rich with the blues.

Wasn't that Pappy Daily's criticism, that Willie was too "bluesy?" Willie remembered meeting Wexler, writing in his autobiography that when he finished his performance at Harlan's party, a stranger came up and said, 'I'm Jerry Wexler. We're starting a country division at Atlantic, and I run it. I'd love to have the album you just sang.' I said, 'I have been looking for you for a long time'.

The first album turned out to be *Shotgun Willie*, not *Phases and Stages*. Willie was allowed to use his band on all the studio sessions along with other musicians of his choice or Wexler's recommendation, specifically the Muscle Shoals musicians, who backed Willie and company on *Phases and Stages*. Needless to say both albums were a revelation to the country music industry and set the stage for Willie's multi-platinum soon-to-come first release for Columbia Records.

Unfortunately, neither of the two Atlantic albums resulted in a major breakthrough for Willie. Jerry Wexler, one of the albums' producers and an executive at Atlantic, blamed his own label for failing to successfully push the records. After the second album, Wexler told Willie, according to Tom Dowd, that he was in the wrong place.

Wexler, himself, wrote in his memoirs that "no one at Atlantic shared my interest in country music." That was why he proceeded to help Willie get away from Atlantic. He said he did not want "to leave Willie dangling," so he "got him an unconditional release." Actually, from the time Atlantic opened its country division in Nashville, it made a major marketing effort only with Willie. Even that thrust was not very well coordinated. Willie's first album did fare better in the marketplace than any of his previous releases.

The second album proceeded to sell much better than any of Willie's previous albums. Unit sales totaled around four hundred thousand copies. Unfortunately, even that level of sales was not enough to keep Atlantic's country music division out of the red. So, Ahmet Ertegun, the label's chief financial officer, made a quick decision to shut the Nashville operation down. Interestingly, years later, Atlantic (by then under the Warner Bros. umbrella) would finally successfully run a country division.

Recently both of Willie's Atlantic albums were rereleased together as a special "gold CD" from Mobile Fidelity, UDCD581. Willie's stay with Atlantic also resulted in one of his early and best "duets," a recording with Tracy Nelson (formerly lead singer with Mother Earth and not a relative) entitled, 'After the Fire Is Gone', originally released on one of her albums in 1974. The song had been a hit for Conway Twitty and Loretta Lynn in 1971. Willie recalled how the duet came about, that:

Bob Johnston was producing her, and he asked me if I'd come in and sing a song with her. He was producing that in Nashville. It was a little rock and roll.

Even more material was recorded but not released at the time. At the *Shotgun Willie* sessions, Willie remembered that "we planned to go in and do one album and just while we were there, things were rollin' pretty good so we did some more things." The "more things" were mostly gospel songs that turned up on the Columbia album, *The Troublemaker*, as well as five other previously unreleased songs, including one written by Leon Russell, and some alternate takes.

Atlantic also failed to release a live album of a June 30, 1974 show Willie did in Austin. The album was actually ready for release with the title, *Willie Nelson Live at the Texas Opry House*. Unfortunately, the company's country division had completely shut down and the album stayed in the vaults until Rhino Records acquired Atlantic's back catalog and released the live set, consisting of eleven tracks, along with the (five) other previously unreleased tracks, as part of their Willie Nelson boxed set in 1993 (the one sold over the QVC home-shopping cable television network). That was the boxed set that featured Willie's first commercial single as well as his Hank Williams tribute album. It was discussed in the section covering Willie's "First Recordings."

Willie recalled how the live album (at the Texas Opry House in Austin) came about, that he "was playin' there and we were pretty hot at that time and Jerry thought it was time to do a live album." The high point of that set came when fiddler Johnny Gimble unexpectedly began playing some Bob Wills fiddle licks enabling Willie to break into the Wills classic, 'Take Me Back to Tulsa'. Willie later said, though it sounded rehearsed, "it sorta happened; it wasn't planned."

According to session notes from the Atlantic archives gathered by Michel Ruppli (and published through Greenwood Press), two shows, one on June 29 and the other on June 30, 1974, were recorded for the projected live album. The entire recording consisted of one hundred and thirteen tracks, a number of which were untitled along with some that were strictly instrumental. Sixty-seven of the tracks came from the first show (June 29) while forty-six came from the second (June 30).

Judging from the track listings, several of the tracks, specifically 'Me and Paul', the medley of 'Bloody Mary Morning' and 'Take Me Back to Tulsa', and 'Truck Drivin' Man', actually came from the first show, the June 29th one. The remainder appeared to have come from the June 30th show, while the medley of 'Funny How Time Slips Away', 'Crazy', and 'Night Life' was crafted together from at least two separate tracks. Some of the gems from those two concert nights, that have remained unreleased, were 'Delta Dawn', Merle Haggard's 'Okie from Muskogee', and the Hank Williams classic, 'Jambalaya'.

The year Willie signed with Atlantic (1973) was monumental to him as that was the year he started his annual Fourth of July picnics. The first was held in Dripping Springs, Texas, and according to Willie, "we had 50,000 show up," even though he had only been "expecting five or six thousand." The picnics would become annual events up to 1980.

The Atlantic signing also coincided approximately with Willie's finally making Austin, Texas (and sometimes Colorado) his permanent base for operating and living. He said that:

> Austin to me represents freedom. Not only Austin, but Texas is still to me the wide open space. There's room to think in Texas. Fortunately no one is in control.

Unfortunately, the following year, 1973, supposedly found Willie so depressed at turning forty without a major recording hit, that he laid himself down "in the middle of Music Row's main drag, hoping a truck would run him over and put an end to his pain." No one did, but of course it was such an odd hour and such an "unbusy" street. The supposed incident made for a great story, but like so much about Willie, it was just another part of his legend, all too similar to the story that had him laying in the street outside Tootsie's in 1962. Regardless of whether either street "scene" ever happened, in a couple of years Willie found himself with an an incredible Columbia deal.

Willie always knew he would make it!
(Photo from Evelyn Shriver Public Relations)

The Atlantic Albums - Album Listings

Shotgun Willie. Atlantic 7262-2. (1973).

Track Listing: Shotgun Willie, Whiskey River, Sad Songs and Waltzes, Local Memory, Slow Down Old World, Stay All Night (Stay a Little Longer), Devil in a Sleepin' Bag, She's Not For You, Bubbles in My Beer, You Look Like the Devil, So Much to Do, A Song for You.

Recording Notes: This critically acclaimed album, released in 1973, was produced by the movers and shakers of Atlantic, Jerry Wexler and Arif Mardin (along with David Briggs). The album was recorded quickly, as an elated Arif Mardin observed, "It's a record, even for Atlantic, thirty-three cuts in one week." It became Willie's best selling album to date, although it did not sell enough to make the *Billboard* pop album charts. Most of the album was recorded in New York, not Nashville, and several top New York studio musicians were used, specifically Dave Bromberg, playing electric guitar on 'Whiskey River'.

A then-unknown Larry Gatlin sang background while Doug Sahm came in and played electric guitar on two cuts, adding harmony vocals to one of them. Friend among friends, Waylon, contributed acoustic guitar (and background vocals) on one song. Johnny Gimble played old-time fiddle on two selections and J. R. Chartwell, swing fiddler, was said to have also assisted, although his name appeared nowhere in the credits. Leon Russell wrote one song for the occasion, 'You Look Like the Devil'. He also contributed 'A Song for You', which he had previously recorded for his debut album, *Leon Russell*, released as catalog number 1001 on his own Shelter Records.

The title song, 'Shotgun Willie' was written by Nelson in his New York hotel room. He said he was pacing the room, "searching for an idea. Finally sat on the toilet and spotted this sanitary napkin envelope I could write on." He wrote the song, chorus first. Susie Nelson said when he played it for her, "by the end of the first verse, I was laughing." She recalled, "even Dad started laughing, although he was red with embarrassment when he was done."

Later, Kris Kristofferson would tell Willie the song was "mind farts." It became the "A" side of Willie's first Atlantic single, rising to number sixty and remaining on the charts for five weeks. The second single, a Bob Wills classic, 'Stay All Night (Stay a Little Longer)', fared quite a bit better, moving up to number twenty-two and staying on the charts for thirteen weeks.

Another Wills piece, 'Bubbles in My Beer', found its way to the album. The song's co-writer, Cindy Walker, said that the great Tommy Duncan called her with a song title he had made up, 'Watching the Bubbles in My Beer'. He told her the song should be about "just remembering and watching the bubbles in my beer."

'Whiskey River' appeared and in time became a fixture in Willie's repertoire. Interestingly the song was written, not by Nelson, but by old pal Johnny Bush. Bush had hitchhiked across Texas with Willie in pursuit of paying gigs long before either one made it big. He was Willie's drummer for a time, before Paul English came along.

Willie also resurrected, for this album, three original songs he had recorded for RCA, 'So Much to Do', 'She's Not for You', and 'Local Memory'. 'So Much to Do' was first recorded by Willie as a Pamper Music "demo," as was another track, 'Slow Down Old World'. He wrote 'Sad Songs and Waltzes' and 'Devil in a Sleepin' Bag' specifically for this project. The 'Sleepin' Bag' song was supposedly inspired by drummer and close buddy, Paul English.

Phases and Stages. Atlantic 82192-2. (1974).

Track Listing: Phases and Stages (Theme), Washing the Dishes, Phases and Stages (Theme), Walkin', Pretend I Never Happened, Sister's Comin' Home, Down at the Corner Beer Joint, (How Will I Know) I'm Falling in Love Again, Bloody Mary Morning, Phases and Stages (Theme), No Love Around, I Still Can't Believe You're Gone, It's Not Supposed to Be That Way, Heaven and Hell, Phases and Stages (Theme), Pick up the Tempo, Phases and Stages (Theme).

Recording Notes: 1974 saw the release of this excellent concept album, which was supposedly negotiated away from RCA Victor by Neil Reshen, then manager for Waylon Jennings and Willie. Willie had written the songs around his final under-contract RCA single, 'Phases, Stages, Circles, Cycles and Scenes'. Integral to the album, the

'Phases and Stages' theme served as the opening and closing piece. It was also interwoven around several of the song selections. Willie revealed:

> the concept is a look at marriage and divorce from the man's point of view on one side and the woman's point of view on the other.

In a reflective moment, he mused that "it was a long time before I ran into any positive relationships between males and females." Relationships had been, he said, "a problem all my life." He also saw that "among a lot of people, it's been the number one problem in the world." So, Willie decided to write an album:

> from both sides, just for the challenge. The man's side is autobiographical, of course. The woman's side? Well, they told me I hit it pretty close. I might have been a girl in a previous life.

The songs all had a point, and not necessarily a hopeless one at that. For example, the song, 'Walkin'', was to Willie,

> a happy song. This person has resolved himself to the fact that this is the way things are and this is what ought to be done about it. Rather than sitting somewhere in a beer joint listening to the jukebox and crying.

Daughter, Susie, said Willie wrote 'It's Not Supposed to Be That Way' for her while they were driving together to Colorado. Waylon concluded that one of the other songs (on the woman's side of the album), 'Pick Up the Tempo', was written "more or less about me and him and our struggles along the way with our music." 'I Still Can't Believe You're Gone', the first single from the album (it stopped at number fifty-one and left the charts after five weeks) was written "about Carlene, Paul English's wife, when she died."

The second single, the venerable 'Bloody Mary Morning', did very well, climbing to number seventeen and remaining chart-bound for thirteen weeks. It has become a crowd-pleaser, especially in Willie's raucous interpretation, one that causes him to "go through a pick every time I play it." 'Sister's Coming Home' went out as the third single but died at number ninety-three and faded after three weeks. It received a new life via Emmylou Harris' traditional folk-sounding rendition recorded in 1979 for her *Blue Kentucky Girl* album.

For this set, Wexler did all the producing with the recording taking place at Muscle Shoals, Alabama. According to Willie,

Jerry Wexler had a brainstorm that he wanted me to go to Muscle Shoals. Since he'd let me do the first one my way, I decided to let him do the second one his way, because he usually knows what he's talking about.

Though the setting was Muscle Shoals, birthplace of many of the greatest R & B records ever, some great country players were on hand, from Fred Carter, Jr. to Conway Twitty's pedal steel guitar player, John Hughey. Johnny Gimble, who played on Willie's first Atlantic album (and toured with him as part of his band from 1979 to 1981), returned to play more great fiddle. Eric Weissberg, famous for his part of the acclaimed 1973 single from the *Deliverance* soundtrack, 'Dueling Banjos', excelled at banjo on 'Down at the Corner Beer Joint'.

Willie and Columbia were very successful together
for almost twenty years.
(Photo from Columbia Records and Evelyn Shriver Public Relations)

"The Troublemaker":

The First Decade of Columbia Solo Projects

In 1975, Willie signed with Columbia Records, through his attorney Joel Katz, who got him "artistic control for that first album" so that he could do it "exactly the way I wanted to do it." Willie proceeded to record *Red Headed Stranger,* an album so different and controversial that it took Waylon Jennings' special personal intervention to convince the Columbia brass to release it. Actually, it was quite a feat that Willie got signed to Columbia at all.

Billy Sherrill, the producer of such top Columbia acts as Tammy Wynette and a notorious over-user of background strings and lush production techniques, opposed the signing. He also opposed the release of the first album. Willie received a contract offer only after CBS president, Bruce Lundvall, overruled Sherrill. Then, upon first hearing the first takes of the first album, Lundvall objected to its release, questioning whether it might "sound better with a couple of strings or background singers." Other CBS brass followed suit, saying things like, "it's a pretty good demo, but..." and asking, "when are you gonna finish it?"

Willie's manager, Neil Reshen, had felt, according to Waylon, that "he might have trouble selling them on the record." So, Reshen brought Jennings with him to New York to "help him explain it." Waylon's specific recollection of Lundvall's reaction was that he said,

> there's some pretty good things here, but this needs to go down to Nashville and let Billy Sherrill sweeten it. Put some strings on it.

Jennings predictably got "pissed" and called Lundvall "a tone-deaf, tin-eared sonofabitch who didn't know nothin'."

That stopped Lundvall who came back at Jennings with the question of "what am I missing?" Jennings tried to explain to him that the sparseness was what thousands and thousands of people came to hear from Willie. So, they sat down and listened again. Lundvall said he still didn't get it, but that he would "release this album just like it is." That was how Waylon helped get *Red Headed Stranger* released.

Willie explained to *Billboard Magazine's* Frederick Burger, that the executives at Columbia:

> thought it wasn't finished. They thought it was underproduced, too sparse, all those things. Even though they didn't like it, they had already paid me a bunch of money for it, so they had to release it under my contract. And since they had money in it, they had to promote it.

In hindsight, he observed that the album:

> sounded to some of the executive ears like it was a demo. They said, 'you can't do anything good in a day and a half, I don't care what you say.' But during that day and a half, I just had the feeling that it was coming together and things were happening right. I thought it was good music. I was not surprised that it did well.

Willie, who had a creative control clause in his contract, also helped get the album released by pledging to give up the clause if the album bombed. Willie knew he was going to succeed. He reflected that:

> when I did the album, I was at a time in my life when things were finally coming together for me. I had the contract I always wanted.

The album went multi-platinum, currently standing at over four million copies sold. As a result, according to Bruce Feiler, writing in his book *Dreaming Out Loud*, the outlaws "yanked Music Row into the Age of the Hippies" and gave Nashville "no choice but to hold its nose and accede to their every demand."

As Willie signed his own personal agreement to record for Columbia Records in 1975, he also signed a deal with the company to release all "future product of artists discovered by Nelson" on the Columbia label using "the Lone Star production logo." Columbia executive Lundvall announced that "first releases under the dual logo will be singles by Milton Carroll and Bill Callery." An ecstatic-sounding Lundvall added that:

Willie is not only a musical giant, but a triumphant forerunner in the contemporary music scene. The launching of the Lone Star label will bring an array of new and vital contemporary country artists to the market.

Reports following the announcement speculated that "some of Nelson's own future product might be released under the dual logo setup."

Though the initial two Nelson albums did appear with the Lone Star logo, the "setup" didn't last too long. By 1978, Lone Star Records signed a distribution deal with Mercury Records. That, in turn, lasted less than a year. After that, Willie did not go back to trying a label. His daughter, Susie, observed that her dad was "definitely lacking in the business department." Even Paul English (Willie's drummer) said he "never took any of his heed in business. I think that Willie's a lousy businessman." To his credit, though, Willie did have the insight to work with a business adviser "par excellent," Mark Rothbaum.

Willie's first decade as a Columbia solo artist was marked by some great and successful album projects, beginning, of course with the *Red Headed Stranger* set. From there Willie was never content to play it safe. With *The Sound in Your Mind*, he hinted at the things to come, a rendition of 'Amazing Grace' to precede his spiritual album, *The Troublemaker*, a Lefty Frizzell song to foreshadow his Lefty tribute album, an old standard to foreshadow *Stardust*, and a great collaborative effort with Steve Fromholz to anticipate his many duet and "guest" projects.

After *Stardust* both shocked and overwhelmed almost everyone, Willie chose to "honor" long-time friend Kris Kristofferson. In 1971, he had been among the first to recognize the unique beauty inherent in Kris' songs, recording, that year, both 'Help Me Make It Through the Night' and 'Sunday Mornin' Comin' Down'. Kris was not the typical country songwriter who came to Nashville knowing not much more than the rudiments of musical expression. His first Nashville mentor, Marijohn Wilkin, owner of Buckhorn Music (where Kris first became a staff writer), remembered that :

Kris had a fantastic mind in addition to his degrees. Everyone is aware more now of his college training, but there was a time when both of us had to keep it hidden. In order to get by here in Nashville, we used to have to hide our backgrounds and just be one of the "pickers." Of course, in time that began to change. Our studies are helping both of us now instead of being a hindrance.

After Kris, Willie paid homage to a set of old favorite Christmas tunes (along with two perfect originals). From there, he turned twice more to the "standards" format (rounding out the decade with *Without a Song*) and concocted a critically acclaimed "concept" album, *Tougher Than Leather*. Then, not surprisingly, he took ownership of an older Elvis song, 'Always on My Mind' while showing he could uniquely re-interpret some classic newer rock songs.

Many of the albums from this first decade sold extremely well, both pop and country, especially, *Stardust* and *Red Headed Stranger*. Overall during his tenure with Columbia, more than three dozen of his albums made *Billboard's* Pop Album Charts (albums on both Columbia and other labels), with many of them reaching a gold (minimum sales of five hundred thousand units) and often a platinum (over one million units) sales certification level. Columbia has acknowledged that, according to their records, he became country music's biggest album seller of all time.

Then too quickly Willie was gone from Columbia, for a myriad of reasons. He was also gone from the country radio airwaves, ostensibly because of his age, even though his concerts to this day have continued to sell out. Willie's reaction to the seeming end of a long run at the top was, "their loss."

Willie loved to "cut and putt!"
(Photo from Will van Overbeek)

The First Decade of Solos - Album Listings

Red Headed Stranger. Columbia Records PCT 33482. (1975).

Track Listing: Time of the Preacher, I Couldn't Believe It Was True, Time of the Preacher Theme, Medley: Blue Rock Montana/Red Headed Stranger, Blue Eyes Crying in the Rain, Red Headed Stranger, Time of the Preacher Theme, Just As I Am, Denver, O'er the Waves, Down Yonder, Can I Sleep in Your Arms, Remember Me (When the Candle Lights Are Gleaming), Hands on the Wheel, Bandera.

Recording Notes: For the first time, with this 1975 Columbia release, a Willie Nelson album hit the national sales chart. *Billboard* first charted it on July 26, 1975 and continued to report that it reached a peak position of number twenty-eight. The album spent a total of forty-three weeks on the *Billboard* best-selling album charts. Eventually it was certified as a multi-platinum seller. Willie had some personal observations on the album, first that:

> it may be the most country thing I've done in some time. Still, it's exactly what I wanted to do and I think it's commercial. Besides, it's the first time I've had full control of everything, the first time a label has taken a finished product and made it work. The title song is years old and I used to sing it to my kids. My wife suggested I build an album around it.

He said that since "the little kids liked it so much," he knew "the big kids would, too." The album proceeded from there. As he related to interviewer Stephen Holden, we were in Steamboat Springs when we started, and by the time we got to Denver, I had most of the album in my head. We already had 'Blue Eyes Crying in the Rain' and I'd written 'Time of the Preacher'. As soon as we reached Austin, I got out my guitar and a tape recorder and put down a rough version.

About the selections on the album he didn't write, he added that they were "old songs I always liked and wanted to go into the studio and record." Song-wise, 'Blue Eyes Crying in the Rain' (ironically not a Willie composition, but written by Fred Rose) was the breakthrough single, reaching number one on the country charts and peaking at number twenty-one on the national pop singles chart. It also garnered Willie his first Grammy award for Best Male Country Vocal Performance.

He remembered the song as "a very different sound for the music industry at the time. The recording was almost oversimplified - but I intended it to be." His guitar playing approach was also quite different. He explained, "I didn't use a pick on that one. Sometimes I use my thumb by itself, to get a softer sound."

The song, itself, after it was written by Rose in 1945, was recorded by several then-current artists, including Roy Acuff, Elton Britt, Ferlin Husky, and Gene Vincent. It did not hit the charts as a single, though, until Willie's recording thirty years later. After Willie resurrected the song, Ace Cannon took an instrumental version, in 1977, to the bottom reaches (number seventy-three) of the charts (and garnered a Grammy nomination).

'Remember Me' was the second single release and it charted at number two. Actually, the full song title was 'Remember Me (When the Candle Lights Are Gleaming)' and it was written in 1939 by Scott Wiseman (of Lulu Belle and Scotty fame). Scott, or Scotty, recalled that he wrote the song during a time when he and Lulu were working a year at radio station WLW in Cincinnati.

He recalled an old mug on a dresser back home when he was a kid. That cup, a memento of the Gay 90's and in some unknown way connected to the courtship of his parents, had embossed on it, in fancy gold letters, the caption, "Remember Me." Years later, Wiseman wrote that,

feeling a bit homesick and sentimental during the bustle of radio shows and road trips, I 'made up' the song while riding in the car to personal appearance jobs. The lyric was not intended to apply to any particular person.

The title song, 'Red Headed Stranger', was one Willie recalled singing to his kids as they grew up. During the kiddie segment of his radio show on KCNC (Ft. Worth) called *Western Express* he very often played 'Red Headed Stranger' (as done by Arthur "Guitar Boogie"

Smith), based on requests and call-in's from the parents. The song, itself, was published in 1953. The lyric writer was Edith Calisch Lindeman and the composer was Carlton Stutz.

Together they also wrote the standard, 'Little Things Mean a Lot'. To the writers then, as it would be later for Willie, 'Red Headed Stranger' was very visual, so much so that Calisch, the lyricist, wrote a teleplay on the song but never produced it. As Waylon saw the song as:

> a gothic Western mystery story that told of a dark rider who rode from town to town trailing his dead lover's horse behind him.

Another of the old songs, 'Down Yonder', by New York pop writer, L. Wolfe Gilbert, almost did not get the chance to become a classic. Gilbert wrote the song in 1920 "in fifteen minutes." He thought then that it would be a hit because singers like Al Jolson and Sophie Tucker liked it. So, he published it himself, which was a bad mistake, because, according to him, the public refused to buy it either on "records or sheet music." He mused that "since I published it myself, it put me out of the publishing business."

Gilbert thought the song was long forgotten. Then, a little more than thirty years later, in 1951, Ralph Peer, who had acquired many of Gilbert's copyrights, began getting sheet music orders for it. What Ralph discovered, in Gilbert's words, was that "a gal named Dell (actually Del) Wood," who demonstrated music for the Kress store in Nashville, "had made a recording of 'Down Yonder' for a nondescript record company called 'Tennessee'." Her recording went on to sell more than three quarters of a million copies.

It was eventually credited with more than a million sales. The Grand Ole Opry's *"Official Opry Picture-History Book"* (published in 1984) claimed it was "the first gold record cut in Nashville." *Country Song Round-up* has listed it as "the biggest-selling instrumental of all time." Because of the fame 'Down Yonder' brought to Wood (real name: Polly Adelaide Hendricks Hazelwood), in 1953 she became a featured performer on the Opry, the first Nashville native to be so honored.

Wood even appeared on the Ed Sullivan Show to showcase her hit recording. After her version, more than twenty-one other recordings of the song followed, including versions by Ethel Smith and Freddy Martin. According to Gilbert, the song stayed:

> on the Hit Parade for eighteen straight weeks, even surviving the Christmas Holidays and 'Rudolph the Red Nosed Reindeer'.

Overall, *Red Headed Stranger* was Nelson's third concept album. The concept was on several levels, the harshness of the Old West, the breakdown of a man when his true love leaves him, and a man's everchanging relationship with his God. Waylon Jennings saw in the album, "the biblical themes of penance and passion." So strong was the concept that it was turned into a major movie (same title as the album) starring Willie and Morgan Fairchild.

The interweaving of old country songs with original Nelson compositions ('O'er the Waves' and 'Bandera') was very successful even on a thematic level. One of the "old" songs, 'I Couldn't Believe It Was True', was co-written by and a big 1947 hit for Eddy Arnold. Its uplifting message fit seamlessly with the theme song (written by Willie), 'Time of the Preacher', and its redemptive meaning.

Willie explained that the line, "the time of the preacher, in the year of '01," referred to an era when ministers were "more admired and looked up to than now." He said that, overall, the song, itself, embodied "the ending of the negative, and the beginning of the positive." The tune became quite familiar even to British audiences as it was featured in a 1985 BBC drama series, *Edge of Darkness*.

Why was the album so important to Willie? He gave a clue to what was behind the album when he revealed "there's a possibility that when I put together the concept album, *The Red Headed Stranger*, I was drawing on experiences from past lives." Each song stood alone yet fit the story/song cycle of the album. Chet Flippo wrote that the effect was "as if the entire album had been written at one sitting."

A San Francisco journalist, Howie Klein, who often wrote for magazines targeted at a gay readership, decided that he could "put Willie's lyrics up against Barry White's as an exponent of the 'gay' experience any day of the week." Willie saw the album as:

> one of my very favorite albums, it came together easily and, while I was doing it, I could see that it would make a good western. I started thinking about it as a movie even before I finished cutting it.

The album went platinum and became one of the "least-cost" best-selling albums ever made. Willie wrote in his autobiography that *Red Headed Stranger* was cut "in three days for $20, 000 with Phil York as the engineer. I mean mixed and fixed and ready to release in three days." He explained that:

> we'd go in the studio about dark and stay until three or four in the morning. The first night we laid all the tracks. The second night we overdubbed and fixed the parts where I blew a line. The third day we mixed it.

As a side note, Willie's kids gave the name, Red Headed Stranger, to a baby deer they adopted in 1983 at their dad's Colorado mountain retreat.

The Sound in Your Mind. Columbia Records PCT 34092. (1976).

Track Listing: That Lucky Old Sun (Just Rolls Around Heaven All Day), If You've Got the Money I've Got the Time, A Penny for Your Thoughts, The Healing Hands of Time, Thanks Again, I'd Have to Be Crazy, Amazing Grace, The Sound in Your Mind, Medley: Funny How Time Slips Away/Crazy/Night Life.

Recording Notes: This album, originally released in 1976, featured Willie recording his first interpretation of a pop standard for Columbia. The song was 'That Lucky Old Sun', though according to the artist who first made it popular, Frankie Laine, it was more of a Western song. Laine wrote in his autobiography that he could hear in the song "a weariness that echoed 'Old Man River'. It wasn't Jazz at all. Instead, it had a Western flavor to it."

Nelson's own writing was also prominent from the title cut, 'The Sound in Your Mind' to the fifth cut, 'Thanks Again'. The medley of his greatest songs at the end was a fitting touch. Also spotlighted was Nelson's own 'Healing Hands of Time', which had been previously released (as a Pamper demo and as an RCA cut), but never in as uplifting a setting as this. It should have become a Nelson standard based on this interpretation alone. He eventually made the song the title cut of his 1994 Liberty Records debut album.

The image of climbing out of a low point and clinging to the "healing hands of time" was especially appropriate to the rebirth of his career on Columbia Records. According to daughter, Susie, the song was written about the breakup of Willie's first marriage. It was obviously a painful song, just as songwriting was often a painful process for Willie, which might help explain why long periods of time went by during which he did not write at all.

Willie once told his daughter that "in order to write songs, he had to dig back into himself and remember a lot of unpleasant things." He explained that,

> there have been times when I dreaded writing the next song, because I already knew what it was going to be about. And I hated to go back to that mentality and live those things again.

Even though songwriting can bring out such feelings, Willie has had to admit that, "I like myself better when I'm writing regularly."

The album's first single, 'I'd Have to Be Crazy', reached the number eleven spot on the country hit lists. The song's writer, Texan Steve Fromholz, also sang on the chorus. That came about when Fromholz said he "went to the studio and taught everybody the song."

Steve said that while he was showing "everybody" how to do the song, Willie said "when it gets to the chorus I want you to sing." Unfortunately, Willie's manager, Neil Reshen, "didn't like it," so an attempt was made to mix out Fromholz's voice. They couldn't get it out, according to Fromholz, so "that's the way it came out. That's a live taping. No overdubs."

The second single, 'If You've Got the Money I've Got the Time', written and first popularized by Lefty Frizzell in 1950, became a huge hit. It went to number one in July 1976, one year after Lefty's untimely death from a massive stroke, and continued Willie's penchant for bringing back great songs. The success of the Frizzell song set the stage for Willie's 1977 tribute to Lefty.

Easily the oldest song on the album and the one with the most varied history, 'Amazing Grace' began as a poem written in the late eighteenth century by converted English slave trader, John Newton. In 1835, Evangelist William "Singing Billy" Walker added music and placed it in his songbook, *Southern Harmony*. The book wound up as the hymnal of choice in churches throughout the South, both black and white, enabling many of the songs, especially 'Amazing Grace', to become immensely popular during the nineteenth and into the twentieth century.

According to the black Gospel singer and composer, Thomas Dorsey, black churches would often embellish the song with a "moaning" style (a vocal expression of the melody without singing the text, because, as Dorsey recalled, "everybody couldn't read back there"). Many older black churches also played it in a compound meter. According to Michael Harris, in his history of "Gospel Blues," the intent seemed to have been to establish the rhythmic beat as "a slow march cadence."

The most popular rendition of the song came in 1970 when folk singer Judy Collins took it to the number fifteen spot on the national pop singles charts (as tracked by *Billboard* magazine). Willie's sparsely recorded version accentuated the plaintive melody yet retained the more rhythmic feel developed in the older black churches. In a 1981 interview, he commented that:

> there's a lot of people who I'm sure experience religious experiences during 'Amazing Grace' and 'Will the Circle Be Unbroken' and 'Uncloudy Day'. They receive religious experiences without even knowing it.

Although *The Sound in Your Mind* (recorded at Autumn Sound Studios in Garland, Texas) was the chronological follow-up to *Red Headed Stranger*, it did not suffer by comparison. *Billboard* named it, in 1976, the best country album of the year. Columbia even repackaged the two albums as a "Specially Priced 2 for 1" set, CGT 38217.

The Troublemaker. Columbia Records PCT 34112. (1976).

Track Listing: Uncloudy Day, When the Roll Is Called Up Yonder, Whispering Hope, There Is a Fountain, Will the Circle Be Unbroken, The Troublemaker, In the Garden, Where the Soul Never Dies, Sweet Bye and Bye, Shall We Gather, Precious Memories.

Recording Notes: Another 1976 album found Nelson singing a set of religious songs. Most of them (except the title cut, 'The Troublemaker', written by Bruce Belland and David Somerville) were old-time gospel standards, showing another side of Willie's ability to reinvent familiar material. 'Uncloudy Day' became the successful single (number four on the national country singles chart) off the album.

Originally written by Reverend J. K. Alwood, the song was a 1925 hit for another Reverend (and evangelist), Homer Rodeheaver. Rodeheaver, born in Union Furnace, Ohio, in 1880, once served as music director for the Billy Sunday Evangelistic Campaigns. 'In the Garden', another of the traditional songs, was arranged by C. Austin Miles and published by Rodeheaver's Publishing Company (ASCAP), one of the oldest publishers of sacred music.

The Carter Family first recorded 'Will the Circle Be Unbroken' as 'Can the Circle Be Unbroken' late in their recording career, 1935. It was their last charting single, reaching number seventeen in August. Though A. P. Carter wrote the main body of the song, the words to the chorus were taken from a 1907 gospel song written by Ada Habershon and Charles H. Gabriel. Over the years, it has become one of those oft-covered songs, recorded by, among others, Joan Baez, Gregg Allman, The Nitty Gritty Dirt Band, and the Neville Brothers.

'Precious Memories' also seemed to have been around almost forever. It was actually written by J. B. F. Wright in 1925. Wright, Tennessee-born in 1877 and a devout member of the Church of God from an early age, claimed to have written songs "when words come spontaneously, flowing into place when I feel the divine urge." Like 'Precious Memories', the traditional song, 'Sweet Bye and Bye', (also known as 'In the Sweet By and By') did have known authors, being originally credited to S. F. Bennett and J. P. Webster.

Although the album was released in 1976, the cuts were all recorded in February 1973 at sessions done for Atlantic (recorded and re-mixed at Atlantic Recording Studios in New York) and the album, *Shotgun Willie*. In fact, this album was actually planned for release in

1973, but Atlantic vetoed the idea because they "did not feel that it was right for his first release." When Atlantic wound down its country operation, Willie was able to keep the cuts and eventually release them on Columbia.

The producer was listed as Atlantic's Arif Mardin. The final album mix was done by Mickey Raphael and Ben Tallent. Guests included Larry Gatlin (guitar/background vocals), Doug Sahm (fiddle/background vocals), Dee Moeller (background vocals), and Sammi Smith (background vocals). The rest of the band consisted of James Clayton Day on pedal steel guitar and dobro, sister Bobbie on piano, Paul (English) on drums, Jeff Gutcheon on organ (giving many of the songs a very "churchy" feel), and Dan "Bee" Spears on bass.

The album charted nationally, reaching number sixty on the *Billboard* album charts, which was amazing for a strictly gospel set. Though it only stayed on the charts for seven weeks, it was eventually certified "gold" in 1986 by the RIAA (Recording Industry Association of America). As Willie once said (to interviewer Jennie Ruggles), "all music is sacred. We carve music up into categories for commercial reasons, but really, that's just business." Nonetheless, the album has remained one of only two Nelson solo sets (the other being *Me and Paul*) that has not yet been rereleased by Columbia on compact disc.

To Lefty from Willie. Columbia Records CK 34695. (1977).

Track Listing: Mom and Dad's Waltz, Look What Thoughts Will Do, I Love You a Thousand Ways, Always Late (with Your Kisses), I Want to Be With You Always, She's Gone, Gone, Gone, A Little Unfair, I Never Go Around Mirrors, That's the Way Love Goes, Railroad Lady.

Recording Notes: Willie chose to tribute a major "honky-tonk" influence, Lefty Frizzell, with his only album release of 1977 (some two years after Lefty's 1975 fatal stroke). "Actually," he recalled,

> I had in mind to do that album earlier, but then when Lefty died, I held on to that idea for awhile. I didn't want anybody to think that I was tryin' to take advantage of the fact that he had died.

Willie had already achieved great success with the Frizzell tune, 'If You've Got the Money...', so it seemed logical to do a full set of Lefty's songs. Admittedly, since Lefty was no longer all over the country charts, it might have seemed a less than commercial idea to combine ten songs either written by or associated with Lefty on an album. Sure enough, CBS producer, Billy Sherrill was quoted as suggesting the album could have been called the "ten songs that killed

Lefty Frizzell." Willie remained serious about the concept, revealing that he:

> felt the same way about Lefty's music that you say some people feel about our music. In other words, it was a religious experience for me to hear Lefty Frizzell sing, 'If You've Got the Money, I've Got the Time'.

Back in 1950 Lefty hit the big time in country music with his first Columbia single, 'If You've Got the Money', sending it all the way to number one. The flip side of that first Frizzell single, 'I Love You a Thousand Ways' also went to number one. Twenty seven years later, in the summer of 1977, that same song went country top ten (number nine) for Willie.

Willie realized the executives at CBS (even though Lefty once recorded for Columbia Records) would probably not be ecstatic, admitting:

> we had a little difference of opinion on the album. They weren't sure what I was trying to do, and obviously, they weren't that familiar with Lefty Frizzell. But I felt that all ten of the songs on the album could be number one songs, because they all were at one time.

Willie revealed another conflict with the executives at his record company, that:

> we had a slight argument over the title of the album. I wanted to call it what it is - 'To Lefty from Willie' - with no pictures, no flair.

Largely because they thought the Frizzell name would have no appeal to a pop audience, CBS wanted to call the album, *Songs for a Friend*. Willie, obviously, won out.

Of the ten songs chosen for the album, the first five came from Lefty's initial two years on top of the business, 1950 and 1951. During those two years, he dominated the country charts with five number one songs. Willie covered three of them, 'Always Late (with Your Kisses)', 'I Want to Be With You Always' (both from 1951), and the album's only single, 'I Love You a Thousand Ways', which Lefty had "composed in the homey surroundings of the Chaves County jail."

Willie also chose to record Lefty's second single (from 1950), 'Look What Thoughts Will Do', as well as 'Mom and Dad's Waltz', which became a moderate country and pop hit for Patti Page in 1961, ten years after Lefty took it to the second spot on the country charts. There were three different stories about how Lefty wrote the overly sentimental

"Waltz" song. Lefty, who should have been the one to know, claimed he wrote it while "holed up and homesick" in a Dallas night club.

His sister, Betty, was insistent that Lefty wrote the song back in their home town of Big Spring. She said only their mother was mentioned in the song's original version. She quoted Lefty as saying, "I guess I ought to put the old man in there, too." That led to the changes that made it 'Mom and Dad's Waltz'. Buddy Griffin, a rhythm guitar player for Lefty, said Lefty wrote it in a hotel room in San Antonio after the release of his first Columbia single.

Lefty stayed with Columbia until the summer of 1972, when the label let his contract run out. He had not done much for them beyond 1964 when his smash hit, 'Saginaw, Michigan' had set both the pop and country world on fire. His last hit of any substance came in 1965 with Harlan Howard's song, 'She's Gone, Gone, Gone'. It peaked at number twelve, the last time Lefty would crack the country music top twenty. Willie covered both that song and Lefty's 1965 follow-up, 'A Little Unfair', co-written by Willie's friend, Hank Cochran.

The final three songs on the album came from Lefty's three years with ABC Records, 1972 through 1974. His recordings of 'I Never Go Around Mirrors' and 'That's the Way Love Goes' were issued by ABC in 1974 on the same single, the "A" side of which peaked at number twenty-five. Both songs came from a productive writing spurt by Lefty and co-writer, Whitey Shafer, during a 1972 recording session.

Shafer said that in order to write 'I Never Go Around Mirrors', they "had to go ahead and drink a few extra more beers 'fore we got into that one too deep." Country singer Ken Mellons told *Music City News* in 1997 that 'I Never Go Around Mirrors' was a song he wished he had written. He said it was "one of my favorite songs" and added that "if I could introduce anyone to traditional country music, this would be the song to do it with."

Willie concluded his tribute with another of Lefty's ABC singles, 'Railroad Lady', which was written by two of Willie's contemporaries, Jimmy Buffett and Jerry Jeff Walker. In 1972, Buffett was signed to ABC (then known as ABC Dunhill). His producer there was a gentleman named Don Gant, who just happened to be Lefty's producer.

That was the connection that got a song from the writer of 'The Great Filling Station Holdup' (Buffett) to the old grizzled "King of Honky-Tonk" (Frizzell). Walker had previously gained songwriting fame with his original 1968 composition, 'Mr. Bojangles', as immortalized by the Nitty Gritty Dirt Band. In spite of its being authored by two very talented writers, 'Railroad Lady' went no further than number fifty-two on the Billboard country charts in 1974, just a year before Lefty's untimely death.

Lefty's brother, David, recalled that, "after Lefty passed away, Willie Nelson did a tribute album to Lefty. I appreciated that." Unfortunately, tribute albums (paying homage to the great artists of another era), once a major "concept" for country artists, had become a dying art by the time of this album's release. Still, Willie was able to take the set to the number ninety-one position on the national pop album charts, a year before his *Stardust* album made him a mega-seller in both the pop and country arenas.

Stardust. Columbia Records CK 35305. (1978).

Track Listing: Stardust, Georgia on My Mind, Blue Skies, All of Me, Unchained Melody, September Song, On the Sunny Side of the Street, Moonlight in Vermont, Don't Get Around Much Anymore, Someone to Watch Over Me.

Recording Notes: 1978 found Nelson releasing his first set of standards, or in his words, "my favorite ten songs." At least, that's always been the "story." So, I asked Willie a detailed, complex question, saying in effect that a lot of thought and research must have gone into the selection of old, classic songs, especially since so many were from long forgotten Broadway shows. He just smiled at the idea and then said, "no, they really were just old favorites of mine."

The album was said to have been partially inspired by the death in 1977 of crooner Bing Crosby. The project, itself, actually began with Willie presenting the idea to Rick Blackburn, then head of CBS/Nashville. Blackburn recalled that Willie called him and said, "I got this idea to take ten of my all-time favorite songs, ... and do those; they're just great songs. What do you think?"

Blackburn admitted his reaction at the time was to tell Willie, "I think what you need to do is write some. To me it just doesn't make sense." He had the "audacity" to propose his own career direction for Willie, saying, "you're a great writer. Go write. Do a 'Luckenbach, Texas' or some damn thing. Stay with the mood that's hot."

Fortunately, Willie's new "mood" made sense to more than three million buyers of the eventual album. For some listeners, this was the first time they had heard such songs. Even Dolly Parton wrote, in her autobiography, that:

> the Broadway sophistication of Cole Porter and Gershwin had never been very big on Locust Ridge. About the only exposure I had ever had to this kind of music was from Willie Nelson's *Stardust* album...

Willie innately knew what the reaction to the album would be. He told Blackburn, during discussions about releasing the album, that:

> my audience right now is young, college age and mid-twenties. They'll think these are new songs, and at the same

time, we'll get the sentiment of the older audience who grew up with those songs but don't necessarily know me as an artist. We'll bridge that gap.

The songs featured Willie, his band, and Booker T. Jones on organ. Booker T. also produced the album. Willie explained that Booker was essential to the album, because "I needed someone like Booker to write and arrange. Once I got with him, it was easy to do the album." Their first meeting came about after Willie bought a Malibu condominium and discovered Booker was his upstairs neighbor.

The entire set of tracks was recorded in Emmylou Harris' Hollywood Hills home using Brian Ahern's Enactron Truck. Willie recalled that "it always felt relaxed when we were workin' around that place over there, it was a great studio." The sales of the album have been phenomenal, reaching a multi-platinum status and beyond, staying on the charts for more than two years.

By 1990, the album had logged more than five hundred and forty weeks on *Billboard's* country album chart. As an aftermath, the following year, 1979, Willie was awarded the highest honor the Country Music Association could bestow on him, the "Entertainer of the Year." The Academy of Country Music gave him the same award that same year.

According to daughter, Susie, Willie "surprised everybody by putting out the *Stardust* album." He didn't surprise her, though. She wrote that:

he said Aunt Bobbie would buy songbooks that had songs like 'Moonlight in Vermont' and 'Stardust' in them, and he would hang around and try to pick his guitar and sing along with her.

His explanation to her was "I thought they were some of the most beautiful songs I'd ever heard. I still do." Willie, himself, said that:

even when I was a teenager, I was singing 'Stardust' and 'Moonlight in Vermont' and all those songs on the *Stardust* album.

Willie explained his love of the classics to a *USA Today* writer,

All of us songwriters try to write songs of this same caliber, but it's difficult if not impossible to do. It's amazing how strong the lyrics and melodies are and how many millions of people are affected by them.

The cut, 'Georgia on My Mind', from 1930 and one of many great Hoagy Carmichael songs, was the first successful single, reaching number one on the country charts in March 1978. It also won Willie a Grammy for "Best Male Country Vocal Performance." Carmichael wrote in his autobiography that:

> what with 'Rockin' Chair', 'Stardust', 'Georgia on My Mind', 'Lazy River', and 'Lazy Bones', to name a few, there was a year or two when my music amounted to about 1.5 per cent of all music played on the air.

He said that "'Georgia on My Mind' was a song that rose in popularity slowly but definitely. It became a hit that musicians liked to play." Ray Charles recorded the definitive version of the song in 1960. He said,

> I wasn't dreaming of the state when I recorded the song, even though I was born there. It was just a beautiful, romantic melody, and I still sing it most nights when I'm performing.

Ray has always been a hard act to follow but somehow Willie's completely different take on the song became the second definitive rendition. On Saturday nights when Georgia's Stone Mountain gets all lit up by a laser light show, they play both versions of the song.

The follow-up single, 'Blue Skies' (the Irving Berlin standard), also went to number one, starting up the country charts in July 1978. It was first introduced to the public in December 1926, as part of a Broadway "flop," *Betsy*, starring Belle Baker. Fortunately, the song was revived by Al Jolson and featured in the 1927 movie widely credited as being the first talkie, *The Jazz Singer*. On March 7, 1986, Willie performed the song for a national PBS audience watching the show, *Irving Berlin's America*, part of the network's *Great Performances Series*.

In the Fall of 1978, the album's third single, 'All of Me', written in 1931 by Seymour Simons and Gerald Marks, reached number three. It had been a number one pop song hit for both Louis Armstrong and Paul Whiteman in 1932 after none other than Belle Baker introduced it in 1931. Later the same year it appeared in the film, *Careless Lady*.

Then Johnny Ray had a hit with it in 1952 after Frank Sinatra sang it in his 1951 movie, *Meet Danny Wilson*. In 1953, Frank recorded it again for his first ten inch long-playing (LP) album for Capitol Records. With versions by artists ranging from Billie Holiday to Ronnie Dove, it has been called "one of the most recorded songs of the century." Its association with Holiday got it featured in Berry Gordy's Diana Ross "bio-film" on Billie, *Lady Sings the Blues*.

1927 was also the genesis year for the title song, 'Stardust', according to its composer, Hoagy Carmichael, who told interviewer Henry Kane that:

> It's 1927. It's nighttime. I'm walking across the college campus. I'm whistling a tune. It's a nice tune. I like it. I love it. I keep whistling it - the opening bars of 'Stardust'.

Carmichael also recalled that the tune made three thousand dollars for him the first year, then five hundred, after which it was almost forgotten until "some of the wonderful Negro bands picked it up."

Mel Torme once described the song as "possibly the single best-known, best-loved popular song of all time." He said "there's something about that song that is so moving I can't resist it." Willie said he doesn't get tired of performing 'Stardust' time and again because it is such a "pretty tricky song to sing and play."

He appraised 'Moonlight in Vermont' as "one of the most beautiful songs I've ever heard." He concluded that "the words don't rhyme at all anywhere in there, but it's still poetic." It was written in 1944 and first recorded by Billy Butterfield and His Orchestra featuring vocals by Margaret Whiting. Whiting had another hit version in 1954.

Kurt Weill, otherwise known for 'Mack the Knife' and 'Lost in the Stars', composed 'September Song'. He originally placed it in his 1938 Broadway musical, *Knickerbocker Holiday*, the first American work he completed after fleeing, in 1933, the growing Nazi dominance of Germany. In structure, it was the kind of musically complex song Willie had grown into, building nine different chords into the first eight measures alone. They were not just simple chords, instead interweaving minor sixths and major sevenths around an A-flat and C-major.

Willie's version, which as a single went to number fifteen, was not the first a country audience had heard. In 1969, Roy Clark had taken the song to the bottom of the country singles top forty chart. On the pop side, the song had been strongly associated with Sinatra, who previously recorded it in 1946, 1961, and 1965.

The painting of starlight (the Plaedis constellation) on the album cover was done by Susanna Clark, a musical and artistic talent and wife of legendary Texas songwriter, Guy Clark. In retrospect, Willie called this "the most exciting album I've ever done." Blackburn characterized it as "a pivotal album for country music" and admitted that it "couldn't have been a better project if we had drawn it on the blackboard, which we didn't." He even acknowledged that "it opened up a whole new audience." Based on its success, CBS put the set out as a picture disc. In England the entire album was rereleased in 1984 on the Hallmark label as *Georgia on My Mind*, with the catalog number SHM 3159.

Willie Nelson Sings Kristofferson. Columbia Records PCT 36188. (1979).

Track Listing: Me and Bobby McGee, Help Me Make It Through the Night, The Pilgrim: Chapter 33, Why Me, For the Good Times, You Show Me Yours (And I'll Show You Mine), Loving Her Was Easier (Than Anything I'll Ever Do Again), Sunday Mornin' Comin' Down, Please Don't Tell Me How the Story Ends.

Recording Notes: Though he once told an audience to "jack off," Kris Kristofferson has been credited with everything from the "hippification" of Nashville to adding a level of literary artistry country songwriting had never experienced. His songs have been recorded by artists as diverse as Roger Miller, Jerry Lee Lewis, and Janis Joplin. He and Willie subsequently became close friends and over the years Willie has recorded many of Kris' finest songs.

For example, Willie cut 'Help Me Make It Through the Night' and 'Sunday Mornin' Comin' Down' when he was on RCA. In 1979, he turned his new recording of 'Help Me Make It Through the Night' (from this album) into a top five country singles charter (number four in early 1980). It was a song not just about love, but overtly about sex, or as Willie observed, "it was the first time anyone in Nashville had taken this direct approach to sex." Country singer Deana Carter recently described the song as being, to her, "almost like English literature put to music."

On the other hand, Dottie West refused to even consider recording the song because it sounded too risque to her. Then-unknown Sammi Smith did the first hit version in 1971 for the tiny Mega label. Her opinion of the song was that it was "a very tender, moving song." She said she saw nothing "scandalous" about it nor did she "see anything distasteful" in the words.

The long-standing friendship between Willie and Kris extended beyond recording and songwriting to movies. In *Songwriter*, they starred as two "close-to-life" musician buddies. In *A Pair of Aces* and *Another Pair of Aces*, they starred as buddies again who walked too close to both sides of the law. Kris and Willie also formed one-half of the "Highwaymen" along with Waylon and Cash. Willie has always expressed great admiration for Kris, telling one interviewer that "Kris made his own rules, did it his own way. That's why I admire and respect him."

The songs on this set were all classic Kris, like 'Loving Her Was Easier', a big hit for Kris and an even bigger one - a top two smash - for Tompall and the Glaser Brothers. Willie loved the song, saying it was "one of those beautifully sad songs that bowl me over." There was also 'For the Good Times', which Ray Price turned into a pop and country sensation (selling more than eleven million copies), much as he had done long before for Willie's 'Night Life'.

Before it became a country standard, there was a time, as Kris recalled, when:

> they wouldn't play 'For the Good Times' because it said 'hold your warm and tender body next to mine...' They thought it was dirty, but now every song you hear has something about a body or touching skin in it.

It was his "sexual candor" that changed country songwriting forever.

Janis Joplin's swan song, her only as well as posthumous number one single, 'Me and Bobby McGee', was one that Kris said he began writing while "driving between Morgan City and New Orleans." He added that it "probably turned over more audience to me than any song I ever had." 'The Pilgrim: Chapter 33' was once dedicated, by Kris, to Johnny Cash and Ramblin' Jack Elliott and, before he was done dedicating, about "half of Nashville."

Willie did all the production work on the album this time. Jerry Reed came in as a musical guest, as did guitarist Albert Lee and Booker T. Jones, who previously produced the *Stardust* album. For marketing purposes, in Australia, the album was released for a time as part of a two record set, paired - one cover - with the *Red Headed Stranger* LP. Willie's biggest live event the same year this album was released was his picnic (4th of July) in Briarcliff, Texas, where he dueted with the "troubadour," Ernest Tubb.

Pretty Paper. Columbia Records PCT/CK 36189. (1979).

Track Listing: Pretty Paper, White Christmas, Winter Wonderland, Rudolph the Red-Nosed Reindeer, Jingle Bells, Here Comes Santa Claus, Blue Christmas, Santa Claus Is Coming to Town, Frosty the Snowman, Silent Night, Holy Night, O Little Town of Bethlehem, Christmas Blues.

Recording Notes/Other Releases: Roy Orbison had a major Christmas hit for Monument Records with 'Pretty Paper', recording it in the Fall of 1963 in London. Willie pitched the song to Roy (in Roy's hotel room) shortly before signing with Monument in 1964, making it perhaps the most successful thing he did "for" that label. After making the song his first recording at RCA, Willie subsequently recorded his tune as the title cut for this perennial Christmas album first released in 1979. Randy Travis recorded a brilliant cover of the song for his holiday set, *An Old Time Christmas*. Glen Campbell also did a version that he included on his best-selling Capitol album, *That Christmas Feeling*.

Willie actually wrote the song about a man who had no legs and got around via a board on top of roller skates. For several years off and on, Willie watched this man sell a variety of items, such as wrapping paper, on the same Ft. Worth street corner. Roy's version went to number fifteen on the American pop singles chart. It also became the only Nelson composition to go top ten in Great Britain, thanks to Orbison's recording.

With both artists on the same label, there was some possibility of writing collaborations between the two. That never happened though the flip side of Roy's 'Pretty Paper' single did feature 'Summersong', a song which, according to Roy's biographer, Alan Clayson, "the pair cobbled together." It was described as boasting "an arresting instrumental preamble reminiscent of Stravinsky."

'Pretty Paper' was one of two Willie originals on this set, the other being the final track, 'Christmas Blues', co-written with Booker T. Jones. Booker T. produced and arranged the set, playing keyboards, as well. In between the two Nelson originals were standard Christmas songs done in the imitable Nelson style. Irving Berlin's 'White Christmas' and Felix Bernard's 1934 classic, 'Winter Wonderland', were featured along with old favorites, 'Jingle Bells' and 'Rudolph the Red-Nosed Reindeer'.

'Rudolph' was first written by an ad copyist for Montgomery Ward catalogs. Johnny Marks, also known as the writer of 'Rockin' Around the Christmas Tree', put on the finishing touches that turned it into one of Gene Autry's most popular numbers, one of his three famous Christmas recordings (all included on this album), along with 'Frosty the Snowman' and Autry's own composition, 'Here Comes Santa Claus'.

Of the three songs, Gene hit first with his own composition, 'Here Comes Santa Claus', in 1947. He said he got the idea for the song when he was Grand Marshall of the Santa Claus Parade in Hollywood. While riding his horse in the parade, he kept hearing the kids say, "here come's Santa Claus!" because Santa's sleigh "was right behind me." With the idea in mind he quickly wrote the song (giving half the credit to his publisher), recorded it, and "sold over a million copies" that first year.

He began looking for a successor to that song to market during a future Christmas season and received an acetate of 'Rudolph, the Red-Nosed Reindeer' from Johnny Marks. Autry remembered that:

> when I first heard it, I didn't think too much of it, but my wife said she liked the song because Rudolph reminded her of the story of the 'Ugly Duckling'.

Gene's wife said she liked the line "where they say they wouldn't let poor Rudolph join in any reindeer games." So, Gene said that since he didn't have anything better, he recorded it, even though he "didn't think it was going to be that big a number." According to Joel Whitburn (of Record Research Inc.), Gene's recording of 'Rudolph' sold over eight million copies, making it "second in the pre-1955 era only to 'White Christmas'."

Berlin's 'White Christmas' has been recorded so often that another version, even by so unique a stylist as Willie, would seem superfluous. Considering that Elvis, Bing Crosby, Mahalia Jackson, Placido Domingo, Otis Redding, and the Beach Boys, among many others have recorded the song, how could there be another interpretation? Berlin said of his Academy Award winner that "not only is this the best song I ever wrote, it's the best song anybody ever wrote." Yet Willie's version stood out very well among the others.

Another cut, 'Santa Claus Is Coming to Town', was actually, according to one of its authors, J. Fred Coots, " written in the middle of a hot July in 1934." It ended up being placed with Eddie Cantor who sang it on his Thanksgiving radio show. According to Coots, "from that one radio plug, 400,000 copies of sheet music were sold between November 27th and December 23rd." And that, of course, marked the beginning of another Christmas standard.

The song, 'Silent Night' (turned into a duet with Connie Smith), was used on a 1984 compilation for Felicity, entitled, *The Austin Christmas Collection*, FR-006 (3rd edition), a "various artists" collection. The same song was used in 1986 on an Epic Records "various artists" compilation, *The Nashville Christmas Album*, FE-40418. In 1990, Willie's previously unreleased version of 'Away in the Manger' was used on an Epic Records "various artists" collection entitled *Voices of the Season Acapella*, EK46074.

That same song was also included on "a very special benefit album," first released in 1993, *Steve Vaus Presents the Stars Come Out for Christmas: Volume V* (Steve Vaus Productions). One of Willie's Christmas cuts also went out in 1991 as part of the charity album, *The Christmas Album: A Gift of Hope*, the proceeds from which went to the San Diego-based Children's Hospital Foundation. The album, produced by Michael Lloyd, featured cuts by Frank Sinatra (accompanied by Frank, Jr. on piano, according to sister, Nancy), Reba McEntire, Kenny Loggins, and a number of other stars.

Willie recorded a number of other Christmas songs during his tenure with Columbia that also went unreleased for quite awhile, until 1994, to be exact, when he and old friend Larry Butler produced and marketed a budget Yuletide set entitled, *Christmas with Willie Nelson*. The collection consisted of ten tracks and came out on the Regency label (Regency Music, Inc. V20037) of Nashville. Willie and Bobbie and five band members played on the tracks with keyboards overdubbed by Butler.

Initial recording was done at the Pedernales Studio. Final recording, engineering, overdubbing, and mastering was done either at Arlyn Studios, The Music Room (in Nashville), or Georgetown Masters. The previously mentioned song, 'Away in the Manger', led off the set, followed by such Christmas standards as 'Deck the Halls', 'It Came Upon the Midnight Clear', 'Joy to the World', 'The First Noel', 'O Little Town of Bethlehem', 'O Come All Ye Faithful', 'We Wish You a Merry Christmas', and 'Silent Night'. Yet another, more-stripped-down version of 'Pretty Paper' closed out the collection.

That newest version of 'Pretty Paper' became the fifth different recording Willie had done of the song. The first was for RCA in 1964. The second was a very different one sung by Willie in German, which along with another track, 'Whiskey Walzer' (also sung in German), could be found on the Bear Family Records 1980 German compilation, *Nashville Stars in Deutschland*, BFX-15040. The third was the standard one Columbia perennially released beginning in 1979. The fourth appeared in 1995 on a Capitol Records anthology, *Superstars of Christmas*, CDP 7243 8 35347 2. It was recorded at Revolution Sound in Nashville and featured production by band member, Bee Spears, the bass player. Since the Regency version, Willie has done two more, one for a 1997 Christmas album he released on small independent label and one for Asleep at the Wheel's 1997 Christmas set, *Merry Texas Christmas Y'all*.

In 1995, Sony Special Products rereleased five cuts from the *Pretty Paper* album along with five Merle Haggard cuts as *Pancho, Lefty and Rudolph*, CT 67296. It was an obvious play on the Rudolph song and the duo's hit single, 'Pancho and Lefty' (which was not included on the compilation). Willie's five cuts were 'Jingle Bells', 'Frosty the Snowman', 'Pretty Paper', 'Silent Night, 'Holy Night', and 'White Christmas'. Like the *Pretty Paper* album, *Pancho, Lefty and Rudolph* has been released each Christmas since then.

Somewhere Over the Rainbow. Columbia Records PCT 36883. (1981).

Track Listing: Mona Lisa, Exactly Like You, Who's Sorry Now?, I'm Confessin' (That I Love You), Won't You Ride in My Little Red Wagon, Over the Rainbow, In My Mother's Eyes, I'm Gonna Sit Right Down and Write Myself a Letter, It Wouldn't Be the Same (Without You), Twinkle, Twinkle Little Star.

Recording Notes: 1981 found Willie releasing a follow-up set of standards. From the traditional children's song, 'Twinkle, Twinkle Little Star' to the Judy Garland calling card, 'Over the Rainbow', he reinterpreted them all with unexpected and excellent results. The first single off the album was the Nat Cole classic, 'Mona Lisa', which peaked at number eleven on the country singles chart.

The song, written by the prolific partners Jay Livingston and Ray Evans, had first appeared in fragments in the picture, *Captain Carey of the U. S. A.* Even though the movie did not create much of a box office splash when it came out in 1949, the songwriters were able to get Cole to record their composition. To most everyone's surprise at the time, the song sold over three million copies, a major impact back in 1950. It also won an Academy Award (Oscar). As Livingston later related,

> 'Mona Lisa' was not even going to be released. Nat King Cole said, 'who wants this? Nobody will buy this.' We went over to see Nat even though he didn't like songwriters to play for him. He was a very gentle man and didn't want to have to say no.

That personal intervention resulted in a classic song.

Lyricist E. Y. "Yip" Harburg spoke of the song he and Harold Arlen wrote in 1938 for Garland to sing in *The Wizard of Oz*. He felt that:

> Harold struck a brave and inspired symphonic theme. It is not a little child's nursery song. It's a great big theme that you could easily build a symphony around.

The song at first bothered Harburg quite a bit "because it was so powerful." So, he added, "we brought it down with those colorful and childlike words."

Just before the movie was to be released, studio heads wanted to cut the song from the score because they thought "it slowed down the action of the first part of the picture too much." Fortunately it stayed in and became, in Judy Garland's words, "symbolic of everybody's dream and wish." The song went on to win the Academy Award for Best Song and stayed at number one on *Your Hit Parade* for seven weeks.

Of the other classic pieces, the team of Dorothy Fields and Jimmy McHugh turned out 'Exactly Like You' toward the end of their partnership, in 1930. It went into and became a big hit for the Broadway show, *The International Revue*. Likewise, the talented duo of Harry Ruby and Bert Kalmar wrote 'Who's Sorry Now' for the Broadway scene of the early 1920's (1923, to be exact).

In 1958, Connie Francis' version of the song became her first top ten pop hit single. She said her father insisted on her recording it even though she thought it was a "lousy old song." Marie Osmond, who sounded somewhere between Connie and Anita Bryant, took the song to the number twenty-nine spot on the country charts in 1975, only fifty-two years after it was first released on record (1923) by Isham Jones and his Orchestra (who turned it into a number three pop hit that year).

On some of the cuts, Nelson shared the vocalizing with Freddy Powers, who had backed him on guitar on other albums. One of their duets was 'I'm Gonna Sit Right Down and Write Myself a Letter', the album's second single, which peaked at number twenty-six on the country singles chart. The song was written in 1935 (by Joe Young and

Fred Ahlert) and first popularized by Fats Waller (the same year). It became a major hit all over again in 1957 for vocalist Billy Williams.

The fact that neither of the album's two singles went top ten, was a drop-off for Willie, who had come off two number one's from the *Honeysuckle Rose* soundtrack. His observation to interviewer Stephen Holden of this album was that:

> the style ... is a little different. For one thing there are no drums, only two rhythm guitars, a bass, a fiddle, and a lead guitar. I tried to use pickers who knew Django Reinhardt's type of music. I've always been a big fan of his. He probably influenced my playing more than anybody.

He obviously succeeded because one review called this album Willie's tribute to Django. Emulating Reinhardt was the main reason he has almost exclusively played a Martin N-20 classical guitar (since 1969), something unheard of in the country music world. He has admitted he began playing such a guitar in order "to find that tone Django was getting."

The guitar, "Trigger" by name, came to Willie thanks to Shot Jackson at Sho-Bud Guitars in Nashville. Willie said he:

> quickly got addicted to it. I love the gut-string sound and I love the fact I can play it with or without an amplifier - it sounds just as good on stage with my band as when I'm sitting on my bus or at home writing songs.

He added,

> I've written a lot of songs on that guitar - basically everything in the last 25 or so years - and I've played a lot of songs on it, so naturally we've bonded quite a bit.

Over the years, "Trigger" (named after Roy Rogers' famous horse) has gotten almost as "shaggy" as Willie, because although "you aren't supposed to use picks on classical guitars," he did it anyway. Willie explained that:

> the guitar has no pickguard to protect its top, so over the years, too many 'Whiskey River's' or 'On the Road Again's' have put a big hole under the soundhole.

That "hole" in his guitar even prompted a question from talk show host Rosie O'Donnell when Willie appeared on her show. His simple reply to her query was that:

this is a classical guitar, and you're not supposed to use a pick because it doesn't have a pick guard. And that's what happens when you use a pick without a pick guard.

To her follow-up question asking if the hole affected the sound, Willie replied, "Yeah, it makes it sound better." He has reinforced the bracing from the inside every year to keep the instrument from collapsing. Otherwise, the hole:

gets bigger every year, but it doesn't hurt the sound - if anything it enhances it - so I've never done anything to close the hole.

It has become as much a trademark as Willie's hair and bandanas. For almost thirty years it has been the basis of his "sound".

The album itself was recorded and mixed at Gilley's Studio in Pasadena, Texas. With another batch of other people's songs, Willie the songwriter faced once again the question of whether his muse had run dry. He answered like always, that he does "go for a long time without writing."

During one interview when the writing subject came up, Willie revealed that he had written a song called, 'I Guess I Can't Write Anymore'. 1981 was also the year that Willie suffered a collapsed lung - in Hawaii - where he was treated with the ancient Kahunas medicine, prayer, and herbal healing approach. The resulting layoff resulted in a number of new songs that became part of the *Tougher Than Leather* album. Willie also held his Fourth of July picnic at Caesar's Palace in Las Vegas.

Always on My Mind. Columbia Records FCT 37951. (1982).

Track Listing: Do Right Woman, Do Right Man, Always on My Mind, A Whiter Shade of Pale, Let It Be Me, Staring Each Other Down, Bridge Over Troubled Water, Old Fords and a Natural Stone, Permanently Lonely, Last Thing I Needed First Thing This Morning, The Party's Over.

Recording Notes: 'Always on My Mind' had been a hit before, for Elvis Presley, a hard act to follow. In 1982, Willie did just that, making the song his own and a best-seller as well (it jumped to number one country and number five pop, ending a mild sales slump for him). It became the title tune for this eclectic album, the highest charting of his career, number two on the national album charts.

Ed Morris, of *Billboard* magazine clearly understood some of the reasons why the album was such a big seller. He saw that Willie:

was huge here and abroad. He began making movies. Willie was everywhere, on all the magazine covers, on The Tonight Show. It's not surprising *Always in My Mind* got the benefit of this media blitz.

When Willie first heard the song, 'Always on My Mind', he said he didn't know Elvis Presley had recorded it (the hit version belonged to Elvis, but Brenda Lee had released it as a single a year before Elvis' version came out). All Willie knew was the song "bowled me over the moment I first heard it, which is one way I pick songs to record." The song was initially brought to Merle Haggard's attention (one of the writers, Johnny Christopher, played it for him during the *Pancho and Lefty* sessions), but he showed no interest.

When Merle didn't pick up on it, Willie, who had listened to it when it was presented to Merle, didn't hesitate to grab it, saying, "that's for me." "I loved the song," Willie later said, "but Merle didn't quite hear it." It was Willie's wife of the time, Connie, and his daughters, who persuaded him to make the song the album title cut as well as the first single from it.

On the strength of the success of both the album and single, *Billboard's* 1982 Year in Music survey listed Willie as the Top Country Artist with both the Top Country Album and Top Country Single. The song and recording won both the single of the year and song of the year awards from the Country Music Association. Willie also won the Academy of Country Music's Entertainer of the Year award for 1982. In 1990, *Billboard* named 'Always on My Mind' the country music single of the decade. The album itself also won album of the year. Willie won another Grammy for Best Male Country Vocal Performance.

Both 'Let It Be Me' and 'Last Thing I Needed First Thing This Morning' followed 'Always on My Mind' as successfully charting singles, each one reaching the number two slot on the country charts in 1982. 'Let It Be Me' was a French popular song by Gilbert Becaud and Pierre Delanoe, with English lyrics added by Mann Curtis. Legendary Texas songwriter Gary P. Nunn penned 'The Last Thing I Needed First Thing This Morning'.

'Permanently Lonely' was a Willie original (he first recorded it for RCA) as was the album closer, 'The Party's Over'. By the time 'The Party's Over' was recorded for this set, it was definitely a Nelson standard, having been first recorded by Willie for RCA and made famous via Don Meredith's use of it on Monday Night football. The Songwriter's Hall of Fame honored Willie's writing by giving him a Lifetime Achievement award the following year, 1983.

Producer Chips Moman contributed three songs to the album. The first was his classic 'Do Right Woman, Do Right Man' (penned with Dan Penn) which Aretha Franklin had taken top forty on the R & B singles chart in 1967. The other two songs were co-written with keyboardist Bobby Emmons, 'Old Fords and a Natural Stone' and 'Staring Each Other Down'.

Two pop/rock million sellers, Procol Harum's 'Whiter Shade of Pale' and Paul Simon's anthem, 'Bridge Over Troubled Water', rounded out the album. Waylon did guest vocals "courtesy of RCA Records" on 'Whiter Shade of Pale'. Willie said they recorded it:

> because we loved the melody as soon as we heard it. I didn't know what the lyrics meant. The melody was infectious and the lyrics were weird and far out enough that I thought they were bound to be good. I couldn't wait for someone to ask me what the lyrics meant. Each time somebody did, I would make up a different story. I had no idea when we recorded the song that it was already a rock classic by Procol Harum.

Tougher Than Leather. Columbia Records PCT 38248. (1983).

Track Listing: My Love for the Rose, Changing Skies, Tougher Than Leather, Little Old Fashioned Karma, Somewhere in Texas (Part 1), Beer Barrel Polka, Summer of Roses, Somewhere in Texas (Part 2), My Love for the Rose, The Convict and the Rose, Changing Skies, I Am the Forest, Nobody Slides, My Friend.

Recording Notes: This was a 1983 concept album similar to *Red Headed Stranger*. The story line centered around Rose and recurring encounters with a convict. Willie told Alanna Nash the album was:

> about a gunfighter who killed this young man, and then got away free. And then he died, and then he was reborn again later as a modern-day urban cowboy, and bad karma caught up with him.

The theme of reincarnation was the strong undertone of this album. Willie told interviewer, Jonathon Kay, that the album "deals with reincarnation." He said he wrote most of the songs while recuperating from a collapsed lung he suffered in Hawaii in 1981. Each of the songs dealt with the strong feelings he was having, "that people come back and do it over again if they screw it up the first time".

The key song, 'The Convict and the Rose', was written in the twenties by Ballard MacDonald. His wife (also on the writing credit) disclosed that her husband wrote the song "tongue-in-cheek." In fact, she continued, he "never expected it to be the hit it was." He even seemed, to her, to be a little ashamed of the song because it was so "syrupy." When he told her the title she recalled laughing until she "read the lyrics for the first time." Interestingly, on the compact disc release, the song was credited to "Duncan-Wills."

The album's lead single, 'Little Old Fashioned Karma', stopped at number ten. The concepts of "karma" and reincarnation were alien to the fundamental beliefs of much of Willie's conservative country audience. However, as he told an interviewer, karma simply meant "a little old-fashioned justice going around." To him, it fit the "Christian belief of doing unto others as you would have them do unto you."

'Beer Barrel Polka', the old Polish-American standard (actually a Czechoslovakian song, 'Skoda Lasky'), was arranged by sister Bobbie Nelson. One of the Willie originals, 'Summer of Roses' dated back to his first concept album, for RCA, *Yesterday's Wine*. For all of his great writing, Willie received, in 1983, the "Lifetime Achievement" award from the National Academy of Popular Music, the first country artist to be so honored. His Fourth of July picnic was staged over three days and several locations, including Syracuse, New York, and Atlanta.

Without a Song. Columbia Records PCT 39110. (1983).

Track Listing: Without a Song, Once in a While, Autumn Leaves, I Can't Begin to Tell You, Harbor Lights, Golden Earrings, You'll Never Know, To Each His Own, As Time Goes By (guest vocal by Julio Iglesias), A Dreamer's Holiday.

Recording Notes: This 1983 collection of ten standard pop interpretations again found Willie's singing framed by sparse yet beautiful arrangements and instrumentation. The title tune, 'Without a Song', written by Vincent Youmans, Billy Rose, and Edward Eliscu (from the musical *Great Day*), had been a huge hit for Paul Whiteman ("the King of Jazz") in 1930. It was one of Youman's signature songs, which he built around a continuing repetition of three or four notes. Willie took his version to number eleven on the country charts, not a high place for him at the time but certainly a high place for an old pop standard.

Though written in 1931, the most memorable rendition of 'As Time Goes By' came in 1942 when Dooley Wilson sang it in the movie, *Casablanca*. Jimmy Monaco and Mack Gordon's 'I Can't Begin to Tell You' was one of their biggest hits, coming from the 1945 movie, *The Dolly Sisters*. A major reason for its popularity was its immediate familiarity to its original audiences, though most of them probably never knew that the song was based on a 1906 hit, 'When Love Is Young in Springtime', written by Rida Johnson Young and Melville Ellis. As Roger Lax and Frederick Smith, authors of *The Great Song Thesaurus*, observed, it was one of many "elegant plagiarisms."

Gordon was responsible for the lyrics to 'You'll Never Know', this time co-written with composer Harry Warren. It turned out to be "no ordinary song," even winning an Oscar for "best song of the year (1943)." According to Warren's biographer, Tony Thomas, "it was instantly popular and within a few months became almost an anthem for the Second World War."

'Autumn Leaves' began its musical life in 1947 as a French song. It soon gained English lyrics by Johnny Mercer though it also became a big instrumental hit for the pianist Roger Williams. 'Harbor Lights' was a 1960 top ten hit for the Platters. Ten years prior to that, it was a top ten hit for five artists in 1950, not the least of which was Bing Crosby. Before that, the song was a top ten hit for two artists in 1937.

'A Dreamer's Holiday' and 'Once in a While' each had strong chart histories, as did 'To Each His Own'. However, the team of Jay Livingston and Ray Evans, who authored 'To Each His Own', said that when it first came out, it was "laughed at." The reaction was, "who wants a song with that title?" It was written for a Paramount picture called, ironically, *To Each His Own*. The man writing the score for the movie, Victor Young, did not want to write the theme song because he wasn't going "to write a song with a dumb title."

After Livingston and Evans wrote the song anyway and "an unknown named Eddie Howard made a record of it that was a hit." The big surprise came when:

> one week in August of 1947, out of the Top Ten records in *Billboard*, five of them were versions of 'To Each His Own'. The first time this ever happened and, so far, the last.

The song sold over a million copies of sheet music alone. Ray Evans explained that:

> this was right after the war. People were coming from overseas and it was sentimental; it caught on a chord. It's become part of our language now: 'To each his own.' And that's because of the song.

Livingston and Evans were responsible for the lyrics of 'Golden Earrings', a late forties hit for both Dinah Shore and Peggy Lee. This time the music was done by Victor Young, the man who did not want to write 'To Each His Own'. It was the theme song for the Ray Milland, Marlene Dietrich film of the same name, *Golden Earrings*.

Once again for this batch of standards, Booker T. Jones did the producing as well as the arranging. The strings were recorded in London using members of the London Symphony Orchestra while the horns were recorded in Hollywood. The rest of the album, utilizing Willie's band, was recorded at the Pedernales Studio, where, according to blues singer Marcia Ball, the piano "is legendary among piano players."

"The Promiseland":

The Second Decade of Solo Projects

Willie's second decade as a Columbia solo artist began with his version of Steve Goodman's classic, 'City of New Orleans'. One of many highlights for the decade was his album, *Me and Paul*, for which he rerecorded many of his earlier compositions. Two further milestones came with a too-often overlooked set of "neglected" standards, *What a Wonderful World*, and Willie's "collaborative" set, *Across the Borderline*. From a 1986 perspective, Willie reflected that Columbia "has let me do what I wanted to do ever since I've been with them."

Willie's own writing during this time was excellent, though he did not record very many new originals. The ones he did write, such as 'I'm Not Trying to Forget You', were outstanding compositions. Often, as on the *Me and Paul* album, a Willie song came from his past catalog because, as he more than once explained, performing and traveling cut into his writing time.

Saleswise, Willie started the decade off with a bang, charting the first single, 'City of New Orleans', at number one. From there, even though it took a while, a sales decline set in, to where Columbia not only refused to release several of his album projects, they made no real effort to re-sign him in 1993, the same year he was inducted into the Country Music Hall of Fame. A 1989 single, 'Nothing I Can Do About It Now', was Willie's last at number one.

That single reflected the unique philosophy that helped Willie get through this turbulent decade (as well as much of his demanding career). He explained that "once you replace negative thoughts with positive ones, you'll start having positive results." Though he "never gave up on country music because I knew what I was doing was not that

165

bad," he only began to experience the success that turned his life around "when I started counting my blessings."

Critically, the solo albums of the second decade (concluded in 1993), could be viewed as a diverse set of efforts. Willie recorded some refreshing (especially for country music) new originals, rerecorded many of his old favorite compositions, and brought to life a whole passel of long-forgotten works through his own unique interpretations of them. In retrospect, Willie's overall tenure on Columbia was marked by great, innovative solo work along with an entire gamut of far-reaching collaboration and cooperative efforts.

Willie, the writer and interpreter-without-peer, also discovered the works of some great songwriters. One was Beth Nielsen Chapman, who by 1998 had become extremely well-known world-wide after Elton John chose her piece, 'Sand and Water' to play during his concerts "in memory of Princess Diana and Gianni Versace." In 1989, Willie had a number one single with her song, 'Nothing I Can Do About It Now'. It was a song way out of the ordinary both in its rendition (by Willie) and its creation (by Beth). Chapman told interviewer Kerry Dexter (for *Dirty Linen*) that:

> I was tortured about that song because, first of all, I had a time period it was due by. He was cutting, and I had to get a song to him by a certain time. Then the worst thing that could have happened, happened: I got the title first. I had the title, I knew this was the title, and I had no idea how to write it. It was like writing backwards. I always write stuff first and say, 'Oh here's this thing, let me name it.' I spent so many hours on that song, and I ended up being very happy with the song and felt like it was very well written... but it almost killed me.

Willie knew that whole creative process only too well.

Don Cusic wrote an expansive analysis of Willie in 1993 (at age sixty), that he had "turned from writing songs of personal trial to crafting lyrics that embrace the broader American experience." Willie, himself, said in an interview that "pure hopelessness is not something I can write about a lot anymore." What Willie did along the way was to discover and rediscover America in song, from its rich folk and ethnic traditions to its well-crafted Tin Pan Alley creations, culminating in the universal themes of Bob Dylan and "a little old fashioned karma coming down."

The Second Decade of Solos - Album Listings

City of New Orleans. Columbia Records FCT 39145. (1984).

Track Listing: City of New Orleans, Just Out of Reach, Good Time Charlie's Got the Blues, Why Are You Pickin' on Me, She's Out of My Life, Cry, Please Come to Boston, It Turns Me Inside Out, Wind Beneath My Wings, Until It's Time for You to Go.

Recording Notes: This 1984 album was highlighted by a masterful interpretation of the Steve Goodman classic train song, 'City of New Orleans', previously a top twenty pop hit for Arlo Guthrie in 1972. Sammi Smith covered it again in 1973 (when it peaked for her at number forty-four on the country singles chart). Though it took Willie back to the number one spot on the country singles charts for the first time since early 1982, one observer wrote that the song's chorus, song, about the train having "the disappearing railroad blues," effectively signalled "the end of the train song."

Goodman recalled the writing of the song, saying it came out of a trip he and his then-new wife took on that very train from Chicago to Mattoon, Illinois. During the ride down, he:

> was just looking out the window, writing down everything I saw - junkyards, little towns that didn't even have a sign to say what they were. Just out of Chicago, there was a bunch of old men standing around tin cans, warming themselves and waving, and it was a cold morning in April.

When Steve showed his song to a friend, that friend advised him to "describe what happened on the train." So, he "sat down and wrote the second verse about the card game and the paper bag." He finished the song with the verse about Memphis, Tennessee, saying it came "strictly from memory," because he figured he:

> couldn't write a song about a train that went 900 miles through the center of the country and stop the song in Mattoon because I was getting off.

As one of many "covers" that Willie has done over the years, it prompted him to observe that:

> I've got a lot of guts. I did 'Georgia' after Ray Charles did it, and I did 'Blue Eyes Crying in the Rain' after Roy Acuff. A good song never dies.

Goodman died of leukemia just two months before Willie's version of the song reached number on. So masterful was his recording that it won a Grammy for "Country Song of the Year."

When the heartfelt love song about equal partnership between the sexes, 'Until It's Time for You to Go', became very popular, most people were surprised to learn that its author was Buffy Sainte Marie, a Canadian Cree Native American. She had been lumped into the folk movement as a protest singer, responsible for such songs as 'Universal Soldier'. She said when she wrote 'Until It's Time for You to Go' that it reflected one of her many sides, in this case her French-Canadian side. "A lot of my songs are French, 'Until It's Time for You to Go', the music is French," she observed.

It also reflected one of her personalities, "myself - I, the woman." It was very much a song from a woman's point of view, intended to be "devoid of conventional female masochism." Perhaps Willie's past experience of writing the woman's point of view about divorce on the *Phases and Stages* album was what made his interpretation of this oft-recorded modern standard ("recorded by everyone from Elvis to Sonny and Cher, " according to Buffy) sound like he understood the point of not being able to own or hang on to someone.

'Cry' was originally written by Churchill Kohlman, a night watchman at the time, who not only composed it but had it recorded by an unknown singer (Ruth Casey) on a "dinky" label, Cadillac. Johnny Ray's subsequent "hit" interpretation of the song has been called one of the most powerful pop recordings ever made. That Willie would even touch the song after such an intense rendition was a credit to his interpretive skills.

As a recorded song, 'Just Out of Reach (of My Two Open Arms)' had an interesting history, both for Willie and others. Willie and one of his friends, Larry G. Hudson, had recorded the song in 1978 for Willie's Lone Star label (when it was being distributed by Mercury Records).

Their version went to number thirty-seven on the country singles chart.

Before that, in 1961 on Atlantic Records, soul singer Solomon Burke had his first big hit with the song. According to author Lee Hildebrand, 'Just Out of Reach' had been "a previous country hit for both Faron Young and T. Texas Tyler that *Billboard* editor Paul Ackerman suggested to producer [Jerry] Wexler." Wexler was not only Burke's producer, but a partner in Atlantic. Hildebrand perceptively noted that it wasn't "the first country tune to be covered by an African-American artist."

The Willie original, 'Why Are You Pickin' on Me', was from his early 1960's writing days. When he was told he seemed to not be writing very much, he equated the hiatus to finally taking a vacation after working so hard writing so many songs for so long. Of the remaining songs, three, 'Wind Beneath My Wings', 'Good Time Charlie's Got the Blues', and 'Please Come to Boston', have become modern pop standards. Chips Moman produced the album and recorded it at his Nashville studio.

Me and Paul. Columbia Records PCT 40008. (1985).

Track Listing: I Been to Georgia on a Fast Train, Forgiving You Was Easy, I Let My Mind Wander, I'm a Memory, She's Gone, Old Five & Dimers Like Me, I Never Cared for You, You Wouldn't Cross the Street (to Say Goodbye), Me and Paul, One Day at a Time, Pretend I Never Happened, Black Rose.

Recording Notes: This 1985 album found Willie doing songs that dated back to his early Pamper "demos" along with his classic 'Me and Paul', a great song, which had been available in many other "Willie" versions (including one for RCA). 'Forgiving You Was Easy' was also a Nelson original. When released as a single, it reached the number one position on the country charts.

Willie actually wrote 'Forgiving You Was Easy' because another song was needed for the 1985 Faron Young/Willie duet album. Then inexplicably, instead of including it on the duet album, he held on to it and cut it as a solo version (waiting until later in the year to release it as a single). Later, he would rerecord the song as a duet with Johnny Rodriguez. He saw it as "sort of a generalized song" and felt:

> I could probably apply it to a dozen situations in my life. As far as the exact reason I wrote it, I don't really remember right now.

'Me and Paul', as the follow-up single, got no higher than number fourteen. That ended Willie's brief stay at the number one spot (with two straight singles). The song selection was pretty much a pastiche with both 'I'm a Memory' and 'One Day at a Time' dating back to Willie's days on RCA. Several of the other cuts originally came out as Pamper Music "demos."

Willie first cut 'I Never Cared for You' in 1964 when he was signed to Monument. He also cut it again while with RCA. Both 'Black Rose' and 'Old Five and Dimers Like Me' were written by fellow Texan, Billy Joe Shaver. Waylon had previously recorded the two Shaver songs (and a bunch more) for his classic 1973 *Honky Tonk Heroes* album.

Even though Willie seemed to not be writing much new material by 1985, he could still come up with highly unusual songs when he chose to. An example was the song, 'They're All the Same', written in 1985 by Willie but done by Cash, because Johnny said he dreamed Nelson had written, just for him, a song having that title. 1985 also saw, for Willie, the birth of Farm Aid, which he said was inspired by a remark Bob Dylan made at the Live Aid concert, concerning the plight of farmers in the United States.

Farm Aid I was launched by Willie with a great deal of publicity and media coverage. The concert and related activities netted approximately ten million dollars and, as a result, became an annual event into the nineties. Willie began serving as President of Farm Aid, writing several articles in national magazines to explain its purpose.

Willie would have appeared at Live Aid. According to the driving force behind the concert, Bob Geldof, Willie "had already agreed to do it through his manager, and had been enthusiastic." Geldof called Willie "a very nice man." It was Kris Kristofferson who had gotten Willie involved by offering to "play either by himself or with Willie Nelson." Then, as Geldof remembered the situation, Kris "kept getting messed around because [promoter] Bill Graham didn't want him on so he pulled out." Subsequently, Willie "had to withdraw." Geldof said that although Willie's manager "offered an excuse," he (Bob) heard "it was because of Bill."

Partners. Columbia Records PCT 39894. (1986).

Track Listing: Partners After All, When I Dream, Hello Love, Goodbye, Heart of Gold, Kathleen, Something in the Way She Moves, So Much Like My Dad, My Own Peculiar Way, Remember Me, Home Away from Home.

Recording Notes: This 1986 album was produced by Chips Moman, who also co-wrote the title cut (with keyboardist and synclavier player Bobby Emmons). Though there was no overall connecting theme, the album was nonetheless enjoyable due to Willie's interpretations of recent classics like Neil Young's 'Heart of Gold' and George Harrison's 'Something'. As the second single from the album, 'Heart of Gold' was only able to peak at number forty-four in the Spring of 1987.

The title cut went out as the first single, reaching number twenty-four earlier in 1987. Of the other selections, Willie presented a great version of his own song, 'My Own Peculiar Way'. His recording of that song dated all the way back to his time on RCA. 'Remember Me' was the third song by that title Willie has done (and they're all different songs). This time the song's author was Stuart Hamblen, who wrote such classics as 'It Is No Secret' and 'This Ole House' (a 1954 number one song for singer Rosemary Clooney, usually remembered today as actor George Clooney's aunt).

One of the other songs entitled 'Remember Me' appeared on the *Red Headed Stranger* album. Its full title was 'Remember Me (When the Candle Lights Are Gleaming)' and it was composed by Scott Wiseman. Willie, himself, wrote a song that has at times been titled simply as 'Remember Me', though its full title was 'Will You Remember Me'. It first surfaced as one of the Pamper "demos."

Crystal Gayle had a 1979 hit with the song, 'When I Dream', written by Sandy Mason Theoret. Johnny Rodriguez, the Tex-Mex singer discovered by Tom T. Hall and who eventually became Willie's son-in-law (for about twenty minutes, as daughter Lana recently recalled), wrote 'Hello Love, Goodbye'. Producer Moman (along with Emmons) also contributed the wistful and insightful 'So Much Like My Dad'. Emmons (with a co-writer, guitarist J. R. Cobb) in turn gave Willie the closing song 'Home Away from Home'.

Incidentally Willie recorded (for Columbia) a total of four songs by the Moman/Emmons team. At first glance, the songs might have seemed like album "filler" because Moman has often been Willie's producer. Yet even after many listenings, the songs hold up as well-written and thoughtful country tunes, which could have become hits with sufficient promotion.

The album was recorded both at the Pedernales Studio in Spicewood, Texas, as well as Moman's Recording Studio in Nashville. Remixing was done at 3 Alarm Studio in Memphis. Johnny Gimble guested on fiddle. A synclavier sound was added to the mix (as played by Emmons, who also played keyboards). Most of the players were great Nashville studio musicians, with Mickey Raphael, from Willie's band, joining in with his unique harmonica playing. Chip's wife, Toni Wine, contributed backing vocals, as did Willie.

The Promiseland. Columbia Records FCT 40327. (1986).

Track Listing: Living in the Promiseland, I'm Not Trying to Forget You, Here in My Heart, I've Got the Craziest Feeling, No Place But Texas, You're Only in My Arms (to Cry on My Shoulder), Pass It on, Do You Ever Think of Me, Old Fashioned Love, Basin Street Blues, Bach Minuet in G.

Recording Notes: Another 1986 album featured Willie's next-to-last big number one solo country single, the title track, 'Living in the Promiseland'. According to the author, David Lynn Jones, the song was inspired by the Cuban migration into Florida beginning back in 1980 as well as by the plight of the Vietnam boat people. Jones said that the initial writing of 'Promiseland' took fifteen minutes.

However, it remained incomplete for about three years until a new publishing deal forced him to complete the song. Within two weeks the song was presented to Willie and accepted. Its socially conscious outlook fit exactly with Willie's personal accomplishments. That same year, 1986, saw the Country Music Federation honor Willie with their Roy Acuff Community Service Award (for all of Willie's major awards, see the appendix on his awards).

Jones also wrote another of the cuts, 'Here in My Heart'. In addition to the two songs, he provided some strong guitar work along with Clint Strong, Paul Buskirk, and Freddy Powers. Waylon's drummer, Richie Albright, guested on drums while Johnny Gimble contributed some very strong fiddle work. Two of Willie's band members, Mickey Raphael and Bee Spears also played while Paul English was noticeably absent.

Willie wrote the second single from the album, 'I'm Not Trying to Forget You', which peaked at twenty-one. Alex Harvey wrote 'No Place But Texas', a paean to that state with sentiments similar to the 1978 Tanya Tucker hit, 'Texas (When I Die)'. Waylon once remarked that Texans "believe that when they die, they go to Willie's house."

The album had its eclectic moments with the inclusion of 'Basin Street Blues', 'Bach Minuet in G', Floyd Tillman's 'I've Got the Craziest Feeling', as well as the lush pop standard, 'Old Fashioned Love'. Overall, the album was entirely produced by Willie and recorded at his Pedernales Studio.

1986 saw Willie continue to busy himself with Farm Aid. The Farm Aid II concert was held in Austin. It turned out to be very successful and that year basically replaced his annual Fourth of July picnic. He also toured heavily, even doing a string of concerts in England where Prince Charles came to see him perform. At mid-year, he was one of many featured guests at Alabama's (the group not the state) fourteen hour "June Jam."

Island in the Sea. Columbia Records CK 40487. (1987).

Track Listing: Island in the Sea, Wake Me When It's Over, Little Things, Last Thing on My Mind, There Is No Easy Way (But There Is a Way), Nobody There But Me, Cold November Wind, Women Who Love Too Much, All in the Name of Love, Sky Train.

Recording Notes: This was the 1987 follow-up to Willie's smash hit album of the previous year, *The Promiseland*. Willie's movie, *Red Headed Stranger*, was also released in 1987 (for a list of all of Willie's major film appearances, see the appendix on that subject). Later that year, in September, the Country Music Hall of Fame presented a multimedia display of Willie's life and accomplishments. He was at the top of the country music world.

Both Frank Sinatra and Willie briefly stopped their busy 1987 schedules to tape a public service announcement for NASA (at the Las Palmas Theater in Hollywood). It was the first time the two had worked together since an ill-fated planned seven day Golden Nugget (Las Vegas) engagement in June 1984. A sudden illness had forced Frank to cancel the show after only one night. Picketers from two local unions, who were on strike against the hotel, had also put pressure on both artists not to do the shows. According to a report in *Variety*, the two unions and other sympathizing unions called Frank and Willie "scabs" after the pair went ahead and performed opening night.

The album's title track (written by Willie) was the featured single and surprisingly it met with disappointing country chart sales action (peaking at number twenty-seven). Bruce Hornsby was the featured guest artist (piano/synthesizer) on 'Nobody There But Me', which he also co-wrote. The song, though a great one, did not connect with country buyers, as it got only as far as number eighty-two on the county charts when released as the follow-up single.

Tom Paxton's original folksong, 'Last Thing on My Mind', was perhaps an odd choice for this album. Actually, Willie had previously recorded the song during a 1976 session which was not released until 1991. The Glaser Brothers also recorded the song. Their version was the one that Porter Wagoner knew when he suggested he and Dolly Parton use it as an uptempo duet number. It became Porter and Dolly's first duet recording and in 1968 a top ten country hit.

The last three songs on the album were co-written by Booker T. Jones, who produced them, as well. Booker T. also played drums, keyboards, acoustic guitar, and bass, giving the latter part of the album a far more "funky" sound than found on most country music albums. Willie's band and some select studio musicians rounded out the album's eclectic musical background.

There was some major songwriting by Willie on this album, including the title cut, 'Wake Me When It's Over' (which he first recorded as a Liberty Records single in 1962 - though it failed to chart when released), and 'There Is No Easy Way'. In addition, Willie resurrected the early sixties piece, 'Little Things', which he co-authored with ex-wife, Shirley. Willie produced the remainder of the cuts on the album with the exception of 'Cold November Wind', produced by guitarist Grady Martin.

In 1987, Willie's Fourth of July picnic was staged on the outskirts of a little privately-owned "town," Carl's Corner, Texas (about sixty miles South of Dallas). Though it was televised live by the cable TV network, TNN (The Nashville Network), Willie said he "went into the tank financially on this Picnic." The lineup was great, though, with Kristofferson, Stevie Ray Vaughan, Don Cherry, Asleep at the Wheel, and Roger Miller among many others. The attendance was also great but the temperature zoomed into the hundreds.

CBS Productions scheduled and shot a Fall 1987 TV special entitled, *Willie Nelson: Texas Style.* Guests were Ray Charles and Bruce Hornsby. The hour long show was Willie's first prime time network television special. Willie also attended the opening of the London Brasserie, a restaurant he co-owned with Ringo Starr and Rolling Stone bassist Bill Wyman. Little Richard and Jerry Lee Lewis were among the guests.

By Fall (actually October), another side of Willie showed itself, his participation in a concert that was called "Cowboys for Indians and Justice for Leonard Peltier." It was a heart-felt expression of his commitment to the cause of Native Americans, a side of him that emanated from his own Native American background, or as he described it, in his autobiography, his "Indian blood - which I got from my mother." So involved was Willie that "they made me Indian of the year in the spring of 1987." In 1988, he received a certificate of appreciation for "devoted and invaluable services rendered to Native American Indians" from the National Association for the Renewal and Unity of Our People.

The concert featured Willie, Kris Kristofferson, Joni Mitchell, and actor/comedian Robin Williams. It was the culmination of highly publicized efforts to free Indian rights activist Peltier, believed by many to have been wrongly convicted of killing two FBI agents. Predictably, the concert drew harsh criticism from the FBI and other law enforcement agencies. One individual who expressed his outrage over the concert proceedings was California state senator, William Campbell, who asked "when will Willie Nelson, Robin Williams, and Kris Kristofferson hold a benefit for them?" By "them," he was referring to "the wives, families, and loved ones of the victims." The "victims" were the ones supposedly killed by Peltier.

The concert's organizer, actor Peter Coyote, felt it was unfortunate such expressions had to come forth, but the cause was just. He said that everyone who participated in the concert was primarily concerned with "something simple - due process." They were not there to take sides in a tragedy. Further, as he elaborated, the cause had the backing of fifty U. S. congressmen, so it wasn't "far from dead center." The slogan, "Free Leonard Peltier," even became an oft-seen bumper sticker.

What a Wonderful World. Columbia Records FCT 44331. (1988).

Track Listing: Spanish Eyes (with Julio Iglesias), Moon River, Some Enchanted Evening, What a Wonderful World, South of the Border, Ole Buttermilk Sky, The Song from Moulin Rouge (Where Is Your Heart), To Each His Own, Twilight Time, Ac-cent-tchu-ate the Positive.

Recording Notes: This 1988 album featured more standards, including a duet with Julio Iglesias on 'Spanish Eyes'. Sales of the duet as a single brought Willie once again into the top ten on the country singles chart (number eight). 'Twilight Time' became the follow-up single, stopping at number forty-one in early 1989. In 1958, it had been a number one pop hit for the Platters.

Of the song selections, 'South of the Border' with both its Western and Spanish tinges proved the most natural for Willie's interpretation and delivery. In 1939, the song had been a big pop hit for Gene Autry (he also sang it in his movie, also entitled, *South of the Border*). Willie once recalled that when he was ten, he "wanted to be a cowboy singer. I wanted to be just like Gene Autry."

The Livingston/Evans composition, 'To Each His Own' appeared for the second time on one of Willie's sets of classics. It had previously been part of the 1983 album, *Without a Song.* As a movie classic, 'The Song from Moulin Rouge (Where Is Your Heart)' dated back to 1953, the year it tied for first place in record sales. The tune came from French composer, Georges Auric.

Once again, Willie paid tribute to two of his biggest influences (as he has stated on many occasions), Johnny Mercer (two songs) and Hoagy Carmichael (one song). The Mercer songs were 'Moon River' and 'Ac-cent-tchu-ate the Positive', a song about which the composer and author Alec Wilder wrote, "the words and music fit perfectly, as, for example, in the release, where the lyric says 'Jonah in the whale, Noah in the Ark'." The "gorgeous ballad," 'Moon River' (co-written with Henry Mancini), won two Academy Awards as part of the 1961 movie, *Breakfast at Tiffany's.*

The Carmichael composition was 'Ole Buttermilk Sky', from the 1946 movie, *Canyon Passage,* in which Hoagy acted in the role of Hi Linnett. Hoagy said that the movie gave him:

a chance to sing several songs and sitting up all night with Jack Brooks, a lyricist, we got a bolt from the blue that turned out to be 'Ole Buttermilk Sky', just handed to me as a gift.

In keeping with the "standards" theme, Willie chose to tackle a more recent Rodgers and Hammerstein classic, the compelling and provocative (for its time) anthem, 'Some Enchanted Evening'. The song was the high point of their Broadway (and movie) musical, *South*

Pacific. In spite of its complexity, musically and lyrically, Oscar Hammerstein wrote most of the words "during a weekend visit to Billy and Eleanor Rose's house in Mt. Kisco [New York]." That may sound like a very short timeframe for writing a great song, but as Willie once said, "the good ones come quickly."

The one song on the album with the most curious history, not only for Willie but for the writers and the artist who initially made it famous, was the title cut, 'What a Wonderful World'. The initial copyright registry on the song credited its authorship to George Douglas (words) and George David Weiss (music). As has often been the case (for rarely explained reasons) concerning song authorship by an industry professional, the name "George Douglas" turned out to be an alias for Bob Thiele. Later copyright information verified this fact.

Thiele was a veteran recording producer who had worked with national acts ranging from Buddy Holly and the Crickets to Teresa Brewer. Another executive who similarly "hid" his compositions was Ahmet Ertegun, founding partner of Atlantic Records. He registered his twelve copyrights, songs like 'Chains of Love', as A. Nugetre (last name spelled backwards) "so as not to embarrass his family."

In the mid-sixties Thiele was working as a producer for ABC Records. He recalled in his memoirs that:

> during the deepening national traumas of the Kennedy assassination, Vietnam, racial strife, my co-writer George David Weiss and I had an idea to write a 'different' song specifically for Louis Armstrong that would be called 'What a Wonderful World'.

At the time, Louis was coming off the biggest hit of his career, his inimitable version of 'Hello Dolly'. Thiele and Weiss wrote their song, the message of which was "the world really is great: full of the love and sharing people make possible for themselves and each other every day." They took it to Louis and his manager, Joe Glazer. After hearing the "demo," both manager and artist became very anxious to record the song as the follow-up single to 'Hello Dolly'.

That's when some very unexpected trouble began. The then president of ABC, Larry Newton, decided that Louis should not be recording a ballad but another up-tempo dixieland-like number. Newton was, in his eyes, simply following an old, usually discredited business axiom that a hit should be followed up by a similar, almost clone-like song. According to Thiele, Newton went to the extreme of believing that if an artist was "lucky enough to have a hit, it invariably had to be duplicated on all subsequent recordings."

Thiele, Louis, and Louis' manager did not agree, so, following their instincts, they went ahead and recorded the song, only to discover Newton became so incensed he first attempted to "cancel the date and fire the musicians." He then, in effect, proceeded to go out of his way to make sure the recording would not sell. In Thiele's words, the single was "personally sabotaged by a bitter vengeful Newton."

That was in the United States. In England, where Newton's push against the single had not extended, the record quickly went to number one. The English success was followed by huge sales in Europe and even South Africa. Soon, most of ABC's foreign affiliates were clamoring for the single. The song eventually became a smash hit almost everywhere in the world, but the United States.

Finally, long after Louis' 1971 death and Newton's departure from ABC (which was subsequently folded into the MCA conglomerate), the single became the big hit Thiele and others thought it would be. Its success was due to its reappearance as part of the 1988 soundtrack for the Robin Williams' film, *Good Morning, Vietnam*. So inspiring was the song once it finally received a large American audience, it became a theme song for a number of self-help and motivational groups.

In the same year, 1988, Willie made the song the title cut of this album. Eight years later (1996), in a most unexpected turn of events, Willie's version of the song reappeared as part of the hit soundtrack from the John Travolta film, *Michael*, the offbeat story of Michael the Archangel returning to earth for one "last blast." It stood out alongside old cuts by Van Morrison, Frank Sinatra, and Bonnie Raitt.

For the album, Chips Moman returned as producer, with two of his family members, Monique and Casey, singing backup. Though the song selections were all pop standards, the album failed to make the national pop album charts, the first time one of Willie's "standards" albums failed to do so. In fact, Willie stopped charting nationally after his 1985 album, *Half Nelson*. It wasn't until 1993 that one of his solo albums, *Across the Borderline*, landed him back on the national pop albums charts.

A Horse Called Music. Columbia Records FCT 45046. (1989).

Track Listing: Nothing I Can Do About It Now, The Highway, I Never Cared for You, If I Were a Painting, Spirit, There You Are, Mr. Record Man, If My World Didn't Have You, A Horse Called Music, Is the Better Part Over.

Recording Notes: This 1989 album featured a strong reading of the Beth Nielsen Chapman song (she did the vocal harmonies, as well), 'Nothing I Can Do About It Now', Willie's final chart-topping solo single. It topped the charts almost three years after his last topper, 'Living in the Promiseland'. So strong was Willie's version that he made it sound like a song he might have written.

Billboard columnist, Marie Ratliff (Country Corner), reported that, "programmers are lauding the return of Willie Nelson to new material that is straight country." By its third week on the chart, Ratliff noted the song had jumped up to number forty-three. She quoted Music Director Tim Wilson (of WAXX Eau Claire, Wisconsin) as saying, "this is the one his fans and others have been waiting for, just Willie doing some good country music."

Music Director Al Hamilton (of KKAJ Ardmore, Oklahoma) added,

> I liked him doing old standards but this is the Willie that does so well in the Southeast. It's the old two-beat stuff that his fans out here love.

The single became Willie's twentieth to hit the top of the charts. It stayed on the charts an amazing twenty-one weeks.

Fred Foster, former president of Monument Records and producer of the album, was the one who obtained the Chapman song. He said he "ran into her in the parking lot and asked her if she had anything uptempo for Willie." She told him, "no, but I'll write something."

The song was one of two written by Chapman that made the album. The other was 'If My World Didn't Have You', which she had written five or six years before "with Willie in mind." Both songs were very impressive because, as Willie explained, "we listened to probably a hundred songs and we did two of Beth Nielsen Chapman's songs."

The title cut by Wayne Carson took a while before it got to Willie but when he heard it, he appraised it immediately as "one of those songs that stand the test of time." He added that "I still think it is one of the greatest songs I've heard in a long time." Carson had written the song with Montana trout-fishing and mountains on his mind.

Kelly Delaney, columnist for *American Songwriter*, noted that the song worked on several different levels. In one sense the lyrics became "a metaphor for the silent song of the soul only we can hear within ourselves." They also told "a story about a man - in this case a cowboy - who above all else is true to himself." The "horse" of the title stood as "a symbol for the individual path this man has no choice but to follow."

After Willie recorded 'There You Are', its co-writer Mike Reid observed that "Willie Nelson makes the song his own, which for the songwriter is the absolute optimum situation." When 'There You Are' was released as the album's second single, it got caught up in a major change made in the demographics of all the *Billboard* charts. Previously *Billboard* had calculated chart position as a combination of radio play and over the counter sales. Then the magazine went to a heavy reliance on airplay data.

When the change was made, 'There You Are' had climbed the charts to number eight, looking to become one of Willie's biggest chart singles in a while. The week following the chart changes, the song came in at the bottom of the top twenty, eventually peaking at number nineteen. That this signalled Willie's fall from grace with radio programmers was probably not a coincidence. Other old time stars dropped out of sight on both the charts and the radio at the same time.

Such a seemingly innocuous change in the reporting of national charts had major implications for the power structure of country music artists. The follow-on single, 'The Highway', fared poorly, peaking at number fifty-four. Though Willie's reign at the top of the country charts was over, the American Music Awards honored him with a Special Merit Award for his contributions to the music industry. He also won, in 1989, the Governor's award from the Nashville chapter of NARAS and a Grammy Living Legend Award.

Of the other album cuts, Willie's own song, 'Is the Better Part Over' was originally done by him as simply a demo. Only his voice and guitar were recorded and, in the words of Foster, they were "a little out of tempo," which gave it a certain amount of "charm." Fred took the tape, added an overture (created by arranger Bergen White), and then dubbed in strings over Willie's original guitar tracks. Willie's version of his own 'I Never Cared for You' reprised a number he originally recorded for Foster at Monument in 1964. The cut, 'Mr. Record Man', dated back to his time with Liberty.

Don Sampson and Skip Ewing wrote 'If I Were a Painting' one afternoon after Don had been inspired by George Harrison's 'Cloud None'. The writers of the song, 'Spirit', revealed they were inspired by an article in *National Geographic*. Their song told of a Native American who lost his family to an attack by invading white men.

Willie stepped up his commitment to farmers in 1989, headlining a benefit at the Bellevue Hotel in Washington, D. C., for the family of Dixon Terry. Terry, a farmer from Greenfield, Iowa, was president of the Family Farm Coalition. He was accidentally killed by lightning while out baling hay. He left his family, a wife and two children, with a debt of three hundred thousand dollars.

In 1989, Willie also branched out into the launching of a cable television venture, The Cowboy Television Network. In May, he appeared on an NBC-TV special, *Kenny, Dolly & Willie: Something Inside So Strong*. It ostensibly "celebrated" the twentieth anniversary of the American moon landing. According to *Variety's* review of the show, Kenny (Rogers), Willie, and Dolly Parton) took turns "singing songs, singing one another's songs, singing together and so on."

Born for Trouble. Columbia Records CT 45492. (1990).

Track Listing: Ain't Necessarily So, (I Don't Have a Reason) To Go to California Anymore, Ten with a Two, The Piper Came Today, You

Decide, Pieces of My Life, It'll Come to Me, This Is How Without You Goes, Born for Trouble, Little Things Mean a Lot.

Recording Notes: Willie's 1990 set featured more from that great songwriter, Beth Nielsen Chapman, who also added harmony vocals. Produced by Fred Foster, this was a very musical album, with strings, synthesizer, acoustic, amplified acoustic, and electric guitar, mandolin, acoustic piano, fiddle, electric sitar, and steel guitar. Most of the recording was done in Nashville at the House of David Studio.

Willie's lead vocals were added later at his Pedernales Studio. Unlike his previous album, none of his own band was present. Instead excellent solo and studio players such as Mark O'Connor, Reggie Young, Bobby Ogdin, Sonny Garrish, Larry Byron, and Eddie Bayers were the prominent backing musicians.

Chapman's 'Ain't Necessarily So' did briefly increase Nelson's single record status, going to number seventeen on the "new" *Billboard* charts. She also wrote 'You Decide' and co-wrote 'It'll Come to Me'. The follow-up single, 'The Piper Came Today', died at seventy and lasted but three weeks. The third single was 'Ten with a Two', which fizzled almost as quickly as its predecessor.

Willie finally recorded the classic 'Little Things Mean a Lot', whose authors, Lindeman and Stutz, composed 'Red Headed Stranger'. Also recorded were two Hank Cochran pieces, '(I Don't Have a Reason) To Go to California Anymore' and 'This Is How Without You Goes'. A Troy Seals song, 'Pieces of My Life' rounded out a wide range of material. Seals, originally from the hill country of Kentucky has written or co-written over two hundred top ten country singles for a variety of artists. Seals first number one country hit, as a co-writer (with Denny Rice), was Conway Twitty's 'There's a Honky Tonk Angel (Who'll Take Me Back in)'.

Willie's 1990 Farm Aid show (Farm Aid IV) was held at the Hoosier Dome in Indianapolis, Indiana, before a sellout crowd of forty-three thousand people. Most of the tickets for the event were sold within the first ninety minutes they were offered. Neil Young was one of the headliners. Willie also spent a good deal of the year touring as part of "the Highwaymen" (Willie, Waylon, Cash, and Kristofferson). The IRS chose to begin their seizure of Willie's properties in 1990.

Across the Borderline. Columbia Records CK 52752. (1993).

Track Listing: American Tune, Getting Over You (w. Bonnie Raitt), (The) Most Unoriginal Sin, Don't Give up (w. Sinead O'Connor), Heartland (w. Bob Dylan), Across the Borderline, Graceland, Farther Down the Line, Valentine, What Was It You Wanted, I Love the Life I Live, If I Were the Man You Wanted, She's Not for You, Still is Still Moving to Me.

Recording Notes: 1993 was the year Willie was elected to the Country Music Hall of Fame and turned sixty, celebrating with a network TV special, *The Big Six-O*. He also released this album, called by at least one major critic, "Willie's finest album in years." It charted nationally, reaching number seventy-five on the *Billboard* pop album charts, the first time in nine years one of his albums had sold that well. By then, Willie had waited three years just to make a successful solo album.

In the interim, specifically Christmas 1991, his son, Billy (Jr.), died. Of all the stresses and crises Willie has survived, this was the one time his sister, Bobbie, worried the most about him. Willie blamed himself for having been an absent father, for having been away so much of Billy's young life when he was "busy trying to pay the rent."

He admitted he had never "experienced anything so devastating in my life." On top of that, Willie also lived through the infamous IRS seizure of most of his property and their subsequent tax bill of sixteen and a half million dollars. Of course, that "experience" never got as bad as one tabloid claimed; Willie never became "homeless." On the bright side, he did win the Academy of Country Music's Pioneer award in 1991.

The album, itself,featured songs and shared performances from some of the great names of pop and rock, Paul Simon, Sinead O'Connor (on the song, 'Don't Give Up', by Peter Gabriel), Bonnie Raitt, and Bob Dylan. Obviously, the album did not come out sounding traditionally country, which was the going "trend" at the time. Simon was present when the album was handed over to CBS officials. He said that "their first reaction was 'It's great, but what is it?'."

Actually it was a project that started out after Willie's manager, Mark Rothbaum, met producer Don Was at a Felix Cavaliere recording session. Mark learned that Don "had always been a huge fan of Willie's." So a meeting was held in Dublin between Willie and Don, which was followed by the first of several recording sessions, eventually leading to the recording of all the tracks on this album.

Originally Dolly Parton was going to sing the duet on the Gabriel song but she couldn't make the session. When the song was initially recorded by Gabriel, Kate Bush had sung the "haunting" refrains. Don Was said he thought it was Parton, not Bush, who had done the singing, hence the request to have her sing with Willie. When she couldn't do it, Was "suggested O'Connor."

That suggestion came at the time Sinead got booed off the Madison Square Garden stage (as part of the aftermath of her ripping up a picture of the pope) during the Bob Dylan Thirtieth Anniversary concert. Willie recalled that,

> that night, after her problems on the stage and everything
> and she was in tears and Kris was all huggin' her up, she was

kinda down. And I went over and I said, 'Now, you're still gonna come sing with me in the mornin', aren't you?' And she kinda laughed and said, 'Yeah.' And she came in and sang her little ass off.

Dylan and Nelson supposedly worked through fax machines to come up with the great song, 'Heartland'. However, Willie blew that tale down in a 1993 interview, saying that it wasn't true, that "we didn't do it by fax." He explained,

> Don Was, who knows Dylan, brought me a tape of the melody he'd recorded, just him humming the tune with the word 'heartland' every now and then. So I took the word and the melody and wrote a song around it.

Dylan shared vocals with Willie on the recording of the song. Willie also recorded Dylan's 'What Was It You Wanted?', which he sang again for the Bob Dylan Thirtieth Anniversary Concert.

Paul Simon, an artist on the scale of Dylan, was also an integral part of the project. Paul had initially tried to get Willie to record his song, 'Graceland', in 1986, just before he recorded it himself. Simon recalled that "I sent him over a cassette, but I never heard from him. I just inferred that it didn't do anything for him."

Willie remembered the tape, saying "I heard it, but I didn't really hear it, you know?" About five years later Simon again asked Willie to record the song. Willie's reply was that "you must be on a mission from God." Nevertheless, Willie agreed to cut 'Graceland', telling Paul, "if you'll produce it, I'll sing on it." There was still a problem in that Willie did not quite understand the song.

Paul explained that Willie "thought it was about Elvis, whereas it's about losing a love, and healing. But I didn't want to say to him, 'You lost a son'." Willie finally did get the song as he sang it in the studio, exulting that "this is a great fucking song. There's a lot more here than 'let's go to Graceland'." With Simon playing guitar, Willie ended up recording not only 'Graceland', but Simon's 'American Tune'.

Some of Nelson's finest recent writing was presented, 'Still is Still Moving to Me' and 'Valentine' (written for son, Lucas). Another Nelson original on the album was 'She's Not for You', which he first recorded for RCA in 1965. What 'Still Is Still Moving to Me' had to say, according to Willie, was that:

> you can't ever be still because even when you're still, your mind is moving, your heart is beating, your vibrations are still going on, nothing stops because you decide to stand still for a moment.

The old Willie Dixon blues, 'I Love the Life I Live', featured Mose Allison on piano and Milt Hinton on bass. Fellow Texan, Lyle Lovett, wrote two songs on the album, 'Farther Down the Line' (Willie said, "I just love that song") and 'If I Were the Man You Wanted'. The cut, 'If I Were the Man', featured backing vocals by David Crosby.

There could have been one more track on this album, a fifteenth song, a live performance of the union standard, 'Solidarity'. Willie explained that, "I took it off because I didn't think it fit in with the other songs." His reasoning was that "most of them are new songs." Did that mean the track was lost forever? Willie didn't think so, saying that "maybe it'll get onto another album, when we're doing that era or those songs." He was also a little politically sensitive, meaning that when he initially recorded the song,

> we were living under the other administration in Washington. I was already swinging at them, with 'American Tune' and 'Don't Give Up', and the Dylan thing, 'Heartland'. That was enough political stuff.

Almost all of the excellent production ('Graceland' was co-produced by Paul Simon and Roy Halee) throughout the album was by Don Was, who said afterward (of Willie) that:

> making a record with him was like going off on a retreat and studying at the foot of a Zen master for about a month. He's this completely gentle, nonjudgmental guy who appears effortless when he sings, but he has distilled the truth down to its most basic form. There's so much to learn from a guy like that, who can hang with a murderer or a U.S. senator and treat everybody the same.

In a recent *Billboard* interview, Was divulged that:

> the people who have influenced me greatly, in the last few years anyway, are like Willie Nelson, Keith Richards, and Bob Dylan. They are three guys who are completely feel-oriented and aren't analytical about stuff.

He elaborated, saying that:

> with Willie, when he sings it great, that's the take. I just listen to his vocal, because if he's singing great, that means everybody's playing the right thing and inspiring him.

Willie's singing was actually what Was admired most,

the way he phrases - he's a fucking genius, man. That's what really got me with Willie. I knew his records, and I knew there was a warmth to him, but when I saw him live and heard what he did with phrases - it's like Jimmy Scott. Willie does the same thing. He staggers the phrase just so far back and yet pulls it out at just the right spot.

When Don was asked if he had "any orphaned children - any records that you made that you loved, that the artist may have loved, that didn't attain the kind of success they deserved," he responded with "the record that I did with Willie Nelson, 'Across the Borderline', I love that record." He elaborated, saying:

that's one of the few records that I play to make myself feel good. I've never felt that that got the proper response. Critics liked it, but it never really caught on with the public.

Was has since produced, for Willie, a reggae album projected for release on the Island label. To Willie, Don is simply "the best producer around, and that covers any kind of music." About Willie, Was also felt "there's something very Eastern in his approach to life. He just doesn't care about the things most people are preoccupied with."

One of Willie's biographers, Lola Scobey, wrote in *Billboard* magazine that "much of Willie's thinking," has centered around "the writings of Kahlil Gibran, Edgar and Hugh Cayce, the Rosicrucians and others." Fellow actor Gary Busey felt that "Willie's like a lighthouse, like a preacher." He is definitely a "strong proponent of positive thinking." To Alanna Nash, he revealed that "I can't be around anything or anyone negative. Just refuse to do it. Haven't got time for it. That kind of things rubs off." He told Country Weekly that:

we just need to keep out of the way and let whatever's supposed to happen, happen. Usually we try to make things happen. But if we just get out of the way, they will.

In my talks with him, he has passed on similar fatalistic yet positive thoughts. He has said that "most of the stuff I've read about me has been true." Joe Casey, promoter of many of Willie's Columbia albums, expressed that Willie "often makes me stop and think about myself, my life and the way I view it." Close friend Kris Kristofferson has seen Willie's mystical qualities up close, saying that:

going to see Willie is almost like going to church in some strange way. There are spiritual touches that ask people to reach for the best in themselves.

"One for the Road":

The Collaboration and Duet Projects

The collaborative and duet projects that Willie did for Columbia were numerous. They were great but in some ways they were also detrimental (sales-wise) because they overexposed him and ultimately made his recorded product so plentiful that sales for individual records dropped off markedly. Nonetheless, the albums were different than any others being done at the time in country music.

His label, Columbia, certainly seemed favorably inclined to Willie's collaborative projects. After all, many of the artists with whom Willie was working, such as Ray Price, Merle Haggard, Jackie King, and Lacy J. Dalton were signed to Columbia (or a subsidiary), so their exposure to the public was increased through being linked to Willie. Columbia artist, Julio Iglesias, though a major international star, received major American exposure with his hit duet single with Willie, 'To All the Girls I've Loved Before'.

Willie was proudest of his Jackie King collaboration, *Angel Eyes*, a major part of "my jazz work" as he called it. Columbia has seemed not to share his view since the label has neglected to rerelease it on compact disc. That has long been a goal of Willie's. Recently, he told me that Jackie has signed with "some small label in San Francisco, I think." He said they have discovered two extra tracks they recorded at the original sessions but didn't release (Willie did not remember why they weren't released). Adding that he hoped the two tracks could be included as "bonus tracks," Willie said that he and Jackie were "negotiating" to get the album rereleased (on CD).

At one point, when Columbia was trying to get Willie to play at a Houston Bob Dylan date, they reportedly offered "to underwrite an album featuring Bob and Willie." I asked Mark Rothbaum about this purported recording and he said there was never any discussion in his presence of a Columbia project involving Willie and Bob. To the best of his recollection, Willie "was asked to be on a Houston show in 1976 or 1977. He came out at the end and did a gospel number."

Some of the duet recordings Willie did proved to be very rewarding for artists who had helped him early on in his career, specifically Ray Price and Faron Young. Ray hired Willie as a bass player in the early sixties while Faron had a number one hit in 1961 with Willie's 'Hello Walls'. Some duet or collaborative projects garnered various awards and recognitions (not to mention that Willie and second wife Shirley started their relationship as a singing "duet").

For example, the Country Music Association awarded Willie and a specific partner their Vocal Duet award three separate times, once with Waylon in 1976, once with Haggard in 1983 and the other with Julio Iglesias in 1984. His and Waylon's single, 'Good Hearted Woman', won the CMA's single of the year award in 1976. The Academy of Country Music named 'Highwayman' its "Single of the Year" in 1985. The collaboration Willie did with Waylon, Jessi, and Tompall in 1976, *The Outlaws*, albeit a compilation or primer, was also named the CMA's Album of the Year in 1976.

In 1979, Willie and Waylon won a Grammy for the Best Country Vocal Performance by a Duo or Group for 'Mamas Don't Let Your Babies Grow Up to Be Cowboys'. Willie's duets with artists like Iglesias and Leon Russell were also very instrumental in opening up the pop market for his music. Will Willie ever give up on working with other artists?

According to a Summer 1996 interview with Merle Haggard, the Hag's (as he's affectionately known) next planned project will involve achieving a totally stripped down sound, with none other than Willie Nelson. He divulged that:

> Willie Nelson and I are planning to do an album together, just the two of us. There's some talk about a record and a tour where Willie and I are by ourselves, with just our guitars, no bands.

In the final analysis, it would be counter-productive to conclude that Willie's many duets and collaborative projects hurt his career. After all, it was just that kind of freewheeling partnering that garnered Willie his reputation as a musician's musician. The friendships he made with artists like Bob Dylan and Bonnie Raitt paid off handsomely with the contributions they and others made to Willie's critically acclaimed and best-selling album, *Across the Borderline*. If Willie hadn't done all that extra recording, he wouldn't have been Willie.

The Collaborations and Duets - Album Listings

Willie and Family Live. Columbia Records CGT 35642. (1978).

Disc One Track Listing: Whiskey River, Stay a Little Longer, Funny How Time Slips Away, Crazy, Night Life, If You've Got the Money I've Got the Time, Mammas Don't Let Your Babies Grow Up to Be Cowboys, I Can Get Off on You, If You Could Touch Her at All, Good Hearted Woman, Red Headed Stranger Medley: Time of the Preacher/I Couldn't Believe It Was True/Medley: Blue Rock Montana/Blue Eyes Crying in the Rain/Red Headed Stranger/Just As I Am, Under the Double Eagle.

Disc Two Track Listing: Till I Gain Control Again, Bloody Mary Morning, I'm a Memory, Mr. Record Man, Hello Walls, One Day at a Time, Will the Circle Be Unbroken, Amazing Grace, Take This Job and Shove It (w. Johnny Paycheck), Uncloudy Day, The Only Daddy That'll Walk the Line, A Song for You, Roll in My Sweet Baby's Arms, Georgia on My Mind, I Gotta Get Drunk, Whiskey River, The Only Daddy That'll Walk the Line.

Recording Notes: Recording this live album at Harrah's, Lake Tahoe, Nevada, April 1978, gave Willie the opportunity to redo many of his earlier songs with his band and put them out to the public to contrast with the earlier overdubbed ones drenched with the "Nashville Sound." Emmylou Harris and Johnny Paycheck were two of the premiere "recording" family members on the album, as released in 1978. Recording was done by Showco, of Dallas, Texas, on their 24 track mobile. Willie did the album production.

'Whiskey River' opened and closed the show. It was also the hit single from the album going to number twelve in early 1979 (remaining on the charts for twelve weeks). Since then, it has been the standard show opener for Willie and his band. Previously, the Nelson original, 'Mr. Record Man' had been used to open his shows.

The track listing for the album, as with so many live releases by top artists, read like a greatest hits roster. There were some unexpected performances, such as the Johnny and Willie duet on Paycheck's classic, 'Take This Job and Shove It'. The country standard, 'The Only Daddy That'll Walk the Line' (a Waylon Jennings staple) was performed as the encore (as well as during the show).

'If You Could Touch Her at All', written by Lee Clayton (also the writer of 'Silver Stallion', which would become a 1990 hit single from the *Highwayman 2* album), was another high point. Three of Willie's renditions of old-time religious songs, 'Will the Circle Be Unbroken', 'Amazing Grace', and Uncloudy Day' also sparkled, as did the "family's" countrified rendition of Lester Flatt's timeless bluegrass song, 'Roll in My Sweet Baby's Arms'.

One for the Road. (Willie Nelson and Leon Russell). Columbia Records CGT 36064. (1979).

Track Listing: Detour, I Saw the Light, Heartbreak Hotel, Let the Rest of the World Go By, Trouble in Mind, Don't Fence Me in, The Wild Side of Life, Ridin' Down the Canyon, Sioux City Sue, You Are My Sunshine, Danny Boy, Always, Summertime, Because of You, Am I Blue, Tenderly, Far Away Places, That Lucky Old Sun, Stormy Weather, One for My Baby and "One More for the Road".

Recording Notes: 1979 brought together Leon, the old rocker, with Willie for an album and some live dates. Willie had learned the full extent of Leon's musical abilities through listening to his daughter's copy of Joe Cocker's *Mad Dogs and Englishmen* album, on which Leon had played a major supporting role. Leon and Willie actually went back somewhat further with similar studio work and road trips.

They even discovered that Leon had backed some of Willie's early sixties Liberty recordings. In 1973, Leon had given Willie two songs for his *Shotgun Willie* album. In 1976, Leon and Mary McCreary got married at Willie's Austin home (Willie and his wife were the only witnesses). Willie sized up his admiration for Russell by saying,

> Leon and I have been friends for years. I'd been trying to figure out a way to make records with him for a long time. I finally talked him into doin' one with me. Leon is just a genius.

On tracks eleven through twenty, all pop standards, Leon both played and arranged the music. Maria Muldaur on vocals and Bonnie

Raitt on slide guitar were featured guests on 'Trouble in Mind'. The Grant Clarke/Harry Akst classic, 'Am I Blue', was originally recorded by Willie when he was on Liberty. Three years earlier, he recorded, solo, 'That Lucky Old Sun' for *The Sound in Your Mind* album.

'Heartbreak Hotel', a number one rock and roll hit for Elvis, became a number one country hit for Willie and Leon. Cutting that particular song "was Leon's idea," according to Willie. He explained further, "I liked the song, and I liked the writer, but he was the one who said we should do 'Heartbreak Hotel'." Actually, Willie had known the writer, Mae Axton, very well and for a long time.

Axton wrote the song with Tommy Durden (with Elvis included on the writer's credits) after Durden showed her an article about a man who left a suicide note with the words, "I walk a lonely street." Axton added a "heartbreak hotel" at the end of that street and within twenty minutes the song was completed. With Mae's ties to Colonel Parker (she worked for him promoting some of the early Elvis tours and records), she was able to get it recorded by Elvis.

Leon and Willie recorded and filmed "a hundred and four or five tracks at Leon's place there in L. A." It was a session without a specific set of songs, during which, as Willie related,

> every time we'd get through with one song, we'd say, 'Well, now what do you want to do?' One of those times, Leon suggested 'Heartbreak Hotel'. It was Leon's feel that we used on that particular record. He was playin' piano at the time, and I sort of followed his lead.

Overall, the album had a very loose, relaxed feel, because, as Willie related, "most of those cuts are just one take." Typical of the collaboration was Willie's observation that they "would sit down at the piano and I'd sing, and we did eighteen songs in one night." Overall, the song selection reached deep across American pop music, from the Gershwin/Heyward *Porgy and Bess* classic, 'Summertime', to Irving Berlin's 'Always', written for his then-girlfriend, Mona.

In 1964, Willie first recorded the Cole Porter Western farce, 'Don't Fence Me in', for RCA. Unfortunately, the track was never released and subsequently "lost." The song dated back to two versions by Roy Rogers and the Sons of the Pioneers, one for the 1944 Warner Bros. flick, *Hollywood Canteen* and the other for Roy's own 1945 movie, *Don't Fence Me in*. So completely did Rogers "own" the song that it became next to impossible to associate it with Porter, composer of sophisticated classics like 'Anything Goes' and 'Begin the Beguine'.

Cole referred to the song as "that old thing" even after it had reached great heights of popularity. One reason he was not enamored with the song was because he did not write the lyric. All he did was to set a "cowboy lament," by a Montana cowpuncher named Bob Fletcher, to music. Only Cole's name appeared on the song credits because he paid Fletcher two hundred dollars for the exclusive rights.

'Danny Boy' from 1913 and 'Let the Rest of the World Go By' from 1919 were two of the oldest songs Willie ever recorded, though Ray Price had brought 'Danny Boy' back to the country charts in 1967. He placed the then fifty-four year old song in the top ten. Both 'Sioux City Sue' and 'Far Away Places' were real "crooner" songs, having been hits for Bing Crosby.

Harold Arlen and Ted Koehler originally wrote 'Stormy Weather' in 1933 with Cab Calloway in mind. It wasn't really a song written for a man, however, so Ethel Waters ended up doing it, even introducing it at the fabled Cotton Club in Harlem. Of the song, she wrote in her autobiography that it was "the perfect expression of my mood." To her it was "the story of wrongs and outrages done to me by people I had loved and trusted." Mel Torme called it "a song for the ages."

Three songs were from artists who had heavily influenced Willie all his life. They were Gene Autry's 'Ridin' Down the Canyon', Johnny Mercer's 'One for My Baby', and Hank Williams' 'I Saw the Light'. According to Hank's wife, he wrote the song as he and his band were pulling into Montgomery after a long tour. They had been afraid of car trouble and not getting home, so when Hank saw the Montgomery airport beacon light, he supposedly said, "we're gonna make it now; I saw the light."

Fred Astaire introduced Mercer and Arlen's 'One for My Baby' in the movie *The Sky's the Limit*. According to Mercer's wife, Ginger, the "mood" of the song didn't "seem to fit Fred Astaire too well in the movie." Frank Sinatra basically did take the song over and, according to Ginger, it did "suit Sinatra down to his dress shoes."

Gene Autry and Smiley Burnette wrote 'Ridin' Down the Canyon' on "their way to Hollywood." That was why Smiley said it took him "three miles" to write the melody. In his autobiography, Gene revealed that he paid Smiley five dollars for the rights to the song.

Hank Thompson's biggest hit ever was 'The Wild Side of Life' in 1952. The song has gone on to be recorded by many, many artists, from Freddy Fender to Waylon and Jessi (Colter). The author said it was a true to life song that he wrote about his wife, who left him after seven months of marriage to return to, "the wild side of life," which meant drinking expensive whiskey instead of a country boy's cheap beer.

Rounding out the album of songs that popped into their heads, Willie and Leon covered the Sarah Vaughan hit, 'Tenderly' and the Tony Bennett number one 1951 chart-topper, 'Because of You'. They even went Western with the Spade Cooley classic, 'Detour'. Overall, Leon (who in 1973 did a country album under the alias, Hank Wilson) and Willie's album encompassed twenty of America's greatest songs, from almost every decade of the twentieth century.

One interesting aside to this album was that Leon became the first to sign Willie's legendary Martin acoustic guitar. How did that "guitar-signing" come about? Willie told Alan Paul of *Guitar World* that it was Leon Russell who first "had me sign my name on his guitar. I asked him why and he said it would be more valuable now." So, Willie had Leon sign "Trigger." After that, Willie recalled,

> I started asking anyone whose autograph I would want to sign it. Roger Miller's on there, as are Johnny Cash and Gene Autry - just a lot of great guys and good friends. My favorite lawyer is on there, too.

San Antonio Rose. (Willie Nelson and Ray Price). Columbia Records PCT 36476. (1980).

Track Listing: San Antonio Rose, I'll Be There (If You Ever Want Me), I Fall to Pieces, Crazy Arms, Release Me, Don't You Ever Get Tired (of Hurting Me), This Cold War With You, Funny How Time Slips Away, Night Life, Deep Water, Faded Love.

Recording Notes: 1980 brought Willie and Ray Price together for a set that featured two great Bob Wills songs, the title song and 'Faded Love'. In 1950, 'Faded Love' had turned out to be Wills' last top ten country single for MGM, following a long run of top sales for that label. On this version, which went to number three on the country charts, Crystal Gayle sang background vocals. Ray and Willie drew on their Bob Wills roots to cover a third song, 'Deep Water', which though associated with Wills (even Wills, himself, felt it was one of several songs that typified "Bob Wills music"), was written by Fred Rose.

The bond between Ray and Willie went back to Willie's playing bass in Ray's band, the Cherokee Cowboys, when Willie needed the money. Willie actually wore a Nudie suit (a fancy, fringed Western suit) when he played in Ray's band. Price had a huge hit with Willie's 'Night Life' and also used 'I Let My Mind Wander' as the B-side of his huge 'Danny Boy' single hit. In his autobiography, Willie disclosed that his mother, Myrle, "always loved Ray Price above nearly everybody else."

By 1980, Price was fading from country stardom so this album and the association with Willie helped to briefly revive his career. Willie has described Ray as "one of the voices I think everybody has to hear." He also wrote that he used to:

> tell Ray Price that I owed him hundreds of dollars in education because I could just stand around and watch what he's do, and then I would know to do the opposite.

The friendship between the two men had been ruptured since the sixties when Willie shot one of Ray's prize roosters (it had been bothering Willie's chickens). Following the shooting, Price vowed to never again record another Nelson song. This collaboration revived the friendship, although Willie once said, perhaps half-kidding, "I reckon shooting that mean rooster didn't cost me but about $60,000 and change." As of 1998, Ray told *Country Weekly* that he and Willie:

> will be getting together in June to do some film work for Willie's new Outlaw cable channel. Willie and I have been friends for a long time, He used to play bass in my band, the Cherokee Cowboys, and he wrote songs for my publishing company. He's a great songwriter and great friend.

The choice of album cuts ranged from Patsy Cline's 'I Fall to Pieces' to the country standard (by Floyd Tillman), 'This Cold War With You', which Willie, himself, had previously recorded for Liberty. The duo revived Price's big 1956 hit, 'Crazy Arms', a song written by Ralph Mooney and Chuck Seals. They also covered Hank Cochran's, 'Don't You Ever Get Tired of Hurting Me', which hit for Price in 1965. It hit again for the pair in early 1981, reaching number eleven.

'Release Me' had been a top ten hit for Ray early in his career (1954) as well as a 1960's pop hit for both "Little" Esther Phillips (1962) and Engelbert Humperdinck (1967). Kitty Wells' top ten country version also in 1954 cemented the song as a standard. Eddie Miller, the tune's principal co-writer, once said that as far as he knew, "the song has sold over 18 million records and has been recorded over 300 times."

The idea for it came from Miller's "playing a one-nighter near San Francisco." He overheard a lover's spat during which the woman said, "if you'd release me, we wouldn't have any problems and everything would be all right." Miller said the line stuck with him because he "had never heard it said like that before." To him, it sounded better than a "dirty word" like divorce. Clearly, "release me" was a "softer way of saying it." It also became the classic way to say it.

Pancho & Lefty. (Merle Haggard/Willie Nelson). Epic Records PET-37958. (1982).

Track Listing: Pancho and Lefty, It's My Lazy Day, My Mary, Half a Man, Reasons to Quit, No Reason to Quit, Still Water Runs the Deepest, My Life's Been a Pleasure (I Still Love You as I Did in Yesterday), All the Soft Places to Fall, Opportunity to Cry.

Recording Notes: Townes Van Zandt had been long heralded as a great songwriter who had recorded critically successful but commercially abysmal albums. It took the 1982 hit single and album by

Merle and Willie to bring Van Zandt's best song, 'Pancho and Lefty', to the public eye.   As the second single from this album, it was a resounding number one, staying on the charts for twenty-one weeks.

The song was brought to the attention of the two men by Willie's daughter, Lana, who played them Emmylou Harris' version off her *Luxury Liner* album.   The song almost didn't get recorded because, according to Susie Nelson, Lana, who was a friend of Townes', told Willie about the song after he and Merle "were all done recording and the band was packing up and putting their equipment on the bus."

Even though Lana had waited so long, Willie agreed to record the song and got the band to unpack and return to the studio. Of all the recording done that day, 'Pancho and Lefty' was the only song that proved difficult to record because of a very complex instrumental bridge that neither Willie nor his guitarist of many years, Grady Martin, could "get the feel of."   It took producer Chips Moman to do the difficult playing.   When it was all completed, not only did Merle and Willie have a hit single and album, they starred in a prize-winning video (produced by Lana) based on the song. Songwriter Townes played one of the "federales" in the video.

Townes' manager, Harold Eggers, said that 'Pancho and Lefty' was the kind of song Townes called a "sky song." According to Eggers, Townes "believed he was a vehicle for the songs - he didn't write them. They came from above." In the case of 'Pancho and Lefty', "Townes woke up and wrote down the words and even the guitar part - all complete." He said the song came to him "through the window of a cheap hotel outside Dallas."

'Reasons to Quit' also succeeded as a duet by having it sound like two old cantankerous men always determined to do things their way. Merle had originally written the song for himself in 1970. It became the first hit single form the album, going to number six in early 1983. Merle's wife of the time, Leona Williams, was the author of 'All the Soft Places to Fall'.

Two Willie originals received new versions, 'Opportunity to Cry', first done by Willie on Liberty (and called an unheralded masterpiece), and 'Half a Man', also originally recorded for Liberty, where it had charted as a single (all the way to number twenty-five). It was during these sessions that guitarist/vocalist/songwriter Johnny Christopher first tried to bring the song, 'Always on My Mind' to Merle's attention. He did, unknowingly at first, get Willie's interest (and how!). Christopher stayed around and played guitar and sang background vocals throughout the album.

Recording-wise, the whole set took only five days to complete. It took another year before the label, Epic, finally released the completed album. The albums in the first shipment became collector's items after it was discovered that "Pancho" was inadvertently spelled

"Poncho." Nation-wide sales of the album pushed it to the number thirty-seven spot on the *Billboard* Top Pop Albums chart in 1983.

In 1983, the album won the Country Music Association's "Album of the Year" award. Willie and Merle also became the CMA's Vocal Duo of the Year in 1983. Merle once said of Willie that he "may be the most influential man of this century in country music." He was also very proud that, in 1987, "Willie sang the hell out of" one of his songs, 'If I Could Only Fly'.

Old Friends. (Willie Nelson & Roger Miller). Columbia Records PCT 38013. (1982).

Track Listing: Old Friends (w. Ray Price), Husbands & Wives, Half a Heart, The Best I Can Give Her, Sorry Willie, When a House Is Not a Home, Aladambama, Invitation to the Blues, When Two Worlds Collide, I'll Pick Up My Heart (and Go Home).

Recording Notes: By 1982, Roger Miller's meteoric pop and country success had all but died. This album was Roger's last big label shot until his Broadway success, *The River.* Actually, it was a natural that Willie and Roger would do something together, since not only were they "old friends" and fellow iconoclasts, Willie stayed in the very same place, Dunn's Trailer Park, when he first moved his family to Nashville, that had inspired Roger's song, 'King of the Road'. According to Hank Cochran, Willie actually lived in the same trailer Roger had, which was the same one Hank lived in when he first moved to Nashville, a trailer that cost Willie twenty-five dollars a month.

Roger also loved to tell "Willie stories," including one about their "wild days" when Willie, "drunk or stoned or both," answered a loud knock on a hotel room door where Roger, Kris Kristofferson, and Willie had been drinking and carrying on too loudly. When Willie saw it was the police, Roger told how Willie "immediately sobered up," telling the cops, "we were writing songs here, sir. And we just didn't realize how loud we were. We'll be quiet, sir." Next, according to Miller, "Willie closed the door and immediately returned to his stupor."

Their rendition of 'Old Friends', including Ray Price (and written by Miller), was as hilarious as any of Roger's Willie stories. As a single, it sold well, going to number nineteen in the summer of 1982. Another Miller composition on the album, 'Sorry Willie', was actually directed at Willie back when it was written in the early sixties. According to Willie, in his autobiography, when his and first wife Martha's marriage was breaking up and the fighting leveled off, the relationship deteriorated into possible infidelities on her part, which Willie didn't particularly care to know about. Willie recalled, there was a rumor I heard on the road that Roger Miller and Martha had something going. I never did ask either one of them if it was true. But Roger wrote a song called 'Sorry, Willie'. Actually I was with Roger the night he wrote the song someplace outside of Tulsa. By then, Martha and I were separated and I didn't care to know what might have happened between them. In fact, I recorded 'Sorry, Willie' on Liberty with Joe Allison. Roger was at the session. It wasn't that I had become broad-minded about such shit as that, but, you know, I wasn't sure of anything. And art is art wherever you find it.

Disc jockey Bif Collie said that even though his wife went off with Willie, he would still play Willie's music because it was his "job to play the best music." That was truly rising above a situation. Yet if Willie did record 'Sorry Willie' with Allison at Liberty, it has never shown up on any compilation or album. That would make the version on this album the one and only recording by Willie of a song that apologized to him for something that may or may not have happened. One Roger composition Willie did cut for Liberty was 'Second Fiddle'. Perhaps that's the song Willie was thinking of, not 'Sorry Willie'.

In the Jailhouse Now. (Willie Nelson & Webb Pierce). Columbia Records PCT 38095. (1982).

Track Listing: There Stands the Glass, Wondering, In the Jailhouse Now, You're Not Mine Anymore, Heebie Jeebie Blues No. 2, Slowly, I Don't Care, Back Street Affair, Let Me Be the First to Know, More and More.

Recording Notes: In 1982 Webb Pierce also received a career shot in the arm with this Willie collaboration. Actually, this was Pierce's last attempt at a comeback after his career had fizzled out in the early 1970's. He went into semi-retirement and died in Nashville in 1991. The title song charted at number seventy-two, the last Webb Pierce appearance on the national sales charts. Leon Russell and Richard Manuel were guest players on the cut.

Webb had previously taken his single version to the top of the country charts in 1955. In fact, most of the songs on this set were Pierce signature songs from his earliest years. Except for 'You're Not Mine Anymore', which peaked at number four in 1954, seven of the songs were chart-toppers, beginning in 1952 with Webb's first number one, 'Wondering', and extending to 1955's, 'I Don't Care'.

Webb had some insights into why some of his songs were hits. For example, he felt that 'Back Street Affair' was very popular because:

there were a lot of people having back-street affairs, and it was something they were keeping hidden. Then when the record came out, it became an emotional outlet for them.

Webb concluded that "there were enough people saying, 'That's us, honey,' that it sold a lot of records." Was it the man saying it, and was it to his mistress or his wife?

Pierce also figured 'There Stands the Glass' would hit "because 75 percent of the people in the world drink." He described it as "the national anthem of barroom songs." The song's hook centered around the lines, "there stands the glass, fill it up to the brim." Their effect on audiences led Webb to conclude, "it's still one of the most-requested songs I've ever recorded."

Yet when Mary Jean Schurz (one of three co-writers) started to write the song, she didn't think there would be "much of a market for the final product." So, she never quite finished it. Then she met with Pierce who became convinced that even in its unfinished state, the song would be perfect for him. He and his wife worked on the song, then they passed it on to Russ Hall. He and, finally, Audrey Grisham finished the piece. Over the concerns of some at Decca, Webb's label, the song went public in October 1953. Just after Thanksgiving it hit the number one spot on the country singles charts.

Willie had fond memories of Webb over the years, saying that:

I liked his swimmin' pool. It was shaped like a guitar. Remember when Ray Stevens got upset because there was so many people comin' by in tour buses lookin' at Webb Pierce's pool, buying 'Webb Water' out of the pool and all that stuff? He was real mad about it, and Webb said, 'Well, you shouldn't have moved next door to a star'.

In the same year this album came out, Willie appeared as "Red" in a made-for-TV movie entitled, *Coming Out of the Ice* (working title: *In the Jailhouse Now*). On the big screen, Willie starred, along with Gary Busey, in the Bill Witliff Western, *Barbarosa*. Willie would later make another TV movie, *Baja, Oklahoma*.

As good as this newest recording was for Pierce, such projects began to damage Willie's career because the duet projects released along with solo albums and compiled collections of all sorts were saturating the market. Since the title cut was an old Jimmie Rodgers song (which he had based on an old blues tune), it was also included on a Jimmie Rodgers tribute anthology entitled, *The Super Stars Salute Jimmie Rodgers*, distributed by the Jimmie Rodgers Foundation as JRF-001.

Take It to the Limit. (Willie Nelson with Waylon Jennings). Columbia Records CK 38562. (1983).

Track Listing: No Love at All, Why Do I Have to Choose, Why Baby Why, We Had It All, Take It to the Limit, Homeward Bound, Blackjack County Chains, Till I Gain Control Again, Old Friends, Would You Lay with Me (in a Field of Stone).

Recording Notes: 1983 found the duo doing country-rock numbers such as the title track. The original Willie song, 'Why Do I Have to Choose' was a number three charting single for Nelson. The song has an interesting history with another music icon, Bob Dylan. Dylan, of course, has always been known primarily as a singer of his own songs, songs around which a generation defined itself.

When he toured, the crowds mainly wanted to hear his famous material. Now and then, Bob would work somebody else's songs into the performance list. As his touring increased, audiences came to realize that Bob knew the works of dozens of great American songwriters, from Jimmie Rodgers to Curtis Mayfield.

Anyway, when Bob took on some heavy touring in 1984 (Rolling Thunder), he began with a long set at the Beverly Theater in Los Angeles. During that performance, after some two dozen of his own songs, he sang 'Always on My Mind', a song with which, of course, Willie had had so much success. Then, towards the end of the evening, he did Willie's 'Why Do I Have to Choose', followed by a standard Willie had recently reprised, 'To Each His Own'.

Dylan followed his performance of 'Why Do I Have to Choose' with eight more at eight different shows on the tour. During that set of live shows, Willie's song was the only non-original that Dylan performed. The song was performed at shows in Switzerland, Germany, Denmark, France, and Italy. Once in France and once in Germany, Bob even closed his show with Willie's song. Then he dropped it and by Ireland, he, fittingly, added Van Morrison's 'Tupelo Honey'.

Willie and Bob's history went further back. In May 1976, when Bob's ongoing Rolling Thunder tour needed a sell-out, or at least a very large audience, at Houston's ten thousand seat Hofheinz Arena, Columbia Records (both Willie's and Bob's label) set about to get Willie to appear there. According to Neil Reshen, then Willie's manager, Columbia offered Willie "in excess of $10,000 as payment to ensure Bob Dylan sold the date." That did it. Willie played but even with his late addition, the arena was "barely three quarters full."

The history of the two artists has stayed intertwined. Bob became involved early on with Willie's Farm Aid. Actually Willie got the idea for Farm Aid from a statement Bob made when the two appeared at Live Aid. At the first Farm Aid concert (held September 22, 1985 at the University of Illinois Memorial Stadium in Champaign), Bob performed six songs, with Willie backing him on three of them. During

1993, they wrote a great song together for Willie's *Across the Borderline* album. Following that, Willie put in a rousing appearance at Bob's thirtieth anniversary special.

Bob always had a great appreciation for country music much the same way Waylon and Willie have had for pop songs, especially the title track, 'Take It to the Limit' (a pop hit by the Eagles). Their version reached number eight on the country charts. Another version of a pop hit (for Simon and Garfunkel), 'Homeward Bound', followed the Eagles song on the track listing. Willie said that "Waylon and I cut the Simon & Garfunkel song 'Homeward Bound' and the Eagles' song 'Take It to the Limit' because they bowled us over."

To juxtapose the "pop" songs, Waylon and Willie reached back into country history for George Jones' 'Why Baby Why', a song that co-writer Darrell Edwards was inspired to write after overhearing a couple having an argument in their car. He watched the woman hit the man over the head with her shoe and then heard the man pitifully ask her, "why, baby, why?" From the time George first took it to number four late in 1955, this great song has had a life of its own.

In early 1956, the unlikely duet team of Webb Pierce and Red Sovine took it to number one. Later on in 1956, Hank Locklin had a top ten version. The ironic capper was that in late 1961, about six months before she sang 'Willingly' with Willie, Shirley Collie (about to become Nelson) recorded a hit duet version of the song with Warren Smith. The song was still not finished being a hit as Charley Pride moved it back into the number one slot in 1983.

Roger Miller's 'Old Friends', which was done a year earlier by Roger and Willie, got a new interpretation from the pair. 'Blackjack County Chains' dated from Willie's days on RCA. To help round out the country flavor, David Allan Coe's song, 'Would You Lay With Me (In a Field of Stone)' (it had been a number one country hit for Tanya Tucker), found its way on to the album. Coe was also one of the background singers. He originally wrote the song as a poem for his brother's wedding, explaining that it was a vow for eternal unity.

Angel Eyes - Featuring the Guitar of Jackie King. Columbia Records PCT 39363. (1984).

Track Listing: Angel Eyes (Willie w. Ray Charles on vocals), Tumbling Tumbleweed, I Fall in Love Too Easily, Thank You, My Window Faces the South, The Gypsy, There Will Never Be Another You, Samba for Charlie.

Recording Notes: Jackie King has long been a jazz guitar great. For close to twenty years, he also taught guitar to private students. Then in 1978 he opened his own Southwest Guitar Conservatory in San Antonio. On this 1984 album, he played generous touches of jazz-inflected runs and chord patterns to go with Willie's singing and playing. The album actually began as a solo King record (in 1983) for which Willie was going to find a label.

However, when Willie heard the cuts, he began to sing over them. Then more cuts were done with Willie singing and playing until it ended up as an album on which Willie did what he had always wanted to do, play and sing "with a good jazz band." Often, he was just the guitar player because, as he reminisced, "it's very enjoyable when the only responsibility you have is playing the guitar."

Two of the tracks were original King songs, 'Samba for Charlie' (an instrumental composed for his son) and 'Thank You' (written for his mother). The rest of the selections, most notably the Bob Nolan (of the Sons of the Pioneers) classic, 'Tumbling Tumbleweed', were standards from a variety of musical genres. Willie was no stranger to the classic songs of Jule Styne and Sammy Cahn. Here, he and Jackie interpreted 'I Fall in Love Too Easily', which Jule and Sammy had written for the Frank Sinatra/Gene Kelly movie, *Anchors Aweigh*.

The two artists picked another standard from a musical (the Sonja Henie 1942 wartime show, *Iceland*), Harry Warren and Mack Gordon's 'There Will Never Be Another You'. The melody has been described as "one of the loveliest Warren ever wrote." The Mitch Parrish and Abner Silver song, 'My Window Faces the South', was one Willie had recorded before (for his second RCA album).

Jackie and Willie's version of the title song, 'Angel Eyes' was another gem. The inimitable Ray Charles joined in on vocals. The tune, itself, was written for the 1953 Ida Lupino film, *Jennifer*. It has been covered by many great vocalists, including Frank Sinatra. As old as the song was, Jackie pointed out that 'Angel Eyes' was completely new to Willie yet amazingly, he "did it right the first time."

Funny How Time Slips Away. (Willie Nelson and Faron Young). Columbia Records PCT 39484. (1985).

Track Listing: Three Days, Touch Me, Congratulations, Half a Man, Hello Walls, She's Not for You, Live Fast, Love Hard, Die Young, Sweet Dreams, (It's) Four in the Morning, Life Turned Her That Way, Goin' Steady, Funny How Time Slips Away.

Recording Notes: Faron was one of the first big names to record a Nelson song. He had great sales success in 1961 with 'Hello Walls' (included here as a duet). On the country charts, the song stayed nine weeks at number one (and went to number twelve on the pop charts). On the day Willie got his first royalty check for the song, he reportedly walked into Tootsie's Lounge and french-kissed ol' Faron.

So happy was Willie with the success of 'Hello Walls' that he said he began to write songs about other house parts, such as 'Hello

Roof' etc. Actually, he did write another "hello" song, 'Hello Fool', for country emcee, Ralph Emery (for years Emery was host of the very popular TNN show, *Nashville Now*. On the flip side of Faron's single release (on Capitol Records) of 'Hello Walls' was another Nelson composition, 'Congratulations', which charted at number twenty eight as 'Hello Walls' hit number one.

Faron recalled when Willie first came to Nashville, "without a penny in his pocket." He added that,

> I think the only money he had was because he'd written one song called 'Family Bible' he sold for fifty dollars. I was down at Tootsie's Orchid Lounge, where me and all the guys hung out. Willie had a crew cut and everything, all young, didn't have all this shaggy beard and all that back in those days. He says, 'I've got a couple of songs I want to sing to you.' He sang me 'Hello Walls' and another thing called 'Congratulations'. I says, 'I'm recording in a couple of weeks, I'll take 'em both'.

What happened next was a quite unexpected, or as Faron recalled:

> so we get in the studio, and everybody started making fun of the song, you know, 'Hello walls, hello guitar, hello microphone.' I said, 'Y'all go ahead and make fun; I think it's a hit record'.

Fortunately, for both Faron and Willie, it was very much a big hit. In 1985, Willie repaid his debt to the "Sheriff" (a nickname Faron got from his 1955 movie debut in Republic Picture's *Hidden Gun*) with this duet project. On the front cover, ironically, was a picture of a clean-shaven Willie with the always clean-shaven Faron.

Four of the cuts were originally top ten singles for Faron in the fifties and sixties, 'Three Days' (1962), 'Goin' Steady' (1953), 'Live Fast, Love Hard, Die Young' (1955), and 'Sweet Dreams' (1956 - preceding Patsy Cline's hit version). 'Four in the Morning', which hit the top of the charts for Faron in February 1972, was the final number one song of his illustrious career. 'Three Days' was written by Willie, though Faron initially got his name on the copyright.

Willie actually wrote all the songs on side one, 'Touch Me', 'Half a Man', and 'She's Not for You', in addition to 'Three Days', 'Congratulations', and 'Hello Walls'. On the album, the writing credits for 'Live Fast, Love Hard, Die Young' went to J. Allison, though the song has also been credited to Floyd Tillman. 'Going Steady' was composed by Faron, while 'Sweet Dreams' came from the pen of Don Gibson, whose top ten hit version of it debuted on the country charts in 1956 two months after Faron's version landed there.

Writer Jerry Chestnut composed 'Four in the Morning' for Faron based on a highly unique request, to avoid, as much as possible, using the letter "S". Faron had been in a car accident that severely injured his tongue. When it came time for him to record again, he still lisped slightly, hence the song guidelines.

Though 'Life Turned Her That Way' (written by Harlan Howard) was neither a hit for Willie nor Faron, it did become a country standard. It was Ricky Van Shelton's 1988 number one version that has kept it so fresh in country fans' minds and proven it to be one of those timeless numbers. Writer Howard said of his creation that:

> I think it kind of fits my philosophy. I do believe that in most relationships, if there's a bad guy, it's the guy. If anybody's gonna cheat, normally it's the guy. If anybody loses their ego and has to go out and get in an affair, it's the guy, in most cases. That's just the way it is. Most of the heartaches in this world seem to occur to women.

Brand on My Heart. (Willie Nelson and Hank Snow). Columbia Records PCT 39977. (1985).

Track Listing: Golden Rocket, I've Been Everywhere, I Almost Lost My Mind, Caribbean, Brand on My Heart, I'm Movin' on, Send Me the Pillow You Dream on, I Don't Hurt Anymore, A Fool Such As I, It Makes No Difference Now.

Recording Notes: This 1985 recording featuring Willie and Hank Snow brought Hank back to country audiences after a long silence. The album included most of Snow's biggest hits. The first track was 'Golden Rocket', written by Hank and a number one hit for him in late 1950. It was a train song in the tradition of Jimmie Rodgers, the artist Snow patterned himself after when he first began recording and performing. It was about one of the "old steam engines" that Hank watched come and go as a child "by going to the little old country station."

Hank's biggest hit, his "signature" song, 'I'm Movin' on', was done by the pair, as well. That song was written by Hank in the forties and initially turned down by his label as unacceptable for recording. After Hank finally got enough "pull" to get it recorded in 1950, it rose quickly to number one on the charts and remained chart-bound for forty-four weeks. So universal was its appeal and singability that almost twenty years later (1972), John Kay (of the rock group Steppenwolf) took his version to the middle reaches of the *Billboard* pop singles chart.

When Hank's original recording of 'I Don't Hurt Anymore' (by Don Robertson and Jack Rollins) was first released as a single in 1954, it became an "instant" smash (topping the country charts for five months). In the first five months it was out, it had "sales approaching six hundred thousand," a very large number of units in those days. Hank chose the song because he "liked the way it fit his strong baritone voice." He also thought the story told by the lyrics "was perfect for the country music market."

Of the other songs on the album, 'Send Me the Pillow You Dream On' had been a 1958 hit (top five), not for Snow, but for Hank Locklin, a Floridian, who wrote the song as well as sang it. 'I Almost Lost My Mind' was a huge 1950 smash for its composer, Ivory Joe Hunter. It was also a hit that year for Nat King Cole and, in 1956, for Pat Boone. The song, 'A Fool Such As I' composed by Bill Trader, was a hit for Hank in 1952. In 1959, it became a huge pop hit for Elvis Presley.

Willie and Hank toured and performed together many times over the years. During one European package tour, Willie got to "know" Hank quite well. One evening during the tour, Hank's fiddler, Chubby Wise, asked Willie to try and figure Hank out. About a week went by until Chubby asked Willie what conclusion he had reached.

Supposedly, Willie said, "there ain't nobody in this whole world that can figure that little bastard out." The two did share a musical kinship, though. Hank once said of Willie that he "has stuck pretty country." In his autobiography, Hank cited Willie as one artist "who stuck to clean lyrics." Hank also related in his book that after he became "discouraged from ever wanting to record again," he continued to hear "of Willie Nelson recording with so many artists."

That made Hank decide "to call him and mention doing an album with him." The result of the phone call was that "my boys and I went to his home on the outskirts of Austin, Texas, and we cut an album together in September, 1984." Hank revealed that he:

> had planned on staying in Texas for three days. I thought it would take that long to record the ten-song album, but things went exceptionally well, and we finished early.

According to Hank,

> we went into the studio around ten on a Monday night and were finished by four the next morning. We had a good time doing the songs, and I remembered just how much fun recording could be. Willie insisted we call the album *Brand on My Heart*, after the song I had written years ago.

As much fun as doing the album was, Hank remembered being "worn out and I never thought I put my best into that album." As far as Hank Snow albums went, "that has been the last thing I ever did."

Jimmie Davis, former Louisiana governor and a country and gospel singer as well, purchased the song, 'It Makes No Difference Now' for a "few hundred dollars" from a cash-strapped Floyd Tillman. Only when the song came up for renewal in 1966, was Tillman able to get half of it back, sharing the copyright with Davis from then on.   Davis originally recorded the tune for Decca in late 1938.

The song went on to have an interesting history for him.   He related that in the early days of his governorship, after he had vetoed a "right-to-work" bill, he came under considerable political heat. Nonetheless, he built and maintained an excellent working relationship with the state legislature by ending each session "with a band at his side."

He said he would say, "Gentlemen of the legislature, what's done is done."   Then he would turn to the band and say, "Give me a 'G' chord, boys," following which he sang, 'It Makes No Difference Now'.   Just as Davis ended those sessions with the song, Hank and Willie used it to close out their album together.   The album predictably did not sell well and Columbia has declined to rerelease it on compact disc.   Bear Family Records packaged the entire album as part of the eight CD collection, *Hank Snow: The Singing Ranger Volume 4*, BCD 15 787 II.

Half Nelson.   Columbia Records FCT 39990.   (1985).

Track Listing: Pancho and Lefty (w. Merle Haggard), Slow Movin' Outlaw (w. Lacy J. Dalton), Are There Any More Real Cowboys (w. Neil Young), I Told a Lie to My Heart (w. Hank Williams), Texas on a Saturday Night (w. Mel Tillis), Seven Spanish Angels (w. Ray Charles), To All the Girls I've Loved Before (w. Julio Iglesias), They All Went to Mexico (w. Carlos Santana), Honky Tonk Women (w. Leon Russell), Half a Man (w. George Jones).

Recording Notes: This set of duets with artists ranging from Julio Iglesias to Neil Young was released in 1985, Willie's tenth year with Columbia.   The duet with Julio, 'To All the Girls I've Loved Before', was a runaway single hit, reaching, by mid-1984, number one and number five on the country and pop singles charts, respectively.   The pair publicly debuted the song at the Country Music Association Awards show in October 1983.   Deborah Miller, vice-president of the William Morris Agency, Julio's booking company, recalled that, prior to the show, Julio "was scared.   It was a tough audience, but the response was just fabulous."

Willie remembered thinking when he first heard Julio, "wow, I've found somebody here!"   He asked his agent to "find out who Julio Iglesias is and see if he wants to cut a record with me."   When Julio was "found," he said he did want to cut a song with Willie.   His biographer described him as "ecstatic."   Willie added that "I didn't know Julio was selling more records at that time than anybody in the world." Another source disclosed it was Willie's wife at the time who turned him on to Julio's singing. She had heard Julio on the radio while in London and thought "his voice would complement Willie's."

According to at least one self-described insider, Iglesias was the one who suggested he and Willie record 'To All the Girls', an Albert Hammond/Hal David composition. It had originally been written for Frank Sinatra. However, Julio's biographer, Daphne Lockyer, quoted Julio's manager, Alfredo Fraile, as saying that Hammond had previously offered Julio the song for a solo recording, but Julio did not like the song at all, or as Fraile recalled about Julio, "being Mr. No at that time he couldn't agree." Fraile said he specifically told Julio, "this song is perfect for you."

Fraile had to work hard to persuade Julio that he should do the song as a duet because it really could work for him and Willie. Once it was a big success, Fraile said, "Julio told me I had been right about it all along." The recording was done in Texas, "at Nelson's own studio." Production was by Richard Perry, known for his work during the seventies with Carly Simon, Martha Reeves, and Art Garfunkel.

It took just one night to record that song and one other, 'As Time Goes By'. After the night of recording, the two men were said "to have had a lavish dinner washed down with two of Julio's infamously expensive bottles of Spanish wine." Then, at 6 AM, Julio and his entourage flew out of Austin.

The song had been extremely difficult for Julio to learn. It took speech coach, Julie Adams, six months to teach him to say "girls" instead of "gulls." Correspondingly, Julio described Willie as "the most natural singer in the world, completely spontaneous." *Cash Box* magazine, a major music industry "trade" publication, noted that "Nelson gives the tune his traditional Texas flavor, while Julio adds a sexy Latin touch to the song." As a result of the single, Willie and Julio were named by the CMA as "Vocal Duo of the Year." The Academy of Country Music honored the recording as its "Single of the Year."

After 'To All the Girls I've Loved Before' hit big, Willie and Julio's duet recording of 'As Time Goes By', cut at the same session, was intended to be the follow-up. It had already been released as part of Willie's 1983 album, *Without a Song*. However, the idea failed to materialize for reasons that have remained vague. It appeared that through a mistake somewhere in the CBS distribution network, the single was shipped prematurely. As soon as some of the major retailers received it, they called CBS, because they had not ordered it and did not know it was an intended release.

Because of those calls, CBS was able to quickly rectify the mistaken shipment by immediately recalling all the shipped singles. They must have been extremely fast in their response because one store owner said he had "never seen a record come and go so fast." CBS also moved hurriedly to counteract any possible publicity damage. A company spokesperson claimed that a warehouse employee, "who didn't know, didn't care, or who was just a goofball, reached in the wrong shelf and shipped out the wrong record."

Was it really the wrong record? Some industry analysts speculated that CBS, at one point, did intend to market the single but that as it got close to release date, a decision was made to hold off. Unfortunately, that decision probably did not get adequately communicated, hence the "unintended" release. Why would such a decision have been made, especially in light of the huge sales totals for 'To All the Girls I've Loved Before'?

There did appear to be a relatively straightforward answer somewhere. Willie was about to release 'The City of New Orleans'. In 1983, he had saturated the market with his own singles and duets with both Waylon and Merle Haggard. CBS may have wanted to pull back on the amount of Willie product to be marketed in 1984.

At the same time, Julio was experiencing great success with a Diana Ross duet on the song, 'All of You'. Indeed, Julio's manager, Fraile, seemed to have favored not releasing 'As Time Goes By'. He said, "we certainly didn't want Julio to end up competing with Julio, because then one of the Julios would have to lose out." It wasn't until 1988 that Willie and Julio recorded together again, on the song, 'Spanish Eyes', for Willie's *What a Wonderful World* album.

Two of the duets on this album, one with Leon Russell (on the Rolling Stones classic 'Honky Tonk Women') and the other with George Jones (on Willie's song 'Half a Man'), had not been previously released, Neither had the track, 'I Told a Lie to My Heart', which featured a crafting of Willie's voice with that of Hank Williams. The Williams performance came from a 78 acetate "demo" he did in 1947 or 1948. The acetate was acquired by the Country Music Foundation in 1983.

Willie and Foundation director Bill Ivey worked to not only enhance Hank's voice and guitar but to add Willie's voice and guitar in the most unobtrusive way possible. According to a *Billboard* article, Ivey added:

> two measures of rhythm guitar to the beginning and one verse
> of rhythm guitar in the middle prior to turning the tape over
> to Nelson.

Ivey said he decided to add the guitar parts because:

> both the beginning and ending of the song were abrupt, and
> Williams' performance contained no empty spaces into which
> Nelson would have been able to fit a solo instrumental.

Though Ivey's additions greatly enhanced the track, he revealed that:

the technical problems of adding guitar to Williams' original 'demo' performance were formidable. The song had been cut direct to a 78 r.p.m. acetate disk, using just one microphone to pick up Williams' voice and guitar.

The "frequency response" was limited which gave Hank's original guitar a less-than-clear "tonal" sound.

As a result, Ivey had to work recording miracles to "downgrade" the clearness of his guitar licks so they would sound similar to the poor quality of Hank's recorded guitar backing. He and engineer Rick McCollister even had to mix in the same background noise behind the new guitar parts as well as duplicate Hank's "somewhat out-of-tune B string." Once they finished the track to their satisfaction, Willie added his vocals at his studio during the winter of 1984. He also added a guitar solo and harmony overdubs. Both Willie and Bill shared production credits.

The royalties Willie earned from the "duet" were donated to the Foundation. The September compact disc release coincided with the Foundation's special Willie Nelson exhibit. In 1989, Joel Whitburn (author of a series of publications on the *Billboard* magazine sales charts) cited Willie as the country artist who had hit the charts with the greatest number of vocal partners (twenty, if Leon Russell and his alter-ego, "Hank Wilson" were counted separately). In 1990, Country Music Foundation Records released the Williams solo performance of the song on the album, *Rare Demos: First to Last*, CMF-067-D.

Highwayman. (Willie Nelson, Johnny Cash, Waylon Jennings, Kris Kristofferson). Columbia Records FCT 40056. (1985).

Track Listing: Highwayman, The Last Cowboy Song, Jim, I Wore a Tie Today, Big River, Committed to Parkview, Desperados Waiting for a Train, Deportee (Plane Wreck at Los Gatos), Welfare Line, Against the Wind, The Twentieth Century Is Almost Over.

Recording Notes: The four personalities, Cash, Kristofferson, Nelson, and Jennings, got together in 1984 in Switzerland to do a Christmas Special. From that came the idea of cutting an album together. After the special was done, Chips Moman had Willie and Cash back in Nashville recording a duet that was projected to round out Cash's forthcoming album. Instead, first Jennings and then Kristofferson came by to visit. According to Jennings, they:

remembered a Jimmy Webb song called 'Highwayman' ... and since we were in the same place at the same time, we did a track on it. Then another, and another.

That 1985 single of Webb's tune about reincarnation spawned this huge selling album, produced by Moman and recorded at his Nashville studio, followed by a popular tour. Both the single and album went to number one on their respective country charts while the album peaked at number ninety-two on the national pop album charts. It also led to two more albums, under the collective name of the Highwaymen.

Initially, Webb had made the song part of his own 1977 Atlantic album, *El Mirage*, where it had garnered some attention. Glen Campbell first covered the song, a couple of years after Webb introduced it. Waylon observed that the song was really "four different people" so being cut by the four of them made "perfect" sense. It won the 1986 Grammy for "Country Song of the Year." It was also voted single of the year by the Academy of Country Music.

Rodney Crowell called 'Highwayman' "one of the most brilliant pieces of writing ever." Webb said the song was first suggested by "a very vivid dream I had in London." It was a dream in which he was being chased "by guys with swords." While the dream inspired the first verse, the song as a whole was about "the kind of people who built this country up." He explained that:

> the first verse is the rogue, the outlaw nation, the highwayman nation. The second verse is the seafaring nation; the trading and growth of a nation, and its subsequent generations adding to that. And then the dam builder is a generation of construction and science and technology. And then the last verse is a spacefarer; he's gonna fly a starship. And so, it's an American allegory.

The Woody Guthrie song, 'Deportee', featured additional vocals by Johnny Rodriguez. Woody wrote the words to the song in 1948 after reading about the crash, in Los Gatos Canyon, of a plane carrying migrant workers being deported back to Mexico. Woody initially performed it as a spoken word chant. It wasn't until ten years later that music was added by schoolteacher Martin Hoffman. After that Pete Seeger began featuring it in concert.

The rest of the song selection on the album turned out to be just as brilliant. There was Cash's 'Committed to Parkview' (recorded as a Willie/Cash duet), Paul Kennerley's 'Welfare Line', and Guy Clark's 'Desperados Waiting for a Train' (a number fifteen charting single for the foursome). Clark wrote the song about a friend of his grandmother's back in his home town of Monahans, Texas. As Clark explained to interviewer Bill DeYoung (writing in *Goldmine*), the friend, named Jack Prigg, drilled oil wells for Gulf Oil and taught nine or ten year old Guy how to whittle, spit, cuss, and drive a car.

All four artists sang together on 'Big River', which Cash wrote in the mid-fifties when he recorded for Sun Records. John disclosed in his autobiography that he wrote it "in the backseat of a car in White Plains, New York." It began "as a slow twelve-bar blues song" and Johnny even performed it that way a few times. Then he played it for Sam Phillips, the head of the Sun label, who said, "we'll put a beat to that." Sam then proceeded to add a "groove" that was "so much more powerful than mine."

The special feature of the version on this album was the inclusion of a "missing" verse. When Cash recorded the song for Sun in 1957, one verse was dropped because the song was deemed to be too long to be a viable commercial single. That verse was added here so that all four singers would have a verse to sing.

'The Last Cowboy Song', written by Ed Bruce, again featured all four singers. Five years earlier it had been done as a duet by Ed and Willie for one of Ed's albums. The long-forgotten Cindy Walker tune, 'Jim, I Wore a Tie Today', inspired by her life in the dust bowl of the thirties, became another Cash/Nelson duet.

Of the four artists involved in the project, only Cash and Willie appeared on all the cuts, including the closing number, 'The Twentieth Century Is Almost Over'. That song was written by Steve Goodman and John Prine, two artists who had been greatly helped on their way by Kristofferson. According to *Billboard's* national album sales charts, the set sold well enough to peak at the number ninety-two spot.

Seashores of Old Mexico. (Merle Haggard/Willie Nelson).   Epic Records PET-40293. (1987).

Track Listing: Seashores of Old Mexico, Without You on My Side, When Times Were Good, Jimmy the Broom, Yesterday, If I Could Only Fly, Shotgun and a Pistol, Love Makes a Fool of Us All, Why Do I Have to Choose, Silver Wings.

Recording Notes: The 1987 follow-up to the *Pancho and Lefty* project found Nelson and Haggard singing much similar and familiar material. 'Why Do I Have to Choose' was featured on the Waylon and Willie collaboration, *Take It to the Limit*, as well as on this album. It was also the only cut written by Willie.

'If I Could Only Fly' was the initial single but it lacked the magic of the previous two Haggard/Nelson singles, 'Pancho and Lefty' and 'Reasons to Quit', going only as far as number fifty-eight. The title cut was written by Merle, who also wrote or co-wrote four of the other nine selections, 'Jimmy the Broom' (with Freddy Powers), 'Shotgun and a Pistol', 'Without You on My Side', and the album closer, 'Silver Wings'.

'Silver Wings' was from 1970 and though a great song, it had never been a hit. The only charting version was done by The Hagers, an underrated twin brother duo who had regularly appeared on "Hee-Haw," the Buck Owens/Roy Clark syndicated television vehicle.

Merle said he wrote the song during a flight halfway across the United States. He told *Country Weekly* interviewer Robyn Flans that:

> it just came to me and it was done by the time we landed in L. A. It didn't knock anybody out. It didn't knock me out, but it was complete. It always had a feeling like maybe people would like to sing it.

The McCartney/Lennon classic, 'Yesterday', sounded great but not "Beatle-esque," being sparse in both production and instrumentation. David Lynn Jones, writer of Willie's 1986 number one hit, 'Livin' in the Promiseland', contributed 'When Times Were Good'. Old mentor and buddy, Hank Cochran, added 'Love Makes a Fool of Us All'.

So, how did Haggard and Nelson initially get together and what has kept them in touch? Willie recalled that:

> we kept runnin' into each other at Lake Tahoe and decided that we wanted to pick and sing together. I knew that he and I wouldn't have any trouble thinking up what songs to do!

Since then, according to Willie,

> Haggard keeps coming up to Tahoe and Reno whenever I'm up there. He lives up there, not far, you know. He comes up and hangs out with me and plays fiddle and guitar.

When Willie was inducted into the Country Music Hall of Fame in 1993, as part of his acceptance speech he spoke about a couple of other artists who deserved the same recognition, Ray Price and Merle Haggard. Merle was inducted in 1994. When statistician and author, Joel Whitburn published, in late 1997, his newest book based on *Billboard* magazine's various sales charts, *Top Country Albums 1964-1997*, he listed the top ten album sellers in country music during that time. The list was topped by Willie with Merle Haggard in second and Waylon Jennings. Merle wrote in his autobiography, that, in his opinion, Willie "changed his image - both to achieve and handle success. Nobody can argue with the results."

Walking the Line. (Merle Haggard, George Jones, Willie Nelson). Epic Records FET 40821. (1987).

Track Listing: I Gotta Get Drunk (w. George Jones), Pancho and Lefty (w. Merle Haggard), Half a Man (w. Merle Haggard), Heaven or Hell, Midnight Rider.

Recording Notes: This 1987 compilation collected previously released numbers by each of the gentlemen (separately and together) and then was made to appear like a cooperative newly-recorded project. Half of the album's ten selections featured Willie, either alone or as part of a duet (as listed above). The Nelson/Haggard cut, 'Half a Man', originally appeared on the *Pancho and Lefty* album, as did, of course, the 'Pancho and Lefty' track.

The Haggard duet on 'Half a Man' was one of three duets Willie did on the song. He shared vocals with both George Jones and Faron Young on separate versions. His first solo recording of the song came out as a Liberty Records single that peaked at number twenty-five.

The 'Heaven or Hell' track came from Willie's *Honeysuckle Rose* soundtrack. He had previously recorded the song for his 1974 Atlantic album, *Phases and Stages* (then it was entitled 'Heaven and Hell'). An earlier version, by Waylon and Willie, was an integral part of the 1976 multi-platinum RCA album, *Wanted: The Outlaws*. That version first appeared on Waylon's RCA album, *This Time*).

The Jones duet (with Willie) on 'I Gotta Get Drunk' was cut for a late seventies Jones album (though it was not released at the time). The track reappeared in 1991 as part of a Jones compilation entitled, *My Very Special Guests*. The final Willie cut was 'Midnight Rider', the Greg Allman song that had been a hit single for him off the *Electric Horseman* soundtrack. The classic Jones and Haggard rendition of 'Yesterday's Wine' also made its way on to the compilation.

Highwayman 2. (Willie Nelson/Johnny Cash/Waylon Jennings/Kris Kristofferson). Columbia Records CK 45240. (1990).

Track Listing: Silver Stallion, Born and Raised in Black and White, Two Stories Wide, We're All in Your Corner, American Remains, Anthem '84, Angels Love Bad Men, Songs That Make a Difference, Living Legend, Texas.

Recording Notes: As the 1990 follow-up to the very successful 1985 *Highwayman* album (and tour), this set spotlighted the song, 'Silver Stallion', written by Lee Clayton. Though a great song, it did not possess the magic of the 1985 album's title song, Jimmie Webb's 'Highwayman'. In the Spring of 1990, 'Silver Stallion' did reach number twenty-five on the country singles chart. Later in the year, the album peaked at number seventy-nine on *Billboard's* top pop album charts, thirteen positions higher than its predecessor.

Willie contributed two songs to the project, 'Texas' and 'Two Stories Wide', as did Kris Kristofferson. Kris' songs were 'Anthem '84' and 'Living Legend'. Cash and Jennings (with Roger Murrah) each added one song to the lineup. For the other songs, the foursome turned to some of Nashville's best, Troy Seals and Bobby Emmons for 'We're All in Your Corner', Rivers Rutherford for 'American Remains', and Don Cook and John Jarvis for 'Born and Raised in Black and White'.

Chips Moman once again produced. Waylon was not entirely satisfied with the end result, however, saying that:

> as an album, it could have used a little more time spent on it. We ran in and out too quick, and we didn't have that one great song. It's hard to find material that goes over with four people, each with strong let-it-all-hang-out opinions.

Clean Shirt. (Waylon & Willie). Epic EK 47462. (1991).

Track Listing: If I Can Find a Clean Shirt, I Could Write a Book About You, Old Age and Treachery, Two Old Sidewinders, Tryin' to Outrun the Wind, The Good Ol' Nights, Guitars That Won't Stay in Tune, The Makin's of a Song, Put Me on a Train Back to Texas, Rocks from Rolling Stones.

Recording Notes: The fourth Waylon and Willie album, from 1991, featured songs that dealt, to a large extent, with looking back over one's life. Bob Montgomery (of Buddy and Bob fame - the Buddy being a young Buddy Holly) produced. The project was actually supposed to have become Waylon's first solo album for his new label, Epic Records (a Columbia subsidiary).

Hen wrote, in his autobiography, that "from almost the first day we were in the studio," Bob wanted "Willie involved in this." Waylon strongly resisted the idea because:

> the minute Willie gets here he's gonna get on that bus, and here comes some of his old smoking and drinking buddies and they're going to have a good time out there.

Waylon felt that the scenario would wind up being:

> Willie coming around a corner and there'll be somebody behind him wailing and Willie will say 'He wrote this song and we're going to do it.' It'll be a dumb fuckin' song and we're stuck with it.

Actually, veteran Nashville songwriter, Troy Seals, dominated the song choices, appearing as co-writer on six of the ten tracks. He and Waylon co-wrote the title track, which, when released as the lead single from the album, peaked at number fifty-one on *Billboard's* country singles chart. Willie was included as one of four co-writers on two of the tracks (the other collaborators both times being Max D.

Barnes, Waylon, and Seals), 'Old Age and Treachery' and 'The Makin's of a Song', while Waylon co-wrote a total of five cuts.

Willie's son, Billy, was co-writer of the very poignant 'Put Me on a Train Back to Texas'. Another "son" also contributed, Eddy Shaver, son of "outlaw" Billie Joe. He fittingly co-wrote the final track, 'Rocks from Rolling Stones'. When the album came out, the only feeling about it from the label seemed to Waylon to be that it "had too many Mexican horns." The album did well enough, sales-wise, to peak at number one hundred ninety-three on the national sales charts.

1991 found Willie marrying his fourth wife, Ann-Marie D'Angelo. He starred with Kristofferson in *Another Pair of Aces: Three of a Kind*, the sequel to their successful movie, *A Pair of Aces*. Willie also appeared Along with Jackson Browne, Rosanne Cash, Queen Latifah, Ziggy Marley and others, he appeared at the Earth Day 1991 concert at Foxboro Stadium in Massachusetts. Late in the year, he signed a deal to become "star-in-residence" at the Ozark Theater in Branson, Missouri, beginning in early 1992.

The theater, right on the edge of the town limits, became known as the Willie Nelson Ozark Theater. Prior residents at the theater had been Mel Tillis and Shoji Tabuchi, both of whom went on to own bigger theaters. Willie did not take ownership of this theater, because as he once said, "I'm not much of a theater owner type guy."

Actually, he came to Branson because theater owner Johnny Harrington "and I are good friends." Willie explained that he "came here because I like him and I liked the idea of being here." What he liked was working a theater that felt "like working in a big club, really, one that doesn't sell alcohol."

Farm Aid picked up again in 1992 with a concert in Texas Stadium, Irving, Texas. John Cougar Mellencamp and the Black Crowes, along with Willie and the other three Highwaymen, appeared. Willie and the Highwaymen also appeared at the "Back to the Ranch" concert in Montauk, Long Island.

"Honeysuckle Rose":

The Columbia and Other Label Soundtracks

Willie got very interested in acting, movie-making, and soundtracks while he was with Columbia. Even before Willie's major soundtrack work for Columbia, his music had been part of a soundtrack album released on RCA. That occurred in 1976 (when he was already signed to Columbia) as part of the movie, *MacKintosh & T. J.*, which starred Roy Rogers in a comeback of sorts.

RCA also used Willie's music in another soundtrack, this time in 1991, for the movie, *My Heroes Have Always Been Cowboys*. The storyline of the movie was adapted from the song of the same title, written by Sharon Vaughan. The soundtrack album featured Willie's 1979 version of the tune (obtained from Columbia, where it had been used initially in *The Electric Horseman* soundtrack) along with songs by other country artists such as Alabama and Lorrie Morgan.

Highlights of Willie's acting and soundtrack accomplishments for Columbia were *The Electric Horseman*, *Honeysuckle Rose*, and *Songwriter*. Both the movie and soundtrack for *Honeysuckle Rose* were not only very successful, they were based on his life "on the road." The Columbia soundtrack for *Porky's Revenge* included his performance of the Elvis classic, 'Love Me Tender'. Willie also was involved in two other projects (on two different labels) that featured his original recordings.

There were times when he appeared in a movie but was not involved in the soundtrack in any way. even though the film did have a separately released soundtrack. One example was *Thief: Music from the Original Soundtrack*, which became a 1981 album release from Elektra (5E-521). The music was done by Tangerine Dream.

Over the years, Willie did become an accomplished actor, either in starring or supporting roles. Two of the critically acclaimed films in which he starred were *Barbarosa* (with Gary Busey) and a remake (for TV) of the John Wayne classic, *Stagecoach*, also starring buddies, Waylon and Johnny Cash.

Bill Witliff, a screenwriter known for his *Raggedy Man* (1981) and *The Black Stallion* (1979) screenplays, helped with the script for *Honeysuckle Rose*, though he said the director refused to see the reality of road life. While working with Willie on *Honeysuckle Rose*, he showed him the script for *Barbarosa*. Witliff remembered that:

> Willie literally stuck his finger in the middle of the script, opened it, read two pages, closed it, and said, 'I want to be that guy.' Then Willie suggested we go to Gary Busey for the other guy, and we made a deal with Marble Arch.

Witliff also directed *Red Headed Stranger* after he and Willie bought the movie back from Universal so Willie could star in it. Universal had been determined that Robert Redford had to be the "red headed stranger" in order for the movie to sell. Just so he could be the "stranger," Willie spent millions of his own money buying back the script, building the sets, and finally, filming the movie. In the end, it established him as a film star.

Where has film stardom taken him? Even with an excruciating road schedule in 1997, Willie landed a part in the Dustin Hoffman/Robert De Niro political thriller, *Wag the Dog*, in which he played a musical character responsible for writing and singing war songs aimed at getting the country behind a trumped-up war with Albania. Though he sang one especially tasteful blues-based song about an old shoe, he did not appear on the accompanying soundtrack album which consisted solely of Mark Knopfler works. Also in 1997, he played a guide (and sang the theme song) in the Joe Pesci/Danny Glover farce, *Gone Fishin'*. Add that to some guest television roles and Willie the actor could be found still going strong.

The Soundtracks - Album Listings

MacKintosh & T. J.: Music from the Original Soundtrack. (Various Artists). RCA APL1-1520. (1976).

Track Listing: Stay All Night Stay a Little Longer (with Waylon Jennings).

Recording Notes: This 1976 soundtrack album featured Willie (and Waylon) singing the Bob Wills classic, 'Stay All Night Stay a Little Longer'. Cowboy matinee hero Roy Rogers was the star of the film. Almost twenty years later, Willie would duet with Roy on Roy's comeback "tribute" album, also recorded for RCA.

The song used in the soundtrack was one Willie had done twice before. His first recorded version came on his debut Atlantic album, while he did the other for his Columbia *Willie and Family Live* set. The RCA cut used on the soundtrack also came out as a single release from the company, SD-1520.

Music from the Original Motion Picture Soundtrack: The Electric Horseman. (Featuring songs performed by Willie Nelson). Columbia Records CK 36327. (1979).

Track Listing: Midnight Rider, My Heroes Have Always Been Cowboys, Mammas Don't Let Your Babies Grow Up to Be Cowboys, So You Think You're a Cowboy, Hands on the Wheel.

Recording Notes: The first part of this 1979 soundtrack, produced by Director Sydney Pollack and Willie (which was why it had the unusual instrumentation featuring French horn and harp), boasted some

215

great Nelson performances. Two of the standouts were 'My Heroes Have Always Been Cowboys' and 'Mammas Don't Let Your Babies Grow Up to Be Cowboys'. When released as a single, 'My Heroes Have Always Been Cowboys' went to number one.

Actually, the song had originally been written for Bobby Bare. The writer, Sharon Vaughan, composed it at the request of her then boyfriend and soon-to-be-husband, Bill Rice, who wanted to present Bare with a cowboy song. When Bare didn't want the song, Waylon eventually recorded it. Later when Jennings was talking with Willie just before the filming of *The Electric Horseman* was scheduled to begin, he suggested that 'My Heroes Have Always Been Cowboys' should become the theme of the movie.

The song got another movie life in 1991 as the title track on the "Original Soundtrack" for the film *My Heroes Have Always Been Cowboys*. The soundtrack album, a "various artists" recording, was released by RCA/BMG as 2338-2-R. Still another life was forthcoming for the song when a version by the Gibson-Miller Band was included on *The Cowboy Way* soundtrack, from a film starring Woody Harrelson.

A Gregg Allman song, 'Midnight Rider', led off *The Electric Horseman* soundtrack. It also became the second single from the album, reaching number six in June 1980. The very tongue-in-cheek 'So You Think You're a Cowboy' was co-written by Willie and old buddy, Hank Cochran.

The other major song on the soundtrack, 'Mammas Don't Let Your Babies Grow Up to Be Cowboys', was very familiar to fans of Waylon and Willie, having previously been a number one country hit for the pair in 1978 (on the RCA label). Much of the rest of the soundtrack (the original score) was comprised of Dave Grusin music. As a promotional tie-in with the film, a promotional LP featuring music and dialogue from the film was released by the Weedeck Corporation, KM-4624.

Voices: Music from the Original Soundtrack. (Various Artists). Planet P-9002. (1979).

Track Listing: Bubbles in My Beer.
Recording Notes: This 1979 soundtrack featured Willie singing 'Bubbles in My Beer', another of the many Bob Wills standards, which Willie, either live or on recording, came to do so well. The song was first recorded by Bob and his band in 1947 when they were on the MGM label. Cindy Walker wrote the original sad lyrics to the song, based on suggestions from Tommy Duncan, the vocalist for Bob's band.

Wills then set the lyrics to a happy-feeling, Dixieland beat and a "lilting rhythm," making the song, in the words of Wills' biographer, Charles Townsend, "almost a satire of a man looking at the bubbles in his beer and thinking of a wasted past." Walker wrote many songs for

Wills, causing Townsend to conclude that the Western themes of her songs "had as much as anything to do with the cultivation of Wills's Western image." In fact, when Columbia Pictures made eight musicals with Bob in the forties, they had Cindy write all the music.

Music from the Original Soundtrack: Honeysuckle Rose. (Willie Nelson & Family). Columbia Records CGK 36752. (1980).

Track Listing: On the Road Again, Pick up the Tempo, Heaven or Hell, Fiddlin' Around (Johnny Gimble), Blue Eyes Crying in the Rain, Workin' Man Blues (Jody Payne), Jumpin' Cotton Eyed Joe (Johnny Gimble), Whiskey River, Bloody Mary Morning, Loving You Was Easier (Than Anything I'll Ever Do Again) (w. Dyan Cannon), I Don't Do Windows (Hank Cochran), Coming Back to Texas (Kenneth Threadgill), It's Not Supposed to Be That Way, You Show Me Yours (And I'll Show You Mine) (w. Amy Irving), If You Could Touch Her at All, Angel Flying Too Close to the Ground, I Guess I've Come to Live Here in Your Eyes, Angel Eyes (Angel Eyes) (w. Emmylou Harris), So You Think You're a Cowboy (Emmylou Harris), Make the World Go Away (Hank Cochran/Jeannie Seely), Two Sides to Every Story (Dyan Cannon), A Song for You, Uncloudy Day (w. Dyan Cannon).

Recording Notes: The semi-autobiographical movie from 1980 spawned this soundtrack album consisting of 23 selections. The album. itself, was recorded using the Enactron truck. Most of the songs were by Willie, with a few by Jody Payne, Johnny Gimble, and Emmylou Harris. Willie said that "the musical part of the character's life certainly parallels mine." Co-star Dyan Cannon did a passable job of singing with Willie when necessary. She also appeared at Willie's 1980 "picnic."

The song, 'On the Road Again', was written when, in Willie's words, he was trying "to show off." The executive producer (Sydney Pollack) and director (Jerry Schatzberg) of the movie were on a plane with Willie talking with him about the music, when, according to Willie, "they wanted a song." It was to be a "touring" song, or one "about people traveling all over the country making music," a topic about which he once said, "after every tour, I swear it'll be my last."

Willie said he picked up "an envelope, or maybe it was an airsick bag" and wrote the "on the road again" chorus. The melody wasn't written until the day it was recorded, which was actually during the filming of the movie. To Willie, melodies come easy, or as he once said,

> melodies are the easiest part for me, because the air is full of melodies. I hear them all the time, around me everywhere, night and day. If I need a melody, I pluck one out of the air.

For such a quickly written song, it won the 1980 Grammy award for Best Country Song and went to number one on the country singles charts in October.   It was also nominated for a 1980 Academy Award in the "Best Song" category.   The second number one single from the soundtrack, 'Angel Flying Too Close to the Ground', was written "during a time when Connie and I were having problems." Willie saw the song as "a good love song" that people were able to relate to "their own love affairs or even to someone who had died." Actually, Willie said that "it has a lot of different meanings to a lot of different people who have no idea why I wrote that song." It was not written specifically for the movie.

In fact, 1976 was the year it was composed.   Willie said he'll often:

> keep a song for a while before I release it. I like to wait until I think it has a chance, because if it's an exceptionally good song and it gets lost in the shuffle, you always wish that you would have waited for a better time to put it out. If you put it out at the wrong time, you've lost a good song.

A lot of very good Willie Nelson originals had previously been wasted on the poor-selling RCA albums.

Once when Willie was asked what his favorite songs were, he answered that they were two songs from *Honeysuckle Rose* (the two big singles, 'Angel Flying Too Close to the Ground' and 'On the Road Again', of course) and 'The Healing Hands of Time'. Willie once played, for a magazine writer (the article appeared in *Vanity Fair*), an unreleased version of 'Angel' that featured an additional verse not on the recorded version. As a recording, the song became Willie's tenth number one single.

Willie gave an "easygoing performance" in the movie, according to one critic.   Another critic, Leonard Maltin, found the movie "appealing." Country audiences did, as well, making it a profitable venture for everyone involved. Producer Pollack said that, as an actor, Willie "was relaxed, he was right on the money all the time, he knew what he had to do." He added that Willie was "incapable of telling a lie, which I think is the mark of a great actor." In his opinion, Willie could become "as big a movie actor as Barbra Streisand."

Music from Songwriter. (Willie Nelson & Kris Kristofferson). Columbia Records PCT 39531. (1984).

Track Listing: How Do You Feel About Foolin' Around (duet), Songwriter, Who'll Buy My Memories, Write Your Own Songs, Nobody Said It Was Going to Be Easy, Good Times, Eye of the Storm (duet),

Crossing the Border, Down to Her Socks, Under the Gun, The Final Attraction.

Recording Notes: Willie's acting and scripting came of age in this 1984 movie that starred him with old buddy Kris Kristofferson. The script was written by Bud Shrake, who would later work with Willie on Willie's autobiography. Sydney Pollack, who was executive producer of *Honeysuckle Rose*, turned up as producer. Lesley Ann Warren, Rip Torn, and Melinda Dillon also co-starred.

Willie starred as a Willie-like character, Doc, a songwriter who had to do it the hard way just to keep life interesting. Kris was his longtime sidekick, Blackie. When all was said and done, film critics Mick Martin and Marsha Porter called the movie "a delight."

Unfortunately, it got lost in a purported "turf war" between executives at CBS Records, who released the soundtrack, and TriStar Pictures, who eventually presented the film. The soundtrack album, never rereleased on compact disc, became the basic remnant of the movie, now rarely seen except on video or late night television. The first side was Willie's "Doc's side."

The culmination of the turf war was actually waged over the use of one of Willie's songs (only one though it was never spelled out which one) in the soundtrack. According to research presented in the book, *Hit and Run*, Walter Yetnikoff, head of CBS (Columbia) Records demanded royalty payments from TriStar Pictures for the use of a Nelson song in the video release of the film, even though Tri-Star was partially owned by CBS. Yetnikoff threatened to sue and even warned that "he would try to block TriStar from making a planned stock offering."

Irving Kaufman, president of TriStar, balked at the request (or demand) and eventually the dispute had to be settled by Yetnikoff's boss, Thomas Wyman, chief executive of the CBS parent company. Wyman eventually ruled that TriStar did not owe CBS Records any royalty payments. Yetnikoff reluctantly accepted the decision but the altercation led to a long adversarial relationship with Kaufman.

The lead cut of the soundtrack was a duet with Kris on 'How Do You Feel About Foolin' Around', a song written by Kris and two co-writers. As the primary single from the album, it sold enough to reach number forty-six on the country singles chart. 'Good Times', a song Willie initially did back with RCA, was reprised for the soundtrack.

'Who'll Buy My Memories', which later became the title for the "IRS Tapes" album, made a strong thematic showing, with its lyrics about the writer's art as commercial product. 'Write Your Own Songs', done also as duets with first Waylon and then Ray Benson, also fit in perfectly. Booker T. Jones produced the soundtrack, which was recorded at Pedernales Recording Studio.

Porky's Revenge: Music from the Original Soundtrack. (Various Artists). Columbia JS-39983. (1985).

Track Listing: Love Me Tender.
Recording Notes/Other Releases: The 1985 sequel soundtrack that followed up a very successful "Porky's," featured Willie singing Elvis' million-selling song from 1956, 'Love Me Tender'. After the song sold so well for Elvis, it became the title song for his first movie. As a single, it became the fifth song he took to the number one spot on the national singles charts. Elvis' version for the movie had an extra verse that was left off the single.

Composing credits for 'Love Me Tender' have always gone to Elvis and Vera Matson, though it was Vera's husband, Ken Darby, who actually wrote the piece. The Ken Darby Trio served as the backing vocalists for Elvis when he recorded the song. It was the first time Elvis recorded without his regular backing musicians.

Darby's music was based on 'Aura Lee', written in 1861 by W. W. Fosdick and George R. Poulton, which went on to become a favorite Union army song during the Civil War. With another set of words, the song was known as 'Army Blue' and became the class song of the West Point 1865 graduating class. As 'Aura Lee', it was sung by Frances Farmer in the 1936 film, *Come and Get It.* The *Porky's Revenge* soundtrack album was also released as CBS 70265.

Honeymoon in Vegas: Music from the Original Motion Picture Soundtrack. (Various Artists). Epic EK 52845. (1992).

Track Listing: Blue Hawaii.
Recording Notes: In the soundtrack of this 1992 film starring Nicholas Cage, James Caan, and a bevy of Elvis impersonators, Nelson performed the old Elvis hit, 'Blue Hawaii', written by two veteran movie songwriters, Ralph Rainger and Leo Robin, better known for songs like 'Thanks for the Memory'. Incidentally, Rainger was killed in a plane crash in 1942. It was a tribute to him that Elvis' 1961 movie featured his (and Robin's) more than twenty year old song. Here it was again in a movie whose premise was that a "living" Elvis continued to perform in Vegas. The theme revolved around a couple who eloped to Las Vegas right in the middle of an Elvis impersonator convention.

The song was initially a hit for Bing Crosby in 1937. It originated as an afterthought to a movie, *Waikiki Wedding* (set in Hawaii), that Bing was doing at the time. Rainger and Robin had completed most of the score for the movie and when the movie was about to open, Robin decided that it "needed a hit song, a simple hit." So, he went to Rainger who promptly told him he was "crazy." In Ralph's opinion, the score already boasted a song, 'Sweet Is the Word for You", which was being "raved about all through the music department."

Robin was not going to be sidetracked. He said to Rainger,

> sit down at the piano, and the first thing that pops into your head, you just write it down and bring it to me, and I'll write it up.

Ralph did just that and played it for Robin, who "jotted some words down to it." Nothing more happened until two months later when the music proofs for the score were sent to Rainger. Ralph saw one of the proofs, and proceeded to tell Robin, "I'm not going to publish this song. This will be a disgrace to us. It's a cheap melody. It's a piece of crap! It'll destroy us."

Robin told him the picture was about to come out and there was no way to stop it. He said he was "willing to take a chance with my reputation." The song and the movie came out as scheduled. The song Rainger thought would be a hit, 'Sweet Is the Word for You' bombed, while, Robin's choice, 'Blue Hawaii' (the supposed "piece of trash"), turned out to be (according to Robin) their "most performed number." Just as it did something to him, he surmised that, "it has something that strikes a responsive chord in the people."

How did the song come to be recorded by Willie? According to Willie's manager, Mark Rothbaum, 'Blue Hawaii' was the first song Don Was produced with Willie. Don and Willie met through Mark and began to work together for the first time in Dublin, Ireland. The very first song they recorded was 'Blue Hawaii'.

Then the Highwayman project got underway and the song got shelved until it turned up as a perfect fit for the *Honeymoon in Vegas* soundtrack. It fell right into place alongside Billy Joel's piano-based version of 'All Shook Up', Dwight Yoakam's stellar performance of 'Suspicious Minds' and Amy Grant's lush remake of 'Love Me Tender', which Trisha Yearwood had also wanted to do. Instead, Yearwood remade 'Devil in Disguise'.

Willie was no stranger to Elvis songs, having recorded, with Leon Russell in 1979, the Elvis million seller, 'Heartbreak Hotel'. In 1985, he sang 'Love Me Tender' on the soundtrack of *Porky's Revenge*. His admiration for Elvis went back even further. He recently said that:

> when I first heard Elvis, I was a disc jockey myself. I was playing all country music or what I wanted to play, really. And I played Elvis all the time. I thought he was a progressive thinker also. I thought he was a progressive musician. In fact, he sort of started what some people called rock and roll. I called it progressive country.

On Elvis, himself, Willie had some definitive insights, telling an interviewer that "in his heyday, when he was really hot, there was an explosion of energy between Elvis and his audience." Willie said he "wasn't a wild fan of Elvis's," but he did admire him as a performer because you could:

> put the man onstage doing his music, and you got something more powerful than the sum of its parts. You got magnetism in action. Maybe it was sexual, I don't know, but if ever a performer could get up onstage and turn a crowd into crashing waves of energy, it was Elvis.

Yet even Elvis had problems with certain audiences, something with which Willie could identify. He told the same interviewer that "Elvis couldn't really whip up a Las Vegas dinner-show crowd on a regular basis." Perhaps that was why, even when Willie was a multi-platinum album seller at the peak of his popularity, he didn't turn to Las Vegas for regular employment. He said he:

> went to see Elvis one night on the strip and I thought, 'What is going on here?' There was Elvis up there working his ass off, and the crowd was just kind of politely exhausted. They clapped and whistled, but you couldn't feel them giving anything back. I felt like jumping up on top of a table and yelling, 'Hey everybody, that's Elvis Presley up there! You should be jumping up screaming.

Gone Fishin': Music from the Original Motion Picture Soundtrack. (Various Artists). Hollywood Records HR-62119-2. (1997).

Track Listing: Down in the Everglades.

Recording Notes: The 1997 movie was not memorable (in fact, one reviewer labeled it the *Ishtar* of the nineties), but parts of the soundtrack were. The score opened with Willie singing 'Down in the Everglades', a very humorous, well-written song, composed by Totch Brown. Randy Edelman scored the picture, conducted the orchestra (he even played a piano solo), and produced the soundtrack album (including Willie's track). Two vocals by the group, The Love Junkies, helped make the music far superior to the on-screen action and acting.

"On the Road Again":

The "Greatest Hits" Compilations

As with all artists, there were the inevitable greatest hits collections. Willie's first "Hits" package was unique for the industry in that all of the tracks had not necessarily been previous "hits." Some were included because they were planned to be "hits" in the future. Some tracks were also included because they were concert favorites.

Willie's Columbia hits packages culminated in 1995 with a three CD "boxed" set, *Revolutions of Time*. Reader's Digest released a five volume collection, the IRS forced two, and Columbia released several in the budget range, as well as two "Super" hits packages. Telstar of England, courtesy of CBS, released, in 1987, one of the best foreign collections.

The IRS-forced collections brought out recordings that probably would not have made it into the commercial marketplace otherwise. That was especially true of *The Hungry Years*, a single disc set that followed the two disc IRS Tapes collection. *The Hungry Years* was full of gems that included tracks done with Emmylou Harris and Rodney Crowell.

Since Willie left the label in 1993, Columbia, recognizing his continuing star power, has mined the catalog of Nelson recordings, releasing several budget collections. The most notable was one they did through the Coyote label, a compilation of recordings with others. Included, for the first time on CD, was his duet with Mary Kay Place, who played aspiring country singer, Loretta, on the TV series, *Mary Hartman, Mary Hartman*. In 1997, Sony Special Products released a collection of standards by Willie.

As a closing note, it is appropriate to say that none of the greatest hits collections has been entirely satisfying because none has had anything new or unique to offer. The boxed set, which was a comprehensive overview of Willie's Columbia recordings, offered no unreleased or alternate tracks. Every single cut had been on a previous album. Columbia needs to go back and thoroughly search their archives to hopefully bring out something that Willie fans and connoisseurs have not heard before or do not have elsewhere on an existing album. Then again, maybe nothing that obscure has ever existed. Yet, even RCA found obscure unreleased stuff on Elvis twenty years after he died.

Willie the movie star!
(Photo from Alive Films and Evelyn Shriver Public Relations)

The "Greatest Hits" Sets - Album Listings

Willie Nelson's Greatest Hits (and Some That Will Be). Columbia Records CGT 37542. (1981).

Track Listing: Railroad Lady, Heartaches of a Fool, Blue Eyes Crying in the Rain, Whiskey River, Good Hearted Woman, Georgia on My Mind, If You've Got the Money I've Got the Time, Look What Thoughts Will Do, Uncloudy Day, Mammas Don't Let Your Babies Grow Up to Be Cowboys, My Heroes Have Always Been Cowboys, Help Me Make It Through the Night, Angel Flying Too Close to the Ground, I'd Have to Be Crazy, Faded Love, On the Road Again, Heartbreak Hotel, If You Could Touch Her at All, Till I Gain Control Again, Stay a Little Longer.

Recording Notes: This 1981 greatest hits package set a new standard for the genre because it included old hits, great performances, great songs, as well as some yet-to-be released singles. Some of the songs had not been singles for Columbia. For example, 'If You (Can) Could Touch Her at All' came out on RCA (in 1978, three years after Willie signed to Columbia) while 'Stay A Little Longer' had been an Atlantic release.

'Heartaches of a Fool' went out as a single in late 1981, settling in at a disappointing number thirty-nine, capping a sales slump for Willie that began in May 1981 with the 'Mona Lisa' single. Though not included here, 'Mona Lisa' had peaked at number eleven, disappointing because it followed the huge number one hit, 'Angel Flying Too Close to the Ground'). Fortunately, the next single would go to number one, 'Always on My Mind' (also not on this set).

With twenty tracks, this was a long album. Fortunately, every cut was a gem to either hear again or for the first time. The selections were also included on a picture disc given out as a promotional tool by HBO (Home Box Office) to drum up support for a Willie and Family show on the cable channel. A full color shot of a bearded Willie highlighted each side of the vinyl disc.

The song, 'Til I Gain Control Again', was written by Rodney Crowell. It was first introduced by Emmylou Harris on her second Reprise album, *Elite Hotel*. Rodney, then a member of her "Hot" band, passed the song along to her after he composed it in 1976. It took until 1983, however, for Crystal Gayle to take it to number one on the country singles chart.

Rodney said the the song was one he wrote "pretty early in my songwriting career and it was just kind of a personal breakthrough." It was an important song for him because:

> it was in the really early stages of when I moved songwriting out of my head and into my heart. That was a really good move for me, because it made my songs more enduring and more acceptable to people.

He explained why that was critical, saying "although our heads may not have much in common, all of our hearts have everything in common."

The version on this album was Willie alone and it was outstanding. Still, the author of the song disclosed in an interview that, "I did this version of 'Till I Gain Control Again' with Willie Nelson that was never released, and it was real good." The version with Rodney was recorded in 1976, but it took until 1991 for it to come out on a set called *The Hungry Years*.

Blue Skies. CBS Records 10025. (1981).

Track Listing: Blue Eyes Crying in the Rain, Georgia on My Mind, All of Me, That Lucky Old Sun, Whiskey River, Always, Moonlight in Vermont, On the Sunny Side of the Street, For the Good Times, Amazing Grace, Stardust, Blue Skies, My Heroes Have Always Been Cowboys, Help Me Make It Through the Night, On the Road Again, Tenderly, Summertime, Unchained Melody, Funny How Time Slips Away, Red Headed Stranger.

Recording Notes: This 1981 release was a British compilation only, never meant for the U. S. market. Several of its tracks were later rereleased in 1987 on a Telstar compilation, *Across the Tracks: The Best of Willie Nelson.* Since some of the cuts were from the *Honeysuckle Rose* soundtrack, this set tied in nicely, as intended, with the movie's showing in and around England. One of the more obscure and rarely rereleased cuts was 'Tenderly', from the Leon Russell duet album.

A Song for You. Hallmark SHM-3127/Pickwick PWKS-578. (1983).

Track Listing: A Song for You, Just As I Am, For the Good Times, Amazing Grace, Stormy Weather, Blue Eyes Crying in the Rain, Help Me Make It Through the Night, Thanks Again, One for My Baby, Loving Her Was Easier (Than Anything I'll Ever Do Again), Moonlight in Vermont, That Lucky Old Sun.

Recording Notes: This late 1983 compilation of CBS (Columbia) material came out in England only. It was an odd assortment of material, culled from his Leon Russell duet album, his albums of standards, and even his "religious" album. 'Thanks Again' from *The Sound in Your Mind* album was both an unusual and welcome rerelease.

His Greatest Hits and Finest Performances: Collector's Edition of Original Recordings. Reader's Digest (CBS Special Products) RBA-133/A. (1987).

Record One (12 of His Greatest No. 1 Hits) Track Listing: To All the Girls I've Loved Before (w. Julio Iglesias), On the Road Again, My Heroes Have Always Been Cowboys, Heartbreak Hotel (w. Leon Russell), Angel Flying Too Close to the Ground, Forgiving You Was Easy, If You've Got the Money I've Got the Time, Blue Skies, Georgia on My Mind, Blue Eyes Crying in the Rain, Pancho and Lefty (w. Merle Haggard), Always on My Mind.

Record Two (Pop Classics - Willie's Way/Country Classics - Willie's Way) Track Listing: Stardust, I'm Gonna Sit Right Down and Write Myself a Letter, Mona Lisa, As Time Goes By (w. Julio Iglesias), All of Me, September Song, Help Me Make It Through the Night, Crazy Arms, (Now and Then There's) A Fool Such as I (w. Hank Snow), In the Jailhouse Now (w. Webb Pierce), Faded Love (w. Ray Price).

Record Three (Willie Sings His Own Songs/The Romantic Side of Willie) Track Listing: Funny How Time Slips Away (w. Ray Price), Little Old Fashioned Karma, Hello Walls (w. Faron Young), Night Life (w. Ray Price), Party's Over, I Love You a Thousand Ways, I'd Have to Be Crazy, Don't You Ever Get Tired of Hurting Me (w. Ray Price), Let It Be Me, Release Me (w. Ray Price).

Record Four (Willie's Favorite "Road" Songs/Willie and Old Friends) Track Listing: The Highwayman (w. Kris Kristofferson, Waylon Jennings and Johnny Cash), I'm Movin' on (w. Hank Snow), City of New Orleans, Desperados Waiting for the Train (w. Kris Kristofferson, Waylon Jennings and Johnny Cash), The Midnight Rider,

Seven Spanish Angels (w. Ray Charles), Reasons to Quit (w. Merle Haggard), Old Friends (w. Roger Miller and Ray Price), I Saw the Light (w. Leon Russell), Take It to the Limit (w. Waylon Jennings).

Record Five (Live in Concert/In a Reflective Mood) Track Listing: Whiskey River, Mammas Don't Let Your Babies Grow Up to Be Cowboys, If You Could Touch Her at All, Good Hearted Woman, Uncloudy Day, Without a Song, Me and Paul, Last Thing I Needed First Thing This Morning, Why Do I Have to Choose, Remember Me.

Recording Notes: This 1987 compilation from Reader's Digest, courtesy of CBS Special Products, featured five LP's with a specific concept for each LP side, such as "12 of His Greatest No. 1 Hits," "Pop Classics - Willie's Way," "Live in Concert," and "Willie's Favorite 'Road' Songs" - well, that's the basic idea. Included was a booklet entitled, "Music Program Notes," which gave an excellent insight into each of the songs. The album was labeled a "collector's edition of original recordings."

Across the Tracks: The Best of Willie Nelson. Telstar Records TCD 2317. (1987).

Track Listing: Always on My Mind, Blue Eyes Crying in the Rain, Until It's Time for You to Go, Unchained Melody, She's Out of My Life, Why Are You Pickin' on Me, I'd Have to Be Crazy, To All the Girls I've Loved Before (w. Julio Iglesias), Mamas, Don't Let Your Babies Grow Up to Be Cowboys, On the Road Again, My Heroes Have Always Been Cowboys, Georgia on My Mind, Let It Be Me, Moonlight in Vermont, Heartbreak Hotel, Help Me Make It Through the Night.

Recording Notes: This was a 1987 compilation, courtesy of CBS Records, UK. It contained sixteen cuts, with a notation for each telling on which album it first appeared. Interestingly, there were three songs from the *City of New Orleans* album (but not the title track) that really weren't "best sellers" by themselves. In fact, the selections were listed as having come from five albums, *City of New Orleans, Always on My Mind, Half Nelson, Willie Nelson's Greatest Hits,* and *Blue Skies,* which was a British compilation, not sold in the United States.

On the Road Again. Columbia Records (CBS Special Products) A/BT 21281. (1989).

Track Listing: On the Road Again, Heartaches of a Fool, One Day at a Time, Me & Bobby McGee, Blue Eyes Crying in the Rain, If You've Got the Money I've Got the Time, Why Are You Pickin' on Me, Can I Sleep in Your Arms, Uncloudy Day.

Recording Notes: A 1989 budget anthology from CBS finally put one of Willie's greatest singles as the title track to an album.   There were nine selections ranging from 'Blue Eyes Crying in the Rain' to 'Uncloudy Day'.   Most were well-known.   It was fitting to bring the lovely 'Can I Sleep in Your Arms' out of an undeserved obscurity,

Yours Always. Columbia Records. (Sony Music Special Products) A 21562. (1990).

Track Listing: Always on My Mind (*), I Never Go Around Mirrors (*), Why Are You Pickin' on Me, Help Me Make It Through the Night (*), Angel Flying Too Close to the Ground, Mona Lisa (*), I'm Not Trying to Forget You, If You've Got the Money I've Got the Time (*), It's Not Supposed to Be That Way, City of New Orleans (*).

Recording Notes: This 1990 budget release from the Special Products division of Sony combined ten past recordings highlighted by 'Angel Flying Too Close to the Ground'.   The two songs associated with Lefty Frizzell and the Kristofferson original gave much-needed depth to the collection.   Opening with 'Always on My Mind' and closing with Steve Goodman's 'City of New Orleans' was also a nice touch.   A 1998 CD from KRB Music Companies (catalog number A28245), entitled *Wanted*, featured (as "six great hits") six tracks (*) from this set.

* = the six tracks from this collection that made up the 1998 set, *Wanted*, KRB Music Companies/Sony Music Special Products A28245.

Who'll Buy My Memories, Vol. 1 & Vol. 2: The IRS Tapes. Columbia Records A2K 52981/2/3. (1991).

Disc One Track Listing: Who'll Buy My Memories, Jimmy's Road, It Should Be Easier Now, Will You Remember, I Still Can't Believe You're Gone, Yesterday's Wine, It's Not Supposed to Be That Way, Country Willie, The Sound in Your Mind, Permanently Lonely, So Much to Do, Lonely Little Mansion.

Disc Two Track Listing: Summer of Roses/December Day, Pretend I Never Happened, Slow Down Old World, Opportunity to Cry, I'm Falling in Love Again, If You Could Only See, I'd Rather You Didn't Love Me, What Can You Do to Me Now, Buddy, Remember the Good Times, Wake Me When It's Over, Home Motel.

Recording Notes: Willie's tax problems and questionable financial advice have all been well documented.   David Beck, of the Knight-Ridder Newspaper syndicate, explained succinctly that:

at a time when he owed $2 million in taxes, he was advised to borrow not $2 million to pay those taxes but $12 million to put into a tax shelter.

While that may have sounded like shrewd advise, it wasn't, because as Beck explained,

when those shelters were disallowed by the IRS, he found himself owing about - well, the total in taxes, interest and penalties, after some heavy negotiation with the feds, is about $17 million.

What was really behind Willie's mountain of tax debt? In a carefully researched article for *Texas Monthly*, Robert Draper concluded that it definitely was not a case "of greed that backfired. It's instead a story of generosity to a major fault." On top of that, as Draper pointed out, Willie was effectively "supporting an entire community" of people who worked for him.

In effect, Willie spent or gave away too much money before paying his taxes. His accounting firm, Price Waterhouse, was supposed to show him how to legally defer his tax debts. Instead, the firm has been charged, in a lawsuit, with giving him not just bad, but deliberately fraudulent, advice.

So, by 1991, he was in "hoc" to the IRS for sixteen or seventeen million dollars, depending on the source, and finally, according to Willie, thirty-two million dollars. His possessions were auctioned off, though fortunately they were often auctioned to a friend who somehow got them back to Willie. The IRS also confiscated some tapes of Willie's songs, ones he had recorded over many years.

This set of tapes was compiled into a two disc album (with production credits going to Willie and Bob Johnston, producer of three albums Bob Dylan recorded in Nashville) and originally sold during 1991 through mail order (exclusively through television marketing by the Austin-based Television Group) to help pay that debt. It was planned that six dollars from each album sale would go to the IRS. Willie's publishers agreed to reduced rates to make this possible. Sony (Columbia) charged only manufacturing costs.

By 1992 Columbia (Sony) began (through its Special Products division) selling the album after it had enjoyed considerable sales success through the mail. All of the songs on the double compact disc were written by Willie (except for 'What Can You Do to Me Now', co-written with Hank Cochran) and featured him singing with only the accompaniment of his own guitar. This marked the first album appearance of the song, 'Jimmy's Road', a favorite of drummer Paul English that Willie wrote in 1967. Paul explained the song, there was this young kid who was playing bass with us named Jimmy Hardeman - real young, 17 or so, awful nice kid. Hell, he hadn't ever been in a fist fight! Well, he got drafted then, right, and they gave him a rifle and expect him to go off shootin' people just cause they told him to. Stupidest thing. Freaked the poor kid out. He ended up in a mental hospital. So Willie wrote this song about it... It was just a sad song about a dumb war, what it did to a friend of ours.

Many of the songs were originally done as Pamper Music demos and many dated back to his days at Liberty, RCA, and Atlantic. The title song was one he remembered writing in Houston just before he went to Nashville. As Willie wrote in his notes, he recorded these "thru the years."

The stark reinterpretation of 'The Sound in Your Mind', first done for Columbia in 1976, gave a much more intimate feeling to the words, especially. The very beautiful, 'I'm Falling in Love Again', appeared again on his 1994 Liberty album. Somehow, the deep, heartfelt song, 'If You Could Only See' appeared for the first and only time on this album.

When the tax debt news hit the public, the tabloids especially picked up on it and began circulating stories about how the whole situation was ruining his life, to the point where one scandal sheet hinted he was homeless and mentally unbalanced. Willie reacted to the "doomsday" tabloid stories with an unusual tongue-in-cheek observation. He told a *Rolling Stone* magazine interviewer that:

I've been calling around looking for one of those suicide machines. I'll go on national TV, hook myself up to that machine and tell everyone I have 'til 7:00 to get $16 million. If I don't, I'm pulling the plug.

That sounded like shades of sarcasm toward the kind of fund raising evangelist Oral Roberts once tried.

He also told the *New York Times* that "I've been broke before and I will be again." He added, with sort of a question, "Heart-broke? That's serious. Lose a few bucks? That's not." About the overall tax problem, Willie has said "there was no criminal intent to hide money." He did admit, however, that "the IRS situation took away my incentive. There was no reason to work if maybe they'd take everything I made."

He explained to Lorianne Crook (of The Nashville Network's Crook and Chase),

I'm not the best business man in the world. I don't think anybody who writes songs and plays can be. I think it's important that you trust someone to do these things for you.

He got to the crux of the matter when he added,

I'm not a tax dodger. Since 1983, I had paid eight million dollars in taxes. I feel like I received some bad advice and it cost me a lot of money.

That prompted Crook to ask Willie what money meant to him. He replied, "It's a tool to get something done." To conclude the interview, he observed that he would rather have a "freezer full of good meat in the winter than to have a closet full of hundred-dollar bills." Willie also told her that "I'm pretty happy with where I'm at. I still have all my fingers left and whatever talent I have." He then quipped, "here's a guy from Abbott, Texas, who picked cotton half his life, and now he owes seventeen million dollars." In an aside to *Time* magazine in early 1998, he admitted that whenever he knew he was going to deal with the IRS, "I made sure I was stoned."

From a 1995 perspective, Willie updated *Rolling Stone* on how the IRS affected him "on a daily basis," saying that:

mentally it was a breeze. They didn't come out and confiscate anything other than that first day, and they didn't show up at every gig and demand money.

Actually, as Willie summarized, "we teamed up and put out a record." In 1993, the tax bill from IRS was finally settled, though the suit against Willie's "advisors," Price Waterhouse, continued. When that suit was filed (for $45 million) by Willie's lawyers in 1990, it charged the company "with fraud over a 10-year period beginning in 1979." Specific damages claimed totalled fifteen million. The language of the suit claimed that:

for over $1 million in advisory fees, Price Waterhouse recommended to him (Willie) investments they said were thoroughly investigated for soundness.

Instead, as the suit alleged, "the firm did not properly investigate the investments and then took steps to conceal its failure to do so." Predictably, the accounting firm denied any "wrongdoing." Their spokesperson and attorney, Allen Young, issued a statement claiming that Price Waterhouse "only did his accounting and taxes. We are not his investment advisors."

The firm was not content with that simple a statement. They went on to say that "Mr. Nelson and his advisors made all of the decisions regarding tax shelters." Further, they stated, "those decisions and the economic consequences that resulted from those decisions were Mr. Nelson's responsibility." So, Willie paid them huge bucks to just do tax returns. They never did any "advising" of any kind.

A number of critics felt this ordeal brought out some of Willie's best efforts. One wrote that "in 1991, Nelson's widely reported tax debts unexpectedly spurred his best work in years." Once the debt was settled, Willie embarked on a tour sponsored by Jose Cuervo and did some Taco Bell ads.

His manager, Mark Rothbaum, thought the tour and ads to be of utmost importance. He commented that,

> people tend to view anyone with tax problems as sick. We felt it was important to let America know Willie was corporately attractive - especially since things between him and the Government are fine now.

Mark could not have anticipated one very important undercurrent; Willie was not looked upon like most people with a tax problem. He wasn't seen as "sick" or as a tax-dodger. Not only did friends "buy back" his property, people all over the country tried to pitch in and help. James White, owner of The Broken Spoke in Austin said that "when Willie had his problem we put a gallon pickle jar on the bar and people started giving donations." That pickle jar mushroomed into a national outpouring or as White recalled,

> before I knew it, the Associated Press put it out on the wire and people were sending in money from all over the country. I told him, 'Hell, I feel like your mailman.' Everyone's offering him the clothes off their back, a place to stay. I even got money from a guy in the Birmingham jail. You don't get more country than that. I sent Willie $10,000 in all. We had to do something to help Willie. He's helped everybody.

By 1993, Willie's debt was reportedly reduced sufficiently for the IRS to finally settle the situation permanently. In a recent CBS Television *Sixty Minutes* profile, Willie said that the thirty-two million dollar debt was reduced to ten million and he was allowed to pay it off over several years. The reporter noted that when Willie pays his taxes for 1997, he will have completely repaid his agreed-upon debt. Willie spoke of being very proud that he did repay and that he didn't declare bankruptcy to get out from under it.

The Hungry Years. Columbia Records (Sony Music Special Products) A22354. (1991).

Track Listing: The Hungry Years, Detour, I'm Ragged but I'm Right, It Wouldn't Be the Same (Without You), Your Memory Won't Die, When I Stop Dreaming, If That's the Fashion, Solitaire, Milk Cow Blues, Linda, The Last Thing on My Mind, She Is Gone, Til I Gain Control Again, Time Changes Everything, Carefree Moments.

Recording Notes: During a 1991 interview with *Vanity Fair,* Willie played a tape of material containing, among other fascinating items, a version of 'Angel Flying Too Close to the Ground' that had an extra verse. There was also another song on the tape the interviewer especially noted, 'Your Memory Won't Die in My Grave', as well as cuts done with Rodney Crowell and Emmylou Harris. The material on the tape was set to go out in 1991 under the title, *The Hungry Years,* as an unadvertised "bonus" addition to the mail-order "IRS tapes."

Its actual release was delayed and a great deal of confusion accompanied its eventual release. Willie said at one point it "never came out." Then late in 1991, the album began a very limited distribution, first through the Columbia House Mail Order Club and most recently as part of Willie's concession stand items, for sale before, during, and after his concerts.

The "tape," itself, turned out to be from a 1976 recording session held at the Studio in the Country in Bogalusa, Louisiana. Unfortunately, the "extra verse" 'Angel' was not included. According to the accompanying notes, the cuts were overdubbed in Nashville in 1978 and then overdubbed again and mixed in Hendersonville in 1991. The album has been included in the "greatest hits" compilation section because of its status as a companion to the "IRS" tapes.

The recording location, Studio in the Country, was built a mile down Highway 436 turnoff after the Highway 21 intersection just outside Bogalusa. In the seventies and eighties, under former owner Gene Foster, who purchased it in 1979, the studio had quite a state-of-the-art reputation. Foster remembered the studio as being "way ahead of its time. It was the first studio to be totally wired for 48-track and video. And back in the early 1970's, that was unheard of." Studio records showed that Willie considerable recording there, in total he "recorded portions of three albums at the studio as well as the entire *IRS* album."

The title song of this collection, 'The Hungry Years', was the first of many musical "departures" for Willie. It was written by the New York-based team of Howard Greenfield and Neil Sedaka. Sedaka was, of course, the fifties rock and roll idol who rode a crest of popularity with hits like 'Oh Carol', 'Calendar Girl', and 'Breaking Up Is Hard to Do'. Signed to Elton John's Rocket Records, Neil re-invented himself in the mid-seventies with two great albums, *Sedaka's Back* and *The Hungry Years.*

One of the cuts on the *Sedaka's Back* album was 'Solitaire', written by Neil with a more recent co-writer, Phil Cody. Karen and Richard Carpenter had a 1976 top twenty pop hit with it and Elvis had a posthumous double-sided top ten country charter featuring it and the Andy Williams hit, 'Are You Sincere'. Andy actually had the first sales success with 'Solitaire' before the Carpenters, but only on the Adult Contemporary charts.

Willie's versions of both Sedaka songs were definitively country, highlighted by his distinctive phrasing and his road band as complemented by fiddler Johnny Gimble and drummer Rex Ludwig. The other "departures" ran the gamut from Sleepy John Estes' 'Milk Cow Blues' to Paul Westmoreland's 'Detour', which Willie and Leon Russell had previously done together on their "duet" album. In the studio, T. J. Clay added harmonica to the 'Milk Cow' cut. When Willie does the song in concert, sister Bobbie often stretches it out with a very bluesy piano solo.

And yes, the album did feature the version of Rodney Crowell's 'Till I Gain Control Again' on which Rodney sang harmony. That was the one Rodney said was "real good" but "never came out." Kimmie Rhodes also sang harmony on the cut. The duet with Emmylou was on the Louvin Brothers' song, 'When I Stop Dreaming'. The Louvin's clear mountain harmonies were big influences on Emmylou and she unfailingly included her version of a Louvin song on most of her early albums.

Willie not only covered Tom Paxton's 'The Last Thing on My Mind' for this set, he redid it in 1987 for the *Island in the Sea* album. He continued his flawless knack for resurrecting older forgotten songs composed by some of country music's greatest writers. His picks ranged from a song that Western film star, Jimmy Wakely, wrote with Fred Rose, 'I Wouldn't Be the Same Without You' to the Wilburn Brothers' 'Carefree Moments'. The Wakely/Rose song had been previously released on the *Somewhere Over the Rainbow* album.

Tommy Collins was a great writer and singer based in Bakersfield, California, who heavily influenced Merle Haggard (he honored him in a song called, 'Leonard'). Here Willie reached deep in the Collins catalog to cover 'If That's the Fashion'. Another Tommy, Tommy Duncan, who worked with Bob Wills, heavily influenced Willie. Willie covered the Duncan song, 'Time Changes Everything'.

Wills was the first to record it and it was a highly personal song for him, coming at a time when his third marriage had broken down completely. Though the lyrics said "time changes everything," Bob told his estranged wife "the lyrics were wrong." According to his biographer, Wills told her that "time had not changed his love for her." Since then both George Jones and the "Hag" have covered the song.

Rounding out the collection was the song, 'Linda' by Jack Lawrence and the classic George Jones autobiographical number, 'I'm Ragged but I'm Right'. The "ragged but right" part served as the title to Jones' classic biography by Dolly Carlisle. The image behind the song could have summarized the lives of many country artists, including both Willie and Johnny Cash. Cash did briefly chart the song in 1983. Though Jones had the writer's credit, Moon Mullican had the first (and only) hit version back in 1961 (it peaked at number fifteen on the country singles chart).

But did George really write the song? In her book, Carlisle quoted George's second wife, Shirley Corley, as saying:

> George didn't write a lot of those songs he took credit for. He didn't write 'Ragged but Right'. Darrell Edwards probably sold it to him. Darrell Edwards wrote most of those songs.

Of course, Darrell and George had been close friends ever since their boyhood days in the Texas big thicket country. Darrell also got co-writing credit on some of George's biggest hits, so he made a good money thanks to George's stardom. Nonetheless, if what Ms. Corley said was true, then someone else got credit for a songwriter's great songs (by buying them - not writing them). Willie definitely knew what that felt like.

The Many Sides of Willie Nelson: 3 CD Set. Columbia Records (Sony Music Special Products) A322736. (1992).

Disc One ("Easy") Track Listing: Always on My Mind, Without a Song, Georgia on My Mind, Stardust, All of Me, Danny Boy, Let It Be Me, Mona Lisa, Blue Skies, Blue Eyes Crying in the Rain, Wind Beneath My Wings, Over the Rainbow.

Disc Two ("Duets") Track Listing: Reasons to Quit (w. Merle Haggard), Slow Movin' Outlaw (w. Lacy J. Dalton), Half a Man (w. George Jones), How Do You Feel About Foolin' Around (w. Kris Kristofferson), Take It to the Limit (w. Waylon Jennings), Seven Spanish Angels (w. Ray Charles), Faded Love (w. Ray Price), Pancho and Lefty (w. Merle Haggard), Hello Walls (w. Faron Young), I'm Movin' on (w. Hank Snow), You're Gonna Love Yourself (in the Morning) (w. Brenda Lee), Heartbreak Hotel (w. Leon Russell).

Disc Three ("Cowboy") Track Listing: My Heroes Have Always Been Cowboys, City of New Orleans, On the Road Again, Mamas, Don't Let Your Babies Grow Up to Be Cowboys, Whiskey River, Red Headed Stranger, South of the Border, So You Think You're a Cowboy, A Horse

Called Music, If You've Got the Money, I've Got the Time, Midnight Rider, Good Hearted Woman.

Recording Notes: With this 1992 three compact disc compendium, Columbia Records' parent company, Sony, showed its determination to make as much money as possible off the Nelson catalog even though they did not renew his contract or release some of his great recent work, such as the Hank Williams tribute set, or the *Just One Love* album. Disc one, subtitled "Easy," was a good cross-section of his interpretations of pop standards, like 'Over the Rainbow' and 'Georgia on My Mind'. The second disc consisted mainly of readily available duets, such as his work with Merle and Waylon; there were no surprises there. The third disc was subtitled "Cowboy," but how that connotation applied to songs like the one by Steve Goodman, 'City of New Orleans', or the Lefty Frizzell classic, 'If You've Got the Money, I've Got the Time', will have to remain a mystery.

The Legendary Willie Nelson. Columbia Records (Sony Music Special Products) BT 23335. (1992).

Track Listings: On the Road Again, Whiskey River, My Heroes Have Always Been Cowboys, I'm Gonna Sit Right Down and Write Myself a Letter, I'm a Memory, Blue Skies, Partners After All, Heartaches of a Fool, Blue Eyes Crying in the Rain, Island in the Sea.

Recording Notes: This Sony Special Products tape was released in 1992 through Southeastern Tape Distributors of Duluth, Georgia. It could only be found in racks of "discount" tapes usually displayed at gas stations, fast food stores, or truck stops. It was Sony's intention, by releasing it through a Southern tape distributor, to reach another avenue of sales (truck drivers, weary vacationers, and even an occasional hitchhiker or two) for Willie's past catalog, now that he had left the company. Nonetheless, it was nice to have 'Heartaches of a Fool', 'Island in the Sea', and 'Partners After All' available on a budget compilation.

Super Hits. Columbia Records CK 64184. (1994).

Track Listing: On the Road Again, My Heroes Have Always Been Cowboys, Blue Eyes Crying in the Rain, Nothing I Can Do About It Now, Georgia on My Mind, Living in the Promiseland, Poncho and Lefty (w. Merle Haggard), Always on My Mind, City of New Orleans, Angel Flying Too Close to the Ground.

Recording Notes: By 1994, Willie had left Columbia to record for the fledgling Justice label, then to go on to the newly-rejuvenated Liberty label. As a parting try for more catalog sales, Columbia released this "hits" package. They did similar ones for other long-time roster artists, like Johnny Cash and David Allan Coe.

There was not a clunker among the set. Indeed, all the cuts had at one time been a number one single on the *Billboard* country singles charts. Starting with the first Columbia single (and first number one), 'Blue Eyes Crying in the Rain', the set culminated with the Beth Nielsen Chapman song, 'Nothing I Can Do About It Now', Willie's final number one for Columbia, which charted in 1989.

Fittingly the collection opened and closed with songs from the movie, *Honeysuckle Rose*. The Merle Haggard duet, 'Poncho and Lefty', appeared, of course, as did 'Always on My Mind'. Surprisingly, some very good number one songs, such as 'Blue Skies' and 'If You've Got the Money I've Go the Time', were not included. Adding those two great cuts shouldn't have created a problem for anyone. Then too, why exclude 'Forgiving You Was Easy'?

Super Hits, Volume 2. Columbia Records CK 67295. (1995).

Track Listing: Ain't Necessarily So, Just Out of Reach, Mammas Don't Let Your Babies Grow Up to Be Cowboys, Stardust, Without a Song, Seven Spanish Angels (w. Ray Charles), Harbor Lights, Remember Me, When I Dream, Let It Be Me.

Recording Notes: The first *Super Hits* collection generated considerable sales for Columbia, peaking on the national album charts at number one hundred ninety-three. It continued to ride the country album charts (from 1994) through 1996. From there it took up residence in the top ten portion of *Billboard's* Top Country Catalog Albums chart. So, the company marketed a "Volume 2" in 1995.

None of the songs were written by Willie. Instead, the emphasis was on some of the standards he had previously recorded. The strong and varied selection was not enough to push the collection on to the national best selling album charts, probably because not enough of the tracks had been big Nelson hits. Four tracks, 'When I Dream', 'Just Out of Reach', 'Stardust' (the title song from his multi-platinum album), and 'Harbor Lights' were not even released as singles.

Only his duets with Waylon Jennings, 'Mammas Don't Let Your Babies Grow Up to Be Cowboys', and Ray Charles, 'Seven Spanish Angels', went to number one on the country singles charts. Two singles that peaked at number two, 'Remember Me' and 'Let It Be Me', were included as was the Beth Nielsen Chapman song, 'Ain't Necessarily So' (which peaked at number seventeen in 1990). 'Without a Song', which peaked at number eleven in 1984, rounded out the collection.

Revolutions of Time ... The Journey 1975 - 1993. Columbia Records (Sony Music) (Legacy) C3K 64796. (1995).

CD One Track Listing (Pilgrimage): Time of the Preacher, Blue Eyes Crying in the Rain, If You've Got the Money I've Got the Time, Uncloudy Day, Always Late (with Your Kisses), Georgia on My Mind, Blue Skies, Whiskey River, Stay a Little Longer, Mr. Record Man, Loving Her Was Easier (Than Anything I'll Ever Do Again), Mammas Don't Let Your Babies Grow Up to Be Cowboys, My Heroes Have Always Been Cowboys, It's Not Supposed to Be That Way, On the Road Again, Angel Flying Too Close to the Ground, Mona Lisa, Always on My Mind, Last Thing I Needed First Thing This Morning, The Party's Over.

CD Two Track Listing (Sojourns): Summertime (w. Leon Russell), Faded Love (w. Ray Price), Night Life (w. Ray Price), Pancho and Lefty (w. Merle Haggard), Old Friends (w. Roger Miller & Ray Price), In the Jailhouse Now (w. Webb Pierce), Everything's Beautiful (In Its Own Way) (w. Dolly Parton), Take It to the Limit (w. Waylon Jennings), To All the Girls I've Loved Before (w. Julio Iglesias), How Do You Feel About Foolin' Around (w. Kris Kristofferson), Seven Spanish Angels (w. Ray Charles), Hello Walls (w. Faron Young), I'm Movin' on (w. Hank Snow), Highwayman (w. Johnny Cash, Waylon Jennings, Kris Kristofferson), Slow Movin' Outlaw (w. Lacy J. Dalton), Are There Any More Real Cowboys (w. Neil Young), They All Went to Mexico (w. Carlos Santana), Half a Man (w. George Jones), Texas on a Saturday Night (w. Mel Tillis), Heartland (w. Bob Dylan).

CD Three Track Listing (Exodus): Nobody Slides, My Friend, Little Old Fashioned Karma, Harbor Lights, Without a Song, Good Time Charlie's Got the Blues, City of New Orleans, Who'll Buy My Memories, Write Your Own Songs, Forgiving You Was Easy, Me and Paul, When I Dream, My Own Peculiar Way, Living in the Promiseland, There Is No Easy Way (But There Is a Way), Ole Buttermilk Sky, A Horse Called Music, Nothing I Can Do About It Now, Is the Better Part Over, Ain't Necessarily So, Still is Still Moving to Me.

Recording Notes: This three disc set was released in 1995 as the quintessential collection of Columbia's Nelson recordings. It was hyped as "the most comprehensive Willie Nelson collection ever assembled." The enclosed book was a gem, quoting from primary interviews, Willie's book, and some excellent articles about Willie. The quotes from other musicians were most enlightening.

Johnny Cash discussed how even he couldn't play "rhythm to Willie's singing." Humorously, the man who would have added strings to *Red Headed Stranger*, Billy Sherrill, noted that Willie had yet to record any of his "83 award-winning songs." Nashville session player and producer, Barry Beckett, had the unusual insight to recognize that blues was the "common link joining" Willie and Carlos Santana.

The song selections consisted of standard material associated with Willie. No alternate tracks or previously unreleased recordings were included. The most welcome track (one that has been relatively unavailable) was the duet with Dolly Parton on her song, 'Everything's Beautiful', from Monument Records (now owned by CBS/Sony).

Quite a few of the duets were from the *Half Nelson* album, songs done with Neil Young, Mel Tillis, and others. However, since the work Willie did with Webb Pierce, Roger Miller, and Hank Snow has yet to appear on CD (though Hank's album with Willie was included on a Bear Family Records boxed set), the appearance of their cuts on this collection was most welcome. Perhaps Columbia will see fit to rerelease those seminal albums. The duet with Kris Kristofferson on 'How Do You Feel About Fooling Around' came from the *Songwriter* soundtrack, another album Columbia has yet to rerelease.

Willie Nelson & Friends. Pure Country/Coyote Sound Cuisine, Inc. Sony Music Special Products PCD-4601. (1996).

Track Listing: Pancho and Lefty (w. Merle Haggard), Take It to the Limit (w. Waylon Jennings), Heartbreak Hotel (w. Leon Russell), How Do You Feel About Foolin' Around (w. Kris Kristofferson), Something to Brag About (w. Mary Kay Place), Night Life (w. Danny Davis and the Nashville Brass), Faded Love (w. Ray Price), Old Friends (w. Roger Miller & Ray Price), Everything's Beautiful (In Its Own Way) (w. Dolly Parton), Highwayman (w. Johnny Cash, Waylon Jennings, and Kris Kristofferson).

Recording Notes: The high point of this 1996 collection was the inclusion of, for the first time on compact disc, the cut 'Something to Brag About', a duet between Willie and Mary Kay Place. Courtesy of RCA came the Willie rendition of 'Night Life' that had Danny Davis and the Nashville Brass overdubbed. Otherwise, the collection was basically culled from disc two (with the exception of the Leon Russell/Willie interpretation of the Elvis classic, 'Heartbreak Hotel') of Willie's Columbia box set, *Revolutions of Time.* Two different pictures have graced the cover of the collection during its first year of release.

Willie Standard Time. Sony Music Special Products A 26915. (1996).

Track Listing: Stormy Weather, Don't Get Around Much Anymore, Ole Buttermilk Sky, Wind Beneath My Wings, I'm Gonna Sit Right Down and Write Myself a Letter, Am I Blue, Unchained Melody, Exactly Like You, Old Fashioned Love, That Lucky Old Sun (Just Rolls Around Heaven All Day).

Recording Notes: This 1996 set was another of Columbia's many attempts to cash in on their extensive Willie Nelson catalog. This time they exploited his recorded standards (as Willie "standard" time would imply). There was, of course, the Hoagy Carmichael classic 'Ole Buttermilk Sky', from Willie's 1988 *What a Wonderful World* album of standards.

From the 1985 *Somewhere Over the Rainbow* album came the Dorothy Fields/Jimmy McHugh chestnut, 'Exactly Like You', a song to which Willie gave an achingly haunting interpretation. The album credits didn't disclose that two of the songs were not Willie solo efforts, but ones he did with Leon Russell. They were the Harold Arlen standard, 'Stormy Weather' and the perennial favorite 'Am I Blue'. Likewise, Freddy Powers assisted on 'I'm Gonna Sit Right Down and Write Myself a Letter', from the 1981 album, *Somewhere Over the Rainbow*.

Two songs, 'Unchained Melody' and 'Don't Get Around Much Anymore' came from Willie's first album of standards, *Stardust*. The 1920's classic, 'Old Fashioned Love' came from *The Promiseland* album, while 'Wind Beneath My Wings' was taken off *The City of New Orleans*. Rounding out the collection was 'That Lucky Old Sun', the Frankie Laine classic, which Willie recorded for his third album, *The Sound in Your Mind*.

Willie Nelson. Time Life Music 3661-2. (1997).

Track Listing: On the Road Again, Blue Skies, My Heroes Have Always Been Cowboys, Always on My Mind, Night Life, Hello Walls, Crazy, Blue Eyes Crying in the Rain, Last Thing I Needed First Thing This Morning, Funny How Time Slips Away, The Party's Over, Touch Me, Me and Paul, Bloody Mary Morning, Stay All Night (Stay a Little Longer), If You've Got the Money I've Got the Time, Man with the Blues, Whiskey River, Angel Flying Too Close to the Ground, Pancho and Lefty (w. Merle Haggard), Forgiving You Was Easy, Nothing I Can Do About It Now, Family Bible, Good Hearted Woman (w. Waylon Jennings), Georgia on My Mind.

Recording Notes: The tracks on this 1997 *Time Life* compilation came mainly from Sony so it has been included in the "Columbia Greatest Hits" section. The twenty-five selections represented one of the best cross-sections of best selling and favorite Willie Nelson music. His original million-selling compositions, 'On the Road Again' and 'Angel Flying Too Close to the Ground' were featured along with later hits like 'Last Thing I Needed First Thing This Morning' and 'Forgiving You Was Easy'.

Also included were Willie's chart-topping interpretations of standards like 'Georgia on My Mind' and 'Blue Skies'. From RCA, came his and Waylon's version of 'Good Hearted Woman'. Newer versions of early classics like 'Night Life', 'Hello Walls', and 'Crazy' were interspersed with crowd pleasers like 'Whiskey River' and 'Bloody Mary Morning'. Some choices were both surprising and pleasing, 'Family Bible', 'Touch Me', and the very long ago 'Man With the Blues' (a 1959 single for "D" records). All in all, this was an inspired collection and one of the best ever put together on Willie.

Willie recorded two legendary albums for Atlantic Records.
(Photo from the Michael Ochs Archives)

"Night Life":

The Columbia Split and Its Aftermath

During his peak years with Columbia, Willie was awarded for sales in excess of forty million units, including cassettes, compact discs, singles, and albums. His best selling album for the label, *Stardust*, went five times platinum (for sales in excess of five million units). Yet an article from *Billboard* that was quoted in a previous chapter made it appear that Columbia was willing to let Willie's contract run out as of 1993. On the surface it also appeared that Columbia refused to release several of Willie's album projects.

What really happened to cause Willie to leave Columbia the year (1993) he turned sixty, after almost two decades with one of the biggest record companies in America? Officially, Columbia said they wanted Willie to stay on the roster. I had a chance recently to talk with Mark Rothbaum, Willie's manager, friend, and advisor, someone who has been around Willie in some capacity for twenty-four years.

The first point Mark made was that he did not see himself as Willie's manager, rather as an advisor because Willie didn't need a manager in the sense of someone telling him what to do. Willie knows what he is doing and what he wants. After that explanation of his place in Willie's business, Mark, who is one of the most personable high-level business people I have ever met, gave me an intensive but enjoyable country music business lesson.

Mark came to work with Willie by being part of former manager Neil Reshen's team. It was Neil, according to Mark, that got Willie the first all important deal with Columbia back in 1975. Neil only stayed with Willie for about four years, from 1974 until "Willie split with Neil in the middle of 1978," following a still unexplained "dispute." Mark had already left Neil by the time Willie and Neil went their separate ways. Soon after the split, Mark was called by Willie to "come back and help."

Fast forwarding to 1993, Mark said he worked on keeping Willie and Columbia/Sony together, but that set of negotiations ended without a signed contract because Sony "wanted to produce Willie themselves." The major factor "was a new management team [at Sony] in Nashville that feared Willie would not accept a Sony producer." They were right, Mark disclosed, "Willie would not allow them to produce him." In his estimation, if there were to be a contract renewal in 1993, "Willie had to allow them to produce him."

The production issue was a major stumbling block for Willie and Mark. Not only did it mean Willie would give up the creative control he had gained back in 1975 (when he first signed with Columbia), it also would have meant no longer working with great independent producers like Don Was. Don had been producing Willie for almost a year and Willie liked his work. In Mark's words, Don had "a plaintive way of producing music" that suited Willie perfectly.

In 1993, Willie had just completed a critically acclaimed album, *Across the Borderline*, produced by Don. Don began working with Willie in February of 1992 after Mark introduced the two in Los Angeles. Mark, a Danbury, Connecticut resident, had stopped by a studio there to visit his Danbury neighbor, Felix Cavaliere, formerly of the rock group, The Rascals. Through Felix, Mark "met and spoke with Don." They found they had a common ground, which was Willie. Mark was Willie's manager and Don "deeply admired Willie." Don felt about Willie as Mark did, that he "is one of the most emotionally deep singers and has a respect for songs."

Looking back, Mark said that he and Willie had a "great working relationship with Sony." The parties "did negotiate" a contract, thus, the negotiations "didn't fall apart." The two parties, Willie and Sony "completed a contract." The contract just wasn't signed because Sony asked "to take away creative control." At that point, Willie (and Mark) simply "chose to go elsewhere. Everyone we had been dealing with at Sony was gone."

What about the alleged refusal by Columbia to release some of Willie's finished album projects? Was that a factor in not re-signing with Columbia? Mark replied that Willie was creating projects so quickly that "no label, not even Columbia, could have accepted that amount of product. The staffs were all overworked because there were so many projects."

The album, *The Hungry Years*, was actually the first completed project by Willie that Columbia refused to release. The refusal came in 1977, a year after recording was completed (in a studio in Louisiana). In 1991, the album finally came out as a budget release. Given that Columbia turned down a project as far back as 1977 would hardly make turning down projects in the 1990's a factor in a 1993 contract negotiation (especially since his contract had been successfully renegotiated in both 1980 and 1983).

Mark delved further into Willie's break with Columbia by explaining how the high levels of popularity country music experienced in the early nineties affected the industry. He described the record sales experienced by country music as being an "anti-rap" and "anti-techno rock" phenomenon. These two types of music "were difficult to get into, lyrically and melodically."

Mark's comments on the basis for country music's new popularity were mirrored by similar statements made by Ken Kragen, manager for Kenny Rogers, Trisha Yearwood, and Travis Tritt, among others. Kragen said it was "the audience that has crossed over." In his opinion, "millions of people" began listening to country music because they "found themselves alienated or at least disinterested in the directions pop music has taken (i. e., rap and hard rock)."

Country music was much easier to listen to, so listeners tuned in and country experienced "a pregnant blip" on the sales charts. The country music record executives that benefited from the expansion of the listening audiences turned around and dropped most of the older higher paid artists from their rosters. They brought in newer, less expensive acts, some of whom have been euphemistically called "hat acts." They were younger and cleaner cut than the old "outlaws" like Willie. The "hat" part came from the big new expensive looking cowboy hats most of them wore.

Mark's view was that Columbia, like most of the other country music labels in 1993, wanted to get older artists off their rosters. He said the new Sony administration in Nashville was "not singling out Willie." They wanted all "the heritage artists" out of the way. Sure enough, artists like Merle Haggard, Johnny Cash, and Waylon Jennings found doors and checkbooks closed at the major Nashville labels.

Jennings, for example, wound up at Justice, the same small independent Texas label that put out a couple of Willie albums following the Columbia departure. The orchestration of major changes in country music was by then coming from the top of the corporate hierarchy, an outside hierarchy of business people Nashville never had before. Country music personnel, who used to rise and fall in terms of hit songs now have to look at business principles such as separate profit centers and development budgets.

The money still flows in country music but most of the attention has been turned to roster pruning rather than innovative music making. Woody Bomar of the Little Big Town publishing house (in Nashville) reviewed the current business of publishing in country music and told Deborah Evans Price of *Billboard* that "publishers might be losing sight of their purpose - delivering hit songs."

In one of my first talks with Mark, he told me it came down to a plain and simple business decision not to pay an older act like Dolly

Parton a million dollars when they could make a decent profit off a newer act that only cost seventy-five thousand dollars. Not only was Willie an older artist who commanded a lot of money, he was not a "hat act." In Mark's words, Willie simply "did not fit in with the sterile image of the new corporate country music."

In any business run by a push to maximize profits, the product becomes controlled so it can be created at least cost. Innovation is only useful as a factor that positively drives sales. Creativity is not useful because it would interfere with keeping all products at a similar low-cost level. Thus, as the major players in the country music business have become able to offer the same low-cost, sound-alike, younger artists, the industry has been able to gravitate towards a predictable profit pie with predictable shares at predictable costs.

Innovation and artistic success is, at best, tolerated only as it positively effects the bottom line. It was no accident that Parton, who had been part of the Columbia roster of artists going into the nineties, found herself in a situation similar to Willie's. In a recent interview captured in a 1997 issue of *The Journal of Country Music,* Dolly answered the question of "why did you leave Sony Music for Rising Tide?" She said, "I was too old for them. They didn't think they could get me played on country radio, and they weren't excited about me."

Like Willie, Dolly made a decision not to re-sign with Sony/Columbia. She explained that:

> at Sony, it was so commercial and so business-oriented. There were not that many musical people there, to be honest. It was more like these Japanese businessmen were putting different people in that I didn't think knew the music that well, and they didn't see in me what I did. My contract was up. And I just didn't want to re-sign. But they might as well have let me go, because they weren't showing any attention. They didn't seem to be shaken when I left.

In the final analysis, Mark said that even though the new corporate Nashville understood the star power Willie still has, they made an "independent decision to go after younger artists." Sony "did not reject" Willie, instead, "Willie split with Sony." Yet even after the split from Columbia/Sony, Willie stayed on top, ahead of most of the newer acts. Mark said they were "happy to be with Island. Chris Blackwell is a great man." Willie called him, "my new best friend."

In mid-1997, the new magazine of the online computer internet ("the web"), *The Web Magazine,* appraised Willie as "the most popular country artist on the Web." They saw that "Nelson's easily the most wired cowboy." Although Willie told me he doesn't "have much to do with all the computers," he does "have an interest in anything that helps country music." He also liked the fact "America

Online ran some Farm Aid ads, which also helped raise promotions and dollars for Farm Aid."

His view was that if the country music consumer was into computers and world-wide networks, then "I'm definitely into them." Over the "web," he has done several live "cybercasts" from L.A.'s House of Blues. To him, "it's exposure. The sound and picture aren't perfect, but it's a new thing and we ought to utilize the tools."   And there you have it, Willie and his fans are living the future.   Sony Nashville has its sterile environment. Country music sales may be off, quite a bit even, but just try getting tickets to a Willie Nelson concert!

As country music moved into 1998, according to *Country Weekly*, fans were more than a little negatively vocal about cost cutting innovations like "short playlists, soundalike artists, cookie-cutter music production" that has made country music "boring." Independent label owner, Pete Anderson, told the magazine that "different used to mean good. Now different is just another way to say no." That's it, rule out innovation, make the product fit into a low-cost formula and the profits will be predictable. There will be no chance-taking (and sudden losses will be averted) but there will be no exciting new creative directions. In the more innovative 1980's (a time period with much larger radio playlists), researcher Ace Collins discovered that Willie Nelson was the "top" radio artist of the decade.

As Collins noted that fact about Willie in his 1998 book, music business analysts were noting a marked decline in country music radio ratings. In the June 13, 1998, issue of *Billboard*, columnist Phyllis Stark (managing editor of *Country Airplay Monitor*) noted that "enough stations clocked in with dramatic losses to raise a red flag." Her observation begged the question of what was going on. In searching for answers, her research brought forth diverse potential answers "ranging from the scientific to the sarcastic."

According to Stark, the concern of music directors like Chris Huff (of Knoxville, Tennessee) was that "nothing has come along" to take the place of "songs that hit in the boom era." Huff noted that while:

> older power gold [titles] continue to test as well as they did when they came out, the '96-'97 power golds seem to be starting to fade.   It seems like they don't have the [longevity]. I haven't found much new product out there that I feel passionate about. And certainly if I can't get excited about new product, how can I expect my audience to?

Country music consultant Keith Hill unequivocally blamed the industry's falling ratings on "a lack of compelling songs." He advised his clients to play a lot fewer "current" songs and rely a lot more on older material. He said that:

there's some real junk out there. On a scale of one to 10, with ten being what we had in 1992, it's about a three. When the water's dirty, don't drink the water.

Not coincidentally, 1993 was the year Columbia Records decided not to continue to reward Willie Nelson (with other companies following suit relative to other older yet still very popular artists) with the same artistic and creative freedom and license he had always had. 1993 was the year that followed the beginning of an audience decline that has continued through today.

A swinging Willie!
(Photo from Will van Overbeek)

The Non-Columbia and Post-Columbia Recordings and Film Career

I'M COMMITTED TO MY MUSIC . . .

Willie made the Country Music Hall of Fame in 1993.
(Photo from the author's private collection)

Willie in concert!
(Photo from the author's private collection and Evelyn Shriver Public Relations)

"Family Bible":

The Non-Columbia Religious Recordings

Willie has always been a very spiritual person, dating from his childhood upbringing in the Methodist religion to his current beliefs, which encompass reincarnation. In a biographical sketch, he revealed that "since we were church-going people my early roots were in gospel tunes." In a more detailed elaboration, he said,

> my grandparents raised me from the time I was about five years old. They were churchgoers. They belonged to the Methodist Church there in Abbott, Texas, and they'd take me and my sister Bobbie with them.

That was "the kind of music I grew up with. I sung it in church all the time."

His daughter, Susie, wrote that Willie told her his grandfather would take him and sister Bobbie "ten miles to Hillsboro for the Wednesday night gospel sing at the county courthouse." According to Willie,

> they'd sing songs out of the old Stamp Quartet songbooks, and they could all sight-read. They'd spend the night harmonizing, just knocking each other out.

Willie told her "that was some of the most beautiful singing he has ever heard." To this day, he has retained a love for gospel music, ending, in Susie's words, "his shows with one or two - 'Precious Memories' or 'Amazing Grace' or other favorites."

His definition of what constitutes gospel music is broader than the generally accepted standard. He told Jennie Ruggles, writing for a 1996 issue of *Body Mind Spirit*, that:

> There may be black blues that we white people try to do, and there's a white gospel that the black folks try to do, and sometimes we can do it all together. B. B. King and I have done 'Night Life' together and that was a wonderful experience. To me, that's as gospel as it gets. That's where I'm at, gospel-wise.

The traditional church music stayed with him as it did with a lot of country artists. Willie explained that many:

> singers and pickers learned to do what we do in church. We learned all the church and gospel songs, so they had to filter into the other music we perform. I know it does mine. When I'm writing songs, I often catch myself using gospel melodies that are similar to those I heard growing up. They're like pop standards. And there are just books and books of them.

He has never hesitated to voice his true standing, "I am religious, even though I don't go to church. I believe in reincarnation." What that belief has meant to Willie is that:

> He made us all in the beginning and since then we've been coming back and forth. First time we came in we knew a lot and we've lost it along the way. Being down here is kinda like goin' through the university: you go through one grade at a time and if you fail, you gotta go back and take those tests again.

He had a point. How could life, as energy, just abruptly end, forever?

When making those observations, the interviewer noted that Willie laughed. Actually, the insights he expressed were not unlike the ones made in *The Tenth Insight* by James Redfield (author of *The Celestine Prophecy*), who wrote that:

> we knew that through wave after wave of successive generations, we would be born into the physical plane, and no matter how long it took, we would strive to wake up, and unify, and evolve, and eventually implement on Earth the same spiritual culture that exists in the Afterlife.

Willie once did consider preaching as a livelihood or calling. "I had considered preaching," he once told Chet Flippo, "but preachers don't make a lot and they have to work hard." He taught Sunday school at his Baptist Church but since he also played the Ft. Worth bars, the church leaders forced him into a choice and the choice was obvious, music. Willie found the hypocrisy to be ironic, noting that, "I was singing to the same people on Sunday morning that I was singing to on Saturday night."

He also considered his forced choice to have come from a personal vendetta. Susie wrote that he:

> couldn't see why it was okay for plumbers and electricians to
> do their work and be accepted as church members, but he had
> to choose between his work or the church.

The result was that Willie never again belonged to a church or had anything much to do with organized religion. Even so, his early exposure to religious music has always been a very obvious factor in his songwriting.

One of his first religious songs was 'Family Bible', which Willie wrote before he attempted to become a professional songwriter in Nashville. He said he was on his way to see his sister, Bobbie, when he came up with the song. Unfortunately, he sold it to Paul Buskirk. Buskirk did get the song recorded by Claude Gray ("The Tall Texan") on Pappy Daily's D label, from whence it reached number ten on the national country singles chart in 1960. It was Gray's first chart single.

From time to time Willie has chosen to record exclusively religious albums. His first was *The Troublemaker* for Columbia (it was also his only religiously-themed album for the label). While signed to Columbia, Willie was allowed to release, on other labels, several projects that were dear to his heart. The projects were all spiritual in nature and for whatever reasons, no doubt a lack of commercial viability being the major one, Columbia did not choose to participate. Fortunately they did not stand in Nelson's way.

In 1980 Willie released his next religious set on the Songbird label, a fledgling Contemporary Christian record company. Songbird has since become part of the much larger MCA Record company, so the cuts have been rereleased in several sets since then. In 1986, he and sister, Bobbie, produced their own album of mostly religious standards, which eventually wound up on K-Tel's subsidiary label, Arrival. The compact disc version came out on Laserlight.

When son, Willie, Jr., (Billie) became committed to a religious album, father Willie became similarly immersed so that the end product was truly a joint effort. The finished package saw the light in 1994, unfortunately after the death of Willie, Jr. It was a touching set of performances with an accompanying video that showed sparks of greatness on the part of Willie, Jr.

Willie and Bobbie again released a religious collection, *How Great Thou Art*, in 1996, this time on the Finer Arts Record label out of Denver, Colorado. Though the release date was 1996, some of the songs had previously appeared on Willie's other religious albums. Specifically, they were his own composition, 'Kneel at the Feet of Jesus', C. Austin Miles' hymn, 'In the Garden' (which had been on *The Troublemaker* album), and Stuart Hamblen's classic, 'It Is No Secret'.

This record was overdubbed!
(Photo from RCA Records and Willie Nelson)

The Religious Recordings - Album Listings

Family Bible. MCA Records MCAC-929. (1980).

Track Listing: By the Rivers of Babylon, Stand by Me, It Is No Secret (What God Can Do), There Shall Be Showers of Blessings, Softly and Tenderly, Tell It to Jesus, Family Bible, In God's Eyes, Revive Us Again, An Evening Prayer, Kneel at the Feet of Jesus.

Recording Notes: Willie's second specifically religious project (the first was *The Troublemaker*, put out in 1976 by Columbia) appeared in 1980 on the new Songbird label, a subsidiary of MCA. It was "specially dedicated to Mama Nelson from Willie & Bobbie." Songbird, with a roster spearheaded by artists like Mylon LeFevre, was MCA's attempt to garner sales from an expanding Christian music market.

Besides 'Family Bible', the title cut and first single (it got as far as number ninety-two on the country charts and died after two weeks), only two songs were Nelson's, 'Kneel at the Feet of Jesus' and 'In God's Eyes'. Though 'Family Bible' officially belonged to Paul Buskirk and others, the song was all Willie. It was inspired by (in the words of Susie Nelson) "the memory of Mama and Daddy Nelson studying the bible by kerosene lantern light."

'Kneel at the Feet of Jesus' was first recorded by Willie for his RCA album, *Willie Nelson and Family*. It was rerecorded for Willie, Jr.'s religious album project (which was finally released in 1994). 'In God's Eyes' became part of that project as well. Previously it was part of the RCA album, *Yesterday's Wine*. 'Family Bible' also first appeared on *Yesterday's Wine*.

Of the other songs, most had been around "forever" or at least so long that they had become part of the public domain as well as included in many fundamentalist church music books. One, 'It Is No Secret', a gospel standard recorded by pop stars such as Elvis and most of the leading gospel artists, had an interesting history. It was written by Stuart Hamblen, who for much of his career played a "really bad" movie "bad" guy while doubling as a gifted songwriter, responsible for gems as '(Remember Me) I'm the One Who Loves You' (from 1950, though a big hit for Dean Martin in 1965).

Then he took a religious turn in his life and joined the Billy Graham organization. His songwriting focus similarly changed as he gradually switched to composing songs like 'It Is No Secret' (1951) and 'Open Up Your Heart' (1955). Hamblen said he wrote 'It Is No Secret' in seventeen minutes, because the topic came naturally to him. When someone asked how he was able to break free from alcohol, he said his response was that, "I didn't do it, fellow, the Lord did it. He can do the same for anybody who'll let him. It is no secret what God can do."

Another "public domain" song, 'Stand By Me' was actually written in the nineteenth century by Reverend Charles Albert Tindley. Dr. Bernice Johnson Reagon described his compositions, of which 'Stand By Me' was one of the most prominent, as "the base upon which the new Black gospel music was developed." She wrote that his songs have become an "integral part of the treasured pool of African American sacred music."

Other Releases: MCA also gave the album a catalogue number of MCA-3258. With the demise of the Songbird label, the company preserved, in 1993, five of the cuts on a Merle Haggard & Willie Nelson budget release, *Gospel's Best*, MCAD-20478. Five more were preserved (along with five additional Haggard tracks) on the 1989 compilation, *The Best of Gospel*, MCAD-20560. In 1994, MCA rereleased the original Songbird set as *Gospel Favorites*, MCAD-20784.

MCA made 'In God's Eyes' the fourth cut, 'Softly and Tenderly' the ninth cut when they rereleased it in 1994. 'An Evening Prayer' was deleted altogether. It was also the only cut of the original eleven not used on the two Willie/Merle budget compilations. On the 1994 rerelease, production credit went to Willie and Bobbie Nelson. On the Songbird release, the same credit went solely to Willie. The only musicians listed were Bobbie on piano and Willie on guitar and vocals. All the cuts were recorded at Autumn Sound in Garland, Texas.

I'd Rather Have Jesus. (Willie and Bobbie Nelson). Arrival NU 719-4. (1986).

Track Listing: I'd Rather Have Jesus, Just a Little Talk With Jesus, Where He Leads Me, Revive Us Again, Sweet Bye and Bye, Old Time Religion, Where the Soul Never Dies, I'll Fly Away, The Lily of the Valley, Are You Washed in the Blood, When We All Get to Heaven.

Recording Notes: Willie and his sister, Bobbie, recorded this gospel album in 1986 in Austin, Texas (Arlyn Studios). Most of the selections were standard old-time gospel numbers. One that was not, 'Where the Soul Never Dies', was written by William Lee Golden of the Oak Ridge Boys, a group which began as a gospel quartet but switched to become one of the all-time most popular country groups.

The group's recording of Golden's song won them a Grammy Award in 1976. Willie's version, dominated by his single voice, gave the song an intimacy that the Oak's barbershop style quartet singing didn't have. The most moving cut, however, was Willie's interpretation of Albert E. Brumley's 'I'll Fly Away', a hymn which was once described by singer Ray Charles as being "the brightest in terms of tempo, and it's a real stomper and hand-clapper." To Brumley's credit, it has earned the distinction of being "the most recorded gospel song in history."

One of the reasons for its great popularity was its close kinship to old time country songs. Brumley, himself, said that he based his song on the first million-selling country song, 'The Prisoner's Song'. He recalled that "it suddenly dawned on me that I could use the world for a prison and heaven for freedom when we pass on." He even described how in one stanza he paraphrased "from the old 'Prisoner's Song'."

He was working in a cotton field at the time he was thinking up the song. He said he felt like he wanted to just "fly out of that cotton field, the way the prisoner in the song wanted to fly out of prison." When he was done he "didn't have any idea it would be a big hit."

Willie sang the song and Bobbie played piano behind him in a way that made it sound like they were back in the hills at an old church in front of a few redeemed believers. Production credits for the whole album went to Bea Spears, who also played bass, and Freddy Fletcher, who also played drums. Mickey Raphael on harmonica was the other supporting musician.

Other Releases: The album was first released on Arrival, a budget label subsidiary of K-Tel Records. K-Tel, itself, had long been a budget "rerelease" label that sold "inexpensive" compilations on about every artist imaginable. In 1990, the "Nelson Gospel Partners" released the album on the Bald Eagle Productions label as NU-719-1. In return for their efforts, they held the 1990 copyright assignment.

A subset of the cuts was also released in 1986 by Arrival as a Willie and George Jones album, entitled *Best of 2 Super Artists Sing Gospel*, with a catalog number BU-1684. The Jones songs did not involve Willie nor did the Willie songs involve George. In 1992, the original Arrival album was rereleased as *Old Time Religion*, Laserlight 12 114, similarly credited to Willie Nelson and Bobbie Nelson. It featured the same cover picture, just more of a close-up.

Peace in the Valley: The Gospel Truth Collection: Volume 1. (Willie Nelson with Willie Nelson, Jr.). Promised Land Music PLMCD-052158. (1994).

Track Listing: Dreaming of a Little Cabin, Family Bible, I Saw the Light, In God's Eyes, My Body's Just a Suitcase for My Soul, Troublemaker, You Can't Have Your Hate and Jesus Too, A Beautiful Life, Kneel at the Feet of Jesus, Peace in the Valley.

Recording Notes: Although this project was only brought to release in 1994, it had its genesis as far back as 1983. Basically, this was the junior Nelson's project (he referred to it as a "Heaven of an album") with Willie in a very active supporting role (only on the cut, Mae Axton's 'My Body's Just a Suitcase for My Soul', did the senior Nelson limit himself to only a minor harmony vocal background with Willie, Jr. dong the lead vocals), though Willie's name got obvious top billing. The liner notes, written by executive producer Robert E. MacDonald, Jr., focused almost exclusively on Willie.

Grant Boatwright of Promised Land Music produced the set and contributed two songs, 'A Beautiful Life' and the rousing 'You Can't Have Your Hate and Jesus Too'. Boatwright had long been on the fringes of the country music industry. His name first popped up in 1966 when he was a singer/guitarist on the college circuit. He soon married Ginger Hammond, with whom he had formed a duo, Grant and Ginger. Their duo led to a group called Red, White and Blue(grass). Ginger said the name stood for "redneck, white trash, and old blue. 'Cause I was the only dog in the group."

The Albert Brumley classic, 'Dreaming of a Little Cabin' stood out as the opening selection of the album. The liner notes said it was Willie's mother's favorite song. More than just a gospel tune, the song was one of many Brumley wrote which focused on a man's love for his mother. It was very sentimental. Brumley was more than once criticized for writing songs that were too sentimental. In answer, he said that "if it comes to the place where Mother and Dad and the old home's not sacred, I'll take my sign down. I'll quit."

Most of the rest of the songs on the album were Willie-centered, with highlights being 'Family Bible', 'The Troublemaker' (which previously appeared on Willie's third Columbia album of the same name), 'Kneel at the Feet of Jesus', and 'In God's Eyes'. Willie had recorded the Hank Williams tune, 'I Saw the Light' in 1979, as part of the album he did with Leon Russell, *One For the Road*. The closing song, 'Peace in the Valley', was written in 1937 by Thomas Andrew Dorsey, the father of Gospel Music and writer of 'Take My Hand, Precious Lord', specifically for Mahalia Jackson.

Dorsey said he wrote 'Peace in the Valley' "just before Hitler sent his war chariots into Western Europe in the late thirties." He was riding on a train bound for Cincinnati and the train passed through a valley where "horses, cows, sheep, they were all grazing and together in this little valley." He recalled a little brook running through the valley and it made him wonder, "why couldn't man live in peace like the animals down there? Out of that came 'Peace in the Valley'."

Willie and Willie, Jr.'s version underscored that desire for peace. The album's release date was especially poignant for the senior Nelson because it followed the suicide of his beloved Willie, Jr. Hopefully, the junior Nelson found the peace he was looking for. An accompanying video captured some vivid moments of father and son together.

Texas Monthly writer Gary Cartwright talked with Willie about losing his son, about how he dealt with the tragedy. Willie told him:

> I just kept on. As it happened, we had a six month gig in Branson, starting New Year's Eve. I had a legitimate reason to cancel all my dates and go bury myself from reality, which is what I felt like doing. But that old survival instinct cut in. So I went to Branson, cussed the place, and threw myself into my work.

Willie has had a strong belief in reincarnation for a long time. He said that as "soon as I read about reincarnation, it struck me just the same as if God had sent me a lightning bolt - this was the truth and I had always known it." Kimo Alo, a priest of the Kahunas (with whom Willie stayed when he recuperated from a collapsed lung in the early eighties), has concluded that Willie is an "old King", brought to earth unite the various native races. Whatever Willie was meant to be, he left interviewer Cartwright with the conclusion that "his life is a series of circles, in which he is continually reincarnated, each version a little better than its predecessor."

How Great Thou Art. (Willie Nelson & Bobbie Nelson). Finer Arts Records (A Division of F2 Entertainment) FA 9605-2. (1996).

Track Listing: How Great Thou Art, Swing Low, Sweet Chariot, It Is No Secret, Kneel at the Feet of Jesus, Just as I Am, Just a Closer Walk With Thee, Farther Along, What a Friend We Have in Jesus, In the Garden.

Recording Notes: Production credits on this 1996 release went to Willie and Bobbie and Freddy Fletcher. The album was dedicated to "the memory of" Michael Fletcher (Bobbie's son), "for his inspiration in the recording of this album." Willie and Bobbie were the two major players, with Jon Blondell credited as the bass player. In 1997, the set was nominated for a Grammy in the category of "Best Gospel Album."

Hearing Bobbie and Willie play together was one of the special treats of this album. According to Willie, he and his sister have played music together since they:

> were very small. She knows instinctively what I'm going to do, and I know that she's going to be there. So there's an understanding there that carries into the studio, and it's very comfortable to have her there because I know what she's going to do. It's going to be right for what I want to hear.

The album was completely recorded at Willie's Pedernales Recording Studio. Many selections were duplicated from previous gospel albums done by Willie and his family. One "new" track was 'Just a Closer Walk With Thee'. In 1950, as recorded by Red Foley, it became one of the first religious songs to double as a country music hit.

The opening selection and title cut, 'How Great Thou Art', was also a new recording, though the song has long been among the oldest in gospel music history. It started life in the mid-1880's in Sweden with the title, 'O Great God'. From there it moved through German and Russian translations to a book of hymns published by the American Bible Society. In 1948, the missionaries Mr. and Mrs. Stuart K. Hine translated the song into English and added a new stanza, thereby gaining credit for authorship of the English version. That was the version that George Beverly Shea recorded in the mid-fifties.

Willie and Bobbie's version, dominated by piano, guitar and bass, brought a quiet reverence to the song and revealed a deep reverence to his God. It was this deep commitment to God that brought Willie to the University Baptist Church in Austin in 1975, at the invitation of the minister. He appeared in tennis shoes and a T-shirt and came to play some songs and answer some questions.

At the end of the service, after dutifully answering those questions and playing songs like 'Amazing Grace' and his own 'Family Bible', Willie and Bobbie broke into one of the songs included on this album, 'Just As I Am'. As he moved through the song, with the congregation softly singing along, Willie let his guitar slide "slackly into his lap, and tears streamed down his rough, bearded cheeks." When Willie ended the song, there was silence and one further question from the minister, "how would Willie want the world to remember Willie Nelson?" Willie gently replied, "Just tell them I meant well."

Gospel music has enabled Willie to reach "out to connect, to let the music do the talking rather than having to stand in front and make a lot of long speeches." He recently told an interviewer for *Body Mind Spirit* magazine, that "this album is the way to get it out there; the music goes right to the bone, there's not a lot of digesting necessary." He observed that, "all music is gospel. All music is sacred."

"Just One Love":

The Post-Columbia Recordings

Ironically, by 1993, the year Willie hit sixty and made it into the Country Music Hall of Fame, he was through with Columbia Records, for a number of reasons. The major one was the expiration of his contract. Though Columbia confirmed the situation, Sony/Nashville's new (as of 1993) Vice President and General Manager (Sony was the parent to Columbia), Allen Butler, was, according to *Billboard* magazine, "quick to add that the company has first option to sign Nelson, and feels certain he will stay with the label."

Butler was quoted as saying, "every indication that I have is that Willie is very much wanting to come back to the label that's been his home for many years." But Willie did not re-sign with Columbia. His view at the time was that he was "between labels." What he was doing was:

placing some music in spots where I can get it heard. This music might not be considered highly commercial by major labels, but I still think it's important enough to come out with.

Specifically he was referring to an album "Grady Martin produced" as well as an "album of Hank Williams songs," and "one with Merle Haggard's band." He concluded that he was:

just glad that there are independent labels around that will gamble on records that don't sound like they're going to go platinum overnight.

It was quite clear that Columbia had refused to release certain recorded product Willie had in the can, specifically, a "set of standards," the Hank Williams tribute, and even an entire album of "old country songs," *Just One Love.*

Reporting in an article for the *Washington Post,* Geoffrey Himes wrote that "no amount of arm-twisting could persuade Columbia to release" a mid-80's "collection of vintage western swing numbers" entitled *Sugar Moon.* That was the "mid-80's" and though Willie "tried again a few years later with an album titled *Willie Sings Hank Williams,* Columbia wouldn't release that one either." In 1994, according to Himes, Willie presented *Just One Love* to Columbia and "once again, Columbia passed on the project."

The "set of standards" (called "a kind of sequel to 'Stardust'") subsequently came out in 1994 on the Texas-based Justice Records as *Moonlight Becomes You.* The tribute became part of the QVC-Rhino three CD set (as did the set with Haggard's band). Later in 1994 and on into 1995, Willie put on a "Moonlight Becomes You" tour. His move to Justice, though short, was musically rewarding because it got him playing again with Paul Buskirk on Paul's *Nacogdoches Waltz* album.

It also got him playing on a jazz album by Justice label-mate and long-time jazz artist, Herb Ellis. Justice was unfortunately too small to successfully move the outstanding set of standards that Nelson had produced. Label President, Randall Jamail, already knew that Willie would not stay with Justice, saying,

> I don't want to give the misimpression that Willie is signed to Justice Records, because that is not the case. I'm sure that Willie will continue to seek out major label opportunities...

According to Jamail, the Justice release came about because Willie has "always wanted to work with an independent, and with me specifically, on this particular project." Then, in late 1994, after Columbia had been telling the press that they felt Willie just "wanted to get some sense of how he was going to be accepted as an artist by the label's new management team" (specifically Allen Butler), Willie moved back to a recently-rejuvenated Liberty Records (a division of EMI), headed by former 1950's rock and roll star, Jimmy Bowen.

The subsequent new album for Liberty, as produced by Bowen, featured "pop" standards along with Nelson standards, surrounded by an array of strings and other sounds. Willie disclosed that:

> EMI Liberty, my new record label, said I should do an album of standards. Like 'Crazy'. I hadn't been looking at those as standards.

Actually, according to *Billboard*, Willie was "signed to both EMI Records' pop imprint SBK and EMI's stand-alone, Nashville-based country label, Liberty Records."

Charles Koppelman, chairman and CEO of EMI Records Group North America, confirmed the arrangement, adding that "both companies can explore every avenue of retail and radio." He further revealed that:

> we're going everywhere with this. Willie Nelson is a blues singer. Whether you listen to 'Night Life' or 'Funny How Time Slips Away', I believe the urban consumer will respond to Willie.

Mark Rothbaum, Willie's manager, confirmed that:

> what it came down to, quite honestly, was there was a stronger sense of commitment from Charles Koppelman and Jimmy Bowen than from the other labels that were interested. In the world of country music, there is generally very little cooperation between the parent label and Nashville, very little across-the-board cooperation and commitment.

He concluded that "with Sony, it was clear that we would have re-signed through the Nashville division."

So, the projected relationship with Liberty was not to mirror the past relationship with RCA. Willie's explanation was that:

> Jimmy Bowen and I were old golfing buddies, and we'd talked about doing an album together for a long time. Charles Koppelman was also very interested in doing the whole 75-piece orchestra number. He does the Frank Sinatra albums, so he knows how to market that kind of record. He wanted me to do some of my old standards in that style, too.

He added that he thought the album would be:

> marketed in a similar way to albums by Sinatra. I would hope they'll service all the country stations, but I don't think they're going to depend entirely on that market.

1994 also saw the release of a Willie/Curtis Potter set that prominently featured the more famous name, Nelson's. The tried and true grouping of Cash, Jennings, Kristofferson, and Nelson toured in 1995 behind a new Highwaymen album, released this time on Liberty. One more Justice album closed out 1995, the lovely *Just One Love*, which

Columbia had declined to release. What was important about this record was that it was solidly country. Justice president, Randall Jamail, exulted that, "like retail, radio is excited that Willie has done a country album."

By mid-1995, the Liberty deal seemed to have gone sour for Willie. In a *Billboard* news feature, his comment on the status of the relationship was, "if you find out, let me know. We get a good thing going with a good label, and it disappears." At the time of Willie's remarks, Liberty executives "could not be reached for comment at press time." To be fair, Liberty was obviously in a state of flux facing the results of the rapid and complete deterioration in Jimmy Bowen's health, due to cancer. Willie and Liberty did not do anything more together at this time.

In 1996, Willie signed with Chris Blackwell's company, Island Records, known mainly for its reggae artists and forays into rock music. In an April, 1996, *Billboard* article, it was pointed out that in its thirty-three year history, Island had never featured a country artist. So, the logical question to ask, was why? The best answer to be gleaned from the article was that it was Willie the label signed and not just a "country" artist. It was projected that Willie's first album for Island, *Spirit*, an all new, all Willie album, due June 1996, would appeal to the cross section of Willie fans, because it featured Willie's band, sparse arrangements, and the first new self-written songs Willie had recorded in some time. How did Island do with *Spirit*? Willie said,

> I experienced a lot of the same things with 'Spirit' that I did with 'Across the Borderline'. I got a lot of great reviews, but sales weren't that impressive. However, I'm told they've planned a whole television campaign for 'Spirit', maybe when the reggae album comes out. As far as I'm concerned, Chris Blackwell is the greatest guy in the world. He's my new best friend.

Then too, Willie's second Island album, due sometime in late 1996 or 1997 or 1998 (Willie said it had been pushed back to early 1997 - though it was completed - so Island could continue to market *Spirit*), was to be a reggae-flavored one, featuring reggae hits and re-done Nelson standards. He told Bill DeYoung, editor of *Scene Magazine*, that the album was to be "called 'One in a Row'. I have a song called that, and it's on there, with a reggae rhythm."

The idea had been kicked around for a long time by Willie and producer Don Was. Johnny Cash, who has lived part time in Jamaica, was also influential in getting Willie to appreciate the easy Caribbean rhythms. Willie remembered how he felt when Was "brought up the reggae idea." He said,

I wasn't sure how it would sound until we went to the studio and cut one of my obscure 60's songs that I think only he remembered, with a reggae band.

That "obscure" song was, of course, 'One in a Row'. For the album, Willie said he also recorded Jamaican artist Jimmy Cliff's 'The Harder They Fall' and 'Sitting in Limbo'. The rest of the songs he did reggae style were his compositions, "old obscure ones." He gave Don Was:

a tape that had about a hundred of these old songs of mine, and he picked out twenty, and I went through that twenty and picked out about ten and recorded them.

The sound was authentic reggae music because "the only two guys on the album who weren't Jamaican" were Mickey Raphael, on harmonica, and Robbie Turner, steel guitarist. The one other song on the album Willie didn't write was authored by Johnny Cash. According to Willie, Johnny "has a place" in Jamaica and "he wrote this song, a story about a Jamaican guy he was talking to there. It's called 'A Worried Man' and it's a great song."

Once Willie got to know a little more about the music and the artists, he observed that:

these reggae guys told me that how they first started playing reggae was by listening to a country station late at night. They could hear the voice and they could hear the melody, but they couldn't hear the bottom, they couldn't hear the bass. So they started putting their own rhythms to these country melodies, which is what these guys told me reggae comes from. So it's not surprising that you can take any country song and do it reggae style.

Willie understood the beginnings of reggae very well. Take a look back at the early material by Bob Marley, Island Records best seller even after his untimely death in the early eighties, and lo and behold there were titles such as 'Wings of a Dove'. So, with the actual release of *Spirit* and the pending release of the "country/reggae" album, Island became the perfect label for Willie, by planning to keep his old fans and add new ones.

In support of *Spirit*, Willie toured heavily in 1996 and 1997. Large crowds, and often sellouts, greeted Willie at most venues. Then came the 1997 version of Farm Aid. The kickoff announcement was jointly made by Willie and Dallas Cowboy owner, Jerry Jones. The concert was scheduled for the home of the Cowboys, the fifty thousand seat Texas Stadium in Irving (a suburb of Dallas).

After just two weeks and only eight thousand ticket sales, the concert was cancelled, even though the guest artist list boasted Neil Young, John Fogerty, and Beck. The cancellation left Willie frustrated yet still wanting to help the independent American farmer. To keep Farm Aid alive, at least for 1997, the promoters moved the event to a smaller location outside Chicago, the New World Music Theater in Tinley Park, Illinois.

Willie explained his feelings about the status of Farm Aid 1997 by saying,

> I'm stubborn. This may be the last one. We might not have any small family farmers out there before it's over. If [the public] doesn't want to do anything about it, then there's no more need for Farm Aid concerts. Sometimes the informing and the entertaining get mixed up. It comes to be just a big party and people have a great time celebrating Farm Aid, and they really don't have any idea why we're there.

The Nashville Network televised the five p. m. (Eastern Daylight Time) show on Saturday October 4, 1997.

Willie's final album of 1997 was fittingly done for the Christmas season. Chet Flippo, writing in his *Billboard* magazine column, appraised the album as a:

> warm, intimate, acoustic, and unconventional approach to Christmas standards and Nelson songs. Bobbie Nelson's church piano stylings work especially well. Gene Autry joins in on 'Here Comes Santa Claus'. The one new Nelson original on the album, 'El Nino' is a lovely Spanish-flavored song and is obviously not about the weather phenomenon of the same name. The set is on Finer Arts Records of Denver.

As Willie closed out the year, the question as to what would be his first new album of 1998 (the reggae one, or another project discussed in 1997, a blues set, or something else) was left in the air. It turned out to not be an internet-marketed set of old songs recorded with his old band, The Offenders.

Willie was also reported to have been working with producer Daniel Lanois. Where was Don Was? Chet Flippo, columnist for *Billboard*, reported that Pat Quigley, president/CEO of Capitol Nashville was talking to Don about an A & R job "at the label." Quigley told Flippo that he envisioned Was "functioning as a 'dean' or 'chancellor' of music for Capitol Nashville." Was had just finished producing two projects for hot label (Capitol) artist, Deanna Carter.

The Post-Columbia Recordings - Album Listings

Six Hours at Pedernales with Special Guest: Curtis Potter. Step One Records SOR-0084. (1994).

Track Listing: Nothing's Changed, Nothing's New, Chase the Moon, Are You Sure, The Party's Over, We're Not Talking Anymore, Turn Me Loose and Let Me Swing, Once You're Past the Blues, It Won't Be Easy, Stray Cats, Cowboys, & Girls of the Night, The Best Worst Thing, It Should Be Easier Now, My Own Peculiar Way.

Recording Notes: This 1994 release was Willie Nelson appearing with Curtis Potter on an album for one of Nashville's strongest independent labels, the Ray Pennington-owned, Step One Records. The company obviously chose to feature the more prominent name, Nelson's, rather than the unknown Potter, though the album was a shared project. Nelson's name made it not only popular stateside, but it became, according to an article in *Billboard*, the company's "first Top 10 project in the United Kingdom."

The musical relationship between Curtis and Willie dated back to 1980 when they worked together on Potter's 1980 Hillside album, *Texas Proud*, HSLP81-101. The Hillside album also included Darrell McCall. Though Curtis had a very country sounding voice and was able to record briefly for Dot Records, he never made the kind of impact on country music he should have, not even with Willie's help.

On this album, Willie did <u>not</u> appear on only three of the cuts, 'Chase the Moon', 'We're Not Talking Anymore', and 'The Best Worst Thing'. Those songs all belonged to Potter's big voice. Of the songs on the album written by Willie, one, 'Are You Sure', was co-written with steel guitarist Buddy Emmons. Two other Nelson songs on the set, 'It

Should Be Easier Now' and 'My Own Peculiar Way', dated back to his days at Pamper Music and the legendary Pamper "demos" (see the earlier chapter on Willie's Pamper Music "demos"). 'The Party's Over' has long been a Nelson standard (since he first recorded it for RCA).

A long-time Nashville songwriter, Mel Holt, wrote a couple of the cuts on the album. Mel has written songs for many established country artists, among them Ray Price, Faron Young, and Hank Thompson, but he never received the corresponding recognition such writing should merit. Step One Records did something about that in 1997, releasing the full length CD, *The Pen of Mel Holt*, SOR-0107. The Willie cut from the *Six Hours at Pedernales* album, 'Once You're Past the Blues', was included as one of fifteen "songs from the vault of Step One Records." The fourteen remaining cuts on the compilation were by Price and Young among many others.

Moonlight Becomes You. Justice Records JR 1601-2. (1994).

Track Listing: December Day, Moonlight Becomes You, Afraid, The Heart of a Clown, Please Don't Talk About Me When I'm Gone, Everywhere You Go, Have I Stayed Away Too Long, Sentimental Journey, The World Is Waiting for the Sunrise, You'll Never Know, I'll Keep on Loving You, You Just Can't Play a Sad Song on a Banjo, You Always Hurt the One You Love, Someday (You'll Want Me to Want You), In God's Eyes.

Recording Notes: After leaving the Columbia label, Willie did this one-shot set of mostly standards for the Justice label, released in 1994 (with two Willie classics, 'December Day' and 'In God's Eyes' opening and closing the set). It was probably his finest set of standard recordings because it mixed long-forgotten ones with others that have rightly become timeless. Some of the songs had experienced previous revivals before Willie brought them back.

For example, the Mills Brothers had a number one hit with 'You Always Hurt the One You Love' in 1944 while Clarence 'Frogman' Henry took it to number twelve in 1961. Isham Jones first cashed in with 'The World Is Waiting for the Sunrise' in 1922. It did not remain forgotten as guitar king Les Paul and his partner/vocalist Mary Ford resurrected it (to the number two spot) in 1951.

One of Gene Austin's last hits for the Victor label was the beautiful Sidney Clare/Sam Stept composition, 'Please Don't Talk About Me When I'm Gone'. Reaching the number three position in 1931, it capped off a very successful career at the top for Austin, whom popular song researcher Joel Whitburn called "the most popular singer of the late 1920s." Toward the end of Johnny Ray's meteoric days as a singing star, he brought the song back and took it top thirty (number twenty-nine).

For the second time in his career, Willie recorded the Frank Loesser tune, 'Have I Stayed Away Too Long'. The first time was for RCA, proving yet again he did do some great and innovative things while with that company. Though the song became a pop classic, it has always been a prime example of a Tin Pan Alley composition that was based in the country "idiom." Mrs. Frank Loesser related that her husband:

> truly enjoyed country music and admired that kind of writing very much. When he wrote 'Have I Stayed Away Too Long?' he was trying to write a song in the country idiom both musically and lyrically.

Of the other standards, Harry Warren and Mack Gordon's 'You'll Never Know' was intended to fit into a "period setting and sound like an old ballad." The period was turn of the century San Francisco.

The song became the Warren and Gordon's biggest success in terms of sales because they "came up with something" that expressed "the feelings of all the war's separated lovers (the song was written in 1943)." When "people immediately started to listen and sing it," the writers said they knew the song "had that certain 'something' we all strive for." Willie knew what a great song it was, having already recorded it for his Columbia album, *Without a Song*.

Two of the other selections were top ten hits from the forties, one being the title song, 'Moonlight Becomes You', a Johnny Burke/Jimmy Van Heusen vehicle from *The Road to Morocco* movie farce starring Bing Crosby and Bob Hope (one of their many "road to somewhere - Rio, Singapore etc." movies). Crosby had a number one chart topper with it in 1943, the same year two orchestra leaders Glenn Miller and Harry James also scored with it. Willie's version was nominated for a 1994 Grammy in the Best Traditional Pop Vocal category. The other forties hit was 'I'll Keep on Loving You', a song by Richard Coburn and Vincent Rose that Connee Boswell took to number twenty-two in 1941

Many great musicians contributed to the sound of the album, among them Johnny Gimble, fiddler extraordinaire, Freddie Powers, rhythm guitar (both he and Gimble added backing vocals to 'Sentimental Journey'), and Paul Buskirk, rhythm guitar and mandola. That's the same Buskirk who years ago bought 'Night Life' and hired Willie as a guitar instructor. Buskirk also co-wrote (with Russell Jackson) 'You Just Can't Play a Sad Song on a Banjo'. Rounding out the roster of players on the album was Paul Schmitt on piano, Dean Reynolds on bass, and Mike LeFebvre on drums. Willie, Buskirk, and Jamail were listed as producers.

In addition to the great mix of songs, the album began with a programmed soundboard, an innovation which was used commercially here for the first time. It featured Nelson commentary for those with the technology to access it. The commentary basically said the album contained "songs that Paul Buskirk and I have been playing for many years."

Forbes Magazine described the new technology, writing that:

Houston's Justice Records, a tiny independent label, has a hot new technology. Justice founder Randall Jamail and colleague David Thompson have a patent pending on a process that allows spoken messages to be heard on a compact disc without interrupting the music.

The album, itself, peaked on the national sales chart at one hundred eighty-eight and, as label president, Randall Jamail proudly noted, got Willie nominated for a Grammy "in the Traditional Pop Vocal category." In 1996, Justice marketed a "sampler" entitled *Justice Country: A Regional Sound*, JR 0011-2, that featured two Willie cuts, 'Afraid' (a Fred Rose song), from this album, and 'Me and Paul', from the RCA album, *Yesterday's Wine*, which was remarketed by Justice.

Healing Hands of Time. Liberty Records 7243-8-30420-2-9. (1994).

Track Listing: Funny How Time Slips Away, Crazy, Night Life, Healing Hands of Time, (How Will I Know) I'm Falling in Love Again, All the Things You Are, Oh, What It Seemed to Be, If I Had My Way, I'll Be Seeing You, There Are Worse Things Than Being Alone.

Recording Notes: The next post-Columbia effort from Nelson arrived in October 1994 as Nelson's first official label became his newest. The Liberty logo had been resurrected as a division of EMI Records. The set featured (a sixty-three piece) orchestrated versions of Nelson standards such as 'Crazy', 'Night Life', 'Funny How Time Slips Away', and the title tune. From the originals, the album segued into a set of timeless classics, ranging from Jerome Kern's 'All the Things You Are' to Sammy Fain's 'I'll Be Seeing You'.

'All the Things You Are' was the "pearl" of a failed Kern/Oscar Hammerstein II musical. It has been critically acclaimed as possibly "the very best song ever written by Jerome Kern." At the time, both Hammerstein and Kern "did not think it would be popular because it was too complex." Kern's biographer, David Ewen, wrote that Kern composed the song "more for his own artistic satisfaction than to woo a public."

What made the song become one of the most-performed standards ever was "Kern's harmonic dexterity." According to music critic William G. Hyland, the song successfully incorporated a device:

known as an enharmonic change, wherein a note is written in two different ways; they sound exactly the same when struck on the piano but perform a different function in the accompanying harmony.

Hyland elaborated that "the effect is startling; it gives the new phrase an entirely unexpected lift." He concluded about Kern's use of the enharmonic device that "in no popular song is it done better."

There was even more to the song, as Hammerstein, the lyricist, explained. In his book, *Lyrics by Oscar Hammerstein II*, he wrote that "one of the best examples of good singing endings" was "the last line of 'All the Things You Are'." It was because "the two notes that are hit by the repetition of the word 'are' constitute the climax of the line."

In 1995, Willie sang the song as part of a PBS Television special broadcast dedicated to Hammerstein. In full dress tuxedo he performed live with a more than sixty-piece orchestra. His unique phrasing and vocal style blended perfectly with the dominating orchestral arrangements. Later the same year, he completely changed styles and approach in front of a CMA Awards show audience (a televised special) and sang, with Dolly Parton, Marty Stuart, Dwight Yoakam, and Merle Haggard, some Roger Miller tunes (in honor of old buddy Roger's election to the Hall of Fame).

Of the other standards Willie chose, the Frankie Carle/George Weiss/Bennie Benjamin work, 'Oh, What It Seemed to Be', had a most unique history. In 1945, Carle wrote the song with his two collaborators and then recorded it with his orchestra (his daughter Marjorie Hughes was the vocalist). For the first half of 1946 it was one of the hottest songs around, selling, in Dorothy Kilgallen's words "more than 100,000 in two weeks."

One final beautiful Nelson original, 'There Are Worse Things Than Being Alone', closed the album. The album, itself, took only three days to record. "We knew all the songs," Willie explained, "there was no reason for it to take much longer than that." Willie, beard neatly trimmed and pony tail prominently contained, appeared on the cover in full tuxedo.

Jimmy Bowen, label president, produced the album. He said, "it was a musical thing that I wanted to do with Willie for half a dozen years. I got it exactly the way I wanted..." Willie was quoted as being very pleased with the album, assessing that "to have [songs I've written] beside these writers is a dream that songwriters have, that very rarely comes true."

As part of promoting the album, Willie appeared on the Howard Stern TV show, which originated in New York. Among the revelations he made to the "shock jock" was that he used "peyote once a year for religious observance," loved bee pollen, and believed in reincarnation. He also revealed that his family history included "bootleggers and moonshiners" and "referred to himself and his first wife as the 'Battling Nelsons'." Willie kept trying to focus on the merits and highlights of his album but Howard kept asking questions like when did he lose his virginity. Incidentally, Willie told Howard that particular loss occurred at age six.

The album touched the listening public well enough for it to peak at number one hundred and three on the national album sales charts. It was all part of a mostly great 1994 for Willie, which found him holding the Farm Aid concert in New Orleans. Earlier in the year, he performed at the New Orleans Jazz & Heritage Festival and in Augusta, Georgia, at the James Brown birthday celebration in the Civic Center (it was birthday number sixty-one, according to the Brown's family records).

Unfortunately, police found Willie sleeping in the back seat of his Mercedes alongside Interstate 35 up near Waco. In the ashtray, there supposedly was the remains of a roach (a marijuana cigarette). So, Willie got arrested on a misdemeanor possession count. He said he was returning to Austin from playing poker in nearby Hillsboro when he pulled off the interstate to avoid some bad weather. Fortunately, after some court time, he got past the allegedly trumped up charge. His comment on the arrest was that "it's all part of life."

The Road Goes on Forever. (Highwaymen). Liberty Records CDP-7243-8-28091-2-8. (1995).

Track Listing: The Devil's Right Hand, Live Forever, Everyone Gets Crazy, It Is What It Is, I Do Believe, The End of Understanding, True Love Travels a Gravel Road, Death and Hell, Waiting for a Long Time, Here Comes That Rainbow Again, The Road Goes on Forever.

Recording Notes: This 1995 reunion, for the third time in ten years, of Cash, Jennings, Kristofferson, and Nelson, showed that the four could still cook musically. All of them seemed to want to be singing lead even when singing together. That approach worked to give the songs a power that couldn't have come from anyone else. Part of the success lay in selecting songs that somehow always worked for the four voices. For example, Waylon said that "a song like 'It Is What It Is' off the third album lets us pass the song around like a hot potato."

The other song choices were just as appropriate, from Nelson's song, 'The End of Understanding' to Steve Earle's 'The Devil's Right Hand' and Robert Earl Keen, Jr.'s title song, 'The Road Goes on Forever'. Besides Willie, each of the three artists contributed a song apiece. Cash's composition (written with son, John Carter Cash) was 'Death and Hell', while Waylon added 'I Do Believe' and Kris gave the group 'Here Comes That Rainbow Again'.

Waylon's view of the album was, "I think it's our best, so far. Three's the charm." Much of the credit belonged to producer, Don Was, who, in Waylon's words, "orchestrates his sessions with the skill of a master conductor." All the work involved with cutting the album and making a corresponding video required "some complex juggling," but:

> through it all, Don was at his ease, moving everything forward, keeping everybody loose and alert, and letting nothing phase him.

Waylon, himself, didn't think the Highwaymen:

> would work with any other configuration. Today the only thing that keeps it together is love. We actually get on each other's nerves and we get in each other's way. We are used to having our own way, and we are strong as a bull as far as character, you know. We are used to having our own way. It would never work with nobody else, I will guarantee you. If we didn't love the music and each other like we do... All of us have our egos, but we don't let them get in the way of the music.

Will there be any more Highwaymen projects? If it were left up to Waylon, the answer would be "no." He recently said that he:

> didn't realize we'd done it ten years. And I guess it's pretty well done for. We're not going to do it any more. I don't intend to. Too many people got involved.

That would be too bad given that this album was daring enough to include an electric sitar (played by Mark Goldenberg).

In his 1997 autobiography, Johnny Cash wrote an incisive retrospective on the group of four, at least from his viewpoint. He said the idea for the grouping came about:

> when I was doing an ABC TV Christmas special in Montreux, Switzerland. The network told me to invite whoever I wanted to be on the show, so I asked Willie, Kris, and Waylon, and off we went to Montreux. We had so much fun, we decided to make a habit of it.

He went on to reveal that "we shot the special in Montreux because it's beautiful there, and snowy, and they have a great musical facility."

About that 1984 special, Waylon remembered that, "as John put it," we all "got along 'handsomely'." He said they started trading songs in the hotel room and finally someone said, "we ought to cut an album." They finally began their first album together after Waylon and Kris visited Willie and John recording a duet together (back in Nashville) under the direction of producer Chips Moman. About Willie, Cash wrote that:

> I don't know Willie that well. I never met him during his Nashville years when he and Faron and the gang were trying to give Tootsie's Orchid Lounge a bad name, and after he left for Texas I didn't spend any significant time with him until we started working together in the Highwaymen (though 'working' isn't quite the word). Even today I can't say I know him very well, either, because he's a hard man to know; he keeps his inner thoughts for himself and his songs. He just doesn't talk much at all, in fact. When he does, what he says is usually very perceptive and precise, and often very funny; he has a beautiful sense of irony and a true appreciation for the absurd. I really like him. He and I have done some two-man shows together recently, just him on a stool with mine, trading songs and jokes and stories. That's fun.

Just One Love. Justice Records JR 1602-2. (1995).

Track Listing: Just One Love, Each Night at Nine, This Cold Cold War with You, Better Left Forgotten, It's a Sin, Four Walls, Smoke, Smoke, Smoke That Cigarette, I Just Drove By, Cold Cold Heart, Bonaparte's Retreat, Alabam, Eight More Miles to Louisville.

Recording Notes: Willie recorded these sides for Justice prior to recording his *Healing Hands of Time* album for Liberty, though Justice did not release them until the summer of 1995. That was the year Willie inducted the Allman Brothers Band into the Rock and Roll Hall of Fame. He had previously had a top ten country hit with their song, 'Midnight Rider'.

Though Justice was a small independent label, it did manage to place the album briefly on the national *Billboard* album charts. Songwriter Kimmie Rhodes was one of the featured artists. She did vocals and background vocals and contributed two of the songs, the title song and 'I Just Drove By', a song about going back to the house where she was child.

Calling this his "honky-tonk" album, all the other selections Willie chose, with one exception, were country classics. That one exception was Chip Young's 'Better Left Forgotten'. The most well-known of the classics were Hank Williams' 'Cold Cold Heart', Tex Williams' 'Smoke, Smoke, Smoke That Cigarette', Cowboy Copas' 'Alabam', and Pee Wee King's 'Bonaparte's Retreat'.

Merle Travis, the co-writer of 'Smoke, Smoke, Smoke' said he wrote the song because:

> Tex Williams needed a song to record and asked me to write him one. He had done such a good job 'The Dark Town Poker Club', I more or less copied that and wrote down these verses.

Tex had his only number one pop and country hit with the song in 1947. It was the first million-selling single for Capitol Records, eventually selling over two million copies.

'Cold Cold Heart' was not only one of Hank's biggest sellers, it crossed over to become Tony Bennett's second number one hit in 1951. Hank's inspiration was wife Audrey, about whom he supposedly said, "she's got the coldest heart I've ever seen." The song was said to have come from those cryptic words.

King once admitted to having used a portion of the tune from an old folk ballad, 'Bonnie Lass of Anglesey', as the basis for 'Bonaparte's Retreat'. He mixed in a little bit of 'Casbah Swing' to create the song which became a 1950 top ten country hit for him. It went to number four on the pop charts for Kay Starr the same year.

Though Jean Shepherd, married to Hawkshaw Hawkins at the time of his death, has pleaded to have Hawkins and Cowboy Copas remembered for more than being the two others killed with Patsy Cline in a 1963 plane crash, the pair unfortunately have come to be thought of mostly for that fact. Copas' only number one country hit had come in 1960 with 'Alabam'. Otherwise his biggest moments had been his appearances on the Opry with none other than Pee Wee King in the forties and that fateful plane crash.

Of the other classics, Eddy Arnold had the second number one single of his fledgling career in 1947 with the fatalistic Fred Rose/Zeb Turner lament, 'It's a Sin'. Marty Robbins achieved top five success with a remake of the song in 1969. 'Four Walls' was written by Marvin Moore and George Campbell. Moore previously wrote Jim Lowe's 1956 number one pop smash, 'Green Door'. In 1957 'Four Walls' became the first number one country hit for Jim Reeves on the RCA label.

Another chestnut, 'This Cold War with You', written by Floyd Tillman in the early days of the real "cold war" between the U. S. and Russia, was first done by Willie in the early sixties during his initial tenure on Liberty Records. Tillman also wrote 'Each Night at Nine' while he was in the Air Force. He said it really was "a song born in the barracks. It was a natural at the time, as easy to write as a letter."

The song was truly a soldier's lament, asking his wife, a thousand miles away, to think of him "each night at nine." While stationed in the states, Tillman knew he was going to be shipped far away because he kept hearing "rumors of overseas shipments ... any day I would be gone." As it ended up, Floyd was very quickly "gone," not overseas, but instead "to New York" where Dave Kapp recorded his song.

Grandpa Jones also placed a song of his on this collection, 'Eight More Miles to Louisville', doing vocals and playing banjo on the track. Grandpa once said about the song that he wrote it:

> back around 1941. At the time, Alton and Rabon Delmore had recorded a song entitled 'Fifteen Miles from Birmingham'. There is no similarity between the two songs, of course, but that's where I got the idea.

Among those in musical support on the album were Grady Martin, guitar and keyboards (he also produced the set), Chip Young, guitar (he did the mixing and served as assistant engineer), various members of Willie's band, Lisa Jones, hammered dulcimer, Buddy Emmons, bass and steel guitar, as well as Pete Wade, guitar. The Fall of 1995 found Willie, Neil Young, John Mellencamp, Hootie and the Blowfish, among others headlining Farm Aid at Louisville, Kentucky's Cardinal Stadium. Willie warmed up for the concert with a variety of live dates, including one at the Valley Forge Music Fair in Pennsylvania. He also toured with the Highwaymen.

Spirit. Island Records (A PolyGram Company) 314-524 242-2. (1996).

Track Listing: Matador, She Is Gone, Your Memory Won't Die in My Grave, I'm Not Trying to Forget You Anymore, Too Sick to Pray, Mariachi, I'm Waiting Forever, We Don't Run, I Guess I've Come to Live Here in Your Eyes, It's a Dream Come True, I Thought About You, Lord, Spirit of E9, Matador.

Recording Notes: Island Records marketed this 1996 album as the first all original Willie Nelson album since 1974's *Phases and Stages* album, meaning it was the first time in over twenty years that Willie wrote all of the songs for one of his own albums. The songs were certainly all new to recording, or were they?

In 1991, Willie spoke with *Vanity Fair* and in the course of the interview, he played the interviewer a tape of material containing, among other fascinating items, a version of 'Angel Flying Too Close to the Ground' that had an extra verse. There was also another song on that tape the interviewer especially noted, 'Your Memory Won't Die in My Grave'. All the material on that tape was supposed to have gone out, in 1991, as an unadvertised companion album to the mail-order set, *The IRS Tapes* (the two CD set later retail marketed by Sony).

When that companion album, *The Hungry Years*, finally did come out in late 1991, it contained 'Your Memory Won't Die in My Grave' but not the "extra-verse" 'Angel' cut. Its release was limited to mail-order and concert sales so the song wasn't heard by very many people. Then came *Spirit* with the 'Your Memory Won't Die' song and eleven other Willie originals. Was *Spirit* an album Willie made altogether in 1995 for release in 1996 on Island?

Willie explained the genesis of *Spirit* to *Billboard*, telling the magazine that as of 1994 (after Liberty released his *Healing Hands of Time* album),

> here I was between labels, looking for someone to put out the 'Spirit' album, which I had already produced myself. In the meantime Don Was is a good friend of Chris Blackwell (Island Records Chairman), and Don wanted to do a lot of Willie Nelson songs reggae style. We decided, why don't we experiment? We took our own money and did our own reggae song. We took real musicians and an obscure song of mine from the '50s. We went to Jamaica to talk to [Blackwell] about the reggae album. I said, 'Hell, while I'm down there, I'm going to take my 'Spirit' album, just on the outside chance that he might be interested.

Once in Jamaica, Willie stayed at the former home of Ian Fleming, the author of the original James Bond books, and sat around listening to music. He said,

> I played Chris the song for the reggae album, which he liked. Then I played him the whole 'Spirit' album, and he said, 'Yeah, I want that, too.

According to Nelson, *Spirit* was comparable to his landmark *Red Headed Stranger* album in its simplicity and mood. His appraisal was that he "wanted the same feel - or as close as I could get - to 'Red Headed Stranger'. And I think we got pretty close." He also revealed that:

> there weren't any amplifiers at all. I just played my guitar into the mike. And it sounds good too - so clean and uninterrupted.

In the final analysis, all except four of the songs on the *Spirit* album were written during a six month period probably in 1995. The four exceptions were written seventeen years ago, approximately 1979 or 1980. One of them, the song, 'I Guess I've Come to Live Here in Your Eyes', was included as part of the 1980 *Honeysuckle Rose* movie and soundtrack. It was not the only song that had been previously recorded, however (on *Phases and Stages*, only 'Bloody Mary Morning' had been previously recorded by Willie - back when he was on RCA).

Willie remembered that "the other three were on an obscure album I recorded that never came out." That sounded like *The Hungry Years*, which did come out (as a Sony "special product") but not exactly when expected. Actually, of the three, 'Your Memory Won't Die' was the only one that was recorded nowhere else but that "obscure" album. Both 'She Is Gone' and 'I'm Not Trying to Forget You' were recorded for Columbia.

'Matador' opened and closed the album, making it more or less the theme. 'She Is Gone' was the first cut shipped to radio stations, with the hope Island could somehow get airplay in a market place which has become, as Willie's peer, George Jones, recently observed, "an industry where youth will be served." Jones put it very bluntly that "there has never been a time when country radio was so disrespectful of its elders." Willie tried so hard to get *Spirit* played that, according to a 1997 report on country radio in *Country Weekly*, "he personally delivered it to a small Arkansas radio station that hadn't received it."

Still, as Charley Pride wrote in his autobiography,

> if you listen to radio in major markets across the country, you'll rarely hear the likes of George Jones, Merle Haggard, Waylon Jennings, Johnny Cash, Loretta Lynn, Willie Nelson, Tammy Wynette, Ronnie Milsap, Mel Tillis, Charley Pride, or anybody else in the business over the age of forty-five.

That's too bad considering that Willie was forty-three at the height of the "outlaw" craze back in 1976. In Willie's mind, he "never had that much airplay." Now in the nineties, he observed, "I'm over 40; country radio has already forgotten about me."

The disturbing trend has not gone unnoticed, fortunately. In a "special report" done in early 1996 for *Country Weekly*, writer Bruce Honick, stated that country radio has "turned its back on the legends who helped make the music as popular as it is today." In fact, he continued, that very subject has "become one of the hottest issues in an art form that celebrates respect for tradition and its elders." In the article, radio station executives were defensively quoted as saying "they're only giving listeners what they want to hear," implying that the public no longer wants to listen to anyone but the young "hunks" who now dominate the airwaves.

Lorianne Crook, formerly one-half of The Nashville Network show (with Charlie Chase), *Crook and Chase*, disputed the view that country music fans only want to hear young stars, saying that

> from what the artists tell me when we do interviews, there is a very strong segment of radio programmers -- I don't know if they're called consultants, I think that's how they're described -- and they are telling the radio stations 'Go young.

Only program the hot new music. Because Merle Haggard
and George Jones are the old-timers, and nobody wants to
listen to them.' Where that attitude came from, I don't know,
but it's so incorrect. I love the new stars, but I would turn on
any station that played Jones and Haggard and Loretta.

According to older, radio-spurned artists like John Conlee, "we're
as busy as ever on the road." So, someone really is still listening, just
not the radio programmers. When Willie released his patently country
album, *Just One Love*, it won critical praise from many country fans and
analysts, but gained no airplay.

Ken Kragen, who managed the career turnaround for Kenny Rogers
and also helped both Trisha Yearwood and Travis Tritt become
superstars, put it a little more bluntly when he concluded that:

> once country got more popular, the stations suddenly
> developed the programming habits of pop stations, in the
> sense that you're only as good as your last record. Regardless
> of how big an artist you are and how long you've been around,
> you're not likely to get airplay anymore if you predate Randy
> Travis.

He understood the frustration of artists:

> like Kenny Rogers, Willie Nelson, and George Jones, who
> continue to record excellent material but find it almost
> impossible to get the records played. Luckily, the fan base is
> still there, so these artists just have to look at the other
> areas, such as touring and acting, to reach them.

So, Willie has continued to tour (to huge crowds) and make movies, like
1997's *Gone Fishin'* and *Wag the Dog*.

Holly Dunn, who turned forty in 1997, had her last top ten huge
country hit in 1987. At forty, Willie had not even become a country
superstar. Yet in 1997, Holly has had to resort to being a country music
disc jockey for radio station WWWW in Detroit, because her third
straight attempt to hit the charts in the last few years met with
failure again due to a lack of radio support. She said she felt like, for
her, "the end was premature." She added that:

> it's so odd that all of my generation and this new generation
> say that our influences were Dolly Parton, Emmylou Harris,
> Willie Nelson, Merle Haggard, Waylon, but those people
> can't get arrested on contemporary country radio.

Many promoters out there, like Pat Garrett in Pennsylvania, would rather book the very profitable big names like Johnny Cash as opposed to losing money on newer acts, the very acts that dominate the play lists of country stations. It wasn't but twenty years prior that Waylon and Willie had the nation's number one country song, 'Good Hearted Woman', while Willie by himself came in at number three with 'Remember Me'.

Willie continues to plug away with the same sound that had him on top of the country world for twenty years. He has always known that:

> I never did really fit into the phases and stages and things that the music always goes through. It would be hard to quit what you're doing and try to conform to what's going on on the radio. It would be too much of a change.

As a result, Willie has found it almost impossible to get airplay. It's not that he couldn't "adapt" his music a little, he simply cannot change the reality of his age. He spoke out in one interview that:

> these days it's ridiculous who-all can't get played. The legends in the business, the people who made it what it is, are not heard.

He said he:

> knew that radio-wise I was getting into a little bit of trouble when I heard some guy say, 'Boy, I wish they'd play some of those old guys again like George Strait ... and Randy Travis'.

In a Spring 1997 interview, he told *Scene* magazine editor Bill DeYoung that gaining radio play has:

> gotten so political that in order to fight that battle you've got to attack it from a higher spot than where I am. You gotta go up there to those guys that program a hundred radio stations.

As no less a writer than Geoffrey Himes observed, in the Fall 1995 issue of *Country Music*, it would be possible to:

> make the argument that Willie Nelson and his contemporaries deserve to be shoved off the country charts by a new generation. After all, they had their day, and there's no reason to prevent younger singers from having theirs just

because Nelson and his cronies are still cranking out respectable records.

Fortunately, Himes saw "one flaw" in the argument. Willie was simply making "the very best music of his entire career" at that time.

The fact that country music has reached (by 1996/1997) "a degree of repetitiveness followed by boredom" has been observed by no less an expert than the executive director of the Country Music Association, Ed Benson. The Kentucky Headhunters likewise concluded that "what's missing from country music today is originality and roots." Narvel Blackstock, manager/husband of Reba McEntire, was recently quoted as saying that "country music is about two inches deep and a mile wide." Someone else has done more than just notice. For quite awhile, Bill Gavin has been airing an "Americana" chart so that "listeners who are bored with today's country-western music" can still hear "the cutting edge sounds of Dale Watson, Joe Ely, Willie Nelson, George Jones, Emmylou Harris, Kelly Willis, and Lyle Lovett."

So, by late summer 1996, Willie was out pushing the *Spirit* album, which did go to number twenty-one on the *Billboard* country album charts. He appeared on the Rosie O'Donnell show in early October, singing a track from the album, 'I Guess I've Come to Live Here in Your Eyes.' Even that beautiful song could garner no radio play. Will Willie quit? Older sister Bobbie stated that, "my brother and I have a need for music. We're driven to it."

Willie was also driven to box heavyweight Randall 'Tex' Cobb in a three round exhibition as part of a fundraiser for amateur boxing. Given all of Willie's varied interests, boxing a heavyweight should come as no surprise but one can't help wonder how such an exhibition came about. Willie said,

> Tex Cobb is a good friend of mine. He called me a few months ago, told me about the event and his involvement and wanted to know if I'd come help him with it.

Tex, on the other hand, said he told Willie, "How'd you like to hit me in the mouth?" When, in Tex's words, "Willie thought this was a great idea," Tex asked him if it would be okay "if people come and watch?" So why did Tex pick Willie for a match? Tex said, "I needed a win."

Augusta. (Willie Nelson & Don Cherry). Coast to Coast Records (An MCM Media Company) CTC 0305. (1995).

Track Listing: My Way, Augusta, One for the Road, Red Sails in the Sunset, Try a Little Tenderness, Tangerine, I Love You for

Sentimental Reasons, Prisoner of Love, Tenderly, Maybe You'll Be There, Don't Go to Strangers, Night Life, Rainy Day Blues.

Recording Notes: This album was an England-only release on a very small label headquartered in Luton. It was licensed from Bellaire Records of Texas. The release date was given as 1995 although the session dates had to be earlier because Don Cherry unexpectedly passed away in 1995. Little was divulged about the cuts, save the titles. The personnel credited was Willie and Cherry, along with Charlie Shaffer as producer, arranger, and Jay Orlando as sax soloist. Don Janicek, of Bellaire Records was listed as executive producer.

Had this album been released ten or fifteen years ago it would have been toasted as one of Willie's most innovative and beautiful "standards" albums.   It began with 'My Way', which was immortalized through Paul Anka lyrics and Frank Sinatra interpretation.   Then it progressed into two standards that had years ago been respectively redefined by Fats Domino and James Brown, namely, 'Red Sails in the Sunset' and Prisoner of Love'.   There the Cherry/Nelson vocal interplay redefined the two songs once again.

'Prisoner of Love' came from talented vocalist Russ Columbo shortly before his tragic death in 1934 at the age of twenty-six. Russ co-wrote the song in 1931 with Leo Robin and Clarence Gaskill. He had a hit with it in 1932, reaching number sixteen. Fourteen years later, Perry Como took the song to the number one spot.

'Red Sails in the Sunset' was a 1935 composition from Jimmy Kennedy and Hugh Williams. Not only was it used in the musical play *Provincetown Follies*, it went on to become the theme song for vocalist Suzette Tarri. Both Bing Crosby and Guy Lombardo had number one hits with it in 1935.

All of the tracks were beauties and beautifully different, especially the title cut, 'Augusta'. Normally, saxophone solos used throughout an album overly dominate. That was not so in this case. Orlando's playing accentuated when appropriate and carried the arrangement to new heights just when it seemed nothing more could be added. 'One for the Road' did not feel like the same song that Willie and Leon Russell once recorded together. It hit a different dimension altogether.

Otis Redding had turned the 1932 standard 'Try a Little Tenderness' (written by Harry Wood, Jimmy Campbell, and Reginald Connelly) into a 1966 pop top forty hit. Willie and Don here turned it into a breezy, jazzy tune for all times. A great song can be done in any variety of ways and will still come through as a great song. That's why, for example, the best thing a rock group like The Black Crowes have ever done was Otis Redding's 'Hard to Handle' as opposed to one of their originals.

Another "tender" song that Willie and Don redefined was 'Tenderly', written in 1947 by Walter Gross and Jack Lawrence for the

Gig Young/Joan Crawford musical film, *Torch Song.* 'Tangerine' came from Willie's favorite, Johnny Mercer. He wrote it in 1942 with composer Victor Schertzinger for the musical film *The Fleet's In* starring Dorothy Lamour, William Holden, and Betty Hutton.

'(I Love You) For Sentimental Reasons' was a top twenty pop hit seven times, with six of those chartings between 1946 and 1947. Nat Cole took it to number one first, followed by Dinah Shore and Ella Fitzgerald (both versions were top ten) and others. Sam Cooke took it to number seventeen in 1958. Two more standards, 'Don't Go to Strangers' and 'Maybe You'll Be There' closed out the amazing variety of classic songs chosen by Willie for this album.

Arthur Kent, Dave Mann, and Redd Evans wrote 'Don't Go to Strangers' in 1954. Although Vaughn Monroe had some success with it as a single, it was one of those songs that became a classic because it was recorded by so many different performers and not due to a definitive hit version. Gordon Jenkins turned 'Maybe You'll Be There' into a number three hit in 1948. Rube Bloom and Sammy Gallop wrote it in 1947.

Closing out the album were two of Willie's "blues" number, 'Night Life' and 'Rainy Day Blues', done in a much lighter, easy-rolling style. The 'Night Life' cut marked about the thirteenth time Willie had recorded the song, either live or in the studio. 'Rainy Day Blues' dated back to a 1959 single he cut in Houston, one that eventually went out on the Bellaire label in the early sixties.

Willie and Don went back quite a way, especially to Willie's 1987 picnic at Carl's Corner, where Cherry was one of the featured guests. Don was going to lead off his part of the show with 'Green Green Grass of Home', a number he had consistently used as his nightclub opener. He frantically went up to Willie and said he'd forgotten the words.

Willie suddenly couldn't remember them either. He recalled that "I could hear the melody in my head, but the words didn't come." He remembered leaving Cherry with his own band of Bee Spears, Grady Martin, Mickey Raphael, and Poodie Locke, all of them singing and trying to remember the words. Cherry has been most well-known for playing a unique style of Jazz trumpet (a small "pocket" trumpet). He was usually a "sideman" and was most remembered for his work with Ornette Coleman.

In retrospect relative to this album, it might seem strange to find Willie in such close musical kinship with a Jazz artist. Yet no less a luminary than Miles Davis told an interviewer in 1981 that "I love the way Willie sings; the way he phrases is great. He phrases sometimes like I do." For his 1981 album, *Directions*, Miles created a piece entitled 'Willie Nelson', specifically "for the rough-voiced middle-aged country balladeer." Miles' biographer, Jack Chambers, described the piece as "a stretch of music that catches the pianoless quintet working over an uptempo riff."

The following year, Miles visited Willie backstage where the two were said to have written a song together, 'Expect Me Around'. When I asked Willie about Miles, he talked about him writing the 'Willie Nelson' song. He added that Miles "visited me back stage once in Las Vegas and then came out and played awhile during one of my shows." But, Willie said, they "never did write a song together."

Miles said Willie's manager, Mark Rothbaum, introduced him to Willie in Las Vegas. Though Miles never made mention of writing a song with Willie, he did reveal, in his autobiography, that "we had a nice time in Las Vegas. I got to know Willie Nelson real well. He was down to earth and cool with me." That was not the extent of their getting together. Miles recalled that:

> after this, Willie came to a place called Red Rocks, in Denver, Colorado, where I was playing. He came to see me play a few times after that.

During the same interview, I asked Willie about the *Augusta* album and what happened to it. He said he was very pleased someone had actually heard of it. As he recalled, "it came out on a small label out of England that didn't have itself together." Unfortunately, they "own the rights to the record" and he didn't think they would ever be able to get it out in the United States. He also didn't think he would be able to get back the rights so another label could put it out in this country.

Willie's manager, Mark Rothbaum said it was essentially "old friend Don's project." So, for the foreseeable future, Willie fans will have to specially order the album from stores that specialize in import albums. As an album, *Augusta* was billed as "an all Texas Project." Cherry was from Wichita Falls, producer Shaffer was born in Houston, and Janicek came out of the small town of Columbus. Saxophonist Orlando was from Detroit but Governor Ann Richards had made him an "honorary" Texan.

Greatest Hits: Live In Concert. BCI (Brentwood Communications, Inc.) Music BCCD 295. (1996).

Track Listing: Georgia on My Mind, Stardust, On the Road Again, You Were Always on My Mind, Angel Flying Too Close to the Ground, Good Hearted Woman, Blue Eyes Crying in the Rain, City of New Orleans, To All the Girls I've Loved Before, Seven Spanish Angels, Luckenbach Texas, Whiskey River.

Recording Notes: What would be next for Willie? In spite of the high hopes for him on Island, late 1996 basically found him free of any label, though he did not actually leave Island. He did reasonably well with *Spirit*, watching it climb the *Billboard* country album charts (it reached number twenty-one by Summer). It was not that he couldn't get someone to sign him, it's that he seemed to revel in going where he wanted to go.

It was announced there would be a forthcoming album of blues songs, entitled *Black Night*, featuring yet another great version of 'Night Life' with one of the bluesiest guitar runs ever on a Willie Nelson track. No label was announced, though it appeared likely Island would pick it up. About the album, itself, Willie told Bill DeYoung that "there'll be a blues album, also on Island." To that he added,

> I used all the Austin blues guys. I'm thinking about calling it 'Black Night', there's an old Jim Witherspoon song, an old standard blues thing, and it came off real good.

More information on the blues album came out in an interview Willie did with Dave Hoekstra (in *Country Song Roundup*). Willie told Dave that he cut the blues album:

> in my studio in Austin, Texas, and I used all the great Austin-based blues musicians. Derek O'Brien playing guitar. George Rains and Riley Osbourne on keyboards. They're the house band at Antone's. We did stuff like 'The Thrill Is Gone' and 'Kansas City' as well as some of my stuff like 'Night Life', which B. B. King and I did for his album.

The Don Was-produced reggae album was projected for a 1997 release. Meanwhile, some older Christmas cuts were released on a budget label out of Nashville. Following that came this set of live material, marketed by two discount companies (initially Brentwood Communications of Westlake Village, California, and nationally by Excelsior Records, with the title *Willie Nelson - In Concert* and the catalog number, EXL 2394). In England, both Charly Records and Hallmark Records released a live set. On Hallmark, the catalog number was 300412 and it was inventively titled, *Live*. On Charly, the title was *Concert* and the catalog number was CDCD-1261.

Though released in 1996, the cuts were from earlier live performances. Without any liner notes, it was impossible to tell exactly the dates of the selections, though the best guess would have to be sometime in 1985. That's because several of the major tracks, 'To All the Girls I've Loved Before', 'City of New Orleans, and 'Seven Spanish Angels' all were popular by late 1984, early 1985.

Some of the cuts had been duets, namely 'Good Hearted Woman' and Luckenbach, Texas' (originally with Waylon), 'Seven Spanish Angels' (studio cut with Ray Charles), and 'To All the Girls I've Loved

Before' (a number one duet with Julio Iglesias when initially put in 1984). On this live set, it was all Willie on those songs, with harmonies from appropriate band members. The closer, of course, was yet another rousing version of 'Whiskey River'.

Hill Country Christmas. (Willie Nelson with Bobbie Nelson). Finer Arts Records FAR 9705-2. (1997).

Track Listing: El Nino (the Christ Child), Away in a Manger, Joy to the World, Little Town of Bethlehem, Here Comes Santa Claus (featuring Gene Autry), Pretty Paper, Hark the Herald Angels Sing, Silent Night, Deck the Halls, White Christmas, El Nino (instrumental).

Recording Notes: During Willie's Columbia Records period, he had one very popular Christmas album, *Pretty Paper*. It was initially released in 1979 and has reappeared every holiday season since then. In 1994, the year after Willie left Columbia, he released another Christmas album, *Christmas with Willie Nelson*, which featured some previously unreleased tracks he had recorded during his Columbia years. The 1994 album went out on Regency, a budget label headquartered in Nashville. Both of Willie's Christmas albums were discussed together as part of one of the sections on his Columbia recordings.

In 1997, using a full page ad in *Billboard* magazine, Willie announced an "all new recording for Christmas 1997." It was entitled *Hill Country Christmas* and introduced "Willie Nelson's original composition 'El Nino (The Christ Child)'." In a late 1997 interview (with Rob Patterson of *Fi* magazine), Willie discussed how the song came about. He explained that he had written:

> this Christmas song, and I didn't know what I was gonna call it. But Gator, my bus driver, said, 'why don't you call it "El Nino"?'

That sounded great to Willie, because:

> there's been so much talk about El Nino in the negative, but El Nino doesn't mean something negative - it's the child, the babe.

In addition to the lead cut, 'El Nino' (instrumentally reprised at the end), the album featured two new (or at least not previously released) tracks, 'Joy to the World' and 'Hark the Herald Sings', both standard Christmas fare. Six of the remaining seven selections had been previously released on either the *Pretty Paper* (Columbia) or *Christmas with Willie Nelson* (Regency) albums. In fact, 'Little Town of Bethlehem', 'Pretty Paper', and 'Silent Night' appeared on both albums. Willie told Patterson that the version of 'Pretty Paper' on this album consisted of "just me and the guitar."

Irving Berlin's 'White Christmas' was on the Columbia album only while 'Deck the Halls' had just been part of the Regency album. Gene Autry's song (co-written by Gene and Oakly Haldman), 'Here Comes Santa Claus', had been on the Columbia album. It appeared here in a different version, featuring the cowboy star himself. Autry turned ninety in 1997 by celebrating at the Autry Museum of Western Heritage. Willie was part of a lengthy guest list, about which one artist said, "Willie Nelson and Glen Campbell are the young 'uns."

Writing in his 1978 autobiography, a much older Autry recalled how and when he, during his cowboy star heyday, came to write the song. It was after the war (World War II), and Autry "was the grand marshall for the annual Hollywood Christmas parade." As Gene recollected,

> the parade route jangled right on down Hollywood Boulevard, leading to what the promoters called Santa Claus Lane.

As the parade progressed with Gene riding towards the front and Santa Claus "in a big sleigh a few rows back," he could "hear the kids ... shouting to each other, 'Here he comes, here comes Santa Claus'."

From that "lane" name and the shouts of the kids, Autry made "a few scribbled notes" and then got together:

> with Oakley Haldeman, then the manager of my music publishing company (set up after the war). In August of 1947, well ahead of the holiday season, we recorded 'Here Comes Santa Claus'. That winter it swept the country, as the first new Christmas song in years.

By the end of the following year, 1948, the song "was an even bigger hit," with new versions out "by Bing Crosby, Doris Day, and the Andrews Sisters, among others."

Gene's story about his song didn't end there. He went on to comment about a most unusual use of the song, in his 1949 Western, *The Cowboys and Indians*. The movie's plot had him as an Arizona ranger, "helping the Navajos defend their land against the palefaces." Somehow, and Gene commented, "please don't ask," the filmmakers "managed to work" his song, 'Here Comes Santa Claus', into the movie's storyline.

The seventh selection on this album, 'Away in the Manger', had been previously released on two compilation albums, the 1990 Epic set, *Voices of the Season Acapella*, and one from 1993, *Steve Vaus Presents the Stars Come Out for Christmas: Volume V* (Steve Vaus Productions). In 1994, the song was rereleased by Steve Vaus Productions as part of a "greatest hits" compilation of *Steve Vaus Presents the Stars Come Out for Christmas*. It was credited to Willie Nelson & the Country Choir.

Willie and Freddy Fletcher produced the album and Finer Arts Records of Denver, Colorado, released it. The label was the same one that in 1996 marketed Willie and Bobbie's gospel album, *How Great Thou Art*. Players on the album included Freddy on drums, Jon Blondell on bass, along with Bobbie on piano and Willie on vocals and guitar. Singer/songwriter Kimmie Rhodes contributed additional vocal backing. Recording and mixing was done at Pedernales Studio. The album, credited to Willie Nelson with Bobbie Nelson, was fittingly dedicated to Billy Nelson and Randy Arlyn Fletcher.

This Christmas album became Willie's final one for 1997. That left open the question of what would be his first new album for 1998? In a late 1997 phone conversation with Mark Rothbaum, I was told that both the blues and the reggae albums were "works in progress." Mark had no direct answer as to which album would come out first. Not long into 1998 (March to be exact), Willie fooled everyone.

According to Ben Ratliff, writing in the March 13, 1998, issue of *The New York Times*, Willie had an about-to-be-released album (produced by Daniel Lanois) entitled, *Teatro*. That was, to begin with, a tentative (though likely final) album title, taken from the name of Lanois' studio, El Teatro, located in Oxnard, California. Ratliff stated in his article that at a previous Wednesday night concert at Tramps in Manhattan, Willie played "a new song," something called 'Somebody Pick Up My Pieces', speculated to have come from *Teatro*.

What was this projected new album? It marked a significant departure for Willie. Lanois was the producer of Bob Dylan's 1997 Grammy award-winning album *Time Out of Mind*. It took a *Billboard* interview with Daniel to reveal the origins of the newest Willie set. *Billboard* columnist Paul Verna wrote that Lanois took a:

> low-key approach with Nelson, recording a few tracks with the artist without necessarily setting out to make an entire album.

Lanois explained that:

> Willie did a song with U2 a couple of years back called 'Slow Dancing' and it's just got something to it that Willie had not had before. So when Bono [U2 lead singer] mentioned this to me, I took an interest and proposed a couple of songs for

Willie to do. Then Willie sent me a tape of a couple of things he'd got going, so we're going to try four tracks and perhaps those four, with 'Slow Dancing', might start building towards a record for him.

Yet even that album did not appear right away. It was finally scheduled for August 1998, the month Willie would be installed into the Texas Hall of Fame. In late April (1998), a news item was released (from Marlo Zoda of a company called CDnow, Inc.) which stated that a new Willie (actually Willie and the Offenders) album could be purchased through the Internet only from April 15 to May 15, 1998. The full title of the set, by default Willie's first of 1998, was *Tales Out of Luck (Me and the Drummer)*. Its street release date was given as May 15, 1998. The label turned out to be "Luck Records" - Luck, Texas, being the name of Willie's Western town).

For web users, there was a bonus. Beginning as of the press release date, anyone could log onto www.audionet.com/willie and hear, with the appropriate software, the album in its entirety. They could also hear, for a very limited time, an interactive, "live one-hour music chat with Willie" through chat.yahoo.com. The service came courtesy of AudioNet, "the largest broadcast network on the Internet," CDnow, Inc., an online music store headquartered in Jenkinstown, Pennsylvania, and Yahoo!, "a global Internet media company" headquartered in Santa Clara, California. Listening to the tracks brought with it a complete listing of the song titles, as well as a short review, written by Dave Looby, which read:

Nelson's new CD showcases his smoky, plaintive voice, set to twangy guitars with the occasional blues riff. The culmination of 42 years of making records, "Tales Out of Luck (Me and the Drummer)" demonstrates that Willie Nelson is still at the top of his game when it comes to country songsmithing.

The album was an enigma. According to Sam Henderson, president of Luck Records,

we are delighted to launch this ground-breaking promotion with AudioNet, CDnow and Yahoo!, who are on the forefront of using the Internet to bring together fans and artists. Through their collaborative efforts, these leaders are re-inventing music marketing to give fans the exclusive opportunity to listen to and buy this new release online before it is available through traditional retail stores. Their innovative approach to marketing and selling music fits perfectly with our strategy at Luck Records to give artists the freedom to explore new ways to create, promote and sell their music.

Zoda's press contained a brief explanation of the genesis of the album. It stated that *Tales Out of Luck*:

> brings Willie Nelson back to his country roots. It features 13 songs written more than 30 years ago -- most were never-before recorded. These songs have been released from the vaults and recorded with The Offenders, Nelson's original band from his Nashville days.

The actual sessions that produced the album's finished cuts featured guest artists like Freddie Powers and Johnny Gimble. Except for the track, 'Me and the Drummer' (though written by Bill McDavid, its title smacked of 'Me and Paul'), the song choices were actually all previously released Willie originals, most harking back to his days of writing for Pamper Music and recording for Liberty and RCA.

In fact, of the twelve other selections (not counting 'Me and the Drummer'), half of them had been commercially recorded for the first time by Willie when he was with RCA, including 'I Let My Mind Wander', 'I'd Rather You Didn't Love Me', 'Something to Think About', 'No Tomorrow in Sight', 'I'm So Ashamed', and 'A Moment Isn't Very Long'. Two had been recorded before that in Houston in 1959 for D Records, 'Rainy Day Blues' and 'What a Way to Live'. Another two, 'Home Motel' and 'You Wouldn't Even Cross the Street to Say Goodbye', were done first for Liberty, though the latter cut was not released until 1996. 'Home Motel' did appear on Willie's second and final Liberty album, *Here's Willie Nelson*. The remaining two cuts had both been previously recorded for Columbia albums, 'I Guess I've Come to Live Here in Your Eyes' and 'Forgiving You Was Easy'.

As it turned out, *Teatro* did not even become Willie's second album of 1998. In June, VH1 (the cable television music channel) announced the release (via the label Johnny Cash recorded for, American), on June 9, 1998, of an album of fifteen songs taken from a June 1997 show Willie and Johnny Cash did for that network. The release (American CK 69416), entitled *VH1 Storytellers: Johnny Cash and Willie Nelson* (the show had the same title), featured Willie and Johnny performing together on '(Ghost) Riders in the Sky', 'Flesh and Blood', 'I Still Miss Someone', and 'On the Road Again'.

Willie also played and sang, by himself, at least two of his classics, 'Crazy' and 'Always on My Mind'. Cash, who wrote the liner notes, added 'Don't Take Your Love to Town' and 'Folsom Prison Blues'. According to the press release, the fifteen tracks came largely from the show with some unreleased (i. e. "unviewed") tracks thrown in.

"Healing Hands of Time":

Willie's Film (and Acting) Career

One of the most amazing aspects of the latter part of Willie's recording career was the turn it took, for him, into feature films. Much has been written about how this came to be and how talented an actor Willie has been. Two film historians, James Robert Parish and Michael R. Pitts, appraised that:

> during the 1980s he starred in some half-dozen Westerns, making him the premiere cowboy star of the decade and allowing him to assume John Wayne's mantle as the top star of this otherwise rather moribund genre.

The announcement of the start of Willie's film career came in a brief news item carried by *Variety*, datelined Austin, January 18 (1976). The blurb stated that:

> country singer Willie Nelson will appear in a western motion picture to be filmed in Texas, but director Michael Michaelian reveals that Nelson will not be cast as a singing cowboy.

Instead, he was slated to:

> play a bounty hunter who falls into a series of misadventures as he pursues a wanted outlaw. Filming of "Gone to Texas" will be begin in April.

It sounded like a good idea but Willie's film debut turned out to be in the Peter Fonda-starring, *Outlaw Blues*, with Richard T. Heffron directing.

As an actor, it would suffice it to say that Willie usually acted as Willie, whether he was the "outlaw" in *Barbarosa* or Robert Redford's manager in *The Electric Horseman*. Nowhere could that be more clearly seen than in the modern-day Western, *Pair of Aces*. Kris Kristofferson played the part of a modern-day Texas Ranger while Willie played a lovable scoundrel with a twinkle in his eye and a basic goodness in his soul. Rip Torn's character was a throwback to the good old days of Western law enforcement. The underlying struggle was between family obligations, devotion to work, and just plain old fun.

In a film career that has spanned more than twenty years, from 1977's *Outlaw Blues* to 1997's *Wag the Dog*, Willie has seen his share of both dismal and inspired film-making. He was fortunate to have worked with and learned on-the-set acting techniques from great stars like Robert De Niro, Robert Redford, Jane Fonda, and Dustin Hoffman. Redford complimented Willie, saying that working with him was "comfortable, like working with your favorite shoe." After "supporting" Redford and Fonda in 1979 (*The Electric Horseman*), he "starred" in the 1980 Warner Bros. picture, *Honeysuckle Rose*.

Some of the movies in which he appeared were great and reflected his convictions and philosophy, such as *Songwriter*. The most critically acclaimed was *Barbarosa*, while the most dear to Willie's heart and mind was *Red Headed Stranger*. *Honeysuckle Rose* was the most biographical while, several, such as *Where the Hell's That Gold!*, were never intended to be more than shallow fun. In two of the worst movies, 1986's *Amazons* and 1997's *Gone Fishin'*, he luckily had only minor roles (in which he did not embarrass himself).

Often Willie was only involved in a movie in the musical sense. For example, in 1975, he sang 'Stay All Night (Stay A Little Longer)' as part of the soundtrack for the Roy Rogers movie (from Universal Studios), *MacKintosh and TJ*. In 1979, his singing was incorporated into the soundtrack of the United Artists picture, *Voices*, a sentimental little film starring Amy Irving, with a "minimal score" (according to a film critic) by Jimmy Webb.

Irving would star the following year, 1980, in *Honeysuckle Rose*. During the filming, she was linked romantically with Willie, though at the time she was married to Stephen Spielberg. According to Peter Biskind, in his book *Easy Riders, Raging Bulls*, Amy did confide that she "fell in love with Willie Nelson," though officially she consistently denied rumors of having an affair with him.

Hank Cochran and Willie together wrote the songs for the 1981 New World flick, *Ruckus* (also known as *The Loner*). The 1984 film, *Welcome Home* (from Columbia Pictures, starring Kris Kristofferson as a Vietnam vet), again featured a Willie song on the soundtrack (during the opening credits). Willie's face was also seen on film in the 1989 documentary, *Superstars and Fast Cars*, another 1991 TV project, *Wild Texas Wind*, and bit parts in various shows such as *Big Country* (1994), *Dust to Dust* (1994), *Starlight* (1996), and the Beach Boys video based on their River North collaborative album, entitled *Nashville Sounds* (1996).

Willie was first and foremost a recording artist, a performer of some of the finest music in American history, and a deep philosophical individual, whose genius could only be roughly estimated. Though he enjoyed acting and making films and the films were mostly enjoyable, his movie career has remained a footnote to his musical accomplishments. Nonetheless, as part of what he has accomplished in a remarkable life, the major film appearances deserved to be chronicled. He wrote in his autobiography, that:

> I do like movie acting and intend to keep doing it. I've learned the secret to movie acting. What is important is to learn your lines and be on time.

He also found out that:

> you really can go make a movie with a minimum of problems if you've got good people around you who know their jobs, and you have the production money in the bank. I have also learned this is almost never the case.

As Willie's recording career appeared to wane in the mid to late 1990's his acting career took a turn toward his being very much in demand. Not only did he appear in 1997's *Wag the Dog*, but in *Gone Fishin'* (that same year). Both films were major box office releases. Also in 1997, Willie appeared (as himself, this time) in a documentary filmed (produced, directed, and written) by Sahinee Gabel and Kristin Hahn, entitled *Anthem*.

Anthem centered around a car trip taken by Hahn and Gabel for much of the year, 1995. According to a review by *Variety*, the two filmmakers hung out briefly with "a flirty Willie Nelson on his tour bus in Texas." Others who made cameo appearances ranged from actor Robert Redford (in Utah) to author Studs Terkel (in Chicago). In 1996, Willie's version of the Louis Armstrong hit, 'What a Wonderful World' was incorporated into the John Travolta film, *Michael*. In 1988, it had been the title cut of one of his solo Columbia albums.

A quick fast forward to 1998 revealed that Willie was penciled in with a part in a movie title, *Half Baked*. Beyond the big screen to the small home screen (television), Willie announced that in 1998,

Kris, Travis Tritt and I will be heading to Almeria, Spain to film a CBS western called *The Long Kill*. Johnny Cash was also going to be in it, but he's not feeling well enough to make it this time.

Tritt told *Country Weekly* how he felt about starring with Kris and Willie in the movie, saying that:

these guys are my heroes. They are tremendous inspirations to me because they've always done exactly what I've tried to do - they've always done their music their own way.

How has Willie assessed his acting career? He told *Country Weekly* that:

like songwriting and performing, acting gives me another way to express myself. I'm not doing Shakespeare, so I don't have to learn to speak with an English accent. I can just talk the way I do talk. I can handle that.

He was both extremely careful and wary about getting into acting in the first place. He very deliberately contemplated taking the role of Robert Redford's sidekick in *The Electric Horseman*, because he had:

seen too many of my musician friends jump into the movies just for the money and glitter. I loved movies, but I didn't want to do just anything. I figured I'd wait for something that was right for <u>me</u>. Truth is, I never know when I'm acting and I wasn't sure I could do it, but I thought it was time for me to find out.

After filming several movies, including *Red Headed Stranger*, he said "this acting may be a hell-of-a-turn of fate, but I confess I like doing it a whole lot."

Pauline Kael, who has been described as "the greatest American movie critic," wrote, of Willie's acting abilities (for the July 29, 1985 issue of *The New Yorker*), that "plainness, naturalness, that's Willie Nelson's style, and he's a master at it - not just in his singing but in his acting, too." She was especially laudatory of his performance in *Songwriter*, noting that not only did he "play his role with considerable bite," he was, as Doc Jenkins, "intense and almost Zen-like in his moment-to-moment decisiveness." From her unique perspective, she saw the effectiveness of "his jazz-inspired musical phrasing" as well as his conscious use of "himself as an icon."

A Synopsis (by Year) of Willie's Film Appearances

1977

Outlaw Blues. Warner Bros. (unnumbered).

Willie's first movie appearance came in this musically-based story of a song-writing ex-convict, played by Peter Fonda, who set out, post-prison, to get back the rights to his songs (from a country star turned politician, no less). They had been stolen and turned into hits. Susan Saint James (co-star of Rock Hudson's television vehicle, *McMillan and Wife*) played the love interest who helped in the fight to regain control of the songs. Shooting was mainly done in Austin, an easy place for Willie to play his bit part. Fonda was supposed to have actually sung his musical numbers.

Renaldo and Clara. Lombard Street Films (unnumbered).

This was to be Bob Dylan's epic film, shot mainly during and around the 1975 Rolling Thunder Review tour. It starred a lot of great performers, including Allen Ginsberg, Joan Baez, and Dylan's then-wife, Sara, as the female lead, Clara. Unfortunately, when the movie first played in early 1978, all 255 minutes, the theaters were almost empty. Bob proceeded to quickly re-edit it down to 112 minutes, leaving, according to Leonard Maltin, "mostly concert footage." The film had its moments, especially when Bob played Bob and then some other role, an ethereal mime type of character.

The cost of the film, the subsequent editing, and other expenses coupled with little return from paying audiences almost bankrupted Bob, sending him out on a seemingly endless set of tours with friends and fellow artists, many of whom appeared as themselves in the original film. Willie was there, too, performing 'Time of the Preacher'. After a brief attempt to screen the edited version, this film has disappeared except for a few "bootlegged" copies.

1979

The Electric Horseman. Columbia/Universal Pictures (unnumbered).
Robert Redford and Jane Fonda starred in this eccentric modern-day Western set in Las Vegas. It was a loosely-interpreted remake of the 1962 film, *Lonely Are the Brave*, that starred Kirk Douglas and Walter Matthau and was itself adapted from Edward Abbey's novel, *Brave Cowboy*. Willie played the roguish manager of Redford's character. Redford's character, in turn, spent much of the movie trying to liberate a horse from an evil corporation that has been force-feeding it a diet of steroids and painkillers.

Sydney Pollack directed the film and co-produced Willie's part of the soundtrack. According to some write-ups on the movie, Willie ad-libbed a great line about finding a woman who could suck the chrome off... well, that's the drift, anyway. He wrote in his autobiography that he got his part after he "just called Sydney Pollack on the phone and asked to be in the movie." He also said that the role enabled him to pick up "a good movie reputation."

As far as the film went, *Variety* summed it up as "a moderately entertaining film, but no screen magic from Robert Redford and Jane Fonda." *Variety* went on to say it was "overlong, talky, and diffused." Critic Leonard Maltin echoed those sentiments, writing that the film was "pleasant, to be sure, but considering the people involved, a disappointment."

Willie Nelson's 4th of July Celebration. Alston/Zanitsch International (unnumbered).
Issued to theaters in 1979, this documentary captured the best of the 1979 picnic, from audience reactions to practicing performers. Leon Russell, Waylon Jennings, and Doug Kershaw were among the guests.

Bob & Ray, Jane, Laraine & Gilda. NBC (unnumbered).
In 1979, the comedy of Bob & Ray (Elliott and Goulding) became a summer replacement special for NBC's *Saturday Night Live*. Three of the *SNL's* regulars, Jane Curtin, Laraine Newman, and Gilda Radner also starred in the special as did, Willie. It was, overall, an odd combination of talent and routines, which ranged from a restaurant that specialized in "toast" to a deadpan reading of Rod Stewart song lyrics. It was popular enough to be rereleased on video for the mass market.

1980

Honeysuckle Rose. Warner Bros. 1043.

Willie played Buck Bonham, an aging country music performer, in this, his first feature film starring role. Dyan Cannon and Amy Irving co-starred. There were some great musical guests, including Emmylou Harris and Hank Cochran. With Willie's band and others, like Johnny Gimble, playing along, the music was out of the ordinary.

Dyan even sang, as did Amy, on a duet with Willie. Interestingly enough, the movie was retitled *On the Road Again* when it was released on TV. During its initial theater distribution, sales were good enough to turn Willie into, as one critic phrased it, "a commercial film entity." James Robert Parish and Michael R. Pitts wrote in their book, *Hollywood Songsters*, that "the film was essentially *Intermezzo* (1939), set in the country."

1981

Thief. MGM-UA M-201305.

Willie made a solid supporting role appearance in this cult flick starring James Caan, Tuesday Weld, James Belushi, and Robert Prosky. In this tense thriller, Caan played a professional jewel thief (safecracker) who joined the mob in order to make one final and very large score. His plan to retire and lead a normal life after that was unfortunately thwarted by his accomplices in crime.

Much of the movie plot focused on the thief's gradual losing of everything he gained. Willie played an ex-convict named Jailbird Okla. The soundtrack was by the rock group, Tangerine Dream. One reviewer complained that the music was "played at an ear-splitting pitch" and completed overwhelmed the accompanying drama. Another called it a "great score."

1982

Coming Out of the Ice. CBS/Playhouse 5519.

Set in Siberia (Russia), this movie, which first came out as a made-for-television film, showcased Willie as a real-life political prisoner, Red Loon, in one of the world's harshest environments. John Savage and Ben Cross also starred. The story was true, about Victor Herman, an American athlete who worked in Stalin-led Russia in the thirties. He was sent to Siberia for refusing to renounce his American citizenship. Susie Nelson summed up the film as being about "some

Americans who had been living in Siberia and how they finally made their way back home." The video version came out in 1987.

Barbarosa. Universal/ITC J2-0035.

Gary Busey, filmdom's Buddy Holly, and Gilbert Roland starred with Willie in this Western story of an aging outlaw who hung out around a Mexican village. Busey played a young farmer turned "badguy," befriended by the Nelson character, while Roland portrayed a rich, vindictive father-in-law. When Bill Witliff, the scriptwriter, first showed Willie the script, he told him the story was about "a blood feud between this old cowboy and a family of Mexicans who cut his ears off."

The direction by Fred Schepisi was excellent. The overall realism of the film was enhanced by its on-location shooting around the Rio Grande. According to a Willie Nelson Museum flyer, this was Willie's favorite film. Poor distribution when it first came out contributed to disappointing ticket sales. It took six years (until 1988) for the film to come out on video.

1983

Willie Nelson and Family in Concert. CBS/Fox 6623-80.

As one of Willie's best and most rousing concerts, it was obviously spurred on by the cameras taking it all in.

The Other Side of Nashville. MGM-UA MV-600351.

This documentary-like film on Nashville as the capital of country music featured Willie and other country music stars.

Hells Angels Forever. Marvin Films/Media M-264.

Shot as a documentary on the legendary motorcycle group (filmed with their cooperation), this film featured performances and appearances by Willie, Jerry Garcia of the Grateful Dead, Bo Diddley, and Johnny Paycheck (as themselves, of course).

1984

Songwriter. Tri-Star Pictures/Goodtimes 4602.

Willie (as Doc) and Kris Kristofferson (as Blackie) starred in this comedy about the foibles of being country songwriters and performers. Their two characters focused most of their efforts on getting even with one of Doc's crooked backers. Rip Torn and Lesley Ann Warren co-starred. *Variety* wrote that Lesley Ann was particularly "radiant as an up-and-coming, but reluctant country/western singer." The original song score was good enough to be nominated for a 1984 Academy Award (Oscar), though it failed to win. Leonard Maltin wrote that the film was "pleasant to watch." The overall critique by *Variety* stated that it was "a good-natured film that rolls along along on the strength of attitudes and poses established outside the picture by its stars."

1985

The Willie Nelson Special. Pioneer PA-92-496/Embassy 1225.
   Special guest Ray Charles highlighted this very well-done network television special.

We Are the World: The Video Event. RCA/Columbia 60475.
   The USA for Africa benefit recording session was released as a filmed event. This was the recording written by Michael Jackson and Lionel Richie. Some of the featured artists included Stevie Wonder, Bob Dylan, Ray Charles, Harry Belafonte, and Waylon Jennings.

1918. PBS/Fox (unnumbered).
   Willie wrote the score for this PBS *American   Playhouse* adaptation of Horton Foote's play detailing the effects that World War II coupled with a flu epidemic had on a small Texas town. Matthew Broderick was the star.

1986

Red Headed Stranger. Alive Films/Charter Entertainment 90153.
   The idea for this project began rolling around in Willie's head in 1975, following the release of the album of the same name. In 1976, he said he talked to Bud Shrake about writing a script (and Shrake immediately said he didn't know how to write "a story where the hero shoots a woman to death for stealing his horse"). In the publicity release for the movie, Willie stated that:

> *Red Headed Stranger* is the movie I've wanted to make for almost a dozen years now -- ever since I started putting together the *Red Headed Stranger* concept album.

The man who eventually became both director and writer, Bill Witliff (Shrake introduced Willie to Bill), said he began:

writing the script nine years ago when the deal called for it to be made in Hollywood with a big budget. They weren't eager to make westerns, especially a religious one about a fall from grace, which would be true to Willie's theme in the album. And we didn't think it should be made any other way. The album is more episodic than a movie can afford to be and we felt the trick was to flesh it out, but do it in a way that would keep all the human elements Willie had in his original concept. Although we never sat down and wrote together, through the years we worked very closely on it.

How did Witliff come to write and direct the picture? Willie explained it was he who had picked Witliff because:

> I'd read his script for *Barbarosa* and I knew he could write the *Red Headed Stranger* the way I'd always wanted to see it. I was sure he could write about this guy, just an ordinary preacher, who has no idea he'd react to things -- like his wife not loving him as much as he loves her -- the crazy way he does. Really, I've been rehearsing to play the part all my life and I just felt he'd know how to write it.

Witliff said he set out to make a film "without any puff in it," very similar to the way early silent film producers made their pictures. He explained that since he had the advantage of both writing and directing, he:

> very consciously went with moving pictures and the emotion in them, rather than with a lot of dialogue to tell the story of the *Red Headed Stranger*. If there's a lot of Willie's own life in that story, I didn't purposely write it in. It was there to begin with in the album.

Willie did allow that "autobiographical parallels are always in the back of my mind when I'm working."

Initially, Robert Redford was to play the "stranger" role. Willie got the part by buying back the rights to the movie. He and Witliff decided to go ahead and make the film themselves, "in good time, our way, and on our own turf." The lead character was a preacher who fought against a very unholy family led a domineering father (played by Royal Dano). The story of the film centered around the concepts of trust and betrayal and the moralistic conflict between sin and redemption, two things Willie said, "I know a lot about."

The preacher tried hard but eventually killed his wife and left the ministry. The very glamorous and beautiful Morgan Fairchild played Willie's philandering love interest/unfaithful spouse.

Katherine Ross played the woman Willie's character eventually learned to love, but not until the pursuing sheriff (played by R. G. Armstrong) left him for dead. Two of Willie's band members, Paul English and Bee Spears, were cast as sons of the character played by Dano. Willie's own grandson, Bryan Fowler (daughter Lana's son), played the son of Ross's character.

According to the movie's press release, the new music for:

> piano, guitar, and harmonica, heard along with the songs from the original *Red Headed Stranger* album, was written expressly for the film by Nelson and recorded at his private studio.

Filming consisted of a thirty-nine day shooting schedule in and around Austin. Though the picture was a critical success, it failed to break even during its initial box office run. That was surprising, considering that, as Witliff recalled,

> we made the picture on a shoestring. In 1980 Hollywood it had been budgeted at $13, 500, 000, and by making it here, at home in Austin, we did it for about 1/7th of that.

Stagecoach. CBS-TV/Starmaker 1072.

A second remake (this time a made-for-TV version) of John Wayne's classic Western (originally done in 1939) starred the four "Highwaymen" (Willie, Johnny Cash, Waylon Jennings, and Kris Kristofferson) along with John Schneider, Elizabeth Ashley, Tony Franciosa, and Anthony Newley. Cash's wife, June Carter Cash, and their son, John, also had brief roles. The movie did not center on one character as it did in the Wayne screenplay, so the remake was actually quite interesting.

The Doc Holliday character, as played by Willie, became a much larger persona, even expounding on Indian rights, in this version. With the four singing stars leading the way, it became the highest rated "made-for-TV" movie of the 1986 season. Willie was hired as executive producer to, in his words, "keep Kris in line." It didn't work. During one interview about the movie, Kris not only said "what a piece of shit" the movie was turning into, he said he wouldn't watch it "if they strapped me in front of a TV set and sewed my eyelids open." In a critical review, Leonard Maltin noted that "the stars made no secret of their disdain for the simple-minded script."

Willie said it was not a happy location. One of the main problems centered on the group of Indians hired for the picture, Apaches straight off the reservation. The movie company wouldn't pay them enough to live on (some had to sleep on blankets in the bushes), so, as Willie recalled, he "was appointed by Johnny Cash to protest to the company." After that the treatment improved.

The movie company made working conditions worse for Willie and the others by continually "bringing us out for shots and changing the scenes." Willie said they would "rehearse all night for a big scene, and the next morning we would get to the set and they had changed their minds." Finally, when it appeared the actors had all walked off, the director got sufficiently "shook" and the picture was completed. The music for the movie was composed by Willie. One of the songs sounded melodically like a mix of the Jimmy Webb composition, 'Highwayman', and the Marty Robbins hit, 'Big Iron'.

The Last Days of Frank and Jesse James. NBC-TV/Vidmark VM-4605.

Another take on the James Brothers legend found Kris Kristofferson, Johnny Cash, and June Carter Cash starring in this made-for-TV movie. Willie made a special guest appearance as an Army general. Leonard Maltin called this movie "an honorable biography of the notorious Wild West hoodlums." He said that Kris and Johnny were "convincingly brotherly."

Amazons. MGM. (unnumbered).

Willie had a bit part in this MGM "B" movie about the legendary tribe of super strong female warriors who dressed in little or nothing. The plot involved a search for a magical talisman needed to help overthrow an evil magician. Willie's name was the most famous of the players involved.

One critic wrote that "the ridiculousness of the fight scenes in this film rivals that of the worst Kung Fu flick." The same critic went on to note that the "silly film was rated R for nudity, violence, and sex." Fortunately it was only seventy-six minutes long, in the tradition of the old Westerns that used to come out of studios like Republic.

Greatest Hits Live. Vestron Musicvideo 5294.

Featured was footage of Willie's performance at the Austin Opera House in Austin, Texas. The songs were all Willie concert favorites from 'Funny How Time Slips Away' to 'Whiskey River'.

1987

Baja Oklahoma. Lorimar (Warner/Orion) ID-5324LO.

In the year after *Red Headed Stranger* was completed, Willie made a brief cameo appearance as himself, singing the title song he co-wrote with author Dan Jenkins (who wrote the novel on which the movie was based), in this critically acclaimed, made-for-cable television (HBO) film. It was briefly released to movie theaters. The story focused on a country "barmaid" with dreams of becoming a country singer.

Featured music in the movie included songs by Willie, Emmylou Harris, and Billy Vera. Leslie Ann Warren starred as the "dreaming" country girl. She gave every bit as good a performance as a small-town Texas barmaid wanting to be in the music business (as a songwriter) as she did in 1985's *Songwriter*. Bob Wills, Jr. played the part of his famous dad, Bob Wills.

Chet Atkins and Friends. HBO 0123.

Willie made a brief appearance on this special honoring Chet's career as a country music icon.

The Greatest Moments in Dallas Cowboys History. PolyGram 085103-3.

Willie sang 'My Heroes Have Always Been Cowboys' in this compiled set of filmed highlights on America's team.

1988

A Vision Shared: A Tribute to Woody Guthrie and Leadbelly. CBS 49006.

More than eighteen top acts participated in this tribute to two of America's finest folksingers. Not only was Willie there, so were Bob Dylan and Bruce Springsteen, both heavily influenced by Woody. Willie sang the old Guthrie song, 'Philadelphia Lawyer', while Dylan picked 'Pretty Boy Floyd' and Springsteen interpreted 'I Ain't Got No Home'. Some of the eclectic acts who honored Leadbelly included Little Richard (with Fishbone) and Taj Mahal.

Where the Hell's That Gold! Mntex/CBS MN5992.

The movie was also called *Dynamite and Gold*, retitled after the "theme" song of the same name. *Designing Women's* Delta Burke and long-time movie bad-guy Jack Elam starred with Willie in this made-for-TV film. It involved a train and a search for stolen gold. Much of the action took place South of the border and most of the story and dialogue was meant to sound "tongue-in-cheek." Fourth-wife-to-be Annie D'Angelo was the make-up artist for the movie.

For the filming, director Burt Kennedy wrote in his 1997 autobiography, *Hollywood Trail Boss: Behind the Scenes of the Wild, Wild Western,* that they used:

> a train outside of Alamosa, Colorado. It was about a two-hour trip up to the location. We would go in trucks and meet the train, and the train would leave early in the morning. But on the way back, when we were through shooting for the

day, we would get in the boxcars, and we would ride back in the train to the station in Alamosa.

Actually, according to Kennedy, who also wrote the script, that "was really the fun part of that picture, riding the train." He went on to say that:

> Willie Nelson was with us, and Willie, Jack Elam, and I would play liar's poker all the way back to the station, which was about three hours, and we did that for about a week. That was fun. The picture wasn't.

There was one more part of the filming that wasn't fun, according to Kennedy, when "we ran off the track." It seemed that "a bunch of us were in the caboose and as we were pulling out of the station, we jumped the track." To Burt and company, it sounded and felt like "an earthquake" and "it just about shook us to death."

Texas Guns. CBS/Starmaker 1118.

This made-for-television film was also entitled *Once Upon a Texas Train*. That was certainly a more colorful and fitting title for a Western in which Willie and a very mature Richard Widmark respectively starred as an outlaw who wanted to rob one more Texas train and the Texas Ranger who wanted to stop him. Willie's character was so bad that he sometimes killed just for fun.

The star of the old TV show, *The Rifleman*, Chuck Connors, and former teen idol, Shaun Cassidy, also appeared in supporting roles. Other name players who took part included Angie Dickinson, Royal Dano, Kevin McCarthy, Stuart Whitman, and *Gunsmoke's* Ken Curtis. A young Dickinson once worked with John Wayne (in *Rio Bravo*) and here, in the twilight of her acting years, she ably supported Willie. Dano had previously played the roguish father who opposed Willie's character in *Red Headed Stranger*.

Burt Kennedy was once again the director. He wrote in his memoirs that the most memorable aspect of making the film was getting the train to appear as if it came into the depot. The depot and train, located in Ely, Nevada, were actually fifty miles apart and separated by a paved highway. Other than that, they were "perfect." Kennedy recalled looking at the situation and saying, "no problem. On the screen, I'll make it work." How did he do it? He said he:

> took a baggage cart from outside the depot and put it in front of the camera at the train locations as a cutting piece and then brought the train in and stopped it. I took the cutting piece back to the depot fifty miles away and shot back over it. That way the train comes into the station and stops on the

screen. On the screen, the train has pulled into the station, and actually, the station is fifty miles away from where the train actually was. It's a trick we use all the time.

Walking After Midnight. Kay Film (unnumbered).

Jonathon Kay, a Canadian filmmaker from British Columbia, produced this unusual film, an "exploration of the emotional and spiritual dimensions of reincarnation." He captured "true personal experiences of today's well-known personalities." Martin Sheen's near-death experience revealed glimpses into some of his past lives while Willie recounted how his interest in reincarnation has affected both his personal outlook and his music.

Other stars who appeared in the movie included George Harrison, Dennis Weaver, James Coburn, and Donovan. *Variety* called it an "imaginatively done" work. The screenplay was accompanied, in 1990, by a paperback book (of the same name) that incorporated most of the on-screen discussions. Willie disclosed that he was sure he had been Mexican in a previous life because he enjoys Spanish music and gets along so well with Spanish people. He also felt his concept album, *Red Headed Stranger*, drew "on experiences from past lives."

1989

In the Hank Williams Tradition. White Star 1659.

This video, a production of the Country Music Foundation (and the Ginger Group), featured film clips of Hank, Sr. along with about an hour's worth of music and interviews (with insightful comments from Hank, Jr.). Original songs by the senior Williams (such as 'Lovesick Blues' and 'Your Cheatin' Heart') were interspersed with some excellent cover versions, among them Emmylou Harris' smiling and animated interpretation of the very touching, 'May You Never Be Alone' and Hank Jr.'s country-rocking rendition of 'Move It On Over'. Willie particularly stood out with 'My Bucket's Got a Hole in It', as did Waylon on 'Turn Back the Years' and Randy Travis on 'I'm So Lonesome I Could Cry'. Topping off all the great performances was an "entire cast" rousing sing-a-long, 'I Saw the Light' (shades of that New Year's day in Canton, Ohio, in 1953 when the audience waiting for Hank reacted to the shocking news of his death by singing together that very song). An old clip of Hank, Sr. singing 'I'll Have a New Life' closed out the video.

Some Enchanted Evening with Willie Nelson. Cabin Fever CF824.

In this concert film, Willie performed for over four hundred executives and friends from the entertainment industry. The emphasis was on live renditions of pop standards. Songs included 'Spanish Eyes', 'Twilight Time', and 'To Each His Own'.

The Real Patsy Cline. Cabin Fever 00008.

Patsy was in top form throughout this documentary covering her life. Two of the highlights were Willie's recollections of Patsy and his evaluation of her performance on 'Crazy'.

1990

Pair of Aces. Warner Bros. 12021.

Willie played a vagabond parody of himself in this made-for-television film that co-starred Kris Kristofferson and Rip Torn. Helen Shaver, whose first movie starring role was as Supergirl, co-starred. The plot was quite good, combining elements of a search for justice with the issue of police corruption.

Willie showed great comedy timing as a wise-cracking but philosophical safecracker. In a cliff-hanger, he and Kris, a modern-day Texas Ranger, captured a serial killer, just as the killer was about to harm Kris' on-screen daughter. In appreciation, Kris' character let Willie's character "get away," hoping never to see him again. In actuality, the "get-away" allowed for the filming of a sequel, which occurred in 1991.

1991

Another Pair of Aces. Starmaker 1153.

Variety's review of this made-for-TV movie saw it as "a good Western." Two other critics, Mick Martin and Marsha Porter, saw the performances as "engaging." Willie, Kris Kristofferson, and Rip Torn reprised their Texas Ranger roles from the 1990 predecessor, *Pair of Aces.* The film, subtitled "Three of a Kind," had some scenes deleted after they were deemed unacceptable for TV. They were later reinserted into the video version.

Joan Severance played an FBI agent who helped the Rangers uncover a vigilante ring and clear the good name of Rip Torn's character. One of the subplots was a very entertaining and sarcastic look at Texas gubernatorial politics. Actor Bill Bixby, star of the TV shows, *The Incredible Hulk, The Courtship of Eddie's Father,* and *My Favorite Martian,* directed. Though the writing was entertaining, suspenseful, and action-filled, the film has not yet inspired a sequel.

1992

Willie Nelson: My Life. Capital Cities/ABC 42067.
The televised version of Willie's life, brought together testimonials, interviews, rare footage, and live music. Musical friends included Waylon, Johnny Cash, and Ray Price. On the back cover of the video, Willie was quoted as saying "everything in this video, both the good and the bad in my life, is the absolute truth."

1993

Willie Nelson: The Big Six-O. Fox/CBS 5934.
Many peer musicians got together to celebrate Willie's sixtieth birthday, among them Paul Simon, Bob Dylan, Neil Young, Lyle Lovett, and Waylon Jennings. Considerable documentary footage on his life was the best feature of this work.

1994

Texas. Republic Pictures. (unnumbered).
Columbia Records compiled the soundtrack (of songs about Texas) to go with a television special put together to coincide with the release of the mini-series, *Texas* (based on the James Michener book). The two Willie cuts were 'No Place But Texas' (from his 1986 Columbia album, *The Promiseland*) and 'Amazing Grace' (from 1976's *The Sound in Your Mind*). The names of the other artists, whose songs appeared on the soundtrack, read like a veritable who's who of Western music, from singing cowboy Gene Autry to Western swing king, Bob Wills. Lee Holdridge wrote additional music for the score.

1995

Big Dreams and Broken Hearts: The Dottie West Story. (No studio). (unnumbered).
This made for TV movie was mainly filmed in Nashville. It used many real life country stars, such as Kenny Rogers, who appeared as a duet partners. Dramatic reenactments of Dottie's life (she was played by Michelle Lee) were interspersed with actual commentary by country performers including Chet Atkins, Loretta Lynn, and Willie. A *Los Angeles Times* critic saw the script as having a "tabloid touch."

1996

Willie Nelson: Down Home. PBS (unnumbered).

This Public Broadcasting System special interspersed live performances by Willie and his band with clips showing Willie picking with friends like Johnny Gimble and Freddie Powers. The highlight was the taping of 'Slow Dancing' with U2. Much of the filming was done at the old Western town Willie built outside Austin and used for the filming of *Red Headed Stranger*.

1997

The Best of Austin City Limits: Country Music's Finest Hour. PBS (unnumbered).

The best clips from this long running series were compiled and released in 1997 along with an accompanying compact disc. Naturally, a segment of Willie's inaugural episode was featured. The song he sang during his segment was none other than 'Blue Eyes Crying in the Rain'.

Gone Fishin'. Warner Bros. (unnumbered).

Willie played a truculent fishing guide (and sang the theme song, 'Down in the Everglades') in this "fishing buddy" farce. Joe Pesci and Danny Glover starred as the New Jersey fishermen pals. Willie's performance was brief but refreshing and almost ethereal in a movie whose theater run was brief, prompted by reviews like the one that said it was "less fun than a fish hook in the eye." Another critic said the actors were allowed to sink "under the weight of slow-moving shtick." Randy Edelman wrote the musical score.

Wag the Dog. (New Line Cinema). (unnumbered).

Willie was brilliantly irreverent in one of his largest recent movie roles in this satirical political thriller. His character was called on to write and sing "pro-war" songs designed to get the country to favor a war with Albania, once part of the Iron Curtain countries. This late-in-the-year film starred Dustin Hoffman and Robert De Niro.

Willie sang an eccentrically-written blues-based song on and off throughout the movie, about an old shoe. An old-looking bluesman (actor) sang with him on occasion during parts of the film. Unfortunately, no complete soundtrack was issued with this cut on it. Instead, a compact disc containing "music from the motion picture" appeared, credited to Mark Knopfler. All eight cuts featured Knopfler on guitars and vocals.

SECTION V
The "Guest" Projects and Tributes

. . . AND I'M HUNG UP ON MY HAT!

Willie and Kris became two of country music's greatest songwriters!
(Photo from the author's private collection and Evelyn Shriver Public Relations)

Willie and Boxcar Willie made quite a pair!
(Photo from Boxcar Willie Theater)

"Whiskey River":

The Prelude for Willie's "Guest" Appearances

One of the most unique aspects about Willie, the consummate artist, has been the numerous appearances (as guest or supporting vocalist or player) he has made on other artists' projects or on "various artists" compilations. Tracking every single performance or guest shot would be never-ending. Sometimes Willie's appearances, like those of other artists such as Bob Dylan or George Harrison, have been under other names or simply have gone uncredited.

At times, Willie has worked on sessions that may never get released, such as some he did with Flaco Jiminez. No official reasons from any source have been forthcoming as to why they have yet to be released. Flaco, himself, praised Willie, saying that guys like him and Ry Cooder were "really easy to work with."

Willie also recorded with Aerosmith. He commented, in his autobiography, that "not long ago the heavy metal band Aerosmith dropped in to cut a record with me, which is kind of a bizarre collaboration." His recording work with artists like Doug Sahm, Larry Gatlin, Bill Pursell (or Purcell), and Bob Moore came by virtue of their appearing on at least one of his sessions. Pursell and Moore respectively played piano and bass for Willie on an RCA session (Moore did so several times). Pursell also played on Willie's first Monument session (Moore was there for both). Other artists with whom he has been linked, recording or session-wise, were Sammi Smith, Cal Smith (as session player), and Ernie Freeman (the arranger).

The purpose of this section has been to track the most well-known (and advertised) cooperative or supporting efforts with other artists. Some compilations have been discovered and noted but not tracked in detail because the cut or cuts appeared originally on another project.

Companies have often taken an original cut and used it on any number of compilations (mostly "various artists" ones). Since the track included was not a unique release these "collections" have been largely ignored.

Willie has recorded with so many musicians, both on their projects as well as his, that it would be almost impossible to say with any exact precision just how many. It would also not be possible to pin down exactly when Willie first recorded with another artist. He has acknowledged he worked on a session for Dave Isbell for Sarg Records back in the mid-fifties (1955, to be exact).

There has been an assertion that prior to working with Isbell, Willie first recorded as a session player on a single track for Fabor Records (catalog number 101), entitled 'I Love You' and credited to Jim Reeves and Ginny Wright. The cut consisted of Wright singing over a spoken recitation by Reeves. It subsequently appeared on a compilation album of early Reeves sides marketed by Guest Star Records (GS-1471). Any specific involvement by Willie has never been documented.

The single track was made in 1953 and released in 1954 when Reeves and Wright were both under contract to Abbott Records. Wright was a gifted singer who appeared regularly on the Louisiana Hayride circa 1954. The tracks were recorded by Fabor Robison, the owner of both Fabor and Abbott Records.

Abbott Records (not named after Willie's birthplace) was headquartered out of Los Angeles, though it recorded mainly artists working out of Louisiana, specifically those with the Louisiana Hayride. The recordings were made after hours at the radio station almost exclusively using session players from the Hayride. Piano player Floyd Cramer was one at the time. Knowing all this about Abbott would make it easier to conclude that it was very unlikely Willie recorded with Reeves while he was with Abbott/Fabor.

There remained the possibility of Willie working on an earlier session, one of Reeves' first for Macy Records. Those recordings, at least one anyway, were done at ACA, the same place where Willie did the 1955 Isbell session. In 1953, Willie was working with bands fronted by Isbell and Johnny Bush, both in and around Houston and San Antonio. Perhaps there was a connection somewhere, although no specific factual information has ever been brought forward. When I asked Willie directly if he ever worked a Jim Reeves session, either in Houston, Louisiana (for Fabor), or even for RCA, he was adamant in saying, "no, I never worked with Jim Reeves on any session anywhere."

In 1961, Willie worked as Ray Price's bass player and not only played for Ray on the road, but in the studio as well. Specifically Willie has been credited as playing guitar on Ray's tribute album to Bob Wills, *San Antonio Rose* and on what has been judged Price's best album, *Night Life*. Willie would not have been a guest artist (even though he was listed as a special guest), of course, but a paid session player or band member instead.

Thus, it would seem most logical to conclude that Willie's first recorded work as a guest artist on another performer's album came on Don Bowman's 1969 RCA set, *Support Your Local Prison*. Willie was also on RCA at the time, as were Waylon and Bobby Bare. The three artists backed Bowman on the album cut, 'Poor Old Ugly Gladys Jones', which also went out as a single (it peaked at number seventy on the country singles chart).

His next major guest shots came in 1974. That was the year he dueted with Tracy Nelson on 'After the Fire Is Gone' and not only sang on one track of fellow Texan Kinky Friedman's 1974 debut set for ABC, but produced the track, as well. Kinky, an Austin friend of Willie's, would later write an excellent piece on him for *Rolling Stone*. Willie's admiration for Kinky's music has continued unabated. He recently told me he had recorded Friedman's classic, 'Ride 'Em Jewboy' (included on a 1997 Kinky tribute disc available on Kinkajou Records).

As a Texas native working throughout East Texas early in his career, Willie personally and professionally came to know some of the greatest Texas artists. Bob Wills was one of the first to inspire him as a performer, an admiration that began soon after Willie helped book Bob into a small Texas venue when Willie was only a teenager. Long tall Texan Billy Walker helped Willie find his first success in Nashville.

Willie has since collaborated with many great Texas artists, either in musical projects, or at the very least by recording their songs. He, with Merle Haggard, was the one who broke Fort Worth native Townes Van Zandt by sending his 'Pancho and Lefty' to the top of the country singles chart. Willie also had significant chart success with songs by Kris Kristofferson and Steve Fromholz. He has even produced tracks for Texas artists as diverse as Kinky Friedman and Jackie King.

Being headquartered in Austin opened the opportunity for Willie to work with each of the best musicians Austin has had to offer, Jerry Jeff Walker, Michael Murphey, Steve Fromholz, Kinky Friedman, and even B. W. Stevenson (though that collaboration took a long time to happen). Projects with fellow Texans (and residents of Austin) have occurred throughout the seventies, eighties, and nineties, involving old friends like Walker, rising stars like Crowell, and songwriting talents like Billy Joe Shaver. West Texas singer/songwriter, Kimmie Rhodes, became the first major artist to enlist Willie in 1996, utilizing his harmony vocals on her debut album for Justice Records.

Willie has always been a country artist, but has never been afraid of tackling anything. People everywhere who love country music have embraced his talents, style, and recordings. For fans of all types of music, Willie has driven home what they innately knew and he learned from playing throughout Texas, that all people are as "at home" with a standard like 'Stardust' as they are with a Western Swing favorite such as 'Faded Love' or the latest top song on the country singles chart. Similarly, Willie has always been as comfortable with pop material and musicians as he has with country songs and artists.

A song is a song and music is music, as Willie has so often proved, which was why he could be at home playing a small Canadian benefit with Ringo Starr as his drummer. Fortunately, he wasn't the only country artist who felt that way. Johnny Cash got Bob Dylan material, such as 'It Ain't Me, Babe', to a mainstream country audience. Dolly Parton turned the "Doc" Pomus and Mort Shuman song, 'Save the Last Dance for Me' into a top ten country hit. Pop stars did the same. Tony Bennett introduced Hank Williams to pop audiences via 'Cold Cold Heart' while Patti Page sold Pee Wee King's 'Tennessee Waltz'.

Still the barriers between pop and country have continued to exist, though not in Willie's mind. Willie works easily with both pop and country artists. In a given year he can record with the Beach Boys and Kimmie Rhodes. The country artists with whom he has worked have run the gamut, on album projects, from Randy Travis to George Jones. On singles projects, he has assisted artists such as Sammi Smith and Pam Rose (on an Epic Records single, 'It's Not Supposed to Be That Way', which made it onto a 1980 Epic "various artists" set, *Best Country Duets*, JE-36547). He even worked with daughter, Susie, on a Delta Records single, 'Once Upon a Time'.

Willie has worked with artists covering many musical venues and parts of the world, from international stars like Julio Iglesias to the "Chairman" of the pop world, Frank Sinatra. One of the first non-country artists with whom he worked was Tracy Nelson (no relation), a fellow Atlantic artist when Willie was with the label. Another rock star, Leon Russell, went way back musically with Willie before Willie finally appeared on one of Leon's albums.

The list with whom Willie has worked grows yearly and more eclectic. Duet partners have ranged from Timi Yuro (with whose parents, restaurant owners, Willie forged a close friendship), to TV star Don Johnson. 1994 saw Willie play in the backing band for jazz artist, Herb Ellis. In 1995, Bobby Charles came out of a recording layoff to involve Willie on three album cuts. 1996 was the year Willie worked with the Beach Boys and appeared on a "new" Carl Perkins project.

During the seventies, eighties, and nineties, it became such a status "thing" to work with Willie that George Burns actually recorded, in 1981, a song entitled, 'Willie Won't You Sing a Song With Me'. George sang about how great it would be for him and his cigar to work with Willie and his guitar. Copies of the song sold well enough for the octogenarian to chart it at number sixty-six and perform it on Dick Clark's *American Bandstand*.

Recently, after an interviewer tried to get young Jakob Dylan to voice his feelings on performing with his famous father, Bob, the question was posed, "well, who would you want to sing with?" Jakob unhesitatingly replied, "Willie Nelson, George Jones, one of those kind of people." Every generation knows an opportunity when they see one.

Then there was a collaboration that was not really a collaboration at all. Parts of Willie's songs, 'On the Road Again' and 'Whiskey River', were used in Jerry Reed's rendition of the song, 'The Bird', with some very funny results on Jerry's 1982 *The Bird*, RCA AHL1-4529. Hal Coleman supplied the vocal imitations that sounded like Willie and George Jones. The lyrics of 'On the Road Again' were changed slightly to "the life I love is making money with my friends."

Many of the Willie "guest" cuts became available on highly unusual compilations. Such cuts often found him attempting something musically out of the ordinary. For a Jimmy McHugh (who for awhile co-wrote with lyricist, Dorothy Fields) promotional EP (Extended Play Record), *Three Guys and a Gal*, released in 1981, Willie was credited along with Nat King Cole, Johnny Mathis, and Shirley Bassey.

In late Fall 1997, an obscure compilation appeared on a Japanese label, according to ICE Magazine. It was a "various artists" tribute to Lowell George, the late founder of Little Feat. Some of George's musical buddies, Californians Jackson Browne and Randy Newman, contributed a track apiece. So did Willie and Tom Folkner. They interpreted 'Willin', a song Little Feat first recorded for their 1978 album, *Waiting for Columbus*. Unfortunately, when the set appeared in the U. S., the Nelson/Folkner track was missing.

Willie has also participated in numerous recordings that wound up only as singles. With Duane Eddy, for example, he and Waylon did the vocals on a remake of 'You Are My Sunshine' for Elektra/Asylum Records. It went out in 1977 and even gained some airplay until the record label inexplicably withdrew it from circulation.

When Willie recorded a duet with Jack Dant on 'My Own Peculiar Way' (released only as a single), it was rumored that Jack was not only an aspiring country singer, he was also Willie's plumber. Actually, Willie told me that Dant was "a shrimp boat operator out of Florida, well, sort of." Then he kind of laughed, leaving it open for conjecture as to what Jack might have used the shrimp boat for.

One of the most unusual guest cuts, even for Willie, came on a song written by U2's Bono, 'Slow Dancing'. According to Bill Flanagan, in his 1995 book on the Irish group, Bono:

> was so excited about the song that the day after he wrote it he told a TV interviewer that he had just written a song for Willie Nelson.

That off-hand remark was picked up by MTV, who broadcast it as news before Bono could get the song to Willie. Bono was quoted as saying,

Can you imagine? Willie Nelson, one of the greatest songwriters alive, hearing me on TV saying I've written a song for him. Without his asking for it! He probably thought, 'Well, fuck you'.

The song was written in the early 1990's, on the heels of U2's successful *Achtung Baby*. When Bono first heard it in his head, Willie's "distinctive, beautiful voice, clear as a bell," was singing it. When a "demo" of the song was completed, Bono sent it to Willie but heard nothing. Bono wondered if Willie ever got the tape. He finally assumed Willie "just wasn't interested, that he didn't like the song." Willie had heard the song, but "simply put it on the back burner."

The story had a happy ending. Not too long after Willie heard the "demo," he flew into Dublin for a concert and got in touch with Bono and the band. He, Bono, and the rest of U2 went into the studio to record 'Slow Dancing'. The resultant vocal duet between Willie and Bono did not immediately appear on a commercial audio recording; instead a video of the two singing together was included as part of the TV special, *Willie Nelson: Down Home*, which circulated on public television during the summer of 1997. The Edge, another member of U2, appraised that:

> the vocals are amazing. The whole thing has a kind of broken quality which I like. It's our job now to finish it but it was a wonderful experience working with him.

Willie has recorded with his own band members, friends, and even his (former) son-in-law. He did live "guest" cuts as part of the Charlie Daniels' Volunteer Jams and Bob Dylan's thirtieth anniversary celebration. Hid duets with both Ernest Tubb and Frank Sinatra were electronically overdubbed. Collaborating artists who publicly commented, such as Julio Iglesias, praised Willie's vocal style, his musicianship, and his incredible interpretive skills. Willie said he did all the different collaborations and duets "for selfish reasons. There are a lot of people whose music and singing I enjoy, and it gives me a chance to sing with them."

As of mid-1998, he had appeared on Leon Russell's third "Hank Wilson" project and contributed a track (actually a duet with Kimmie Rhodes) to a Walter Hyatt tribute album compiled for Shanachie Records. Hyatt was a highly respected Texas singer/songwriter who was one of the passengers killed on the heavily publicized Valujet crash in the Florida Everglades. In his *Billboard* column of June 13, 1998, Chet Flippo discussed the album and the family's confidential settlement with the airline. The title of the "soundtrack" (as Flippo called it) was *Deep in the Heart of Texas*.

"Forgiving You Was Easy":

The Guest Appearances with Country Artists

Lily Dale. (Darrell McCall). Columbia KC-34718. (1977).

Darrell McCall was one of those projected country stars who never quite made it. It wasn't for the lack of trying, especially considering he had Willie working with him on 'Lily Dale' and 'Please Don't Leave Me' for his 1977 Columbia release. The 'Lily Dale' single, an old Bob Wills classic written by Bob's brother Billy Jack Wills, reached number thirty-two on the country charts for the duo, after making its debut on the charts in March 1977. *Cash Box* magazine named it the Best Duet of 1977.

Darrell came from Hillsboro, Ohio, and began as lead tenor with the Little Dippers. As a country artist, he toured with Faron Young and Ray Price and co-wrote (with Lamar Morris) 'Eleven Roses', turned into a hit by Hank Williams, Jr. Even with Willie's backing, McCall was unable to get beyond being a footnote in country music history. Maybe it was because he was viewed as "hard country."

Aimin' to Please. (Mary Kay Place). Columbia KC-34718. (1977).

Mary Kay Place was a regular on the TV show, *Mary Hartman, Mary Hartman*, appearing as Loretta, a would-be country singer. In real life Mary Kay did a 1977 album which had Willie working with her on 'Something to Brag About' (reviewed as a "duet revival of the blue-collar classic"). Bobby Braddock wrote the song and it was initially a hit, of sorts (reaching the number eighteen chart spot), for the pairing of Charlie Louvin and Melba Montgomery in 1970, seven years after the Louvin Brothers disbanded and five years after the older of the two brothers, Ira, died in a car crash.

When released as a single for Mary Kay and Willie, the song worked its way up to number nine on the country charts, selling enough to remain on the charts for sixteen weeks, well into early 1978. That was her last best-seller. Prior to the duet single with Willie, she had a solo single, 'Baby Boy' (her first outing), reach number three on the country chart and number sixty on the pop chart. Recently, she resurfaced as a very talented supporting actress in the movie, *The Rainmaker*.

Volunteer Jam III and IV. Epic Records E2 35368. (1978).

Charlie Daniels, who can play fiddle, mandolin, guitar, and banjo was born and raised in North Carolina. Turning to music at an early age, he experienced his first songwriting success when Elvis recorded his composition, 'It Hurts Me'. From there he made his reputation as a bandleader with hits like 'Uneasy Rider' and 'The Devil Went Down to Georgia. In 1974, he staged, at the War Memorial Auditorium in Nashville, a charity event that he called a "Volunteer Jam."

It became an almost yearly event, featuring some great names in country and Southern rock. For two of the late seventies events, Willie appeared and did three selections. The first was 'Good Hearted Woman', featuring Willie and band, while the second was a "Blues Medley," consisting of 'Funny How Time Slips Away', 'Crazy', and 'Night Life'. Toy Caldwell of the Marshall Tucker Band joined in on the 'Night Life' segment of the medley, just one of a multitude of different settings in which the song has been recorded by Willie.

For his third and final performance on the record, Willie joined with the 1977 Jam Band, Caldwell, Bonnie Bramlett, Daniels, and Mylon LeFevre to sing the Carter Family classic, 'Will the Circle Be Unbroken'. Willie's performances were from the 1977 Jam while the album, itself, was released in 1978. The performances were recorded on January 8th at the Municipal Auditorium in Nashville. Other artists on this set included, beyond those already mentioned, Wet Willie, Sea Level, Papa John Creach.

Ed Bruce. MCA MCA-3242. (1980).

Ed Bruce (with then-wife, Patsy) wrote the song, 'Mammas Don't let Your Babies Grow Up to Be Cowboys', a commercial and critical success for Willie. Here, Willie returned the favor by appearing with Bruce on 'The Last Cowboy Song' for Ed's self-titled 1980 album. The song was co-written by Bruce and Ron Peterson and first went out as a Bruce single, MCA 41273. It peaked at number twelve on *Billboard's* country singles chart.

In 1995, the cut was included on *The Best of Ed Bruce*, Varese Sarabande Records VSD-5566. In addition to being a top-notch songwriter, Ed has also done some acting, doing his best work as part of the television series, *Maverick*. He also had a small part in the film, *The Last Days of Frank and Jesse James*, which starred Willie, Johnny Cash, and Kris Kristofferson.

Bill Monroe & Friends. MCA (Masterfonics) MCA-5435. (1983).

Willie contributed guitar and also appeared on the song, 'The Sunset Trail' as one of bluegrass legend Bill Monroe's friends for a December 1983 MCA release entitled, *Bill Monroe & Friends*. Waylon was another of the "friends." He guested on the song 'With Body and Soul'. Johnny Cash, John Hartford, Oak Ridge Boys, Ricky Skaggs, Barbara Mandrell, the Gatlin brothers, Emmylou Harris, and Mel Tillis rounded out the highly impressive selection of Monroe's musical "friends." The album was rereleased in 1992 (budget cassette only with same title) as MCA Special Products MCAC-949.

Friendship. (Ray Charles). Columbia CK 39415. (1984).

Willie sang a duet with Ray Charles on 'Seven Spanish Angels' for Ray's 1984 album, *Friendship*. It became a hit country single, reaching number one in early 1985 and lingering on the charts for an astounding twenty-seven weeks. After that, it became the featured title song on Ray's 1989 "hits" compilation, *Seven Spanish Angels and Other Hits*, Columbia CK 45062.

Producer Billy Sherrill edited out part of the song, which may or may not have helped make it a hit. It certainly affected the storyline. Sherrill explained that:

> the song was like two movements. One of 'em was the 'Seven Spanish Angels' thing, and the boy and the girl and the soldiers comin' and shootin'. Then, it went into some sort of a refrain and another melody that explained it all - why the angels, why there were seven, and all that.

To Sherrill, this was all too much so he called the songwriter, Troy Seals, and said "this is like a book, not a song." As a result, Sherrill only recorded part of the song, wiping out "the whole other end," leaving the listener "in the dark about what it meant." Billy concluded that the mystery "contributed to the beauty of the song."

Willie spoke once of the special relationship he had with Charles, recalling how Ray invited him up to his hotel room for a game of chess. When Willie walked in the room it was dark. Ray had the board all set up, a braille board. Needless to say, Willie was soundly trounced. Later, when Ray asked him how he enjoyed the game, Willie asked if next time he could have some light. In 1991, Willie sang

'Busted' with Ray on Ray's *50 Years in Music* Fox TV special, which aired in October.

New Patches. (Mel Tillis). MCA MCA-5472. (1984).

In 1984, Mel Tillis recorded his second album for MCA during his second time around at the label. Willie was one of the backing artists for Mel, who was one of the early group of writers, including Roger Miller and Hank Cochran, with whom Willie hung out. In his autobiography, Mel said Willie was not only his friend, but called him "Mr. Country and a great songwriter."

Their duet, 'Texas on a Saturday Night', also appeared on Willie's duet album, *Half Nelson*. The song was written by Raymond "Mundo" Earwood, of Del Rio, Texas. It was Earwood's most successful song, the result of a career that saw the would-be country star crack the country singles top twenty chart only once in almost ten years of struggling with minor independent labels. He even charted the same song twice, for two different labels.

Country Livin'. (Rattlesnake Annie/Annie McGowan). Rattlesnake 2020/Columbia Records B6C-40678. (1985).

Rattlesnake Annie (McGowan) was born Rose Ann Gallimore and first went to Nashville in 1954 as part of the Gallimore Sisters trio. By then, she had barely attained the age of thirteen. She was a part Cherokee (and part Scotch-Irish) artist from West Tennessee (the town of Puryear), who, after one failed marriage, tried again with a rancher/schoolteacher named Ed "Max" McGowan. They settled in Texas near the Brazos River.

From there she got to know Willie while settling into the Austin music scene beginning around 1969. She recalled that when she:

> first saw him in a bar in Grand Prairie; there was about twelve people there. I sure liked what he was doin' so I went up to him afterwards and we talked and played songs for each other. We've been friends ever since.

She was actually billed, for awhile, as "the female Willie Nelson." That was mainly due to her (in the words of a Columbia press release):

> bluesy tone, behind-the-beat phrasing, stripped-down musical settings, guitar work, and unconventional life-style.

The *Austin American-Statesman* viewed her comparison to Willie as "a tribute to her versatility."

In 1974 she began her own label, Rattlesnake Records and released her first single the same year. Her second self-produced and released album, *Country Livin'*, from 1986 (released on her Rattlesnake Records), featured a duet with Willie on the cut 'Long Black Limousine'. The song was one of those that get recorded by a substantial number of artists even though there never was an actual hit version.

The best it ever did was to reach number seventy-three when released by Jody Miller in 1968 for Capitol Records, as a disappointing follow-up to her top five hit, 'Queen of the House'. Written by Bobby George and Vern Stovall in 1962, it has been recorded since then by everyone from Glen Campbell to Elvis Presley. Annie's recording of the song was done at Willie's Pedernales Studio with part of the production work being done by his daughter, Lana.

When Annie signed with Columbia Records in 1987, four of the tracks from *Country Livin'* made it on to her debut album for the label, *Rattlesnake Annie.* One of the four tracks was was the duet with Willie. For her Columbia Records "biography," Willie wrote,

this is Rattlesnake Annie, international superstar, known all over the world. How come you never heard of her?

Son of the South. (David Allan Coe). Columbia FC-40028. (1986).

David Allan Coe spent much of his younger life incarcerated in the state of Ohio, where he was born. For that reason, he considered himself the original country music "outlaw". His big break came when he signed with Shelby Singleton's Plantation Records. In 1973, Tanya Tucker took his song, 'Would You Lay with Me (In a Field of Stone)' to number one on the country singles charts. That led to a long-term contract with Columbia Records.

Willie was a featured musician on David's 1986 breakthrough album for Columbia, Son of the South, which also included Waylon Jennings, Jessi Colter, Karen Brooks, and Dickey Betts. Their duet, 'I've Already Cheated on You', co-written by Willie and David, reached number fifty-six on *Billboard's* country singles chart in 1986. The song was also included on Coe's *Super Hits Vol. 2* package for Columbia (CK 67568). One of Coe's most successful singles for Columbia came in 1976 with the tribute song, 'Willie, Waylon and Me'.

Can't Run Away From Your Heart. (Lacy J. Dalton). Columbia FC-40028. (1986).

Willie did a guest appearance with Lacy J. Dalton (real name Jill Lynne Byrem) on 'Slow Movin' Outlaw' (written by Dee Moeller) for her 1986 album, *Can't Run Away from Your Heart*. Their duet also appeared on Willie's *Half Nelson* album. Though hailing from

Pennsylvania, Lacy possessed a "voice so unique it rises above the rest" in country music, according to Billy Sherrill. As she began her career, she was often an opening act for the Willie Nelson show.

She once said she wouldn't mind looking like Willie. She rhetorically mused that,

> wouldn't it be great to be a woman and be just like Willie Nelson? I've often thought, 'God, would that be great, to be the first woman out there with wrinkles and not trying to cover it up.' Wouldn't that be a wonderful thing?

Montana Cafe. (Hank Williams, Jr.). Warner Bros. WB 25412-2. (1986).

The only son of the legendary Hank Williams, Hank Williams Jr. became an artist with his own award-winning sound. His 1986 album entitled, *Montana Cafe*, featured Willie on the Hank, Sr. classic, 'Mind Your Own Business'. Also appearing on this cut along with Willie were Reba McEntire and Reverend Ike. The three helped make this one of the most rousing covers of a Hank, Sr. song. As a single, it went to number one on the country charts in December 1986.

The producer, Jim Ed Norman, suggested turning the recording into an "event" record, something which Warner Bros. very much wanted from Junior. To the label, an "event" record was one that created excitement due to the combination of famous names involved. The first famous name specifically requested by Hank, Jr. was the Reverend Ike.

He was asked to sing the part involving a preacher. Ike consented to do the recording but asked not to do the "preacher" verse. Instead, Willie (the "preacher" in *Red Headed Stranger*) came in to do (in a Chicago studio) that verse. One of Hank, Jr.'s associates, Barry Beckett, traveled to various locales to record two of the other "names," Reba and Tom Petty.

Heroes and Friends: Randy Travis Duets. Warner Bros. 9-26310-2. (1990).

Randy Travis came out of North Carolina to score big on the country charts with 'On the Other Hand' and 'Forever and Ever, Amen'. Despite his talent and traditional country sound, it took close to eight years of trying in Nashville for Randy to make it big. His biographer, Don Cusic, wrote that he never got discouraged. According to Randy,

> I didn't ever worry about making it. After all, I had heard all the stories about how long it took someone like Willie Nelson to finally break through.

After several outstanding albums, he released this 1990 country duet collection. In addition to duets with artists like George Jones and B. B. King, he and Willie sang together on the standard, 'Birth of the Blues'.

The song, done originally by Harry Richman, appeared back in 1926, not as a "blues" song, but as part of a show, *George White's Scandals of 1926*. Paul Whiteman and His Orchestra enjoyed the first "number one" hit version of the song during the same year, 1926. On the track, Willie played solo guitar, while, among other excellent backing artists, Denis Solee added clarinet, Mickey Raphael played harmonica, and Barry Beckett joined in on piano. A trend-setting country album, it has sold enough copies to be certified a "platinum" seller.

Roy Rogers Tribute. (Roy Rogers). RCA 3024-2-RRE. (1991).

Talent manager, Stan Moress, first approached Roy about making an unusual 1991 tribute in which Roy sang with a gallery of country stars in rerecording his biggest hits. Richard Landis produced the set for RCA. The Ohio-born Roy (real name Leonard Slye) was 79 at the time, and, as Landis observed, "I defy you to find any other 79-year-old man singing like that."

Roy sang with Willie on the song, 'Rodeo Road', an Allen Shamblin/Chuck Cannon composition. Roy also sang with artists ranging from Randy Travis to Clint Black. The duet with Black, 'Hold on Partner', became a single that peaked in the top fifty on the country singles chart.

The success of the album was the greatest for Roy in many years, peaking at number one hundred thirteen on the *Billboard* national album sales charts. For Rogers, it was the culmination of a career that transcended Western films, a spot as lead singer of Sons of the Pioneers, and a long marriage and partnership with the "Queen of the West," Dale Evans.

The Song Remembers When. (Trisha Yearwood). MCA Records MCAD-10911. (1993).

Former "demo" singer Trisha Yearwood hit it big in 1991 with a hit single on MCA Records. Within two years she not only had more hits but a major biography, *Get Hot or Go Home*, written by Lisa Gubernick. She has recorded solo and with other major talents, including duets with Don Henley and Garth Brooks.

In 1993, Willie sang harmony vocals with her on the cut (written by Kimmie Rhodes), 'Hard Promises to Keep', for her 1993 album, *The Song Remembers When*. In 1996, he sang harmony on the same song with the song's author (for the author's debut album on Justice Records).

Willie also played solo acoustic guitar on Trisha's rendition of his own song, 'One in a Row'.

50 Years of Makin' Music. (Charlie Louvin). Playback Records PCD 4505. (1993).

In 1993, an obscure record (on Playback Records of Miami, Florida) by one of Country Music's greatest names, Charlie Louvin, appeared without publicity and with little or no chance to make a sales splash. Country music in 1993 had no place for legends like Loretta Lynn and Merle Haggard, let alone Mr. Louvin. The tracks were recorded (engineered by Ronny Light and Don King - not the boxing promoter) at Nashville's Reflections Studios and The Cypress Room. Jack Gale produced and wrote the liner notes. In them, he wrote that this was "truly a 'country event' ... Totally awesome!" In his part of the notes, Louvin wrote that:

> getting to record with Willie, Waylon, George, Charlie, Tanya, Crystal and Melba has been the greatest thing to ever happen to me.

That was obviously a publicity statement but amazing nonetheless. Charlie for years, with brother Ira, was one-half of one of the greatest country harmonizing duos ever. They influenced many artists, chief among them Emmylou Harris. She rarely failed to include a Louvin Brothers tune on her early albums. After Ira died, Charlie tried to carry on, recording solo and with artists like Melba Montgomery and Jim and Jesse.

On this album, Charlie recorded with guests Charlie Daniels, Waylon Jennings, Tanya Tucker, and of course, Willie. In fact, Willie and Waylon together joined Charlie on the cut, 'Makin' Music', while Willie dueted with Charlie on 'This Darn Pen'. Charlie once said that as his voice got older it started to waver, making it harder to stay on key. That was not evident here as he was in great voice. So was Willie. Although Charlie no longer rated the pick of the best Nashville songs, some of the selections were quite good. The one he did with Tanya, 'Takes Love to Know Love' was by Paul Overstreet, while Opry veteran Johnny Russell wrote 'Ain't You Even Gonna Cry', which Charlie did solo.

The Last Country Song. (Hermann Lammers Meyer). Desert Kid Records DK 96008. (1997).

1997 brought forth one of the strangest collaborations, Willie, along with Norma Jean, Johnny Bush, Buddy Emmons, and Jimmy Day, working with Europe's top country singer, Hermann Lammers Meyer on his album, *The Last Country Song*, consisting of "20 great songs." Meyer, known as an excellent steel player, was named the European Country Music Association's European Artist of the Year and Male Vocalist of the Year (for 1996). He also received the "European Album of the Year" award from the association.

Willie's main part in the album consisted of a duet with Meyer on 'The Part Where I Cry', which Willie fans would have no problem recognizing as coming from his early writing days at Pamper Music. Willie and Porter Wagoner's former female partner, Norma Jean also assisted Meyer on the Ernest Tubb classic, 'A Little Bit of Everything in Texas'. Additionally, Meyer recorded (with the help of Texas Dance Hall musician Clay Blaker) Willie's 'Sad Songs and Waltzes'. Earlier in 1997, when Meyer toured the U. S., Blaker opened for him.

Production was done by Meyer and Jurgen Koop with Jimmy Day and Tommy Hill. The majority of the tracks was recorded at Pedernales Studio with the rest cut at Starday Studio in Nashville. Reviewer Mike Gross (a dee-jay for WSHU-FM, Fairfield, Connecticut) called the album "a musically beautiful and conceptually exciting project." Anybody wanting the album could send twenty dollars cash or check to Desert Kid Records, Drosselweg 15, 26871 Aschendorf - Germany or send a fax to ++49 4962 338. The owner of Scotty's Music (314 427-7794) said Hermann has become internationally renowned as a very good steel guitar player.

Everybody's Got a Song. (Donnie Fritts). Oh Boy Records OBR-017CD. (1997).

This album had been in the works and ready for release for quite some time before it finally came out on John Prine's Oh Boy record label. In 1995, it was set to circulate via the Dakota Arts label (the Oh Boy release was actually produced under license from Dakota Arts). Willie was just one of a large coterie of guests that included Prine, Kris Kristofferson, Waylon Jennings, Delbert McClinton, Lucinda Williams, Tony Joe White, Lee Roy Parnell, Dan Penn, and Spooner Oldham. The latter two have been long-time songwriting collaborators.

Fritts, sometimes called the "Elegant Alabama Leaning Man" (Jerry Wexler wrote in the album's liner notes that he gave Donnie the nickname), has been in and around country music as an artist, though mostly a songwriter, for over twenty years. He was one of many writers who hung out at Tompall Glaser's studio (sometimes called Hillbilly Central) and was even lumped into the "outlaw" category at times. His best known song was '(My Life Would Make a) Damn Good Country Song', cut by Jerry Lee Lewis for Mercury Records in 1975. When released as a single, it managed to climb to number sixty-eight on the country singles chart.

In addition to being a staff writer for Combine Music early in his career, Fritts also managed to land a few small parts in various Sam Peckinpah movies. He recorded a duet with Dan Penn on 'Adios Amigo', which made its way onto the Arthur Alexander tribute album, *Adios Amigo*, Razor & Tie RT 2814. It was a song Donnie co-wrote with Arthur when they were both writers for Combine Music.

On this album, Fritts seemed to have finally gotten it together with great songs, great band, and great collaborators. It was too bad the record didn't make it to a major label. Willie's contribution was to share lead vocals with Donnie and play acoustic guitar on the cut, 'The Oldest Baby in the World'. The song, co-written by Prine and Fritts, was about a little girl suffering from the disease that causes a person to age ten times faster than normal. Bobby Bare and Billy Swan were part of the background vocals on the track.

Willie did an electronic duet with Hank!
(Photo from the author's private collection)

"Sweet Memories":

The Duets and Collaborations with Texas Artists

Kinky Friedman. ABC ABCD-829. (1974).

Kinky Friedman originally released his first album for his second label, ABC, in 1974. His debut album went out in 1973 on Vanguard Records. Willie was slated to produce the entire ABC debut album for Kinky, but the label had other ideas, moving the recording site from Texas to Los Angeles while handing production responsibilities over to Steve Barri.

As it was, Willie's did produce and contribute background vocals to 'Miss Nickelodeon'. Kinky said that Willie also "sang backup with Waylon Jennings and Tompall Glaser on 'They Ain't Making Jews Like Jesus Anymore' (Willie was also listed as producer)." In Kinky's view, their singing together was "an event which has never happened before or since."

Willie's contributions to Kinky's debut ABC album marked probably the second time he was prominently featured on someone else's album as a guest (as opposed to being a hired hand as he was with Ray Price). The album artist, Richard "Kinky" Friedman, was born in Palestine, Texas (quite a few miles south of Dallas), and has become known for both his highly individualistic recordings and his suspenseful mystery novels as well. The album was rereleased in 1994 on Varese Sarabande as VSD-5488.

In new liner notes written for the Varese Sarabande rerelease, Kinky recounted the initial recording work done on this album. He said that "twenty years ago," he and Willie "left Austin to record this album in Nashville." With guest appearances by Waylon Jennings, Tompall Glaser, and Billy Swan among others, the:

iconoclastic endeavor was close to fruition when we got a call from ABC Dunghill's offices in Hollywood. They pulled the plug on the Nashville sessions, assigned a new producer to the project, and moved the whole thing to Los Angeles.

As a result, the album reflected "two diverse sensibilities, one Hollywood, and one Nashville." Actually, the Kinkster knew the album was in trouble when he looked up and "saw the new producer painting his fingernails with a smooth coat of clear polish." From there, though it took a while, Friedman became a best-selling novelist.

On the book-writing side, Kinky recently told *Texas Monthly* that he made Willie the central character of his tenth (and as of 1997, his newest) novel, *Roadkill*. To do that novel, Kinky traveled extensively with Willie and his band and family aboard the Nelson bus, the Honeysuckle Rose. From that vantage point, he was able to observe much of what had been going on in country music recently, saying that:

> the changing landscape of country music has made major-label support and generous radio airplay almost a thing of the past. For many legends of country music, this trendy tidal wave toward Nashville poster boys and modern, youthful 'hat acts,' plus the inevitable pull of the old rocking chair, has meant the end of careers that were supposed to last forever. In the midst of all this, like a diamond among the rhinestones, Willie Nelson stays on the road.

To him, Willie was:

> a storybook gingerbread man; born into poverty, rich in the coin of the spirit, ephemeral and timeless, fragile and strong, healing the broken hearts of other people and sometimes, just maybe, his own as well. Yesterday's wine for Willie includes personal tragedies, Internal Revenue Service audits, and a somewhat geriatric band that could be dubbed the Shalom Retirement Village People yet to this very day undeniably takes no prisoners.

What Kinky admired most about Willie was "his Zen-Texan approach to inevitable triumphs and defeats." In a *USA Today* interview, Kinky added that "Willie is a jet-set gypsy. It's a spiritual tonic traveling with him." As far as being a character in a murder mystery, he related that Willie "thought it might be worth a shot." Later, after the book came out, he revealed to *USA Today* that "*Road Kill* readers told me they're happy to find out Willie is the kind of person they thought he was."

About the same time the book went out, Kinky released a collection of his songs done by other artists, entitled *Pearls in the Snow*, on Kinkajou Records. Two of the "other artists" were Willie and Waylon (separately not together). The collection was marketed as a "tribute" album. Willie's contribution was his interpretation of Kinky's song, 'Ride 'Em Jewboy'.

Swans Against the Sun. (Michael Martin Murphey). Epic PE-33851. (1975).

For Michael Murphey's 1975 album, *Swans Against the Sun*, Willie contributed vocals on the cuts, 'Renegade' and 'Rhythm of the Road' (along with other vocalists, John Denver, Tracy Nelson, Jeff Hanna, Charlie Daniels, and Murphey). Murphey, from Dallas, was at one time a staff writer for the publishing company that supplied many of the songs done by the Monkees. He also had a unique memory of Nelson from the days when Willie first moved back into the Austin Music scene.

That was the first time he ever saw Willie, at the Armadillo World Headquarters, a former National Guard Armory turned premier performance showcase. He recollected that, "we saw this short-haired, clean-shaven guy wearing a sharkskin suit walk in." Just about everyone there was immediately suspicious of the individual. "We thought he was a narc," was the way Murphey remembered the reaction to their first sight of none other than Willie Nelson.

Gypsy Boy. (Billy Joe Shaver). Capricorn CPN-0192. (1977).

Willie appeared on 'You Asked Me to' with Billy Joe Shaver, the legendary songwriter, from Corsicana, Texas, known for great songs but not much commercial success as a performer. The album was released in 1977. Prior to this album, one of Shaver's biggest successes was writing (or co-writing) all but one of the songs on Waylon's 1973 album, *Honky Tonk Heroes*.

Ain't Living Long Like This. (Rodney Crowell). Warner Bros. BSK-3228. (1978).

Willie appeared on 'Song for the Life' with Crowell on this great 1978 Warner's album that didn't sell much but was a critical success and helped establish Rodney as a great songwriter. The song, according to Rodney, was the:

> first song I ever wrote that I kept. I wrote it when I was very young, and it was writing into the future about maturing. When it was finally a hit record, a couple of summers ago, I

had lived to the age that I was writing about. That was something I enjoyed.

Rodney, from Houston, Texas, was a member of Emmylou Harris' Hot Band, married to Rosanne Cash (they subsequently divorced), and responsible for classics like 'Til I Gain Control Again', recorded by Willie in 1976 and 1978.

Charlie's Shoes. (Billy Walker). Quicksilver DEC DECP-02. (1983).
      In 1983, when Billy Walker recut his 1962 Columbia hit, 'Charlie's Shoes' and released it along with some other songs on a small "indie" label, Willie joined him as a featured performer. In 1961, on Columbia, Walker turned Willie's 'Funny How Time Slips Away' into a top twenty-five hit, though it wasn't the first Willie song he recorded. In 1959, Billy cut 'The Storm Within My Heart'. He also recorded 'Mr. Record Man'.
      Early in Willie's career he stayed with Walker, a fellow Texan from the small town of Ralls, while Billy appeared on an Ozark Mountain radio show. Billy remembered those days, including the first time he met Willie, saying,

> I knew Willie in Texas. I was on radio in Waco, and he came from Abbott, right outside of there. And sometimes he used to come and watch me perform live on the radio.

Later, after Walker had moved to Nashville and Willie came there, too, Walker remembered asking him, "what are you doing here?" He said Willie told him he was there because "nobody's buyin' songs in Ft. Worth" and that he was living in "that old 1950-model gray Buick."
      Billy told him to "get your gear and come on out to my house." Willie proceeded to live "out there with me for about three months." Walker recalled taking Willie "around, tryin' to get him a songwriting job." During that time, Willie had written 'Crazy' and Billy had "cut a demo on it over at Starday Studio, tryin' to show the guy what kind of songs Willie Nelson was writing." According to Walker, the "guy" said he didn't "think that song'll ever sell."
      So, Walker went and achieved a "big" hit on Willie's 'Funny How Time Slips Away' (his single actually peaked at number twenty-three on the country singles charts in late 1961). His success with the song occurred less than a year before Jimmy Elledge, whom Walker once described as "a guy who sounded like a black woman," took it to number twenty-two on the pop singles charts. Walker also, in 1961, put a "hold" on 'Crazy'. That meant he had the exclusive right to record the song sometime in the ensuing months.

It was then, in Walker's words, that Hank Cochran "came to me and said, 'Owen wants to cut 'Crazy' on Patsy Cline. Would you let go of it?'" Walker obviously didn't want to let go of the song, but he related how Hank got him to do just that. Walker said,

> Hank promised me that he would find me another song, which he did, which sold a million records for me, 'Charlie's Shoes'.

Full Circle. (Johnny Rodriguez). Epic FE-39583. (1985).

When Johnny Rodriguez attempted a 1985 major label comeback, he included a duet with Willie on Willie's song, 'Forgiving You Was Easy'. Johnny previously had experienced great success on Mercury before substance abuse sidelined his career. Here, Willie backed the man who became a son-in-law by marrying his daughter, Lana.

Though a Mexican-American, Johnny had comparable country roots to Willie, having been born in Sabinal, Texas. They had a similar sense of propriety, with Johnny going to Willie to ask for his daughter's hand in marriage. Johnny, in one quote, also pretty well summed up Willie's theory of songwriting, saying that "Willie Nelson told me one time, 'All you gotta do is be honest and make it rhyme'."

During one interview I had with Willie, Lana was there. When she walked in, he said, "did you know Lana was married to Johnny?" Then he laughed and said, "yeah, for about twenty minutes." Lana looked over and laughed as well, adding, "no, it was more like eighteen minutes, the longest eighteen minutes of my life."

Box Car Willie. (Box Car Willie). Dot Records MCA-39052. (1986)

Box Car Willie made his country singles chart debut in 1980. He was already pushing fifty years of age. In 1981, he was voted the Most Promising Male Vocalist by *Music City News*. As of 1986, he was signed to Dot, then an affiliate of MCA.

This 1986 Box Car Willie on Dot featured two Willie Nelson collaborations. Willie played acoustic and lead guitar and sang a duet on 'Boxcar's My Home', a Box Car Willie original. On 'Song of Songs', co-written by Box Car, Willie just sang the duet part.

The two cuts showed up again on a 1986 MCA Records compilation of Box Car Willie recordings, *King of the Freight Train*, MCAD 20544. Box Car Willie was the stage name of Lloene Martin of Sterret, Texas, the son of a railroad worker. Martin adopted the hobo persona after years of trying to break big-time into the music business, as a dee-jay and impressionist.

American Music. (Bugs Henderson and the Shufflekings). Bingo Pajama 22222/Flat Canyon Records FC 01012. (1988).

It took until 1988 before Willie again appeared on an album by a fellow Austin artist. That was when he performed with Bugs Henderson and his group on their *American Music* album as released, first on the Bingo Pajama label, then by Flat Canyon Records of Evergreen, Colorado. It was recorded live at the Prohibition Room in Dallas.

Willie was one of twelve soloists (the album credits listed him as number ten) on the cut, 'Honky Tonk', the legendary instrumental written by Bill Doggett and three other co-writers). Other "soloists" on the cut included Johnny Winter and Jimmy Vaughan. The album itself was a nostalgic and creatively outstanding effort credited to one of the more fun-loving groups in the Austin music scene. Overall sales of the album were steady yet slow but substantial enough to get the album rereleased in 1993.

Tu Amigo. (Little Joe (Hernandez)). Columbia CK 46229. (1990).

In 1990, Columbia Records attempted to move Little Joe, a Tex-Mex favorite, into the mainstream. Willie got involved with his Pedernales studio being used for some of the album's recording and by doing lead vocals and playing guitar on 'Marie' and 'You Belong to My Heart'. The latter cut was also included on a 1993 Sony Disco compilation, *Lo Mas Grande de Little Joe*, CDB-80870/2-469538.

My Very Special Guests. (George Jones). Epic EK 35544. (1991).

This 1991 George Jones compilation for Epic Records featured a number of his duets with other musicians. Leading off the set was a collaboration with Waylon Jennings on Willie's song, 'Night Life'. Fellow-Texan (born near Saratoga in the East Texas "Big Thicket" country) Jones also did a duet with Willie on 'I Gotta Get Drunk'. It was a great version of the Nelson song, which could be heard in an earlier version (Willie alone) on an RCA "live" Willie Nelson album. The cut featuring George and Willie was actually intended for an earlier Jones album involving "guest stars."

Live at the Philharmonic. (Kris Kristofferson). Columbia Records (Sony Music Special Products) AK 52415. (1992).

Willie joined Kris Kristofferson (from the audience) for several live shows in New York back in 1972. On December 2, 1972, one of the shows was recorded but not released until 1992. At this concert, Willie's part included 'Funny How Time Slips Away', 'Night Life', 'Me and Paul', and a rousing version of 'Mountain Dew'.

One thing about Willie's guest singing of 'Night Life' at Kris' concert was that it was one of more than a dozen (depending on whether the RX cut compiled on a United Artists collection is counted or not) recorded versions of the song, which featured Willie. The first version was, of course, the Rx single done way back in 1959. Willie also did four live versions and seven other studio recordings, the most recent being on the 1995 album, *Augusta,* he recorded with Jazz-master Don Cherry.

He did a duet of it with Ray Price, sang a refrain of it for a Toy Caldwell album, and performed it at one of Charlie Daniels' Volunteer Jams. He did one live and one studio version of it for RCA and Columbia. His Columbia studio version was part of a medley done on *The Sound in Your Mind* album. The Rhino box contained a live cut of Willie singing it at the Texas Opry House. Another studio version appeared on his 1994 Liberty album, *The Healing Hands of Time.*

It was also planned to be a cut on a projected future "blues" album. Performance-wise, Willie has sung the song with a variety of artists, not necessarily country ones. In a 1996 interview, he spoke of doing 'Night Life' with none other than B. B. King (their recorded duet of the song did appear on B. B.'s 1997 *Deuces Wild* album). Another live performance (at the US festival) was featured on the CD-ROM, *Willie: The Life and Music of Willie Nelson,* Graphix Zone GZ10760.

For a 1991 Sony compilation, *Kris Kristofferson: Singer/Songwriter,* A2K-48621, featuring Kris' greatest performances and the greatest covers of his songs, Willie contributed 'Help Me Make It Through the Night'. Kris, from Brownsville, Texas, appeared with Willie on the *Songwriter* soundtrack, on all of the Highwaymen efforts, and on Monument's *...the Winning Hand* project. One of Willie's finest albums was his 1979 tribute to Kristofferson.

The Legendary Ernest Tubb & Friends: Rainbow at Midnight/The Legendary Ernest Tubb & Friends: Waltz Across Texas. (Ernest Tubb & Friends). Laserlight 12/118/12 115. (1992).

Ernest Tubb, born in Crisp, Texas, a hamlet in Ellis County, rose from those impoverished farm community beginnings to become one of the biggest Texas names in country music. The widow of Jimmie Rodgers, Carrie, helped him begin his career, to the point of giving him one of Jimmie's Martin guitars and even touring with him for a short time. In 1940, he began recording with Decca, the label with whom he stayed for thirty-five years. The company that bought Decca, MCA, showed no qualms in letting Ernest slip off their artist roster in 1975.

In the late 1970's (1977 and 1978), a project began that involved rerecording Ernest Tubb singing his major works. Steel guitarist and studio owner, Pete Drake, spearheaded the project for his own label, First Generation Records, although he had hoped to sell the finished product to a major label, though initially Drake had told Tubb the sides were being recorded "for a mail order project." Tubb had fought emphysema since the early 1960's and by the late seventies, the disease was more pronounced, so recording was slow and laborious.

The project was actually completed in stages. The first stage resulted in a ten cut album on First Generation Records, FG LP 001, entitled *Ernest Tubb: The Living Legend*. It was released in December 1977. The cuts were all Ernest and backing musicians, often including Harold Bradley on bass and sometimes piano.

Almost a year later (August 1978), as Ernest recalled the occasion, "they called me in the office - I thought presumably to listen to the playback of what we'd done last night." Instead, to his surprise,

> they started playing something I'd done last year - 'Waltz Across Texas'. I thought maybe they'd made a mistake till I heard Willie Nelson come in singing on it!

To his further amazement, he discovered, as the tape played, that:

> about seven different people - Willie Nelson, and Waylon Jennings, Johnny Paycheck, Loretta Lynn - they had come in and recorded with me on those tapes.

Tubb confessed that he "was really surprised, a very, very nice surprise, to think those people wanted to come in and do that." How had all this come about? In a 1980 interview with Bill Oakey, Tubb spoke about the adding of the various duets, saying:

> it got started when Waylon and Willie said they wanted to make a record with me. We just weren't available at the same time to do it. So Pete Drake, my producer, invited them to the studio to sing on a few tracks that I had finished. Pete called me back to do some more songs, and then he sprang the surprise on me.

It was actually in July of 1978 that Willie and others had juggled their schedules and gone into Drake's studio to add their voices, where appropriate, to at least one of the many tracks Drake had recorded on Tubb up to that point (August 1978). Charlie McCoy (harmonica) and Charlie Daniels (lead guitar) were also listed as being on that cut. In addition to 'Waltz Across Texas', Willie's voice was overdubbed (along with an amazing steel solo by Speedy West) on to 'You Nearly Lose Your Mind', a song Tubb wrote but which owed substantial debt to Jimmie Rodgers.

On February 9, 1979, Drake's First Generation label issued a twenty track Tubb album, fittingly entitled, *The Legend and the Legacy Volume 1*, FG 0002 (and TV 1033). The album was introduced at a sixty-fifth birthday party for Ernest held at the Exit/In in Nashville. This time many of the overdubbed sides were featured. Willie's electronic duet with Ernest was one of those overdubs released for the first time. Drake continued to hope that all the guest artists would entice a major label to pick up the album or at least distribute it. That didn't happen.

Instead, a small Canadian label, Cachet Records, a company that specialized in TV marketing, released, also in 1979, a twelve track subset of the twenty cut First Generation (FG 0002) album. Because Ernest had been such a rousing success at Willie's 1979 Fourth of July picnic, Cachet chose to release the Willie/Ernest cut, 'Waltz Across Texas' as a single. Amazingly, it reached number fifty-six on the country singles chart as Cachet 3001. The Cachet album "rose to upper-chart levels" and became, according to Irwin Stambler and Grelun Landon's *Country Music: The Encyclopedia*, "one of the top-50 best-selling LP releases of the year."

The label also released one other single, Cachet 4507, 'Walking the Floor Over You', which had been completed with "friends" Merle Haggard, Chet Atkins, and Charlie Daniels. It fared a little better than the Willie/Ernest one, reaching number thirty-one. Led by those two singles the album went "gold," selling over $500,000 worth of copies (or 50,000 units). It was also the last Ernest Tubb album to reach any national sales chart.

Willie and Ernest's 'Waltz Across Texas' cut also appeared on other collections containing some number of the Drake-produced cuts. In 1989, Ray Pennington's Step One Records released a thirty track CD. It was entitled *The Ernest Tubb Collection: The Last Recordings of His Greatest Hits*, catalog number SOR-0049. Guest artist and publisher credits (for each song) were given but there were no writer credits or liner notes.

In 1995, Intercontinental Records of Council Bluffs, Iowa, issued (via Excelsior) ten of the First Generation cuts as *A Tribute to a Legend: Ernest Tubb*, EXL 7135. The cuts were listed as being from 1982 and First Generation Records. The first cut was the Willie/Ernest duet on 'Waltz Across Texas'.

Eventually five albums worth of material were recorded. Most of it did not see release during either Drake's or Tubb's lifetime. It wasn't until 1992 that Ernest's widow, Rose, agreed to license all the tracks (overdubs and all) to Laserlight, a California label that specialized in budget compilations. Laserlight released the tracks as a five volume set entitled, *The Legendary Ernest Tubb & Friends* (12-115 through 12-119).

The 'Waltz Across Texas' cut naturally appeared on the first volume, appropriately entitled *The Legendary Ernest Tubb & Friends: Waltz Across Texas* (12-115). Then came the first appearance of Willie's (and Waylon's) electronically-added vocal on 'You Nearly Lose Your Mind', on the fourth volume, *The Legendary Ernest Tubb &*

Friends: Rainbow at Midnight (12-118). Willie's vocals for this were also taped in July (or possibly September) 1978.

One of the "other voices" belonged to Waylon Jennings. Waylon remembered the Tubb project with the observation that he sang "on an album of his once, though he wasn't there." Waylon's view of the process was that "they had his voice on tape, and at the part where I was supposed to come in, he'd say 'Aw, sing it, Waylon'."

Sure enough, when it came time for Willie's part on 'Waltz Across Texas', Ernest could be heard saying, "now let me hear you, Willie boy." As famous as that song finally became, it almost didn't get finished. After it had been partially written by Tubb's nephew, Talmadge Tubb, the song laid around Ernest's den "for about eight or ten years." One day he:

> dug it out and started fooling with it and liked it, so I rewrote the chorus and added a verse, and I decided to do it for my own pleasure, because it's about my home state of Texas.

Then, even after it was finished, recorded, and released as a single in 1965, it barely broke into one of the top forty spots on the *Billboard* country singles charts. peaking at number thirty-five. By the end of his career, however, Ernest was finally able to acknowledge that "it's become a classic." According to Tubb's biographer, Ronnie Pugh, Mrs. Drake "plans more repackagings of this material, one at least without any guest vocal overdubs." In 1997, in England, the original twenty cut First Generation album was released on Edsel Records as EDCD 517. The English label dropped the "Volume 1" part of the title.

Willie's payback of his debt to Ernest came in 1979, when he booked Tubb as part of his 1979 Fourth of July picnic. Tubb's last recording session was in 1982 and like his hero, Jimmie Rodgers, he finished that session, according to his long-time pianist, Johnnie Walker, resting on a cot, overcome with his illness. The session involved his singing with Hank Williams Jr. and Waylon on the cut, 'Leave Them Boys Alone', released in 1983 on Hank's *Man of Steel* album. Ernest lingered two years before dying in 1984 (of emphysema).

Nacogdoches Waltz. (Paul Buskirk). Justice Records JR 1701-2. (1993).

Texan Paul Buskirk was the bandleader for whom Nelson played when first starting out. Buskirk bought and owned some of Willie's first songwriting successes, most notably, 'Family Bible' and 'Night Life'. Though the song sales became a huge windfall for Buskirk and not Willie, the two men have remained friends.

Willie wrote in his autobiography that, "believe it or not, I never harbored any resentment toward Paul." In 1993, Willie played guitar on Buskirk's 1993 Justice Records album, the same label which released Nelson's first post-Columbia album. Willie revealed that:

> Paul Buskirk was my mentor. He taught me a lot about life and music. He's one of the top musicians I've ever seen in my life. He knows his instruments and knows what he's doing and is able to tell you what he's doing and then play it again exactly the same way, if he wants to.

As for himself, Willie said that he never knows "where I'm going or what I'm going to do and sometimes it comes out right."

Lost Train of Thought. (Ray Wylie Hubbard). Dejadisc DJD-3223. (1995).

Though Hubbard was born in 1946 in Soper, Oklahoma, he was also raised in Oak Cliff, Texas (near Dallas). He attended the same high school, Adamson, as Michael Martin Murphey, with whom he did some coffee-house gigs early in his career. B. W. Stevenson and Steve Fromholz also attended Adamson High. After the gigs with Murphey, Ray got to know Jerry Jeff Walker and wrote 'Up Against the Wall, Redneck Mother' for him. Walker's version eventually became a "progressive country" classic without ever being a hit single.

In the mid-seventies, Ray had a shot at being a major label star with Warner Bros. but the album he did for the company failed to sell, so since then he has recorded and marketed a number of independent label releases. In 1978, according to Roy Kasten, writing in the Seattle, Washington-based magazine, *No Depression,*

> at the request of Willie Nelson and his fledgling Lone Star Records, Hubbard cobbled together demos he had scattered across Texas.

The result was an album called *Off the Wall*. It was one of about half a dozen that went out on the label. Supposedly, Hubbard agreed to put out the album because he was conditionally promised a good-sized budget and producer for the follow-up. As Kasten found out, "when Nelson signed to CBS, the condition was moot."

In 1992, he cut this set at both Sound Logic Studios in Garland, Texas, and Willie's Pedernales Studios in Pedernales, Texas. He put it out on the Misery Loves Company label and for three years it was available only at his concerts. Then in 1995, Dejadisc picked it up and released it nationally (via their newly-instituted program of rereleasing classic but relatively unknown independent albums).

The album featured an all-star crew of Austin musicians beginning with Willie and Bugs Henderson. Among the many other Austin-based musicians were Terry 'Buffalo' Ware, Bobby Chitwood, and Becky Lane. With Ray and band, Willie performed the song 'These Eyes'. One reviewer wrote that the end result sounded like "a perfect Willie Nelson-style ballad."

Fire to Fire. (Tanya Tucker). Liberty Records D 108291. (1995).

Almost twenty-five years after a thirteen year old Tanya Tucker took the country world by storm, two of the most unique voices from Texas got together as a duet on the title track, 'Fire to Fire', of this album. A review in the May 1995 issue of *Music City News* noted that "helping Tucker heat it up is longtime friend Willie Nelson." In the album credits, Tanya wrote "thanks for the fire, Willie."

Tanya had almost nothing to say about the record in her autobiography except that it "didn't do much," even though she felt it was a "good and solid" album. According to her, it was unfortunately released at "one of those times when upheaval at a record label affect artists and their projects, usually in an adverse way." Jimmy Bowen had resigned as president of Liberty, due to a diagnosis of cancer, about the time the album was released. As a result, a very "soulful sound for a story about one night of love" (in the words of the reviewer at *Music City News*) came and went, overlooked by potential listeners when the album failed to make a sales impact.

West Texas Heaven. (Kimmie Rhodes). Justice Records JR 2201-2. (1996).

West Texas Heaven was the first album by a very gifted Texas singer/songwriter (from Lubbock, Buddy Holly's home town), Kimmie Rhodes, to gain any recognition in the United States (in 1996). Her previous album (from 1989), *Angels Get the Blues*, had been released only in England on the Heartland label, even though it had been recorded at the legendary Sun studios in Memphis. Her debut album, *Kimmie Rhodes and the Jackalope Brothers*, came out in 1981 but went nowhere, as did the 1985 follow-up, *Man in the Moon*.

West Texas Heaven was critically acclaimed and featured two vocal performances by Willie on 'Hard Promises to Keep' and 'I Never Heard You Say'. Waylon Jennings and Townes Van Zandt also guested. Another highlight of the album was the theme song for the Shirley MacLaine/Ricki Lake movie, *Mrs. Winterbourne*. Previously, one of Kimmie's first major album appearances came as both a writer and performer on Willie's Justice Records album, *Just One Look*.

"One Voice":

The Appearances with Non-Country Musicians

Tracy Nelson. Atlantic SD-7310. (1974).

Soon after joining Atlantic Records, Willie did a duet with Tracy Nelson (former lead singer of Mother Earth, from Madison, Wisconsin) on the old Conway Twitty and Loretta Lynn song, 'After the Fire Is Gone'. It was included in this 1974 Tracy Nelson album and has also been included in the Rhino/QVC package, *The Classic, Unreleased Collection.* As a single release, the song reached number seventeen on the country charts. Its appearance there was sandwiched in between Willie's final two charting singles for Atlantic.

The writer of the song, L. E. White, was employed by Conway's publishing company at the time, but he said he did not write the song with the boss in mind. Actually, the writer remembered that he wrote the song when he was in Gatlinburg, Tennessee. He was, of all things, "looking at a fireplace where the fire was out."

He recalled that somebody said to him, "Boy, it looks cold in there, don't it?" That made him think in terms of a song, or as he said he thought to himself, "there's nothing colder than ashes after the fire is gone." He added that:

> that was about all there was to that, so I wrote it and showed
> it to Conway and he didn't like it all for about a year.

Then Conway decided the song would be perfect as a duet with singing partner Loretta Lynn. In 1971, their version went straight to the top of the country singles chart.

Timi Yuro Today. Ariola 205.006. (1982).

In 1982, Willie "underwrote"and produced an attempted comeback album by Timi Yuro. It was released only on the German label, Ariola. Yuro was best known for the hit single, 'Hurt', covered by many artists including Elvis. Once described as a "troubled" little girl with a big voice, she reached the 1980's suffering from throat problems (cancer of the throat that eventually required tracheotomy surgery) that necessitated several operations.

Willie sang (even did a duet) and played, with his band, on all the songs, most of which were written by him. The entire album was recorded at his Pedernales Studio. The duet they did together was on Willie's song, 'There Is No Easy Way But There Is a Way'. As the tape closed, Timi thanked Willie by saying, "Thank you, Jesus, for Willie Nelson and his family."

Early in her career (back in 1963 when both she and Willie both recorded for Liberty), Yuro recorded a number of Nelson tunes, including 'Are You Sure?' and 'Permanently Lonely'. In 1989, after being out of the business for several years following the bout with throat cancer, Timi recorded another album of Nelson songs, several of which were duets with Willie. These cuts were not issued until 1991 and then only briefly as a "mail-order" release, blocked in large part due to a series of legal wrangles.

1100 Bellaire Place. (Julio Iglesias). Columbia CK 39157/9C9-39928. (1984).

In 1984, Willie did a duet with Julio Iglesias on 'To All the Girls I've Loved Before'. The cut was included as part of this album which proved to be Julio's breakthrough album in the American market. It also appeared on Willie's *Half Nelson* album for Columbia.

Julio also contributed a guest vocal on 'As Time Goes By', a cut on Willie's 1983 *Without a Song* album. The pair recorded another duet, on the song, 'Spanish Eyes', for Willie's 1988 album, *What a Wonderful World*. Willie revealed that with Julio, "it was his singing that attracted me."

Heart Beat. (Don Johnson). Epic OE-40366. (1986).

In 1986, Don Johnson, the actor, filmed a special that became a TV show and video. The soundtrack was subsequently turned into an album, on which Willie contributed vocals for the Bob Seger song, 'Star Tonight'. That cut also featured fellow-Texan Stevie Ray Vaughan on guitar.

Vaughan's biographers, Joe Nick Patoski and Bill Crawford referred to the recording as "the goofiest gig he [Stevie Ray] had ever done." After noting the other stars involved, such as Ron Wood and

Dickie Betts, they termed Johnson's album, a "vanity record." Johnson was, of course, the *Miami Vice* headliner, turned *Nash Bridges* star. Incidentally, Willie did a guest shot on one of the 1997 Bridges episodes.

In 1998, the Razor & Tie label rereleased the album "with six bonus tracks," according to *ICE: The CD News Authority*. The news release from *ICE* stated there still was "an impressive list of guests: Stevie Ray Vaughan, Willie Nelson, Ron Wood, Bonnie Raitt, and Dweezil Zappa." The outstanding songwriters, whose songs Johnson and his guests recorded, included Tom Petty, Bob Seger, and Jeff Daniels. Daniels also played guitar on the album.

Night Bird. (Jackie King). Columbia FC-40396. (1986).

In 1986, Willie furthered his work with guitarist Jackie King when he played guitar on the cuts 'Supermotion' and 'Fireshaker'. King previously appeared on Willie's Columbia album, *Angel Eyes*. Although Jackie grew up in San Antonio, Jazz became his primary musical love early in life. Beyond their studio work, some of the best playing Jackie and Willie have done together came on the 1981 Austin City Limits tribute to Django Reinhardt.

Master of Suspense. (Jack Walrath). Blue Note 46905. (1987).

More Jazz work followed as Willie was featured on the Hank Williams song, 'I'm So Lonesome I Could Cry' for a 1987 album by saxophonist and band leader (with his septet) Jack Walrath. Willie also guested on the old Eddy Arnold hit, 'Bouquet of Roses'. This time the backing consisted of trumpet, piano, and Willie's guitar.

Walrath was said to be a "talented player with a tough almost percussive sound." That suited Willie, the superb rhythm guitarist, perfectly. Walrath had a long history in Jazz, playing with Charlie Parker and Charlie Mingus, as well as fronting his own band on some excellent Blue Note albums.

Havana Moon. (Carlos Santana). Columbia FC-38642. (1987).

Willie recorded his vocal for a cut that appeared on a Santana album, 'They All Went to Mexico', at his Pedernales studio in Texas. Carlos wrote in the liner notes to this 1987 release that he was grateful to meet the great Willie Nelson and doing this song made him "infinitely more receptive to the contribution of country and western music." The song, written by Greg Brown, also made its way onto the *Half Nelson* album.

Chalk Mark in a Rain Storm. (Joni Mitchell). Geffen GHS-24172. (1988).

Willie shared vocals with Canadian folk-rocker, Joni Mitchell, and contributed additional background vocals to the cut, 'Cool Water', the Sons of the Pioneers classic (with revised lyrics by Joni). It was featured on her 1988 Geffen Records album. Willie was familiar with Joni's music, having recorded 'Both Sides Now' when he was with RCA (as the title cut of an album).

Rainbow Down the Road. (B. W. Stevenson). Amazing AMCD-1020. (1990).

Big B. W. Stevenson (the initials stood for Buckwheat, though his real name was Louis) came from Dallas and had been big in the United States years before (on RCA) when 'My Maria' (co-written with Daniel Moore) went top ten in 1973. He was also the first to chart the song, 'Shambala'. Unfortunately, he died April 28, 1988, following heart surgery, at the age of thirty-eight. By 1990, a posthumous release credited to him had been relegated to a small Canadian label. Fellow Texan, Willie, did a duet with B. W. on the title cut.

Toy Caldwell. (Toy Caldwell). Cabin Fever Music CFM9012. (1992).

Willie was one of the featured performers, doing guest vocals on his own composition, 'Night Life', on a solo 1992 release by the late Toy Caldwell. Caldwell was formerly the lead guitarist of the Marshall Tucker Band, a seventies group from South Carolina. This was truly a star-filled recording with Gregg Allman also doing guest vocals, Charlie Daniels playing the fiddle, and Ace Cannon appearing on saxophone, among others.

Another Country. (The Chieftains). RCA Victor 09026-60939-2. (1992).

In 1992, Ireland's finest musical group recorded an album with Chet Atkins, Emmylou Harris, Ricky Skaggs, The Nitty Gritty Dirt Band, Don Williams, and Willie Nelson. Willie did the vocals on a Leadbelly song, 'Goodnight Irene'. The song was recorded in April of 1992 in Dublin, with Kris Kristofferson and others backing him.

The 'Goodnight Irene' collaboration came about after the group's founder Paddy Moloney met backstage with Willie, Kris, and Waylon to seek their assistance on the recording. The three had just finished performing at the Point Depot as part of the Highwaymen. The session was set for two days later, which happened to be Good Friday, when the bars in Dublin were all closed.

Moloney recalled telling the three American artists "not to worry if they wanted a pint of Guinness or something as I'd organize it." As far as the results of the session, Moloney said,

> we did it in two takes. I had the arrangements made out for the song including a new introduction piece. Willie Nelson told me that my introduction was the best version of the song he'd ever heard.

Another member of The Chieftains, Matt Molloy, "was thrilled to play with Willie Nelson." Willie had long been "one of his favorite singers." In fact, one of Molloy's proudest possessions became the picture of him with Willie taken during "the session in the music room at Matt Molloy's." Molloy said about Willie that:

> to watch him deliver a song was really something. It was all done very quickly. He sang it twice and that was it. And to boot he brought in Kris Kristofferson to do backing vocals which was an unexpected pleasure. They were just dead on.

As it turned out, when the session was over, Moloney "took the country musicians to a nearby bar which had agreed to open its doors on Good Friday especially for the occasion."

The 30th Anniversary Concert Celebration. (Bob Dylan). Columbia Records C2K 53230. (1993).

In 1992, Bob Dylan celebrated his thirtieth year in the recording business with a televised special that captured a tribute concert at Madison Square Garden in New York. A whole host of stars, from Eric Clapton to Neil Young, came to congratulate Bob and sing his songs. A double CD album resulted which was released in 1993.

Willie was on hand to do a masterful version of 'What Was It You Wanted', one of the cuts from his 1993 album, *Across the Borderline*. Don Was played bass behind Willie. Willie proceeded to play guitar and sang with Kris Kristofferson on 'I'll Be Your Baby Tonight', a song Bob wrote in 1970 for his *New Morning* album. Willie was also part of the "everyone" who came back out to sing 'Knockin' on Heaven's Door' toward the end of the program.

On October 19, the day after the concert was recorded, Bob recorded his vocals for the 'Heartland' track (which became a duet with Willie). Don Was produced the session for Bob, which was held at New York's Power Station studio. 'Heartland' was a collaborative writing effort by Bob and Willie.

Texas Swings. (Herb Ellis). Justice Records 1002. (1994).

Willie was featured on another Jazz release, from 1994. This time it was with Herb Ellis, a renowned guitarist with a long recording history, specifically for Concord Records. Ellis began his career with Oscar Peterson. Often, he tended to play "tempos at an easy jog."

Over the years he played with such greats as Joe Pass and Red Mitchell. At his best, he was "swinging and hard-hitting." With Willie and other sidemen, this album was rhythmic, filled with intelligent guitar riffs, and often as mellow as a late night supper club.

The sessions, on which Willie played, came about after the founder of Justice Records, Randall Hage Jamail, lured Ellis, a native of Farmersville, Texas, back to Texas to record. According to famed Jazz writer and critic, Nat Hentoff, there "always was a tangy Texas sound in Ellis's jazz." So, Jamail, as Hentoff recalled,

> put together a session with Ellis and three former Texas Playboys - the ceaselessly surprising fiddler, Johnny Gimble, drummer Tommy Perkins, and pedal steel guitarist Herb Remington.

Hentoff added that the session also included "Willie Nelson on acoustic guitar, violinist Bobby Bruce, bassist Tommy Alsup, and pianist Floyd Domino." Jamail, wrote Hentoff, sensed that:

> the excitement of the recording was almost childlike. Everybody was having such a good time.

Who wouldn't have a great time playing Western swing?

Duets II. (Frank Sinatra). Capitol 28103. (1994).

Early in his career, as Willie was searching for a unique vocal style, he emulated the famous Sinatra phrasing. He wrote that when he first heard Frank,

> Sinatra's style caught my attention at once. I listened to his phrasing and admired his breath control. Somebody had taught him how to breathe.

Over the years Willie has sung a number of songs associated with Frank. In 1994, he and Frank sang a duet on the classic 'A Foggy Day' for the second of two Sinatra duet albums. Both albums raised quite a stir because the duets were recorded over phone lines.

Frank recorded his vocals at Capitol Studios in Hollywood. The other artists recorded their duet parts in a studio of their choice. Willie's was done at the Pedernales studio. The duet parts were transmitted via telephone lines to another studio and "mixed" with Frank's original vocals, achieving the final results heard on *Duets* and *Duets II.*

The song, 'A Foggy Day', was a George and Ira Gershwin work, first introduced by Fred Astaire in the 1937 film, *A Damsel in Distress.* The scene in the picture during which Fred sang the song actually had fog swirling about him. After Fred's film performance, the song, a humorous and affectionate tribute to the city of London, became part of the Sinatra repertoire for over forty years. This arrangement was by composer Johnny Mandel. The album, itself, sold well enough to peak at the number twenty-nine spot on the national album sales charts.

Wish You Were Here Right Now. (Bobby Charles). Stony Plain Records SPCD 1203. (1995).

Legendary singer/songwriter, Bobby Charles from Louisiana, was the author of the Bill Haley classic, 'See You Later, Alligator' and recorded briefly for Chess Records without much success. Here, in 1995, he recreated, with the help of Willie, Fats Domino, and Neil Young, some of his past brightest moments as well as created some new ones. Willie was guest vocalist and played acoustic guitar (with Neil Young) on 'I Remember When'.

He also played acoustic guitar on 'Ambushin' Bastard' and 'I Don't See Me', contributing some solos on the latter cut. The genesis of this album went back to 1984 and a planned album on Bobby's own label, Rice & Gravy, which he operated near his hometown of Abbeville. Willie and Neil recorded guest spots back then on a number of tracks for Charles' never released set entitled, *Lil' Cajun.*

The tracks featuring Willie and Neil were then intended to be released sometime in the early 1990's on an album called *I Wanna Be the One* (also slated for release on the Rice & Gravy label). That one likewise never came out. Finally a number (though supposedly not all) of the Willie and Neil tracks came out on the 1995 collection, *Wish You Were Here Right Now.*

How did all of this come about? According to Charles, he took the Neville Brothers, who had always wanted to meet Willie, to one of Willie's concerts in New Orleans. In a surprise move, they walked out on stage, unannounced and sang behind Willie. Charles said that after the show they got on a bus and started talking.

It was then that Willie told Charles he "wanted to play something with me, and said I should come to his studio." Charles suggested the Neville Brothers be included, too. The date was set for April 15, the only off day Willie had for about the next six months. Unexpectedly, the Neville's backed out.

Willie's manager tried to call it off, but Charles said he still wanted to do it, so when the time came, he, along with Neil Young, showed up. Neil had a 1928 Martin guitar once owned by Hank Williams. According to Charles, "Neil had never met Willie, and that night they started putting together Farm Aid." That was 1984 and the Farm Aid I concert took place in September 1985.

One of the most interesting things about Bobby Charles the songwriter is that he cannot play a musical instrument, not even the guitar, though Chuck Berry once tried real hard to teach him back when they were both signed to Chess. Further, Charles doesn't even know chords by name, but he does know what the music in his head should sound like. Charles said that during one of the sessions,

> Willie was hitting a wrong chord on one song. Maybe not wrong, but it didn't sound right to me. I mentioned it to him. He said, 'Well, which is the right one?' I said, 'I don't know. You'll have to play me the ones you know and I'll tell you when you hit it.' He started going through chords, and he and Neil Young were looking at each other laughing. He hits one, and I said, 'That's it!' Neil said, 'He's right.'

So, Willie the guitarist extraordinaire played the right chord from his extensive memory of chords. That enabled the recording of one particular song to be finished. It was a song written by a man who could not play a note of music but who knew what he heard.

Stars and Stripes: Vol. 1. (The Beach Boys). River North Nashville Records 51416 1205 2. (1996).

Willie sang with Brian Wilson and the Beach Boys on the song, 'The Warmth of the Sun'. It was part of an interesting project, released in late summer 1996, that melded the Beach Boys music with admiring country stars ranging from Lorrie Morgan to James House, who had been the opening act for recent Beach Boys concerts. Other country performers included Junior Brown and Sawyer Brown. Willie's involvement, according co-producer Joe Thomas, brought the whole project together; he was "the catalyst for the project."

Thomas said that when he proposed getting Willie Nelson to work on this most recent Beach Boys album, Mike Love replied that "if you can deliver Willie Nelson to me, I can deliver Brian Wilson to you." Next, Brian Wilson told Thomas, "I'll produce this record if you can get Willie Nelson to record 'Warmth of the Sun'." Before long, the Beach Boys went to the Pedernales Studio to cut the song with Willie. The recording was completed at Sound Stage in Nashville. Nelson was excited about doing the song, saying that:

> I've known those guys for a long time, Brian and Love were fans, and vice versa. So they all came down to Texas. They

gave me one of their best songs. I think 'Warmth of the Sun' is a beautiful song, and they put the finishing touches on it. Those guys can sing. I think this was a natural mix.

The Beach Boys loved it, too. Thomas recalled that:

when Willie sang the first lines, the guys gave him a standing ovation, and we knew right there it would work. The Beach Boys became background singers then and there.

In the liner notes, the Beach Boys acknowledged that Willie "has been an inspiration throughout the years."

Go Cat Go! (Carl Perkins). Dinosaur Entertainment 76401-84508-2. (1996).
When Carl Perkins lost his connection to his own song, 'Blue Suede Shoes', and Elvis took off with it, he became recognized as a musical "pioneer," but not a superstar like Elvis. He was famous for his rockabilly hits at Sun Records and for having several of his songs covered by the Beatles. Their version of 'Matchbox' went to number seventeen on the pop singles chart in 1964.
Unfortunately, about the only things most stores ever stocked by him were his "greatest hits" collections. Then Carl wrote his autobiography which came out in 1996, followed by a compilation of new and old Carl, some old "covers," and some interesting work with other artists, including Paul Simon, John Fogerty, and Willie Nelson. Willie appeared with Carl on three very good and quite diverse cuts.
The best was their duet on Carl's 1975 song, 'Wild Texas Wind'. Bono, Johnny Cash, Tom Petty, and Willie shared vocals with Carl on a recent Jim Garland "working man" song, 'Give Me Back My Job'. Willie's final contribution was playing guitar on Carl's remake of his old hit, 'Matchbox'.

Polka! All Night Long. (Jimmy Sturr). Rounder Records CD 6077. (1996).
Though Jimmy Sturr and band tackled some pretty eclectic material on this album, with the help of Cajun accordion player, Jo-El Sonnier, the Jordanaires, and Willie, he insisted they will never try to become a country group. They will always remain a Polka band. In his excellent liner notes, Elijah Wald, a free-lance music writer quoted Sturr as saying that:

polka is a very general type of music that has been popular for a lot of years, only they don't call it polka. Louisiana calls it Cajun; Tex-Mex calls it Tejano; back in the swing era, they called it Texas swing.

That's why he and his band were completely at home with Bob Wills material as well as a Cajun fiddle number and an old English novelty number. Willie did the vocals on three songs associated with Wills, one of them an old "public domain" favorite, 'Tavern in the Town'. The other two were 'Big Ball's in Cowtown' and 'All Night Long'. Willie fit right in with the band's style. As Sturr pointed out, Willie "actually started out in a Texas polka band."

In a recent *Billboard* article, after completing his latest project (which included guest appearances by Bill Anderson and Flaco Jiminez), Sturr appraised his feelings on the prior album in which he worked with Willie. He said,

the one before this one was with Willie and we were thrilled with it. It won a Grammy and everything.

Sturr further revealed that:

what I'm trying to do is get a greater base of audience, and the way I like to do it is recording with Willie, recording with Bill Anderson and Flaco.

Willie told an interviewer that he:

ran into Jimmy Sturr several years ago on the road. He'd heard about me being in a polka band when I was a kid. I was raised up all around polka music. I've always loved it; it's so lively.

Working with Willie has brought Sturr a lot of new fans and even an appearance on the Opry. He has almost singlehandedly been working and traveling to keep authentic polka music alive in this country. He began as a clarinet prodigy in his hometown of Florida, New York, where his family was "100% Irish" but where most of the rest of the town was Polish. At 48, he has had his own band (or some form of it) for over thirty-seven years.

In that time he has won seven Grammys and cut almost one-hundred albums. His band had the distinction of being the "first big band" to ever appear on the Grand Ole Opry. A special guest at one of his Opry appearances was none other than Willie, who proceeded to perform on-stage at the Opry for the first time in approximately twenty years.

Deuces Wild. (B. B. King). MCA Records MCAD-11711. (1997).

In the review of Willie's appearance on a live Kris Kristofferson album, it was noted that Willie had recorded a dozen different versions of his classic song, 'Night Life'. In performance, he has sung it literally hundreds, perhaps thousands, of times. One of the people with whom he had sung, but not recorded, the song, was B. B. King. Willie was quoted as saying that singing it with B. B. was "a wonderful experience." Fans of both artists would have been in for quite a treat had the performance been recorded and released commercially.

On November 4, 1997 (national release date), fans got that treat after all, when, as part of B. B.'s album, *Deuces Wild*, there was a cut of the famous blues singer and Willie singing, of course, 'Night Life'. The album, itself, boasted a number of famous guest artists, from English guitar legend, Eric Clapton, to country-rock artist Marty Stuart. In an article featured in the October 25, 1997, issue of *Billboard*, King talked briefly about the guests on the album, saying, "Clapton I have known for a long time; we're friends. Willie Nelson, we're friends." He went on to say that guest artist Bonnie Raitt was also a friend but that he didn't know some of the others, such as rap artist Heavy D and Van Morrison.

MCA marketing director, Michael Solomon, said that discussions were underway with MCA Nashville president Tony Brown "about radio exploitation of the Stuart and Nelson tracks." If that worked out, maybe Willie could get some radio play being denied him and others because of their age. B. B., at 72, sounded a lot like Willie when he told *Billboard*, "I won't stop, because what else would I do? People talk about retiring. People who retire die." Similarly, Willie recently told *Country Weekly*, "some of us just won't go away - me, Merle, Billy Joe Shaver and Hank Williams Jr."

In an interview with Jas Obrecht, of *Guitar Player* magazine, B. B. had some very "from-the-heart" thoughts on Willie. He appraised him as:

> one of the greatest people I know on this planet. Oh, I love the man. He done things for people, and nobody give him credit for a lot of it. Like the Farm Aid and all that - this was from the bottom of his heart. He didn't have to do that. He hadn't been in trouble or nothing at that time. He was just trying to help people, and then later it seemed like some rapped on him. But to me he is an angel on this earth. He is a great, great man. Not only that, he is a hell of an artist and one of the nicest people I know.

B. B. added, when asked about Willie's guitar, "I just love it. he wore a hole in it, yes, and he can really play it, man." According to Dave

Rubin, writing in *Guitar* magazine, B. B. actually recorded 'Night Life' for a solo album back in 1966. Recently, B. B. told Rubin that:

> I was in Nashville right after I recorded 'Night Life' the first time. I was playing a place called the Exit Inn, and I was feeling real good, had a few drinks, you know, and was getting into 'Night Life'. When I got to that part about 'Listen to the blues ...' the bridge part of it, I looked up and saw Willie Nelson staring at me, and almost fainted. But he came backstage after the show and complimented me on it and thanked me for doing his tune. We have been good friends ever since.

In his autobiography, B. B. said that Willie's 'You're Always on My Mind' and Lionel Richie's 'Three Times a Lady' were his favorite songs. Because of that, he wrote, people said he had "corny taste." He said he didn't care what people thought, he just likes "what I like." The fact that 'Always on My Mind' was far and away Willie's best selling solo single put B. B.'s tastes clearly in line with a huge portion of the American popular music audience.

The country music superstar in his sixties!
(Photo from Evelyn Shriver Public Relations)

"Pick Up the Tempo":

The Multiple Collaborations with Select Artists

Pasture Prime. (Asleep at the Wheel). Stony Plain 1086. (Undated).

Western Standard Time. (Asleep at the Wheel). Epic EK 44213. (1988).

Asleep at the Wheel's Tribute to the Music of Bob Wills and the Texas Playboys. Liberty Records CDP-7-81470-2. (1993).

Merry Texas Christmas, Y'all. (Asleep at the Wheel). High Street Records 72902-10355-2. (1997).

Asleep at the Wheel has, for more than twenty years, ranked as a great Western Swing group in the tradition of Bob Wills and the Playboys. The group never became a Wills clone, because they also mixed in a considerable amount of blues and "jump" band sounds. As a band, Asleep at the Wheel has always been largely based on the talent of Ray Benson. Over a more than twenty-five year period the band has prospered, through personnel and label changes and grueling tour schedules. Willie was the one who convinced Ray to finally and irrevocably move his group to Austin.

In 1973 the group released their first album for United Artists, *Comin' Right at Ya'*. Their producer was Tommy Allsup. He had previously worked with Willie when both were with Liberty in the early sixties. A fiddle player, Buddy Spicher, whom the band had hired to work on some dates with them, told the group about Tommy. Benson recalled that:

since I'd already seen his name on some Willie Nelson records, that's all it took for me to want to work with him.

By 1974, according to Ray, Willie Nelson and Doug Sahm had persuaded the band to relocate to Austin, Texas.

Willie's first project with the band was a duet with Benson on the Nelson original, 'Write Your Own Song'. It was included on the undated album, *Pasture Prime*, from the tiny Stony Plain label. This was just one of many commercial recordings Willie made of the song, both as a duet and solo. In 1985, MCA released abridged (budget) versions of this set, both simply titled, *Asleep at the Wheel*, MCA-30036 and MCAD-20840, with the 'Write Your Own Song' included both times.

In 1988, after the band signed with Epic Records, Willie contributed vocals to the cut, 'Chattanooga Choo Choo', on their classic album, *Western Standard Time*. In 1992, the cut led off Asleep at the Wheel's greatest hits package for Epic, entitled *The Swingin' Best of Asleep at the Wheel*, EK 53049. It was interesting to hear a Western swing version of the song, considering that it was originally written by Harry Warren and Mack Gordon for the 1941 movie musical, *Sun Valley Serenade*. It was featured as a production number, at the end of the film, with Dorothy Dandridge singing while the Nicholas Brothers tap-danced.

When Benson put together the band's 1993 Bob Wills tribute, Willie participated with Jody Nix, Huey Lewis, and Ray Benson on 'Ida Red'. He was featured on the cut, 'Still Water Runs the Deepest', a song written by one of the original fiddle players in the Texas Playboys, Jesse Ashlock. Ashlock also wrote 'The Kind of Girl I Can't Forget'. Benson, in the song's liner notes, wrote that, on 'Still Water Runs the Deepest', "this might be how Willie would have sounded singing with the Texas Playboys." Ray also complimented Willie, calling him "the premier songwriter of our era."

In the August 1974 issue of *Country Music*, Willie recalled the Playboys and those two songs, in an article entitled, "A Tribute to Bob Wills." He wrote about the time when "Tommy Duncan came to sing" with Wills. In Willie's view, Bob and Tommy:

> turned out to be a very good combination. They started doing 'Still Water Runs the Deepest' and 'The Kind of Girl I Can't Forget', and all those Bob Wills classics like 'Faded Love'.

'Ida Red', as a song, was so old that no clear record as to its authorship. It has seen many reincarnations. Chuck Berry's song 'Maybellene' was actually 'Ida Red' with a few musical changes and obviously a whole set of different lyrics. Berry's biographer, Howard DeWitt wrote that "it was Wills' version which apparently influenced young Chuck Berry." Benson wrote that 'Ida Red' "was a favorite of

Bob Wills fans for years" and that it "epitomizes the <u>fiddle</u> sound" of the band. In cutting the song for this project, Ray said Willie and Huey Lewis "were ready to sing, so how could I turn them down?"

Overall, the album featured eighteen cuts, because, as Benson said,

> so many artists volunteered. It was all a matter of who was available and who was willing. Well, everybody was willing.

He added that:

> when we began planning this album, I asked all the participants if they had a favorite song they wanted to do. Some did, some didn't, so I tried to suggest certain tunes that I thought they would like and would fit their vocal style.

From that came Dolly Parton singing 'Billy Dale' (originally 'Lily Dale'). Ray wrote that "when Dolly asked me what song I was considering for her, this was my immediate response." Other participating artists included Suzy Bogguss, Garth Brooks, George Strait (a contemporary purveyor of the Texas "Western Swing" style pioneered by Wills), as well as Johnny Gimble and Eldon Shamblin, together with Chet Atkins and Vince Gill.

Gimble was long the fiddler extraordinaire with the Texas Playboys. Even after Leon McAuliff and Leon Rausch took over leading the band following Wills' incapacitation due to a stroke, Gimble continued as a featured performer. Willie and Johnny have also joined forces often over the years.

The album itself reflected lots of hard years of great playing. In Benson's words,

> when I came up with the idea to do this album, it wasn't like I just 'thought' it up one moment and then went and did it. I had been waiting to do this record for over 20 years.

David Zimmerman's review of the album for *USA Today* touted it as "a likely candidate for album of the year. If you're from Texas, make it the decade." So successful was this album from the start, that in 1994, Liberty included it, in its entirety, in their Asleep at the Wheel box set, *Still Swingin'*, CDP-7243-8-30284-2.

Willie's work with the group was not done. In 1997, he appeared on their Christmas album, *Merry Texas Christmas, Y'all*, along with another (and almost as "aged") Texan, Don Walser. The pair and the group combined to create an overly harmonized treatment of 'Silent Night'. Willie also sang with the group on yet another interpretation of his classic, 'Pretty Paper'. Whether the listener was from Texas or not, the upbeat, "swinging" treatment of Christmas standards had to bring a new sense of joy to the holidays.

This Time. (Waylon Jennings). RCA APL1-0539 (AYL1-3942). (1974).

Ol' Waylon. RCA AFL1-2317 (AYL1-5126). (1977).

Black on Black. (Waylon Jennings). RCA AHL1-4247. (1982).

Waylon and Company. RCA AHL1-4826 (AYL1-5433). (1983).

Waylon Jennings Greatest Hits. RCA AHL1/PCD1-3378. (1979).

With Waylon Jennings, Willie has done some of his most expressive cooperative work. Additionally, he tried to get Waylon to not move to Nashville. Their relationship dated back to the time when Waylon was first starting out in the entertainment business in Phoenix, Arizona. It was late 1965 or early 1966 and Waylon was considering moving to Nashville. Willie advised against it but Waylon went anyway, as part of the same RCA Victor company that already had Willie on its artist roster.

In his autobiography, Waylon recalled that his first encounter with Willie was in Phoenix. It came during the time Waylon was the headliner at J.D.'s. He was making good money. He was also coming off the recording of an album for the fledgling independent label, A&M, founded by Herb Alpert and Jerry Moss.

Chet Atkins and RCA were attempting to contract with Waylon to come to Nashville and begin recording for the label. Waylon wrote that:

> I'd thought long and hard about leaving Phoenix, even asking another RCA artist passing through town what he thought of moving. His name was Willie Nelson...

Why did Waylon ask Willie, beyond the fact that Willie was in town and was an RCA artist?

Willie was "a fellow Texan" and he had "just gotten his start recording as an artist in his own right." Further, Willie "liked my singing and I liked his." So they met. Waylon wrote that "Willie came to town and sent word he wanted to meet me." According to Waylon, Willie was then "appearing across town at the Riverside Ballroom." Waylon said he:

> went over to the Adams Hotel and spent the afternoon finding out how much we had in common, asking him about

Nashville and what I might expect. He had just moved there. I told him I had a good deal at J. D.'s. By then, I was up to maybe fifteen hundred dollars a week, clear.

What was Willie's response to Waylon's "dilemma?" Willie told Waylon, "don't move, and if you do, let me have that job!"

Willie had a similar recollection about their first meeting, writing in his autobiography that:

> on a running tour in 1965, I stopped in Phoenix, where the hottest act in town was a kid named Waylon Jennings. I went to catch his show, and afterwards we shared a bottle of tequila and he asked my advice on his career.

Willie said that he told him,

> whatever you do, Waylon, stay away from Nashville. Nashville ain't ready for you. They'll just break your heart.

Waylon did, of course, sign with RCA and move to Nashville, or as Willie put it, "Waylon did what any good songwriter would do."

Singing together on Willie's song, 'Heaven or Hell', an unpremeditated duet on 'Luckenbach, Texas', and further work on writing 'Good Hearted Woman', were among the high points of their friendship and working together status. Waylon once told (Lorianne) Crook and (Charlie) Chase (of *The Nashville Network*) that Willie was "truly a 'free spirit,' one of the few he has ever known." Waylon also wrote about Willie, that:

> he'll give you everything, say yes to anybody, trust that events will turn out fine in the end.

When Waylon and Jerry Bradley put together *The Outlaws* compilation for RCA, they naturally included two previously recorded Waylon and Willie duets as well as two Willie originals. Then came the 1978 follow-up album, *Waylon and Willie*. One more RCA duo album, *WWII*, along with two on Columbia, *Take It to the Limit* and *Clean Shirt* (actually on Epic), have also resulted.

When Willie left RCA to join Atlantic, Waylon bluntly told RCA executives, "you lost him," (pointing to Willie's picture in the office of one RCA executive) during his own efforts to gain a more beneficial contract renewal. For a time, the pair shared a New York-based manager, Neil Reshen, who helped the two gain better contracts and more artistic freedom. Neil, at times, has been credited with coining the term, "Outlaws" (as has Hazel Smith, most recently with *Country Music* magazine) in reference to his clients.

For several of Waylon's RCA projects, Willie contributed background music, sometimes guitar, but usually vocals, most often in terms of a duet. The first contribution occurred in 1974 on Waylon's *This Time* album as a duet on the song, 'Heaven or Hell'. That was the same song Willie wrote and recorded as 'Heaven and Hell' in 1974 on his *Phases and Stages* album for Atlantic Records.

Willie produced Waylon's *This Time* album, played guitar on four cuts while singing with him on 'Heaven or Hell'. That same cut made it onto *The Outlaws* compilation. Besides 'Heaven or Hell', three other songs on the *This Time* album were written by Willie. Waylon related, in his autobiography, that *This Time* was "one of my first under the WGJ logo." The album was actually recorded in October 1973 and:

> Willie played guitar on it and helped me put it together along with a couple of his songs: 'Heaven or Hell' and one of my personal favorites, 'It's Not Supposed to Be That Way'.

'Pick Up the Tempo' and 'Walkin'' were two other Willie originals Waylon picked for the album, which Willie co-produced along with Waylon. For the sake of clarification, "WGJ" stood for "Waylon Goddamn Jennings" Productions.

In 1977 Willie again joined in on a Waylon project, *Ol' Waylon*, singing with him on 'Luckenbach, Texas', a Chips Moman/Bobby Emmons composition. It was "a spur-of-the-moment decision" that got Willie's voice on the recording (as part of the final verse, with a couple of self-generated lyric changes). Waylon recalled that,

> Willie stumbled in the studio, and I said, 'Why don't you sing with me on this?' I was cuttin' it, and he came in and put his voice on it. That's the way all those things were. They were inspirational, you might say.

The concept for the 'Luckenbach, Texas' song had its genesis back in 1972 when J. R. "Hondo" Crouch, part-owner of the real but tiny West Texas "town" of Luckenbach, hosted the first annual Luckenbach World's Fair. That fair was headlined by Willie and other Austin-based musicians.

More than twenty-thousand people showed up throughout the event. In 1976, Crouch declared Luckenbach to be the center for the Non-Buy Centennial, a humorous cut at the highly commercialized American bicentennial celebration going on all over the country. Moman and Emmons heard about all that was emanating from the microscopic Texas town and were moved to write the famous song, even though they had never been anywhere close to it.

After Waylon and Willie recorded the song and took it to number one on the country singles chart, writer John Davidson observed that Luckenbach became:

> a happening, a replay of the sixties for the sort of people who had stood by and watched angrily or enviously while students and hippies broke all the rules.

As many as four thousand people a week visited Luckenbach for several years after the song came out. Once again, Willie (and Waylon) had taken country music to listeners who would normally not have paid attention to that kind of music.

In 1982, the third Waylon project with Willie's involvement, *Black on Black*, had Willie singing on 'Just to Satisfy You'. The song had its beginnings when an old friend of Waylon's and fellow disc jockey, Don Bowman, called Waylon while he was still in Phoenix and asked him if he "wanted to collaborate." According to Waylon,

> about the first thing he brought over was 'Just to Satisfy You'. He had a verse and a melody, and we went ahead and finished that. It happened so quick, I thought that can't be any good.

Bowman was the first to record the song. Then Bobby Bare wanted to record it, but Chet Atkins had him record something else. That was just as well because the version by Waylon and Willie has become the definitive one.

Waylon initially recorded the song when he was signed to A & M Records. A few years later, when it came time to record it for RCA, Waylon said that "Willie wanted to do that song. It was his idea more than mine." As a single, the RCA cut went to country number one in early 1982 and then to number fifty-two on the pop charts.

'Just to Satisfy You' was also included on the 1983 collection, *Waylon and Company*. "The Company" part of the album encompassed, in addition to Willie, talents as diverse as Tony Joe White, James Garner, Ernest Tubb, and Emmylou Harris. As late as 1993, RCA repackaged 'Just to Satisfy You' as part of a Waylon anthology, *Only Daddy That'll Walk the Line: The RCA Years*, 66299-2. An earlier 1979 *Greatest Hits* collection compiled by RCA on Waylon featured three of the cuts (all number one smashes) that Willie and Waylon recorded together, 'Good Hearted Woman', 'Mammas Don't Let Your Babies Grow Up to Be Cowboys', and 'Luckenbach, Texas (Back to the Basics of Love)'.

Quarter Moon in a Ten Cent Town. (Emmylou Harris). Warner Bros. BSK-3141. (1978).

Light of the Stable: The Christmas Album. (Emmylou Harris). Warner Bros. 3484-2/BSK-3484. (1980).

Roses in the Snow. (Emmylou Harris). Warner Bros. BSK-3422. (1980).

Duets. (Emmylou Harris). Reprise Records 25791-2. (1990).

Emmylou Harris has become one of the best singers in the music business, especially as a harmony vocalist. Her harmony career began with the recordings and live shows she did with progressive country-rocker, Gram Parsons. Gram had been a member of the Byrds and was largely responsible for the sound they achieved on *Sweethearts of the Rodeo.*

Prior to her affiliation with Gram, Emmylou was a "folk rocker" for a small New York label, Jubilee. After Gram, she recorded a set of albums for Reprise and Warner Bros. that were consistently among the most beautiful and eclectic in the country field. In addition to recording she served as a past President of the Country Music Association.

As a great harmony vocalist, she has probably recorded with more artists than anyone else in recent memory, everyone from Dolly Parton to, yes, Willie Nelson. She sang for Willie on several occasions. The especially outstanding set was on the *Honeysuckle Rose* soundtrack.

In addition to using Willie on four of her albums, Emmylou has also recorded many of his songs. The most memorable cover was her version of 'Sister's Coming Home'. Willie has returned the favor several times, either as a guitar player or singer or both. Overall, the blending of two voices never sounded better than when Willie's was intertwined with Emmylou's.

Emmylou's 1978 album, *Quarter Moon in a Ten Cent Town,* had Willie singing a duet with her on 'One Paper Kid'. The cut had only her and Willie's voices, her acoustic guitar, and Mickey Raphael's harmonica. Two years later, in 1980, when she was recording her classic Christmas album, Willie came in and did harmony background vocals, joining voices with Ricky Skaggs on the Rodney Crowell song 'Angel Eyes (Angel Eyes)'. The album was rereleased on compact disc in 1992.

One of Willie's guitar backups for Emmylou came on her 1980 *Roses in the Snow* album. He played "gut-string guitar" on the traditional song, 'Green Pastures'. It was arranged by her producer (and then-husband), Brian Ahern. Emmylou remembered that track well, saying that Brian felt it was "really important that we stick to our guns ... and make a record that is pure in its style." She said, the only left-field thing that he allowed me on the record was Willie Nelson's solo on 'Green Pastures.' Which is still one of my favorite guitar solos, of anything.

Emmylou Harris' label, Reprise, collected, in 1990, her duets with other artists such as Neil Young, Roy Orbison, and of course, Willie. The two sang their version of the Nanci Griffith song, 'Gulf Coast Highway'. This same cut was also included on Emmylou's major boxed-set retrospective put out by the label in 1996. Emmylou once said that "if America only had one voice, it would be Willie's."

Support Your Local Prison. (Don Bowman). RCA LSP-4230. (1969).

Still Fighting Mental Health. (Don Bowman). Lone Star L-4605. (1979).

On the Road Too Long. (Don Bowman). Lone Star LB-1000. (1981).

Willie founded the Lone Star label back in 1975 after his many years of frustration working directly for major labels like RCA and Atlantic. He worked out a deal with Columbia (CBS) to market and distribute his projects. At that point Lone Star was only used for his recordings.

By 1978 CBS had decided it didn't want to market anyone on the label but Willie. So, Lone Star was moved to a distribution pact with PolyGram (Mercury) for the release of any of Willie's product not picked up by Columbia (specifically a collection of his earlier "demo" tapes) as well as projects from other artists. The resulting flow of money enabled Willie, during 1978 and 1979, to sign artists and support their recording efforts even though they were not great "commercial" entities.

Somewhere around six non-Willie albums were released. For some of the first releases, Willie got involved, not only behind the scenes, but with the music, as well. The label soon folded (midway through 1979) and the release of Willie's albums continued through Columbia Records. In addition to the approximately six albums, the label released some singles, including one featuring Larry G. Hudson and Willie singing 'Just Out of Reach of My Two Open Arms' and 'Warm and Tender Love'.

The label, though fun, folded pretty quickly, primarily because it was run as a company that made great records, not a commercial business with one eye on the bottom line. That, of course, was what Willie said he hated about record companies, that they were run by people who managed money but couldn't tell a hit record from anything else. In Willie's opinion, the label just sort of died because Mercury "wasn't sure what to do with the music or how to classify it."

The first major artist to be signed to the label beyond Willie was Don Bowman. Bowman was a top country humorist. In 1967, he was voted CMA Comedian of the Year. He was also a songwriter of some talent, writing 'Just to Satisfy You' with Waylon. Prior to that, he had enjoyed a modicum of success as a disc jockey (working for a time at a radio station with Waylon Jennings). Though not thought of as an actor, he did appear in a number of "quickie" grade "B" country music films with Ferlin Husky, *Hillbillies in a Haunted House* and *Hillbillies in Las Vegas.*

Willie, Waylon, and Bobby Bare were all involved on Don's 1969 RCA album, *Support Your Local Prison.* They sang on 'Poor Old Ugly Gladys Jones', a song Don co-wrote with Waylon. The track was recorded June 20, 1968 with Chet Atkins producing. In 1969, it became a Bowman RCA single "A" side, peaking at number seventy. Willie did the liner notes for Don's 1967 RCA album, *Almost Live*, LSP-3646.

After Don was signed to Lone Star, Willie, along with Waylon, worked closely with him to produce and record his first album for the label in 1979, *Still Fighting Mental Health.* That album was also the company's first non-Willie album after being picked up by Mercury in a distribution deal. The major cut, 'Willon and Waylee', did get some radio play and was otherwise hilarious. When first marketed, the single went out with a letter introducing the "new" label. Waylon, Willie, and Bowman sang together on that track as well as on 'East Virginia Blues', and 'Hot Blooded Woman', two other album cuts.

Willie did background for the second and final Bowman release on Lone Star. According to *Variety*, the Lone Star label, as distributed through PolyGram, folded in 1979. According to label information, this album appeared (on the Lone Star logo) in 1981. By 1981, Willie was using the Lone Star logo off and on for some of his specific projects.

Together Again with Special Guest Willie Nelson. (Johnny Bush). Delta DCA-1139/DLP-4072. (1982).

Time Changes Everything. (Johnny Bush). TCE. (1994).

The Offender's Reunion. (Willie Nelson, Jimmy Day, Johnny Bush, David Zettner). J & M Productions 0955CS. (1997).

Willie's drummer of long-standing has always been Paul English. Yet, for awhile, with a backing group known as "The Record Men," Johnny Bush played drums behind Willie. He and Willie went back to the days when they were both starving deejay's who had to hop a freight train to work because they couldn't afford a car.

Zeke Varnon, a Willie friend from boyhood also recalled that he and Willie used to "hop" freight trains. Once they were able to throw their stuff on a train but couldn't get on themselves, thereby losing all their gear. Willie said that in those days their gear probably consisted of one or two tee-shirts.

Bush was actually born John Bush Shin III on February 17, 1935 in Houston, Texas. That's why the writing credit for his most famous composition, 'Whiskey River', was usually given to Shin, not Bush. As a drummer, Johnny was known for his adaptation of Buddy Harman's "shuffle beat," which Buddy developed in the mid fifties as part of Ray Price's band.

In 1953, a year after Willie got married for the first time, he went to San Antonio to play in Bush's band, The Mission City Playboys. Johnny played in at least two incarnations of Willie's "band," and at one point Willie was "exclusively managed by Johnny Bush and the Hillbilly Playboys." Both Bush and Willie played in Ray Price's band.

Willie's memory of his relationship with Bush goes back to his first band. Willie recounted that:

> the Offenders is the name of the group that I first put together. We went on the road and for some reason we decided to call ourselves the Offenders. Johnny Bush, who has gone on to have a lot of record sales and hits on his own, played drums for us back then. David Zentner played the bass and Jimmy Day played steel guitar.

Then in a strange coincidental development, sometime in 1995, Willie returned from a tour to find the members of his first band laying down some tracks in his studio. What else could Willie do but join in. As he described it,

> I came home a few weeks ago and those guys were in the studio just recording this song. We wound up doing a lot of the older songs and a couple of new things. I'm trying to sell it to somebody.

Unfortunately, the Highwaymen tour and his own projects such as the *Spirit* album diverted Willie and the project remained dormant until 1997.

Then some of the tracks came out on the tiny J & M label out of Buda, Texas, bearing the title, *The Offender's Reunion*. The label, itself, had become known mainly for its sporadic releases of Jimmy Day product. That was the only American label which would release the finished album. In October 1997, the Bear Family label of Germany released the set under the title (of one of the songs on the album), *Can't*

Get the Hell Out of Texas. When announced in the music press, the album was billed as "a reunion of Willie Nelson's first group featuring the man himself."

Willie was one of four people who got top billing as band members, the other three being Day (steel and vocals), Bush (drums and vocals), and David Zettner (bass). Four others, Jimmy Day, Jr. (lead guitar and acoustic rhythm), Floyd Domino (piano), Johnny Gimble (fiddle - with fiddle solos), and Ron Knuth (fiddle) were listed as "special guest Offenders." Day did the arranging and producing while the recording was done at Willie's Pedernales Studio in Spicewood. Not only did Willie play in the band, he did the vocals on 'I'm So Ashamed' and yet another version of his classic 'Rainy Day Blues'.

In the mid-sixties, Bush went from Willie's band to Ray Price's band, where he stayed for three years, absorbing a lot of Ray's vocal sound. During that time, Ray recorded Johnny's song, 'Eye for an Eye'. From there, Bush became a drummer and band leader in his own right. In fact, he became that rarity of rarities in country music, a drummer who could be a lead singer. He was even once billed as the "Country Caruso." Unfortunately, vocal problems (a major throat disorder diagnosed as spastic dysphonia, a rare neurological problem) threatened to stop him from singing. Though he eventually regained about seventy percent of his range, he never made the major commercial breakthrough he richly deserved.

Bush's biggest break as a recording artist came in the mid-sixties when "Willie paid for a session that yielded the album [title track] and single, 'Sound of a Heartache'." The song and album went out on Stop Records. In 1967 and 1968, Bush's first three chart singles for Stop were songs written by Willie, 'You Oughta Hear Me Cry', 'What a Way to Live', and 'Undo the Right' (which went top ten).

Willie, as "special guest" appeared on three cuts for Johnny's 1982 release on the Delta label, the aptly named, *Together Again with Special Guest Willie Nelson.* All of the cuts with Willie were released as singles, beginning with 'You Sure Tell It Like It Is, George Jones'. 'The Party's Over' (Willie's composition) and 'The Sound of a Heartache' comprised a two-sided Johnny/Willie single. Their duet on 'The Party's Over' also came out as the "A" side of a single for the Merit label, which was credited to Johnny Bush and Friend, obviously Willie.

The album, itself, was filled with mainly slow-paced, vintage country songs. The exception was Paul Simon's 'Still Crazy After All These Years'. John Morthland once wrote that, in his opinion, Bush "is one of the best interpreters of Willie Nelson's honky-tonk classics."

Both Willie and Hank Thompson appeared on Bush's 1994 small label (TCE) release. As beautiful as the album was, there was little market for it. The tracks were all recorded at Willie's Pedernales studio. As it was being finished, it became one of many items the IRS seized in a raid to obtain enough property to pay off tax claims against Willie. Because of the seizure, its release was held up for two years.

A Man Must Carry on. (Jerry Jeff Walker). MCA MCA-2-6003. (1977).

Reunion. (Jerry Jeff Walker). Southcoast Records (MCA Records) MCA-5199. (1981).

Jerry Jeff Live at Gruene Hall. Rykodisc RCD-10123. (1989).

Jerry Jeff Walker has always had a reputation as a great songwriter and after Willie immortalized the Austin music scene, Walker became as big a part of it as many others. With that proximity to Willie, the two naturally were able to work together several times. Jerry Jeff was not born either a native Southerner or Texan, but his songs and playing have made that fact a non-reality, as he has come to sound so Texan that he could probably fool even himself by now.

Actually, Walker was born and raised in the Catskill Mountains area of New York state. His first commercial breakthrough was as the writer of the Nitty Gritty Dirt Band hit, 'Mr. Bojangles'. That fame resulted in an Atlantic Records contract. His recordings didn't prove to be commercial at the time, so he retreated to places like Key West.

The early seventies brought him to Austin and a contract with MCA Records. In 1974, he played at Willie's Fourth of July picnic. Though he never did sell albums in the mass grosses that record companies demand, several of his albums, such as *Viva Terlingua* reached "legendary" status and have finally been rereleased on compact disc. He even rated a "greatest hits" (*Great Gonzos*) compilation, put together by the label.

In 1977, Willie appeared on the last two tracks of the live side of a two record Jerry Jeff album, *A Man Must Carry on*. He played guitar, and sang on 'Up Against the Wall, Redneck'. Willie was also credited with "spelling of the word, 'mother'." On the final cut of the album, 'Will the Circle Be Unbroken? (Reprise)', Willie sang and played only. The album became a Jerry Jeff classic, and in 1996, both volumes were rereleased by MCA as MCAD-11565/6. It was also Walker's highest charting album, peaking at the number sixty spot on the *Billboard* Pop Album charts in mid-1977.

In 1981, Willie played acoustic guitar on the cut 'For Little Jessie' for Jerry Jeff's *Reunion* album. The "Jessie" was said to have been Jerry Jeff's daughter. Then in 1989, Willie did guest vocals with Walker on the Steve Fromholz song, 'Man with the Big Hat', for the *Jerry Jeff Live at Gruene Hall* album on Rykodisc (which was originally released on the Tried and True label as TTMC-1698). In 1991, both Willie and

Kris Kristofferson were the primary guests on the inaugural show of Walker's weekly TNN show, *The Texas Connection*.

With a Little Help From My Friends. (Hank Cochran). Capitol St-11807. (1978).

Make the World Go Away. (Hank Cochran). Elektra 6E-277. (1980).

Several close friends have stayed in touch with Willie over the years and recorded with him on occasion. Hank Cochran was Willie's first Nashville friend. He also became, in effect, his songwriting mentor and often partner.

Cochran was from Greenville, Mississippi. Actually, he was born Garlan Perry in Isola, Mississippi, in September 1935. He made his way West winding up in California in 1954. For quite awhile there, another Cochran was better known than he was. That was Eddie Cochran (whose real last name was Cochrane).

Though they were not related, they did form the short-lived duo, the Cochran Brothers. In 1960, Hank moved on to Nashville, where he became one of the greatest country songwriters ever. He was one of the first people Willie met in Nashville. After Willie impressed Hank as a songwriter with immense, untapped talent, they became fast friends.

Hank believed in Willie enough to get him signed (on a royalty draw of fifty dollars a month) to Pamper Music. Hal Smith, the owner did not want to spend any more money on staff writers, so Hank, as the story goes (collaborated by Willie and Hank), gave up his fifty per month raise to cover the cost of signing Willie. After the signing, Hank visited Willie and family in their run-down trailer and they all ended up crying (from happiness and relief, of course).

Hank was also the best song pitch-man in the business, so he was great to work for. In that capacity, Hank was instrumental in getting 'Crazy' to Patsy Cline. It helped that Hank co-wrote one of her hits, 'I Fall to Pieces'. Even as Pamper's song pitcher, Hank always made sure he got his own material recorded.

There was the legendary tale about Hank pitching songs to Burl Ives. He supposedly pitched everyone else's songs first and after he was sure Burl had heard so many he couldn't remember them all, Hank sang his own songs. Those Burl remembered and recorded. Two of them wound up being Burl's biggest hits, 'A Little Bitty Tear' and 'Funny Way of Laughing', so Burl made out well.

Hank helped get Willie placed on Liberty. Willie's first top ten single for the label, 'Willingly' (recorded as a duet with the then soon-to-be Mrs. Nelson, Shirley Collie), was written by Hank. He even got Willie set up as Pamper's West coast office manager. That didn't last long because Willie wasn't cut out for office work.

Over the years, Willie became much more successful as a performer and recording artist. Hank only had sporadic luck with recording, but when he needed Willie, Willie was there to assist on two of Hank's most important album projects. Willie also got Hank into his movie, *Honeysuckle Rose*, doing the classic (by Hank, of course) 'Make the World Go Away'.

For awhile, Hank was married to country star, Jeannie Seely. She recorded, for Monument Records, a "12 song salute to Hank Cochran." For the liner notes, she expressed that his songs were "some of the best songs of our era." She also had a number of friends express their feelings following her notes. Willie wrote that Hank "made a rough and almost impassable road a great deal smoother for me and many others like me."

On one of his final albums for Capitol, *With a Little Help From My Friends*, released in 1978, Hank assembled a talented backup group consisting of Willie, Merle Haggard, Jack Greene, and Jeannie Seely. There was also a "write-up" on the album by Willie. After the album's release, later in 1978, the Cochran and Nelson duet, 'Ain't Life Hell' became a Capitol single. Another track on the album featured Merle Haggard and Cochran singing a tribute to Nelson, entitled 'Willie'.

It stayed on the charts five weeks, peaking at number seventy-seven. The cut appeared again in 1994 on the Liberty "various artists" compilation, *Classic Duets*, CDP-7243-8-30851-2-5. On that same compilation was the 1962 duet, 'Willingly', between Willie and second wife, Shirley Collie.

For his 1980 Elektra album, *Make the World Go Away*, Hank and Willie worked together on five songs. One of them was a harmony duet on a reprise of 'Little Bitty Tear' (originally a hit for Burl Ives). As a single, it became a top sixty country hit.

The other four cuts with Willie were 'A-11', 'Sally Was a Good Old Girl', 'I Fall to Pieces', and 'You Comb Her Hair Every Morning'. Willie added a little harmony to 'Love Makes a Fool of Us All'. Additionally, Hank recorded Willie's song, 'Angel Flying too Close to the Ground'. Willie did not appear on that cut. The two men have stayed in touch and worked together since then. Hank co-wrote a song, 'Patsy' (a tribute to Patsy Cline), for a recent project, *Desperate Men - The Legend and the Outlaw*, he did with fellow songwriter Billy Don Burns.

In the final mix, it was Hank alone singing the song, but initially the song featured vocals by Willie Nelson. According to Hank,

> we had a hell of a duet, but something just wasn't right. My wife and everybody said to take him off because they didn't think it needed anyone else, so that's what we did.

That's what Hank said. When I asked Willie about this recent duet with Hank (that got erased), he skirted the subject, saying simply, "I helped Hank out a lot."

Searchin' for Gold. (Larry Butler). Three Star 32735. (1990).

The Difference Between Men and Boys. (Larry Butler). Zak-Tone ZT-32732. (Undated).

Larry Butler, with whom Willie worked over the years, was one of those artists who, for a long time, stayed just on the edge of the country music scene. Butler and his wife, Patsy, ran various clubs over the years as he tried his hand at leading bands and writing songs. Butler wanted very much to be a performer in his own right. He got his shot as a recording artist on two small independent Texas labels.

Each time, Willie was there to help out. Willie did a guest shot on two cuts, 'My Mama's Waltz' and 'Big Balls in Cowtown', the Bob Wills classic, for a 1990 Butler album, *Searchin' for Gold.* Willie also appeared (sang and played) on Larry's undated (but relatively recent) release for a small independent label, Zak-Tone.

Their friendship and mutual trust went all the way back to the time before Willie tried his hand at songwriting in Nashville. Willie tried to sell Larry some songs, including 'Mr. Record Man', offering him the rights for a mere ten dollars. Butler gave him fifty dollars outright instead, not wanting to take the song away from Willie.

When Larry turned down the offer to buy the songs, Willie asked him if he liked them. Larry's reply was that he loved them, but he wouldn't take another man's song. He told Willie that the songs "are to good for you to sell like this." Luckily for Willie, Larry did lend him enough money (fifty bucks) to see him through yet another trying financial time. Susie Nelson wrote that Butler's loan helped the family get an apartment in Pasadena, on the outskirts of Houston.

Additionally, Butler gave Willie a job with his band at the Esquire Club. Willie also went to work as the "sign-on" disc jockey for a Pasadena, Texas, radio station, Soon after that, according to Willie (writing in his autobiography), he cut his "two 45 rpm records for Pappy Daily."

It was at the Butler's 21 Club that Willie said he first spied the woman who became his third wife, Connie Koepke. He described seeing her in the audience as "classic eye contact, lightning across a crowded room." He told Jimmy Day to "get that blond for me." It wasn't long before Connie was expecting and second wife Shirley was suing for divorce. Patsy revealed that, until 1985, the last time Willie played at their club was 1969, "the night he first met Connie."

In 1994, Larry's name turned up on a Willie project, a Christmas album released on the budget label, Regency. He was listed, along with Willie, as the producer. The keyboard overdubs on the album were also credited to Larry. What he and his staff accomplished was to pull together a number of recordings Willie had done of Christmas songs, while at Columbia, and turn them into a very enjoyable, cohesive album.

For Jimmy Day Fans Only: Rare Recordings by Jimmy Day. J & M Productions [demo]. (undated).

Jimmy Day and the Texas Outlaw Jam Band. J & M Productions [pre-release edition]. (undated).

In the more than thirty year period they've known each other, Jimmy and Willie have often worked together, most notably as part of Willie's backing band, The Record Men (along with Wade Ray and Johnny Bush). Day also supplied the "snap rhythm" effect on Willie's Hank Williams tribute (released on the Rhino box set that was discussed as part of the section on Willie's first recordings). Not only was Jimmy an on and off part of Willie's band, especially in the mid-sixties, he also backed on occasion or played in the bands of Ray Price, Johnny Bush, Ernest Tubb, Lefty Frizzell, Jim Reeves, Ferlin Husky, George Jones, Charlie Louvin, and Don Walser. His long and illustrious career culminated in his elections into the International Steel Guitar Hall of Fame (1982), the Texas Steel Guitar Hall of Fame (1986), and the Texas Western Swing Hall of Fame (1994).

Late in his career, Jimmy began to record his legendary steel guitar playing for the tiny company, J & M Productions of Buda, Texas. As Willie has been prone to do with many long-time musical and personal friends, he played on a couple of the projects, both of them instrumental recordings. The first was a collection Jimmy recorded of a montage of his "rarest" recordings. Willie played on 'The Way You See Me' and 'Rainy Day Blues'.

The album came out as a "demo." Whatever the further intent was for the collection, it has remained available only in this initial state, as a cassette obtainable through mail order or select distributors. One outlet that has readily stocked the album was Scotty's Music of St. Louis (314 427-7794).

The other project on which Willie played came out as *Jimmy Day and the Texas Outlaw Jam Band,* also on the J & M label. It appeared in a special "pre-release edition" and has remained in that format, as a cassette one may order through the mail or request from specialists such as Scotty's Music. The album was described, on the cover, as a "live" instrumental set recorded at Arlyn Studio in Austin - i. e. no separations, no headphones. The selections ranged from Billy Strayhorn's 'Take the "A" Train' (made famous by Duke Ellington and his orchestra) to the classic big band hit of 1940, 'Tuxedo Junction'.

Day hailed from Tuscaloosa, Alabama. He began his career as the steel guitarist for Webb Pierce, who did much of his playing then at the Louisiana Hayride. In the Spring of 1952, he did a few shows with Hank Williams. By November, Hank had approached Day asking him to join a new band he was going to start touring with in early January of 1953. Jimmy went over to his mom's house that New Year's day. She was listening to the radio and told him, "Hank's dead." Jimmy remembered just sitting there while "everybody was very sad."

Jimmy's tenure on the Hayride opened up for him the opportunity to work with a very young charismatic musician just beginning to tear up the Southern circuits, Elvis Presley. Early in 1955 (while appearing on the Hayride), Elvis added D. J. Fontana, Floyd Cramer, and Jimmy in with his other two musicians, Bill Black and Scotty Moore to form a six piece group. Throughout 1955, they played most of Elvis' shows that way.

Then when Elvis left for Hollywood in 1956, he asked all five of the players to go with him. Both Day and Cramer declined to go because they wanted to move on to Nashville and the Grand Ole Opry. Reminiscing about that fateful decision not to stay with Elvis, Jimmy said, "it would have changed rock 'n' roll forever. Rock 'n' roll would have had a steel guitar."

Jimmy did very well for himself despite the missed Elvis opportunity. Close friend and producer, DeWitt Scott, appraised that:

> in the minds of many people, Jimmy is the best. When you listen to Jimmy playing a slow ballad, you will hear sounds no other player can duplicate. He just seems to melt into the steel and squeezes the pedals to milk every sound he can with his phrasing.

Country music historian, Rich Kienzle, saw in Day's pedal steel work, "a different, more flexible sound that permitted his pedal changes to be used almost as rhythmic device." He achieved a "chord-based sound" that made effective use of the pedal to "create rhythmic, swirling chords that came out on the beat." Kienzle wrote that the best examples of Day's later work came on Willie's Atlantic Records album, *Shotgun Willie*. He was just as great on Willie's Hank Williams tribute, bringing with him the experience of having played behind Hank on some shows in the spring of 1952. In fact, Hank had asked Jimmy to join a new band that was going to tour with him starting a few weeks after New Year's 1953.

Old Ways. (Neil Young). Geffen GHS-24068. (1985).

Farm Aid at the Superdome. (Neil Young with Crazy Horse). Tornado TOR065. (1994)

In 1985, Willie did a duet with Canadian rocker Neil Young on 'Are There Any More Real Cowboys' for Neil's *Old Ways* album. The album became one of several that Geffen Records considered "non-commercial" Neil Young sets. Young's biographer, John Robertson, wrote that *Old Ways* showed how close Neil had become "to country veterans like Willie Nelson and Waylon Jennings."

The label sued Neil, the artist, charging he was deliberately withholding better material and sticking them with inferior releases, or "unrepresentative" product, as his albums for Geffen were called. Young, on the other hand, felt that Geffen Records interfered with his creativity. In 1987, Geffen elected to free Young from his recording contract. That was after Neil told the company:

> the longer you sue me for playing country music, the longer I'm going to play country music. Either you back off or I'm going to play country music forever. And then you won't be able to sue me because country music will be what I always do, so it won't be uncharacteristic anymore.

It was too bad that Geffen couldn't foresee just how popular and "money-making" country music was going to become less than ten years down the road, thanks to stars like Garth Brooks and Leann Rimes.

On July 4, 1985, Neil appeared at Willie's picnic in Austin and sang, among a host of other songs, 'Are There Any More Real Cowboys' as a duet with Willie. Nine days later Neil was at the Live Aid benefit show in 1985 when Bob Dylan made his famous remark to the effect that some of the money should go to the American farmer. That was the comment that precipitated Willie's Farm Aid efforts. Neil almost immediately became one of the leading supporters of Farm Aid,

> recruiting rock musicians (including Dylan) for the first Farm Aid concert, and performing there himself with Harvesters.

In mid-July 1985, Neil and Willie filmed a video for their single 'Are There Any More Real Cowboys'. While making that video, the two first discussed "the possibility of staging a concert to benefit American farmers." At the first Farm Aid concert, Young opened the show by performing 'Are There Any More Real Cowboys' with Willie. Because of all the rock and country artists who played at the show, Farm Aid I was able to raise approximately nine million dollars "to help alleviate the financial problems of American farmers."

Later in 1985, Neil flew to Washington to lobby senators to support Iowa Senator Tom Harkin's Farm Policy Reform Act. Neil stayed involved with Farm Aid and at the 1993 concert, he not only performed Ian Tyson's 'Four Strong Winds' with Willie, he came back for an encore duet with Nelson on 'Are There Any More Real Cowboys'. In 1994, a bootleg album of his performance at the event (held in the Superdome) surfaced, featuring a lengthy and spirited version, done with Willie, of the Bob Dylan song, 'All Along the Watchtower'.

Stop All That Jazz. (Leon Russell). Shelter SR-2108. (1974).

Legend in My Time: Hank Wilson Vol. III. (Leon Russell). ARK 21 61868 10022 2. (1998).

Willie played rhythm guitar on the Tim Hardin composition, 'If I Were a Carpenter', for the original 1974 release of Russell's *Stop All That Jazz* album. The 1990 compact disc rerelease (DCC Compact Classics SRZ-8011) of that album added two bonus cuts. The first featured Willie and Leon doing a vocal duet (with Willie also on rhythm guitar) on the old Roy Acuff signature song, 'Wabash Cannonball'. The second had Willie playing rhythm guitar (only) on the Rolling Stone classic, 'Wild Horses'.

All three cuts were recorded at the same time and place, Pete's Place (the Pete being steel guitar player Pete Drake) in Nashville. Among the premier session players were (in addition to Drake) Linda Hargrove and Edwin Scruggs, acoustic guitars and John Cale, electric guitar. 'Wabash Cannonball', featuring Willie and Leon (performing as Hank Wilson), hit number ninety-one (lasting for two weeks) on the country singles charts in 1984. Its original album appearance came in 1984 on Leon's *Hank Wilson, Vol. II* album, Paradise PRL-0002. That album did not sell very well and has remained out of print, making this extended release of *Stop All That Jazz* the best place to find the cut.

Hank Wilson, Vol. II and *Stop All That Jazz* were not the only recordings on which Willie and Leon worked together. Their musical relationship extended back to Willie's days at Liberty and forward to their critically acclaimed duet album on Columbia, *One for the Road*. Fortunately, it didn't end there. In 1998, Leon revived his Hank Wilson persona for *Legend in My Time: Hank Wilson Vol. III*. Willie was very much involved, dueting with Leon on two cuts, the George Jones favorite, 'He Stopped Lovng Her Today' and Merle Haggard's anthem, 'Okie from Muskogee'. The album featured a very innovative technological breakthrough, audio liner notes, which could be listened to by pausing on track one and pushing rewind.

"Without a Song":

The Cuts on "Various Artists" Compilations

All American Cowboys. Kat Family FZ-38126. (1983).

In 1983 on this compilation, *All American Cowboys,* from the small independent label, Kat Family, Willie sang with Jeannie Seely on 'You've Been Leaving Me for Years'. He also did 'I Would Have Loved You All Night Long' and 'What Can You Do to Me Now'. That was one of two 1983 "various artists" compilation appearances for Willie, the other being a representative sampling from five years (1972-1976) of the Kerrville (Texas) Folk Festival.

Texas Folk and Outlaw Music: Kerrville Festivals 1972-1976. Adelphi AD-4122/3. (1983).

Willie performed 'The Party's Over' on a 1983 collection of performances from the "legendary" Kerrville, Texas festivals, a town already known as "the home" of Jimmie Rodgers (he built a "mansion" there though his birthplace was Meridian, Mississippi), the blue yodeler. The cut dated from the early seventies. Many artists such as Michelle Shocked got their starts at this gathering, which tended to feature singer/songwriters. Previously, in 1973, Willie's cut was included on the first volume of selections gathered from the Festival entitled, *Kerrville Folk Festival 1973, Vol. 1,* PSG PSG-24.

They Come to America. A&M WR-98334. (1986).

Willie contributed a track, 'Let America Be America Again', to a 1986 compilation, the purpose of which was "to benefit the restoration of the Statue of Liberty." As a project, it was the only one of its kind to be "officially licensed" by the Statue of Liberty/Ellis Island Foundation. It featured across the board performances from Waylon Jennings, Glen Campbell, Sandi Patti, The New York Philharmonic Orchestra, and even the late Kate Smith.

Renegade Heart. (Don Steele). Catholic Comm. Svcs. CCS-1986. (1986).

Willie contributed 'Those Healing Hands of Time' to a special 1986 release from Don Steele. It was a very limited release intended to benefit a Catholic charity. As such, it has become one of Willie's rarest releases.

Folkways: A Vision Shared: A Tribute to Woody Guthrie and Leadbelly. Columbia Records CK 44034. (1988).

In 1988, a video and companion soundtrack album was compiled to honor two great artists of folk music, Leadbelly and Woody Guthrie. Contributing artists ranged from Bob Dylan to Little Richard. Willie added his unique interpretation of Guthrie's 'Philadelphia Lawyer'.

The song actually began life as 'Reno Blues'. Woody wrote it sometime late in 1937 to sing on a radio show he was doing with Lefty Lou (Maxine Crissman) for KFVD Los Angeles. He got the idea from a listener, who, according to Woody's biographer, Joe Klein, sent him "a press clipping about a cowboy who killed a lawyer in a fight over a woman in Reno."

The music was based on an old folk song, 'The Jealous Lover'. As time passed, Woody's song came to be referred to either as 'Reno Blues' or 'Philadelphia Lawyer'. The song also became one of the few he wrote that was covered by a country musician or musicians.

In this case, the artists were The Maddox Brothers and Rose (Rose being sister Rose Maddox). In 1947 (the year his son Arlo was born), Woody was informed that the country group was going to record his ten year old ballad. They did and according to country music historian, Barry McCloud, it was one of two songs that made "the biggest impact" for them.

For a 1996 interview with Joe Ross (published in *Bluegrass Unlimited*), Rose recalled the song. She said that in 1949, their "biggest was 'Philadelphia Lawyer'." She said they tried to sing the song during their 1949 debut on the Grand Ole Opry, but they couldn't "because they had to get clearance on it, and they didn't have time to get clearance." So, in 1949, a song by the left-wing people's poet, Woody Guthrie, might have made it onto a Grand Ole Opry show, but for a legal complication.

Red Hot + Country. Mercury 314-522 639-2. (1994).

As an AIDS Benefit from a select group of country artists, the 1994 collection, *Red Hot + Country,* boasted a duet between fellow Texan Jimmie Dale Gilmore and Willie on Nelson's standard 'Crazy'. Many other artists ranging from Johnny Cash to Mary Chapin Carpenter contributed tracks to this anthology. On each track, the artist or artists were asked to perform the song in a style which had influenced them.

For example, Cash picked 'Forever Young', a Bob Dylan original. Others reached back to Jimmie Rodgers and the Carter Family. Some were more contemporary, such as the Nanci Griffith track including Jimmy Webb on his song, 'If These Old Walls Could Speak'. All in all, this was a very eclectic collection.

Don Was produced the set, remembering that right from the start, "everything clicked." He said, "at first we played it very safe." Then when it became "obvious it was gonna work, we became more adventurous." At that point Was did some "pretty radical reworkings" of specific songs, especially the duets by Lyle Lovett and Al Green and Trisha Yearwood and Aaron Neville.

Mama's Hungry Eyes: A Tribute to Merle Haggard. Arista 18760. (1994).

In 1994, a tribute to Merle Haggard was put together. It found Nelson singing Merle's classic, 'Today I Started Loving You Again'. Willie was no stranger to Merle's song, having recorded it for a 1971 RCA album. He was quoted in the notes as saying,

> Merle Haggard is a great musician... and this sort of goes unnoticed - but listen to Merle pick... what more can I say, Merle and I are Poncho and Lefty...

Haggard told Robyn Flans of *Country Weekly* that he wrote 'Today I Started Loving You Again' three weeks after he had first spoken those same words to then-wife, Bonnie Owens, and she had replied, "damn, that sounds like a great song." It was after a show when Bonnie had gone out to get Merle some food that he sat down:

> in the middle of the bed in my shorts. While she was gone, I wrote the song on a paper bag that I tore in the middle and spread out. She came back up, I grabbed my guitar and sang it for her and she started crying.

Other highlights of the album, in addition to Willie's contribution were Emmylou Harris' rendition of 'Mama's Hungry Eyes' and the Clint Black (he sounds amazingly like the Hag at times) version of 'I Take a Lot of Pride in What I Am'. The net proceeds and royalties from sales of the album were donated to Second Harvest, a nation-wide network of food banks.

Come Together: America Salutes the Beatles. Liberty Records CDP-7243-8-31712-2-4. (1995).

A 1995 (part pop, part country) compilation tribute to the Beatles featured Willie doing the Lennon-McCartney tune, 'One After 909'. The song was written by John and Paul in 1957, six years before their "overnight" rise to international fame and superstardom. John told *Playboy* magazine that he wrote it "when I was about seventeen. I lived at 9 New Castle Road. I was born on the ninth of October, the ninth month." At one point, after the Beatles had recorded the song, John apologized for the words, explaining that he had always meant to rewrite them.

The non-country artists on the set were Delbert McClinton, David Ball, Phil Keaggy, Huey Lewis, and Susan Ashton & Gary Chapman. Along with Willie, Tanya Tucker, Randy Travis, and Chet Atkins led a contingent of all-star country artists. Prior to the release of the album, Willie was featured on a video of the song he contributed. Willie has said that in his early days he would often perform a Bob Wills tune and a Beatles song on the same venue.

Tower of Song: The Songs of Leonard Cohen. A&M Records 31454 0259 2. (1995).

Willie sang 'Bird on the Wire' on a 1995 "various artists" tribute to legendary Canadian singer/songwriter, poet, and novelist Leonard Cohen. The classic song had been previously "covered" by artists ranging from Joe Cocker to Judy Collins. Willie's interpretation added new dimensions to the piece.

Other artists on the compilation were Sting, Tori Amos, and Don Henley, putting Willie in some pretty "heady" company. He and Trisha Yearwood were the only "country" artists included. Overall, the album sold well enough to peak at number one hundred ninety-eight on the national album sales charts.

One Voice. MCA Records MCAD11403. (1996).

This 1996 compilation was the culmination of a Michael Omartian production project for the 1996 Atlanta Summer Olympic games. Omartian wrote the lead track, 'Atlanta Reel '96' and produced all but one of the rest of the tracks, including 'We Must Believe in Magic', a duet between Willie and rockabilly country artist Marty Stuart, who also played twelve string guitar and mandolin on the cut. The song itself was written by Bob McDill and Allen Reynolds. Other album highlights included the Amy Grant/Patty Loveless interpretation of 'Every Kinda People' and 'From a Distance' by the unlikely trio of Nanci Griffith, Raul Malo, and Donna Summer.

The Best of Austin City Limits - Country Music's Finest Hour.
Columbia/Legacy Records CT 065007. (1996).

Austin City Limits has been a Public Broadcasting Service mainstay show since 1975 when it first aired as a Willie Nelson pilot. That original broadcast was produced by the Station Program Cooperative. The exposure it gave Willie came at the same time he finally broke loose as a major country music star and was obviously an important factor in his emergence. As Bill Arhos, the executive producer of the show, said, "it's not like we made Willie a star, but we took the dust cover off him at the right time."

From the original pilot show, Willie has been a frequent performer over the years. One of his most famous shows was a "landmark project called 'Swingin' Over the Rainbow'." That special paid tribute to Django Reinhardt as well as Western Swing guitarists, Zeke Campbell and Eldon Shamblin.

There have been a number of televised programs put together to sample the "best" of the long-running and very popular show. In 1996, Columbia Records, through it Legacy imprint, compiled this "best of" audio set (cassette and compact disc - there was also a companion video) that featured artists and their songs ranging from Merle Haggard and 'Silver Wings' to Asleep at the Wheel and 'Boogie Back to Texas'. Obviously for so many years of great music, a fifteen song retrospective would seem to be far too limited a summation.

It would be perfect, for example, to have an audio version of that great Willie tribute show to Reinhardt. For now, however, Willie has been represented on this compilation by his live 1976 version of 'Blue Eyes Crying in the Rain'. The excellent and informative liner notes were also by Mr. Nelson.

In them, he wrote that his contribution to this compilation was 'Red Headed Stranger' and then proceeded to reminisce about the song, revealing that "I had no idea it was going to become the biggest hit of my career!" He recalled that he:

> did the very first pilot show for *Austin City Limits* in 1974, and was glad to be part of the launching.

In closing, he acknowledged that "I'm glad that we're both still around and doin' well!" In 1998, Willie appeared on the show as a major part of a Townes Van Zandt tribute.

The Songs of Jimmie Rodgers - A Tribute. Egyptian Records/Columbia
CK 67676. (1997).

Willie's musical friend and collaborator, Bob Dylan, was the
"impetus" behind this intensely felt Jimmie Rodgers tribute album, the
first release on Bob's new Egyptian label (distributed by Sony). Bob
wrote the liner notes, stating that Mr. Rodgers was "one of the guiding
lights of the twentieth century." In them, he gave Jimmie due credit as
being "par excellence with no equal." He succinctly concluded that
Rodgers' message was "all between the lines" and that Jimmie
delivered it "like nectar that can drill through steel."

Seeing Rodgers as "the man who started it all," Dylan brought
together a roster of songs and artists that ranged from his own cover of
'My Blue Eyed Jane' (remember my "blue-eyed son?"), featuring
production by Daniel Lanois and backing by Emmylou Harris, to Mary
Chapin Carpenter's rendition of 'Somewhere Down Below the Mason
Dixon Line', featuring "cheesy travel guitar" by John Jennings. Willie,
with Byron Berline on fiddle, Jim Keltner on drums, and Don Was
producing, did a mesmerizing version of 'Peach Pickin' Time in
Georgia'. Other compilation highlights were Dwight Yoakam's
version of 'T for Texas' and Van Morrison's eclectic interpretation of
'Mule Skinner Blues'.

Willie's choice was a song about which Rodger's "fiddler,"
Clayton "Pappy" McMichen said,

> yes, I wrote the words and music to 'Peach Pickin' Time in
> Georgia' and played it on the Victor recording with him with
> Slim Bryant on guitar.

Rodgers, as band leader and top name, did get co-writing credit.
McMichen, one of the best fiddlers in early country music, worked with
Rodgers on his major recordings, yet was more than a mere band member,
recalling that he took care of Jimmie "to the point of administering
morphine shots." Clayton once described Jimmie as being "very high-
strung, yet he was full of fun."

Rodgers had been previously honored by a number of tribute
albums, most notably Merle Haggard's *Same Train - A Different Time:
A Tribute to Jimmie Rodgers*. Bob purposely stated that he:

> didn't see any point to making a record like Merle Haggard's,
> so I had to find another way to get Jimmie's music out there.

He did it by bringing together a number of performers and letting each
one choose:

the song they wanted. Everybody was free to suggest their choice. I could hear the influences in the music in just about all the performers on the record, one way or another.

Ironically, Bob was turned onto Rodgers' music by another tribute album, one by Hank Snow. Bob recalled that,

when I was growing up, I had a record called *Hank Snow Sings Jimmie Rodgers*. That's the first clue I had that Jimmie was unique.

Upon hearing the songs, he:

could tell they were from a different period of time, and I was drawn to their power. On the surface their lyrics seemed funny and bright, but underneath they could be alarmingly dark and dreary.

Snow was indeed an ardent admirer of Rodgers, recording not one but four tribute albums (though one was a ten inch LP) dedicated to the memory of Jimmie, the singing brakeman.

Heritage. Six Degrees/Island Records 314 524 434 2. (1997).

1997 continued to be a busy year for Willie the collaborator as he contributed one track to this "various artists" venture consisting of interpretations of traditional and folk music by contemporary artists including Mary Chapin Carpenter, Bela Fleck, Mavis Staples, John Hartford, Tim O'Brien, and many others. The collection came out on an Island Records subsidiary label, Six Degrees. Island, of course, was the reggae label that issued Willie's *Spirit* album.

The project's mover and shaker was Darol Anger, a former member of the Turtle Island String Quarter, an innovative chamber ensemble. In an interview with Derk Richardson (for *Strings* magazine), Anger called *Heritage* a collection of "some of my favorite American folk material." He added that:

it started out as kind of a hobby project to test my home studio, and it became, with the encouragement from some friends of mine at this new record company, Six degrees, a gigantic, many-headed beast, with many people I know - and some people I've never met - playing on it.

Willie sang the vocals to 'Hard Times Come Again No More' while backing himself on guitar along with David Grisman on mandolin, Philip Aaberg on piano, and Anger, on violin. The song was written by Stephen Foster in 1855. Actually he wrote the words to his own adaptation of a melody from a traditional black church song.

Foster's brother, Morrison, wrote that Stephen he had been fond of the "singing and boisterous devotions" he had heard in a "church of shouting colored people" when he was a boy and had:

> stored up in his mind 'many a gem of purest ray serene,' drawn from these caves of negro melody.

Those gems became two songs, according to Stephen, 'Hard Times, Come Again No More' and 'Oh! Boys, Carry Me 'Long'. Foster's biographer, William W. Austin, felt that the words to 'Hard Times' were derived from writings by Charles Dickens that had a similar sentiment.

Darol Anger wrote, in the notes to the CD, that "the sentiments of the lyric" will always "be with us." According to Anger, Willie's manager suggested the song, which fit quite well with the overall theme of the project, to show "traditional music as a river connecting the present with our parents, grandparents and on back." The "river" song was none other than 'Shenandoah', which opened and closed the set, as sung by Jane Siberry.

The project took over a year and a half to complete. Sometimes there were serious time constraints, as with getting Willie's cut done. Anger remembered that Willie "was available only for a two-hour period between ten and noon on one day." With Darol's careful "mapping" of people's time, he completed a critically acclaimed collection of "stuff that I love," a set of tunes that "have all stayed with me a long, long time."

The IRS was relentless!
(Photo from Will van Overbeek)

"Heartland":

The Sideman/Supporting Player Appearances

A Rumor in My Own Time. (Steve Fromholz). Capitol ST-11521. (1976).

Willie played lead guitar on 'Knockin' on Wood' for the 1976 major label effort by Steve Fromholz, a legendary Texas songwriter from Temple, Texas, in the class of Guy Clark and Rodney Crowell. Fromholz was briefly signed to Willie's Lone Star label in the late seventies. The label released his album entitled, *Just Playin' Along*, in 1979, though Willie did not participate in the making of that album, save for being the label owner.

The Fromholz song, 'Man With the Big Hat' was done by Willie and Jerry Jeff Walker on Jerry's *Live at Gruene Hall* album. One of Fromholz's songs, 'I'd Have to Be Crazy' was a hit single for Willie in 1976. Steve's voice was on the recording because, in the studio, Willie asked him to sing along on the chorus. In 1983, on the Felicity label, Steve and Willie released a single called 'Hondo's Song'.

Bare. (Bobby Bare). Columbia KC-35314. (1978).

Willie backed old friend, singer-songwriter Bobby Bare, on this album, Bare's first for Columbia. Waylon Jennings was another of the friends who appeared with Bobby on the album. Prior to this effort, Bare, a native of Ironton, Ohio, had already had a dozen top ten hits for both RCA and Mercury. His most famous single featured his rendition of the country classic, 'Detroit City' (written by Danny Dill and Mel Tillis).

A Legendary Performer. (Chet Atkins). RCA CPL1-2503. (1978).

A number of Chet Atkins friends and RCA label-mates (all of the artists on the Nashville roster - billing themselves as "Some of Chet's Friends"), including Willie, got together to do an improvised song, 'Chet's Tune', with Chet. The cut finally appeared on a 1978 RCA compilation. Chet, of course, was one of Willie's two main producers when he was with RCA. He also became, on an international scale, one of the best guitarists ever, ranking up there with Les Paul and Django Reinhardt.

The song, itself, was written by Cy Coben specifically as a tribute to Chet. Recording was done April 6, 1967. Each artist sang a short phrase. Willie's was "from Montreal to San Antone" and he sang after Waylon sang his part. Porter Wagoner followed Willie. Though Floyd Cramer played piano, Chet did not join in on guitar. Jerry Reed did, however, and true to Chet's proclivity for strings, there were three violins, a cello, and a viola in the background.

If You Think I'm Crazy Now. (Geezinslaw Brothers). Lone Star L-4606. (1979).

Of the various country acts signed to Willie's Lone Star label, during the seventies, when it was distributed by PolyGram, the Geezinslaw Brothers were an outrageously talented and funny country comedy group. They recorded for the label for a short time. Willie's grandson was in the group (the nucleus of which was two long long-time friends, Austin natives Sam Allred and Raymond Smith, not brothers) during their Lone Star tenure. For their 1979 album, Willie played guitar behind the group. The Geezinslaws also appeared at a number of Willie's picnics.

My First Album. (Jody Payne & the Willie Nelson Family Band). Kari KARI-5000. (1980).

Willie's band has always been a talented lot, so it has been no surprise that some have recorded their own albums. One of Willie's hopes in opening his own studio was to be able to record deserving musicians who couldn't get a studio break elsewhere. Who could be more talented to record than one's own band members?

Jody Payne has always seemed to have been Willie's guitarist. At the time he went to work for Willie, he was married to singer Sammi Smith and "playing in her band." Willie said he "really liked the way he played backup, and I liked the way he sang harmony." Payne was a member of Willie's road band long before that road band was able to do studio recordings with the boss.

He has been on virtually all of Willie's Columbia recordings, except where a producer brought in studio players of his own. In return,

Willie did background vocals for "family member" Payne on 'There's a Crazy Man' and 'Uncle Pen' for his 1980 album. By being a band member of long standing, Jody got his motion picture break in *Honeysuckle Rose*. In 1992, Willie played lead guitar on a single cut recorded by Jody of a song, 'Heart of the Matter' that Jody tried to market on his own Jody Payne label (SS-101).

Floyd Tillman and Friends. Gilleys MG-5004. (1981).

Johnny Lee, Willie, Merle Haggard, and Ernest Tubb joined Floyd Tillman in 1981 on one of his last albums, recorded on Mickey Gilley's short-lived label.   Willie once said that Tillman, from Ryan, Oklahoma (though he grew up in Texas), was one of "the three writers who've probably influenced me the most." The other two were Johnny Mercer and Hoagy Carmichael. He was quoted as saying (in 1981) that he'd love to do a Floyd Tillman album. With material like, 'Slippin' Around', that would be a rich album indeed.

Incidentally, when Tillman first took 'Slippin' Around' to the charts in 1949, his version reached only to number five. Then, not one but two covers, the first by Ernest Tubb and the other by the team of Jimmy Wakely and Margaret Whiting (their version also hit number one pop), proceeded to hit country number one after Tillman's. Tillman has unfortunately been forgotten (in spite of his 1984 Country Music Hall of Fame induction) among the rush of "new country" sounds.

However, back in 1949, as *Billboard* magazine noted, the only country artist of the time to approach Hank Williams' ability to get his country songs to later hit in "the pop field," was:

> Floyd Tillman, who had three songs that switched from
> country hits on Columbia to pop hits elsewhere on wax within
> a 16 month period.

For example, his song, 'It Makes No Difference Now', became a major national crossover hit for Bing Crosby in 1941. 'I Love You So Much It Hurts' was a top ten hit for the Mills Brothers in 1949.

We Are the World. (USA for Africa). Columbia USA 40043. (1985).

In 1985, Willie was again part of a multiple artist setting (along with Dylan, Michael Jackson, and too many others to list), this time to sing together on the single and title cut of the album, *We Are the World*. The song was recorded and marketed for the purpose of helping to alleviate starvation in Africa. Lionel Richie, Michael, and Quincy Jones were the primary movers behind the project.

Jammin' with J. R. and Friends. (J. R. Chartwell). CA LA-0003. (1985).

A 1985 album by the swing fiddler and fellow Texan, J. R. Chartwell, was recorded at Willie's Pedernales studio and featured Willie as guest performer. J. R. also was said to have worked with Willie on one of the Atlantic albums. This set was marketed by CA Records and Films of San Marcos, Texas.

Feel the Fire. (The Family Brown). RCA/Canada KKL1-0564. (1985).

In 1985, Willie worked with one of the premier Canadian maritime groups, The Family Brown. He appeared on the cut, 'Together Again', featured on their Canadian-only album. Maritime music is really country music as played in the Canadian maritime provinces.

Still Within the Sound of My Voice. (Glen Campbell). MCA MCAC-42009. (1987).

For Arkansas-born Glen, this 1987 album was a major attempt to return to past chart glories, such as the albums he made for Capitol. Those albums featured some of Jimmy Webb's best material, songs like 'Wichita Lineman' and 'Galveston'. The title cut for this set, 'Still Within the Sound of My Voice', was another Webb composition.

Steve Wariner sang the duet part with Glen on one of the cuts, 'The Hand That Rocks the Cradle'. According to Glen, the song originally came from Charley Pride, who was going to do the duet part once Glen cut his part. At the time, Charley was between labels after getting bumped from RCA.

Then Charley got a new contract with a smaller company. He decided not to do the duet, so Steve got the call. Emmylou Harris sang with Glen on the cut, 'You Are'. The "background vocals" on the album were done by Willie and Lee Greenwood along with Glen, himself, and Curtis "Mr. Harmony" Young (as he was billed in the credits).

Glen made the point in his autobiography that "recording legends" such as Charley Pride, Loretta Lynn, and Willie Nelson, among others, no longer "even have recording contracts." He felt like country music had gotten away from the "thoughtful lyrics" of the past. He noted that of all the songs today's country fans counted among their favorites, most were "historical ones."

A country boy from Delight, Arkansas, Glen worked his way from acclaimed session guitarist, to traveling member of the Beach Boys, into a career as a country artist that culminated with the 1975 hit, 'Rhinestone Cowboy'. For a time, he even had his own TV show, *The Glen Campbell Goodtime Hour*. But as with too many artists, as they've aged, their sales have dropped. In 1985, Glen returned with an

HBO special, *The Silver Anniversary of the Rhinestone Cowboy*, which featured Willie as a special guest.

Duck Soup: Dead Solid Perfect. Pedernales Records. (1994).

Willie was one of the guest artists for this low-budget album set recorded at his Pedernales studio. According to *ICE* magazine, it was set for a 1994 release date. They reported on it because of Willie's involvement. Not much else was forthcoming about this set except the imminent release date. When I asked Willie's manger, Mark Rothbaum, about the recording, he said he wasn't even aware of it.

Hand to Mouth. (Mickey Raphael). En Pointe 0006. (Undated).

Mickey Raphael, out of Dallas, has been a long-standing member of Willie's band, in Willie's words, "a great harmonica player." They first met outside a Dallas recording studio when Mickey was a teenager. Raphael has said that in some ways, Willie practically raised him.

Willie recalled that Mickey came up to him and said "he was our new harmonica player." Mickey said that when he first:

joined Willie's band, I really didn't know anything about country music. I'd never listened to it at all.

Thanks to his studying a number of harmonica players like Charlie McCoy, Mickey's playing grew to an innovative level, initially on the *Red Headed Stranger* album, where he added some especially distinctive yet subtle "echo" sounds from his harmonica to 'Blue Eyes Crying in the Rain'.

Guitarist Grady Martin impressed on him "the importance of tunefulness." Mickey explained that was why:

on 'Georgia on My Mind', which is in the key of C, I use a D-minor harp - it's a natural minor scale - and I can play the melody line just the way Willie sings it, whereas on an F Marine Band, I'm really just playing licks along with the song.

He added that:

with Willie I try to play a lot of rhythm stuff and a lot of string-line things behind him so it's not just hot licks, so that you don't get burned out on it.

Of the boss, Mickey once said, "Willie Nelson is a modern day Shakespeare who travels around with a band of gypsies." He could not ever envision leaving Willie's band, in which he has also played diatonic organ, saying,

> we work all the time. He has a loyal band because he in turn is very supportive of the people he works with. He's not like other touring pros who hire a new band all the time.

Willie was one of the featured musicians, including Paul Butterfield and Lee Michaels, on Mickey's first, only, and undated album release. Butterfield and saxophonist King Curtis were both once listed by Mickey as two of his biggest influences.

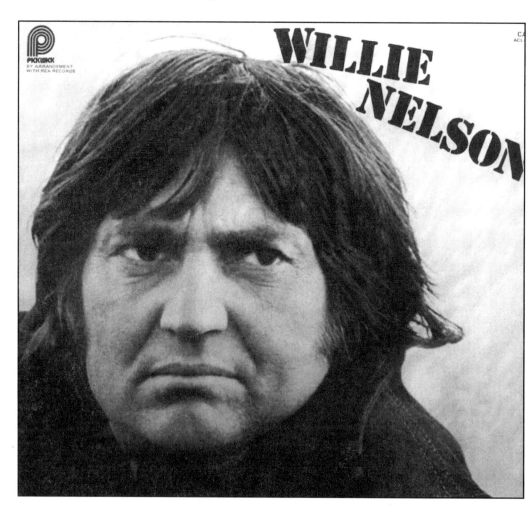

A budget album!
(Photo from RCA Records and Willie Nelson)

"Sorry, Willie":

The Willie Nelson Tributes

Tribute albums have long been a tradition in country music. In past years it was almost a requirement for a then currently hot artist to pay homage to the preceding star or stars who had either been influences or instrumental in getting one's career started. Hank Williams has been feted by various tribute albums more than a hundred times while Jimmie Rodgers has received more than half a dozen.

Loretta Lynn has acknowledged her debt to Patsy Cline, Dolly Parton has honored her early mentor, Porter Wagoner, and Del Reeves has remembered Jim Reeves. Some Hall of Fame artists, however, like George Jones, have never even rated one tribute, even though recently the budget label, K-Tel, threw together some of Johnny Paycheck's old renditions of George Jones songs and called it a "tribute."

Willie has done tributes to Kris Kristofferson, Lefty Frizzell, and recently, Hank Williams. He has said that he would love to do full albums of Bob Wills, Floyd Tillman, and George Jones music. Recently, Willie was the recipient of an "alternative" tribute, which served to show how universal his music has become.

Before that, Columbia compiled (in 1981, after Ray had signed with Dimension Records) a Ray Price set of Ray singing five Willie and five Kris Kristofferson cuts, entitled, "A Tribute to Kris and Willie." It was interesting to find Ray associated with Willie songs in 1981, because even though Willie wrote one of Ray's early hits, 'Night Life', and learned to play bass in Ray's band, they had a major falling out when Willie killed one of Ray's prized roosters (for more on the incident, see page 191).

Even though the two men talked about and tried to justify the incident, Ray at the time swore he would never record another Willie song. He didn't for a long time. The two men did reconcile. Even then, it would be hard to visualize a singer of Ray's caliber not recording songs as great as the ones Willie has written continuously over the years.

Surprisingly, the Price compilation and the "alternative" tribute have been the only full albums devoted to Willie's music as done by other artists. The covers of Willie's individual songs number in the hundreds, ranging from Joe Hinton's soulful version of 'Funny How Time Slips Away', that was titled only as 'Funny', to Roy Orbison's perennial holiday version of 'Pretty Paper'.

The pure universality of Willie's songs comes clear when the variety of artists who covered them is considered. For instance, Ray Price first took 'Night Life' up the charts, but since then the song has been "covered" by Roy Orbison, Al Hirt, Doris Day, Lawrence Welk, Marvin Gaye, Aretha Franklin, and perhaps the greatest blues singer of all times, B. B. King. Maybe the song really was too "bluesy."

Elvis covered 'Funny How Time Slips Away' and not just once. His first studio recording of the song came on June 7, 1970 and was included on the 1971 album, *Elvis Country*. In 1972, he included the song on his live album, *Elvis as Recorded at Madison Square Garden*. Another live version, done April 14, 1972 in Greensboro, South Carolina, was included on the 1972 documentary, *Elvis on Tour*. An alternate mix was released on the RCA Record Club album, *Elvis Memories*.

Willie certainly looked different when he first started out!
(Photo from the Michael Ochs Archives)

The Tributes to Willie Nelson - Album Listings

A Tribute to Willie and Kris. (Ray Price). Columbia Records PC 37061. (1981).

Track Listing: Night Life, The Healing Hands of Time, Crazy, I'm Still Not Over You, Funny How Time Slips Away.

Recording Notes: Many country artists have been feted by other admiring country performers. In Willie's case, Ray Price was the admirer. In this 1981 compilation (put together by Columbia, not Ray), Ray saluted Willie by singing five of his best songs.

Of those songs, 'I'm Still Not Over You' and 'Crazy' had formed a two sided hit single for Ray in 1967, reaching number six and number seventy-three, respectively. 'Night Life' had gone to number twenty-eight as the "B" side of Ray's number two smash, 'Make the World Go Away'. Kris Kristofferson and five of his songs were saluted on the other side of the album.

Twisted Willie. (Various Artists). Justice Records JR 0009-2. (1995).

Track Listing: Time of the Preacher (Johnny Cash), Three Days (L7), Shotgun Willie (Tenderloin), Bloody Mary Morning (Supersuckers), She's Not for You (Mark Lanegan), Devil in a Sleepin' Bag (The Presidents of the United States of America), I've Seen All of This World I Care to See (Jerry Cantrell), Pick Up the Tempo (Best Kissers in the World), Still Is Still Moving to Me (Jello Biafra with Life After Life), I Never Cared for You (Waylon Jennings), Hello Walls (The Reverend Horton Heat), I Gotta Get Drunk (Gas Huffer), The

Ghost (Steel Pole Bath Tub), Sad Songs and Waltzes (Jesse Dayton), Home Motel (X), Angel Flying Too Close to the Ground (Kelley Deal with Kris Kristofferson).

Recording Notes: Willie came up to two with this 1995 "various artists" tribute put together by his former label, Justice. Artists on the compilation ranged from The Reverend Horton Heat to Johnny Cash, whose rendition of 'Time of the Preacher' was said by one reviewer to be definitely on the par with Willie's superb version. For a unique approach, check out Jello Biafra's rendition (with Life After Life) of 'Still Is Still Moving to Me'.

Of the album, itself, Willie mused that:

> they all surprised me. I was amazed that they chose some of those songs, because some of them are really obscure.

He added that:

> I'm always glad to see guys coming from every direction, especially if they take a song of mine and stretch it. They can't hurt it. If it's a good song, it'll still be a good song. If it's not, it never was.

He further elaborated that the "guy from Alice in Chains [Jerry Cantrell] did a great rendition of an old song of mine, 'Came to See'." He said he talked to him about the track and learned that "he did it in his bathroom." Overall, Willie was quite "amazed" about the song selection because "some of these songs were written before these guys were born."

Randall Jamail, Justice Records President and "longtime Nelson compadre," produced this tribute with Donnell Cameron engineering. It was Danny Bland, manager of Supersuckers, who first approached Jamail with the "Twisted Willie" concept. Bland saw Willie as:

> an example of what a musician should be. A lot of musicians who've been around for a while have turned into oldies acts, but he just keeps getting more vital as he goes along.

The first important fact about the album was that each cut was recorded live, with minimal overdubs, and (the kicker in this day and age) "without digital effects." Cameron, the engineer, was quoted as explaining that he and Jamail:

> share a similar philosophy of recording, in that we believe the fewer electronics you put between the microphones and the tape machine, the better.

Jamail reinforced Cameron's outlook, saying,

> the fun and creativity of recording and mixing is utilizing things that save the emotion and the mood of the music.

Jamail also said that it was their:

> intention to have the artists interpret these songs as if they were a part of their own repertoire. The only way to tributize Willie was to let these kids do whatever the hell they thought these songs should be. That's what Willie did 30 years ago.

He concluded with a philosophy that neatly summed up why this became an almost perfect tribute album, perhaps the best that has been done in the genre. He said simply that:

> for them to do anything other than reinvent the song in a way that is consistent with the type of music they are making would have been a sham to Willie.

So they proceeded to do some mighty weird things, but all in an effort to create or enhance specific moods.

For example, Jamail wanted Cameron to run Jesse Dayton's "really big vocal sound" on 'Sad Songs and Waltzes' "through a notch filter" to make it sound "weird and messed up." In the end, to achieve the sufficiently strange effect Jamail wanted, they ran it "through a Leslie." On Steel Pole Bath Tub's rendition of 'The Ghost', Jamail had the drums put through one speaker, creating the feeling that the drums sounded "real far away." Cameron thought the idea "worked well with the arrangements."

Another of the artists (on the song 'Angel Flying Too Close to the Ground'), Kelley Deal wanted "to use only guitar feedback and a sewing machine for her track." The sewing machine was used to achieve "a rhythmic bottom" for the track. The machine's sound was built into "a series of tones that take the song into a very spooky kind of place." Cameron said they recorded the sewing machine first and wound up with seven tracks of feedback and a mix that was "a mess."

In came, of all people, Kris Kristofferson. He turned "the mess" into a harmonica part and a vamp vocal, which was run through the Leslie cabinet, creating a recording that "became what it became" minus the feedback. The harmonica became the only musical instrument used on that cut. When Willie heard the cut, he said, "they're destroying the melody." But, he was smiling when he made the observation.

Soundgarden's Kim Thayil played guitar for Johnny Cash's version of 'Time of the Preacher'. According to Willie, when the guitar solo was finished, Cash asked Thayil, "what was the philosophy behind that solo you played?" The answer from Thayil was that "the intention was to destroy the melody."

Overall, the tracks were recorded at many different studios, ranging from one in Seattle to Willie's own Pedernales Studio. One track, 'I've Seen All of This World I Care to See' (a song Willie said was about "the night I laid down in the street outside Tootsie's"), by Jerry Cantrell, was recorded in Cantrell's bathroom by guitar tech Darrell Peters. The location where a particular track was made was not as crucial to Jamail as the equipment used.

He disclosed that he considers "the critical issue for the kind of records" he makes is "the interaction between the musician, the musician's instrument and the microphone." Judging from this album, Jamail makes superb records. Willie was not strictly an observer on this project; he played and sang on both the Horton Heat and Supersuckers tracks. He also revealed, "I like what they've been doing."

Farm Aid has become Willie's passion.
(Photo from HBO and Evelyn Shriver Public Relations)

"Red Headed Stranger":

A Willie Nelson Retrospective

It was no coincidence that country's glory years of the seventies through late eighties coincided with Willie's most prolific years. He reached out to America with his music and resurrected American music, popular song, jazz, blues, and folk. In 1975, he became one of the few country performers to be awarded the Handy Award (from The Blues Foundation), for "keeping the Blues alive in Country Music."

Today country music is not the same. In a 1994 article for *American Heritage,* Tony Scherman described "the generation of George Jones, Merle Haggard, Willie Nelson, and Waylon Jennings" as the "last great infusion of country-music creativity." Those four artists represented the last set of fans who "lived" the experiences written about in the music. Today, fans can "choose" to like country music or not, so the music must appeal to people who have no underlying reason to identify with it. To Scherman, that meant "goodbye to country music."

The creation of a "new" country music designed to have an "across the board" appeal, caused Scherman to conclude that "authenticity" had become a "meaningless criterion." *New York Times* columnist Bruce Feiler specifically charged that country music has now become "more removed from black America than at any time in its history." He concluded that there was not only "a negligible black presence in Nashville" but that it reflected "the new reality of the industry."

Writing in 1998, a reviewer for *Dirty Linen,* a magazine devoted to Folk and World music, saw the same disturbing problem Feiler had discussed. Char R. Leslie-Miller began with the analysis that (in 1994), a would-be black country music artist, Cleve Francis, had:

presented to the Country Music Foundation a 1993 Harris poll of radio listeners that found that 24 percent of the listening audience for country radio was African American.

Leslie-Miller went on to point out that, in spite of the presentation of those numbers, "little has been done about the sorry state of country radio programming" and, as a result, country radio remains "the whitest spot on the dial." Sadly, Leslie-Miller concluded,

> even though country music is as 'black' as all the other American musics, you would never know it by watching TNN [*The Nashville Network*].

The "new" reality Feiler described has also deliberately excluded, against their wishes of course, older "heritage" artists like Charlie Pride, Merle Haggard, and Willie Nelson. Today, country music, with its emphasis on "hunks" and "models" has digressed to a level similar to the one it was in when Willie and Waylon's "outlaw" movement shook it to its knees and out of its bland "sameness" lethargy. As a musical form, it has moved "far from its rural roots." It just experienced a year in which sales and radio listening dropped considerably, with sales down at least eleven percent, perhaps because of too many "hat" acts "doing formula songs."

How far down did country go? By 1994, the year following Willie's departure from Columbia, a country music video producer (who remained anonymous) stated that:

> lyrically, most of what you hear on the charts and in the dance clubs now is just fodder, an utter triumph of style over substance. It's music made for the moment, completely trivial and completely forgettable.

One country music analyst, Clark Parsons, writing in *The Journal of Country Music*, related country music's problems to those experienced in pop music several years ago. He asked, somewhat rhetorically,

> what happened to pop music when the record labels and artists became overly preoccupied with spectacle, lights, hamming, and appearance?

He answered his own question, concluding that "a large portion of the fans ultimately became alienated from the artists and stopped caring." He further warned that "if country acts ... continue to view themselves as stars instead of artists, they're headed for the same kind of trouble pop ran into."

But is it the "acts" who have been driving country music away from its peak position with fans everywhere or is it the record companies? Mark Rothbaum, Willie's manager and advisor recently made the rhetorical comment that, "why should record companies pay Dolly a million when they can pay new acts seventy-five thousand." That is especially true when the labels can successfully market such "new acts." Unfortunately the quality suffers all the way around, especially the quality of the songs.

To Johnny Bush, speaking with Austin newspaper columnist and critic Don McLeese, "it's marketing." He rhetorically asked "why Ray Price and Merle Haggard's and Willie's crowds are still sellouts, and they're not being played on the radio." He answered his own conjecture by describing a Fort Worth disc jockey he knew as "a sweet young lady" who plays "exactly what she's told to play."

Max D. Barnes, who has co-written countless songs recorded in the past by Willie, Vince Gill, Alan Jackson, and Randy Travis among others, observed that record companies have been:

> signing people and wanting them to be a writer so they can control the copyrights. Those guys can't necessarily write well, but they have a record deal, so they get with other writers or they try to write themselves. Consequently the music suffers.

From his viewpoint, "fans are screaming out for better acts, better quality of songs." It was no coincidence that in 1997, Jimmy Bowen, former head of Nashville-based Liberty Records, wrote of country music in a similar vein. He concluded that:

> the music today suffers from a disturbing conformity. You listen to country radio for a couple of hours, and you can't tell whose records you've heard. So much of it sounds the same.

By 1997, the downward spiral of country music was not lost on some of the younger artists who had talent and wanted the same results John Michael Montgomery wanted, "to show a creative side that I haven't had time to do before." What did Montgomery do to create (for release in early 1998), in his words, "one of the most unique albums that I've ever done?" It was quite simple. John Michael "went back and pulled out roots and influences from the Outlaw country days of Willie and Waylon." He may yet help to propel country music back to a place of prominence through a rediscovering of his and the music's roots.

In spite of Willie's seemingly complete banishment from country radio, he has never turned bitter nor has he turned on country music. He has continued to be positive in his outlook, even with respect to the industry, especially its huge impact overseas. Prior to a major tour of several European countries where he has maintained huge followings, he told *Country Weekly* that:

> I've seen country music acceptance in the international marketplace grow by leaps and bounds over the years. They love country music.

Willie recalled that the first time he went to Europe:

> was in the early '60s when Waylon Jennings and I went over there with Hank Snow. Hank Snow was big over there. He had people staying up all night in parking lots to get tickets to his show. I thought it was incredible that people could sing word for word with Hank as he sang each song.

Hank, of course, was a long-term veteran of country music who evolved his musical creations from Jimmie Rodgers-like songs to many classic and trend-setting individualized works. However, early on in his career, his most original material was rejected. For example, in 1949, his label, RCA, told him that a song he had written (which much later, obviously became a country standard), 'I'm Movin' On', "was not a song we should record."

Like Hank, the country music sound Willie has made never had any creative shortcomings - it was not only dynamic, it also set trends. Perhaps that's why he and Hank found it so effortless to record an album together in 1984. Willie's sound has been a wellspring of creativity to which artists of all generations have readily returned for inspiration and new beginnings. Willie wrote his own standards and interpreted some of the greatest songs written by the best writers in all genres of popular music. His recordings have consistently been unique and personal yet filled with familiarity.

Whether they were his own or others, he has always had a way with songs, even when he first started out. In an interview for *No Depression*, Don Walser and Johnny Bush were discussing Willie's style. Walser conjectured that Willie may not be a great singer, but he sure could "sell a song." Bush explained that Willie was really "pitching songs and he wanted to make sure you heard every word." When a disc jockey asked Bush (about Willie's interpretation of Johnny's song, 'Whiskey River') if he thought Willie would "ever learn to sing it right," Bush replied, "I hope not." What Bush knew was that no matter how Willie chose to do a song, his version hit home with the vast majority of listeners.

His personal recording vision has unfolded over a forty plus year period, beginning with a 1955 audition tape. Today those recordings have filled more than two hundred different album collections. The history of Willie Nelson's recording career has been Willie singing himself while he sang America. He recently told an interviewer, "it's like me and a song - we have an edge on the rest of the people."

Songwriting has been a major factor in setting Willie apart from so many other country stars. In 1980, he told an interviewer that:

> 99 percent of what I write has come from my own experience. A person could probably start from my first song and go all the way to my last - if he knew what to look for - and write my autobiography.

Because of the deep personal nature of many of his songs, Willie has been unwilling to let them die. He told me he would love nothing more than to go back to his old albums and pick out his forgotten original songs and rerecord them. As he believed in his music, so have others.

Outside the music world Willie had another edge, a giving, spiritually philanthropic side. He "got" from the world and he gave back, completing what Deepak Chopra called the spiritual law of giving and receiving, which is manifested by keeping "the abundance of the universe circulating in your life." He never forgot those who helped him on the way up, either.

Horace "Hoss" Logan, formerly the voice and almost everything else for the Louisiana Hayride, the weekly radio show which showcased the early careers of talents like Elvis Presley and Hank Williams (he also appeared on the show when his career went into decline), had a very telling personal insight into Willie's "memory." In the early sixties, when Willie was signed to Liberty Records, he regularly appeared in Dallas at the Big D Jamboree (broadcast from the Sportatorium) and at Dewey Groom's Longhorn Ballroom, then one of the largest country nightclubs in Texas. About Groom, Willie told Logan (which Hoss recounted in his 1998 book about the Hayride) that:

> back when I didn't have two coins to rub together and really needed some work, he'd always make a spot for me at the Longhorn - and he always paid me, too.

Not long before Groom retired, his club had declined into hard times and the number of patrons dropped considerably. Nonetheless, even into the early eighties when Willie was commanding huge fees for live performances, he went and played at the Longhorn every few months. When Logan asked Willie how Groom could afford him, Willie answered that "I stay pretty busy these days, but whenever Dewey Groom wants me, I'll be there. And I'll play for whatever he can afford."

That was the same Groom who, according to Willie, swore he wouldn't book Charley Pride or any other black performer into his club. In an extraordinary move, not only did Willie give Pride his first big touring break (agreeing to book him in 1967 as part of what, in Pride's words, became known as "The Willie Nelson Show"), he got Groom and Pride to sleep (drunk and passed out, of course) on the same bed together after getting Charley up on the Longhorn stage.

The way Willie told the story (in his autobiography), the chain of events began when he got drunk one night at the Longhorn while watching Johnny Bush perform. Pride was also there (in the audience). Sufficiently drunk, Willie got onstage and told the crowd they ought to hear Charley sing. He got Pride to the microphone amidst gasps from the audience, especially Groom. Looking at the crowd, he said he knew:

> something special was called for at that moment, so I grabbed Charlie and laid a big kiss on his lips, and once the crowd recovered they listened to Charlie and went crazy for him.

After the show, Willie remembered that he, Pride, Groom, and others went to the motel room and "partied and played songs all night long." Eventually Groom passed out drunk on the same bed with Charley. Willie's summation was that "Dewey sure never had no more prejudice about booking Charlie Pride."

Pride noted, in his autobiography, that after the tour with Willie, doors were opened for him in country music. He said it "dispelled a lot of anxieties about the race factor." Not only did Willie humorously disarm potential racial problems, he even kissed Charley again. Pride recalled a stop in San Antonio during which, in front of a bunch of fans, Willie yelled to him, "Hey, Supernigger, come over here." In front of the whole crowd, Willie grabbed him and kissed him. Charley said "that broke everybody up."

For quite a while after that "kiss," Charley remembered that "Willie called me 'Supernigger'." He saw no problem in Willie's use of the term because, in his mind, it was an effective way:

> of disarming any racists who might be around, a way of taking the language of rancor and throwing it back at them as humor, the way Redd Foxx often did. In the same way that profanity is enfeebled by overuse, the buzzwords of hate can be neutralized by mocking them.

Charley credited Willie as one of several "established singers, who took a chance by taking me onstage with them."

Willie also never lost sight of the importance of his fans. With every concert, even in 1998, he was still making new ones. Two Iowans wrote to *Country Weekly* that when he appeared in Sloan, Iowa, "we wanted to find out why Willie is a legend." Though they had "never been Willie Nelson fans," the two acknowledged, "he showed us. For close to three hours he sang, played guitar and captured the hearts of everyone there." It didn't stop at the end of the concert, according to the two Iowans, as "afterwards, this warm, kind and gentle man visited with fans and obviously loved meeting them."

Another big area for Willie's giving back was to the farmer, an important cause because of its tangible results in saving both families and a key segment of the American economy. In 1987, *Billboard* reprinted part of an interview that Willie did with Jane Ayres for her book, *Hearts of Charity*. One of the key points of the interview was Willie's statement that "if you're looking for a hero, the farmer is it. And farmers can use all the help you can give them."

Willie, "with John Cougar Mellencamp and Neil Young to help me," established Farm Aid to "help farmers help themselves." The goal became to raise money, provide legal assistance, advice hot lines, and much more, including the ability to "network with farmers and farm organizations around the U. S. and develop ideas of what needs to be done." Farm Aid has been a charitable effort that appealed to conservative and liberal forces alike. As country singer, John Conlee, a previous participant in Farm Aid, observed,

> with the help of Willie and others, we brought the family problems to the forefront and some changes began to take place. I'm not a radical or a rebel, but I will stand up and speak my mind on issues that I feel affect me, my family and others, and the farm crisis was, and remains, one of those issues.

Willie boiled the issues to one basic premise, that "we shouldn't jerk the farmer off his land."

During much of the time Willie was raising money to help save the American farmer, the U. S. government (the IRS, specifically) was after him for massive amounts of back taxes. The irony of the situation was not lost on comedian Sam Kinison who joked that, "oh man - poor Willie. See, he thought he owed *Texas*." According to Sam (courtesy of his brother Bill), that was why Willie threw his Fourth of July party every year for free. Then one day,

> the government said, 'No, you don't owe Texas. You owe taxes.' 'What? What are you talking about? I thought I owed Texas.' 'No, you owe taxes, Willie. Seventeen million.' 'Oh fuck, man. I threw that party every year for free!'

Though Farm Aid has been Willie's most visible cause, it was not his only one. Being that he is part Cherokee, the plight of the Native Americans has always been dear to him. In early February 1998, Willie, through his publicist Evelyn Shriver, announced that he had joined with the Kickapoo tribe of Kansas to co-found a satellite television network dedicated to Native American heritage and culture and old-time country music shows.

Willie said he would supervise the channel's programming with a goal of presenting a mix of Indian music and dancing, historical documentaries, along with country music television shows from the 1950's and 1960's. Shriver's announcement underscored the fact that this was something Willie has "talked about for years." The country TV shows will come from his own extensive collection of over seven hundred episodes of *The Porter Wagoner Show* (featuring Dolly Parton) and three hundred and fifty hours of the Wilburn Brothers Show (which featured Loretta Lynn).

How did this venture come about? Willie told Scott Lenz (in 1998) that:

fifteen years ago, I bought a library of these videotapes from Norman Lear. He had a whole shit-slew of 'em - 700 half-hour shows of Porter Wagoner, all the Wilburn Brothers stuff, Del Reeves, Billy Walker, Ralph Emery's *On the Road*, Jerry Lee Lewis and Dolly Parton specials. There's around 1400 hours. We've been 24-hours-a-day since February, and you wouldn't believe the hundreds of letters we've received.

Willie had an ulterior motive. Not only did he want the country music fan to see these old shows, he wanted the latest young performers to view them as well. Willie explained,

I think these up-and-comers should watch this channel and see how the old-time professionals country artists really worked. People like Johnny Cash, Kitty Wells and Roger Miller were very charismatic. I think the young people could learn a lot.

From Willie's point of view, it would allow the younger artists to go back "20, 25 years and compare this music then to the way it is now." What would they come to understand? According to Willie, "there's really no comparison. Everything was so good back then, and it's all watered down now."

So, with Farm Aid, Native American television programming, and over two-hundred live dates per year, Willie the artist and humanitarian is alive and well and more vital than most men half his age. In the interviews I have had with him on his career, he has often said, "I don't want to spend too much time on this." I can't say that I blame him - he has so much else to do.

The Appendices

Willie and Willie, Jr. made a great spiritual album together!
(Photo from Promised Land Music and Evelyn Shriver Public Relations)

Willie was always a great live performer!
(Photo from the Michael Ochs Archives)

The Singles and Their Chart Positions (to 1993)

Given that Willie's singles have been among the major reasons why he rose to place among the greatest artists in Country Music, their chronicling is of great importance. Where to start on a Willie Nelson singles discography was the first question. He was said to have written his first song when he was sixteen years old, or seven, or twelve. According to his own recollection, his first completed song was 'Storm Within My Heart', composed when he was twelve yet containing imagery far beyond his young years. He even put together a songbook of his own works while still in his teens.

On two of his earliest songs, 'What a Way to Live' and 'Misery Mansion', a co-writer was listed by the name of "Craig." In daughter Lana's book, the "co-author" credit was specifically given to Hank Craig. I asked Willie about this. He adamantly shook his head and replied, "no, there was no co-writer. I wrote those songs myself." Willie did say he wrote the song with Jack Rhodes. According to Willie, Jack was a dee jay in and around the Houston area at the time.

Since none of his first songs became singles, this listing was begun with three singles that were actually recorded first, though they were not all released when cut. The singles in question were the ones on the Sarg label. The owner of that indie label out of Luling, Texas (south of Austin), Charlie Fitch, received Willie's first audition tape in 1955. According to Fitch, the tape sat on the shelf for 25 years, when it was finally released as a collector's item (after Willie became "real popular"). Also from Sarg were two 1955 singles credited to Dave Isbell with Willie on guitar.

The first commercial release by Willie was literally put together (in all facets) by Willie himself. When he was a disc jockey in

Vancouver, Washington, he utilized the station's facilities to record, in 1957, two songs (one written by Willie). He used Starday in Nashville (Willie said he used Houston-based Pappy Daily's "D" Records) to manufacture the sides and sold them wherever he could, using his own show to plug the record. He sold about five hundred copies, making them a rare Willie Nelson collectable.

The owner of Sarg rightly stated that the audition song sent to Sarg was later rerecorded and released on Pappy Daily's "D" label. That would be 'The Storm Has Just Begun'. It was coupled with 'Man With the Blues' on the "A" side and released out of Houston in 1959. "D" Records released a follow-up Nelson single in 1960.

By 1962, Willie released his first single for Liberty Records. It went nowhere, but his second, a duet with Shirley Collie, 'Willingly', went country top ten. Willie appeared to be on his way. His own single, 'Touch Me' reached the number seven spot on the country charts in 1962. Then his sales fizzled. He experienced four uneventful years, broken by 1966's top twenty charter, 'One in a Row', a Willie original. Two years later, a non-country song (and non-original) took him and RCA to number thirteen. That was it until 1975, when Willie hit number one with his first Columbia single. After that, what a string it was until age (in the minds of radio programmers) caught up with him.

After Willie left RCA (for Atlantic and then Columbia), the label had a top ten hit with one of his recordings, 'If You Can Touch Her at All', but none while he was signed to the label. How is that for irony? While he was still with RCA, the highest any of his singles reached was number thirteen and that song wasn't even a country song. The top ten single RCA achieved on Willie actually peaked at the number five spot in March of 1978 at the same time his Columbia single, 'Georgia on My Mind' reached number one.

RCA sure knew how to sell Willie's records after Columbia made him a household name. In spite of all the criticism leveled at Willie's RCA material, maybe it really was "commercial." After all, it sold well (very well) for others, such as Patsy Cline and Faron Young. In February 1979, the company pushed the previously released 'Sweet Memories' up the *Billboard* country singles charts to number four.

The number thirteen song RCA had on Willie, while Willie was still under their recording contract, was 'Bring Me Sunshine', which peaked in December 1968. 'One in a Row' went country top twenty (nineteen) in 1966. In 1967, Willie almost hit the top twenty (twenty-one) with 'Blackjack County Chain' and in 1968, he almost did it again with 'Little Things', which charted at number twenty-two.

On Atlantic, it looked like Willie could have broken through. His second release, 'Stay All Night', reached number twenty-two in 1973, while his fourth, 'Bloody Mary Morning' hit number seventeen. Unfortunately, the relationship with Atlantic ended all too soon, when Atlantic decided it no longer wanted to be in the country music business.

In Willie's case, the public never really caught on to him (or had the chance to) until he hit the number one slot with his first single for Columbia, the old Fred Rose standard, 'Blue Eyes Crying in the Rain'. That single also went almost top twenty on the pop charts, reaching number twenty-one. From that hit song forward, Willie found an almost unparalleled acceptance, by the fans, of himself and his creations. It wasn't until fourteen years later, 1989, that he stopped having a major impact on the country singles charts. Since then, he didn't necessarily lose touch with his audience, just the radio people who concluded he was too old to continue to sell singles on the air. Willie's history of selling singles was nonetheless amazing, even in a medium where fan loyalty has been shown to be higher than in almost any other musical genre.

His tenure with Columbia was definitely the most fruitful. There he had a phenomenal run of twenty top ten country hits through 1986. During that time even more singles were marketed from the days when he was on either RCA or Liberty. Quite a few of them charted, often competing with his latest Columbia release. Many of his Pamper "demos" came out as singles, though they did not chart.

With other artists, he had an additional ten (on Columbia or affiliate label) top ten sellers. Beyond that, two of his Columbia singles went top twenty on the pop charts. 'Always on My Mind' reached number five, 'On the Road Again' hit twenty, and one of the singles he did with Julio Iglesias, 'To All the Girls I've Loved Before', reached number five.

When chronicling Willie's singles, there has always been the question as to just what constitutes a Willie Nelson single, one with Willie alone or one which featured a Willie appearance or duet. For the purposes of this listing, all of Willie's major appearances, duets, and single performances have been documented, down to the ones on the Justice label, which featured a Willie Nelson soundboard. So, duets with Hank Williams Jr., for example, have been listed along with ones on which Willie merely played.

In 1977, at the height of the "outlaw" craze, Willie was at least part of seven singles. Even though he was signed to Columbia, he sang the last part of Waylon's 'Luckenbach, Texas (Back to the Basics of Love)' RCA single (actually RCA made three single releases of this song) and had two post-contract solo RCA singles, 'You Ought to Hear Me Cry' and 'I'm a Memory'. He also had his own Columbia single, 'I Love You a Thousand Ways', along with appearances on singles by Darrell McCall ('Lily Dale') and Mary Kay Place ('Something to Brag About'). Finally, Willie and Larry Trader's label, Double Barrel Records, released one of Willie's Pamper "demos" as a single, 'Pride Wins Again'. It came off the *1961* album, the first of numerous collections consisting of some portion of those tracks.

1990 was another year when Willie was involved with a great many singles. For Columbia, there were three Highwaymen singles (one was a combination consisting of 'American Remains' and 'Texas') and three solos, 'The Highway', 'Is the Better Part Over', and 'Ain't Necessarily So'. He dueted with Emmylou Harris on the Reprise Records single, 'Gulf Coast Highway' and sang with Waylon on the song, 'If I Can Find A Clean Shirt', for Epic Records.

In late 1989, his single, 'There You Go', had gone top ten (number eight) when *Billboard* changed its method for computing chart position. The emphasis went from an equivalent combination of airplay and sales to a heavier reliance on airplay alone. That change effectively knocked the single down to number nineteen. So, depending on which chart method used, Willie either charted top ten for the last time with that single or just barely made it into the top twenty.

If that single were not counted then Willie (by himself) last reached the top ten with his previous single in 1989, 'Nothing I Can Do About It Now'. That single ended a dearth of three years during which Willie (by himself) went without a top ten single. The previous top ten single came in 1986 with the David Lynn Jones song, 'Living in the Promiseland' (it reached number one).

When Willie left Columbia in 1993, his chart-topping days, at least for single records, were all but over. In fact, early 1991 was, for all intents and purposes, the time period that ended his more than fifteen years of topping (or at least prominently riding up and down) the singles charts. For Columbia alone, Willie had twenty-three top ten country singles (again depending on which chart method was used).

1991 was one of those "watershed" years for country music. A new generation of stars like Garth Brooks and Mary Chapin Carpenter had pretty much taken over domination of the charts. Old standbys and standouts like Willie Nelson, George Jones, Dolly Parton, and Merle Haggard, found themselves drastically diminished in their presence at the top rungs of the chart. Because of their advancing years, they could not get enough air time to sell their latest singles.

There were of course, other reasons why Willie's chart strength ended. He was overexposed as far as radio and over the counter sales with all his own singles and guest appearances on other people's projects. His battle with the IRS also took him away from recording at that particularly crucial time.

Also, by 1988, Willie was more connected, in the public's mind, with pop standards (even 'Heart of Gold') than new country songs. A *Billboard* column written by Marie Ratliff in June 1989 observed that "programmers are lauding the return of Willie Nelson to new material that is straight country." The "new material" was Beth Nielsen Chapman's 'Nothing I Can Do About It Now'. That song was his last number one hit.

It reached number one after a previous release, the standard, 'Twilight Time' had bottomed out at number forty-one. Unfortunately, Willie's time at the top of the best-selling lists was just about over. His personal run of charting singles was effectively concluded as of 'The Piper Came Today', which entered the charts in January 1991. Later in August, Waylon and Willie did peak with their Epic single (73832), 'If I Can Find a Clean Shirt', at number fifty-one.

The number of Willie singles was, in a word, voluminous. He recorded his own, he did duets, he backed other musicians or made guest appearances. In order, year by year, the following list captured all of those appearances on singles. The first commercial single was the one he made for his own Willie Nelson Records in 1957. Fortunately, he's still making them, up to and including one for Island Records in 1996.

No artist has ever charted all the singles he or she made. Elvis Presley and the Beatles probably came the closest. Willie Nelson, on the other hand, made so many diverse singles, obscure ones, ones to help other artists careers, in short, ones done for any number of reasons. As a result, he didn't chart anywhere near as many singles as he made.

Still, he charted some great ones, from his own compositions to interpretations of pop standards for a country audience, songs like 'Georgia on My Mind'. He went top ten country, either by himself or with someone else, more than forty times (forty-three through 1991). He even had a top five pop hit ('Always on My Mind').

Many of the songs that became chart successes for Willie were ones he either wrote or co-wrote, like 'Angel Flying Too Close to the Ground', 'On the Road Again', 'Forgiving You Was Easy', 'Why Do I Have to Choose', and 'Little Old Fashioned Karma'. For himself, his originals produced seven top ten country hits, five of which reached number one. He also wrote many for prominent country and pop stars from Patsy Cline and Faron Young to Linda Ronstadt and Roy Orbison. In fact, nine of his songs went top ten country for other artists and one even went top ten pop ('Crazy' by Cline).

Faron had only one number one song in the sixties and it was Willie's 'Hello Walls'. The only top twenty pop hit Faron ever had was with that same Willie song. Early in her career, Patsy hit either number one or two with four straight single releases; one of them was 'Crazy'. 'Crazy' also took her onto the pop top ten chart for the only time in her career. In 1977, Linda Ronstadt hit the country top ten with her rendition of 'Crazy', one that many people felt was the ultimate interpretation, at least according to her biographer.

After Claude Gray achieved top ten status on a small indie label (a highly unusual feat) with Willie's 'Family Bible', it earned him a major label shot with Mercury Records. Joe Carson, of Brownwood, Texas, was projected to be a "big" star for Liberty Records, beginning in 1963. Liberty picked a great song for his debut single, Willie's 'I Gotta Get Drunk', and Joe took it into the country top forty. His next two singles also sold well. Unfortunately, he was tragically killed in a car accident in early 1964.

Johnny Bush, "the country Caruso," was relegated for most of his career to independent, mostly regional, labels (except for two short years with RCA). In 1968, Willie's song, 'Undo the Right' was strong enough to earn him a top ten ranking on the country singles chart even though it came out on the tiny Stop Records label. After Bush signed with RCA in 1972, he hit the country top twenty with his original composition, 'Whiskey River', which Willie later on turned into his own signature song, almost always opening and closing his live shows with it (not counting any encore after a standing ovation).

Willie's 1971 album, *Yesterday's Wine*, and title song were considered by many to be among his finest work. The album was certainly one of the first, if not the first, concept albums in the history of country music. Regardless of its critical acclaim, neither the album nor the single featuring the title song sold well for Willie and RCA. The single barely dented the chart, peaking at number sixty-two.

Then in 1982, two country superstars, George Jones and Merle Haggard cut their own rousing version of the song for Epic Records and it zoomed right to number one on the *Billboard* country singles chart. Producer Billy Sherrill recalled that Merle brought the song to the session and George "didn't care what he sang." In fact, Merle brought in most of the songs for the sessions. The success of 'Yesterday's Wine' as done by the Jones/Haggard team showed what a little promotion and the addition of famous names could do for a great song.

Two singles, one by country talk show host Ralph Emery and the other by Ben Colder (Sheb Wooley's humorous nom de plume) were actually "answer" songs - to Faron's rendition of 'Hello Walls', though Willie remained listed as the primary writer (Wooley was listed as co-writer on 'Hello Walls No. 2'). The 1961 "answer" by Emery, 'Hello Fool', turned out to be Ralph's only country single hit (going top five on the *Billboard* country singles charts). The Colder satire reached number thirty in 1963.

'Hello Fool' had a very interesting genesis as Skeeter Davis, then married to Ralph, recalled. On page 216 of her autobiography, *Bus Fare to Kentucky*, she wrote that:

> Faron Young had a song out at that time called 'Hello Walls', written by a virtually unknown writer named Willie Nelson. Someone from the West Coast sent me an answer to 'Hello Walls'. It was a clever, catchy recitation-type song in which the walls answered the man. Appropriately, it was called 'Hello Fool'.

Though the song was sent to her "with the intention of my recording it," Skeeter said it "made me think of Ralph immediately."

When she told him her idea of having him record the "answer" song, he listened to the song and "loved it." According to Skeeter, he:

> detected the hit potential and began raving about how it could be the break he had been looking for. A split second later, he began complaining that nobody in town would record him and that he could not possibly find the money to back him, and so on.

At that point, Skeeter told him that if nobody else would do it, she would pay for it because she wanted him to be happy. As Ralph had thought, nobody would record him, so Skeeter "rented studio time at Starday and hired Pete Drake to produce the record." When she and Ralph took their "professional product" to Joe Allison at Liberty Records, he "loved the idea of 'Hello Fool' and signed Ralph to a contract with Liberty Records.

The end result was that "Ralph had a hit," which "restored his pride" and changed his whole attitude. Skeeter wrote that they were happy after that for quite a while. She wished things could have stayed that way but that's another story. The story for Willie was that his songs, as singles for himself and others, changed the face of modern country music.

<u>Note:</u> See page 414 for chart legend.

The Sarg Records Singles

Label/Number	Date/Chart	Title (Side A/Side B)	Rank/Weeks
108-45	1955	No Longer Afraid/Satisfied or Sorry (Dave Isbell, with Willie on guitar)	nca
109-45	1955	Let's Do It Up Brown/A Make Believe Christmas (Dave Isbell, with Willie on guitar)	nca
260-45	1955	When I Sang My Last Hillbillie Song/A Storm Is Just Begun (Audition Tape)	nca

The Willie Nelson Records Single

45/15-628	1957	No Place For Me/The Lumberjack	nca

The "D" Records Singles

D-1084	1959	Man with the Blues/The Storm Has Just Begun (with the Reil Sisters)	nca

D-1131	1960	What a Way to Live/Misery Mansion	nca
D-1179	1961	Man with the Blues/The Storm Has Just Begun	nca
Betty 5702	1964	What a Way to Live/Misery Mansion	nca
Betty 5703	1964	The Storm Has Just Begun/ Man with the Blues	nca

The RX Single

RX 502	1959	Night Life/Rainy Day Blues (appeared as Hugh Nelson)	nca
Bellaire 107	1959	Night Life/Rainy Day Blues	nca
Bellaire 107	1963	Night Life/Rainy Day Blues	nca
Oldies 64-6756	1964	Night Life/Rainy Day Blues	nca
American Gold 7601	1976	The Original Night Life/ Rainy Day Blues	nca
Bellaire B-5000	1976	Night Life '76/Man with the Blues	nca

The Pamper Music "Demos" Singles

Double Barrel LT-1961-7	1977	Pride Wins Again/Is There Something on Your Mind	nca
Lone Star 703	10/28/78 (C)	Will You Remember Mine/ The End of Understanding	67/5
Delta Records DS-11571/2	1982	Pride Wins Again/Burning Both Ends of the Candle	nca
Casino WN-008	1984	The Ghost/Go Away	nca
Paula 442	n/d	I Can't Find the Time/A Moment Isn't Very Long	nca

The Liberty Records Singles

55386	1962	The Part Where I Cry/Mr. Record Man	nca
55403	3/17/62 (C)	Willingly/(Our) Chain of Love (w. Shirley Collie)	10/13
55439	5/26/62 (C)	Touch Me/Where My House Lives	7/13
55439	6/23/62 (P)	Touch Me/Where My House Lives	109/2
55468	1962	You Dream About Me/Is This My Destiny (w. S. Collie)	nca
55494	1962	Wake Me When It's Over/ There's Gonna Be Love in My House	nca

55532	4/6/63 (C)	Half a Man/The Last Letter	25/5
55532	3/30/63 (P)	Half a Man/The Last Letter	129/1
55591	1963	Take My Word/Feed It a Memory	nca
55638	1/18/64 (C)	You Took My Happy Away/How Long Is Forever	33/3
55661	1964	Am I Blue/There'll Be No Teardrops Tonight	nca
55697	1964	River Boy (Original version)/Opportunity to Cry	nca
56143	12/13/69 (C)	I Hope So/Right or Wrong	36/9
S7-18486	1995	It Is What It Is/The Devil's Right Hand (Highwaymen)	nca
S7-18584	1995	One After 909 (Willie)/Yesterday (Billie Dean)	nca

The United Artists Singles

UA-641	1963	Night Life/Rainy Day Blues	nca
UA-XW771-Y	3/27/76 (C)	The Last Letter/There Goes a Man	46/7
UA-X1254-Y	11/25/78 (C)	There'll Be No Teardrops Tonight/Blue Must Be the Color of the Blues	86/3
UA-XW1165	1978	Hello Walls/The Last Letter	nca
Capitol X-214	1978	Hello Walls/There'll Be No Teardrops Tonight (SSS)	nca

The Monument Records Singles

45-855	1964	I Never Cared for You/You Left Me (A Long Time Ago)	nca
WS4-03408	12/11/82 (C)	Everything's Beautiful in Its Own Way (w. Dolly Parton)/Put It Off Until Tomorrow (Parton & Kris Kristofferson)	7/20
WS4-03781	4/9/83 (C)	You're Gonna Love Yourself in the Morning (w. Brenda Lee)/What Do You Think About Lovin' (Parton & Lee)	43/9

The RCA Records Singles

47-8484	1964	Pretty Paper/What a Merry Christmas This Could Be	nca
47-8519	5/8/65 (C)	She's Not for You/Permanently Lonely	43/5
47-8594	1965	Healing Hands of Time/One Day at a Time	nca

47-8682	10/16/65 (C)	I Just Can't Let You Say Good-bye/And So Will You My Love	48/2
47-0825	10/1/66 (C)	One in A Row/Good Times	19/13
47-8801	1966	Columbus Stockade Blues/He Sits at My Table	nca
47-8852	1966	I'm Still Not Over You/I Love You Because	nca
47-8933	1966	One in a Row/San Antonio Rose	nca
47-9029	1966	Pretty Paper/What a Merry Christmas This Could Be	nca
47-9100	3/4/67 (C)	The Party's Over/Make Way for a Better Man	24/16
47-9202	6/24/67 (C)	Blackjack County Chain/Some Other World	21/11
47-9324	10/21/67 (C)	San Antonio/To Make a Long Story Short (She's Gone)	50/9
47-9427	2/10/68 (C)	Little Things/I'll Stay Around	22/11
47-9536	6/15/68 (C)	Good Times/Don't You Ever Get Tired of Hurting Me	44/8
47-9605	9/7/68 (C)	Johnny One Time/She's Still Gone	36/7
47-9684	12/21/68 (C)	Bring Me Sunshine/Don't Say Love or Nothing	13/14
47-9778	1969	Pretty Paper/What a Merry Christmas This Could Be	nca
47-9798	3/14/70 (C)	Once More With Feeling/Who Do I Know in Dallas	42/9
47-9903	11/28/70 (C)	Laying My Burdens Down/Truth Number One	68/2
47-9931	1970	Pretty Paper/What a Merry Christmas This Could Be	nca
47-9951	2/6/71 (C)	I'm a Memory/I'm So Lonesome I Could Cry	28/11
47-9984	1971	What Can You Do to Me Now/Kneel at the Feet of Jesus	nca
74-0162	1971	Jimmy's Road/Natural to Be Gone	nca
74-0542	10/23/71 (C)	Yesterday's Wine/Me and Paul	62/7/4
74-0635	2/19/72 (C)	The Words Don't Fit the Picture/A Moment Isn't Very Long	73/2
74-0816	1972	Phases, Stages, Circles, Cycles and Scenes/Mountain Dew	nca

JH/PB-10429	11/15/75 (C)	Fire and Rain/I'm a Memory	29/11
JH/PB-10529	12/27/75 (C)	Good Hearted Woman/ Heaven or Hell (w. Waylon) (Waylon's 'Sweet Dream Woman' on some "B" sides)	1/17
JH/PB-10461	1975	Pretty Paper/What a Merry Christmas This Could Be	nca
JH/PB-10529	2/7/76 (P)	Good Hearted Woman/ Heaven or Hell (w. Waylon)	25/12
JH/PB-10591	4/17/76 (C)	I Gotta Get Drunk/Summer of Roses	55/6
JH/PB-10591	4/17/76 (P)	I Gotta Get Drunk/Summer of Roses	101/4
JB/PB-10924/ GB-11757	4/16/77 (C)	Luckenbach, Texas (Back to the Basics of Love) (w. Waylon)/ Belle of the Ball (Waylon solo)	1/18
JB/PB-10924/ GB-11757	5/7/77 (P)	Luckenbach, Texas (Back to the Basics of Love) (w. Waylon)/ Belle of the Ball (Waylon solo)	25/16
JH/PB-10969	5/14/77 (C)	I'm a Memory/It Should Be Easier Now (w. Darrell McCall)	22/11
JB/PB-11061	9/10/77 (C)	You Ought to Hear Me Cry/ One in a Row	16/13
G/J/PB-11198	1/21/78 (C)	Mamas Don't Let Your Babies Grow Up to be Cowboys/I Can Get Off on You (w. Waylon)	1/16/15
G/J/PB-11198	2/11/78 (P)	Mamas Don't Let Your Babies Grow Up to Be Cowboys/I Can Get Off on You (w. Waylon)	42/10
JH/PB-11235	3/18/78 (C)	If You Can Touch Her at All/ Rainy Day Blues	5/15
JH/PB-11235	4/1/78 (P)	If You Can Touch Her at All/ Rainy Day Blues	104/3
JH/PB-11465	2/10/79 (C)	Sweet Memories/Little Things	4/14
JB/PB-11673	8/18/79 (C)	Crazy Arms (Willie)/Hurri- cane Shirley (Bobby Bare)	16/13
JH/PB-11893	2/2/80 (C)	Night Life (w. Danny Davis & the Nashville Brass)/ December Day	20/12
JH/PB-11999	5/17/80 (C)	Funny How Time Slips Away (w. Davis & the Nashville Brass)/The Local Memory (Willie solo)	41/8

GB-11995	1981	Sweet Memories/If You Can Touch Her at All	nca
JH/PB-12254	6/27/81 (C)	Good Times/Where Do You Stand	25/12
JK/PB-12328	10/3/81 (C)	Mountain Dew/Laying My Burdens Down	23/12
PB/JK-13073	3/13/82 (C)	Just to Satisfy You (w. Waylon Jennings)/Get Naked With Me (Waylon solo)	1/18
PB/JK-13073	4/3/82 (P)	Just to Satisfy You (w. Waylon Jennings)/Get Naked With Me (Waylon solo)	52/9
JK/PB-13319	10/23/82 (C)	Sittin' on the Dock of the Bay (w. Waylon Jennings)	13/15
47-0891	1982	The Party's Over/Bring Me Sunshine	nca
PB-13465	1983	Lucille (Waylon Jennings solo)/Medley of Hits (including Willie/Waylon duet 'Good Hearted Woman')	nca

The Atlantic Records Singles

45-2968	7/14/73 (C)	Shotgun Willie/Sad Songs and Waltzes	60/5
45-2979	9/29/73 (C)	Stay All Night/Devil in a Sleeping Bag	22/13
45-3008	2/16/74 (C)	I Still Can't Believe That You're Gone/Heaven and Hell	51/5
45-3020	4/6/74 (C)	Bloody Mary Morning/Phases and Stages	17/13
45-3228	12/7/74 (C)	Sister's Coming Home/Pick Up the Tempo	93/3
45-3334	1974	Heaven and Hell/I Still Can't Believe That You're Gone	nca
OS-13178	1974	Shotgun Willie/I Still Can't Believe That You're Gone	nca
OS-13179	1974	Bloody Mary Morning (Willie solo)/After the Fire Is Gone (w. Tracy Nelson)	nca

The Columbia Records Singles

| 3-10176 | 7/19/75 (C) | Blue Eyes Crying in the Rain/Bandera | 1/18 |
| 3-10176 | 8/30/75 (P) | Blue Eyes Crying in the Rain/Bandera | 21/18 |

3-10275	1/3/76 (C)	Remember Me/Time of the Preacher	2/15
3-10275	1/3/76 (P)	Remember Me/Time of the Preacher	67/8
13-33326	1975	Blue Eyes Crying in the Rain/Remember Me (When the Candle Lights Are Gleaming)	nca
3-10327	5/1/76 (C)	I'd Have to Be Crazy/Amazing Grace	11/13
3-10383	7/24/76 (C)	If You've Got the Money I've Got the Time/The Sound in Your Mind	1/15
3-10453	12/18/76 (C)	Uncloudy Day/Precious Memories	4/14
13-33346	1976	If You've Got the Money I've Got the Time/Uncloudy Day	nca
3-10588	7/30/77 (C)	I Love You a Thousand Ways/Mom and Dad's Waltz	9/12
3-10704	3/25/78 (C)	Georgia on My Mind/The Sunny Side of the Street	1/16
3-10704	5/27/78 (P)	Georgia on My Mind/The Sunny Side of the Street	84/6
3-10784	7/15/78 (C)	Blue Skies/Moonlight in Vermont	1/13
13-33362	1978	Georgia on My Mind/Blue Skies	nca
3-10834	10/21/78 (C)	All of Me/Unchained Melody	3/14
3-10877	12/23/78 (C)	Whiskey River/Under the Double Eagle	12/12
13-33403	1978	All of Me/Whiskey River	nca
3-10929	4/14/79 (C)	September Song/Don't Get Around Much Anymore	15/12
13-02166	1978	September Song/On the Road Again	nca
3-11023	7/7/79 (C)	Heartbreak Hotel/Sioux City Sue (w. Leon Russell)	1/13
3-11119	1979	Trouble in Mind/One for My Baby (and One More for the Road) (w. Leon Russell)	nca
1-11126	11/10/79 (C)	Help Me Make It Through the Night/The Pilgrim: Chapter 33	4/14
13-33404	1979	Heartbreak Hotel (w. Russell)/Help Me Make It Through the Night (Willie solo)	nca

13-03476	1979	Pretty Paper/White Christmas	nca
AE7-1182	1979	White Christmas/Blue Christmas	nca
AE7-1183	1979	Rudolph the Red-Nosed Reindeer/Pretty Paper	nca
AE7-1775	1979	Pretty Paper/White Christmas	nca
1-11186	1/12/80 (C)	My Heroes Have Always Been Cowboys/Rising Star (Love Theme)	1/14
1-11186	2/9/80 (P)	My Heroes Have Always Been Cowboys/Rising Star (Love Theme)	44/10
1-11257	5/3/80 (C)	Midnight Rider/So You Think You're a Cowboy	6/15
1-11329	8/9/80 (C)	Faded Love/This Cold War with You (w. Ray Price)	3/15
1-11351	8/30/80 (P)	On the Road Again/Jumpin' Cotton Eyed Joe (Johnny Gimble solo)	20/20
1-11351	9/6/80 (C)	On the Road Again/Jumpin' Cotton Eyed Joe (Johnny Gimble solo)	1/16
11-11405	12/6/80 (C)	Don't You Ever Get Tired of Hurting Me/Funny How Time Slips Away (w. Ray Price)	11/14
11-11418	1/10/81 (C)	Angel Flying Too Close to the Ground/I Guess I've Come to Live Here in Your Eyes	1/14
11-02000	4/18/81 (C)	Mona Lisa/Twinkle Twinkle Little Star	11/12
18-02187	7/25/81 (C)	I'm Gonna Sit Right Down and Write Myself a Letter/Over the Rainbow	26/11
18-02558	11/14/81 (C)	Heartaches of a Fool/Uncloudy Day	39/10
53/18-02741	3/6/82 (C)	Always on My Mind/The Party's Over	1/21
53/18-02741	3/6/82 (P)	Always on My Mind/The Party's Over	5/23
18-02681	6/5/82 (C)	Old Friends (w. Roger Miller & Ray Price)/When a House Is Not a Home	19/16
53/18-03073	8/14/82 (C)	Let It Be Me/Permanently Lonely	2/17

53/18-03073	8/7/82 (P)	Let It Be Me/Permanently Lonely	40/12
13-03123	1982	Angel Flying Too Close to the Ground/Mona Lisa	nca
13-03124	1982	Heartaches of a Fool/ Midnight Rider	nca
13-03125	1982	My Heroes Have Always Been Cowboys/I'm Gonna Sit Right Down and Write Myself a Letter	nca
38-03213	1982	Slowly/Back Street Affair (w. Webb Pierce)	nca
38-03231	10/9/82 (C)	In the Jailhouse Now/Back Street Affair (w. Webb Pierce)	72/5
38-03385	12/4/82 (C)	Last Thing I Needed First Thing This Morning/Old Fords and a Natural Stone	2/20
38-03674	3/12/83 (C)	Little Old Fashioned Karma/ Beer Barrel Polka	10/18
38-03965	6/18/83 (C)	Why Do I Have to Choose/ Would You Lay with Me (in a Field of Stone)	3/21
38-04131	10/8/83 (C)	Take It to the Limit/Till I Gain Control Again (w. Waylon)	8/19
38-04131	10/8/83 (P)	Take It to the Limit/Till I Gain Control Again (w. Waylon)	102/1
38-04263	12/24/83 (C)	Without a Song/I Can't Begin to Tell You	11/16
38-04217	3/10/84 (C)	To All the Girls I've Loved Before (w. Julio Iglesias)/I Don't Want to Wake You (Julio solo)	1/20
38-04217	3/3/84 (P)	To All the Girls I've Loved Before (w. Iglesias)/I Don't Want to Wake You (Julio solo)	5/21
38-04495	1984	As Time Goes By (w. Iglesias) /You'll Never Know (Willie solo)	wdrwn
38-04568	8/18/84 (C)	City of New Orleans/Why Are You Pickin' on Me	1/25
38-04652	11/3/84 (C)	How Do You Feel About Foolin' Around/Eye of the Storm (w. Kris Kristofferson)	46/11
38-04847	4/13/85 (C)	Forgiving You Was Easy/You Wouldn't Cross the Street (to Say Goodbye)	1/22

38-04881	5/18/85 (C)	Highwayman (Willie, Waylon, Kristofferson, Cash)/ The Human Condition (Willie and Johnny Cash)	1/20
38-05566	1985	Are There Anymore Real Cowboys (w. Neil Young)/ I'm a Memory (Willie)	nca
38-05594	9/14/85 (C)	Desperados Waiting for a Train (Willie, Waylon, Kristofferson, Cash)/The 20th Century Is Almost Over (Willie & Cash)	15/18
38-05597	9/14/85 (C)	Me and Paul/I Let My Mind Wander	14/19
38-05677	1985	Slow Movin' Outlaw (Willie & Lacy J. Dalton)/They All Went to Mexico (Willie & Carlos Santana)	nca
38-05749	1985	I Told a Lie to My Heart (Willie and Hank Williams)/ Slow Movin' Outlaw (Willie and Lacy J. Dalton)	nca
38-05834	3/29/86 (C)	Living in the Promiseland/ Bach Minuet in G	1/20
38-06246	8/9/86 (C)	I'm Not Trying to Forget You/ I've Got the Craziest Feeling	21/17
38-06530	12/6/86 (C)	Partners After All/Home Away from Home	24/13
38-07007	3/21/87 (C)	Heart of Gold/So Much Like My Dad	44/11
38-07202	7/11/87 (C)	Island in the Sea/There Is No Easy Way	27/12
38-07636	1/9/88 (C)	Nobody There But Me/Wake Me When It's Over	82/3
38-08066	9/17/88 (C)	Spanish Eyes (w. J. Iglesias)/ Ole Buttermilk Sky (Willie solo)	8/19
38-08395	1988	Living in the Promiseland/ Forgiving You Was Easy	nca
38-08406	1988	Highwayman/Desperados Waiting for a Train (Willie, Waylon, Kristofferson, Cash)	nca
38-68541	1/21/89 (C)	Twilight Time/ Ac-cent-tchu-ate the Positive	41/8
38-68923	6/10/89 (C)	Nothing I Can Do About It Now/If I Were a Painting	1/21

38-73015	10/8/89 (C)	There You Are/Spirit (*)	8/19/23
CSK-1649	1989	Nothing I Can Do About It Now (CD Promo)	nca
38-73249	2/24/90 (C)	The Highway/Spirit	52/13
38-73233	3/3/90 (C)	Silver Stallion/American Remains (Highwaymen 2)	25/14
CSK-73233	1990	Silver Stallion (Highwaymen 2) (CD Promo)	nca
38-73374 (T)	1990	Is the Better Part Over/Mr. Record Man	nca
CSK-73374	1990	Is the Better Part Over (CD Promo)	nca
38-73381	1990	Born and Raised in Black and White/Texas (Highwaymen 2)	nca
CSK-73381 (CD Promo)	1990	Born and Raised in Black and White (Highwaymen 2)	nca
38-73518	12/15/90 (C)	Ain't Necessarily So/I Never Cared for You	17/20
38-73572	1990	American Remains/Texas (Highwaymen 2)	nca
38-73655	1/19/91 (C)	The Piper Came Today/I Don't Have a Reason to Go to California Anymore	70/3
38-73749	3/16/91	Ten With a Two/You Decide	45/12
CSK-73749	1991	Ten With a Two (CD Promo)	nca
74993	1993	Graceland (CBS album cut)	70/1
38-77184	1993	Still Is Still Moving to Me/Valentine	nca

The Epic Singles

34-03494	1/15/83 (C)	Reasons to Quit/Half a Man (w. Merle Haggard)	6/18
34-03495	1983	Reasons to Quit (w. Haggard) (one sided budget single)	nca
55/34-03842	4/30/83 (C)	Pancho and Lefty/Opportunity to Cry (w. Haggard)	1/21
07400	9/19/87 (C)	If I Could Only Fly/Without You on My Side (w. Haggard)	58/5
34-73832	1990	If I Can Find a Clean Shirt/Put Me on a Train Back to Texas (Willie and Waylon)	51/10
34-74024	1991	Tryin' to Outrun the Wind/The Makin's of a Song (Waylon and Willie)	nca

The Religious Singles

MCA/Songbird 10/4/80 (C) MCA-41313		Family Bible/In God's Eyes	92/2
Arrival NU-719-5	1987	I'd Rather Have Jesus/Just a Little Talk with Jesus (w. Bobbie Nelson)	nca

The Post-Columbia Justice Records Singles

JR 1601 2N1	1993	December Day (soundboard)	nca
JR 1601 2N2	1993	Afraid (soundboard)	nca

The Singles with Other Artists

RCA 47-9229	1967	Chet's Tune (Some of Chet's Friends)/Country Gentleman (Chet solo)	nca
RCA 74-0133	5/17/69 (C)	Poor Old Ugly Gladys Jones (Don Bowman w. Willie, Waylon, & Bobby Bare)/Boll Weevil Airlines (Don solo)	70/5
Atlantic CY-4028	8/17/74 C	After the Fire Is Gone (w. Tracy Nelson)/Whiskey River (Willie solo)	17/11
Epic 50214	1975	Rhythm of the Road (Willie & Michael Murphey)	nca
Epic 9-50184	1/24/76 (P)	Renegade (Murphey & Willie)/A Mansion on the Hill (Murphey solo)	39/7
Elektra E-45359	1976	You Are My Sunshine (Duane Eddy & Willie)/From 8 to 7 (Duane solo)	nca
Columbia 3-10480	3/12/77 (C)	Lily Dale/Please Don't Leave Me (w. Darrell McCall)	32/13
Columbia 3-10644	11/19/77 (C)	Something to Brag About (w. Mary Kay Place)/Anybody's Darlin' (Place solo)	9/16
Capricorn CPS-0286	3/11/78 (C)	You Asked Me to (w. Billie Joe Shaver)/Silver Wings of Time (Shaver solo)	80/5
Capitol 4635	10/14/78 (C)	Ain't Life Hell (Hank Cochran w. Willie)/I'm Going With You This Time (H. Cochran & Friends, w. Willie)	77/5
Lone Star 701 (LSR-2003)	1978	Willon and Waylee (Don Bowman w. Waylon and Willie)/Power Tool Song (Don solo)	nca

Lone Star 702	10/14/78	Just Out of Reach of My Two Open Arms/Warm and Tender Love (w. Larry G. Hudson)	37/10
Cachet CLS-3001/ CS4-4501	6/2/79 (C)	Waltz Across Texas (Ernest Tubb & Willie)/Jealous Loving Heart (Tubb & Johnny Cash)	56/6
Epic 9-50819	1/5/80 (C)	It's Not Supposed to Be That Way (w. Pam Rose)/We're Gonna Try It Tonight (Rose solo)	52/7
MCA MCA-41273	7/5/80 (C)	The Last Cowboy Song (w. Ed Bruce)/The Outlaw & the Stranger (Bruce solo)	12/15
Elektra E-47062	11/8/80 (C)	A Little Bitty Tear (w. Hank Cochran)/He's Got You (Hank solo)	57/9
Crescent C80-002	1980	My Own Peculiar Way (w. Jack Dant)/I Just Started Stopping (Trying to Quit Loving You) (Dant solo)	nca
Kari KARI-117	2/28/81 (C)	There's a Crazy Man (Jody Payne & W. Nelson Family - Willie on backing vocals)	65/6
Kari KARI-122	1980	Uncle Pen (Jody Payne & W. Nelson Family - Willie on backing vocals)/Lovin' and Feelin' (Payne & W. Nelson Family)	nca
Warner Bros. WBS-49239	1980	Green Pastures (w. Emmylou Harris/Wayfaring Stranger (Harris solo)	nca
Columbia 4-42287	1982	Charlie's Shoes (Willie & Billie Walker)	nca
Rattlesnake RS-4000	1982	Long Black Limousine (w. Annie McGowan aka Rattlesnake Annie)/Lullaby (Annie solo)	nca
Delta DS-1139-5S	1982	Together Again (w. Johnny Bush) (Promo)	nca
Delta DS/ DTA-11391 -PS	1982	You Sure Tell It Like It Is George Jones (w. Johnny Bush)/ Adrianna's Song (Bush solo)	nca
Delta DS-11393/4	1982	The Party's Over/Sound of a Heartache (w. Johnny Bush)	nca
Delta DS-1175 -1/2	1982	Once Upon a Time (w. Susie Nelson)/Let's Stay Home (Susie solo)	nca

Felicity UR-4385	1983	Hondo's Song (Steve Fromholz & Willie)/Come on Down to Texas (Fromholz solo)	nca
Paradise PR-629	10/27/84 (C)	Wabash Cannonball (Hank Wilson aka Leon Russell w. Willie)/Tennessee Waltz (H. Wilson solo)	91/2
Columbia 38-04715	12/15/84 (C)	Seven Spanish Angels (Ray Charles w. Willie)/Who Cares (Ray & Janie Fricke)	1/27
Merit M-2502	1984	The Party's Over (Johnny Bush w. Willie)/Whiskey River (Bush solo)	nca
Columbia US7-04839	3/23/85 (P)	USA for Africa: We Are the World (Quincy Jones/46 artists w. Willie)/Grace (Jones)	1/18
Columbia 38-06227	8/2/86 (C)	I've Already Cheated on You (Willie &. David Allan Coe)/Take My Advice (Coe)	56/8
Warner Bros. 7-28581	10/11/86 (C)	Mind Your Own Business (w. Hank Jr.)/My Name Is Bocephus (Hank Jr.)	1/19
EMI-America B8319	1986	Hands Across America/ We Are the World	nca
Reprise PRO-CD -4002	1990	Gulf Coast Highway (Emmylou Harris & Willie) (CD Promo)	nca
Jody Payne SS-101	1992	Heart of the Matter (Jody Payne w. Willie on guitar)	nca

Chart Legend: (C) = *Billboard* Country Singles, (P) = *Billboard* (Hot 100) Pop Singles, nca = no chart activity (as of 1993), wdrwn = withdrawn from the market almost immediately after release.

* = the asterisk for the single 'There You Are' meant that it had two "highest" ranks on the *Billboard* country chart. The first number showed that the single initially went to number eight. The second number showed that on the charts following, which were "new" charts, or charts in which the ranking was figured more on airplay than a combination of sales and airplay, the highest rank for the single became number seventeen.

The Songs Written by Willie Nelson Alone.
And So Will You My Love, Angel Flying Too Close to the Ground, Any
Old Arms Won't Do, Ashamed, Bandera, Bloody Mary (Merry)
Morning, Blue Rock Montana, Both Ends of the Candle, Broken Promise,
A, Buddy, Building Heartaches, Changing Skies, Congratulations,
Country Willie, Crazy, Darkness on the Face of the Earth, December
Day, Denver, Devil in a Sleepin' Bag, Did I Ever Love You, Down at
the Corner Beer Joint, El Nino (The Christ Child), End of
Understanding, The, Face of a (the) Fighter, The, Follow(ing) Me
Around, Forgiving You Was Easy, Funny How Time Slips Away, Ghost,
The, Go Away, Goin' Home, Good Times, Half a Man, Happiness Lives
Next Door, Healing Hands of Time, Heaven and Hell, Heebie Jeebie
Blues No. 2, Hello Walls, Hold Me Tighter, Home Is Where You're
Happy, Home Motel, How Long Is Forever, (How Will I Know) I'm
Falling in Love Again, I Am the Forest, I Can Cry Again, I Didn't Sleep
a Wink, I Don't Feel Anything, I Feel Sorry for Him, I Feel That Old
Feeling, I Gotta Get Drunk, I Guess I've Come to Live Here in Your Eyes,
I Just Can't Let You Say Goodbye, I Just Don't Understand, I Just Dropped
By, I Let My Mind Wander, I Never Cared for You, I Still Can't Believe
You're Gone, I Thought About You, Lord, I'm a Memory, I'm Going to
Lose a Lot of Teardrops, I'm Not Trying to Forget You (Anymore), I'm
Still Not Over You, I'm So Ashamed, I'm Waiting Forever, If You Could
Only See, If You Could See What's Going Through My Mind, If You
Really Loved Me, In God's Eyes, Is the Better Part Over, Is There
Something on Your Mind, Island in the Sea, It Could Be Said That
Way, It Should Be Easier Now, It's a Dream Come True, It's Not for Me
to Understand, It's Not Supposed to Be That Way, Jimmy's Road, Kneel
at the Feet of Jesus, Laying My Burdens Down, Let Me Be a Man, Let's
Pretend, Little Old Fashioned Karma, Local Memory, The, London,
Lonely Little Mansion, Man With the Blues, Mariachi, Matador, Me
and Paul, Message, The, Moment Is Not (Isn't) Very Long, (A), Mr.
Record Man, My Kind of Girl, My Love for the Rose, My Own Peculiar
Way, New Way to Cry, A, No Love Around, No Place for Me, No
Tomorrow in Sight, Nobody Slides, My Friend, O'er the Waves, On the
Road Again, Once Alone, One Day at a Time, One in a Row, One Step
Beyond, Opportunity to Cry, (Our) Chain of Love, Part Where I Cry,
The, Party's Over, The, Permanently Lonely, Phases & Stages (Circles,
Cycles & Scenes), Phases and Stages (Theme), Pick up the Tempo,
Pretend I Never Happened, Pretty Paper, Pride Wins Again, Rainy
Day Blues, Remember the Good Times, Right from Wrong, Sad Songs
and Waltzes, She Is (She's) Gone, She's Not For You, Shotgun Willie,
Sister's Comin' Home, Slow Down Old World, So Much to Do, Some
Other Time, Someone Waiting for You, Something to Think About,
Somewhere in Texas (Part 1), Somewhere in Texas (Part 2), Songwriter,
Sound in Your Mind, The, Spirit of E9, Still is Still Moving to Me, Storm
Within My Heart (Has Just Begun), The, Suffer(ing) in Silence, Summer

of Roses, Take My Word, Texas, Thanks Again, That's Why I Love Her So, There Are Worse Things Than Being Alone, There Goes a Man, There Is No Easy Way (But There Is a Way), There's Gonna Be Love in My House, These Are Difficult Times, Things to Remember, Time of the Preacher, Time of the Preacher Theme, Too Sick to Pray, Touch Me, Tougher Than Leather, Two Sides to Every Story, Two Stories Wide, Valentine, Waiting (Wastin') Time, Wake Me When It's Over, Walkin', Washing the Dishes, We Don't Run, What Do You Want Me to Do?, When I Sang My Last Hillbillie Song, When We Live Again, Where Do You (We) Stand?, Where My House Lives, Where's the Show, Who'll Buy My Memories, Why Are You Picking on Me, Why Do I Have to Choose, Will You Remember (Mine) (Me), Within Your Crowd, Wonderful Future, Wonderful Yesterday, A, Words Don't Fit the Picture, The, Write Your Own Songs, Yesterday's Wine, You Dream About Me, You Left (Me) a Long, Long Time Ago, You Ought to Hear Me Cry, You Took My Happy Away, You Wouldn't (Even) Cross the Street to Say Goodbye, Your Memory Won't Die in My Grave.

The Songs Written by Willie and a Co-writer.

Are You Sure (w. Buddy Emmons), Blame It on the Time(s) (w. Hank Cochran), Christmas Blues (w. Booker T. Jones), Everything But You (w. H. Cochran), Family Bible (w. Buskirk, Breeland, Gray), Good Hearted Woman (w. Waylon Jennings), Heartaches of a Fool (w. Breeland, Buskirk), Heartland (w. Bob Dylan), I Can Get Off on You (w. Jennings), I Can't Find the Time (w. H. Cochran), I Want a Girl (with Paul Buskirk), I'd Rather You Didn't Love Me (w. Gray, Breeland), I'll Stay Around (w. H. Cochran), I've Already Cheated on You (w. David Allan Coe), Little Things (w. Shirley Nelson), Makin's of a Song, The (w. Max D. Barnes, Jennings, Troy Seals), Misery Mansion (w. Craig), Night Life (w. Buskirk, Breeland), Nobody Said It Was Going to Be Easy (w. M. Raphael), Old Age and Treachery (w. Max D. Barnes, Jennings, Troy Seals), Pages (w. Shirley Collie Nelson), Pullamo (w. Steve Pulliam), She's Still Gone (w. Shirley Nelson), Shelter of Your (My) Arms, The (w. Shirley Collie Nelson), So You Think You're a Cowboy (w. H. Cochran), Stay Away from Lonely Places (w. Don Bowman), Summersong (w. Roy Orbison), Three Days (w. Faron Young), To Make a Long Story Short, She's Gone (w. Fred Foster), Too Young to Settle Down (w. Jack Rhodes), Undo the Right (Wrong) (w. H. Cochran), What a Way to Live (w. Craig), What Can You Do to Me Now? (w. H. Cochran), Who Do I Know in Dallas (w. H. Cochran), You'll Always Have Someone (w. H. Cochran)

The Album Chart Positions (through 1992)

What was released under Willie's name and what was actually bought by the public, especially throughout the country, revealed what was important to those fans. Obviously, it was the Columbia material, though albums Willie did with Tracy Nelson, Leon Russell, Waylon Jennings, and Roy Rogers sold well. Some of the soundtracks sold quite well, as did his Merle Haggard and Julio Iglesias projects. Prior to the Garth Brooks phenomenon, Willie had become the biggest album seller in the history of country music.

The highest Willie went on the national album sales charts was number two with the *Always on My Mind* set. His involvement, along with dozens of other artists, on the *We Are the World* album, got him associated, at least, with a number one album. His next highest album was not *Stardust* or *Red Headed Stranger*, but the soundtrack from *Honeysuckle Rose*. *Stardust* provided Willie with his longest chart residency, one hundred and seventeen weeks.

Willie's first national album chart appearance on his own came in 1975 with *Red Headed Stranger*, though 1974 saw him reach the charts as part of Tracy Nelson and Leon Russell albums. Listed below, from 1974 through 1992, are the albums with which or as part of which Willie made chart appearances. On some, next to the title is a letter in parentheses for which there is an explanation at the end.

As of 1992, Willie's final album chart appearance came with *Half Nelson*, highlighted by his Julio Iglesias number one duet, 'To All The Girls I've Loved Before'. He did chart again after 1992 with *Across the Borderline*, *Super Hits*, and *Moonlight Becomes You*, but given his abrupt dismissal from the radio airwaves (due to advancing age - hey, didn't anyone hear about the ninety-eight year old woman graduating

417

from high school?), his days of being country music's top album seller effectively ended as of 1992.

Chart Albums Done with Others

Label/Number	Date	Title/Sales Status	Highest Rank/ No. of Weeks
Shelter 2108	6/22/74	Leon Russell: Stop All That Jazz	34/16
Atlantic 7310	10/19/74	Tracy Nelson	145/5
Epic 33851	12/6/75	Michael Martin Murphey: Swans Against the Sun	44/13
RCA 1321	2/7/76	Wanted!: The Outlaws (w. Waylon Jennings, Tompall Glaser, and Jessi Colter) (P)	10/51
RCA 1520	4/17/76	MacKintosh & T.J. (Original Soundtrack)	189/4
RCA 2317	5/21/77	Ol' Waylon (P)	15/33
RCA 2686	2/4/78	Waylon & Willie (P)	12/29
Col. 35642	12/2/78	Willie and Family Live (P) (various guests)	32/55
Col. 36064	6/30/79	One for the Road (w. Leon Russell) (G)	25/18
Col. 36476	6/14/80	San Antonio Rose (w. Ray Price) (G)	70/25
RCA 4247	3/6/82	Waylon: Black on Black	39/23
RCA 4455	10/30/82	WWII (w. Waylon) (G)	57/22
Monu. 38389	1/15/83	... The Winning Hand (w. Brenda Lee, Dolly Parton, and Kris Kristofferson)	109/14
Epic 37958	2/12/83	Pancho & Lefty (w. Merle Haggard) (P)	37/53
Col. 38562	4/23/83	Take It to the Limit (w. Waylon) (G)	60/16
Col. 39363	6/16/84	Angel Eyes - Featuring the Guitar of Jackie King	116/7
Col. 39157	9/1/84	Julio Iglesias: 1100 Bel Air Place (P)	5/34
Col. 39531	11/10/84	Music from Songwriter (w. Kristofferson)	152/5
Col. 40043	4/20/85	We Are the World (various artists) (P)	1/22
Col. 40056	6/1/85	Highwayman (w. Waylon, Johnny Cash, and Kristoferson) (G)	92/35

Col. 39990	10/12/85	Half Nelson (G)	178/3
Col. 45240	3/17/90	Highwayman 2 (w. Waylon, Cash, and Kristoferson)	79/13
Epic 47462	8/3/91	Clean Shirt (w. Waylon)	193/3
RCA 3024	11/9/91	Roy Rogers Tribute (various artists)	113/9
Epic 52845	8/29/92	Honeymoon in Vegas: Music from the Original Motion Picture Soundtrack (various artists) (G)	18/24

Solo Chart Albums

Label/Number	Date	Title/Sales Status	Highest Rank/ No. of Weeks
Col. 33482	7/26/75	Red Headed Stranger (P)	28/43
Col. 34092	3/20/76	The Sound in Your Mind (G)	48/15
Col. 34112	10/16/76	The Troublemaker (G)	60/7
Col. 34695	7/9/77	To Lefty from Willie	91/12
Col. 35305	5/13/78	Stardust (P)	30/117
Col. 36188	11/17/79	Willie Nelson Sings Kristofferson (P)	42/25
Col. 36189	12/1/79	Pretty Paper (P)	73/8
Col. 36327	1/12/80	Music from the Original Motion Picture Soundtrack: The Electric Horseman (G)	52/25
Col. 36752	9/6/80	Music from the Original Soundtrack: Honeysuckle Rose (P)	11/36
Col. 36883	3/21/81	Somewhere Over the Rainbow (P)	31/23
Col. 37542	9/19/81	Willie Nelson's Greatest Hits (and Some That Will Be) (P)	27/93
Col. 37951	3/20/82	Always on My Mind (P)	2/99
Col. 38248	3/19/83	Tougher Than Leather	39/20
Col. 39110	11/26/83	Without a Song (P)	54/34
Col. 39145	8/4/84	City of New Orleans (P)	69/26
Col. 40008	3/30/85	Me and Paul	152/7

Sales Status: (P) = Platinum and multi-Platinum (where appropriate); (G) = Gold.

The trade association for record companies, RIAA (Recording Industry Association of America) awards Gold, Platinum, and Multi-platinum sales certifications based on the following criteria:

Gold - for an album, sales must exceed one million dollars (manufacturer's wholesale prices) and half a million units.

Platinum - for an album, sales must exceed one million units and two million dollars (manufacturer's wholesale prices).

Multi-platinum - for an album, each additional one million units in sales (ex: double platinum for another one million units over platinum).

Listing of RIAA (Recording Industry Association of America) Certifications for Album Sales

Gold (1976); Platinum & Multi-Platinum (1986); *Red Headed Stranger*
Gold & Platinum (1976); Multi-Platinum (1985); *Wanted: The Outlaws* (with Waylon Jennings, Tompall Glaser, and Jessi Colter)
Gold & Platinum (1978); Multi-Platinum (1985); *Waylon & Willie*
Gold & Platinum (1978); Multi-Platinum (1984); *Stardust*
Gold (1978); *The Sound in Your Mind*
Gold (1979); *One for the Road*
Gold (1979); Platinum (1980); Multi-Platinum (1990); *Willie and Family Live*
Gold (1980); *The Electric Horseman*
Gold (1980); Platinum (1992); *Willie Nelson Sings Kristofferson*
Gold & Platinum (1980); Multi-Platinum (1992); *Honeysuckle Rose*
Gold & Platinum (1981); *Somewhere Over the Rainbow*
Gold (1981); Platinum (1982); Multi-Platinum (1986); *Greatest Hits (and Some That Will Be)*
Gold & Platinum (1982); Multi-Platinum (1984); *Always on My Mind*
Gold (1982); Platinum (1989); *Pretty Paper*
Gold (1983); *San Antonio Rose*
Gold (1983); *WWII*
Gold (1983); Platinum (1984); *Pancho & Lefty*
Gold (1984); Platinum (1994); *Without a Song*
Gold (1984); Platinum (1994); *City of New Orleans*
Gold (1986); *The Troublemaker*
Gold (1986); *Highwayman*
Gold (1987); *Half Nelson*
Gold (1989); *Take It to the Limit*
Gold (1996); *Super Hits*

The Music Awards

Anyone having a tenure approaching Willie's had to deserve more than a few awards. Add to that longevity, the creativity and trend-setting nature of his writing and recordings, and the number of awards should have turned out to be numerous. They did. On the musical side, he received major awards from NARAS, CMA, and ACM. The ultimate honor came in 1993 when he was inducted into the Country Music Hall of Fame, one of three "Hall of Fame" awards - the others being the Songwriter's Hall of Fame and the *Playboy Magazine* Hall of Fame.

Another crowning achievement was his Global Sales Award for sales of singles, albums, cassettes, and CD's in excess of 40,000,000 units. Until the advent of Garth Brooks, Willie was country music's all-time top album seller. He took the emphasis off singles by showing the industry that country albums could sell well enough to make the national pop charts.

His musical recognition came from beyond country music. He won the Handy Award (named for blues composer, W. C. Handy) from the Blues Foundation for keeping the blues alive in country music. He was even awarded a "doctorate," Doctor of Armadillology, that is. His Farm Aid and Native American activism have garnered him numerous accolades. The State of Texas has also amply honored its native son.

One award really tickled him and that was the "Living Legend" award. After he received it (in 1996), he asked the award-givers, "how do you find someone every year?" He mused that perhaps it means, "we're glad you're still alive." Then he wondered, "do they go through a list and ask, 'who's living?'." If that was the case, he definitely wanted "the legend list." Even though 1997 found him shunned by radio programmers because of his age, he still impressed the awarding agencies, receiving a Grammy nomination for his *How Great Thou Art* (even though it was released on a small independent label) in the Best Gospel Album category.

NARAS (National Academy of Recording Arts & Sciences)

Grammy Award Winners
1975: Best Country Vocal Performance, Male; 'Blue Eyes Crying in the Rain'
1978: Best Country Vocal Performance, Male; 'Georgia on My Mind'
1978: Best Country Vocal Performance by a Duo or Group (with Waylon Jennings), 'Mammas Don't Let Your Babies Grow Up to Be Cowboys'
1980: Best Country Song (Songwriter's Award); 'On the Road Again'
1982: Best Country Vocal Performance, Male; 'Always on My Mind'
Grammy Living Legend Award
Governor's Award - from the Nashville Chapter of NARAS, 1989

Grammy Award Nominations (Nominees)
1974: Best Country Vocal Performance, Duo or Group (with Tracy Nelson), 'After the Fire Is Gone'
1976: Best Country Vocal Performance, Male; 'I'd Have to Be Crazy'
1976: Best Inspirational Performance; 'Amazing Grace'
1979: Best Country Vocal Performance, Male; 'Whiskey River'
1979: Best Country Performance by a Duo or Group with Vocal (with Leon Russell); 'Heartbreak Hotel'
1979: Best Inspirational Performance (with Leon Russell); 'I Saw the Light'
1980: Best Country Vocal Performance, Male; 'On the Road Again'
1980: Best Inspirational Performance; *Family Bible*
1981: Best Country Vocal Performance, Male; *Somewhere Over the Rainbow*
1982: Record of the Year (Chips Moman, producer); 'Always on My Mind'
1982: Best Country Performance by a Duo or Group with Vocal (with Waylon Jennings); '(Sittin' on) The Dock of the Bay'
1983: Best Country Performance by a Duo or Group with Vocal (with Merle Haggard); *Pancho and Lefty*
1983: Best Country Performance by a Duo or Group with Vocal (with Waylon Jennings); *Take It to the Limit*
1984: Best Country Vocal Performance, Male; 'City of New Orleans'
1984: Best Country Performance by a Duo or Group with Vocal (with Julio Iglesias); 'As Time Goes By'
1985: Best Country Vocal Performance, Male; 'Forgiving You Was Easy'
1985: Best Country Performance by a Duo or Group with Vocal (with Kris Kristofferson, Waylon Jennings, and Johnny Cash); 'Highwayman'

1990: Best Country Vocal Collaboration (with Kris Kristofferson, Waylon Jennings, and Johnny Cash); *Highwayman 2*

1994: Best Traditional Pop Vocal; *Moonlight Becomes You*

1997: Best Gospel Album; *How Great Thou Art*

1997: Best Traditional Recording: 'Peach Pickin' Time in Georgia'

CMA (Country Music Association)

1976: Single of the Year (with Waylon Jennings); 'Good Hearted Woman'

1976: Album of the Year (with Waylon Jennings, Tompall Glaser, and Jessi Colter); *Wanted: The Outlaws*

1976: Vocal Duo of the Year - with Waylon Jennings

1979: Entertainer of the Year

1982: Single of the Year; 'Always on My Mind'

1982: Album of the Year; *Always on My Mind*

1983: Vocal Duo of the Year (with Merle Haggard)

1984: Vocal Duo of the Year (with Julio Iglesias)

ACM (Academy of Country Music)

1982: Entertainer of the Year

1982: Album of the Year; *Always on My Mind*

1984: Single of the Year (with Julio Iglesias); 'To All the Girls I've Loved Before'

1984: Tex Ritter Award (with Kris Kristofferson); *Songwriter*

1985: Single of the Year (Highwaymen); 'The Highwayman'

1991: Pioneer Award

Hall of Fame Inductions

Induction 1973: Songwriters' Hall of Fame; from NSAI (Nashville Songwriters' Assn. Int.).

Induction 1983: Music Hall of Fame; from *Playboy* Magazine.

Induction 1993: Hall of Fame; Country Music Hall of Fame and Museum.

Billboard Magazine

1982: Top Artist Country; Top Country Album (*Always on My Mind*); Top Country Single ('Always on My Mind')

1984: Top Country Single (with Julio Iglesias); 'To All the Girls I've Loved Before'

1990: Country Music Single of the Decade; 'Always on My Mind'

American Music Awards

1977: Favorite Single, Country

1982: Favorite Male Artist, Country; Favorite Single, Country (tied with Anne Murray)

1983: Favorite Album, Country; Favorite Album, Pop/Rock

1984: Favorite Male Artist, Country

1985: Favorite Male Video Artist, Country
1986: Favorite Video, Duo or Group, Country (Highwaymen); Favorite Video Single, Country (with the Highwaymen); Favorite Male Artist, Country; Favorite Single, Country, Special Award of Appreciation
1987: Favorite Male Artist, Country
1989: Special Merit Award; music industry contributions

Individual Awards

Certificate of Citation; from The Texas House of Representatives.

Proclamation: "Willie Nelson Day" (July 4, 1975); from The Texas Senate.

The Handy Award, for keeping the Blues alive in Country Music; from The Blues Foundation, 11/17/1975.

Commission as Honorary Texas Ranger; from The State of Texas, 1978.

Commission as Admiral in the Texas Navy; from The State of Texas, 1978.

Lifetime Achievement Award; from NAPM (National Academy of Popular Music), 1983.

Lifetime Achievement Award; from the Songwriters' Hall of Fame (NSAI), 1983.

Special Agricultural Tribute Award; by the Triumph of Agriculture Exposition, 1986.

The Ernest Tubb Humanitarian Award, 1987.

The Roy Acuff Community Service Award; from the Country Music Federation. 1988.

Certificate: In Appreciation of Devoted and Invaluable Services rendered to Native American Indians; The National Association for the Renewal and Unity of Our People, 9/5/1988.

Vocal Group Award (Highwaymen); from German American Country Music Federation, 1993.

Minnie Pearl Award; from *The Nashville Network/Music City News*, 1995.

Living Legend Award; from *The Nashville Network/Music City News*, 1996.

The Complete Willie Nelson RCA Sessionography

FROM THE ORIGINAL RCA SESSION LOGS

Was RCA ever a "good time" for Willie?
(Photo from RCA Records and Willie Nelson)

Willie recorded pop and country for RCA!
(Photo from RCA Records and Willie Nelson)

Willie Nelson's RCA Session Information

The Chronological Session List

Session date: November 12, 1964 6 to 9PM; (C & W Singles) Producer: Chet Atkins, Engineer: Chuck Seitz

Songs recorded:
RWA4-1596 Pretty Paper
RWA4-1597 What a Merry Christmas This Could Be (Howard/ Cochran)
RWA4-1598 Healing Hands of Time
RWA4-1599 Talk to Me

Session personnel: Willie Nelson - leader/guitar, Henry P. Strzelecki - bass, Kenneth A. Buttrey - drums, Hargus Robbins - piano, Velma Smith - guitar, Pete Drake - steel guitar, Jerry R. Hubbard - electric guitar, Jerry Smith - vibes

Additional backing: Priscilla A. Hubbard, Dolores Edgin, Harold R. Ragsdale (aka Ray Stevens), Raymond C. Walker

Session notes: 'Pretty Paper' came out as the "A" side of a Christmas single. It has since been on several anthologies. 'What a Merry Christmas This Could Be' only appeared on a "various artists" Christmas collection. 'Talk to Me' has yet to be released by RCA or an affiliate. This version of 'Healing Hands of Time' (one of three times Willie recorded the song for RCA) did not come out on an album.

Session date: December 3, 1964 9:30 AM to 12:30 PM; (German recordings) Producer: Chet Atkins, Engineer: William Vandevort

Songs recorded (by Bobby Bare):
RWA4-1637 Alle Clausen Dass Ich Gluecklich Bin (Scharfenberger - Busch)
Songs recorded (by Willie Nelson):
RWA4-1638 Whisky Walzer (Mayer - Hertha)
RWA4-1639 Don't Fence Me In (Cole Porter)

Session personnel: Floyd Cramer - piano/leader, Murrey M. Harman, Jr. - drums, Ray Edenton - guitar, Henry P. Strzelecki - bass, Harold R. Bradley - guitar, Hargus Robbins - harpsichord

Additional backing: Anita Kerr, Dorothy Dillard, Louis Nunley, William G. Wright, Jr.

Session notes: The recording of the Porter song, 'Don't Fence Me in' was "lost" by RCA. One hour was spent on Bare's track and two on Willie's.

Session date: December 4, 1964 2 to 5 PM; (German recordings) Producer: Chet Atkins

Songs recorded (by Bobby Bare):
RWA4-1637 Alle Clausen Dass Ich Gluecklich Bin (Scharfenberger - Busch)
Songs recorded (by Willie Nelson -Vocal overdubs):
RWA4-1640 Little Darling (Pretty Paper) (Nelson - Claus Ritter)
RWA4-1638 Whisky Walzer (Mayer - Hertha)

Additional backing: Anita Kerr, Dorothy Dillard, Louis Nunley, William G. Wright, Jr.

Session notes: No musicians were listed as present during this session. It was for tracking only (with additional backing added). The Willie songs were released as a foreign RCA single, 47-9621.

Session date: January 12, 1965 2 to 5 PM; (C & W Singles) (C & W Album: *Good Times*) Producer: Chet Atkins (with Felton Jarvis on 'Ashamed'), Arrangements and Copyist: Anita Kerr, Engineer: Wm. Vandevort

Songs recorded:
SWA4-1048 Permanently Lonely
SWA4-1049 Healing Hands of Time
SWA4-1050 Ashamed

SWA4-1051 She's Not for You

Session personnel: Willie Nelson - leader, Jerry G. Kennedy - electric guitar, Murrey M. Harman, Jr. - drums, Velma W. Smith - guitar, Henry P. Strzelecki, Hargus Robbins - piano, Pete Drake - steel guitar

Additional players: Brenton B. Banks, Solie I. Fott, Lillian V. Hunt, George Binkley, III - violin, Martin Kathan (or Katahn) - viola

Additional backing: Anita Kerr, Dorothy A. Dillard, William G. Wright, Louis D. Nunley

Session notes: 'Permanently Lonely' and 'Ashamed', wound up on the 1968 album, *Good Times*. 'She's Not for You' was first released as a single and on the 1977 album, *Before His Time*.

Session date: April 7, 1965 6-9 PM RCA's Studio A; (C & W Album: *Country Willie: His Own Songs*) Producer: Chet Atkins, Engineer: Jim Malloy

Songs recorded:
SWA4-2371 Are You Sure
SWA4-2372 Night Life
SWA4-2373 Mr. Record Man
SWA4-2374 Healing Hands of Time

Session personnel: Willie H. Nelson - leader/guitar, Henry P. Strzelecki - bass, Murrey M. Harman, Jr. - drums, Jerry R. Hubbard - electric guitar, Pete Drake - steel guitar, Ray Edenton - guitar

Session notes: Jerry R. Hubbard became known as Jerry Reed. This version of 'Healing Hands of Time' wound up on Willie's first RCA album, the 1995 compilation, *The Essential Willie Nelson*, and the expanded twentieth anniversary edition of *The Outlaws* album.

Session date: April 8, 1965 6-9PM RCA's Studio A; (C & W Album: *Country Willie: His Own Songs*) Producer: Chet Atkins, Engineer: Jim Malloy

Songs recorded:
SWA4-2379 Funny How Time Slips Away
SWA4-2380 My Own Peculiar Way
SWA4-2381 One Day at a Time
SWA4-2382 It Should Be Easier Now
SWA4-2383 Darkness on the Face of the Earth

Session personnel: Willie Nelson - leader/guitar, Henry Strzelecki - bass, Jerry K. Carrigan - drums, Jerry G. Kennedy - electric guitar, Velma Smith - guitar, Pete Drake - steel guitar

Session date: April 9, 1965 6-9PM RCA's Studio A; (C & W Album: *Country Willie: His Own Songs*) Producer: Chet Atkins, Engineer: Jim Malloy

Songs recorded:
SWA4-2384 Buddy
SWA4-2385 Hello Walls
SWA4-2386 So Much to Do
SWA4-2387 Within Your Crowd

Session personnel: Willie Nelson - leader/guitar, Bob L. Moore - bass, Murrey M. Harman, Jr. - drums, Jerry G. Kennedy - electric guitar, Velma W. Smith - guitar, Jerry R. Hubbard - electric guitar, Pete Drake - steel guitar

Session notes: The cut, 'Buddy', recorded April 9, 1965, was not used on this first album. It was held and then used on the 1968 set, *Good Times*.

Session date: August 17, 1965 10 PM to 1 AM; (C & W Singles); (Remakes) (C & W Album: *Good Times*) Producer: Chet Atkins (with Felton Jarvis on 'Did I Ever Love You' and 'Down to Our Last Goodbye'), Arrangements: Harold R. Ragsdale, Copyist: John Ragsdale, Engineer: Jim Malloy

Songs recorded:
SWA4-2660 Did I Ever Love You
SWA4-2661 And So Will You My Love
SWA4-2662 I Just Can't Let You Say Goodbye
SWA4-2663 Down to Our Last Goodbye

Session personnel: Chet Atkins - guitar/leader, Harold R. Ragsdale - piano

Additional players: Brenton Banks, Lillian Hunt, Kenneth Goldsmith, Solie Fott, Sheldon Kurland, Martin Kathan - violin

Additional backing: Priscilla A. Hubbard, Dolores D. Edgin, Mildred Kirkham

Session notes: This version of 'I Just Can't Let You Say Goodbye' was not released by RCA until the 1988 compilation, *All Time Greatest Hits, Vol. 1*. Only two tracks were made part of the *Good Times* album,

'Down to Our Last Goodbye' and 'Did I Ever Love You'. 'And So Will You My Love' was the "B" side of a 1965 RCA single. Both 'Down to Our Last Goodbye' and 'Did I Ever Love You' were placed on Willie's Camden album, *Good Ol' Country Singin'*.

Session date: December 15, 1965 6-9PM Studio A; (C & W Album: *Country Favorites: Willie Nelson Style*) Producer: Chet Atkins, Engineer: Jim Malloy

Songs recorded:
SWA4-2946 Fraulein (Lawton Williams)
SWA4-2947 I Love You Because (Leon Payne)
SWA4-2948 I'd Trade All of My Tomorrows (Jenny Lou Carson)
SWA4-2949 Making Believe (Jimmy Work)
SWA4-2950 Home in San Antone (Floyd Jenkins)
SWA4-2951 Don't You Ever Get Tired (of Hurting Me) (Hank Cochran)

Session personnel: Willie Nelson - leader, Hargus Robbins - piano, Jimmy Wilkerson - vibes, bass guitar, Wade Ray -fiddle, Grant C. Shofner - rhythm guitar, Buddy (Elmer) Charleton - steel guitar, Leon Rhodes - electric guitar, Jack Drake - bass, Jack H. Greene - drums

Session date: December 16, 1965 6-9PM Studio A; (C & W Album: *Country Favorites: Willie Nelson Style*) Producer: Chet Atkins, Engineer: Jim Malloy

Songs recorded:
SWA4-2956 Columbus Stockade Blues (Jimmie Davis and Eva Sargent)
SWA4-2957 Seasons of My Heart (George Jones/Darrell Edwards)
SWA4-2958 Heartaches by the Number (Harlan Howard)
SWA4-2959 Go On Home (Hank Cochran)
SWA4-2960 My Window Faces the South (Abner Silver - Mitchell Parish)
SWA4-2961 San Antonio Rose (Bob Wills)

Session personnel: Willie Nelson - leader, Hargus Robbins - piano, Jimmy Wilkerson - vibes and bass guitar, Wade Ray -fiddle, Grant C. Shofner - Rhythm Guitar, Buddy (Elmer) Charleton - Steel Guitar, Leon Rhodes - electric guitar, Jack Drake - bass, Jack H. Greene - drums

Session notes: Cal Smith was scheduled as rhythm guitarist on the 15th and 16th. His name was replaced by Grant Shofner, his real name. Like Shofner, several of the players at the session had previously been in Ernest Tubb's band.

Session date: March 1, 1966 2 to 5 PM; (C & W/Pop Singles) Producer: Felton Jarvis, , Engineer: Jim Malloy

Songs recorded:
TWA4-0654 I'm Still Not Over You
TWA4-0655 San Antonio Rose (Bob Wills)
TWA4-0656 Columbus Stockade Blues (Jimmie Davis & Eva Sargent)
TWA4-0657 He Sits at My Table (Chip Taylor)

Session personnel: Jerry Hubbard - leader/electric guitar, William McElhiney - contractor and trumpets, Floyd Cramer - vibes and piano, Bob Moore - electric bass and upright, Murrey Harman - drums, Billy Sanford - electric guitar, Karl Garvin - trumpet

Additional players: Kenneth Goldsmith, Lillian Hunt, Brenton Banks, Solie Fott, Martin Kathan, Sheldon Kurland - violin, Harvey Wolfe - cello

Additional backing: Dolores Edgin, Mary E. Greene, Mildred Kirkham

Session notes: 'I'm Still Not Over You' and 'He Sits at My Table' were placed, in 1968, on *Good Ol' Country Singin'*. Willie cut the other two tracks for singles. He had previous recorded versions of the two songs for albums.

Session date: June 8, 1966 6 to 9:30 PM; (C & W Album: *Make Way for Willie Nelson*) Producer: Chet Atkins, Engineer: Jim Malloy

Songs recorded:
TWA4-0978 A Wonderful Yesterday
TWA4-0979 The Party's Over
TWA4-0980 One in a Row
TWA4-0981 Make Way for a Better Man (Cy Coben)

Session personnel: Willie Nelson - leader, Johnny B. Shinn - drums, Buddy Emmons - steel guitar, Roy M. Huskey, Jr. - bass, Hargus Robbins - piano, Wade Ray - bass, Jerry Hubbard - electric guitar, Velma Smith - guitar

Additional players: Brenton Banks, Lillian Hunt, Sheldon Kurland - violin, Solie Fott - violin

Additional backing: Margaret E. Willis, Judy P. Johnson, Mary E. Johnson, Anna Johnson

Session notes: 'The Party's Over' was not used on this album, but instead on the album for which it served as the title track, *The Party's Over.* 'A Wonderful Yesterday' was not used until the 1968 album *Good Times.*

Session date: 2 Sessions (Live Recording) - July 9, 1966, 6PM to 12PM; Panther Hall, Ft. Worth, Texas (C & W Album: *Country Music Concert*) Producer: Felton Jarvis, Engineer: Al Pachucki

Songs recorded:
TWA5-1111 Introduction: Bo Powell
TWA5-1111 Willie Introduces Band
TWA5-1111 Medley: Mr. Record Man/Hello Walls/One Day at a Time
TWA5-1112 Medley: The Last Letter (Rex Griffin)/Half a Man
TWA5-1113 I Never Cared for You
TWA5-1114 Yesterday (John Lennon - Paul McCartney)
TWA5-1115 Touch Me
TWA5-1116 Something to Think About
TWA5-1117 I Just Can't Let You Say Goodbye
TWA5-1118 How Long Is Forever
TWA5-1119 Night Life
TWA5-1120 Medley: Opportunity to Cry/Permanently Lonely
TWA5-1121 My Own Peculiar Way

Session personnel: Willie Nelson - leader, Jerry Stembridge -rhythm guitar, Wade Ray - bass, John Shinn - drums

Session notes: This album would be rereleased as *Willie Nelson Live* in 1976. The drummer, John Shinn, became known simply as Johnny Bush.

Session date: November 28, 1966 10 AM to 1PM; (C & W Album: *Make Way for Willie Nelson*) Producer: Felton Jarvis, Engineer: Jim Malloy

Songs recorded:
TWA4-1520 Have I Stayed Away Too Long (Frank Loesser)
TWA4-1521 Some Other World (Floyd Tillman)
TWA4-1522 If It's Wrong to Love You (Bonnie Dodd/Charles Mitchell)
TWA4-1523 Have I Told You Lately That I Love You (Scotty Wiseman)
TWA4-1524 You Made Me Live, Love and Die (Floyd Tillman)
TWA4-1525 Born to Lose (Frankie Brown aka Ted Daffan)

Session personnel: Willie Nelson - leader, John Shinn - drums, Jerry Smith - piano, Jerry Hubbard - electric guitar, Velma Smith - rhythm guitar, James Day - steel guitar, Roy M. Huskey, Jr. - bass

Session date: November 29, 1966 (10 AM to 1 PM); (C & W Album: *Make Way for Willie Nelson*) Producer: Chet Atkins (except Tender Years - Felton Jarvis and Chet Atkins), Engineer: Jim Malloy

Songs recorded:
TWA4-1526 What Now My Love (Becaud-Sigman-DeLanoe)
TWA4-1527 Lovin' Lies (Troy Martin - Pete Pyle - Dorothy Chapman)
TWA4-1528 Teach Me to Forget (Leon Payne)
TWA4-1529 Tender Years (Darrell Edwards)
TWA4-1530 A Mansion on the Hill (Hank Williams - Fred Rose)
TWA4-1531 Something to Think About

Session personnel: Willie Nelson - leader, John Shinn - drums, Jerry Smith - piano, Jerry Hubbard - electric guitar, Velma Smith - rhythm guitar, James Day - steel guitar, Roy M. Huskey, Jr. - bass

Session notes: Two tracks, 'Tender Years' and 'Something to Think About', were not used on this album, but instead went on Willie's first Camden album (from 1968), *Good Ol' Country Singin'*, the release of which was scheduled for May 1968 but was put into suspension.

Session date: February 22, 1967 10 AM to 1 PM; (C & W Singles) Producer: Chet Atkins, Engineer: William Vandevort

Songs recorded:
UWA4-2202 Blackjack County Chain (Red Lane)
UWA4-2203 Don't Say Love or Nothing
UWA4-2204 You Ought to Hear Me Cry
UWA4-2205 I Don't Feel Anything

Session personnel: Thomas Grady Martin - leader/electric guitar, William P. Ackerman - drums, Jerry D. Smith - piano, Velma W. Smith - rhythm guitar, James C. Day - steel guitar, Henry P. Strzelecki, bass

Additional backing: William G. Wright, Louis D. Nunley, Priscilla A. Hubbard, Dorothy A Dillard

Session notes: 'Blackjack County Chain' was initially released as a single (it charted). In 1981, it was included on the album, *The Minstrel Man*, in overdubbed form. 'Don't Say Love or Nothing' was released only as the "B" side of a single. This version of 'I Don't Feel Anything' remained unreleased as Willie rerecorded the song June 2, 1970, for the *Laying My Burdens Down* album. 'You Ought to Hear Me Cry' was held until 1977 when it was released as a single (which charted) and included on the *Before His Time* album, also released in 1977.

Session date: June 13, 1967 10 AM to 1PM; (C & W Album: *The Party's Over*) Producer: Chet Atkins, Engineer: Jim Malloy

Songs Recorded:
UWA4-2518 Hold Me Tighter
UWA4-2519 I'll Stay Around (Nelson - Hank Cochran)
UWA4-2520 A Moment Isn't Very Long
UWA4-2521 The Ghost
UWA4-2522 No Tomorrow in Sight

Session personnel: Willie Nelson - leader, John B. Shinn - drums, Jerry Smith - piano, James Day - steel guitar, Thomas G. Martin - electric guitar, Jerry Hubbard - electric guitar, Roy Huskey, Jr. - bass

Additional players: Brenton Banks, Howard Carpenter, Sheldon Kurland, Solie Fott - violin, Marvin Chantry - viola, Harvey Wolfe - cello

Session date: June 14, 1967 10 AM to 1 PM; (C & W Album: *The Party's Over*) Producer: Chet Atkins, Engineer: Jim Malloy

Songs recorded:
UWA4-2523 There Goes a Man
UWA4-2524 Go Away
UWA4-2525 Once Alone
UWA4-2526 The End of Understanding
UWA4-2527 To Make a Long Story Short (She's Gone) (Nelson - Foster)
UWA4-2528 Suffer in Silence

Session personnel: Willie Nelson - leader, John B. Shinn - drums, Jerry Smith - piano, Jimmy Day - steel guitar, Thomas G. Martin - electric guitar, Jerry Hubbard - electric guitar, Roy Huskey, Jr. - bass

Additional players: Brenton Banks, Solie Fott, Sheldon Kurland, Howard Carpenter - violin, Marvin Chantry - viola, Harvey Wolfe - cello

Session notes: 'The Party's Over', master number TWKM (TWA4)-0979 and title cut of *The Party's Over and Other Great Willie Nelson Songs*, was recorded 6/8/66 at the *Make Way for Willie Nelson* sessions.

Session date: August 9, 1967 10 AM to 1PM; (C & W Album); Producer: Chet Atkins, Engineer: Jim Malloy

Songs recorded:
UWA4-2664 Truth Number One (Aaron Allen)

UWA4-2665 When I Don't Have You
UWA4-2666 Someday You'll Call My Name (Jean Branch - Eddie Hill)
UWA4-2667 Wild Memories

Session personnel: Grady Martin - leader and electric guitar, Jerry Carrigan - drums, Jerry Smith - piano, Harold Bradley - rhythm guitar, James Day - steel guitar, Roy Huskey, Jr. - bass, Ray Stevens - vibes, Chet Atkins - guitar

Session notes: This session started out as the first of three for the *Texas in My Soul* album, but only one track, 'Truth Number One', was released by RCA or an affiliate. It came out only as the "B" side of a single.

Session date: August 10, 1967 10 AM to 1PM; (C & W Album: *Texas in My Soul*) Producer: Chet Atkins, Engineer: Jim Malloy

Songs recorded:
UWA4-2668 San Antonio (Jerry Blanton)
UWA4-2668 Texas in My Soul (Zeb Turner - Ernest Tubb)
UWA4-2670 Travis Letter (William B. Travis)
UWA4-2670 (continued) Remember the Alamo (Jane Bowers)
UWA4-2671 Beautiful Texas (W. Lee O'Daniel)
UWA4-2672 There's a Little Bit of Everything in Texas (Ernest Tubb)

Session personnel: Grady Martin - leader/electric guitar, Ray Stevens - organ and vibes, Murrey Harman, Jr. - drums, Jerry Smith - piano, Ray Edenton - rhythm guitar, James Day - steel guitar, Roy Huskey, Jr. - bass, Chet Atkins - guitar

Session notes: Two cuts, 'Travis Letter' and 'Remember the Alamo' were recorded as separately but were "continued" (run) together as one with one master number. That kept the total number of tracks on the album at ten. On the Bear Family rerelease of the album, they were listed as separate selections. Zeb Turner was listed as co-writer on 'There's a Little Bit of Everything in Texas', but his name was crossed off. In Ronnie Pugh's Ernest Tubb discography, Tubb was listed as sole author.

Session date: August 11, 1967 9:30 AM to 12:30 PM; (C & W Album: *Texas in My Soul*) Producer: Chet Atkins, Engineer: Jim Malloy

Songs recorded:
UWA4- 2673 Who Put All My Ex's in Texas (E. Rabbitt/T. Moon/L. Lee)
UWA4- 2674 Dallas (D. Stovall/Groom)
UWA4- 2675 The Hill Country Theme (Cindy Walker - Glenn Paxton)
     (From Lyndon Johnson's Texas)
UWA4- 2663 Streets of Laredo (P. D.)

UWA4- 2676 Waltz Across Texas (Billy T. Tubb)

Session personnel: Grady Martin - leader/electric guitar, Ray Stevens - organ, vibes, Murrey Harman, Jr. - drums, Jerry Smith - piano, Ray Edenton - rhythm guitar, James Day - steel guitar, Roy M. Huskey, Jr. - bass

Session date: December 12, 1967 10 AM to 1 PM; (C & W Singles) (C & W Album: *Good Times*) Producer: Felton Jarvis, Engineer: Tom Pick

Songs recorded:
UWA4-3078 December Day
UWA4-3079 Pages (Nelson - Nelson)
UWA4-3080 Little Things (Nelson - Nelson)

Session personnel: Thomas Grady Martin - leader/guitar, Chester Atkins - guitar, Roy M. Huskey, Jr. - bass, James C. Day - guitar

Session notes: All the tracks were used on the 1968 album, *Good Times*.

Session date: March 27, 1968 2 to 5 PM; (C & W Singles) (C & W Album: *Good Times*) Producers: Chet Atkins and Felton Jarvis, Engineer: Bill Vandevort

Songs recorded:
WWA4-1982 Good Times
WWA4-1983 She's Still Gone (Nelson - Nelson)
WWA4-1984 Sweet Memories (Newbury)

Session personnel: Willie Nelson - leader, Thomas G. Martin - guitar, Chet Atkins - guitar, Roy M. Huskey, Jr. - bass

Session notes: All the tracks were used on the *Good Times* album. 'Sweet Memories' became the title cut, in overdubbed form, of a 1979 album. The overdubbed version was also on *The Best of Willie Nelson*.

Session date: July 8, 1968 10 AM to 1 PM; (C & W Singles) Producers: Chet Atkins and Felton Jarvis, Engineer: Al Pachucki

Songs recorded:
WWA4-3208 Johnny One Time
WWA4-3209 Jimmy's Road
WWA4-3210 Bring Me Sunshine

Session personnel: Grady Martin - leader/guitar, Murrey Harman - drums, Bill Pursell - piano, Ray Edenton - guitar, Chester - guitar, Roy Huskey, Jr. - bass

Session notes: 'Johnny One Time' was released only as a single (which did chart) until 1984, when it was included on the album, *Don't You Ever Get Tired of Hurting Me*. 'Bring Me Sunshine' was also released first as a single and then as part of the 1988 compilation, *All Time Greatest Hits, Vol. 1*. 'Jimmy's Road' was only released as a single.

Session date: July 18, 1968 2 to 5 PM; (C & W Singles) (Overdub) Producers: Felton Jarvis (Chet Atkins and Felton Jarvis produced 'Bring Me Sunshine'), Engineer: Al Pachucki

Songs recorded:
WWA4-3286 Johnny One Time
WWA4-3287 Jimmy's Road
WWA4-3288 Bring Me Sunshine

Session personnel: Felton Jarvis - leader, Brenton Banks, Lillian Hunt, Sheldon Kurland, Solie Fott - violin, Howard Carpenter, Martin Kathan - viola, Howard Cruthirds - cello

Session notes: Ten days after Willie cut these tracks (July 8), Jarvis added the strings. After that, each cut was released as a single.

Session date: November 5, 1968 10 AM to 1 PM; (C & W Album: *My Own Peculiar Way*) Producers: Chet Atkins and Danny Davis, Arrangements (and conducting): Bergen White, Copyist: George Tidwell, Engineer: Al Pachucki

Songs recorded:
WWA4-4990 I Let My Mind Wander
WWA4-4991 I Just Don't Understand
WWA4-4992 I Just Dropped By
WWA4-4993 The Local Memory

Session personnel: Bergen White - leader, Murrey M. Harman, Jr. - contractor, drums, David Briggs - piano, Jerry Hubbard - electric guitar, Wayne Moss - electric guitar, Charles R. McCoy - guitar, piano, vibes, Bob L. Moore - bass

Additional players: Byron Williams, Brenton B. Banks, Lillian V. Hunt, Akira Nagai, Solie Fott, Martin Kathan, George Binkley, III - violin, Gary VanOsdale, Marvin D. Chantry - viola, Byron Bach - cello

Additional backing: Dorothy A. Dillard, William G. Wright, Jr., M. Jeanine Ogletree

Session date: November 6, 1968 10 AM to 1 PM; (C & W Album: *My Own Peculiar Way*) Producer: Chet Atkins, Arrangements (and conducting): Bergen White, Copyist: George Tidwell, Engineer: Al Pachucki

Songs recorded:
WWA4-4994 Natural to Be Gone (John Hartford)
WWA4-4995 Love Has a Mind of Its Own (Dallas Frazier)
WWA4-4996 I Walk Alone (Herbert Wilson)
WWA4-4997 It Will Come to Pass (Don Baird)

Session personnel: Willie Nelson - leader, Bergen White - contractor, Jerry Carrigan - drums, David Briggs - piano, Thomas Martin - electric guitar, Wayne Moss - electric guitar, Charles McCoy - piano, vibes, Bob Moore - bass

Additional players: Byron Williams, Brenton Banks, Laurence Harvin, Jo L. Parker, Stephanie Woolf, Suzanne Parker - violin, Martin Kathan, Solie Fott - viola, Byron Bach - cello

Session date: November 7, 1968 10 AM to 1 PM; (C & W Album: *My Own Peculiar Way*) Producer: Chet Atkins, Arrangements (and conducting): Bergen White, Copyist: George Tidwell, Engineer: Al Pachucki

Songs recorded:
WWA4-4998 My Own Peculiar Way
WWA4-4999 The Message
WWA4-5000 That's All (Merle Travis)
WWA4-5001 Any Old Arms Won't Do (Nelson - Hank Cochran)

Session personnel: Willie Nelson - leader, Bergen White - contractor, vibes, celeste, Wayne Butler - tenor sax, trombone, Jerry Carrigan - drums, David Briggs - piano, Thomas Martin - electric guitar, Wayne Moss - electric guitar, Bob L. Moore - bass, Donald Sheffield - trumpet, George Tidwell - trumpet, Norman Ray - baritone sax

Additional players: Byron Williams, Brenton Banks, George Binkley, Carol Walker, Pierre Menard, Lillian Hunt - violin

Session date: November 12, 1969 10 AM to 1 PM; (C & W Album: *Both Sides Now*) Producer: Felton Jarvis, Engineer: Al Pachucki, Technician: Milton Henderson

Songs recorded:

XWA4-2607 Bloody Merry Morning
XWA4-2608 Pins and Needles (Floyd Jenkins)
XWA4-2609 Everybody's Talkin' (Fred Neil) (from the United Artists
     motion picture "Midnight Cowboy")
XWA4-2610 Crazy Arms (R. Mooney - C. Seals)

Session personnel: Willie Nelson - leader/guitar, Jimmy Day - bass,
David Zettner - guitar, Billy English - drums

Session notes: On 1/15/70, two cuts, 'Everybody's Talkin'' and 'Pins and
Needles' were overdubbed.

Session date: November 13, 1969 10 AM to 1 PM; (C & W Album: *Both
Sides Now*) Producer: Felton Jarvis, Engineer: Al Pachucki, Technician:
Milton Henderson

Songs recorded:
XWA4-2611 I Gotta Get Drunk
XWA4-2612 Wabash Cannonball
XWA4-2613 One Has My Name (the Other Has My Heart) (Eddie and
     Dearest Dean - Hal Blair)
XWA4-2614 Who Do I Know in Dallas (Nelson - Hank Cochran)

Session personnel: Willie Nelson - leader/guitar, Jimmy Day - steel
guitar, David Zettner - bass, Billy English - drums

Session date: November 18, 1969 10 AM to 1 PM; (C & W Album: *Both
Sides Now*) Producer: Felton Jarvis, Engineer: Al Pachucki, Technician:
Roy Shockley

Songs recorded:
XWA4-2615 Both Sides Now (Joni Mitchell)
XWA4-2616 It Could Be Said That Way
XWA4-2617 Once More with Feeling (Shirley Nelson)

Session personnel: Willie Nelson - leader/guitar, Jimmy Day - steel
guitar, bass, David Zettner - bass, guitar, Billy English - drums

Session notes: On 1/15/70, 'Both Sides Now' was overdubbed.

Session date: January 15, 1970 10 AM to 1 PM; (Overdub) (C & W Album:
Both Sides Now) Producer: Felton Jarvis, Engineer: Al Pachucki,
Technician: Roy Shockley

Songs recorded:
XWA4-2608 Pins and Needles (from 11/12/69)

XWA4-2609 Everybody's Talkin' (from 11/12/69)
XWA4-2615 Both Sides Now (from 11/18/69)

Session personnel: Norbert "Curly" Putnam - bass, James Isbell - bongos

Session dates: June 1, 1970 10 AM to 1 PM; (C & W Album: *Laying My Burdens Down*) Producer: Felton Jarvis, Engineer: Al Pachucki, Technician: Roy Shockley

Songs recorded:
ZWA4-1572 Following Me Around
ZWA4-1573 Minstrel Man (Eddie Rager/Stan Haas)
ZWA4-1574 Where Do You Stand?
ZWA4-1575 When We Live Again

Session personnel: Willie Nelson - leader, Jerry K. Carrigan - drums, David P. Briggs - piano, Jerry Stembridge - rhythm guitar, Herman B. Wade - electric guitar, Norbert Putnam - bass

Session date: June 2, 1970 10 AM to 1 PM; (C & W Album: *Laying My Burdens Down*) Producer: Felton Jarvis, Engineer: Al Pachucki, Technician: Roy Shockley

Songs recorded:
ZWA4-1576 If You Could See What's Going Through My Mind
ZWA4-1577 Happiness Lives Next Door
ZWA4-1578 I've Seen That Look on Me (A Thousand Times) (Harlan
    Howard - Shirl Milete)
ZWA4-1579 I Don't Feel Anything

Session personnel: Grady Martin - electric guitar/leader, Jerry Carrigan - drums, David Briggs - piano, Jerry Stembridge - rhythm guitar, Norbert Putnam - bass

Session notes: 'If You Could See What's Going Through My Mind' has remained unreleased by either RCA or any of its affiliates.

Session date: June 3, 1970 2 to 5 PM; (C & W Album: *Laying My Burdens Down*) Producer: Felton Jarvis, Engineer: Al Pachucki, Technician: Mike Shockley

Songs recorded:
ZWA4-1580 Laying My Burdens Down
ZWA4-1581 How Long Have You Been There (Dee Moeller)
ZWA4-1582 Senses (Glen Campbell/Jeannie Seely)

Session personnel: Thomas G. Martin - leader/electric guitar, Jerry Carrigan - drums, David Briggs - piano, Jerry Stembridge - rhythm guitar, Norbert Putnam - bass

Session date: November 19, 1970 2 to 5 PM; (C & W Album: *Willie Nelson and Family*) Producer: Felton Jarvis, Arrangements: Glen Spreen (on 'Sunday Mornin' Comin' Down' and 'What Can You Do to Me Now?'), Engineer: Les Ladd, Technician: Roy Shockley

Songs recorded:
ZWA4-1946 Sunday Mornin' Comin' Down (Kris Kristofferson)
ZWA4-1947 What Can You Do to Me Now? (Nelson - Hank Cochran)
ZWA4-1948 The Loser's Song (Cindy Walker)

Session personnel: Felton Jarvis - leader, Jerry Carrigan - drums, David Briggs - piano, Jerry Stembridge - guitar, Herman Wade, Jr. - guitar, Norbert Putnam - bass, David Zettner - guitar, Glen Spreen - organ, George Tidwell - trumpet, Don Sheffield - trumpet, Dennis Good - trombone, Terry Williams - trombone, Eberhard Ramm - french horn, David Elliott - french horn, Farrell Morris - percussion, Billy Puett - flute, Skip Lane - flute

Additional players: Sheldon Kurland, Brenton Banks, Albert Coleman, George Binkley - violin, Marvin Chantry, Gary VanOsdale - viola, Byron T. Bach - cello, David Vanderkooi - cello

Session notes: The Cindy Walker composition, 'The Loser's Song', was recorded for this album but not used. It has not yet been released by RCA or an affiliate.

Session date: November 20, 1970 2 to 5:30 PM (One-half hour overtime); (C & W Album: *Willie Nelson and Family*) Producer: Felton Jarvis, Arrangements: Glen Spreen (on 'I Can Cry Again', 'I'm a Memory', and 'That's Why I Love Her So'), Engineer: Les Ladd, Technician: Roy Shockley

Songs recorded:
ZWA4-1949 Fire and Rain (James Taylor)
ZWA4-1950 I Can Cry Again
ZWA4-1951 I'm a Memory
ZWA4-1952 That's Why I Love Her So

Session personnel: Felton Jarvis - leader, Jerry Carrigan - drums, David Briggs - piano, Jerry Stembridge - guitar, Herman Wade, Jr. - guitar, Norbert Putnam - bass, David Zettner - guitar, Glen Spreen - organ

Additional backing: Ginger Holladay, Lavernge Moore, Temple Riser

Session date: November 24, 1970 10 Am to 1 PM; (C & W Album: *Willie Nelson and Family*) Producer: Felton Jarvis, Arrangements & Copyist: Glen Spreen, Engineer: Al Pachucki, Technician: Roy Shockley

Songs recorded:
ZWA4-1953 Yours Love (Harlan Howard)
ZWA4-1954 Kneel at the Feet of Jesus
ZWA4-1955 Today I Started Loving You Again (Haggard - B. Owens)
ZWA4-1956 I'm So Lonesome I Could Cry (Hank Williams)

Session personnel: Felton Jarvis - leader, Jerry Carrigan - drums, David Briggs - piano, Jerry Stembridge - guitar, Herman Wade, Jr. - guitar, Norbert Putnam - bass, Glen Spreen - organ, George Tidwell, Don Sheffield - trumpet, Dennis Good, Terry Williams - trombone, Eberhard Ramm, David Elliott - french horn, Weldon Myrick - steel guitar

Additional players: Sheldon Kurland, Brenton Banks, Albert Coleman, George Binkley - violin, Marvin Chantry, Gary VanOsdale - viola, Byron T. Bach, David Vanderkooi - cello

Additional backing: Mary E. Greene, Mary Holladay, Ginger Holladay

Session date: May 3, 1971 10 AM to 1 PM; (C & W Album: *Yesterday's Wine*) Producer: Felton Jarvis, Engineer: Al Pachucki, Technician: Roy Shockley

Songs recorded:
AWA4-1445 Where's the Show/Let Me Be a Man
AWA4-1446 In God's Eyes
AWA4-1447 These Are Difficult Times/Remember the Good Times

Session personnel: Felton Jarvis - leader, Willie Ackerman - drums, Jerry Stembridge - guitar, Herman Wade, Jr. - guitar, Roy M. Huskey, Jr. - bass, David Zettner - guitar

Session notes: The master number for 'Where's the Show' was AWA4-1444. It became part of master no AWA4-1445 because only ten sides were allowed on the album. The resulting medley was given master number AWA4-1445 so the numbers could run consecutively.

Session date: May 3, 1971 2 to 5 PM; (C & W Album: *Yesterday's Wine*) Producer: Felton Jarvis, Engineer: Al Pachucki, Technician: Roy Shockley

Songs recorded:
AWA4-1448 Yesterday's Wine
AWA4-1449 Summer of Roses
AWA4-1450 December Day
AWA4-1451 Will You Remember?

Session personnel: Felton Jarvis - leader, Jerry Carrigan - drums, Jerry Stembridge - guitar, Dave Kirby - guitar, Weldon Myrick - steel guitar, Roy M. Huskey, Jr. - bass, David Zettner - guitar

Session notes: 'Will You Remember?' was not used on this album, instead it was placed on the album *The Words Don't Fit the Picture.*

Session date: May 4, 1971 10 AM to 1 PM; (C & W Album: *Yesterday's Wine*) Producer: Felton Jarvis, Engineer: Al Pachucki, Technician: Mike Shockley

Songs recorded:
AWA4-1452 Me and Paul
AWA4-1453 Wonderful Future
AWA4-1454 It's Not for Me to Understand
AWA4-1455 Wake Me When It's Over

Session personnel: Felton Jarvis - leader, Hargus Robbins - organ, piano, Jerry Stembridge - guitar, Herman Wade, Jr. - guitar, Weldon Myrick - steel guitar, Roy M. Huskey, Jr. - bass, David Zettner - guitar, Norman K. Spicher - fiddle

Session notes: 'Wonderful Future' and 'Wake Me When It's Over' were not used on this album, but placed on a later album, *The Willie Way.*

Session date: May 4, 1971 2 to 5 PM; (C & W Album: *Yesterday's Wine*) Producer: Felton Jarvis, Engineer: Al Pachucki, Technician: Mike Shockley

Songs recorded:
AWA4-1456 Goin' Home
AWA4-1457 Help Me Make It Through the Night
AWA4-1458 Family Bible
AWA4-1459 Rainy Day Blues

Session personnel: Felton Jarvis - leader, Jerry Carrigan - drums, Jerry Smith - piano, Jerry Stembridge - guitar, David Kirby - guitar, Weldon Myrick - steel guitar, Roy M. Huskey, Jr. - bass, David Zettner - guitar, Bobby Thompson - banjo, Charlie McCoy - harmonica

Session notes: 'Help Me Make It Through the Night' and 'Rainy Day Blues' were not used on this album. The former was placed on *The Willie Way* and the latter went on *The Words Don't Fit the Picture.*

Session date: October 19, 1971 2 to 5 PM; (C & W Album: *The Words Don't Fit the Picture*) Producer: Felton Jarvis, Engineer: Les Ladd, Technician: Mike Shockley

Songs recorded:
AWA4-1884 If You Really Loved Me
AWA4-1885 The Words Don't Fit the Picture
AWA4-1886 What Do You Want Me to Do
AWA4-1887 Stay Away From Lonely Places (Nelson - Don Bowman)

Session personnel: James Burton - leader/guitar, Jerry Carrigan - drums, Charles McCoy - vibes, harmonica, Jerry Stembridge - guitar, David Kirby - guitar, Hargus Robbins - piano, Weldon Myrick - steel guitar, Henry Strzelecki, bass

Session notes: 'What Do You Want Me to Do' was not used on this album, but on *The Willie Way.* Don Bowman's name was typed in as co-writer for 'Stay Away from Lonely Places', but was crossed off by hand.

Session date: October 21, 1971 2 to 5 PM; (C & W Album: *The Words Don't Fit the Picture*) Producer: Felton Jarvis, Engineer: Les Ladd, Technician: Mike Shockley

Songs recorded:
AWA4-1888 Good Hearted Woman (Nelson - Waylon Jennings)
AWA4-1889 Home Is Where You're Happy
AWA4-1890 My Kind of Girl
AWA4-1891 I'd Rather You Didn't Love Me

Session personnel: Charles F. Jarvis - leader, Jerry Carrigan - drums, Hargus Robbins - piano, Charles McCoy - vibes, harmonica, Jerry Stembridge - guitar, David Kirby - guitar, Weldon Myrick - steel guitar, Henry P. Strzelecki, bass

Session notes: 'Home Is Where You're Happy' and 'I'd Rather You Didn't Love Me' were not used on this album, but on *The Willie Way.*

Session date: October 26, 1971 2 to 5 PM; (C & W Album: *The Words Don't Fit the Picture*) Producer: Felton Jarvis, Engineer: Al Pachucki, Technician: Roy Shockley

Songs recorded:

AWA4-1892 Undo the Right
AWA4-1893 One Step Beyond
AWA4-1894 I Want a Girl (Nelson - Paul Buskirk)

Session personnel: Charles F. Jarvis - leader, Jerry Carrigan - drums, Hargus Robbins - piano, Jerry Stembridge - rhythm guitar, David Kirby - electric guitar, Weldon Myrick - steel guitar, Henry Strzelecki, bass

Session notes: Two cuts , 'Undo the Right' and 'I Want a Girl', were not used on this album. 'Undo the Right' was placed on *The Willie Way*. 'I Want a Girl' has yet to be released by RCA (or an affiliate).

Session date: October 28, 1971 2 to 5 PM; (C & W Album: *The Words Don't Fit the Picture*) Producer: Felton Jarvis, Engineer: Les Ladd, Technician: Mike Shockley

Songs recorded:
AWA4-1932 Country Willie
AWA4-1933 You Left a Long, Long Time Ago
AWA4-1934 London
AWA4-1935 A Moment Isn't Very Long (Nelson/Breeland/Gray)

Session personnel: Charles F. Jarvis - leader, Jerry Carrigan - drums, Hargus Robbins - piano, Jerry Stembridge - rhythm guitar, David Kirby - guitar, Weldon Myrick - steel guitar, Henry P. Strzelecki, bass

Session notes: Two cuts, 'You Left a Long, Long Time Ago' and 'A Moment Isn't Very Long' were not used on this album, but on *The Willie Way*.

Session date: April 25, 1972 10 AM to 1 PM; (Pop Album) Producer: Felton Jarvis, A & R Representative: Joan Deary, Engineer: Al Pachucki

Songs recorded:
BWA4-1342 Phases, Stages, Circles, Cycles and Scenes
BWA4-1343 Pretend I Never Happened
BWA4-1344 Sister's Coming Home
BWA4-1345 Down at the Corner Beer Joint
BWA4-1346 I'm Falling in Love Again

Session personnel: Willie Nelson - leader/guitar, Paul English - drums, Dan Spears - bass

Session notes: 'Phases, Stages, Circles, Cycles and Scenes' went out as Willie's final RCA single (under contract), though it failed to chart. The rest of the cuts have not been released, to date, by either RCA or a subsidiary. All of them were later rerecorded for Atlantic Records and appeared on his second album for the label, *Phases and Stages*. This and the following session were done for a "pop" album.

Session date: April 27, 1972 2 to 5 PM; (Pop Album) Producer: Felton Jarvis, A & R Representative: Joan Deary, Engineer: Al Pachucki

Songs recorded:
BWA4-1347 Who'll Buy My Memories
BWA4-1348 No Love Around
BWA4-1349 Come on Home
BWA4-1350 Mountain Dew (B. L. Lunsford - S. Wiseman)

Session personnel: Willie Nelson - leader/guitar, Paul English - drums, Dan Spears - bass

Session notes: 'Mountain Dew' was used on *The Willie Way*. The other cuts have not been released by either RCA or an affiliate. A "Listing Notice" from July 15, 1982 noted that 'Mountain Dew' had vocal accompaniment by the Lea Jane Singers added as part of its inclusion on *The Best of Willie* collection.

Session date: November 10, 1975; (Stereo MOR Single Release) Producer: Chet Atkins

Songs recorded:
RWKS-1596-1 Pretty Paper (PB-10461-A)
RWKS-1597-1 What a Merry Christmas This Could Be (Harlan
    Howard - Hank Cochran) (PB-10461-B)

Session notes: Done three years after Willie left RCA, this session's sole purpose was to convert the two 1964 tracks into stereo format.

Session date: March 2, 1976 10 AM to 1 PM; (Pop Album) (No Producer Credit Shown), A & R Representative: Jerry Bradley

Songs recorded:
FWA4-0769 Introduction - Bo Powell
FWA4-0769 I Gotta Get Drunk (remixed version for album use)

Session notes: There were instructions to "note title change from: *The World of Willie Nelson*" to *Willie Nelson Live* (APL1-1487, APS1-1487 and APK1-1487). Another note read, "this album will contain an additional selection 'I Gotta Get Drunk'." Under Specific Cover Approach, was the notation "new art to be completed in Nashville."

Session date: July 28, 1977; (Stereo Country Single Release) Producers: Felton Jarvis and Chet Atkins (on 'One in a Row') and Chet Atkins (on 'You Ought to Hear Me Cry')

Songs recorded:
UWKS-2204-1 You Ought to Hear Me Cry (from the "Willie/*Before His Time*" album. APL1-2210)
TWKS-0980-1 One in a Row (from the "Willie/*Before His Time*" album. APL1-2210)

Session date: November 28, 1978 10 AM to 1 PM Music City Music Hall; (Pop Album: *Sweet Memories*) (Overdub) Original production: Felton Jarvis, A & R Representative/Overdub production: Pat Carter, String Arrangement: Mike Leech, Engineer: Bill Harris

Songs recorded:
WWA4-1984 Sweet Memories (Newbury)
AWA4-1451 Will You Remember?
UWA4-3078 December Day
AWA4-1455 Wake Me When It's Over
AWA4-1457 Help Me Make It Through the Night (Kris Kristofferson)

Session personnel: Sheldon Kurland - leader/violin, Roy Christensen - cello, Terry McMillan - harmonica, George Binkley III, Marvin Chantry, Carl Joseph Gerodetzky, Lennie Haight - violin, Suzee Waters - vocal accompaniment (on 'Sweet Memories' and 'Help Me Make It Through the Night')

Session notes: This version of 'Sweet Memories' went in 1979 as both a single and album title cut, and as a cut on *The Best of Willie Nelson*.

Session date: 1981; (Overdubs) (Album: *The Minstrel Man*) Mastering: Randy Kling, Randy's Roost, Technical Data: John T. "Killer" Johnson, String Arrangement: D. Bergen White, Overdub & Remix Engineer: Bill Harris, Assistant: David DeBusk

Session personnel: Vocal accompaniment - The Jordanaires, String performances - The Shelly Kurland Strings

Session notes: The purpose of this session was to add strings and vocal accompaniment to ten previously released tracks and release them together as a 1981 album, *The Minstrel Man*.

The Notes and Sources

Johnny once married Lana!
(Photo from Happy Shahan/John Lentz Personnel Management)

The Red Headed Stranger!
(Photo from Alive Films and Evelyn Shriver Public Relations)

The Source Listings and Bibliography

An Introduction

The purpose of this book has been to review, critique, report on, discuss, and analyze, especially from an historical viewpoint, the recording career of Willie Nelson, Hall of Fame country music artist. As such, every pertinent word that he and others spoke about that career and the music on which it was built became an integral part of presenting every possible slant or viewpoint. Additionally, every conceivable viewpoint or historical factor on critical musical pieces he recorded became integral to the analysis.

Presenting and discussing all these disparate quotations and sources formed the backbone of this book. The source material ranged from the author's notes on private conversations, notes from other writers, quotes from various books, encyclopedias, periodicals, journals, trade press magazines, album liner notes, and newspapers. The origin of each quotation and the full bibliographic listing pertinent for each noted entry is presented herein.

Work on this book began in the early nineteen-eighties as part of a plan to present the complete discographies of major country music figures on-line through the world net. The work on Willie Nelson became so detailed and complex that a book with a companion web-page became a more plausible format. Once the major work was done on the discographical entries, the work was presented to Mr. Nelson who said that it greatly assisted him in his efforts to go back and rerecord many of what he considered his lost masterpieces of song.

I would like to thank all those who made photographs, press information, and original insights available. They included Mark

Rothbaum, the Evelyn Shriver Agency, Bill DeYoung, editor of the *Scene Magazine* (and writer of several great Willie features), Steve Lindsey of MaxAmor Productions, and the people at the Michael Ochs and the Country Music Hall of Fame Archives. I would like to especially thank the curators of the Performing Arts and Music collections at the University of Florida. The marketing departments at the various companies for whom Willie recorded or wrote, especially RCA, Columbia, Sony Tree, and Justice Records, who kindly sent me everything they possessed, have my eternal gratitude.

Part I. The Willie Nelson Source Material

All the quotes about and information on Willie Nelson came from the following books, papers, news columns, and articles, except where another source has been specifically noted or where the author directly quoted Mr. Nelson or others close to him, such as individuals who work or worked with him or have been involved with his recordings.

Articles in Periodicals and Collections

Ackerman-Blount, Joan. "Sister Bobbie's Amazing Grace," *Esquire*, Volume 96, Number 2, August 1981, pp. 82-83.

Allen, Bob. "Interview: Willie Nelson," *The Journal of Country Music*, Volume VIII, Number 2, 1980, pp. 3-14.

Allen, Nelson. "The Texas Scene," *Country Music*, Volume 5, Number 2, November, 1976, p. 8.

Allen, Nelson. "Is It Goodbye to Willie's Picnics?," *Country Music*, Volume 5, Number 2, November, 1976, p. 13.

Altman, Billy. "Tacos, Tequila and Taxes," *The New York Times*, April 4, 1993, Section 2, p. 32.

Apter, Bill. "*Countrybeat* Interview: Willie Nelson," *Countrybeat Magazine*, Winter 1993, pp. 42-46.

Axthelm, Pete. "Willie Nelson: King of Country Music," *Newsweek*, Volume XCII, Number 7, August 14, 1978, pp. 52-57.

Axthelm, Pete. "Songs of Outlaw Country," *Newsweek*, Volume LXXXVII, Number 15, April 12, 1976, p. 79.

Baird, Robert. "The King of Conjunto," *Stereophile*, Volume 19, Number 12, December 1996, pp. 122-125.

Ball, Aimee Lee. "On Stage, Backstage...and Heart-to-Heart with Willie," *Redbook*, Volume 156, Number 6, April 1981, pp. 31, 73-76.

Bane, Michael. "Willie: The Gypsy Cowboy Goes Hollywood," *Country Music*, Volume Seven, Number Seven, May 1979, pp. 24-28.

Bane, Michael. "Willie Nelson," *Country Music*, Number 154, March/ April, 1992, pp. 52-53.

Bane, Michael. "20 Questions with Willie Nelson," *Country Music*, Number 160, March/April, 1993, pp. 48-49.

Bane, Michael. "Cowboys Don't Sing the Blues, " *Country Music*, Number 128, November/December 1987, pp. 34-38.

Barnard, Russ. "Willie Nelson's Family and Friends," *Country Music*, Number 170, November/December 1994, pp. 42-46.

Bloom, Steve. "Gatewood & Willie," *High Times*, Number 195, January 1991, pp. 34, 66-69.

Bloom, Steve, Steve Hager, and John Holmstrom. "The *High Times* Interview: Willie Nelson," *High Times*, Number 185, January 1991, pp. 13-16.

Blount, Roy, Jr. "Wrasslin' with This Thing Called Willie Nelson...," *Esquire*, Volume 96, Number 2, August 1981, pp. 78-87.

Bowen, Jimmy. "Nashville: Here They Come!," *EQ: Project Recording & Sound Techniques*, Volume 3, Issue 1, April 1992, pp. 36-42.

Breskin, David. "Willie Nelson," *Musician*, Number 45, July 1982, pp. 40-48, 84-85.

Buchalter, Gail. "Willie Nelson: Makin' Music...Havin' Fun," *Country Song Roundup*, Volume 32, Number 248, March 1980, pp. 13-14.

Burger, Frederick. "Red-Headed Stranger: The Movie Willie Dreamed, Struggled and Plotted for a Decade to Bring to the Big Screen," *Billboard*, Volume 98, Number 41, October 11, 1986, pp. W-4, W-16, W-17.

Cain, Linda. "Not Just Another Willie Nelson Interview," *Country Music*, Volume 8, June 1980, pp. 58-62.

Carr, Patrick. "The Man Who Beat the System," *Country Music*, Volume Four, Number Five, February 1976, pp. 22-26.

Carr, Patrick. "Willie Nelson: Farm Aid's Founder," *Mother Earth News*, Issue Number 105, May/June 1987, pp. 42-45.

Carr, Patrick. "Waylon and Willie Go to a Party," *New Times*, Volume 10, Number 4, February 20, 1978, pp. 63-64.

Carr, Patrick. "Catching Up with Ole Willie," *Country Music*, Number 123, February, 1987, pp. 24-28.

Carr, Patrick. "The Outlaws Revolution Revisited," *Country Music*, Number 180, July/August 1996, pp. 30-34.

Cartwright, Gary. "A Star Is Reborn," *Texas Monthly*, Volume 25, Issue 3, March 1997, pp. 126-128, 140-144.

Cartwright, Gary. "Willie at 65," *Texas Monthly*, Volume 26, Number 4, April 1998, pp. 98-102, 129-132.

Castro, Peter. "Talking With ... Willie Nelson," *People Weekly*, Volume 44, No. 9, August 28, 1995, p. 21.

Chintala, John. "Chet Atkins: A Half-Century of Guitar Excellence," *Discoveries*, Issue 119, April 1998, pp. 42-51.

Clark, Rick. "The Mix Interview: Chet Atkins," *Mix*, Volume 21, Number 7, July 1997, pp. 24--32, 225.

Coffey, Kevin. "Indelible Ink: The Life and Times of Ted Daffan," *The Journal of Country Music*, Volume 16, Number 2, pp. 25-34.

Cooper, Mark. "Cheer Up, It Might Never Happen," *Q: The Modern Guide to Music and More*, Number 82, July 1993, pp. 68-71.

Cronin, Peter. "Nelson's 'Stardust' Sequel to Emerge on Texas Indie," *Billboard*, Volume 105, Number 50, December 11, 1993, pp. 10, 138.

Davis, John T. "The Making of Willie's Special," *Austin American-Statesman*, January 18, 1983.

DeCurtis, Anthony. "Willie Nelson: Farm Aid II a 'Success'; Farm Aid III May Be Postponed Until Next Year," *Rolling Stone*, Issue Number 481, August 28th, 1986, p. 38.

Deitz, Roger. "Willie Nelson's Martin N-20," *Acoustic Guitar*, Volume 5, Number 2, Issue 26, September/October 1994, p. 130.

Deitz, Roger. "On the Road Again: With Two New Breakthrough Albums, *Across the Borderline* and *Moonlight Becomes You*, Willie Nelson Is Back on Top," *Acoustic Guitar*, Volume 5, Number 2, Issue 26, September/October 1994, pp. 42-52.

Delaney, Kelly. "Horse/Music Are Metaphors," *American Songwriter*, Volume 10, Number 5, July/August 1996, pp. 28-29.

Dellar, Fred. "How to Buy ... Willie Nelson," *Mojo*, Issue 42, May 1997, p. 140.

De Rakoff, Sophie. "The Electric Horseman: Willie Nelson's Always on My Mind," *Paper*, February 1995, pp. 40-41.

Dexter, Kerry. "Beth Nielsen Chapman: The Song's the Thing," *Dirty Linen*, Issue Number 76, June/July 1998, pp. 32-35.

DeYoung, Bill. "The Man in Black," *Players*, April 8, 1993, pp. 18-21.

DeYoung, Bill. "Willie Nelson: One in a Million," *The Gainesville Sun: Scene*, October 13, 1995, pp. 12-13.

DeYoung, Bill. "Willie Nelson: Funny How Time Slips Away," *Goldmine*, Volume 21, Number 1, January 6, 1995, pp. 16-48, 68-74, 135-142.

DeYoung, Bill. "Pioneer Days in High Springs; A Chat with Willie Nelson," *The Gainesville Sun: Scene*, May 2, 1997, pp. 4, 10.

DeYoung, Bill. "Guy Clark," *Goldmine*, Volume 23, Number 7, Issue 435, March 28, 1997, pp. 14-15.

Dick, Stephen. "Inside a Classic Song," *Acoustic Guitar*, Volume 8, Number 1, Issue 55, July 1997, pp. 39-41.

Dunn, Janice. "Interview from Rolling Stone," *Rolling Stone*, March 9, 1995, p. 34.

Easley, Greg. "Wail on, Willie!: Willie Nelson Talks to Bubba," *Bubba Magazine,* Fall 1993, pp. 14-20.

Editors of *Billboard,* the. "Willie Nelson Belongs to Fast School of Writing," *Billboard: The World of Country Music,* October 30, 1965, p. 46.

Editors of *Billboard,* the. "Willie Nelson OK Following Collapse," *Billboard,* Volume 88, Number 9, February 28, 1976, p. 49.

Editors of *Billboard,* the. "10,000 Fans Fete Nelson in Abbott," *Billboard,* Volume 85, Number 47, November 24, 1973, p. 28.

Editors of *Country Music,* the. "Summer Country '74," *Country Music,* Volume Two, Number Thirteen, September 1974, pp. 34-36.

Editors of *Country Weekly,* the. "Willie Nelson, a Narc?," *Country Weekly,* Volume 3, Number 47, November 19, 1996, p. 5.

Editors of *International Musician,* the. "AFM to Honor Willie Nelson at Convention," *International Musician,* Volume 83, Number 12, June 1985, pp. 1, 17.

Editors of *Music City News.* the. "What Song Do You Wish You Had Written?," *Music City News,* March 1995, p. 17.

Editors of *Music City News.* the. "Artists Join Statue of Liberty Campaign," *Music City News,* August, 1986, p. 14.

Editors of *Music City News,* the. "Willie's Farm Aid II: A Lot of People, But Little Money," *Music City News,* August 1986, p. 3.

Editors of *Music City News,* the. "New Willie Exhibit Comes to Hall of Fame," *Music City News,* Volume XXIII, No. IV, October 1985, p. 68.

Editors of *New Country,* the. "The Best of *New Country*: The Talk of the Town: 1996," *New Country,* April 1997, pp. 29-34.

Editors of *Redbook,* the. "Talking with Willie Nelson: 'It's Not Easy Being Married to a Man Like Me'," *Redbook,* Volume CLXIV, Number 2, December 1984, pp. 30-34.

Editors of *Time: The Weekly Newsmagazine,* the. "The Ballad of Willie's Woes," *Time: The Weekly Newsmagazine,* Volume 137, Number 6, February 11, 1991, p. 67.

Editors of *Time: The Weekly Newsmagazine,* the. "Harvest Song: Willie Plans a Benefit," *Time: The Weekly Newsmagazine,* Volume 126, Number 12, September 23, 1985, p. 32.

Editors of *Time: The Weekly Newsmagazine,* the. "Q & A: Willie Nelson," *Time: The Weekly Newsmagazine,* Volume 151, Number 1, January 12, 1998, p. 96.

Editors of *U. S. News & World Report,* the. "Willie Nelson," *U. S. News & World Report,* Volume 109, Number 21, November 26, 1990, p. 22.

Editors of *Variety,* the. "Willie Nelson, Nashville Guru," *Variety,* Volume 295, Number 4, May 30, 1979, p. 75.

Editors of *Variety,* the. "Nelson Sues Accounting Firm," *Variety,* Volume 295, Number 4, May 30, 1979, p. 75.

Editors of *Variety*, the. "Court Rules Nelson Can't Hide Tax Flap from Press Inquiry," *Variety*, Volume 321, Number 8, December 18, 1985, pp. 1, 95.

Editors of *Variety*, the. "Singer Willie Nelson Due for Film Debut," *Variety*, Volume 285, Number 11, January 19, 1976, p. 7.

Editors of *Variety*, the. "Willie Nelson Buries His Lone Star Label," *Variety*, Volume 295, Number 6, June 13, 1979, p. 65.

Editors of *Variety*, the. "Anthem," *Variety*, July 28/August 3, 1997, p. 58.

Farinella, David John. "'Twisted Willie': Randall Jamail Plays Outside the Rules," *Mix*, August 1996, pp. 163, 182-186.

Feiler, Bruce. "Has Country Music Become a Soundtrack for White Flight?" *The New York Times*, October 20, 1996, p. 38.

Fine, Andrea J. "Willie Nelson's a Hit - as a Boxer," *Country Weekly*, Volume 3, Number 52, December 24, 1996, pp. 8-9.

Finger, Bill. "Bascom Lamar Lunsford: The Limits of a Folk Hero," *Southern Exposure*, Volume II, Number 1, pp. 27-37.

Fish, Scott K. "Paul English: On the Road with Willie Nelson," *Modern Drummer*, Volume 5, Number 3, May 1981, pp. 18-20, 67-74.

Flans, Robyn. "Talkin' Recordin' with Merle Haggard," *Mix*, August 1996, pp. 162, 172-180.

Flans, Robyn. "Cowboy Hero Gene Autry at 90: 'I've Had a Great Life'," *Country Weekly*, Volume 4, Number 45, November 11, 1997, pp. 52-52.

Flippo, Chet. "Willie Nelson's New York Country Sessions," *Rolling Stone*, Issue Number 132, April 12, 1973, p. 14.

Flippo, Chet. "The Saga of Willie Nelson," *Rolling Stone*, Issue Number 269, July 13, 1978, pp. 45-49.

Flippo, Chet. "The Great Willie Nelson," *Rolling Stone*, Issue Number 289, April 19, 1979, pp. 87-88, 90.

Flippo, Chet. "Nashville Scene," *Billboard*, Volume 109, Number 51, December 20, 1997, p. 25.

Friedman, Kinky. "It's Not Supposed to Be That Way," *Rolling Stone*, Issue 599, March 7, 1991, pp. 73-76.

Friedman, Kinky. "My Willie," *Texas Monthly*, Volume 25, Issue 9, September 1997, pp. 56-64.

Fruin, Deborah. "The Healing Hands of Time," *Country Fever*, Volume 1, Number 1, August 1992, pp. 42-47.

Gates, David. "Red Headed Survivor: With the IRS Off His Back and a Startling New Album, Willie's on the Road Again," *Newsweek*, Volume CXXI, Number 12, March 22, 1993, pp. 66-67.

George-Warren, Holly. "Road Warrior: His Troubles Behind Him, Willie Nelson and His Battered, Beautiful Guitar Take to the Highway Once More," *Country Guitar*, Winter 1994, pp. 16-20, 25.

George-Warren, Holly. "Growing Up Country: Ten Legends Speak," *The Journal of Country Music*, Volume 19, Number 1, pp. 10-18.

Gill, Jerry H. "Guilt, Grace and Willie Nelson," *The Christian Century*, Volume XCVIII, Number 27, September 9, 1981, pp. 877-879.

Gilyard, Burl. "Willie Nelson: Across the Borderline," *Request*, April 1993, pp. 50-51.

Gleason, Holly (interview by). "The Record That Changed My Life," *Musician*, October 1994, p. 42.

Greco, Mike. "Memories of a Texas Childhood," *American Film*, Volume VI, Number 8, June 1981, pp. 25-30.

Green, Doug, and Martha Hume. "Texas: Deep in the Heart of Country Music," *Country Music*, Volume 4, Number 12, September 1976, pp. 35-45.

Grein, Paul. "The Long-Playing, Hit-Studded Record of One of the Most Prolific and Successful Artists in Music History," *Billboard*, Volume 98, Number 41, October 11, 1986, pp. W-10, W-14.

Guterman, Jimmy. "Paid in Full," *CD Review*, April 1993, pp. 68-69.

Hackett, Vernell. "Willie Nelson's a Natural in *The Songwriter*," *American Songwriter*, Volume 1, Number 2, October, 1984, pp. 20-22.

Hackett, Vernell. "Songwriters Write Desperate Album," *American Songwriter*, Volume 11, Number 3, March/April 1997, p. 7.

Hackett, Vernell. "Harlan Howard ... In the Beginning," *American Songwriter*, September/October 1990, p. 7.

Hackett, Vernell. "Different Directions," *American Cowboy*, May/June 1997, pp. 30-31.

Hackett, Vernell. "The Jimmie Rodgers Musical Legacy:," *American Songwriter*, Volume 11, Number 6, September/October 1997, pp. 16-17.

Hackett, Vernell. "Willie Nelson: Recording Songs by New Writers," *Country Song Roundup*, Volume 41, Number 365, December 1989, pp. 8-13.

Hainer, Cathy. "With Friedman, a Willie Nelson Trip Takes a Kinky Turn," *USA Today*, Thursday October 16, 1997, p. 10D.

Hajari, Nisid. "Free (Wheeling) Willie: 10 Stupid Questions," *Entertainment Weekly*, Number 330, June 7, 1996, p. 67.

Halbersberg, Elianne. "Picture Perfect with Waylon and Willie," *Country Song Roundup*, Vol. 48, No. 435, August 1996, p. 60.

Halbersberg, Elianne. "One-on-One with America's Greatest Singer/Songwriter ... Willie Nelson," *Modern Screen's Country Music*, Volume 91, Number 8, July 1997, pp. 54, 78-79.

Hall, Michael. "The Great, Late Townes Van Zandt," *Texas Monthly*, Volume 26, Issue 3, March 1998, pp. 110-113, 160-161.

Halverson, Tiffany A. "Tanya Tucker: Fire to Fire," *Music City News*, Volume 32, Number 11, May 1995, p. 46.

Harden, Lydia Dixon. "Waylon & Willie," *Music City News* (from an Internet reprint), August 1995, p. 3.

Harrigan, Stephen. "Deconstructing Willie: The Taco as Imperialist Symbol," *Utne Reader*, Number 59, Sept./Oct. 1993, p. 127.

Harris, Pat, and Danny Proctor. "Faron Young: 1932-1996," *Music City News*, Volume 34, Number 8, February 1997, pp. 20-24.

Harris, Pat. "Gibson USA Presents Stargazing," *Music City News*, July 1994, p. 93.

Harris, Stacy. "Willie Nelson: On Picnics and Things," *Country Song Roundup*, Volume 30, Number 228, July 1978, pp. 10-11. 36-37.

Hatlo, Jim. "On the Beat: Willie's Legendary Guitar Continues to Deteriorate as the Years Roll By," *Frets Magazine*, Volume 10, Number 12, Issue Number 118, December 1988, pp. 18-19.

Haydan, Rick, and Catharine S. Rambeau. "Legends Turned Off by Radio - But They Won't Be Silenced," *Country Weekly*, Volume 4, Number 43, October 28, 1997, pp. 18-25.

Haydan, Rick. "Radio Revolution," *Country Weekly*, Volume 4, Number 48, December 2, 1997, pp. 23-25.

Hentoff, Nat. "Willie Nelson: Country 'Outlaw'," *The Progressive*, Volume 45, Number 1, January 1981, pp. 46-47.

Herbert, T. Walter. "Willie Nelson and Herman Melville on Manhood: *Pierre* and 'The Red-Headed Stranger'," *Texas Studies in Literature and Language*, Volume 35, Number 4, Winter 1993, pp. 421-439.

Herndon, John. "For the Sake of the Song: The Musical Legacy of Townes Van Zandt," *Acoustic Guitar*, Volume 7, Number 11, Issue 53, May 1997, pp. 38-39. 42-43.

Hickey, Dave. "Outlaw Blues," *Country Music*, Volume Five, Number Five, February 1977, pp. 22-27.

Hickey, Neil. "On the Road with Willie Nelson: 'If There Is a Hatchet, Let's Bury It'," *TV Guide*, Volume 31, Number 41, October 8, 1983, pp. 36-39.

Hilburn, Robert. "Willie Nelson: The Landmark Career of the Red-Headed Stranger," *Billboard*, Volume 98, Number 41, October 11, 1986, pp. W-2, W-18, W-19.

Hilburn, Robert. "There's Still a Need for Farm Aid III, but We May Have to Take It to Washington First," *Billboard*, Volume 98, Number 41, October 11, 1986, pp. W-8, W-21.

Hilburn, Robert. "Nelson Avoids the Country Bland Wagon," *Los Angeles Times Calendar*, November 23, 1976, p. 68.

Hilburn, Robert. "Willie Nelson, Country Music with a Concept," *Los Angeles Times Calendar*, March 17, 1974, p. 54.

Hilburn, Robert. "Willie After the IRS and on the Road to 60," *Los Angeles Times Calendar*, March 17, 1974, p. 54.

Himes, Geoffrey. "Willie Nelson: Outlaw Gets Some Justice," *Washington Post,* August 6, 1995, p. G11.

Hirshberg, Charles, and Robert Sullivan. "Witnesses: Willie Nelson, There Are No Laws," *Life: The Roots of Country Music,* pp. 66-67, 72.

Hoekstra, Dave. "Flood of Willie Nelson Product Plumbs Depths of Creativity, *Chicago Sunday Sun-Times,* October 1, 1995.

Hoekstra, Dave. "Willie Nelson: Songs Are Born," *Country Song Roundup,* Volume 50, Number 443, April, 1998, pp. 36-37.

Holden, Larry. "Ray Price Still Flying High (If Not Far) After 50 Years in Country," *Country Weekly,* Volume 5, Number 17, April 28, 1998, pp. 50-53.

Holden, Larry. "Willie Nelson's 65 Years Go By in Just a Cotton-Picking Minute," *Country Weekly,* Volume 5, Number 16, April 21, 1998, pp. 10-13.

Holden, Larry. "Country Music Storms An International Stage, " *Country Weekly,* Volume 5, Number 18, May 5, 1998, pp. 16-21.

Holden, Stephen. "Willie Nelson, Voice of America," *High Fidelity,* Volume 31, Number 3, March 1981, pp. 81-84.

Holden, Stephen. "Nelson in Black Tie, With Strings," *The New York Times,* February 16, 1995, p. C21.

Holley, Debbie. "Nelson Inks Sponsor Deal with Cuervo; Tour Set," *Billboard,* Volume 104, Number 10, March 7, 1992, pp. 27, 29.

Holley, Debbie. "Highwaymen Are Hitting the PPV Concert Path," *Billboard,* Volume 104, Number 10, March 7, 1992, p. 27.

Honick, Bruce. "Why Doesn't Radio Play the Old-Timers Anymore?," *Country Weekly,* March 12, 1996, pp.18-23.

Honick, Bruce. "'Mr. Guitar' Celebrates 50 Years of Recording," *Country Weekly,* November 19, 1996, p. 21.

Honick, Michelle Broussard. "Jimmie Rodgers' Continuing Influence: From Dylan to Walser, His Influence Remains," *American Songwriter,* September/October 1997, p. 22.

Hood, Phil. "Jackie King," *Frets,* Volume 6, Number 12, Issue Number 70, December 1984, pp. 39, 48-49.

Hoskyns, Barney. "The Buddha of Texas," *Mojo,* Issue 14, January 1995, pp. 18-20.

Huff, W. A. Kelly. "A Thematic Analysis of Willie Nelson's Song Lyrics," *Popular Music and Society,* Volume 18.2, Summer 1994, pp. 91-124.

Hume, Martha. "Waylon & Willie in New York: Outlaws Corralled," *Rolling Stone,* Issue Number 261, March 23rd, 1978, pp. 20-21.

Hunter, Glenn. "Willie Cleans Up His Act," *Country Music,* Volume Five, Number Six, March 1977, p. 16.

Jaffe, Thomas, editor (written by Christopher Palmeri). "Plugola," *Forbes Magazine,* Volume 153, Number 6, March 14, 1994, p. 20.

Jones, David H. "Studio in the Country Is Alive and Well," *offBEAT*, Volume 10, Number 12, December 1997, pp. 26-27.

Kasten, Ray. "Put Down the Gun," *No Depression*, September-October 1997, p. 42.

Kienzle, Rich. "The Quiet Man: Playing Behind Willie Nelson Is One of the Most Accomplished Guitarists in Country Music History: An Appreciation of the Great Grady Martin," *Country Guitar*, Winter 1994, pp. 22-23.

Kingsbury, Paul. "Once More With Feeling: A Conversation with Dolly Parton," *The Journal of Country Music*, Volume 19, Number 2, pp. 31-37.

Kirby, Kip. "Willie Comes to Grips with 'Half Nelson': Singer's Latest Duet Album Is Unusual Even for Him," *Billboard*, Volume 97, Number 35, August 31, 1985, pp. 62, 66.

Kirby, Kip. "Monument Launches 'Winning Hand' Push," *Billboard*, Volume 94, Number 46, November 20, 1982, pp. 37, 42.

Kirsch, Bob. "Willie Nelson: He Twice Almost Quit," *Billboard*, Volume 87, Number 47, November 22, 1975, pp. 39, 42.

Kyle, Dave. "Waylon Jennings - Settin' It Straight," *Vintage Guitar Magazine*, June 1997, pp. 90-94, 102.

Leigh, Spencer. "Willie Nelson: One of Country Music's Most Popular, and Prolific, Performers of the Last Two Decades, Who Has Picked Up a Large and Loyal Following in This Country," *Record Collector*, Number 84, August 1986, pp. 20-25.

Lenz, Scott. "Full Nelson: Big Willie on the Industry, His New TV Channel and IRS Backlash," *Grammy Magazine*, Volume 16, Number 2, April/May 1998, pp. 28-29.

Leslie-Miller, Char R. "Various Artists: *From Where I Stand: The Black Experience in Country Music*," *Dirty Linen*, Issue Number 76, June/July 1998, p. 65.

Lindsay, Joe. "Willie Nelson: The Albums," *DISCoveries*, Volume 1, Number 6, November 1988, pp. 93-95.

Lotito, Mark, Jimmy Vivino, and Allen Bloomfield. "B. B. King," *20th Century Guitar Magazine*, March 1998, pp. 122-127.

Love, John. "Willie Nelson and His Sweet Sound of Success," *Cosmopolitan*, Volume 189, Number 6, December 1980, pp. 62-66, 124-126, 131.

Maier, Ann, and Steve Dougherty. "Back in the Groove Again," *People Weekly*, June 21, 1993, p. 53.

Martin, Gavin. "All My Excess Was in Texas," *New Musical Express*, May 15, 1993, pp. 32-33.

McCall, Cheryl, with photography by Harry Benson. "Life Visits the Colorado and Texas Retreats of the Private Willie," *Life*, Volume 6, Number 8. August 1983, pp. 76-82.

McCall, Cheryl. "Willie's Hit Album Goes Big Screen," *Life*, Volume 9, Number 8, August 1986, pp. 56-62.

McConnell, Frank. "On the Road Again: Willie Nelson's Sprezzatura," *Commonweal*, Volume CXII, Number 17, October 4, 1985, pp. 532-534.

McDonald, Glenn. "Honky-Tonk Browsin'," *The Web Magazine*, Volume 1, Number 7, July 1997, pp. 32-33.

McLeese, Don. "Still Wanted: They Gave Country a Rock 'n' Roll Attitude in the '70s," *New Country*, September 1997, pp. 38-40.

McLeese, Don. "The Country Caruso and the Pavarotti of the Plains Contemplate Their Careers as Classic Crooners: Johnny Bush & Don Walser: Horse Opera," *No Depression*, May-June 1998, pp. 56-62.

Miller, Townsend. "Willie Nelson," *BMI: The Many Worlds of Music*, Issue 4, 1976, pp. 36-37.

Mr. Bonzai. "Willie Nelson: Deep in the Heart," *Mix*, Volume 16, Number 11, November 1992, pp. 127-128, 156-157.

Morris, Edward. "Will Willie's 'Masters' Plan Go Willy-Nilly?," *Billboard*, June 22, 1991, p. 52.

Morris, Edward. "Willie Nelson 'IRS' Set Aimed at Aiding Taxing Situation," *Billboard*, June 22, 1991, p. 52.

Morris, Edward. "RCA Is Bullish on 'Cowboys' Set: Aims to Lasso Big Sales for Soundtrack," *Billboard*, March 2, 1991, p. 44.

Morris, Edward. "Farm Aid Rolls on, but Public Focus Changes," *Billboard*, Volume 104, Number 7, February 15, 1992, pp. 1, 88.

Morris, Edward. "IRS Gives Willie a Sweet 60 Present," *Billboard*, Volume 105, Number 7, February 13, 1993, p. 86.

Morris, Edward. "Nelson Pitches Boxed Set on QVC: Exclusive Package Features Rarities," *Billboard*, Volume 106, Number 7, February 12, 1994, p. 18.

Morris, Edward. "Rogers & Co. Back on Happy Trails," *Billboard*, September 21, 1991, pp. 56-58.

Nash, Alanna. "Willie Nelson Talks to Alanna Nash," *Stereo Review*, Volume 43, Number 5, November 1979, pp. 68-70.

Nash, Alanna. "Willie Nelson: To Hell and Back," *TV Guide*, Volume 40, Number 47, Issue Number 2069, November 21, 1992, pp. 22-24.

Nelson, Pat. "Lone Star Label Launched in Texas: Willie Nelson Boss," *Billboard*, Volume 90, Number 26, July 1, 1978, pp. 14, 59.

Nelson, Willie. "Why the Farmer Needs Your Support," *Billboard*, Volume 99, Number 38, September 19, 1987, p. 9.

Nelson, Willie. "A Tribute to Bob Wills," *Country Music*, Volume Two, Number Twelve, August 1974, pp. 68-73.

Newcomer, Wendy. "Jessi Colter's Still Looking to Make History," *Country Weekly*, June 3, 1997, p. 50.

Newcomer, Wendy. "Life's Changing Very Quickly for Travis Tritt the Family Man," *Country Weekly*, Volume 5, Number 16, April 21, 1998, pp. 20-23.

Newman, Melinda. "Willie Nelson Shows His 'Spirit' on Island Debut," *Billboard*, Volume 108, Number 17, April 27, 1996, pp. 13-14.

Newman, Melinda. "2 EMI Imprints Team with Willie," *Billboard*, Volume 106, Number 44, October 29, 1994, pp. 1, 107.

Oakey, Bill. "Ernest Tubb: Legend and Legacy," *Country Song Roundup*, Volume 32, Number 248, March 1980, pp. 28-30, 40.

Obrecht, Jas. "B. B. King: 'Deuces Wild'," *Guitar Player*, Issue 37, Volume 32, Number 1, January 1998, pp. 58-70

Pareles, Jon. "From Two Great Voices, a New Message," *The New York Times*, April 4, 1993, Section 2, p. 32.

Patoski, Joe Nick. "Pssssst: Steve Fromholz Says He's Nutty As a Fruitcake," *Country Music*, May 1977, pp. 30-32.

Patterson, Rob. "A Great Spirit Enjoys an Uncloudy Day," *New Country*, Volume 3, Number 4, April 1996, pp. 30-37.

Patterson, Rob. "*Fi* Interview: Willie Nelson," *Fi: The Magazine of Music & Sound*, Volume 3, Number 2, February 1998, pp. 20-25.

Paul, Alan. "Willie Nelson's Martin N-20: 'Trigger'," *Guitar World*, Volume 17, Number 1, January 1997, p. 107.

Platts, Robin. "Jimmy Webb Sings Jimmy Webb," *Discoveries*, Issue 112, September 1997, pp. 36-39.

Pond, Neil. "Willie Nelson: Singer of Songs, Star of the Silver Screen - and now - Man of Letters," *Music City News*, Volume 26, Number 3, October 1988, pp. 20-22.

Pond, Neil. "'Austin City Limits' Launches 10th Season: Public Broadcasting's Hour-Long Music Showcase Defies Its Early Skeptics," *Music City News*, Volume XXII, Number IX, March 1985, p. 12.

Pond, Neil. "Willie Nelson's Casting Call," *Music City News*, Volume XXIII, Number IV, October 1985, pp. 66-67.

Pond, Neil. "Willie No 'Stranger' to TV, and Oak Meets a 'Deere' & Mel McD. Helps Say Thanks," *Music City News*, Volume 24, Number 12, June, 1987, p. 67.

Pond, Neil. "25 Movers and Shakers: The Most Influential Country Stars of All Time," *Country America*, Volume 5, Issue 5, March 1994, pp. 31-48.

Pond, Neil. "Dynamic Duos: Then & Now," *Country America*, Volume Six, Number Nine, July/August 1995, pp. 43-51.

Pond, Steve. "Willie Rides Again," *Live!*, Volume 1, Number 2, March 1996, pp. 52-57.

Price, Deborah Evans. "Two Nelson Releases for July 4: Rhino, Justice Collaborate on Promotion," *Billboard*, Volume 107, Number 27, July 8, 1995, pp. 8, 92-93.

Price, Deborah Evans. "Are Pubs Becoming Labels' Farm Teams?," *Billboard*, Volume 110, Number 22, May 30, 1998, pp. 40, 50-51.

Rambeau, Catharine S. "Willie Nelson - He's the Legend Who Never Quits," *Country Weekly*, Volume 4, Number 20, May 20, 1997, pp. 50-53.

Ratliff, Marie. "Country Corner," *Billboard*, June 24, 1989, p. 24.

Ratliff, Ben. "Standard Road Menu but a New Dessert," *The New York Times*, Friday, March 13, 1998.

Reinert, Al. "King of Country," *The New York Times Magazine*, March 26, 1978, pp. 20-28, 33, 50-53.

Reinert, Al. "Bringing It All Back Home," *Texas Monthly*, Volume 4, Issue 8, August 1976, pp. 102-103, 131.

Richardson, Derk, with photography by Rory Earnshaw. "Anger's Passion: Darol Anger Trades the Camaraderie of the Quartet for the Producer's Chair," *Strings*, Volume XII, Number 5, Issue 67, January/February 1998, pp. 46-51.

Rife, Joanne. "The Great God of Guitar," *San Francisco*, Volume 23, June 1981, pp. 42-44.

Rollins, Cathy, and J. J. Syrja. "Willie Nelson," *Goldmine*, Number 64, September 1981, pp. 19-20.

Rosen, Richard J. "Rick Visits Don Was," *Stereophile*, Volume 20, Number 6, June 1997, pp. 97-105.

Rosenbaum, Ron. "The Ballad of Willie Nelson," *Vanity Fair*, Volume 54, Number 11, November 1991, pp. 210-216, 233-240.

Rowland, Mark, with photographs by Jay Blakesberg. "A Thousand Miles from Nashville: Dwight Yoakam Meets Willie Nelson," *Musician*, Issue No. 210, May 1996, pp. 24-33, 74.

Rubin, Dave. "B. B. King," *Guitar*, Volume 15, Number 3, January 1998, pp. 54-67.

Ruggles, Jennie. "Willie Nelson: The Eclectic Horseman," *Body Mind Spirit*, Volume 15, Number 6, October - December 1996, pp. 62--65.

Sanderson, Jane. "Talking With ... Chet Atkins," People Weekly, Volume 49, Number 3, January 26, 1998, p. 29.

Saviano, Tamara. "John Michael Montgomery Shows a Different Side," *Country Weekly*, Volume 5, Number 14, April 7, 1998, pp. 12-14.

Schmuckler, Eric, editor. "The Tax Shelter Blues," *Forbes*, Volume 146, Number 6, September 17, 1990, p. 14.

Scobey, Lola. "The Red-Headed Stranger - The Secret of Its Power," *Billboard*, Volume 98, Number 41, October 11, 1986, pp. W-6, W-22.

Scoville, Dennis, and Lisa Sorg. "King for a Day, " *No Depression*, November-December 1997, pp. 72-76.

Sebree, Dave. "On the Road Again: Harmonized Soloing," *Country Guitar*, Winter 1994, pp. 84-85.

Shaw, Russell. "Odd Couple: Willie Nelson Says Duet with Julio Iglesias Was His Wife's Idea," *Billboard*, Volume 96, Number 12, March 24, 1984, p. 49.

Shelton, Robert M. "Doing Theology with Willie Nelson," *Theomusicology*, Volume 8, Number 1, Spring 1994, pp. 254-265.

Shrake, Bud. "The Songwriter Is the Stranger," *Billboard*, Volume 98, Number 41, October 11, 1986, pp. W-6, W-21.

Skelly, Richard. "Marcia Ball," *Goldmine*, Volume 23, Number 19, Issue 447, September 12, 1997, pp. 14-15.

Smith, Kevin. "Sarg," *Goldmine*, Volume 19, Number 19, Issue 343, September 17, 1993, pp. 134-135, 169, 173.

Smucker, Tom. "Willie Nelson's Historical Burden," *The Village Voice*, Volume XXV, Number 52, December 24-30, 1980, p. 67.

Standish, David. "Saint Willie: In Every Audience There Are Those Who Come Not Just to Hear but to Be Healed," *Playboy*, Volume 28, Number 4, April 1981, pp. 176, 214-220.

Stevens, Dale. "Marty Robbins Talks of Willie Nelson and Parton," *Cincinnati Post*, August 26, 1978, p. 15.

Streissguth, Mike. "Cindy Walker: You Do Know Her Songs," *The Journal of Country Music*, Volume 19, Number 1, pp. 7-9.

Sylvester, Bruce. "Texas Troubadours: Billy Joe and Eddy Shaver," *Goldmine*, #426, November 22, 1996, p. 15.

Thrasher, Sue. "Country Music -- From Hillbilly to Hank Wilson," *Southern Exposure*, Volume II, Number 1, pp. 3-16.

Turok, Paul. "Hold the Applause: A Social History of the Classical Audience from Court Composers to the Three Tenors," *Pulse!*, Number 108, September 1992, pp. 38-41.

Verna, Paul. "For Lanois, Work Is Center Stage," *Billboard*, Volume 110, Number 14, April 4, 1998, pp. 28-29.

Von-Frederick, Teresa Taylor. "Willie Nelson: Very Much at Home," *McCall's*, Volume CXV, Number 8, May 1988, pp. 92-97.

Ward, Ed. "Willie Nelson: Breakthrough of a Lone-Star Legend," *Rolling Stone*, Issue Number 204, January 15th, 1976, p. 18.

Williams, Nancy. "Willie Weds Morgan Fairchild: 'Red Headed Stranger' Films in Texas," *Music City News*, Volume XXIII, No. IV, October 1985, p. 68.

Witchel, Alex. "Where the Cowboy Hangs His Hat: On the Road with Willie Nelson," *The New York Times*, February 23, 1995, pp. C1, C10.

Wood, Gerry. "Acuff Award Honors Willie for Farm Aid," *Billboard*, Volume 99, Number 7, February 14, 1987, p.73.

Wood, Gerry. "Spotlight on Willie Nelson," *International Musician*, Volume 79, Number 20, August 1980, pp. 9, 12.

Wood, Gerry. "A Day in the Nightlife of Willie Nelson: Country Music's Rebel Finds Pleasure in the Grind of One-Nighters on the Road," *Billboard*, Volume 91, Number 24, June 16, 1979, pp. 56-57.

Wood, Gerry. "Willie Cooks Up Another Winner: Cool Breezes, Hot Acts at 14th Picnic," *Billboard*, Volume 99, Number 29, July 18, 1987, p. 35.

Wood, Gerry. "The CBS Story - Flowing with the Changing Currents of Brilliance," *Billboard*, Volume 98, Number 41, October 11, 1986, pp. W-8, W-14.

Wood, Gerry. "Willie Nelson's Lone Star to Collaborate with Col Label," *Billboard*, Volume 87, Number 48, November 29, 1975, p. 52.

Wood, Gerry. "Nelson Changing January?," *Billboard*, Volume 87, Number 49, December 6, 1975, p. 28.

Wood, Gerry. "Farm Aid IV Set for Hoosier Dome," *Billboard*, January 20, 1990, p. 55.

Woodard, Josef. "States of Being," *Jazziz*, Volume 14, Number 6, June 1997, pp. 50-54, 80.

Zimmerman, David. "'Asleep at the Wheel' Revs Up Bob Wills Tribute," *USA Today*, November 2, 1993, p. 8D.

Book Chapters

Axton, Mae Boren. "Willie Nelson," in *Country Singers: As I Know 'Em*. Introduction by Biff Collie. Austin, Texas: Sweet Publishing Company, 1973. 384 p. List of fan club presidents and artists.

Bane, Michael. "The Austin Angle," and "Outlaw Blues," in *The Outlaws: Revolution in Country Music*. New York: Doubleday, 1978. 154 p.

Bart, Teddy. "Willie Nelson: Are There Any Basic Rules for Writing a Good Song," in *Inside Music City, U.S.A.* Nashville: Aurora, 1970. 164 p.

Brown, Charles T. "Willie Nelson," in *Music U.S.A.: America's Country & Western Tradition*. Englewood Cliffs, New Jersey: Prentice-Hall, 1986. 215 p. Discography, bibliography, index.

Carr, Patrick, editor. "Modern Country," in *The Illustrated History of Country Music*. Garden City, New York: Doubleday, 1979. 359 p. Index.

Cook, Bruce. "Willie Nelson's Roller Coaster," in *Welcome to Branson, Missouri: The Town That Country Built: Your Complete Guide to a Rip-Roaring Toe-Tapping Good Time*. New York: Avon Books, 1993. 260 p. Branson guide.

Dellar, Fred, Alan Cackett, and Roy Thompson. "Willie Nelson," in *The Harmony Illustrated Encyclopedia of Country Music*. Special Consulting by Doug Green, Country Music Foundation. Foreword by Ricky Skaggs. New York: Crown Publishers, 1986. 208 p. Index.

Escott, Colin. "Billy Walker: Cross the Brazos at Waco," *Liner Notes*, Billy Walker Boxed Set, Bear Family Records, BCD 15 657 F1.

Field, Kim. "Mickey Raphael (1951 -)," in *Harmonicas, Harps, and Heavy Breathers: The Evolution of the People's Instrument*. New York: Simon & Schuster, 1993. 344 p. Bibliography, index.

Flippo, Chet. "Outlaws Willie and Waylon," in *Everybody Was Kung-Fu Dancing: Chronicles of the Lionized and the Notorious.* New York: St. Martin's Press, 1991. 292 p.

Gaillard, Frye. "Putting the Audiences Back Together" and "In the Wake of Johnny Cash," in *Watermelon Wine: The Spirit of Country Music.* New York: St. Martin's Press, 1978. 236 p.

Green, Douglas B., and Bob Pinson. "Music from the Lone Star State," in *The Illustrated History of Country Music.* Edited by Patrick Carr. Garden City, New York: Doubleday, 1979. 359 p. Index.

Hatlo, Jim. "Willie Nelson," in *Country Musicians.* Edited by Judy Eremo. Foreword by Roy Clark. New York: Grove Press, 1987. 151 p.

Hickey, Dave. "Letter from Austin," in *The Best of Country Music: Volume I.* Edited by the Editors of *Country Music Magazine.* New York: KBO Publishers, 1974. 128 p.

Kernaghan, Eileen, and Jonathon Kay. "Willie Nelson and James Coburn: A Little Old-Fashioned Karma Coming Down," in *Walking After Midnight.* Preface by Ringo Starr. New York: Berkley, 1990. 217 p. Bibliography.

Kingsbury, Paul, editor. "Outlaws and Rockers," in *The Country Reader: Twenty-Five Years of the Journal of Country Music.* Foreword by Chet Flippo. Nashville: The Country Music Foundation Press/Vanderbilt University Press, 1996. 333 p. Bibliography

Linedecker, Cliff. "Willie Nelson: Reincarnation and the Mystery Schools," in *Country Music Stars and the Supernatural.* New York: Dell, 1979. 317 p.

Lomax, John, III. "The Coming of the Outlaws," in *Nashville: Music City USA.* New York: Harry N. Abrams, 1985. 224 p. Bibliography, index.

McCloud, Barry, and contributing writers. "Willie Nelson," in *Definitive Country: The Ultimate Encyclopedia of Country Music and its Performers.* New York: Berkley, 1995. 1132 p.

Meyer, Ray. "Lost Train of Thought," in *All Music Guide to Country.* Michael Erlewine, Vladimir Bogdanov, Chris Woodstra, Stephen Thomas Erlewine, editors. San Francisco: Miller Freeman Books, 1997. 221 p.

Mockus, Martha. "Queer Thoughts on Country Music and k. d. lang," in *Queering the Pitch: The New Gay and Lesbian Musicology.* Edited by Philip Brett, Elizabeth Wood, Gary C. Thomas. New York: Routledge, 1994, p. 266.

Morthland, John. "Contemporary Country," in *The Best of Country Music.* Garden City, New York: Doubleday & Company, 1984. 436 p.

Nash, Alanna. "Willie Nelson," in *Behind Closed Doors: Talking with the Legends of Country Music.* New York: Alfred A. Knopf, Inc., 1988. 553 p.

Reid, Jan. "Willie the Lion," in *The Improbable Rise of Redneck Rock.* New York: Da Capo, 1974. New edition 1977. 342 p.

Rovin, Jeff. "Willie Nelson," in *Country Music Babylon.* New York: St. Martin's Press, 1993. 279 p.

Shestack, Melvin. "Nelson, Willie," in *The Country Music Encyclopedia.* New York: Thomas Y. Crowell Company, 1974. 410 p. Discography.

Stambler, Irwin, and Grelun Landon. "Nelson, Willie," in *The Encyclopedia of Folk, Country & Western Music*. Introductory essay by William Ivey. New York: St. Martin's Press, 1969. 902 p. Bibliography.

Tucker, Ken. "9 to 5: How Willie Nelson and Dolly Parton Qualified for 'Lifestyles of the Rich and Famous'," in *Country: The Music and the Musicians*. Edited by Paul Kingsbury and Alan Axelrod. New York: Abbeville, 1988. 595 p. Discography, bibliography, index.

Books and Papers

Allen, Bob. *Waylon & Willie: The Full Story in Words and Pictures of Waylon Jennings & Willie Nelson*. New York: Quick Fox, 1979. 127 p. Discographies.

Bane, Michael. *Willie: An Unauthorized Biography of Willie Nelson*. New York: Dell Publishing Co., Inc., 1984. 253 p. Index.

Cusic, Don, editor. *Willie Nelson: Lyrics 1957- 1994*. Foreword by Willie Nelson. New York: St. Martin's Press, 1995. 215 p.

Fowler, Lana Nelson, compiler. *Willie Nelson Family Album*. Foreword by H. M. Poirot. Amarillo, Texas: H. M. Poirot & Company, 1980. 154 p. (unnumbered). Catalog of songs, discography.

Kienzle, Rich. *Willie Nelson: Nashville Was the Roughest...* Hambergen, Germany: Bear Family Records, 1998. 71 p.

Nelson, Susie. *Heart Worn Memories: A Daughter's Personal Biography of Willie Nelson*. Austin: Eakin Press, 1987. 228 p.

Nelson, Willie, with Bud Shrake. *Willie: An Autobiography*. New York: Simon and Schuster, Inc., 1988. 334 p. Index.

Scobey, Lola. *Willie Nelson: Country Outlaw*. New York: Kensington Publishing Corp., 1982. Reprinted 1984. 414 p.

Wildman, Sherman, and Kent. *The Willie Nelson 'Cooked Goose' Cookbook and IRS Financial Advisor*. Atlanta: Longstreet Press, 1992.

Willie: The Life and Music of Willie Nelson. Irvine, California: Graphix Zone GZ10760, 1996.

Witliff, Bill, written and directed by. *Willie Nelson: Red Headed Stranger*. An Alive Films Release. [Publicity packet].

Part II. The Music Source Books

Much of the information about the various songs discussed in this book came from a variety of sources. Additionally, many of the quotations used came from sources not cited in the previous two parts. In the event my detailed citings failed to include an appropriate bibliographic entry, I apologize in advance, and add that it had to be inadvertent, that the author has my sincerest regret, and if any individual would notify me of any oversight, through my publisher, I will make every effort to fix such an oversight in future editions.

Ackland, Diana, and Janie Freeburg, editors. *Texas*. Boston: Houghton Mifflin Company, 1996. 411 p.

Allen, Bob. *George Jones: The Saga of an American Singer*. Garden City, New York: Doubleday, 1984. 291 p.

Allen, Bob, editor. *The Blackwell Guide to Recorded Country Music*. Oxford, England: Blackwell Publishers, 1994. 411 p.

Amburn, Ellis. *Dark Star: The Roy Orbison Story*. New York: Carol Publishing Group, 1990. 283 p. Bibliography, discography, index.

Atkins, Chet, with Bill Neely. *Country Gentleman*. Foreword by William Ivey. Chicago: Henry Regnery Company, 1974. 226 p.

Austin, William. *Susanna, Jeanie, and the Old Folks at Home: The Songs of Stephen C. Foster from His Time to Ours*. New York: Macmillan, 1975. 420 p. Index.

Autry, Gene, with Mickey Herskowitz. *Back in the Saddle Again*. Garden City, New York: Doubleday, 1978. 252 p. Discography, filmography, index.

Bach, Bob, and Ginger Mercer, editors. *Johnny Mercer: The Life, Times and Song Lyrics of Our Huckleberry Friend*. Tribute by Irving Berlin. Secaucus: Lyle Stuart, 1982. 252 p. List of published songs, movie contributions.

Bergreen, Laurence. *As Thousands Cheer: The Life of Irving Berlin*. New York: Penguin Books USA, 1990. 658 p. Chronology of songs, bibliography, index.

Bernard, Shane K. *Swamp Pop: Cajun and Creole Rhythm and Blues*. Foreword by Carl A. Brasseaux. Jackson: University Press of Mississippi, 1996. 264 p. Timeline and discography, suggested listening, bibliography, song title index, subject index.

Biskind, Peter. *Easy Riders, Raging Bulls: How the Sex-Drugs-and-Rock 'n' Roll Generation Saved Hollywood*. New York: Simon & Schuster, 1998. 506 p.

Bordman, Gerald. *Days to Be Happy, Years to Be Sad: The Life and Music of Vincent Youmans*. New York: Oxford University Press, 1982. 266 p. Index.

Bowen, Jimmy, and Jim Jerome. *Rough Mix: An Unapologetic Look at the Music Business and How It Got That Way*. New York: Simon & Schuster, 1997. 302 p.

Brahms, Caryl, and Ned Sherrin. *Song by Song: 14 Great Lyric Writers*. Bolton, England: Ross Anderson Publications, 1984. 282 p.

Bufwack, Mary A., and Robert K. Oerman. *Finding Her Voice: The Saga of Women in Country Music*. New York: Crown Publishers, 1993. 594 p.

Byron, Janet. *The Country Music Lover's Guide to the U.S.A.* New York: St. Martin's Press, 1996. 245 p.

Cahn, Sammy. *I Should Care: The Sammy Cahn Story*. New York: Arbor House Publishing Co., 1974. 318 p. Songography, index.

Campbell, Glen, with Tom Carter. *Rhinestone Cowboy: An Autobiography*. New York: Villard Books, 1994. 253 p. Discography.

Carlisle, Dolly. *Ragged but Right: The Life and Times of George Jones*. Chicago: Contemporary Books, 1984. 250 p. Discography, index.

Carmichael, Hoagy, with Stephen Longstreet. *Sometimes I Wonder: The Story of Hoagy Carmichael*. New York: Farrar, Straus and Giroux, 1965. 313 p.

Carmichael, Hoagy [Hoagland]. *The Stardust Road*. Bloomington: Indiana University Press, 1946. Copyright renewed 1974. New edition 1983. 156 p.

Cash, Johnny, with Patrick Carr. *Cash: The Autobiography*. New York: Harper Collins, 1997. 310 p. Discography by John L. Smith.

Charles, Ray, with David Ritz. *Brother Ray: Ray Charles' Own Story*. Discography by David Ritz. New York: The Dial Press, 1978. 340 p.

Choron, Sandra, & Bob Oskam. *Elvis!: The Last Word: The 328 Best (and Worst) Things Anyone Ever Said About "The King"*. New York: Carol Publishing, 1991. 103 p. Index.

Clayson, Alan. *Only the Lonely: Roy Orbison's Life and Legacy*. New York: St. Martin's Press, 1989. 257 p. Discography, index.

Collins, Ace. *The Stories Behind Country Music's All-Time Greatest 100 Songs*. New York: Boulevard Books, 1996. 283 p.

Collins, Ace. *The Country Music Book of Lists*. New York: St. Martin's Press, 1998. 181 p.

Cook, Bruce. *The Town That Country Built: Welcome to Branson, Missouri*. New York: Avon Books, 1993. 260 p.

Cooper, Daniel. *Lefty Frizzell: The Honky-Tonk Life of Country Music's Greatest Singer*. Boston: Little, Brown and Company, 1995. 224 p.

Crook, Lorianne, & Charlie Chase, with Mickey Herskowitz. *Crook & Chase: Our Lives, the Music, and the Stars*. New York: William Morrow and Company, 1995. 202 p.

Cusic, Don. *Randy Travis: The King of the New Country Traditionalists*. New York: St. Martin's Press, 1990. 210 p. Bibliography, discography, index.

Daley, Dan. *Nashville's Unwritten Rules: Inside the Business of Country Music*. New York: The Overlook Press, 1998. 351 p.

Daly, Marsha. *Julio Iglesias*. New York: St. Martin's Press, 1986. 131 p. Index.

Dance, Stanley. *The World of Earl Hines*. New York: Charles Scribner's Sons, 1977. 324 p. Chronology, bibliography, index.

Davis, Miles, with Quincy Troupe. *Miles: The Autobiography*. New York: Simon & Schuster, Inc., 1989. 431 p. Index.

Davis, Skeeter. *Bus Fare to Kentucky: The Autobiography of Skeeter Davis*. Secaucus: Carol Publishing Group, 1993. 338 p. Discography, index.

Dawidoff, Nicholas. *In the Country of Country: People and Places in American Music*. New York: Pantheon Books, 1997. 294 p.

Dellar, Fred, and Richard Wootton. *The Country Music Book of Lists*. New York: The New York Times Book Co., 1984. 175 p.

Denisoff, R. Serge. *Waylon: A Biography*. Discographies by John L. Smith, compiler. Knoxville: University of Tennessee Press, 1983. 375 p. Index.

Dickerson, James. *Goin' Back to Memphis: A Century of Blues, Rock 'n' Roll, and Glorious Soul*. New York: Schirmer Books, 1996. 279 p.

Duff, Arleigh. *Y'all Come: Country Music: Jack's Branch to Nashville*. Austin: Eakin Press, 1983. 188 p.

Dunkleberger, A. C. *The Life Story of Roy Acuff: King of Country Music*. Nashville: Williams Printing Co., 1971. 137 p.

Ellison, Curtis W. *Country Music Culture: From Hard Times to Heaven*. Jackson: University Press of Mississippi, 1995. 314 p. References, index.

Emery. Ralph, with Tom Carter. *Memories: The Autobiography of Ralph Emery*. New York: Macmillan, 1991. 278 p.

Emery. Ralph, with Tom Carter. *More Memories*. New York: G. P. Putnam's Sons, 1993. 288 p.

Endres, Clifford. *Austin City Limits: The Story Behind Television's Most Popular Country Music Program*. Austin: University of Texas Press, 1987. 136 p.

Eng, Steve. *A Satisfied Mind: The Country Music Life of Porter Wagoner*. Nashville: Rutledge Hill Press, 1992. 464 p. Sources, discography, index.

Eng, Steve. *Jimmy Buffett: The Man from Margaritaville Revealed*. New York: St. Martin's Press, 1996. 364 p. Discography, reference, index.

Escott, Colin. *Tattooed on Their Tongues: A Journey Through the Backrooms of American Music*. New York: Schirmer Books, 1996. 243 p. Index.

Ewen, David. *The World of Jerome Kern: A Biography*. New York: Henry Holt and Company, 1960. 178 p. Selected recordings, index.

Farr, Jory. *Moguls and Madmen: The Pursuit of Power in Popular Music*. New York: Simon & Schuster, 1994. 319 p.

Feiler, Bruce. *Dreaming Out Loud: Garth Brooks, Wynonna Judd, Wade Hayes, and the Changing Face of Nashville*. New York: Avon Books, 1998. 406 p.

Flanagan, Bill. *U2: At the End of the World*. New York: Delacorte Press, 1995. 536 p.

Flanagan, Bill. *Written in My Soul: Conversations with Rock's Great Songwriters*. Chicago: Contemporary Books, 1987. 472 p. Index.

Foster, Morrison. *My Brother Stephen*. Indianapolis: Foster Hall Library, 1932. 55 p.

Geldof, Bob. *Is That It?: The Autobiography*. New York: Weidenfeld & Nicolson, 1986. 360 p.

Gentry, Linnell. *A History and Encyclopedia of Country, Western, and Gospel Music*. Foreword by Tex Ritter. Nashville: Clairmont, 1969. 598 p.

Gilbert, L. Wolfe. *Without Rhyme or Reason*. New York: Vantage Press, 1956. 240 p. Index.

Glatt, John. *The Chieftains: The Authorized Biography*. New York: St. Martin's Press, 1997. 331 p. Discography, index.

Graham, David. *He Walks with Me: The Religious Experiences of Country Music Stars*. New York: Simon & Schuster, 1977. 210 p.

Green, Benny. *Let's Face the Music: The Golden Age of Popular Song*. London: Pavilion Books, 1989. 234 p.

Griffin, Nancy, & Kim Masters. *Hit & Run: How Jon Peters and Peter Guber Took Sony for a Ride in Hollywood*. New York: Simon & Schuster, 1996. 496 p.

Grissim, John. *Country Music: White Man's Blues*. New York: Coronet, 1970. 299 p.

Gubernick, Lisa Rebecca. *Get Hot or Go Home: Trisha Yearwood: The Making of a Nashville Star*. New York: William Morrow and Company, 1993. 365 p.

Hagan, Chet. *Country Music Legends in the Hall of Fame*. Nashville: Thomas Nelson, 1982. 256 p.

Hagan, Chet. *Grand Ole Opry: The Complete Story of a Great American Institution and Its Stars*. New York: Henry Holt and Company, 1989. 346 p. Index.

Haggard, Merle, with Peggy Russell. *Sing Me Back Home: My Life*. New York: Times Books, 1981. 287 p.

Haislop, Neil, Ted Lathrop, Harry Sumrall. *Giants of Country Music*. New York: *Billboard* Books, 1995. 257 p.

Hammerstein, Oscar II. *Lyrics*. Preface by Richard Rodgers. New York: Simon and Schuster, 1949. 215 p.

Harris, Michael W. *The Rise of Gospel Blues: The Music of Thomas Andrew Dorsey in the Urban Church*. New York: Oxford University Press, 1992. 324 p. Bibliography, index.

Hefley, James. *How Sweet the Sound*. Wheaton, Illinois: Tyndale House, 1981. 320 p.

Hemphill, Paul. *The Nashville Sound: Bright Lights and Country Music*. New York: Simon and Schuster, 1970. 289 p. Index.

Hentoff, Nat. *Listen to the Stories: Nat Hentoff on Jazz and Country Music*. New York: HarperCollins, 1995. 220 p.

Heylin, Clinton. *Bob Dylan: A Life in Stolen Moments: Day by Day: 1941-1995*. New York: Schirmer Books, 1996. 403 p. Bibliography.

Hicks, Darryl E. *Marijohn: Lord, Let Me Leave a Song*. Foreword by Brother Joe Dee Kelley, Pastor, Brentwood Assembly of God Church. Waco, Texas: Word Books, 1978. 159 p.

Hively, Kay, and Albert E. Brumley, Jr. *I'll Fly Away: The Life Story of Albert E. Brumley*. Branson, Missouri: Mountaineer Books, 1990. 126 p.

Holloran, Carolyn. *Your Favorite Country Music Stars*. New York: Popular Library, 1975. 283 p.

Horstman, Dorothy, *Sing Your Heart Out, Country Boy*. Foreword by Frances Preston. Nashville: Country Music Foundation, 1975. 331 p. Bibliography, discography, index of songs.

Hume, Martha. *You're So Cold I'm Turnin' Blue: Martha Hume's Guide to the Greatest in Country Music*. New York: Penguin, 1982. 195 p.

Humphries, Patrick. *Paul Simon: Still Crazy After All These Years*. New York: Doubleday, 1988. 193 p. Discography, bibliography.

Hurst, Jack. *Nashville's Grand Ole Opry: The First Fifty Years 1925-1975*. Introduction by Roy Acuff. New York: Harry N. Abrams, 1975. New edition 1989. 364 p. Discography.

Hyland, William G. *The Song Is Ended: Songwriters and American Music, 1900 - 1950*. New York; Oxford University Press, 1995. 336 p. Index.

Jennings, Waylon, with Lenny Kaye. *Waylon: An Autobiography*. New York: Warner Books, 1996. 418 p. Selected discography, index.

Jones, Margaret. *Patsy: The Life and Times of Patsy Cline*. Foreword by Loretta Lynn. Discography by Don Roy. New York HarperCollins, 1994. 335 p.

Kael, Pauline. *For Keeps: 30 Years at the Movies*. New York: Penguin, 1996. 1291 p. Index.

Kane, Henry, as told to. *How to Write a Song*. New York: Avon, 1962. 224 p.

Kennedy, Burt. *Hollywood Trail Boss: Behind the Scenes of the Wild, Wild Western*. Foreword by Jack Elam. New York: Boulevard, 1997. 177 p.

Killen, Buddy, with Tom Carter. *By the Seat of My Pants: My Life in Country Music*. New York: Simon & Schuster, 1993. 316 p.

King, B. B., with David Ritz. *Blues All Around Me: The Autobiography of B. B. King*. New York: Avon Books, 1996. 346 p. Discography, awards, index.

Kingsbury, Paul. *The Grand Ole Opry History of Country Music: 70 Years of the Songs, the Stars, and the Stories*. Foreword by Dolly Parton. New York: Villard Books, 1995. 257 p.

Kinison, Bill, with Steve Delsohn. *Brother Sam: The Short, Spectacular Life of Sam Kinison*. New York: William Morrow and Company, 1994. 315 p.

Klein, Joe. *Woody Guthrie: A Life*. New York: Random House, 1980. New edition 1982. 476 p. Index.

Kragen, Ken, with Jefferson Graham. *Life Is a Contact Sport*. New York: William Morrow and Company, 1994. 202 p.

Laine, Frankie, and Joseph F. Laredo. *"That Lucky Old Son": The Autobiography of Frankie Laine*. Prelude by Irving Stone. Ventura, California: Pathfinder Publishing, 1993. 295 p. Discography, index.

Lax, Roger, & Frederick Smith. *The Great Song Thesaurus*. New York: Oxford University Press, 1984. 665 p.

Leamer, Laurence. *Three Chords and the Truth: Hope, Heartbreak, and Changing Fortunes in Nashville*. New York: HarperCollins, 1997. 450 p. Bibliography, index.

Lewis, George H., editor. *All That Glitters: Country Music in America.* Bowling Green, Ohio: Bowling Green State University Popular Press, 1993. 340 p.

Lockyer, Daphne. *Julio Iglesias: The Untold Story.* Secaucus, New Jersey: Birch Lane Press, 1997. 311 p. Index.

Logan, Horace, with Bill Sloan. *Elvis, Hank, and Me: Making Musical History on the Louisiana Hayride.* Foreword by Hank Williams Jr. Introduction by Johnny Cash. New York: St. Martin's Press, 1998. 274 p. Index.

Lord, Bobby. *Hit the Glory Road!* Nashville: Broadman, 1969. 143 p.

Lucaire, Luigi. *Howard Stern A to Z: A Totally Unauthorized Guide.* New York: St. Martin's Press, 1997. 249 p.

Malone, Bill C. *Southern Music American Music.* Lexington: The University Press of Kentucky, 1979. 237 p.

Malone, Bill C. *Country Music U. S. A.: A Fifty Year History.* Austin: University of Texas Press, 1968. 422 p. Bibliography, index.

Malone, Bill C. *Stars of Country Music: Uncle Dave Macon to Johnny Rodriguez.* Foreword by D. K. Wilgus. Urbana: University of Illinois Press, 1975. 476 p. Index.

Mason, Michael, editor. *The Country Music Book.* New York: Charles Scribner's Sons, 1985. 421 p. Index.

McCloud, Barry. *Definitive Country: The Ultimate Encyclopedia of Country Music and its Performers.* New York: Berkley, 1995. 1132 p.

Meyerson, Harold, and Ernie Harburg. *Who Put the Rainbow in the Wizard of Oz?: Yip Harburg, Lyricist.* Ann Arbor: University of Michigan Press, 1993. 454 p.

Millard, Bob. *Country Music What's What.* New York: HarperCollins, 1995. 249 p. Index.

Millard, Bob. *Country Music: 70 Years of America's Favorite Music.* New York: HarperCollins, 1993. 328 p.

Morthland, John. *The Best of Country Music.* Garden City, New York: Doubleday, 1984, 436 p.

Morton, David C., with Charles K. Wolfe. *DeFord Bailey: A Black Star in Early Country Music.* Discography compiled by Charles K. Wolfe. Knoxville: The University of Tennessee Press, 1991. 245 p. Sources, index.

O'Brien, Ed, with Robert Wilson. *Sinatra 101: The 101 Best Recordings and the Stories Behind Them.* Foreword by Sid Mark. New York: Boulevard, 1996. 167 p.

Oermann, Robert K., with Douglas B. Green. *The Listener's Guide to Country Music.* New York: Facts on File, 1983. 137 p. Bibliography.

Oermann, Robert K. *America's Music: The Roots of Country.* Atlanta: Turner Publishing, 1996. 240 p.

Osborne, Jerry. *55 Years of Recorded Country/Western Music.* Edited by Bruce Hamilton. Phoenix: O'Sullivan Woodside, 1976. 164 p.

Parish, James Robert, and Michael R. Pitts. *Hollywood Songsters: A Biographical Dictionary*. New York: Garland, 1991. 826 p.

Parton, Dolly. *Dolly: My Life and Other Unfinished Business*. New York: HarperCollins, 1994. 338 p. Discography.

Patoski, Joe Nick, and Bill Crawford. *Stevie Ray Vaughan: Caught in the Crossfire*. Discography compiled by Craig Keyzer. Boston: Little, Brown and Company, 1993. 313 p.

Peterson, Richard A. *Creating Country Music: Fabricating Authenticity*. Chicago: University of Chicago Press, 1997. 222 p.

Price, Steven D. *Take Me Home: The Rise of Country & Western Music*. New York: Praeger Publishers, 1974. 184 p. Biographies, bibliography, discography, index of names, index of song titles.

Pride, Charley, with Jim Henderson. *Pride: The Charley Pride Story*. New York: William Morrow and Company, 1994. 302 p.

Reavis, Dick J. *Texas*. Photography by Will Van Overbeek. Oakland: Compass American Guides, 1995. 330 p.

Riese, Randall. *Nashville Babylon: The Uncensored Truth and Private Lives of Country Music's Stars*. New York: Congdon & Weed, 1988. 290 p. Bibliography, index.

Robertson, John. *Neil Young: The Visual Documentary*. London: Omnibus Press, 1994. 160 p.

Rodriguez, Elena. *Dennis Hopper: A Madness to His Method*. New York: St. Martin's Press, 1988. 198 p.

Rogers, Jimmie N. *The Country Music Message: Revisited*. Fayetteville: University of Arkansas Press, 1989. 268 p. Index.

Roland, Tom. *The Billboard Book of Number One Country Hits: Country Music's Chart-Topping Records, Artists, and Songwriters*. New York: *Billboard* Books, 1991. 584 p.

Rooney, James. *Bossmen: Bill Monroe & Muddy Waters*. New York: The Dial Press, 1971. 159 p.

Rothel, David. *The Singing Cowboys*. San Diego: A. S. Barnes, 1978. 272 p.

Rovin, Jeff. *Country Music Babylon*. New York: St. Martin's Press, 1993. 90 p.

Schlappi, Elizabeth. *Roy Acuff: The Smoky Mountain Boy*. Gretna, Louisiana: Pelican, 1978. 289 p. Discography, bibliography, index.

Schwartz, Charles. *Cole Porter: A Biography*. New York: Dial, 1977. 270 p.

Sedaka, Neil. *Laughter in the Rain: My Own Story*. New York: G. P. Putnam's Sons, 1982. 253 p. Discography, list of songs.

Shannon, Bob, and John Javna. *Behind the Hits: Inside Stories of Classic Pop and Rock and Roll*. New York: Warner Books, 1986. 254 p. Index .

Sheff, David. *The Playboy Interviews with John Lennon & Yoko Ono*. Edited by G. Barry Colson. New York: Playboy Press, 1981. 193 p.

Shelton, Robert, and Burt Goldblatt. *The Country Music Story: A Picture History of Country and Western Music.* Secaucus: Castle Books, 1966. 256 p.

Sinatra, Nancy. *Frank Sinatra: An American Legend.* Santa Monica, California: General Publishing, 1995. 367 p. Filmography, index.

Snow, Hank, the Singing Ranger, with Jack Ownbey and Bob Burris. *The Hank Snow Story.* Note on the recordings by Charles K. Wolfe. Urbana: University of Illinois Press, 1994. 555 p. Index.

Stelzer, Dick. *The Star Treatment.* Indianapolis: Bobbs-Merrill, 1977. 213 p.

Stokes, Niall. *Into the Heart: The Stories Behind Every U2 Song.* New York: Thunder's Mouth Press, 1996. 144 p.

Streissguth, Michael. *Eddy Arnold: Pioneer of the Nashville Sound.* New York: Simon & Schuster, 1997. 290 p. Sessionography, bibliography, index.

Strobel, Jerry, editor. *Grand Ole Opry: WSM Picture-History Book.* Nashville: Opryland USA, 1984. 168 p.

Sulpy, Doug, and Ray Schweighardt. *Drugs, Divorce and a Slipping Image: The Unauthorized Story of the Beatles' "Get Back" Sessions.* Princeton Junction: The 910, 1994. 31.7 p.

Tassin, Myron, and Jerry Henderson. *Fifty Years at the Grand Ole Opry.* Foreword by Minnie Pearl. Introduction by Mother Maybelle Carter. Gretna, Louisiana: Pelican Publishing, 1975. 112 p.

Thiele, Bob, as told to Bob Golden. *What A Wonderful World: A Lifetime of Recordings.* Foreword by Steve Allen. New York: Oxford University Press, 1995. 168 p.

Thomas, Tony. *The Hollywood Musical: The Saga of Songwriter Harry Warren, the Man Whose Melodies Are Sung More Than Those of Any Composer Other Than Irving Berlin.* Foreword by Bing Crosby. Secaucus, New Jersey: Citadel Press, 1975. 344 p.

Tichi, Cecelia. *High Lonesome: The American Culture of Country Music.* Chapel Hill: The University of North Carolina Press, 1994. 318 p. Bibliography.

Tillis, Mel, with Walter Wager. *Stutterin' Boy.* New York: Rawson Associates, 1984. 270 p. Discography, index.

Tosches, Nick. *Country: Living Legends and Dying Metaphors in America's Biggest Music.* New York: Charles Scribner's Sons, 1977. New edition 1985. 252 p.

Townsend, Charles. *San Antonio Rose: The Life and Music of Bob Wills.* Discography and Filmography by Bob Pinson. Urbana: University of Illinois Press, 1976. New edition 1986. 395 p.

Trischka, Tony, and Pete Wernick. *Masters of the 5-String Banjo: In Their Own Words and Music.* New York: Oak Publications, 1988. 413 p. Discography.

Tucker, Tanya, with Patsi Bale Cox. *Nickel Dreams: My Life.* New York: Hyperion, 1997. 345 p. Discography.

Vassal, Jacques. *Electric Children: Roots and Branches of Modern Folkrock.* New York: Taplinger, 1976. 270 p.

Vaughan, Andrew, author and compiler. *Who's Who in New Country Music: A Complete Guide to the Modern Country Sound.* Foreword by Ricky Skaggs. New York: St. Martin's Press, 1989. 128 p.

Wacholtz, Larry E. *Inside Country Music: A Behind-the-Scenes-Look at Songwriting, Arranging, Producing, Recording, and Promoting a Career in the Country Music Industry.* New York: *Billboard* Publications, 1984. New edition 1986. 254 p. Index.

Wade, Dorothy, and Justine Picardie. *Music Man: Ahmet Ertegun, Atlantic Records, and the Triumph of Rock 'n' Roll.* New York: W. W. Norton & Company, 1990. 303 p. Index.

Wexler, Jerry, and David Ritz. *Rhythm and the Blues: A Life in American Music.* New York: Alfred A. Knopf, 1993. Introductory essay by David Ritz. 334 p. Selected discography, index.

Whitburn, Joel. *Joel Whitburn's Top Country Singles 1944-1988.* Menomonee Falls, Wisconsin: Record Research, 1989. 535 p.

Whitburn, Joel. *Joel Whitburn's Top Pop Albums 1955-1992.* Menomonee Falls, Wisconsin: Record Research, 1993. 968 p.

Whitburn, Joel. *Joel Whitburn's Pop Memories 1890-1954: The History of American Popular Music.* Menomonee Falls, Wisconsin: Record Research, 1986. 535 p.

White, Mark. *'You Must Remember This...': Popular Songwriters 1900-1980.* Foreword by David Jacobs. London: Frederick Warne, 1983. 304 p. Bibliography, index.

Wilder, Alec. *American Popular Song: The Great Innovators, 1900-1950.* Edited with an introduction by James T. Maher. Foreword by Gene Lees. New York: Oxford University Press, 1972. 536 p. Index.

Wills, Rosetta. *The King of Western Swing: Bob Wills Remembered.* New York: *Billboard* Books, 1998. 224 p. Bibliography.

Wolfe, Charles K. *Kentucky Country: Folk and Country Music of Kentucky.* Lexington: The University Press of Kentucky, 1982. 199 p.

Wolfe, Charles K. *Tennessee Strings: The Story of Country Music in Tennessee.* Knoxville: The University of Tennessee Press, 1977. Reprinted 1981. 118 p.

Zelade, Richard. *Hill Country.* Houston: Gulf Publishing Company, 1997. 635 p.

Zollo, Paul. *Songwriters on Songwriting.* New York: Da Capo Press, 1997. 641 p.

They were known by their first names.
(Photo from RCA Records and Willie Nelson)

About the Author

Steven Opdyke

Steven Opdyke currently resides in Gainesville, Florida, where he works as a performing arts consultant. He earned a Masters degree from the University of Florida. His experience in the music business was as a staff lyricist, first for Big Seven Music, a subsidiary of Roulette Records of New York, and then for Glaser Publications of Nashville, Tennessee, owned by Tompall and the Glaser Brothers.

Previously, he has been a systems designer and Manager of Management Information Systems for a banking conglomerate. In 1991, he became the performing arts consultant at the University of Florida's Belknap Collection for the Performing Arts. He has also written articles on both systems design and music personalities, several discographies, and a book on the all the books about Elvis Presley, *The Printed Elvis*, a 1998 publication.